BRIDGES
of
MEMORY

BRIDGES
of
MEMORY

CHICAGO'S FIRST WAVE
OF BLACK MIGRATION

TIMUEL D. BLACK JR.

*WITH FOREWORDS
BY JOHN HOPE FRANKLIN
AND STUDS TERKEL*

NORTHWESTERN UNIVERSITY PRESS
EVANSTON, ILLINOIS

DUSABLE MUSEUM OF AFRICAN AMERICAN HISTORY
CHICAGO, ILLINOIS

Northwestern University Press
Evanston, Illinois 60208-4170

DuSable Museum of African American History
Chicago, Illinois 60637

First paperback printing 2005

Printed in the United States of America
10 9 8 7 6 5 4 3 2 1

ISBN 0-8101-2315-0

Frontispiece: Outside a movie theater (Russell Lee,
Library of Congress, Prints and Photographs Division,
FSA/OWI Collection, LC-USF34-038808-D, 1941)

Publisher's Note
Northwestern University Press has been honored to
work with Timuel D. Black Jr. on this groundbreaking
oral history of the first wave of African-American migration from the American South to Chicago. The
book's title, *Bridges of Memory*, describes well the art
of oral history. Memory, like all things human, is influenced by emotion and perception, both of which
can change over time. Occasionally in the text, minor
details and the spellings of place-names, businesses,
and people's names have been corrected. But for the
most part, the book's editors have let Tim and the interviewees speak for themselves, and the result is a living
history rather than a static record of events.

Bridges of Memory is not meant to be a scholarly
account of African-American migration to Chicago.
Rather, it is a lively first-person story of how a thriving
community arose in Chicago, a story told in the voices
of those who created the community. The hope is that
their memories, however accurate or however hazy,
will enable readers to appreciate the accomplishments
of the past and gain understanding that will help them
to face the challenges of the future.

Library of Congress Cataloging-in-Publication Data
Black, Timuel D.
    Bridges of memory : Chicago's first wave of Black
migration / Timuel D. Black Jr. ; with forewords by
John Hope Franklin and Studs Terkel.
        p. cm.
    Includes index.
    ISBN 0-8101-1362-7 (alk. paper)
    1. African Americans—Illinois—Chicago—
Interviews.   2. African Americans—Illinois—
Chicago—History—20th century.   3. African
Americans—Migrations—History—20th century.
4. Migration, Internal—United States—History—
20th century.   5. Chicago (Ill.)—Biography.
6. Chicago (Ill.)—Social conditions—20th century.
7. Chicago (Ill.)—Race relations.   I. Title.
F548.9.N4 .B55 2003
977.3'00496073'00922—dc21

                                        2003009753

The paper used in this publication meets the mini-
mum requirements of the American National
Standard for Information Sciences—Permanence of
Paper for Printed Library Materials, ANSI Z39.48-1992.

*The author wishes to thank Elizabeth Hollander and the Monsignor John J. Egan Urban Center at DePaul Univer-
sity, Sunny Fischer and the Richard H. Driehaus Foundation, Warren Chapman and the Joyce Foundation, and Judith Hochberg and Judith Types for their contributions to this book. Thanks also to Muriel Chandler, Gene and Es-
tella "Tedda" Walsh, Sadie Hampton, Bridgette McCullough, and Sherry Fox.*

CONTENTS

FOREWORD

JOHN HOPE FRANKLIN

Timuel Black's collection of interviews covers much ground, both in terms of the places of origin of many of those he interviewed and in terms of the times that they migrated to the city. It is reminiscent of Jacob Lawrence's *Migration Series*, in which he observed in the first and most celebrated panel, "During the World War there was a Great Migration North by Southern Negroes." They did not all settle in Chicago, but the "city of great shoulders" certainly attracted its share. They established firm roots, created their own progeny, and became pillars of the community. These Chicagoans did not have an easy time. Life for them was no crystal stair, but they persevered. They not only developed strategies to cope with their adversities, they also built religious, social, and economic institutions, many of which continue to flourish.

Chicago is not lacking in accounts of the growth of the African-American population and the problems it has encountered along the way. They range from robust broad-gauged treatments such as *Black Metropolis*, by St. Clair Drake and Horace Cayton, to definitive monographs of institutions such as *History of the Chicago Urban League*, by Arvarh Strickland. What has been lacking is the personal testimony of the experiences of living individuals, struggling, coping, and thriving in Chicago. An insufficient number of Chicagoans have had the opportunity to tell their own stories, their triumphs and tragedies, their victories and defeats as only *they* can tell them. Tim Black has provided this opportunity for people from many walks of life. *Bridges of Memory* constitutes the personal testimony of many who were the key figures in the history of Bronzeville, the "Black Metropolis," or by whatever name Black Chicago was called.

In *Bridges of Memory* we have the saga of many Chicagoans whose narratives tell us that the story of the City on the Lake would not be complete without their voices. Some are well known, some are not. They all have their stories, all worth telling because they add mightily to our understanding of the central themes of Chicago's history. Without these narratives Chicago's history would not be complete. We are deeply indebted to Tim Black for making them available to us in *Bridges of Memory*.

FOREWORD

STUDS TERKEL

What Zora Neale Hurston did in the thirties, capturing the voices and visions of ex-slaves and their children, Tim Black has done with the grandchildren and their younglings. Hurston's turf was the Deep South; Black's territory is Chicago's Bronzeville.

Timuel Black, one of Chicago's most eminent educators, has for the past several years, in the manner of an old-time family doctor, paid house calls on old friends, some of whom were schoolmates, as well as the generation of their children. In so doing, he has "turned the corners of my mind" in rekindling some of his own memories as well.

It is a revelatory work, exploring hitherto uncharted territory: an oral history from unexpected sources. When St. Clair Drake and Horace Cayton gave us the classic *Black Metropolis*, they astonished us in revealing the history of Chicago's black South Side community, its "Black Belt." What Black has done, in informal conversations, is enthrall us with the long-buried memories of living individuals, some barely surviving, others still feisty and full of salt. Chicago, for the great many arrivals from the South, was, in the words of the old spiritual, the "City Called Heaven." It was the place where you needn't step off the sidewalk if a white passed by; the place where there were jobs in the stockyards and steel mills. It was in the blues Jimmy Rushing sang: "I'm goin' to Chicago, sorry I can't take you. . . ." Of course, they did come with families, bag and baggage, riding the day coaches of the Illinois Central. They came to Bronzeville by the thousands, multitudes, enriching the remarkable community with song as well as muscle, with art as well as the strong arm; but, mostly, with hope that their children would be better off than they had ever been.

In so many instances, despite one barrier or another they "got over." But it was a hard road, a long haul. The city was not what they had in their fond dreams envisioned. There was a race riot in 1919 when a black kid was stoned to death for

swimming in white waters. It was a city of restrictive covenants, of official brutish-
ness, of less than benign neglect. Yet, with miraculous obstinacy, they "got over."

What makes Tim Black's oral history so compelling are the memories that surprise. One that especially fascinated me was the remembrance of Wayman Hancock
(the father of Herbie Hancock, the gifted and celebrated musician). Of his family's
migration to Chicago, he says, "They were strikebreakers." It was during the days
when the stockyards and the steel mills were flourishing; when the industrial unions
were being formed; when the owners fought them tooth, nail, and with scabs. (What
is so beautifully ironic is that many of the African-Americans so imported subsequently became some of the most fervent union advocates and leaders.)

What further holds me in this work is that most of the subjects are not the blue
collars, but doctors, lawyers, bankers, judges, businesspeople—"successful." Yet, in
the telling of the tales, there have always been those obstacle courses to overcome,
the indelible racism to surmount. What Tim Black has succeeded in telling us is
that the barriers are still there, especially for the new arrivals from the rural South,
strangers in a strange land.

As Alex Haley, in putting *Roots* together, visited Gambia, the home of his fore-
bears, and spoke to the griots, the storytellers, so Tim Black has revisited his home-
land, Chicago, and found a mother lode with his griots.

INTRODUCTION

"What was ain't no is no mo'"—that's what my ex-slave grandmother used to say. Sometimes it meant one thing—sometimes it meant another, but whenever she spoke those words, my parents listened, and I did too. It's been a while—a long, long while—since I've heard her voice, but somehow, even today, if I listen very carefully, I can still hear an echo of those words I first heard when I myself was very young. Many things have changed, and the voices that I hear are not her voice, but they are voices that in these passing years have also come to mean so very much to me.

Even when I listen to a popular song such as "The Way We Were" as it was interpreted by Gladys Knight, I hear not only the voice of the singer herself but also our voices—the voices of all the people I knew and still know—and now I want to share those voices with you and also with your children's children so that they will be able to hear what I heard and know what once was known not only to me but to an entire community as well.

Every time I think about my grandmother's words or hear a song sung in a certain way, my mind drifts back to the old neighborhood in Chicago that I grew up in, once called the "Black Belt" or the "Black Metropolis" and now popularized as "Bronzeville." Call it what you will, it was and is characterized descriptively and accurately as "a place populated mostly by people of African-American descent." Its boundaries at present are roughly Twenty-sixth Street on the north, Sixty-seventh Street on the south, Cottage Grove on the east, and the Dan Ryan Expressway on the west.

Yes, just as the song says, certain memories of people and places still "light the corners of my mind." Through the years I was fortunate enough to have many friends, but several stand out among all the others as being my closest friends. Their names are William "Billy Boy" Green, who later became the first black agent for the U.S. Internal Revenue Service, Carl Cotton, who became a highly regarded taxidermist at the Field Museum (also maybe a first for a black at any major museum), and Charles White, who became a graphic artist of national acclaim. But the guys that I had the most fun with in my world of "the way we were" were Carl "Carlos the Cool" Caldwell, Cleophas "Tally Ho" Smith, Robert "Bob" Carroll, Lonnie Young,

Lester Reed, and Albert "Al" Ingram. We all grew up together. We all "hung out" together. We all played softball, hardball, basketball, football, and tennis together. A little later we used to hang out in "Dad's Very Safe Poolroom" together. If one of the guys did not have enough money—and that "one guy" was usually me—to go to the places we wanted to go, the other guys would "pot-up" so that he would not miss the fun. Since none of us in those early days had cars of our own, we either walked or caught one of the jitney cabs that ran up and down the Strip, and we spent our spare time just being together walking, talking, laughing, and sometimes attempting to whistle in harmonic parts that sounded almost perfect to our untrained ears.

Sometimes there were demonstrations of rivalry in some of the more tawdry hangouts such as one of the dance halls or poolrooms, but other members on both sides of those conflicts were usually there to make certain that matters got settled peaceably. Even as rivals, we all knew each other through school, sports, and other activities. Perhaps it was not perfect, but we had a lot of fun in those days. As teenagers most of us worked not only to have money for our fun but also to supplement our parents' meager incomes—as far as we were concerned all income was family income. Some would say we were poor, but we were never "poverty stricken." We knew "the sun was going to shine in our back door someday." That was the way we were.

It is in respect for those memories that I decided in 1988 to record and preserve some of the recollections of people who have lived in Chicago for a long time. Psychologists tell us that the mind's recollection of the past is necessarily selective, and its tendency is always to choose only the most pleasant of those past memories and experiences, unconsciously avoiding the pain of recalling the ones that are unpleasant. Nonetheless, I have chosen to believe that these recollections of "the way we were" should endeavor to be a mixture of both the pleasant and the unpleasant. As a matter of fact, it seems to me that these two aspects of experience complement each other and that both are necessary for a complete understanding of what life is all about.

The demand for me to do some writing on this subject came from my two children, about twenty years ago, when they both came to me and said, "Dad, you have been so active and done so much, why don't you write a book about your life?" They then handed me a pen and a legal-sized pad with which to start the process. Because I was so busy with my teaching and social-action activities, however, I kept putting it off until, at my retirement dinner in March of 1989, my fellow members of Black Faculty in Higher Education issued me a check and a challenge to go ahead and write the book. The check as well as the challenge propelled me to buy an almost obsolete word processor with which to begin what I was certain would prove to be an arduous task.

It may seem to be a bit too sentimental to some, but it is very important to me to give recognition to the fact that the driving force and deciding factor in making this renewed commitment to this project was a conversation with my son, Timuel Kerrigan Black, when he revealed to me that his HIV infection had turned into AIDS. Immediately after informing me about this tragic situation, he attempted to be cheerful and asked me, "Dad, how are you coming along with that book?" He died from kidney failure due to AIDS on March 8, 1993, and now I realize I must finish this work as I promised him that I would. He was a fine son, and I cherish his memory and will always miss him so much.

Another force driving me along toward the completion of this project has been the realization, as I talk to more and more young black people under the age of forty, of just how little they know of the interesting, important, and somewhat glorious past history of the life of black people in Chicago during the 1920s, 1930s, 1940s, and even the 1950s and 1960s. All life for this present generation seems to have started when they were born, and their experience is focused entirely on the present and those places where they are now living, those activities they are currently in the midst of doing, and those events they have most recently seen on television. What better way to broaden their knowledge and understanding and possibly even their vision of what life might be than to hear or read about the full spectrum of experience from those who have already lived it and have survived to talk about it in clear and meaningful detail? In these conversations there will be found some valuable learning experiences that deal with the transition from an evil, unequal, and very often brutal South to a very often evil, unequal, and psychologically brutal North. How does one survive and stay humane and sane in such an environment? Black people of my generation learned these particular lessons from their parents, as well as older relatives, friends, and neighbors, and then they modified that information they had received to fit the specifics of their own immediate needs. It is a truism and also a fact that "there is nothing new under the sun," but just a change and difference in form and style. It seems to me that, back in high school, my freshman physical science class taught me that in ultimate reality nothing is created and nothing is destroyed—it only changes in form. It is those "changes in form" that continue to be such a fascinating field for both study and active participation.

The goal that I set for myself in this oral history project was to do a series of interviews with a relatively large number of people who grew up in Chicago. The purpose was to create a full and representative range of subjective information that all of us can review, examine, criticize, modify, or even reject. This process of personal evaluation may serve to help the present and future generations to understand the distinctive qualities of the individual lives as well as the collective life of black folk in Chicago, whether it be organized, unorganized, or even disorganized.

It is important to note and understand that much of the physical history of black Chicago—"Black Metropolis" or "Bronzeville" if you prefer—has been destroyed by the wrecker's ball. Places such as the Regal, the Savoy, the Vendome, Poro College, the YWCA, and many other monuments of both physical historical significance and treasured personal memory have been erased. In most cases nothing but vacant lots remain. All are gone—yes, all are gone except in the individual and collective memories of those of my generation who saw and enjoyed them. How could we know as much as we do about Egyptian, Greek, or Roman civilizations if all the places like the pyramids, the Parthenon, and the Colosseum had been totally destroyed? What would still exist as models on which we could build our own towns and cities and places of culture and entertainment? Would we have had to go elsewhere—perhaps to some place as far away as Australia—to learn about the actual process of social and cultural evolution and to study the dynamics of social and cultural organization in relation to social and cultural chaos and breakdown? Ah, but fortunately for all of us the individual and collective memories of every period of life will always continue to be available for our instruction if only we can learn to be wise enough to devise a suitable method for preserving them. The only reason why we know so much about the richness of African life in the distant past is because the storyteller or griot was given the responsibility for carrying the experiences, traditions, and expectations of both the past and present on to the next generation and to generations beyond for all to hear and remember and utilize within the context of their own lives.

In attempting to gain some insight to that past as it pertains to the present and our visions of the future, I am utilizing one of the field techniques developed in cultural anthropology by becoming a "participant observer" as well as an information gatherer. I have selected individuals that I believe are well informed and articulate about their own lives and also the physical, social, and cultural environment that has surrounded and still surrounds them. This approach, which anthropologists call the "emic" approach, allows the person being interviewed to carve out the rules of the interview as he or she desires by determining according to his or her point of view the time, the place, the length, and the number of permissible interruptions that will occur during the conversation, as well as, if desired, the right to ask the interviewer certain personal and specific questions. In this type of process the interviewer makes no personal judgmental comment on the interviewee's point of view or style of narration. He simply encourages the conversational flow or at most asks leading questions. "Uh-huh," "My Lord," and "Can you imagine that?" are pretty good examples of this technique, which is also my own personal way of assuring the interviewee that I am very interested in what he or she is telling me and that I want to know more. As a matter of fact, this process is almost like encouraging gossip. The idea is to come as close as possible to an informed but informal conversation between friends, and in this regard it is important to understand that I have known the majority of my interviewees most of their lives and most of my own as well. Because of this, they are usually quite comfortable, honest, and candid with me. After all, we have shared the same time span of life in the same community. We are all active participants in the same general African-American social, economic, religious, and political culture. More specifically we are all African-Americans who have grown up in Chicago and have shared much of the same experiences inside the ghetto as well as the challenges outside of it.

For an outsider, in order to get the same or even similar results, this task would be much more difficult—if not impossible. My friend Leon Dash, a veteran journalist on the staff of the *Washington Post*, tells me that it took him four years to get the real facts behind the Rosa Lee story that recently won him a Pulitzer prize in reporting. The reason for this was that, even though he is an African-American, he was considered to be an outsider to that community. In other words, he had to earn and gain the confidence and respect of the people that lived in that depressed section of Washington, D.C., before they would stop lying to him about their lives and come forth with what was really the truth. Fortunately for us all, he was a sympathetic participant observer who had patience and took the necessary time to wait for those true stories to emerge.

I have the advantage of having already put in my "four years plus" before asking any of my interviewees to tell me their stories. As a matter of fact, I have personally lived through many of their stories myself. Much of what they say is at least part of my own story as well. I am quite fortunate that in growing up I hung out with all kinds of people, and apparently I was acceptable to them, so they responded to my request for taping our conversations willingly and enthusiastically. I think they wanted our story to be told by an insider, someone they knew and had known for a long, long time.

This work, *Bridges of Memory*—and it is work—is also a labor of love for me. In essence it is not really about the economic, social, or cultural history of black Chicago, because for me those are secondary considerations, though not unimportant. This work is a collection of the oral memories of some of the people who participated in helping to make and shape those institutions as the result of their opportunities or lack thereof. Each of these sets of recollections reveals the specifics of personal struggle for survival in what was very often a hostile environment. These individuals and their predecessors did not come to Chicago with institutional development in mind. They and their families came to Chicago in order to escape from an oppressive, restrictive environment in the South of the United States. They did bring certain valuable experiences and skills with them, but mostly they brought their hopes and dreams for what they hoped would be a better world for themselves, their children, and those who would follow in future generations. Therefore, what I have done and am doing is not to study set categories of institutional development, but instead to record and examine the strategies for survival that have been developed by certain specific categories of people during the course of their lives.

The first of these categories is composed of people of my own generation or older who ranged roughly at the time of their interviews from sixty-five to one hundred years old. It was necessary for me to do these interviews quickly because we are all moving along, and for some of us time is already at a premium. By now I have already recorded on audiotape over 125 of these conversations, and, of course, there remain many, many more people with whom I would like to speak. It is my understanding that Steven Spielberg has a project in which he has been able to videotape interviews with 75,000 of the remaining 300,000 survivors of the Holocaust. I only wish I had his time, talent, and money because my own people are survivors of another kind of historical holocaust that will also be lost if their voices are not recorded in significant depth and detail.

The second category is composed of individuals from the generation after that first generation, ranging at the time of their interviews approximately from thirty-five to sixty years of age. This includes the so-called baby boomers and the youngsters who were teenagers during the days of what is loosely labeled the "civil rights movement." Many of these younger people are former students of mine.

The third category is the children of that second generation. As it stands, I know quite a bit more about those first two generations. In regard to this third generation, which may prove to be the most interesting of them all, I must admit that at present I know almost nothing at all, and as yet no one else does either.

At this point, in regard to the information that has been gathered, I have not attempted to develop any specific social scientific theories, and I have not made any firm and final judgments or evaluations, but I am convinced that eventually certain definable conclusions about personal, family, community, and institutional indicators will emerge from the content and context of these interviews. That's where the scholars may want to take over and make their own kind of contribution. Maybe even I will attempt to become a scholar myself at that point when it occurs sometime in the not-too-distant future.

BRIDGES
of
MEMORY

WILLIS THOMAS

CIVIL RIGHTS AND LABOR LEADER

I first met Willis Thomas in 1957 at DuSable High School at the annual Chicago election of local NAACP officers. After the 1954 U.S. Supreme Court decision of Brown v. Kansas Board of Education outlawing de jure *segregation in public schools, there was a great social movement determined to eliminate all* de facto *forms of racial segregation that were still existing all over the United States in our local public schools. The nominal leader of the group in Chicago that was dedicated to achieving this goal was the late Willoughby Abner, who was president of the local chapter of the NAACP and also a Midwest regional official for the United Automobile Workers. As a result of the escalating social, educational, and political pressures of that time, with the active support of Mr. Thomas's hotel and dining car waiters' union and several other local union groups as well as other advocates for public school desegregation, Mr. Abner organized picket lines around Mayor Richard J. Daley's City Hall and the central office of the Chicago Board of Education. In doing this, he hoped to highlight the fact that the mayor, more than any other individual, was responsible for the current state of affairs by his choosing segregationist Benjamin Willis to replace integrationist Herold C. Hunt as the general superintendent of Chicago Public Schools. Daley's immediate response to this was to gather together all of the black political and religious forces that were dependent on his Democratic "machine" for patronage and prestige and get them to take out a massive number of memberships in the local branch of the NAACP in order to overpower Mr. Abner and his colleagues from within their own organization. As the result of this strategy,*

Daley's forces won, and the NAACP's former militancy in Chicago was transformed into another political tool for Daley's use, thereby rendering the NAACP ineffective for fighting the racial problems that still existed for black people in Chicago.

Although Willis Thomas had been solidly on the side of Mr. Abner in that struggle, he continued to remain active in the NAACP, working as best he could to help that organization recover its lost strength and promise. It never happened, and from that 1957 takeover by Daley's forces until the present, the Chicago chapter of the NAACP has never again been the force for equality and social justice that it was before that '57 election of its Daley-sponsored officers.

Undeterred, Mr. Thomas has continued to work vigorously as a civil rights and labor leader here in Chicago and on the national level as well.

———

TB: I'm honored, Mr. Thomas, I'm really honored to have you willing to spend some time with me. Mr. Thomas, what I'm trying to do is to recapture in their own words as much of people's lives as they care to talk about, so let's go ahead and talk about where you were born and some of your early childhood experiences that you would like to share.

WT: Well, I was born in 1903.

TB: So you're now ninety-two years of age.

WT: Yes, ninety-two.

TB: My gracious!

WT: And how old are you?

TB: I'm seventy-six. I've been around a little while too!

WT: And you'll be around for a long time. Hopefully.

TB: Yes, I hope that I can match you. Where were you born?

WT: In Arkansas.

TB: And what part of Arkansas were you from?

WT: Helena.

TB: Helena! I was in the army with several fellows from Helena.

WT: Oh, is that right? Well, there in Helena my father was what they called a "planter." They called farmers "planters" at that time *if* they employed others. That is, if they had other people working on their farms with them. If it was less than that and just their own families were working the land, then they called them "sharecroppers." But my father, he always had control over large farms, you know.

TB: What were your early educational experiences like?

WT: Well, we lived in a rural area, and the local schools were very poor, and to go to a private school was very difficult.

TB: So you lived outside of Helena, and it was a rural environment. What kind of crops did you grow?

WT: Cotton and rice.

TB: Anything else?

WT: Yes, livestock.

TB: Was your father born in Helena?

WT: Yes, both my mother and father were born there.

TB: How old were they when they passed?

WT: They both were around seventy.

TB: So they had relatively long lives for people living at that time.

WT: That's right. There was a lack of hospitals and very few doctors—so you had to be healthy in order to survive.

TB: Were there any doctors who were black?

WT: There were only a few black doctors, but at least there were some.

TB: Well, you must have come from good stock, as is indicated by your parents and yourself as well!

[*Laughter.*]

WT: Yes, and I think they stayed healthy because of all the things that *weren't* available. What they ate was mostly fresh and wholesome.

TB: How many brothers and sisters did you have?

WT: Oh, I had three brothers and two sisters—so there were four boys and two girls. My oldest brother, George, when he died, his age was probably sixty-five or so. And my kid brother died here in Chicago at about forty-five or fifty.

TB: How long did you stay in Helena? What age were you when you left?

WT: Oh, about twenty.

TB: So you left about 1923.

WT: Yes, that's right.

TB: Why did you leave?

WT: Well, my sister went to Omaha, and she married a man there, and she praised it as a place to live because she liked it so well. At that time I had just about finished high school, and I liked what I heard of what she had to say about the opportunities that were there. My mother also encouraged me to go there because her hope was always that I was going to be a college professor, and I promised my mother that I would—so I said, "Well, I'll go with my sister to Omaha, and I'll finish my high school education at Central High School—and then I'm sure I'll be able to qualify for Tuskegee." Tuskegee was the place where I wanted to go and complete my education.

TB: You promised your mother that you would stay in school?

WT: Yes, I was considered a very bright student in those days and was expected to finish high school as head of the class—the class valedictorian and so forth—but, anyway, to make a long story short, my brother was also living in Omaha at this time, and he was working as a "captain" in a restaurant and already making a pretty good living for himself. One day he asked me to come on down to the restaurant, and when I got there, I liked what I saw, and they offered me a job, and I accepted. I'd never heard of people making the kind of money they offered me, and, of course, there were also tips and other benefits—so I said to myself, "Well, I'll just skip this one semester at Central High, and then I'll go back to school. After I graduate, then I'll go down to Tuskegee and satisfy my mother," and also, of course, satisfy my own great desire to further my education.

TB: Those were your plans. What actually happened?

WT: Well, they had given me a "co-captain-ship" at the restaurant, and I was doing so well that one day when I passed by this showroom where they sold new Fords and Lincolns, I walked right in there and decided to buy a car. By then, my wages were increased, and, of course, there were those gratuities as well—so I could afford to do what I was doing, but when the salesman asked me about my age, and I told him I was nineteen, he said, "Well, I can't sell you a car!" And I said, "Why not? I've got the money." And he said, "Because you're not of age, young man. Where's your father? He'll have to sign the papers for you." So I went back home, and I told Dad, and he said, "See, I told you—you're not a man yet."
[*Laughter.*]
And I said, "But I've got the money." And he said, "I appreciate that. I really do. You're doing all right—but money isn't everything, and you're still, you know, not a man yet." But, even so, he went down with me to the showroom and signed the notes!

TB: And this is in 1924, 1925, around that time?

WT: Yes, so I thought I had just about all the money I needed, and I wanted to go right on being a waiter.

TB: Yes, I can understand.

WT: And I did quite well. As a matter of fact, I did *exceptionally* well. There was a broker—Mr. Botham—who was a regular customer at the restaurant and, as a result of his request, the management of the restaurant selected me as a "special" waiter.

TB: Now, as a "special" waiter, you mean you were selected to wait on special parties?

WT: Yes.

TB: What you might call "the big shots"!

WT: That's it! Now you have it!
[*Laughter.*]

And this same man—Mr. Botham—he traveled a lot in his work, and he came through Chicago one time on his way back to Omaha, and when I saw him, he said, "Willis, you know, I stopped at that place called the Palmer House, and that guy that used to be the captain here at this restaurant is now the catering manager there at the Palmer House, and he says that those guys that are working there, they are really making a lot of money." Well, that sounded interesting to me, but I said, "Oh, I can't go to Chicago. I understand it's very difficult to get a job there. Jobs are pretty scarce." So he said, "Well, I travel around quite a bit, and the next time I have to go to New York or whatever, I'll stop over in Chicago and check things out." And so he stopped at the Palmer House on his way back from Omaha, and the man there says, "Well, of course, I remember Willis. Have him come over here, and I'll see what I can do for him." So I came to Chicago. Got the job and went right to work.

TB: What year was this when you first came to Chicago?

WT: I guess that was in the forties, and the first year I was there, they had a system at that time in which, no matter what category of work you were in, the management used to give you a gold button for courtesy and efficiency. But one of the requirements for this was, you had to have at least one year of employment before you could qualify—and you still might not get one even after your tenth or fifteenth year or whatever because you had to have at least "X" number of customers who would say, "I like this man or this woman, this girl or this boy, because they are courteous, and in my opinion they seem to do a very good job. Their work speaks well for the Palmer House." And the first year that I was there I won that gold medal!

[*Laughter.*]

TB: And that was because you met all of those qualifications.

WT: Of course, but at that time you also had discrimination there in the Palmer House between black and white, if they were waiters and waitresses or cooks or anybody else—and to get this award, everyone had to qualify on that one same basis. The only restriction, you know, was that you had to have been there at least one year.

TB: My observation was that most of the waiters at the Palmer House at that time were blacks.

WT: Yes, that is correct.

TB: You know I went there myself in those early days—not too many times, only occasionally—and I used to marvel as to how efficient and courteous they all were and the sense of pride they seemed to have about working in that place. And apparently they were doing fairly well financially because some of them had children, and most of those children went to college.

WT: Also you must keep in mind that there was discrimination almost everywhere, which made it very difficult to get a job of any kind, let alone a *good* job. They were hard to find—and if you didn't get on the railroad—

[*Laughter.*]

And even most of our black lawyers, they all started somewhere along that line, working for the railroad, because there was really nothing else. What I mean is you couldn't go into your father's insurance company.

TB: No.

WT: And you couldn't get a partnership in your father's bank.

TB: That's right. So what you're saying is that the Palmer House was not only a stepping stone but also in its own way a kind of elitist situation for the people that were working there.

WT: Yes, it really was. And then, eventually, we started talking about organizing the people working at the Palmer House. For better pay, to get better wages and benefits, you need to form a union—and so I spoke with A. Philip Randolph and several others about what we should do to get started.

TB: This was still in the forties?

WT: Yes, it was. Well, history moves on, but there were a lot of misunderstandings about what we were doing.

TB: In attempting to unionize?

WT: Yes, and the things that they did to me personally at that time—

TB: It was a hard time.

WT: Yes, you see at that time a substantial number, maybe even a majority, of black people who were working in America in hotels and restaurants, they felt that by forming a nondiscriminatory union I was taking jobs away from the black people and giving those jobs to the whites. But what they didn't understand was that, in reality, I was taking from the whites and giving increased opportunities to the blacks! When they said that the white guys were going to be taking their jobs, what they didn't seem to realize was that the white guys *already* had the best jobs, and they had the best jobs because you had a discriminatory situation—and that had to change!

TB: And because of what you did, it changed.

WT: Yes, but you can never get people to accept change—changes of any sort—unless they can identify with a common interest.

TB: That's right.

WT: But, when I first came to Chicago, at that time in the hotels black waiters and white waiters just didn't work together.

TB: It wasn't allowed by the management.

WT: And, of course, in the South, blacks and whites, they didn't even drink out of the same water fountain — but it's not that way today.

TB: Yes, and it was people like you who helped to change all of that.

WT: We *did* change it!

TB: That's right.

WT: We *did* change things.

TB: Yes, you did.

WT: And now, today, you have black workers and white workers all working together in the same room.

TB: Yes.

WT: And every man working in every hotel in Chicago has a pension.

TB: And that was not so before.

WT: No, not until we negotiated a contract in which *all* employees — whether white or black or green — anybody that works in a hotel or restaurant now gets a pension; and that is because of the contract that I negotiated with Colonel Crown down in his house in Evanston.

TB: Colonel Henry Crown?

WT: Yes, Henry Crown. Not his son, but the old man, and we became friends, and one time when we had lunch together, he said, "You know, Willis, nobody — not a single white man — has ever before invited me to his house for a meal." And then later on he invited me to come to New York City and stay at the Waldorf.

TB: At that time he was on the board of directors of the Waldorf-Astoria, wasn't he?

WT: Yes, and when I got there, they put me in a suite that was right next to where General MacArthur was staying.

TB: You had a suite just off from where MacArthur had his?

WT: Yes, and remember: I'm just a boy from Arkansas!

[*Laughter.*]

But, you know, right now black people, they're back in the streets again, and now it's about issues such as affirmative action, and you get people like Jesse Jackson speaking up and saying, "The jails are going to get filled tonight." But, well, now, in my opinion, you're not making any progress by filling the jails. They've already filled the jails with black men! As a matter of fact, now it's mostly blacks that are in those jails.

TB: And relatively few whites.

WT: That's right, in the past we, blacks, were placed in jail because we were denied our civil rights — but now we have our civil rights. We can vote now. We can do many other things.

TB: And we no longer have to go to jail to change things!

WT: Absolutely!

TB: You can change things now because you have struggled to obtain the right. Even now, you—as an individual—might still have only a little bit of power, but if all those little bits of power are put together, then it becomes collective power—which is what the union movement was—and in that way, eventually, you can bring about all the changes that you believe are necessary.

WT: That's right.

TB: Now, when the civil rights movement emerged, you met Dr. King, didn't you?

WT: Yes, I met Dr. King.

TB: And that was important—that was *very* important—because as I look at it the civil rights movement is a continuation of the labor movement in many ways.

WT: Yes, but in my remembrance the majority of Martin Luther King's active supporters were not labor people.

TB: Yes, that's true, particularly in the South.

WT: In fact, I don't think that there was any outstanding union support for Dr. King—except, of course, from the Pullman porters.

TB: Led by A. Philip Randolph.

WT: That's right, and then there were some other labor guys who were really outstanding in terms of raising funds.

TB: Yes, guys like Charley Hayes over at the packinghouse who helped raise some money. Later on, you got involved in real estate, didn't you?

WT: Well, when I went to California, I made a couple of very valuable purchases of what they call "units" out there.

TB: Here we call them "apartment buildings."

WT: Yes, and what Dempsey Travis was trying to do was to get me to stay with him in real estate, but I felt that I had done well enough already.

TB: Yes, but, perhaps, you as a person with some experience in real estate development wouldn't mind commenting on the fact that at least a third of all the land on the old "Black Belt" here on the South Side is now vacant and belongs to the city. And I'm also beginning to notice that most of our black-owned real estate companies are no longer in existence—except for those owned by Dempsey and maybe a couple of others.

WT: It that right?

TB: Yes, almost all of them are gone—retired or whatever—and nobody has picked up the slack. You can just walk up and down the street now on King Drive or Michigan Avenue and see all those beautiful old brownstones and graystones standing empty and deserted.

WT: Yes, that's true.

TB: And much of the neighborhood is emptied out because the gangs have chased all of the good people away. Now it is wide open, and I wonder why wouldn't some young black professionals—or nonprofessionals but experienced people—come back here and start redeveloping that area?

WT: Well, up until recently, you could buy those properties inexpensively by the block, but now I don't think much of anything is still available anymore. I think that some young white guys—along with their friends and parents—have just about taken all of it up for themselves.

TB: It's sad for me to see such a great opportunity taken away once again by white real estate speculators and developers.

WT: What has happened to this new generation? Maybe you know. We paid the price. We were there. We are *still* here. But where are they? What are they doing with their lives?

TB: They're confused—even those that have Ph.D.s and master's degrees and M.B.A.s. They seem to have lost their sense of identity—both as individual people and as members of a group—and now they're busy chasing something that they will never obtain. Every time they buy a big car, they want to buy another bigger car, and it becomes popular for everyone to get a bigger car like that—so you're never going to get in front of the game.

WT: It sounds like they don't understand the system.

TB: Yes, that's it. They don't understand the system *at all*.

WT: They don't understand either the *economics* of the system or the *politics* of it, but I understand *both*, and I was prepared to pay the price on my end for what needed to be done.

TB: Yes, you did, and we all should be grateful to you for what you accomplished.

July 23, 1995

WARREN KIRKLAND
(AND MR. RHODES)

STREET-SAVVY CHICAGOAN

I met Mr. Kirkland through the recommendation of his daughter, who is a success-ful investment broker. As indicated in this narration, he was living in a privately owned senior citizens retirement home, where most of the other residents were white. (Musician Herbie Hancock's parents also lived in that same complex.) The build-ing is located in a southwest suburb quite near to Chicago. However, since most of the residents are aged, and sometimes physically infirm, very few are able to leave the retirement home to go anywhere. Mr. Kirkland voiced his discomfort at being confined to a place that, though physically comfortable, was what he termed a rather racist social environment. As indicated in his narrative, Mr. Kirkland was a man of quick temper and very strong personal and racial feelings. His growing up in Chicago and his early experiences as a streetwise operator gives one the impression of a strong-willed man with great personal courage and a deeply felt commitment to his family and to his race.

His account of one of his encounters with the law gives an idea of his style and temperament. Because of my interest in the way he related his past and present life, I wanted to do another session with him, but to my great regret he passed before that was possible. Mr. Rhodes just had a few comments to make and then he was inter-rupted and "shooed" away by Mr. Kirkland.

TB: How long have you been out here, Mr. Kirkland?

WK: Almost two years. This is a nice place you know, but, hell, me — I don't have no car, and transportation is bad, you know. When you are not accustomed to shit like this, it's just hard.

TB: Where were you living before you moved out here?

WK: At Seventy-ninth and King Drive. I lived there for over forty years.

TB: And Mr. Rhodes, how long have you been here?

R: Oh, I've only been here a little over six months.

TB: So this is new for you too. I'm going to have to come back to talk with you a little bit. You must know a lot about Chicago.

R: Oh, I've been here practically all my life.

TB: And how old are you now?

R: Eighty-seven.

TB: Mr. Kirkland, where were you born?

WK: I was born in the city of Chicago.

TB: Now, Mr. Kirkland, when you were born, where did your folks live at that time?

WK: At Thirty-first Street and Rhodes.

TB: Do you remember what that neighborhood was like back then?

WK: Yeah, we were living in a two-flat building in a cold-water apartment.

TB: "Cold-water apartments" — that means you had to heat your water to take a bath.

WK: And sometimes you had to take a bath in the kitchen.

TB: In a big old tin tub — a "galvanized" tub.

WK: And we had a few relatives who lived around there. One of then, his name was Montgomery. You might have heard of him.

TB: Yeah, I might have heard the name.

WK: Well, he sold ice and wood, and he rented horses. He also sold moonshine down there around Thirty-seventh and Rhodes.

TB: Are you a native of Chicago too, Mr. Rhodes?

R: No, I'm from Iowa.

TB: OK, well, I'm in good luck to be talking with gentlemen of your generation who didn't come here from down in the South.

WK: Don't make no difference where you come from. You'd be surprised how people holler about prejudice and everything, and you'd figure it was the whites that was prejudiced against us, but we are also prejudiced against ourselves. In fact, you have more blacks that's more prejudiced, and they're ignorant on top of that! But you got more poor people than you got any nationality in the world. They are all over, and they immigrate them all to here. We always get the bullshit. Even out here. What I mean is that the government has this contract, and they are all of them fighting over it now.

TB: Over Social Security?

WK: Yes, Medicare and all that.

TB: All of that's up for grabs.

WK: That's because it's 90 percent Republicans now. We don't have no backers any-more, and everybody is stealing.

TB: And the rich are getting richer.

WK: That's because they stick together on every damned thing. It ain't too much you can do.

TB: What about education?

WK: Years ago, when I was going to school, they didn't give a damn whether you went or not so long as they had a quota there so that the state government would pay them for the kids.

TB: What was the first school you went to?

WK: I went to Willard.

TB: At Forty-ninth and St. Lawrence. I went to Willard too.

WK: Then you ought to know me, man!

TB: Well, I'm a little younger. Pretty soon I jumped across the boulevard and wound up at Burke. You remember Burke School at Fifty-fourth and what was then South Park? We probably know some of the same people.

WK: Do you know Papa's at Fifty-eighth and Prairie? That's where Dave Sanders and them niggers were over there, man. Red's Tavern is still down there. He's my buddy, and all them — what you call them? — "entertainers," they used to drop in there at Thelma's. Even Lena Horne. You wouldn't think that neighborhood was ever the way it once was. Even the Willard School is boarded up now.

TB: Yes, it's boarded up. I don't know what they are going to do with it.

WK: Remember that building down there at Fifty-eighth and Indiana where they had Chinese food?

TB: Yes, they called it Round the Alley.

WK: Yeah, Round the Alley. It was a light brick building.

TB: Duke and all the musicians used to stop in there when they were in town.

R: That was right on the corner at Prairie. We used to go upstairs there and gamble. They had a poolroom upstairs, and, boy, it was something! What was the name of that cop who used to be around there?

TB: Two-Gun Pete.

R: That's right. Two-Gun Pete! Guys would hang around out in front, and then someone would say, "Two-Gun Pete, I want this corner cleared."

TB: And he'd get it cleared too.

R: But then, when he'd come upstairs, we'd be shooting dice on the pool table, and he would leave us alone. I remember one time Two-Gun Pete arrested ten guys over here on Forty-eighth Street, and he marched them from Forty-eighth and Cottage Grove all the way to the police station at Forty-eighth and Wabash. They were marching along all ten of them, and Pete was in the back. Then, when they got to the station, they marched right in, and the sergeant said, "What do you guys want?" That's when they looked back behind them, and old Pete ain't nowhere to be seen!

TB: He told them to go, and they just went.

R: That's right. They were too scared to look back.

TB: That's because they knew that Pete would shoot them if they did!

R: Then there was that guy Joe—what's his name—who had that poolroom on Fifty-fifth?

WK: The Chicago Poolroom—that's where old Pete used to go in there and whip niggers on the head.

TB: All that's probably been torn down now.

R: No, it's not torn down.

WK: The Arabs got a grocery store right there where it was at Fifty-fifth.

TB: Well, before that, that's where the Twentieth Ward Organization used to be. That was Ken Campbell and those guys, but upstairs there used to be a place called the Golden Lily, didn't there?

R: The Golden Lily, yeah. I couldn't think of that till now.

TB: There was so much going on back then. Down the street was the Rhumboogie.

WK: Back then the Jones boys were over there on Forty-seventh where the Apollo Theater was. They had a regular casino there, and they had a bad nigger from St. Louis, St. Louis Kelly. He was the bouncer over there at their gambling house.

TB: St. Louis Kelly, he had quite a reputation for being a rough kind of guy.

WK: That's right. Later on he went over to the DeLisa. And over there at Vincennes and the alley where the Jones boys had their five-and-dime store. When I was a kid, that used to be where the Bowman Dairy kept the horses that they used to deliver milk. That was over on the north side of the street, and I used to go work there in the morning and deliver milk for them. I had one of them bikes with a big basket on it, and I could deliver their milk all over their damned streets from Hyde Park all the way to Cottage Grove. Back then, you would go anywhere, and you weren't ever bothered by nobody taking your butt off.

TB: When you tell kids today about delivering milk, they don't even know what you're talking about.

WK: Well, I don't see how in the hell people could have forgotten all these things.

TB: So, back then, before and after school you were out there making money whenever you could without getting into any kind of trouble.

WK: Yeah, but you know sometimes you have to take a rap for a person.

TB: Yeah, I sure do. I know a guy by the name of Bobby Redcross who took something for Billy Eckstine when he had some trouble.

WK: Eckstine was a syndicate man back then before he played for Earl Hines. I never will forget some of the records he made: "Jelly, Jelly," "Break My Mama's Stove Down." Back in them days, entertainers like him and even Duke or Louis Armstrong, they didn't have no place to stay. A lot of them musicians weren't even making fifteen dollars a day.

TB: They weren't big time yet. So, after you went to Willard, where did you go to high school?

WK: I went to Phillips and Dunbar, and also Lawson as well. I was always doing things wrong.

TB: Well, a lot of folks were doing things wrong. You weren't by yourself. The Depression was on. What were you doing back then?

WK: I was working for the city, and one time I had a fire on my truck. I don't know how it got started, but sometimes you'd haul stuff like old oil cans and things you ain't supposed to haul. You did that sometimes to make a couple of extra dollars. Well, anyway, the damned thing caught fire, and when you get a fire like that on a truck that belongs to the city, you just get the fire department and let them worry about how to put that fire out—so I called them on a public phone, and this cat down there downtown say he ain't going to put the fire out! So I drove over to the fire station, and I dumped all that mess right there. Man, you should have seen the way it poured! Well, you talk about fast, but you never seen nothing faster than all of them damned white firemen hustling around to their hoses and trying to put that little fire out! We just sat across the street looking at them and enjoying the show.

TB: Now comes the war.

WK: Yes, and when that damned war broke out, now some of those niggers was fighting about why don't they put niggers in the army. That's one hell of a time for Uncle Sam to get himself unprejudiced. It just don't make no sense to me. None at all, and, no matter what happens, you got to have common sense.

TB: Oh, yeah, otherwise you'll just be upset all the time.

WK: And you'll also wind up in a whole lot of trouble. You got to get to know yourself, and you must always act according to yourself and not someone else.

May 22, 1995

THOMAS ELLIS
AND EDITH ELLIS

WOODLAWN RESIDENTS

I met Mr. and Mrs. Ellis while having lunch with my brother at Army & Lou's on East Seventy-fifth Street. They seemed like they would be an extremely interesting couple to have a longer conversation with, and so I scheduled an oral history session with them. They were living in the southwest section of the community of Woodlawn, and they had lived there as husband and wife for many years. This was the neighborhood that the great black scholar E. Franklin Frazier called "the most middle-class Negro community in the country." Maybe the reason that he made that observation was because he had lived in Woodlawn during the period he was a Ph.D. student in sociology at the University of Chicago. At that time (this was in the early thirties), he was not allowed to live in any of the University of Chicago dorms or anywhere else for that matter in either Hyde Park–Kenwood or southeast Woodlawn.

The Ellises were very cordial to me and quite informative about their life together in Chicago, the many prominent friends they have had, and their various life experiences. Those of us who grew up in the Douglas–Grand Boulevard area often tended to think of "Woodlawners" as somewhat snobbish and aloof, as well as more economically fortunate than we who were "strangers" to their neighborhood. We believed back then that people living in Woodlawn were somehow different from us, even though we all went to the same schools and places for entertainment and social affairs, and some of us even had relatives and friends who were living in that neighborhood. This indicates the kind of biases that can develop and accumulate when there is social and physical isolation among people even if they come from the same racial or ethnic background.

TB: I'm speaking to Thomas Ellis, an old school friend of my brother, Walter Black, and to his wife, Edith Ellis. Mrs. Ellis, where were you born?

EE: In Waynesburg, Georgia. That's about thirty miles from Augusta and ninety from Savannah.

TB: If I may be so presumptuous, may I ask you when?

EE: In 1929.

TB: And when did you first come here to Chicago?

EE: Well, I came to visit in '52, and then I went right back home. I came back to Chicago again in '55.

TB: And when were you born, Mr. Ellis?

TE: I was born in 1914.

TB: In 1914! Jesus Christ, you look well! In Chicago?

TE: Yeah, in Chicago.

TB: Your mother and dad, where were they born?

TE: My father was born here in 1882.

TB: He was a native. And your mother?

TE: My mother was born in St. Joseph, Michigan.

TB: That's not so far away. Did you know your grandparents?

TE: I knew my grandparents on my father's side.

TB: Where were they born?

TE: My grandfather was an African. He was a slave. They brought him to Ohio, and that's where he learned a trade. He learned upholstery. That's what he did to earn a living. He passed in 1922. And my grandmother, she was from New Orleans.

TB: Was she born free or in slavery?

TE: She was born free.

TB: But your granddad was from the African continent. He became a slave after being deported. You know, when I was on the island of Goree, off of Dakar, in Senegal, some of the blacks that were there in our group could not bring themselves to set foot on Goree. Their emotions were so strong that they couldn't even look out at it from out on the ocean because they had to face the fact that in earlier days somebody in their ancestry walked out of that portal in chains, never to return, and they just cried, but it wasn't proper for them to do that, and so I said to one girl, "No, you've got to go look at this. You've got to take this back home where you came from. No, you're going to come here and look at this." You can just feel what kind of place it once was while you're there, and, of course, you can't help but get strong feelings. You know your imagination just runs in a certain tragic direction, but you must never forget that one day some of your own ancestors were forced to leave that place in chains.

[There are several moments of silence.]

TB: Well, coming back to you, Mr. Ellis, do you know where you were born in Chicago? What were your first memories of Chicago?

TE: I was born at 4419 Dearborn. My first memories? Let me see. Well, my father worked downtown, and the way the Loop looked in those days, it looked like the sidewalk had little round pieces of glass in it that would reflect the sunlight. I also remember being on the elevated. That was one of my very first memories.

TB: So, even as a child, you used to go downtown?

TE: Yeah, I used to go downtown with my father. My brother and I would go downtown with him on Saturdays while he was working. He was working in a place with a lot of steel balls. I don't know what kind of place it was, but it was up near Van Buren Street.

TB: So how many of you were there in the family?

TE: There was three of us. My youngest brother was born in 1927. My oldest brother was born in 1913. My father bought a home out in Englewood at 6039 May in 1920. That was an all-white area then. Yeah, there wasn't but two black families in that entire block. Back then the black families mostly lived on Ada Street.

TB: Yes, there was always a little patch of black folks who lived in Englewood.

TE: That was on Ada. My auntie was the next black person to move into the neighborhood when she moved in on Aberdeen. That was a Jewish section. See, there was a lot of those little "sections" around there. There were Jews out there, there were Swedes out there, and there were Irish. We used to go to that Jewish church up on the corner near Sixty-first and May on Saturdays. It's not a Jewish church now, but when we were just kids, we used to make fires for Jewish people, who couldn't do anything like that on Saturdays. And then up on the corner of Sixty-first and May there was a Swedish church where we went sometimes with the fellow who lived next door.

TB: So, after you had the initial friction and all, you became friends with all kinds of kids.

TE: Oh, yeah, except we weren't too well liked when we went over to Ogden Park. Wouldn't go into the swimming pool.

TB: Where did you go to school?

TE: We went to Copernicus School. That was all white then.

TB: For me that was foreign territory when I was growing up in the old Grand Boulevard area.

TE: We also moved down into that same area a little later. We moved to 3120 Calumet, right across the street from Ralph Metcalfe's home. We had a good many problems at first with the kids that lived in that neighborhood because we weren't used to playing with black kids, and for a while it looked like they didn't take to us, but Ralph kept things together for us. He was older than us. He was a senior when I went to Tilden in '29.

TB: He had been a track star at Tilden before you got there.

TE: He was well known even then, and he could go anywhere in any of those white-owned stores if he wanted to make a purchase.

TB: So you moved from Englewood to the old Douglas neighborhood. What was that like, as you recall? How old were you then?

TE: I was about eight or nine when I went to Douglas School. Remember the Branham boys, John and Joe? They lived next door to the Olivet Baptist Church. That was when L. K. Williams was pastor. Those little boys would go off and fight white guys too!

TB: Yes, they would. Their father was assistant pastor at Olivet. Joe now has a son of his own who does some work as a curator for the Chicago Historical Society among other things. I remember back then those two brothers used to come back to Phillips all the time just to show off. They were good-looking guys, I suppose, and they were pretty full of themselves. So what was the rest of the neighborhood like back then?

TE: Well, you know, the neighborhood was fairly nice around Thirty-first Street in the area where we lived.

TB: My folks used to have friends who lived in a tall apartment building near there. I don't think it was the Ellis building. It was on that part of Calumet though or maybe it was on South Park. I remember it was a nice place. The neighborhood was nice, except for the guys. They had to get used to you, and you had to get used to them. Do you remember any people from the Douglas neighborhood?

TE: I remember Ernest Griffin. He was in my brother's class. As a matter of fact, he was in his class when they were at Tilden Tech.

TB: Yeah, I recently had an interesting conversation with him. One of his nieces is a doctor—a psychiatrist—in Washington, D.C., and another one, Barbara, was married to Robert Lawrence, the first black astronaut. Remember how he got burned up in a fire about fifteen years ago? It's little noted that this first black guy preceded the black guy who later went up into space by quite a little bit. Ernie himself is quite a guy. He knows a lot of things that most people don't about the Civil War.

TE: Yeah, I know he does. I remember when that family had their funeral establishment on Michigan at Thirty-first Street.

TB: Yes, one of those graystones. Do you happen to remember the South Park Methodist Episcopal Church at Twenty-ninth and Prairie?

TE: Yeah, I used to go down there and play basketball.

TB: Did you play with Willie "Hutch" Hutchinson? Did you know Peter King or any of those guys?

TE: Yeah, Peter King, he was one of my old-time buddies. He liked to play over at Phillips.

TB: He was a little older than me, but he taught me a lot of stuff. He was a nice guy. I was like you—except that I came from Fifty-first Street to play over there at Phillips. I was like a stranger there because I was living "way out south"—at least they thought it was—at Fifty-first and Michigan.

TE: You and I weren't too well taken by those guys.

TB: No, so I had to make friends quick. And I did.

TE: So did I.

TB: As I remember it, the movie house in that neighborhood on the Thirty-first block was called the Avenue, and I used to go there quite a bit. I don't know why, but I went. The Avenue was just a place where many of the young people went all the time.

TE: At one time they used to have vaudeville there.

TB: That's the reason! Now I remember! It was because they had vaudeville there, and I could see some of the things there that I wouldn't be able to see at the Met and, of course, the Regal wasn't built yet.

TE: And also because the Met didn't allow blacks in there.

TB: Not for quite a while, even though we lived nearby in the neighborhood. Did you ever go to the Vendome?

TE: Yes. Erskine Tate was there. They had a pit band.

TB: First time I saw Louis Armstrong was at the Vendome. My mother took us down, and Louis was there. Earl Hines was playing in his band, and Ethel Waters was singing. All those stars-to-be came through there at the Vendome. And then there was the State Theater. Do you remember the Mecca Building and what it was like?

TE: Oh, yeah, that was at Thirty-third and State. I've never been in there, but my father had some friends that used to live there.

TB: It was a nice place. A lot of professional railroad people—some of whom were white—lived there. I've heard that some of those old-timers who were white lived in that neighborhood before blacks began to move in there—that's a long time ago—and they stayed on because they thought of that place as being a kind of architectural gem. Did they have any black teachers at Douglas School at that time?

TE: I don't think so, as I can recall. The first black teachers that I can recall were at Forrestville. We had moved several times. We moved to Thirty-third and Giles.

Then we moved onto Indiana Avenue across from the *Defender*. Then we moved to 4518 Champlain, and that's when I went to Forrestville. But at that time Forrestville only went to sixth grade because they still had the junior high school. I went to that junior high from 1927 to 1930, and I still remember Mrs. Bousfield's daughter because her daughter and I were in the same class. They lived on Forrestville near Forty-sixth Street, the second house from the corner.

TB: Yeah, that was a nice block. That was very much like Washington Park Court. Washington Park Court and Forrestville—those were the high muckety-mucks! [*Laughter.*]

You know, some of the younger people whose grandparents or great-grandparents lived in those blocks are coming back and recovering some of that area. They are renovating it, and now it's beautiful once again. One family I visited had six generations that had lived in there, but then the space was all cut up and divided, and now this woman and her husband have restored it to its original condition. There's just this one family living there now. That house has got about nine rooms and four baths!

TE: The house we lived in at 4518, they've torn that down. As a matter of fact, they tore down most of the buildings in that block when they built that housing development.

TB: And that housing development's right around the corner from what used to be the Grant AME Church that's now on Drexel.

TE: You're not talking about Ebenezer?

TB: Ebenezer also. It had a big congregation back then, and its architecture is still gorgeous. Inside it's beautiful. It's a landmark. So at least they can't tear it down, and that's good! Once that building had been an old synagogue.

TE: That's where we went to Sunday school. My mother taught Sunday school there. You've heard of Gus Mebank, haven't you? He used to be our Sunday school teacher. And back in those times the Regal wasn't there. The Regal didn't come along until 1928, I think.

TB: My brother, Walt, and I and our little gang—we used to roast potatoes in the place where the Regal was later built. It was a vacant lot then. We used to go out to Forty-seventh Street, you know, where the vendors had all the stuff they were selling outside, and we would steal a few potatoes from them—they didn't care. They didn't seem to worry about it.

TE: That's because they couldn't catch you! [*Laughter.*]

TB: Yes, I guess that's what it was! But, anyway, you graduated from Forrestville, and then you went to Phillips. Forrestville was very crowded at that time, wasn't it?

TE: Yes, and it only went to sixth grade.

TB: It was so crowded because back then all of us were moving all the time! First white folks moved out, then black folks would move in. We even had something called "Moving Day," which was in September and sometimes also in April. That's when the white folks would be leaving and the black folks would be coming in. It was kind of prestigious to do that because our community was constantly expanding, and we were always moving farther south.

TE: Yeah, but there were also a lot of pockets where blacks weren't allowed. On Oakwood Boulevard, for instance, there were no blacks. A lot of white schoolteachers lived on Oakwood Boulevard, and a lot of black schoolteachers lived on Thirty-third Street at Cottage Grove. On the corner of Thirty-third and Cottage there was a Greyhound Bus depot, and across the street from that there used to be a little park-like setting for homes that was close to the lake.

TB: That's Groveland Park. That's been restored. It's very nice. A number of people live down there, but I can't remember any names right offhand that you would know. The only one I can think of right now is Jerry Butler, the singer, and his family, but they're not from the South Side. Jerry is originally from the North Side.

TE: The reason I know about that area is because I used to sell the *Defender* in that neighborhood. I can still remember getting my papers from Mrs. Wimp at the *Defender* office—she looked just like a white woman.

TB: The Wimp family, they all looked like they were white, but you knew they weren't because Ed was a colonel in the Eighth Regiment of the Ninety-second Division, which was all black in its composition. His wife, Kay Davis, you know, sang with Duke. She was his last wife. After he passed, she comes back here each year to attend the opera season. That Mrs. Wimp you're talking about was his mother.

TE: This might have been another lady, but, anyway, I would go there, and she would give me the papers in advance.

TB: Oh, that's right, she'd hand out the papers to you, and then you'd bring the money back to her later.

TE: Sometimes if I had the money, I'd give it to her then. If I didn't have it, then I'd bring it back to her later.

TB: Well, that shows a big difference in trust as compared with today.

TE: I knew David Kellum too. I worked for him.

TB: Mr. "Bud Billiken." He started the Bud Billiken parade that is still popular every year.

TE: That's right. They don't give him enough credit for starting that.

TB: If I ever get a chance to publish, I'm going to give him the credit that he deserves. I had a long conversation about that with his son, James.

TE: Mr. Kellum was distribution manager for the *Defender*, and I used to go down there and stuff copies of the newspaper into plain envelopes so that he could send those papers to the South. They had to put them in envelopes like that so the white folks wouldn't recognize them.

TB: And sometimes they'd give copies of the *Defender* to the porters to take with them on the trains going south just to make sure that those papers got there. What kind of a guy was Dave Kellum?

TE: He was strict, and he didn't take any foolishness off of young fellows out there who were standing in line and waiting for their papers. He had his stick, and he'd use it, but if you acted all right, he'd do things to help you.

TB: Now, Kellum's offices, they were located on the Thirty-fourth block on Indiana Avenue in a building which later became the Dawson headquarters. Was the printing press right there in the building?

TE: They had a Linotype, and I started working on that Linotype in 1946.

TB: Were you in the union?

TE: No, but I was trying to get into it.

TB: Well, at that time the *Defender* was still a great paper . . .

TE: Yes, it stood for something.

TB: I looked forward to reading the *Defender* as well as selling it. That was how I made my weekend money to go to the show and whatever other little things I wanted to do. Walt was always aggressive, and he'd pull me along with him. So, in the summertime when we weren't going to school, he'd sell vegetables in the alley, you know, hustling. And I had to be with him because I couldn't deny that we needed the money. In that way he kind of helped me to learn how to deal with money a little bit. So, now you go to junior high. Do you remember any of the people that were there?

TE: Roosevelt Hudson.

TB: Rosey just passed about two months ago. He played with the Globetrotters.

TE: We used to play together at the Boys Club. We had a team on Thirty-sixth Street called the Giles Athletic Club, and we went to the Wabash Y and to the Boys Club to try to beat their teams.

TB: Yeah? That was hard to do. They were tough guys to beat.

TE: We couldn't come out of there winning nothing! Charles Gant, he was my right-hand buddy. He tried to encourage me to join the Boys Club and get in a club group and win a game once in a while. You see, that's how he went to college. His whole squad from the Boys Club went to Xavier.

TB: Let's see. There was Gant, Cleve Bray, McQuiter, LeRoy Rhodes . . .

TE: LeRoy Rhodes did the smart thing—he got himself an education.

TB: Yes, he went on down to Xavier, and he never came back. I used to see his brother, Tealee, who was a good ballplayer too.

TE: Yeah, Tealee also played with us. I haven't heard from him since I left the Government Printing Office, and that's been quite a while.

TB: Yeah, those places like the Boys Club and the Y were where you could always have a good time—and also learn something. All those older guys were like our big brothers.

TE: They were all my friends.

TB: Yes, but they were tough guys, and they knew how to keep us in line. We came right after you. We were like the second wave of guys at the Club. Walt played at the Y. He never played around the Club. He used to play with a team at the Y called the Ottawas. They even had a church league in those days. I think all the churches had a team of their own.

TE: When I played at the Y, it was mostly against outside teams. Englewood Reds, Englewood Grooves. Remember George Ray? George played with a team up around Coleman School.

TB: Yes, Coleman School had a good team. I think they were sponsored by a funeral director, and they were called Hi Flyers, Hot Stuffers, Big Stompers, or something like that.

TE: At that time the gym at Coleman School was open to anyone. You could just go in and play anytime you wanted. That's how I got into basketball. Later on I started going to the gyms around Forty-fourth Street, Forty-fifth Street, and then the ones around Forty-eighth and Dearborn.

TB: Do you remember the Rosenwald Building?

TE: Well, it was for the people that had a little bit more than we did. It was high class. Now, of course, it's a slum.

TB: It really makes you sad to go through there and see what it has become.

TE: They used to have festivals at the Rosenwald. They were nice.

TB: It was very nice. They had that inner court and an inside garden. Well, so when you graduated from junior high, you went to Tilden. What kind of experience was that?

TE: Well, to me it was a new kind of experience, because now you were dealing with folks who were calling you "nigger." This is in 1930, '31, '32, and it was hard for me for a while because it was mostly white. There was only fourteen of us who were black in our class. I think Walt and me were about the first black basketball players in that school's history.

TB: Walt dropped out of school for a couple of years, and then he went back.

TE: By then they were interested in getting blacks to play basketball because they'd won the championship with a star black player.

TB: Yeah, first you had Walt, and then you had the Murphy twins, George and Chester. George and Chester went straight on over to the University of Chicago and became All-American; they were white as you know.

TE: Walt went to the University of Illinois and he wasn't allowed to play on the team there either.

TB: Lou Boudreau was their star player, but, even so, he couldn't make the coach take Walt to help make the team better. Boudreau told him, "If Walter Black doesn't get on that team, it's only because of racial prejudice."

TE: Well, they found out later on what they missed. Now the black schools can't get good players because the white ones gobble them up so fast.

TB: Yeah, now they recruit them from all over the country. A winning team makes a difference in the attendance, and when the attendance goes up, they make more money. Now, back then Tilden Tech was considered to be college preparatory. Whether or not the guys actually went on to college, that was another thing, but at least if they graduated, they were prepared to go on to engineering.

TE: They were prepared for a lot of things. See, you could also learn a machine trade there. A lot of fellows left there and went right out to the steel mills and got better jobs than their parents had out there because they were trained to work on the machines. I went into a printing company—Macintosh—which was a small place down at Twenty-seventh and South Park.

TB: That was a pretty good operation.

TE: But I left them. See, there weren't no jobs for guys like us downtown at that time. You didn't work downtown if you were black. It was only *after* the war that I was able to go downtown and get a job.

TB: What was the religious life of the community like when you were growing up?

TE: Well, I went to a lot of churches, but I went to them to play basketball.

TB: Oh, you went for basketball. I went for pretty girls!
[*Laughter.*]

TE: There was another fellow in my class at Tilden. He went to Quinn Chapel and we had a little singing group. I really couldn't sing a note, but I tried to learn.
[*Laughter.*]
And we also had a baseball team in that church . . .

TB: You know I am trying to think of the name of that church at Thirty-seventh and Indiana where Dinah Washington sang.

TE: That was St. Luke's. St. Luke's had a basketball court right in the Sunday school room!

TB: Yeah, I played on their junior team when Reverend Lewis was our sponsor. What do you remember about the Great Depression years—1929?

TE: Well, '29 and up until '35, '36 was rough. There wasn't anything like jobs. You didn't even have to worry about trying to find jobs because there weren't no jobs to be found. The best thing you could do was go down there to the post office and get those applications, fill them out, and that was it. You had to wait, and some people got lucky and got hired at times. So, during that time, I was just more or less just hustling. Washing cars, selling papers—that kind of thing. For a time I worked out at London Dairy over on Stony Island. Ever heard of London Dairy? They didn't pay me much, but they would tell me to drink all the milk I wanted! [*Laughter.*]

TB: During that time, none of us had any money. We just hustled as best we could, and somehow we got through it all. At least we all got along, and there wasn't any violence between us.

TE: The first time I even recognized violence was a possibility was when it was perpetrated on me. It was 1935. Before then any neighborhood I went into selling my papers, nobody ever bothered me. Then one night I was going to make some money up there at Forty-sixth and Vincennes, and some fellows were waiting around outside. When I opened the door, they tried to come in with me, and so I slammed the door, and one of the guys stuck a knife right through the door and stabbed me in the chest! So I ran over to a doctor I knew up there on Forty-seventh Street, and he took me to Provident Hospital, and Provident sent me to the County Hospital, and when I got there, they looked at me like they thought I was going to die, but the next morning I was still living, and so they brought me out, and I started working again.

TB: They kept you a whole night at County? Well, why wouldn't they give you emergency treatment at Provident?

TE: No money.

TB: You didn't have the money *or* they didn't have the money?

TE: I didn't have any money, and my folks didn't either.

TB: Your folks didn't have any money! They were asking you questions like that when you were badly wounded?

TE: Oh, yeah, they wanted money first. They also did that same kind of thing, as I recall, when my daughter swallowed a lot of aspirin. We lived in the Ida B. Wells housing development, and we rushed her up there to Provident, and they kept her up there until I went back home and got some money.

TB: What year was this?

TE: This had to be in 1946, '47.

TB: This was after you came out of the service?

TE: I wasn't in the service. When they called me, I already had four kids, and besides that I also worked at Douglas Aircraft, which was out there where O'Hare is now.

TB: Oh, you were exempt? I didn't realize that.

TE: Before that I had been working for Duesenberg. I'll never forget—it was in September, and that heat was burning my back and that cold air coming out the window was blowing across my chest, and so I finally said, "Well, I just can't take

this anymore." You know all the time I was working there I would always have to walk home because everything I was wearing was so dirty I couldn't sit down anywhere. I couldn't even get on a streetcar looking like that. That was because everything was so filthy there, and you couldn't change clothes, and so everyday I had to have on something different, and I'd have to walk home. Well, that's why I went out to apply for a position at Douglas Aircraft, and they sent me to school. I was sitting up there learning how to rivet, about then I saw them lathes they had there, and so I asked my instructor, "They got lathes out here, don't they?" He said, "Yeah, they're teaching machinists how to use them." I said, "Well, I went to school for that." So he called over to the other office, and he said, "One of our boys here has training in lathes. If you have an opening there, I'll send him over." So, when I heard that, I told him, "Well, why don't you leave out calling me 'boy' and just say 'young man' instead?" Well, he did that. He had to do that because Roosevelt had already passed that bill—this was 1942 or '43—that they couldn't discriminate against people in government work. So he sent me out there, and they signed me up before they even saw me, and by then it was too late!
[*Laughter.*]
And when I got there, all them white folks just walked up and down that aisle looking at me. That aisle was long, from here to way back there, and all those people were just watching me and waiting for me to make a mistake, but I had been trained as a machinist at Tilden, and I could read blueprints and do everything that was required for the job. So I started out pretty good, and they didn't give me any trouble.

TB: Did the personal relationships get any better?

TE: Oh, yeah, relationships got better because more blacks began to come to work out there. Just not in my department. There was only about three blacks in that department.

TB: Now, at that time you were living in Ida B. Wells.

TE: We lived in Ida B. Wells for one year. That was in 1941, and it was nice. At that time Mr. Brown was the manager.

TB: Yes, Oscar Brown Sr.

TE: They washed the windows every two weeks. Someone on your floor had to clean the back hall, and you had to clean the front hall—whichever way it went. The apartments had to be kept clean, and the kids couldn't just go out and tear up the playground. It only got risky after we left.

TB: Well, I knew a lot of guys who lived there back then. Did you know Nugie Watkins?

TE: Yeah, Nugie used to live south. We were out at Douglas together, and we played on the same team.

TB: It seems like we know a lot of the same people. You guys were just better players than me, and so I had to come along and just look! But, yeah, that was the quality of tenant that was selected for Ida B. Wells. I remember that I was wishing that I could get in, but I wasn't married yet, and I think you had to be married or something.

TE: You had to be married and have at least one child.

TB: Then they caught me and put me in the army. Yeah, but I still remember the playground they had back there. What's the name of that playground? They named it for the congressman who was before Oscar DePriest. By the way, what do you remember about the politics of that period that we're talking about?

TE: Well, Bill Dawson was the strong arm in politics back then, but I wouldn't let these precinct captains of his into my house. You know I didn't want to be bothered with them because I didn't appreciate the type of person he was. You see, he was leaning on Daley, and Daley was leaning on him. I used to try to get into politics myself. I tried to get a job with William B. King, and so I coached the Camp Fire Girls because that was his wife's pet project. They had a basketball team and a baseball team, and I coached their basketball team, but I finally had to leave them because we had raised ninety dollars to get uniforms for the team, and then one of his cohorts came by and took all the money! So I said, "No more of that kind of stuff!" That was a lot of money in those days.

TB: So, during the war, you were working in a strategic industry, but now the war is over. What was Chicago like at that time?

TE: It was pretty hard getting a job after the war because most of the places were holding jobs for the veterans coming back. I was trying to get into the machinists' union because that was the latest thing, and I said, "Naw, I'd better go back to printing. I can't stand this machine anymore." The first job I got was in a Jewish printing plant on the other side of Halsted Street, but they didn't seem to like me much there because I just couldn't get those Jewish characters together in the right kind of order. So I started working with another fellow on Lake Street, but I was just filling vacation spots. So from there, I got a job in the neighborhood at a local press at Sixty-third and Langley, and I worked there for about five years from 1945 to 1950.

TB: Now that the war is over, you are beginning to get some new folks in the neighborhood. What is your impression of the newcomers flooding into the city?

TE: Things began to change for everyone because, you know, you couldn't just stand around on Sixty-third and Cottage Grove for very long without the police wanting to know what you were doing. It was mostly a white area, and a lot of white businesses were out there, but, of course, it looks like a ghost city now.

TB: Yes, it does look that way, but there used to be a lot of fine entertainment around there.

TE: Yeah, the Circle Inn used to be right on the corner of Cottage Grove and Sixty-third. But then, when I graduated from high school, the prom was held at the Trianon, which was also near there, and they didn't allow blacks to go there.

TB: Yeah, I think the first time blacks went in there was when some white guys bought bids for the blacks. That was Earl Strayhorn and his class. You know Judge Strayhorn, Joe Robichaux, and those guys? Well, some white guys bought the bids and gave it to the black guys, and that was the first time they were able to go to the Trianon.

TE: Yeah, but that kind of thing didn't happen till a little later. Our guys just didn't get to go to the prom!

TB: Now, didn't you say that you first came to Chicago in 1953, Mrs. Ellis?

EE: I only came here to visit then.

TB: What was your impression of the city at that time?

EE: Well, being from a small town, at that point it was just too big for me. Too many things, you know, were going on. I had been raised in a little town, and I just wasn't accustomed to the size.

TB: But it was kind of exciting, wasn't it?

EE: Well, I suppose it was kind of exciting in one sense, but, on the other hand, it was also kind of lonely because I wasn't accustomed to being around a whole lot of people that I didn't even know.

TB: Do you mean without you knowing who they are?

EE: Yes, you don't know who they are. You don't even know your neighbor. As for me, I wasn't accustomed to going out the front door. We always went out the back door. Even now, when you go down South, you can be on your porch or walking by, and people will speak to you regardless of whether they know you or not. So it was kind of hard for me to get accustomed to that kind of coolness that people have up here . . .

TB: Yes, but at least you had relatives here.

EE: I just had an adopted sister here. I didn't have any blood relatives here at all.

TB: And where was she living?

EE: She was living at Seventy-second and Wabash.

TB: So you decided to go back home.

EE: Yes, and I moved back here again in '65.

TB: And then what did you do?

EE: I came back here again and lived with my adopted sister. She had children, and I came back here to stay with them while she and her husband went to school. The first outside job that I got was packaging liquor in a liquor store. Later I went to work over at Goldblatt's at Thirty-fifth and King Drive.

TB: In the shopping center there?

EE: Yes, and I was there as a salesperson and then as department manager until '71 when I transferred and went to the warehouse at Fortieth and Kedzie. I was department manager there until I was laid off in 1981.

TB: How did you and Mr. Ellis meet?

EE: Well, you know, he and I are both members of St. John's Church at Forty-eighth and Michigan. He was an insurance agent at the Met [Metropolitan Assurance Company] at that time, and we would talk quite frequently, and one day I told him that I was looking for a job, and he told me that one of the young ladies that was working at the Met as a receptionist was going to leave. So I went down there and applied for the job.

TB: What was that place like? Did they still have field agents?

EE: Yes, they had agents when I got there. In fact, they've still got them—one at Eighty-sixth and Cottage Grove, and there's another one at Ninetieth and Ashland.

TB: Did they have any agents out of town?

EE: They had one in South Bend, and they had one in Ohio. Those were the branch offices.

TB: Who was the president at that time?

EE: Anderson Scheich.

TB: And general counsel?

EE: Hollis Riggs. He was one of the nicest persons I ever met at the Met. Everybody else was kind of like just employees, and they remained like that, to me. But his door was always open if you wanted to talk to him. He would always listen to what you'd have to say.

TB: Was Jack Isbell there at that time?

EE: Yes, James Isbell was there. Every so often before I left, he would come down, and we would visit together for a while.

TB: Well, Jack Isbell brought me into the business. He and I grew up in the same neighborhood. He's not well now. He had a heart attack.

EE: I am sorry to hear that.

EE: Yes, every so often before I left, he would come down and they would all visit together.

TB: Do you remember Poro College? It was located right down the street from the Met, and they bought all that property where Poro College used to be. As it happens, I met Madame Walker's great granddaughter in Indianapolis about two months ago, and she's writing a story about her great-grandmother.

TE: C. J. Walker, the hair lady?

TB: Yes, when a young girl graduated from high school, she could go straight over there to Poro College and learn how to do hair. They could always get a job back then, when we had so many beauty parlors all around the neighborhood.

TE: Do you remember Bacon's Casino, where they had outdoor dancing?

TB: Yes, that building is still standing, and now we're trying to save it. Warren Bacon's uncle used to own that place, and he also lived across the street, but then, during the war, Mrs. Coles—Robert Coles's wife—created a USO center there and the soldiers who came in from out of town and wanted someplace to go, they would stop there and have a good time. But what I remember most about Bacon's was that they used to have breakfast dances. What were the breakfast dances like?

TE: I only went to a couple. They were nice, but my folks didn't think I ought to be taking a date out that early in the morning.

TB: How early was it?

TE: Around six o'clock in the morning!

[*Laughter.*]

TB: You know I remember that sometimes Walter would get up real early, and he'd start to get dressed up, and I would think, "Where in the world is this crazy man going this time of morning! Why doesn't he just go back to bed and sleep!" But lots of people would go to those breakfast dances and apparently all of them had a good time. Bacon's was a swinging place, but it was kind of exclusive. You know, not just everybody went there. It wasn't like the Savoy. Did you get there when the Savoy was still going, Edith?

EE: No.

TB: It was already closed down, I suspect. Do you remember the Binga Arcade?

TE: I remember hearing about it, but I don't think I was ever there.

TB: It was very nice. It was where the Illinois Institute of Technology is now.

TE: Yeah, I know where it was. I did go to the Warwick because Nat Cole was playing there.

TB: My high school classmates—Nat Cole and Tony Fambro. Back then we didn't even know that Nat could sing.

TE: Because in school all he did was play the piano. I used to go up to his house. A fellow I knew who played trumpet would also go and practice up there. They lived at Forty-third and Calumet in that big tall building.

TB: He surprised everybody when he became a singer, but he told me that out in California he had to turn singer or starve.

TE: Yeah, the band broke up out there because they were going to starve to death. All those guys had to go off and try to make it for themselves.

TB: Well, Chicago has certainly been a very interesting place for me to look back on, but when I look at the kids here today, you can see that they have just about given up having hope. As poor as we were living in this big city and never knowing what's going to happen next, even so, we always had the hope that it was going to get a little better. But now these youngsters seem to have just given up hope.

EE: They don't care. They don't learn anything, and they just don't care.

TE: Yeah, but in some ways some things are now a little better. Remember back in those times we've been talking about there weren't even any black businesses over there on Forty-seventh Street.

TB: No, except for the Palm Tavern.

TE: Well, even before the Palm Tavern, Morris's Eat Shop came along in there, and I'm trying to think of the name of the guy who had the haberdashery next to Morris's Eat Shop. He was the first black in there because he looked like a white man.

TB: Yes, he did. What was his name? I saw his name somewhere recently. He was a nice guy, and we would go out of our way to patronize him. I think he later got drafted.

TE: Then, of course, Scotty came along.

TB: Scotty Piper, yes! Later on he campaigned in his own way for Harold Washington, and then, after that, he became ill. I went to his funeral. He was Catholic and his service was at Corpus Christi. Do you remember when we couldn't go to Corpus Christi?

TE: That's right. Not only Corpus Christi. You also couldn't go to that Catholic church there on Oakwood Boulevard—Holy Angels. The only Catholic church for blacks was St. Elizabeth. So I sometimes wonder why any of our folks ever converted!

[*Laughter.*]

TB: Well, Chicago in those years that we are talking about underwent a lot of changes, but the South Side was always a place where young people, in particular, used to come during the summertime to have a good time.

TE: Well, when we were coming up, even the white folks were coming over to our area for entertainment, but they aren't coming over here anymore, and if *we* want entertainment, we got to go out to where the entertainment's at.

TB: That's because they bought the entertainment away from us, and yet there used to be so many places down here.

TE: The North Side is where the local bands are playing now. If you want to hear them, that's where you have to go.

TB: Well, we've still got one of those places here on Seventy-ninth Street near the lake.

TE: Is that Alexander's?

TB: Alexander's, yeah. Have you been there? That's just once a week, and you always see the same people. I don't get there very often, but I know some of the guys like Eddie Johnson. I went to grammar school with Eddie. But in the old days, if people came to visit you, you could say, "Let's go out for a while," and then you'd just put on your clothes, and walk, maybe, two blocks, and all the places that you wanted to go to were right close by. There was entertainment and all kinds of music. Whites would come in, and you wouldn't pay them any attention. They just came in. Do you remember the night when Joe Louis won the championship? Benny Goodman was playing in town that night at the Eighth Regiment Armory, and Lionel Hampton and Teddy Wilson were part of Benny Goodman's band, and Joe wanted to hear the music. So, after the fight, Joe walked over from Comiskey Park over to the Armory, and when he got there, the place just went wild! Joe Louis walked over and came right on in. Can you imagine Michael Jordan doing anything like that?

TE: I didn't get to go that night because I was working, but once we went to a banquet at the YMCA, and Joe Louis came in, and he was wearing his Golden Gloves suit. That was big stuff then! Well, everybody sat down at the table, but before the minister could even say the blessing, Joe was already starting to eat!

TB: And Joe really could eat too!

[*Laughter.*]

Did you know that his wife, Marva, has moved back to that old building where they used to live at Forty-third and Michigan?

TE: Yes, at 4316/18, the six-flat.

TB: Well, she's remodeled the place, and people say they sometimes see her puttering around in the garden next door. It's nice to have her back.

TE: It's too bad she ever left.

June 14, 1995

FRED SMITH

FROM TEXAS TO CHICAGO

Fred Smith was born in rural Texas and came to Chicago as a young man. I met Mr. Smith through a longtime friend, Eddie Casey, who has also participated in these oral histories and has since passed away (1999). Mr. Smith's remembrances of his early years in rural and later urban Texas and his incentives to move to Chicago—the "Promised Land, Land of Hope"—give the reader insights into the experiences and opinions of a young man coming to Chicago during the first Great Migration, as well as the trials, tribulations, and triumphs that occurred during his long lifetime in Chicago. His stated memories seem to be typical of the migrants of that period. Despite disappointing and frustrating personal experiences, he always managed to retain a core of optimism and remained true to the dreams and hopes that motivated him to create a successful career for himself. Now he too has passed on to that everlasting "Promised Land" where, perhaps, the rest of his dreams will be fulfilled.

TB: When were you born, Fred?

FS: I was born April 14, 1897.

TB: Where?

FS: In the great Lone Star State of Texas.

TB: Where in Texas?

FS: I was born near a little town four miles east of another little town called Kosse. That's about midway between Dallas and Houston, Texas.

TB: I don't know where that is, but I know where Dallas and Houston are. I've been to both of those places. What were your parents doing?

FS: I was raised on a farm.

TB: What kind of farm?

FS: A big Texas farm. It was 487 acres, to be exact, and we had everything on that farm. We were a large family. I had seven sisters and four brothers, and I'm the baby of the group. My oldest sister was married before I was born. I can also point out that both my parents had been slaves.

TB: Were they born in Texas?

FS: No, my father is from Louisiana, and my mother is from Mississippi. My mother was born in 1854. She died in 1929 at the age of seventy-five.

TB: Was she in Chicago or Texas?

FS: In Texas. My father was born in 1850, and he died in 1930.

TB: So they both were born into slavery?

FS: Yes, my father was thirteen when Abraham Lincoln signed the Emancipation Proclamation. I told my father, I said, "Father, you were a slave, were you not?" He said, "Yes, but how did you know?" I was reading about slavery and learned that they had some they called "houseboys." So I figured at the tender age of thirteen, my father no doubt was a houseboy. As a matter of fact, my real name is not Smith. When some slaves were freed, they took their master's name, and my father's people took their master's name, which was Smith. My real name is Sterling, but I didn't know that until one of my brothers who did some research on slavery found out. He took up the name Sterling as his middle name. So his name was Clarence Sterling Smith. He's dead now.

TB: How long did you stay in Texas after you were born?

FS: I left Texas in 1928, but let's back up for a moment. I quit college in 1917 and took an exam to become a railway mail clerk. One of my schoolteachers wrote me a letter, and he said that he was taking the examination for railway mail clerk, and he asked me to take it along with him. I was going to Prairie View State College, but I took that test, and I passed it. Well, I'm back in school now, and so I forgot all about that test until another friend of mine, he too had passed that test and been appointed as a railway clerk—so I wrote the Civil Service Commission in Washington to ask if I was still on their list. I knew I had passed because they had sent the results by postal authority. That was a five-hour examination. It started at 9 A.M. and lasted until 2 P.M., but I just rushed on through the thing, and by twelve, I was out and gone. My professor also passed, but he did not get appointed because he was not eligible for the job. So, anyway, I wrote the Civil Service Commission, and they told me that I had been appointed, and a few days later I received my permission slip, and, after that, I stayed in the service for almost ten years.

TB: All this time was in Texas?

FS: Yeah. I was stationed in Houston, Texas.

TB: What was Houston like at that time in terms of race?

FS: Houston was like all the other southern cities. They were very prejudiced—some more so than others—and Houston was especially bad, as I soon found out—so I left Houston and took another run out of San Antonio, Texas. I'm on a big run now from Houston to Dallas.

TB: So you're a railway clerk?

FS: Yes, I ran the Railway Mail Service in the summer of 1918. They were paying the big sum of seventy-five dollars a month. They sent me from Houston to La Monte, Missouri, as a relief clerk.

TB: What could you buy for seventy-five dollars in those days?

FS: Anything you wanted. Just to show you, at seventy-five dollars a month, I was taking classes along with schoolteachers, doctors, and lawyers. I stayed in the service, but I left this big run because I didn't see any future there for me. At that time they were in the process of developing what they called "The Magic Valley." I could see in my mind how that was going to be when it was developed. They had a little one-man run then going almost to the valley, but when they saw that was happening, they built a railroad that extended on out into the Rio Grande Valley. Anyway, I took the little run 'cause I knew when it was developed it would really be something, and when they expanded the train into the Rio Grande Valley, I was on the first scheduled train out of there, and I stayed on that run. Later on, when mail began to increase, I got a larger car, and they gave me a helper. They reclassified the run and changed it from a Class A job to Class B job, and I stayed there until 1926 or 1927. In the meantime, my brother had bought a poultry farm. He became an expert in poultry, and he told me that I would make more money with eggs than I would on the road. So I began to spend quite a bit of time there with him, but when Uncle Sam found out about that, he said, "You have another business, and now you have an alternative. You can either remain in the service or relinquish your other business." And that's when I left the railroad and devoted my full time to the poultry farm. We had hundreds and hundreds of white-legged hens, but there were no roosters. We specialized in eggs only. Then the Depression began to come in 1928, and my brother had to reduce the size of the farm, and there was nothing there for me to do—so I said, "Well, I think I'll go back to school," and that's why I came to Chicago. It was for school.

TB: That was when?

FS: The year 1929. I didn't know anyone here but one man, Roscoe Simmons. So I contacted him, and he said, "Where were you headed to?" and I said I was going on to Detroit. He said, "I was hoping you'd come here to stay, and I would be able to put you right into City Hall."

TB: Who was Roscoe Simmons?

FS: Well, today he would be classified as a civil rights leader, and back then he seemed to know just about everybody. He was a very wise man, and if he said he would put you in City Hall, believe me, you'd go to City Hall.

TB: Who was the mayor here then?

FS: Big Bill Thompson was the mayor in 1929. He was Chicago's last Republican mayor. So, anyway, I didn't go to Detroit. I stayed right here, but I couldn't go to school and work as well. That's why when Roscoe Simmons said, "What are you doing?" I said, "I'm not doing anything. I can't even find no work," and he said, "Did you ever hear of the Illinois Central?" And I said, "What is that?" He said, "That's a railroad. Did you ever work on a railroad?" So I told him, and he went over to the telephone inside City Hall, and he came back out with a note and said, "Take this note down to the train station and give it to a man named Incres, and he'll know what to do." So I gave that note to Incres, and he said, "Come back here tomorrow at two-forty-five." That's how I got my first job on a railroad.

TB: Where was Mr. Simmons living then?

FS: I don't know.

TB: Where was his office?

FS: I don't know, but I saw him again years later on a train. He got on that train in Hollandale, Mississippi, and I heard a lady yell that this was his hometown, but I don't know for sure. Then a little later I saw an ad in a newspaper that they wanted an experienced mail clerk here in Chicago, and so I answered the ad, and it was for a bank back there on La Salle Street. I think the name of that bank was the Republican National Bank, but it's not there anymore. So, anyway, I applied for this job, and I am the only black face among all the people trying to get work there. This employer was so cruel he wouldn't even ask anybody to have a seat. He would just ask what kind of work you been doing and then say, "We can't use you!" Then he said, "I'm going to lunch now, but I'll be back in a while"— and when he came back and saw that I'm the only one still there, he said, "Well, have a seat, young man. What kind of work have you been doing?" And I said that I was in the Railway Mail Service. He said, "The Railway Mail Service? Why did you leave a job like that?" I said, "Well, if I'm on a job, and I reach the top inside of ten years, then it's just too small a job for me." Why I told him that is because I had read an article about how to be interviewed. "Always interview yourself, and form questions in your mind that you figure an employer might ask you." So I figured he might ask me that kind of question, and I was prepared and had already made that answer up. Then he asked me, "How long have you been in Chicago?"

I said, "Oh, about six months"—and he goes, "Oh, my goodness, from the way you were talking, I was hoping you had been here at least five years." Well, that was in 1929, and that bank is not there anymore. I learned in later years, I think, the bank was absorbed into the Continental Bank. I don't know for sure. Anyway, I retired from the railroad on February 1, 1965, and on February 17 of the same year I went to work for the Continental Bank here in Chicago doing the same type of work I had tried for back in 1929. Things do change. So I stayed there until I retired in 1979.

TB: What was Chicago like in terms of the black population back then when you first came to Chicago?

FS: Well, when I was new here, I do know there were a lot of black folks working in City Hall. As a matter of fact, there were so many black folks there that they called it "Uncle Tom's Cabin." I don't know what type of work most black people were doing, but there were certain parts of Chicago that we just didn't go in. I don't think we went east of Cottage Grove. When I first came here in 1929, I got me a job at a hotel in Hyde Park in the place where that high school is now. One day I got to work a little early, and so I stopped at a sandwich shop that was nearby, but they wouldn't wait on me. They just looked at me and laughed.

TB: This is Hyde Park in 1929?

FS: Yeah.

TB: What was life like back then in terms of the people you were around, the nightlife as well as the day life?

FS: When I first came here in 1929, there was a nightclub nearby where Earl Hines was playing, and I used to go in there and sit by myself because I didn't know anybody.

TB: That was in the hotel you were in, wasn't it?

FS: Nearby. I was living at the hotel, and Earl Hines was performing at Asia World. So I just rode over there with somebody else, but way back then for most people Wrigley Field was the biggest thing going.

TB: It was almost new, wasn't it?

FS: Yeah, and I used to see people lined up blocks away just trying to get into Wrigley Field. Well, I didn't have any money or anything, but I had a girlfriend, and she wanted to go to Wrigley Field. I had to tell her, "I ain't got any money," and she said, "Well, then, I'll give you some of my money." So this girl gave me a ten-dollar bill, and I took her and her aunt to the ball game, and I never did give her no change! Right after that was the war, and so I started working on the railroad again. I went to work for the Pennsylvania Railroad because they had a training school over there, and then I went back over to the Illinois Central and stayed at IC until I retired in 1965. That was thirty-five years I was with them.

TB: What was your run?

FS: I ran from Chicago to New Orleans. The big train was the Panama Limited. Illinois Central had the Panama Limited, and Pennsylvania was also involved with the Limited. New York Central had their Twenty-Six Limited and Santa Fe had their Chief. That was the time when people would really want to ride the train. All the VIPs would ride the deluxe service. We even had barbers and maids on that train. That was just before World War II started, and when they gave me a promotion. I advanced to steward in control of the car, but I would have made more money back when I was waiting tables.

TB: So you made less money getting promoted than you did before the promotion?

FS: Yes, that's right. When the VIPs were riding trains, we always knew who was going to be there because it was a "reservation" train. We always knew how to prepare for them. If I made a trip from Chicago to Miami, Florida, and didn't get back with at least one hundred dollars' worth of tips, then it was a bad trip. That's why I finally gave it up. It was because during the war when I was working as a steward, I wasn't making enough money, and I had to hire such bad help. When the war was going on, you couldn't get no good help. None were available.

TB: The best guys were in the army.

FS: That's right. I even had to hire a waiter who had epilepsy, and he was subject to a seizure anytime. Well, one time it happened, and when it did, I kept him with me on an all-night trip just to bring him back. Some of the help that we hired were also a bunch of thieves. They would steal from me, and so myself and the other men got together and had a meeting. I said, "I know what I am going to do. I am going to charge everything to them." All the pop and things they had, I said, "This is all yours, but at the end of the trip you must return my merchandise or pay me the money for them." Before that time I would always come up short. This one guy, I would always give him two dollars to make change, but one day, just to test him, I gave him two dollars and ten cents. I said, "Now, be sure to count it because I made a mistake once." Well, he counted it, but he didn't say a thing, and then the next day I gave him a dollar and ninety cents. He counted it out and said, "You are a dime short," and I said, "Yes, but yesterday I was a dime over."

TB: That was clever.

FS: These new guys, they would come on the train and not even know enough to introduce themselves. Now, at this time we had five waiters and three cooks. So to this new waiter I said, "Are you going with us?" He said, "Yeah," and so I told him to take the first passenger that comes in the car for dinner. At that time we had an all-silver service—such as silver compotes to serve juice packed in ice—so, anyway, this boy brought that juice out and spilled it right on the passenger's lap, and so I told that lady to go have her suit cleaned and send the bill right here to us and we would take care of it for her. Then, when the meal was over, I tried not to embarrass this waiter. I tried to treat him the way I would like myself to be treated by him—so I called him over to the side and told him, "You have made two mistakes today," and he said "What was that other mistake?" I said, "Well, the first mistake you made was you didn't know anybody in the crew and you didn't even introduce yourself. If you are new and you don't know anybody's name, ask and then introduce yourself and especially make friends with the passenger man, but now I don't want to discuss this with you anymore." Well, I didn't see that boy for five or six weeks, but when I did see him, he said, "You put me on the right track," because before that he thought it was the best thing to do to just pretend that you know something that you didn't really know.

TB: Now, because the railroad industry at that time had the responsibility of transferring both civilians and soldiers all over the country, did you become unionized?

FS: We didn't become unionized until 1936. Before we were unionized, they worked us like slaves. You got a pay of twenty-four and one-fourth cents per hour, with unlimited hours and no kind of accommodations whatsoever. We would run from Chicago to Florida, and when you'd serve your last meal, you'd have to clean up the dining cars and then sit down right where you were in order to get any kind of sleep. When we finally got organized in 1936, the first thing they did was to put dormitory cars on the train with hot and cold running water for us. We also got vacations with pay and an increase in salary.

TB: The dining-car waiters and the sleeping-car porters were almost all blacks, weren't they?

FS: Yeah, where I worked at they were all black.

TB: How did you all get organized? Do you remember?

FS: The conditions were bad until A. Philip Randolph started organizing the porters, but when we tried to organize here we were having some difficulty because the white railroad unions were not receptive about taking us in. You see, there are two types of railroad unions: operators and nonoperators. We were classified as nonoperators, but the nonoperators union didn't want to take us in, and the only way we got organized was to organize through the hotel and restaurant employees union.

TB: You organized under the AFL?

FS: Yeah.

TB: Now, at that time the railroad industry was kind of centered here in Chicago, wasn't it?

FS: Yes, at that time Chicago was the center.

TB: How did it happen that Mr. Randolph, who was from New York, became the union manager here in Chicago?

FS: I don't know just how Randolph got involved, but Randolph never was a worker. He knew where we needed some help, and he became a good railroad union manager for us. Mr. Phil Randolph could be called the father of the FEPC [Fair Employment Practices Committee].

TB: In fact, you could also almost call him the father of the civil rights movement.

FS: Yes, when he threatened the march on Washington, that was when Franklin Roosevelt issued direct orders to create the FEPC.

TB: That was Executive Order 8802, and the year was 1941! Mr. Randolph was a very unusual man in that he was a scholar, but he also had deep roots and sympathy for ordinary working people.

FS: In my opinion, Mr. Randolph was a man of high character with good principles, and he wouldn't ever sell you out, and we do have a lot of so-called leaders who would sell you out and often did just that.

TB: You said you came from a large family. Are any of your sisters or brothers still living?

FS: All of them are gone.

TB: Did you have any children?

FS: I had one son, and he died in 1982. He had two sons—so I have two grandsons. One of my grandsons works for the state, and he is thirty-eight years old. I also have some nieces—the youngest niece is seventy-three. She is around the same age as you. She was born April 3, 1918.

TB: That was a great year!

FS: I talked with her just last night. She lives in Waco, Texas. She has a master's degree in library work, and she worked in the library in Atlanta, Georgia, until 1983. I was there once and spent a week with her, but I spent most of my time right there in the library.

TB: They have very fine archives in the library there.

FS: Oh, yes. This man that I call "Mr. Coca-Cola" gave them ten million dollars, and they added on some more money from somewhere and built an eighteen-million-dollar library, and to tell you the truth, if you like going to a library, don't miss going to this library!

TB: I've been there!

FS: It's what I call an "inspirational accuracy" library.

TB: Well, that's because you've got those colleges and universities there.

FS: Yes, this library serves kind of like an umbrella for five or six schools—Spelman, Morehouse, Brown, Clark, and Atlanta University—so, anyway, I went to the archive section, and I said to the young lady that was there, "I recall my brother made a speech, and he quoted a part of what Booker T. Washington once said: 'Let you drop your bucket down where you are,' or something like that," and she said, "Oh, yes, would you like to see the book?" Well, I read the book, and she took that book and Xeroxed parts of it for me. What Booker T. Washington was saying was that there were two ships that embarked, and one ship said to the other ship when it ran out of water, "My men need water," so the other ship sent a message back to "cast down your bucket down where you are because you are now at the mouth of the Amazon River, and you can fill your bucket with freshwater right there where you are."

TB: He made that speech in Atlanta in 1895.

FS: A lot of people don't like Booker T. Washington.

TB: That's because they're confused.

FS: They think that he just wanted to see us all become blue-collar people, but that's not true. All he was telling us was don't give up, keep up, keep up with God, and God will provide.

TB: You know, some people believe that during that period Booker T. Washington and W. E. B. DuBois were at odds with one another, but if you read them carefully, you'd find that they really weren't too far apart.

FS: Well, even today, we still have different approaches to solve our problems even though our objectives might be exactly the same.

TB: Were you here in Chicago when the Garvey Movement was very active? Did it ever amount to much for people around here?

FS: Well, I recall who Marcus Garvey was, but I was in Texas at that time.

TB: If you look at Chicago, Mr. Smith, and compare it to the many places you've been and were to make a comparison, how would you compare life in Chicago for black people with all these other places?

FS: Let me see, are you asking me where would I like to be?

TB: You could answer it that way if you want to.

FS: If I had my choice, if I was a younger person, I would live in Atlanta, Georgia. It doesn't have that aggressive attitude that I have found here in Chicago. In a place like this, they want everything too quick.

TB: Yes, but sometimes change comes slowly. Even here.

FS: Well, if you traveled throughout the country like I did, you could see some of those changes right while they were taking place. Take a place like Memphis, Tennessee, for instance. In their railroad station they had two separate waiting rooms. The white folks were downstairs, and the black folks were upstairs, and the waiting room for the black folks was also the custodial room. They had signs everywhere you looked marking everything "colored" or "white," but then some changes came along, and the next time I came through they had taken all those signs off the walls and left behind spots on those walls that looked just like they were freshly painted!

[*Laughter.*]

That's just one of the small things you noticed, and, as time went on, we continued to progress, but, as late as the late sixties, I went back to my wife's home in Natchez, Mississippi, and all that you saw was our young people mopping floors and washing dishes. Then, when I went back down there in 1971, some of those same people that were mopping floors and washing dishes, now they were payroll clerks, bank clerks, and so on, and things had really changed.

TB: What about the changes you might have witnessed here in Chicago?

FS: Well, when I first came to Chicago, I thought this was the best place. There were some prejudices here, but not so much as other cities. I came here on the train and coming here was really quite an experience. I met all these people, and almost everyone that I talked to was coming to Chicago for one reason or another: to get better jobs, more pay, better housing. Now, don't get me wrong, after that union thing came through with the railroad, my pay and benefits were pretty good considering the fact that I was black—which was then termed "nigger"— but there was still that need for more, especially when there was a family to consider, but my family was excited about coming to Chicago. They had heard so many things about the big city with the bright lights, and they wanted to see those lights! But when I came to Chicago, things were not all roses and candy. There were hard times, what with finding an apartment that I could afford with the pay that I was getting and then bringing my family there, and that also meant buying new furniture, clothing. You see, it was a totally different lifestyle here, including even things like the clothing, and I wanted my family to look like all the rest of the people here in the city. Things here were pretty much as Booker Washington and Garvey explained it. There are racial prejudices everywhere: If you're black, I guess, the phrase is "stay back," but if you're white, then it's "all right." With the many racial movements that were going on, things got pretty rough even for Chicago. I thought to myself there had to be a change for the better someday, and you know what? That change did come. To you or to some of the younger ones, it might seem that it came a little late, but to me it changed in time with the way life was.

TB: Why do you say that?

FS: You see, I worked for twenty-four cents an hour on the railroad, and at the time that was pretty good pay for a black person. Then I went from twenty-four cents an hour to fifty cents an hour, and, boy, I thought I was living high on the hog, and when I got up to a dollar an hour, no one could tell me anything! Back then, you could buy a lot of things with that kind of money. But look at the way things are today. People make thousands, even millions of dollars in a twelve-month period and still talk about how hard it is to make ends meet.

TB: What do you remember most vividly about those many days you worked on the railroad?

FS: The railroad was one of the fastest ways to get places, especially when you wanted to travel a distance. Well, back then, it was really the only way. There were cars, but for blacks, well, most of us couldn't afford a car or even a horse. Sometimes we had a mule, and you were considered to be doing good when you had a mule and wagon, but the railroad was the most popular thing. When you made a stop at the depot to make pickups, everyone standing on the platform seemed to be so proud just to be there, like it was God's greatest gift to man to travel on the rail system. Sometimes we served some of the greatest people in the world on the train, and some of them were very good to us. I remember one time a big-shot white man gave me a real gold coin just for letting him know that he was about to lose his wallet, but then there was another time when I told a young man that his watch was coming out of his pocket, and he told me to "mind your own business, nigger"—so you see we met all kinds of people on that railroad track.

TB: What have you seen changed today about the railroad system that was once your way of life?

FS: Well, now the railroad system is much better. You don't need people to serve you. Blacks don't have to sit in one car and the whites in another. Everyone sits together, thanks to all the racial movements that went on. You don't ever have to say, "Yes, sir," or "No, sir," to anyone that you don't want to say it to, and you can refuse to service any person. You can go from car to car without being asked, "What are you doing in here, nigger?" In fact, the word "nigger" no longer seems to exist as part of our spoken vocabulary. Well, we know it's still there, but we went from that to "African-American," and now we are "black," and we're proud to be black. I used to think I would be better off if I were white, but now I am glad to be black, and I am proud of it!

December 20, 1994

REPRESENTATIVE CORNEAL DAVIS

FORMER ILLINOIS STATE REPRESENTATIVE

A state representative for twenty-seven years, Corneal Davis was born in rural Missis-sippi as the son of a white landowner and an African-American ex-slave mother. Due to the racial restrictions in Mississippi at that time, no legal marriage was possible for his parents. Even so, it seems that he grew up having more privileges and personal se-curity than most other African-American youngsters in that region during that era. After his graduation from high school, his father offered to pay all his expenses if he would go to an eastern white university and not disclose his African heritage. Corneal Davis refused that offer, saying he would never insult and deny his mother in that way, and he chose instead to attend Alcorn A&M College, where he met many other students also of a mixed racial background.

After his college experience, Mr. Davis joined other black troops in the racially seg-regated army during World War I. Because they were denied the opportunity to fight as combat troops by General John "Black Jack" Pershing in "the fight to save democ-racy," they were transferred into the French army as combat troops under Marshals Foch and Petain. They spent more time on the front lines of battle than any other unit of the American Expeditionary Forces (AEF), and then they returned home to find racism was as flagrant as ever.

Hoping to find "the promised land, the land of hope," Mr. Davis left Mississippi and came to Chicago in 1919 during the Chicago race riot in July of that year. Al-though the economic opportunities were much less than he had expected, he entered politics quite soon after his arrival under the Republican leadership of Second Ward

Ald. Oscar DePriest, who a few years later in 1928 would become the first black member of the United States Congress since 1901. When the focus for political participation and leadership for blacks in Chicago shifted from the Republican Party to the Democratic Party in 1936, Mr. Davis likewise changed his political affiliation and became an even more outspoken, articulate, and effective defender of civil rights for black people. He was elected to the Illinois State Assembly and served as its longest-serving member until his retirement.

Though he was ninety-two years old and in a wheelchair when we had our conversation, he was still vigorous, articulate, and very informative about his memories of his experiences in the South and in Chicago. He remained a true fighter for freedom, justice, and equality until his death in 1997.

TB: I guess you already know why I'm here. I'm here because I would like to learn a little something about your family's history and your own as well.

CD: Well, first of all, let me tell you something about my father's older brother, Uncle John Davis, because he was old enough to be able to help General Grant when Grant came down to Mississippi, and back then my father was only about nine years old, so there wasn't much he could do, but Uncle John was already sixteen or seventeen, and that's when they had one of the great battles that was fought down there before Grant ever got to Vicksburg, and it was called the Battle of Milliken's Bend, but I don't know whether you know anything about that or not.

TB: Oh yes, I do. That's part of my history as well.

CD: Well, the Battle of Milliken's Bend was a battle where the slaves were fighting the masters, and they had some whites that were fighting alongside them, and so when the rebels issued an order that there would be no prisoners taken, that meant that anybody that was captured at Milliken's Bend, even if they was white, they would be hung and killed, and so they fought this serious battle, and after that Grant decided that he was going to have to go back to Memphis because, you see, he knew he was going to have to use gunboats to take Vicksburg away from the rebels.

TB: Why did he need to use gunboats? Didn't he have enough soldiers?

CD: Well, it was because, if you know anything at all about Vicksburg, then you know that the fort they have there is way up high on top of one of the highest hills, and so that's why Grant decided that he was going to have to use gunboats to get in there, but in order for him to get in there up close with those gunboats he would also have to dynamite the Mississippi River because you know the Mississippi River in its natural bed is really at least three miles away from Vicksburg, and now, a lot of people don't know about this, but what he decided to do is that he would use some of the blacks that were fighting with him to lay that dynamite, and the reason that he did that is because he thought those rebels wouldn't suspect that people that looked like slaves would ever be doing anything like that, and so what Grant did was he got them to lay down three miles of dynamite from the Mississippi River all the way down to Washington Street in Vicksburg!

TB: All three miles in just one night?

CD: Yes, and all night long those black guys, they had laid down that dynamite for him, and that is how he dynamited the Mississippi River, and when the rebels woke up the next morning, the river was running right up to their front doors! Well, today that's what we call "Grant's Canal," but, back then, those rebels, they didn't allow you to call it "Grant's Canal," and they would kill you if you did, but, anyway, now that river was running all the way down to Mulberry Street below Washington, and so Grant, he came on in there between them two hills with them gunboats of his all ready to knock out that fort, and that's how he got in there, but the important thing for us to remember is that blacks, they are the ones who laid that dynamite! And then, when they had that battle there, seventeen thousand Americans were killed, and four thousand of them were black, but, even though there are no names on any of those graves, my father knew where his brother John—Uncle John—was buried, and we used to go out there on what you call Decoration Day, and we'd put a flag there on his grave, and I sometimes wonder if maybe it is still there, but I just wanted you to know that my father's older brother is buried out there in that cemetery and that there were seventeen thousand of them that were killed there in that terrible battle!

TB: And four thousand of them were black! Some free and some slaves?

CD: Some free and some slaves.

TB: But they were all black men fighting for their freedom.

CD: Yes, they thought they were fighting for their freedom, and they thought that they had won it, and they did, but then there was that Hayes-Tilden deal, and that's when they were lied to and tricked into losing it again because, you see, this Tilden was a man who was a prosecutor in New York, and he had made quite a name for himself by prosecuting those gangs in New York City and all that sort of stuff, and so he decided to run against Rutherford B. Hayes for the presidency, and he did, but the results of that election were so close that the election was thrown into the House of Representatives because it had been declared a tie, and so the rebels, they made a deal with Hayes that they would give him the votes he needed to win if he would just withdraw all them government soldiers out of the South.

TB: And those federal soldiers that were stationed down there, many of them were black as well as white, weren't they?

CD: Yes, and ever since the end of the Civil War, they had had both black and white soldiers that were stationed down there to keep those damned rebels in their proper place, and now those rebels, of course, they didn't like that at all, and so they made this deal with Hayes, and he took it, and most of the people down there and everywhere else for that matter, they didn't know nothing about that damned deal that Hayes was making, but I'm sure that you know how and why it was that they didn't know.

TB: Yes, first they double-cross us, and then they try to cover up what they've done.

CD: And so that's just exactly what happened, and there in the House of Representatives those rebel representatives from down south, they voted all their votes to make Hayes the president of the United States over Tilden, and so that's how Rutherford B. Hayes, he got to be president, but now, even though he was president, he knew damned well they were still going to kill him if he didn't keep his word to them, and so the next thing that he did—one of his first administrative things—was to withdraw all the soldiers, black and white, from out of the South, and that's what broke things up down there because now black people, they had no protection for themselves! None whatsoever!

TB: And is that when Jim Crow came in and the Ku Klux Klan came out in force?

CD: Well, the old rebel army, that was the Klan, and, yes, that's when they started all the killing and everything else. It was a real reign of terror, and up to that time we had already elected I don't know how many black congressmen, although it was at least either ten or twelve, but those were the last black congressmen we ever had down there after that just because we was voting Republican for Hayes, and now he's double-crossed us and done made a deal to withdraw all them soldiers from out of the South.

TB: And many of those soldiers were black.

CD: Like I said, a lot of them soldiers were black, and so they took them all out and left us down there without any proper protection, and that's why when somebody tells me about that separate-but-equal law, I always say, "I come from down in Mississippi. So don't tell me nothing about that separate-but-equal law. That's the thing that killed my Uncle John Davis, who's buried down there in Vicksburg!"

TB: May I ask you, Mr. Davis, when were you born?

CD: I was born in 1900, and now I've passed my ninety-first birthday, and the reason you see me get this color that I got is because, even though my grandfather was as black as anybody else's grandfather, he was married to this white woman, and she was the old master's daughter, and that's why my grandfather's daughters, they all came out looking so light, and when they started to grow up a little, all the white men down there, they wanted to have my grandfather's three daughters, and he tried his best to keep them away from them, but that was always his biggest worry, and it was a constant struggle, and then one day down there this white guy, he grabbed my mother, and there just wasn't nothing she could do about it. He just took her, that's all, and so my grandfather knocked him in a ditch, and that's when he had to leave because if he didn't, they were going to kill him for sure, and he had to leave everything behind, which meant not only his daughters but everything else he had, including all the land he had cleared and now owned, half of which was in Mississippi and half was in Louisiana, because, in those days, if you cleaned up new ground, then that land was yours, and my grandfather even had a title to it, but he had to leave all that land behind just because he knocked somebody in a ditch who deserved what he got and much worse than that, if you want to know the truth! So, well, whoever my father was, he was white, and one of my mother's sisters, she also had children by this same man, but she never told me his name.

TB: You never even knew your father's name?

CD: No, and I didn't want to, but then, when I got older and I was preparing to go off to school up to Tupelo, that was when this other white guy who said he was a friend of my father, he comes over and says to me, "You can't go to school in Tupelo because that's where your father's own family lives, and he don't want you there, but if you want to go up north, your father will pay for all your school and everything, but you've got to stay away from here and go all the way up to New York!" Now, that's what my father told his white friend, and that's what his friend told me, and that's when I told him, "So what he wants is for me to go away and leave my mother? Well, you just tell that so-and-so that I don't know who the hell he is, and I don't never want to know his name because if I learn who he is I will kill him—damn me if I don't kill him!" So, of course, I didn't go to New York or anywhere else for a while, and that man who is my father, he never gave me anything, and I wouldn't have taken nothing from him even if he did, but then, a little later on, my mother, she got married, and pretty soon I had a sister, and so my mother had to get a job, and she was working for five dollars a week, and she would work all day and then come home and take a little washing to do at night because I think that she was getting about two dollars a week for doing things like that, and that was why I decided to join the army when I was just seventeen years old. My mother couldn't take care of us and send no two children to school and pay for our food and our clothes and our rent and all that kind of stuff for no six or seven dollars a week. She just couldn't do it, and she just couldn't do it because no one could!

TB: You said that you went into the army. When did you go?

CD: I went into the army in 1917 when I was seventeen years old, and I enlisted down there at Beachwood, and the man they had down there, he says to me, "You ain't nothing but seventeen years old, and you got to be at least eighteen to join *this* army! So why don't you just go home and wait a little bit longer." Well, that's the way the law was, and so now what am I going to do? But then this same guy, he says, "Do you *really* want to go?" And so I say, "Hell, yeah, I want to go because I need to go somewhere where I can make some money, and I can't make nothing down here, and my mama can't take care of no kids and feed them and send them to school and pay no rent and all that with her having only five or six dollars a week. She just can't do it, and I don't want her to do it, but I don't want her to know that I'm joining." And so he said, "Well, I'm going to put you down in this book as 'C. A. Davis.'" And so that's the name I was enlisted under, C. A. Davis, and my mother, she didn't know I was in the army until somebody told her, "You know that boy of yours, he went down to Beachwood, and he enlisted," and so that's when she went down there and tried to get me out, but when my mama gets down there, they say to her, "What you say his name was? We ain't got nobody here by the name of *Corneal* Davis," but I was there all right, although not for very long, because this was World War I, and that was when President Wilson was making all them speeches about how doing what is right is more precious than peace and how we must now all fight for that thing which is right, and he kept on making them speeches like that until he convinced the Congress to declare the war!

TB: Did you go overseas?

CD: Oh, yeah, and the first thing you know they sent us right over to fight in them old trenches over there, and that's when they gave us some of them machine guns for us to fight with, and those were something that was new back then, and so they showed us how to load the ammunition belt through the gun so that you wouldn't put your finger up there in the wrong place and get your damned finger torn off!

TB: Which unit were you in?

CD: Well, pretty soon they took me out of that machine gun thing, and they put me in the medical corps because a lot of those black men that they was drafting, they couldn't read or write, and they had to be trained how to use a stretcher or even put on a bandage and things like that, and so they put me in there because at least I had gone into my last year of high school, and I had a little education, and so they thought that I could train them, and I did.

TB: And your job in the army was to train those recruits?

CD: Yes, I had to train them because our job was to bring the wounded from off the battlefield, and that's what we did, and I trained those men and taught them how to put tourniquets on and how to use a stretcher, and I had to even teach them how to crawl through all that mud and hitch up the wounded onto those stretchers and pull them back on in, and that was a hard and dangerous job for us to do, and what made it even harder was that some of those soldiers—especially those white guys who were Marines—they didn't even want black people like us to come anywhere near them, but we were the ones who still had to go out there when they got shot and bring them back off the battlefield!

TB: Without your help, they would have died out there.

CD: And without our help, they wouldn't have won that war because let me tell you something that a lot of people don't know, and that is that we didn't even start to winning World War I until our black troops got over there, and what's more our people have also helped this country win every darn war they ever had! Do you hear what I'm saying?

TB: Yes, and black troops also stayed out there on the front lines of combat much longer than any other group and, in that way and others as well, they helped to supply what's called a "margin of victory" because victory would not have been possible without those contributions that they made.

CD: Well, of course, it wouldn't, and I suppose it was another "margin of victory" like that when those black soldiers in the Fifteenth New York Infantry came in there and chased them Germans out of France, and most people don't know about this either, and this is the fact that it was also black soldiers that chased them Germans out of Belgium as well, but in order for us to be able to do something like that we had to fight under the French.

TB: Rather than the Americans?

CD: That's right, and here we were supposed to be fighting for this country and making it safe for democracy and all of that, but they had to take a French general and put him in charge of all the black soldiers before they would let us chase them Germans out of Belgium, and that's just what we did. We marched right up to those barbed wires that them Germans had put up there between Belgium and the French territory, and ninety-nine of our black men died right there on those wires, but the rest of us, we tore them damned wires down and ran those Germans out of Belgium, and I know all about what happened because I was right there when we doctored the ones that survived and buried the other ones that didn't!

TB: When you came out of the army, what did you do?

CD: Well, when I came out of the army, all of my people, they had already left Mississippi because, just before then there was a boy in Vicksburg that I used to play with who was named Hamilton, and one day they picked him up because some white woman said she had been raped or something, and they took that boy who was completely innocent, and they hung him up on a tree, and that's when the black people all started leaving Vicksburg because they wasn't ever hanging black people like that in Vicksburg before then, and so my mother, she sent me this newspaper with the article in it about this boy that had been hanged, and she knew I knew him, and so in her letter to me she said, "Son, we are leaving."

TB: She sent you that letter while you were still in the army?

CD: Yes, and I was still drawing my army pay and sending her part of it, and that was why she had enough money to leave there, and so she left there and came up here to Chicago while I was still in the army, and that was because of all that lynching that was going on down there, and do you know that none of that would have happened if those Republicans, they had not got rid of the army down there?

TB: Yes, but let's get back to your own story.

CD: But that's also part of my continued history because when I got out of the army, that's why I came here to Chicago.

TB: Is this 1919 or 1920?

CD: I came back here in August of 1919, and the reason I was so late in getting back here was because I came back with a service-connected disability that I got over there having to do with the fact that my feet was all knocked out from being in all those trenches and battlefields, and so, they were paying me a little for these service-connected disabilities that I had, but that just wasn't enough for me to live on, and so I went over to this employment office that they had for servicemen to go to down there on Van Buren Street, and I went in there to register and gave them my name and filled out a form they had, and then they sent me around to about three different places to where I might be able to find a job, and so I went to all those places, and at each one of them I had to fill out another application, and each one of those had a place on it where I always wrote in the word "colored."

TB: In reference to your race?

CD: Yes, I always put "colored" on there in reference to my race, and then the man I gave it to would go back with that thing to some office or another and come back and say to me, "Sorry, but we don't need nobody today," and so then I'd go back there again the very next day, and the man would say, "I seen you were in here yesterday, didn't I?" And I would say to him, "Well, you said you didn't need no-body *yesterday*—so what about today?" And I did that same thing three times at three different places, and I got three answers—all of which was "no"!
[*Laughter.*]
And so, after the third and last time of that kind of thing happening to me, I came back to see that fellow in the employment office, and I walked right up to him

and asked him to tell me what the hell is going on, and so he went over to where the telephone was, and, well, what he said I don't exactly know, but he was talking to the people that he had sent me to, and he must have raised hell with them because when he came back, he looked at me, and he says, "Listen, I'm going to ask you something. Are you colored?" And so I says, "Hell, yes, I am colored!" And then he says, "Well, I'm going to send you out somewhere once again, but this time will you do something for me?" And I say, "What?" And he says, "This time when they give you an application like that, you just write 'American' on there and don't write nothing else. Don't you write no 'colored' on there. Write 'American' if you really want to get that job!" And so I told him that I would do what he said, and so he sends me over to an office that's near to where they used to have that old Illinois Central terminal, and when I got there, I do exactly what he tells me, and I write "American" on that application just like he said, and that's the way I got my first job here in Chicago, but ain't it a shame that after I've been soldiering and risking my life for this country, now I can't put down "colored" and even get myself any kind of a job in a city like this?

October 20, 1991

LILLIE LODGE BRANTLEY

PHILLIPS/DuSABLE ALUMNI COUNCIL FOUNDER

Lillie Brantley was a pleasure to be around. She was cheerful, efficient, informed, and worked hard for the causes in which she believed.

I first met Lillie in 1980 when I joined the '35–'39 Phillips/DuSable High School Alumni Council. We are a group of people who graduated from that building, which was located across the entire 4900 block of Wabash on the east and of State Street on the west. Back in the fall of 1934, there had been a fire at the Wendell Phillips High School, which was located at Thirty-ninth Street and Prairie. The building at Forty-ninth and Wabash was originally being constructed as a separate high school designed to keep the rapidly growing black high school population contained within the narrow ghettoized area known as the "Black Belt" or the "Black South Side." Then, when the fire destroyed a portion of Phillips High, a decision was quickly made by the powers in charge to move the entire school to the new building, which would now be called New Wendell Phillips High School. That name remained until June of 1936 when a group of historically knowledgeable black women demanded that the new building be named after the first known nonindigenous settler in this area—now known as Chicago—who was a black man whose name was Jean Baptiste Pointe Desaible (now known as DuSable). Hence the inclusion of members of those earlier classes with our own into our combined '35–'39 alumni group. Lillie Brantley was one of the founders of this group, and until she passed, one of its most efficient organizers and sustainers. The time spent with her in this conversation is invaluable to a clearer and more concrete understanding of what it was like to be a young African-American woman growing up on the South Side of black Chicago.

LB: I was born in Midville, Georgia, in August of 1921, and I came here when I was four or five years old in about 1925 or 1926. We lived on the South Side on Thirty-ninth Street. If you recall, there used to be an ice house there on Thirty-ninth Street. I think it was near Cottage Grove.

TB: Do you remember the circumstances that brought your family up north at that time?

LB: Well, down south my father said the white people controlled everything. When he and the other farmers had their crops all in and they took them to town to sell in order to get nails or grains for the next year or something like that, the white people would tell them how many bushels they would net from their acres and that would determine just how much credit they would get. But, because my father could read and write and count, he would go around and let the other farmers know how much they were really supposed to get. Naturally, the white people resented that, and so he knew that in due time he would have to leave. That's when he made up his mind to come north. So he came first, and then, by degrees, all my brothers and sisters came. There were five girls and three boys. We were all brought up here in shifts, and I'm the third from the youngest.

TB: Do you remember your grandparents at all?

LB: No, I only met some of my father's brothers, but after dinner in the evenings, my father would tell us about his parents and his grandparents. We would always say, "Papa, tell us about the South." He told about the unity that existed for him with his sisters and brothers. We were always taught that you must first learn to live with your sisters and brothers because in doing that you would also know how to relate to other people and to get along. It was a story without an end.

TB: What do you remember about your mother?

LB: I don't remember her at all. My mother died when I must have been in about first or second grade in school. My father died before I finished high school.

TB: So, you don't remember personally any of the South?

LB: No, and I only went back there after I was eighteen because I had made a promise to myself after listening to my father's stories to go back to Augusta and talk to his sister. Her name stuck out in my mind, Lorena Jones. She had fourteen children, and when I went there, they took me around to meet all the other relatives.

TB: Augusta is also the home of Paine College, which is a prominent AME college in the South. In fact, it has quite a few of its graduates living here in Chicago now. So, eventually your entire family came up north and settled on Thirty-ninth

Street between Cottage Grove and, let's say, Langley—in that general area. What do you remember about it?

LB: It was still relatively a poor neighborhood, predominately black. I started kindergarten there at Drake School.

TB: Which was then at Twenty-sixth and Calumet. I'm guessing that most of the young people who were from the South were also going to Drake when you were there. What kind of work did your dad do?

LB: He worked for the Santa Fe Railroad. He worked in the yards.

TB: That was almost within walking distance from where you lived.

LB: Yes, my father walked to work many days. A lot of times they gave the workers some of the fruits and vegetables that would come in on the boxcars. If a crate was broken, they'd give what was inside to him, and he'd bring it back home with him. That's how we got a lot of food!

TB: You were close together with your brothers and sisters in terms of the spacing, weren't you? Most of them were older?

LB: We ranged from two years to two and a half years apart, and that's about it. I'm third from the bottom.

TB: When your mother passed, you had two sisters who were younger than you.

LB: Yes, I think I had just started to school. I can still remember all the help and support that was given to us by a neighbor of ours from Olivet Church.

TB: Your family went to Olivet?

LB: That's right, Olivet was quite a church. Dr. L. K. Williams was the reverend. Reverend John Branham was his assistant, and he had two sons, the Branham boys.

TB: Yes, John now has a church in California and the other brother, Joseph, has a son, Charles Branham, who is doing some research over at the Harold Washington Library. Charles teaches at the University of Illinois and Northwestern. He was raised in Memphis after his father and mother separated. You know, his father had a church of his own at Sixtieth and St. Lawrence or something like that. But these Branham boys, they were good-looking. They went to Phillips, but they used to hang around DuSable.

LB: They went around with my older sisters.

TB: John was younger than Joseph, and they both went on to Grambling and from there they went to Virginia State and to Morehouse. Back then, the Olivet Church was also kind of a cultural and social center, wasn't it?

LB: Yes, it offered everything. I would go to church every day but Saturday, and the only reason I didn't go there then was that there was nothing going on. The rest of the week we had our youth groups, and we visited other churches and joined in various activities. We even organized a club that involved other churches, regardless as to their denomination, and we called it the Olivet Progressive Society. At one time we had over one hundred in membership, and that club has continued to this day. When Reverend Jackson came in and the members were disbanded from Olivet, that club did not dissolve because that club was something that Dr. Williams told them they could continue to have. Reverend Jackson disagreed and said it could no longer meet at the church because the members were not all members of Olivet. But we all had the same cause, which was to worship and to socialize.

TB: Reverend Williams was killed in an airplane accident, as I remember, in 1940. I think he was traveling on behalf of the Republican candidate Wendell Willkie, and he was killed going to Michigan to make a speech. There was a lot of mourning for him. My mother was a great admirer of his.

LB: Yes, he was a great man. The dissension started after Reverend Jackson came in at Olivet. We were accustomed to having financial meetings with the deacons in charge and making reports concerning the finances of the church, but he didn't want the members to have access to those financial reports and to take any kind of an active part—so he started eliminating the deacons that did not go along with him, and at the last meeting we had, he dismissed so many deacons that naturally their entire families left with them. Then all the other people, they also started leaving.

TB: Whereas Reverend Williams had encouraged active participation, Reverend Jackson discouraged that kind of independence.

LB: That's right. He was the one who had to take charge of everything, and we had not been accustomed to that. If you asked a question about the finances of the church, that became a big no-no at that time, and anybody that disagreed with him had to go!

TB: So the membership began to decline, particularly the young membership.

LB: We had a group called the Herald. They were the officers of all of the circles of the church, and they disagreed with Reverend Jackson—so they were all voted out. Only the people who agreed with him remained!

TB: So, the membership of the church, young and old, began to just vanish from the congregation of one of the great black churches in the United States.

LB: That's right.

TB: Now, the reason I'm pressing you for your memory of Olivet is because in the period that we're about, that early part of the twentieth century—at this period, Olivet was like a haven in the storm for some people, and it was like a port of entry for many other people. In other words, people who were newcomers to the city could trust Olivet's programs to embrace them and coach them and send them along. For a long time it was a kind of center for the community.

LB: Yes, and they also would help people find jobs. Reverend Williams never turned you away. People could come with their problems to him, and he would always have the time to listen. As a matter of fact, we had so many various programs that a lot of young people were employed right there in the church.

TB: Another little bit of history on the church itself, the building. Before John D. Rockefeller donated so much money to the University of Chicago and they moved to the Midway, that building had been the chapel for what was then the University of Chicago when it was located along Thirty-first Street. Back then, the University of Chicago was just a small Baptist college and Olivet was its original chapel.

LB: That's right, because I did hear my sisters and my father say how they used to walk to the old church up on Thirty-first Street.

TB: So it has a Chicago history as well as black history. What was your maiden name? Did your dad ever marry again?

LB: Lodge, I was always Lillie Lodge, and my father never married again. He said that he wanted to keep us all together, and under his guidance, my sisters and brothers, we raised each other, see? We were told to do what the older ones said without asking any questions, and that's how we were. We had moved from Thirty-ninth Street down to Twenty-fourth Street, and then we went to Douglas School. During that period of years, we made several other moves, and we finally ended up at Thirty-second and Vernon where we lived with one of the members of Olivet Church because she had a house with enough space. She rented several rooms to my father, and then also he paid her to watch us while he went to work with my older sisters and brothers. That's when I went to Douglas. Both of the principals at Drake and Douglas were white, and the faculty was mixed black and white in Douglas. Douglas became overcrowded during that time, and so Douglas was divided up, with the first grades through the sixth grades staying there at Douglas while seventh through eighth grades went to a place at Twenty-sixth and Calumet. We were only there a couple of years, but that's where we graduated from—Twenty-sixth and Calumet. It wasn't open as a school very long. Now it's a clinic once again.

TB: Now it is part of the Mercy Hospital complex at Twenty-sixth and Wabash, but, historically, it was the old South Division High School, and out of South Division High School grew Wendell Phillips. There were so few high school students in Chicago at that time that they had only two divisions. One was South Division, and one was North Division. That was South Division. When the neighborhood grew, they needed a larger school, so that's when they built Wendell Phillips in 1903. My sister went to Phillips in 1920 or '21, and at about that same time, Bishop Carey's son, Archibald Carey Jr., also went to Phillips, among many other people.

LB: When we were going to Phillips, that's when they had these old potbellied stoves they used to heat the classrooms.

TB: It was cold as could be! I mean, your backside would be freezing even though your stomach was warm!

[*Laughter.*]

What had happened was that they gerrymandered the lines so that all the black kids would have to go to Phillips

LB: We had been enrolled at Phillips to come in that September, and then the fire occurred.

TB: That would have been September of 1935.

LB: That's right. We were looking forward to going to Phillips, and then the fire happened, so they sent us over to DuSable. Mrs. Bousfield was also over there at Phillips, as the principal. They transferred a lot of those teachers from Phillips over to DuSable.

TB: It was then called New Phillips. I was on the basketball team, and some of us, Jack Cosey included, we went downstate to play basketball as the team from the New Wendell Phillips High School, but then the next semester, I think, they changed the name to DuSable High School. Anyway, you went to DuSable in 1935?

LB: Yes, we were the first full class to graduate from DuSable.

TB: Chuck Davis was also one of the early ones to graduate from DuSable. He went on to become a very important person, and the late piano player, Clyde Winkfield, also graduated in that early group, but what were your own experiences during those years at DuSable?

LB: It was very crowded, but I liked the school. I was very active in school. I was a secretary for Walter Dyett, and I was also in the chorus. There were a lot of good programs there, but there were class distinctions, socially, and at that time, we were prejudiced within ourselves. The lights went together, and the browns went together.

TB: So you were selective and selected by the various groups that existed at DuSable, socially and academically, and you got involved with the famous Captain Dyett. Who are some of the musicians that you remember from that period that were in the band?

LB: I didn't know any of them personally, but one fellow that I admired was Edward Stovall. After he graduated, he came back to DuSable in order to continue to work under Walter Dyett. He was in the army, and he played the trumpet.

TB: Were you involved in any of the famous Dyett "Hi-Jinks" productions?

LB: No, not actually. I was always in the little operettas and various programs like that in the chorus under Mildred Bryant-Jones. She was a very meticulous person. One thing that she had a fetish about was, if you spoke to her, you didn't walk around her desk to talk to her but needed to stand in front of her. She kept you at a distance, and, boy, would she chew you out if you'd go around and talk in her face! You must always be a lady in her class. You mustn't talk loud but talk very low. If you were in her class, she would also give you little auditions to be sure that you could really sing. But, even so, she was a brilliant lady, and you learned quite a bit—and not just about singing! You had your music book in her class, and you learned theory as well.

TB: At that time the National Youth Administration had a program for young people who might have needed financial assistance to stay in school.

LB: That's right. The NYA was there to help pay your class fees and various things like that. They also had the NYA chorus.

TB: Did you know any of the young men who joined the Civilian Conservation Corps?

LB: I know of some, but they were not at the school. They were on the outside. I think the CCC got them jobs working on the part of the Outer Drive which was being built at that time.

TB: Yes, and those young men got good, rigid discipline. They made a little money and that kept them off the streets, and that saved a lot of those young men. As a matter of fact, a lot of those boys also went to work up in Skokie. At that time Skokie was just one big swamp, and these young men helped to clear it. So the work they did, as far as I can remember, was useful work.

LB: Very useful, and I think it's unfortunate that we don't still have some type of program like that anymore. We wouldn't have so many gang problems if young people actually worked.

TB: What was life like on the South Side, as far as you can remember, growing up?

LB: My activities were very limited because I was not allowed to go to dances and various things. The only time I went it had to be an "invitational," because my father was very strict, and, in turn, my sisters were just the same. So they would escort me to various things. Otherwise, I wasn't permitted to go. In fact, when I was growing up, almost all of my activities would stem from the church.

TB: After your family stopped going to Olivet, where did you go then?

LB: We went to the First Presbyterian Church because my sister, who helped to raise me, lived over in Woodlawn.

TB: When you graduated from DuSable in '38, what did you do?

LB: I went to Wilson Junior College, and after I graduated from Wilson, I worked for about two years for Cook County Public Aid, and then I went to the Board of Education, where I started as an internal account treasurer in the finance department.

TB: So then you transferred your membership to the First Presbyterian Church, and you moved away from the old neighborhood.

LB: Yes, but you know, it's amazing how you find that when you have lived in a neighborhood like that, even though you move away, you still stay in touch through the years. When I was living at Twenty-fourth Street and Twenty-sixth Street, in that area, Oscar Brown and his older sisters and brothers were in school with my older sisters and brothers—and Ernest Griffin. His mother and father knew my mother and father. They lived at Twenty-ninth and Ellis, and his father owned the Bell Funeral Home on Michigan Avenue, and that funeral home was originally a part of Olivet Church.

TB: When did you get married?

LB: In '48, and then we moved in with my husband's aunt at Forty-ninth and what is now King Drive, and then from there we went to Sixty-first and Greenwood.

TB: Were your children born while you were living there at Sixty-first Street?

LB: No, we were living at Seventy-first Street when my son was born and in Woodlawn when my daughter was born. My husband and I purchased the building, and we still had white tenants when we moved in there, but then that neighborhood changed right before your eyes. Everybody in that area used to take pride in the upkeep of their homes, and they had the block clubs, but all those things gradually went down.

TB: Yes, I remember that. Yes, I noticed the change, because I was doing a lot of work with St. Clair Drake and with some of the people at the University of Chicago that were kind of watching those rapid neighborhood changes and saying that overnight you might look up and it would be all gone! And with South Shore it was even quicker. Those neighborhoods didn't ever get a chance to stabilize. So, now, at the present time you have two children and some grandchildren as well, don't you?

LB: Yes, I have two grandchildren, my daughter's children. She went to Hyde Park in 1968. That was just after her father died in 1967. She graduated from Hyde Park High School with honors, and then she got a scholarship to Lake Forest College. When she graduated from Lake Forest, she received her bachelor's degree in social studies. After that, she taught social studies at DuSable for five years, but when her husband received a job at Lake Forest College in admissions, they moved up to Lake Forest because the college provided housing. She had her first child, and then she started teaching in Lake Forest in several other schools. Then they moved from there to Evanston, and now she's teaching in Evanston at Chute. She received her master's, and now they're doing quite well. My son was born in 1956. He went to Chicago State. When he finished, he joined the Air Force and went in as a paramedic. So he was with the medical unit, and they sent him to Cambodia, and then he came back and went with the ambulance paramedics. Then he went from there to join the police as a regular policeman on the Task Unit. Not too long ago he broke his leg, and he has been injured several times, but, even so, he still likes his work on the police force.

TB: My best friend, Billy Williams, who has since died, his son also decided he wanted to go to work on the police force, and that's what he does, and he also enjoys his job, but you know, it's hard for me to figure out why anybody would choose to be on the police force. Howard Saffold also loved it. He retired not because he had to but because he thought he'd do some writing, and he should because he was with Harold Washington during some very important times. Tell me, Lillie, going back through these years, coming to Chicago, growing up on the South Side, who are some of the important people you remember?

LB: Well, I'll say the Griffins and some of the other people that were poor and on our level, but they succeeded. They made it. It was very important to me to succeed in whatever you strived to do. When I was teaching at DuSable, I used to tell the kids that were on the wrong road—that would say to me, "I don't have a mother" or "I don't have a father"—"Well, that doesn't matter because I didn't have one either." It has to be within you to want to strive for better things, and that's what I have always felt and believed to be true.

TB: What do you believe was the source of that conviction? Was it your religious background?

LB: Yes, of course, but also very instrumental in my life was my sister's husband. When she married, it was just after my father died, and she felt, "Well, I now have the responsibility for my sisters and brothers—so I can't get married. Not now because that would be like getting married with the responsibility for an entire family," and her husband, he told her, "I didn't ask you what your problems were. I asked you to marry me. I already know what your problems are, and I also know that together we will find a way to solve them." And so from the first day they were married they immediately had three children: me, my brother, and my other sister. Her husband never ever refused us anything that we wanted just so long as it was something that would better our lives. His name was Milton McCloud, but we called him "Uncle Mack," and he always had a smile for us. I used to go to him and get my carfare for school, and then on the weekends I would go back to him and get seven cents or whatever so I could get something or do something, but he taught you that if you borrowed you should always be sure of what you wanted. If I would say, "Uncle Mack, loan me a nickel or a dime," he would say, "Are you *really* sure you want to borrow it . . . or do you want me to give it to you?" And if I said "borrow," then, believe me, I had to pay it back!
[*Laughter.*]

TB: He was teaching you discipline and responsibility. How did he earn his living?

LB: He was a butcher, and when I first met him, he was on Forty-fifth and Cottage at the grocery store, and then he went to Forty-seventh near Evans in a grocery store there. Then he got a job at Jewel, and he ended up as one of the supervisors for Jewel. Before he left Jewel and retired. Whenever Jewel opened a store, he would go there and set it up, do the hiring and all of that. He was quite a man with Jewel before he retired. He had come from Hattiesburg, Mississippi, and he didn't even have a high school education, but he wanted that. So, when one of the white men in the South asked him if he would drive him north, my brother-in-law did exactly that. He drove that guy up north, and he never went back. He went to Phillips—their evening school, and he graduated from Phillips.

TB: It's very important for young people to remember that generation of migrants from the South, those people who came here because they felt there were better things, and then they worked to make things better. They had relationships with one another that helped inspire the younger generation. That's the reason I was asking you about these "role models" as they call them now—they were heroes! Your sister and her husband, it is wonderful the kind of commitment that those people made.

LB: I also tell my kids about my father, Wiley Lodge. He taught himself math so he could figure out the acreage and not be cheated. When my sister was going to high school, and when she had problems with her algebra, my father would help her, and I would listen—I was smart at listening—and he said to her, "There's no problem to this. All you have to do is read." Now they're stressing reading, but my father taught us the same thing years ago. He said if you can read, you can do anything. He believed that if you acquire knowledge, which is something you can never get too much of, then prejudice vanishes. If you have something to offer the world, they will forget what color you are because they will need you. He said when you leave this Earth, you should feel within your lifetime that you have contributed something to the world. I remember he used to make these big cardboard multiplication tables of from one to twelve, and there was always a contest, and all the kids in the neighborhood—oh, they loved Mr. Lodge!—they'd sneak by from their homes and repeat the tables for him. Whatever he gave them, it wasn't much. It could have been a penny or a nickel, but they would come and compete to see who would be the first one to learn the tables from one to twelve. And then if it wasn't that, it was something else, but it was always a process of learning. They loved him, and that has stuck with me. You can never acquire too much knowledge. We'd run home with our report cards, and if it was the average, a G or something like that, he would look at it, and he'd say, "You only got a G? Anybody can get a G. You just didn't put forth enough effort." And then he'd say, "When you went to school, you were not cold, and you were not hungry, and so at least you could listen. If the teacher explained it, why didn't you get it? If you can read, why didn't you get it?" He didn't pressure us, but he always made you feel that you could do better and get more. He preached to us that women must excel because women are supposed to use their brains. "Men may have to use their back because they may not have any other alternative, but a woman must learn to use her head and not her back." And his penmanship! He would sit and write for hours because back then he would be able to make extra money writing for people. In fact, his penmanship was so perfect, we could never sign our own report cards because we couldn't write that good! He was a very polished man. You'd never know he wasn't a college graduate.

TB: Yes, there was an attitude and an air about the men and women of that generation. They were in their own way kind of aristocratic.

LB: Yes, that's right. He was a very proud man. When I told him about getting some assistance at school, he said, "I am your father, I will provide." People used to tell him in church, "Mr. Lodge, you can get public aid." Oh, no! That was an insult. "I provide for my family"—and he always did the best that he could to provide for us. I remember one of the neighbors would say, "They don't have anything," but we were clean, and we were proud! We washed that same dress every day! But I always think now that if he hadn't set such high standards, then we would have had nothing to work for. It kept us trying to climb higher on the ladder.

TB: Well, just by observation, Lillie, I would say that for the years that you've lived there have been ups and downs, but in general life has been good to you. It shows.

LB: Well, I would say, looking back to our era, it was hard coming up, but now I'm proud. I'm proud even of all the problems because they made a better person out of me. They gave me a better insight into life and a better way to raise my children and the determination that was necessary. I'm proud of what I learned because it helped me to instill certain principles in my children, and I know they will make an even more successful and better life than I did. I can see in my daughter the family principles that have been instilled from one generation to another. She is now instilling those same principles in her own children. That's the basic foundation, I would say, for blacks. We must maintain this family unity and have those same shared basic principles so that our children will know they have a goal they must attain. You can live by all kinds of rules and regulations in society, but you still need to have those basic foundations within your own family—and right now we need to re-create that unity and love within our families so we won't have so many broken homes without either a mother or a father. It is very important for a home to have them *both* living there.

TB: Listen, thanks so much, Lillie, I've enjoyed borrowing this time.

September 9, 1991

ROBERT COLIN

POLICEMAN AND CIVIL SERVANT

I first met Bob Colin in 1979 when I moved to my present apartment in a co-op fifty-three-unit building at Forty-ninth and Drexel Boulevard. He was, as his narrative indicates, an extremely interesting and sophisticated gentleman. He often spoke with me about his experiences in Chicago from the age of fourteen until the time of his death seventy-eight years later. During that long period of time, he was not only a policeman and local government employee but was also a pioneering black star football player at what was back then an almost all-white Englewood High School and later went on to Northwestern University as one of the first blacks on its football team.

He was always a vigorous and informed participant in local, state, and national politics, while also raising a family and still finding time to enjoy the exciting nightlife of the South Side at its various theaters and nightclubs. Bob Colin not only witnessed some of the changes that have occurred on the black South Side of Chicago but in a very positive way helped to make some of those changes happen.

His widow, Mattie Smith-Colin, has continued for many years to be the culinary columnist for the Chicago Defender.

TB: Robert, tell us something about where you grew up.

RC: We always lived in a white neighborhood. I was born in Indianapolis, and so was my sister and a younger brother. When I got my birth certificate, it had "white" on there. See, the doctor was white, and he didn't pay no attention to color at that time. He served all the people in the community. I remember him because he still took care of Mother until we moved from there in 1919. Back then, he was still driving a horse and buggy, and anytime he was in the neighborhood, he'd stop by. It was one of those things he did. His office was just a few blocks from us. When we lived there in Indianapolis, I doubt whether it was even 1 percent black. Black people lived all over town, east, west, north, south—anywhere where they could get a place to live. The grammar schools were segregated, but not the high schools, because they didn't have enough blacks to go to their own high school. By the time we moved from there, there were only two high schools there: Shortridge and another school. After 1930 black people began to quarry in from the South because of the jobs that were available.

TB: I remember Crispus Attucks High School because it was the home of a great basketball player, Oscar Robertson. I was teaching at Gary's Roosevelt High School at that time, and so I lived in Gary for a little while. It was like a northern southern country town.

RC: I started carrying papers when I was eight or nine years old. My father made enough to take care of the family in those days, but most things were cheap anyway, and my father also always had a hustle on the side. On Saturday my mother would cook a big thing of chitlins and he'd go up to the tavern near where he worked, and the guy that owned that place would let him sell those chitlins in there—and, shoot, he'd sell out every Saturday! But he always took good care of the family, and things were so cheap back then, you know. We could get beans for two cents a pound. We didn't have the chain stores like they do today, and even when the first chain stores came along, they used to have bins where you could buy dry beans, dry foods, and stuff like that. My dad used to take me to buy a new pair of shoes for a dollar and a half! But then came the war and that's when inflation set in. Prices kind of kept going up until they got to be the way they are today. The war started in 1914, and I had two brothers. One was at Indiana University, but my oldest brother wasn't in school, and so he was drafted and went off to camp. My second-oldest brother served by taking training in ROTC at Indiana University, and those guys, they would've gone too if the war had lasted. Well, in 1914, I was just nine or ten years old, and I wanted to go to war so bad I could taste it, you know? Man, when we were in grammar school, I wanted to go to war, but the war ended in 1918, and I'm going to tell you a story. You won't believe this, but I used to hustle newspapers. They didn't have no newsstand in those days in Chicago or anywhere else. Well, when the war ended officially, there in Indianapolis, the whistles in the factories started blowing about two or three o'clock in the morning—so I got up, put my clothes on, and went downtown to get the papers. I sold those papers until daylight, and then I saw there was a little white

kid who was selling flags, and he couldn't handle those flags fast enough! They were giving him a quarter, fifty cents, even a dollar for those flags of his—so when he got through, I went over there, and I said, "Where did you get those flags?" He said, "Come home with me," and I took my little pennies that I had made by selling newspapers—I must have had about two or three hundred—and I invested them in flags! I bought all the flags I could buy, and I came back out there and sold all those flags. Then I had to go back and get more flags, and I just kept going back and forth, see. Well, I left home at two o'clock in the morning, and I didn't get back until nine o'clock that night. We had a telephone at that time, and I should have called, but I was so busy making money I didn't even notice the time. Back home, you know, they were worried because they didn't know what had happened to me. From two o'clock in the morning until nine o'clock at night, and I hadn't been home at all! So, when I get home, my father says to me, he says, "Where have you been?" and I said, "Well, I was selling newspapers," and then I said, "and I was also selling flags." He said, "Well, take your pants off. I'm gonna give you what you deserve for worrying us that way." Well, in those days we wore slacks, and when I took my britches off, money went everywhere!
[*Laughter.*]
And so my father said, "Where did you get all this money?" I guess I had about three hundred dollars, and back then my daddy wasn't making even ten dollars a week! You see, we were paying two cents for those flags and selling them for a quarter, fifty cents, or a dollar, whatever they would give you when they bought those flags. Ha! Well, my father, he took all that money, and, I swear, that's when we moved to Chicago! And he didn't whip me either!
[*Laughter.*]

TB: So then you all came here in 1919 just about the period of the race riot?

RC: Well, we came here in May, and when the riot started, we were at 4933 Wabash. Before then, we were temporarily for a few days at Fortieth and State. That's where my father's sister lived. Anyhow, the riot—let's see—it was in July, and I ought to have been about fourteen years old, I think. That riot took all the religion out of me and all the patriotism as well because of what they did to blacks. You know State Street was the main street for us back then, and they were out there pulling blacks down State Street with their cars and then shooting those blacks right out there in the street!

TB: And at that time State Street was the main street in the black community?

RC: Yeah, it ran right through the entire area where blacks lived, what few blacks there were. You know some black people also lived on Dearborn, Federal, State, and Wabash. Of course, not too many lived on Michigan Avenue because Michigan was white all the way through. When we came, down around State and

Thirty-fifth Street was the main area for blacks to live. They were mostly in that area, and that area started, as I understand it, around where the Dearborn Station was. It was just mostly blacks in there, and then they moved south and they kept going down further south, but the fact was that when we moved in on Wabash, our next-door neighbors on one side were white. Later on, the few whites on that block eventually moved out.

TB: Were you living south of the area where the riot occurred?

RC: Well, it kind of forked out. There was more activity around Thirty-fifth and State, but all along State Street there was shooting, and, in fact, when the state militia came in, they stayed in the Farren School during the time that they were here, and that was just a block away from us.

TB: Yeah, at Fifty-first and Wabash.

RC: But that riot, it wasn't just Chicago. It was Detroit, Cleveland, all over.

TB: Even East St. Louis.

RC: Yeah, and you know what the problem was? They didn't want blacks to come north to work.

TB: How did they end the riot?

RC: Well, they stopped it by force. That's when they called the militia in, but the hatred has been there ever since — and, you know, it was even there before then for that matter, and it is still there. Even with all the things that have happened, even with Washington having to become the mayor and all that business.

TB: What about the black neighborhoods, what the *Defender* calls the "Black Belt"?

RC: Yeah, well, I don't know if the *Defender* started it or who started it, but it was known back then as the "Black Belt," but I don't think that you can say you had more black businesses there then than you have today. Back then, most of the businesses were either barbershops or beauty parlors, you know? In the twenties, there was one black who had three drugstores in the black community. He had one out on Forty-fifth and State, and another one down at Thirty-fifth Street, but I think he had three. This was in the twenties, and the problem that blacks had was that whites owned all the business property, and a lot of times they wouldn't rent to blacks. I mean, we also had a few grocery stores or delicatessens, but at that time blacks had more businesses down in the South than they had up here in the North because segregation was so complete in the South. You know, I started going down to Hot Springs in 1959. That was the first year I went down there, and at that time there were two black hotels, and they both did good business, but after '65, when they broke the segregation laws for restaurants and for public places, then these hotels went out of business. Blacks would rather go to the white hotels! That's the difference between the black community and other communities. Take the Hungarians. They will come over here, get together, and the first thing they do is go into business because over here they are free to do things like that here which they weren't, maybe, over there, but blacks have neglected their own business and stopped serving themselves. Now they don't ever serve themselves! You know, it's a funny thing about the Europeans that come in here. They work together. Now the Arabs, they are coming into our community and opening businesses, but not us. If blacks would ever learn how to work as a community together, then nobody like that could come into our neighborhood and do business if we didn't want them to.

TB: Yes, if we could just learn to work together.

RC: But black people, most of them, they haven't learned about business. They think the only way to make a living is to get a job! Don't they know that sometimes you can also work for yourself! There's a thousand ways to make money *if* you learn how to do it, but blacks are just negative about business.

TB: At one period of your life, you were a salesman, weren't you?

RC: Yes, I was a salesman. I worked for Continental Liquors for two or three years. The guy that owned the Continental was bootlegging during Prohibition, and when the law changed again—it went into effect in '20 and then it went out in spring of '33—a lot of those bootleggers, they had money and went right into legitimate businesses. Most of them had black salesmen because of the communities where they had their distribution houses. That was one of the main reasons that they had to hire black salesmen. By the time I went to work for them, there were only about four or five distribution houses. When they had started back in '33, there must have been forty distribution houses, but they gradually went out of business through competition. So in 1935 I decided to join the police department out in Robbins.

TB: Do you remember when Robbins started?

RC: No, I think Robbins started before I came to Chicago. I think it was a black guy by the name of Robbins that started that town, you know, and I think he started that town back in the teens, 1914, 1915, 1916, something like that.

TB: I remember my father talking about, "Let's try and buy something out in Robbins," but my mother never could see that.

RC: Well, when I went out there, I was still selling liquor, and I took the job with the police only part-time. I started not to take it, but a friend of mine—the guy that influenced me—he had connections there, and he just kept begging me, and he said, "Now, listen, you could do most of the people some good out here." That was because their police department at that time was volunteer, as was the fire department. There was only one or two of them that were on salary. All the rest of them were mostly volunteers. When I signed on, I only got two hundred fifty dollars a month for being the chief! But that was all right because I was also still working as a liquor salesman, and I had a lot of time on my hands. That was because in that liquor business you sold all your merchandise on Monday and Tuesday. See, when you'd go in Monday, the guy would give you the order for what he needed, and that was the end of that. What he sold on the weekend, you'd fill up again for him, and that was it. So on Monday and Tuesday I made at least sixty calls or more like that, and I'd work from about eight o'clock in the morning, just as soon as I could get out there, because they could open at seven, until nine or ten o'clock at night. You understand? Just taking orders. And on Tuesday I'd come out just as early but I didn't usually work quite as late, and maybe I'd be through by three or four o'clock. Whatever they sold over the weekend, they would replace that merchandise, and then there was no more business for the rest of the week. So you had Wednesday, Thursday, Friday, Saturday, and Sunday as times when you didn't have nothing to do. Well, of course, the company wanted you to do "missionary" work. You know, to go around and generate some new business, and then they would also have a company meeting on Thursday afternoon. A lot of guys, they made so much money, the company felt that they should make them work a whole week, and even when they weren't selling nothing they should at least be doing some of that "missionary" work. As I remember it, we had a Greek guy over there that made more money than the owners, but, of course, he supplied every Greek grocery store, bar, and restaurant in Cook County!

TB: So you didn't stay very long in Robbins?

RC: Well, there was too much factional fighting and messing around. I couldn't stand it. I even went to printers that printed that type of merchandise for the county and the city, and I had some arrest books and arrest slips printed up and set everything up for those people, but then they would just lose them and never even use them.

TB: How big was Robbins when you left?

RC: Robbins must have been about seven or eight thousand. They were all homeowners, and some of them had businesses out there. They had only one tavern in the community, and the guy who ran it was one of the local politicians, and he violated all the laws because he stayed open just as long as he wanted to!

TB: Robbins is adjacent to some other black towns, isn't it?

RC: Well, there's another town just south of Robbins that has a black mayor today: Harvey, Illinois. They have a black mayor, but Harvey wasn't completely black. There were whites there too.

TB: There are some pretty large factories around there, aren't there?

RC: Well, you had factories all around there, but there were none in Robbins. When Robbins got that incinerator plant burning all the garbage, the towns around there tried to stop it, but they weren't successful. But in general, in Robbins they had nothing much to tax except property.

TB: Now, when you joined the Chicago Police Department, what were the major problems that a law enforcement officer had to face in the district where you worked?

RC: Well, when I went into the department in June 1935, even though Prohibition had ended two years before, they still bootlegged, and that was a big problem for us.

TB: Even after Prohibition had ended?

RC: Yeah, you still had the bootleg joints that were still existing that sold the stuff because they could sell it cheaper, since they weren't even paying any taxes on it, but of course, they eventually were wiped out. Remember when Prohibition started? It was January 16, 1920. At twelve o'clock that night, the moment when Prohibition started, they opened up all the speakeasies!

[*Laughter.*]

They just opened the doors, and everybody walked right in! In fact, it became even more pleasant to buy liquor because now there were more taverns than there were when it was legal, and so, you see, it was a major problem for the federal department to try to control what was happening. It was so massive, and most people had such disrespect for the law. These guys were bootlegging for fourteen full years, and those racketeers in the bootleg business, they would fight each other all the time, but most of the time they didn't bother anybody else. What happened was that the government had a problem that they couldn't do nothing with—and the only way for them to solve that problem was to bring Prohibition to an end, and that's exactly what they did.

TB: What about the entertainment, Bob, in the black community back then, as you remember it?

RC: Well, during that period, say in the twenties and thirties, the entertainment was controlled mostly by Jews where blacks were concerned. In fact, that was also true even where whites were concerned. Jews completely controlled the recording business in the black community in the twenties and thirties. In those days, recording equipment would only run you about five thousand dollars or so because back then things were so cheap, and so those guys set up companies to record and sell black music.

TB: Labels like Okeh and Vocalion?

RC: Yeah, they were probably all Jewish outfits. Blacks didn't really get into the thing until they started in Detroit, and that was very late in the business.

TB: Yes, in the sixties.

RC: Back here in Chicago a lot of blacks were still making songs that sold for fifty dollars flat, and then the guys who made the recording, they would turn around and sell a million of them and get to keep all the money! Those guys down here, my wife worked for them for a while. Shoot, they didn't do nothing but rob the blacks. They were brothers. They are dead now.

TB: What about the quality of the live entertainment?

RC: Oh, live entertainment. What they called "black and tan" that meant whites could come into the black community, to any place they wanted for that matter, even though you might still be barred from their community, you know?

TB: Uh-huh. But whites could always freely come into and roam around in the black community.

RC: Yes, and back then practically all the policemen were white. Even when I left the police department, fifteen years later in 1950, there was still less than 1 percent black in the entire police department.

TB: And almost none in the command office.

RC: I think Bluett was acting commander. He was on the list for promotion, but they promoted all the others until they finally got down to him, and then, when they finally made him commander, he was ready to retire. He had been acting commander for six or seven years, and the guys under him were responsible for him getting made commander because they kept clamoring for him to stay on and get the promotion he deserved. You know, when I left the job, I think there was only one black sergeant and no lieutenants.

TB: Was that sergeant a guy named Bob Harness?

RC: Yeah. But you know something else? When I first went on the job, there were a lot of Polish policemen, and they couldn't even read and write. They couldn't make a report out, and those were the guys they mostly put in the black community. They walked the streets—you know?—and they couldn't even write their own names!

TB: How did they get the job?

RC: Politics. When I took the exam, if I had had three hundred dollars to give someone I could have gone to work maybe six months ahead of the time that I finally went to work, you know. That's how bad politics were. The common, ordinary policeman was nothing more than a guard. He'd just walk the beat, and that was it.

TB: The job for police officers today must be considerably more stressful now than it was back then.

RC: Yeah, when I was there, even then, we had a little narcotic problem but not like today. Most of it back then was just marijuana.

TB: Heroin hadn't come in yet?

RC: No, not commonly among the street people. People with money may have been using heroin and whatnot. You know, entertainers and those kind of people, but it wasn't a problem in the black community. Now, on the other hand, marijuana has always been a problem, all the time, because you could grow it yourself. You can get the seeds and grow it in a pot or in a box, just like any plant that you have in the house.

TB: I used to know the beat cop in our neighborhood. Every neighborhood had a neighborhood cop like that.

RC: Yeah, but that was prior to 1950. You know, the various improvements that have come along have always aided crime as well. See, you know, say back in 1920, it took you half a day to go fifty miles.

[*Laughter.*]

Some son of a bitch committed a crime, and he had no way to get away, but now a guy can hold up a bank here, and in five hours he can be in Detroit. Just get in a car and get on a highway, and in a half hour you could be in Gary, and in another five hours you can be three hundred miles away!

TB: And these guys have two-way radios now, and they can pick up all the police signals.

RC: Yeah, they can do just like these truck drivers out on the highway. These truck drivers listen to the police calls, and they got a code to tell each other where the police are out there on the highway. These guys are warning each other all the time, you know, "slow down."

[*Laughter.*]

TB: Well, things have certainly changed in the black community since you first arrived in May of 1919.

RC: Well, of course, today it's difficult to designate a black community because blacks are living almost all over the city. See, Rogers Park has a lot of blacks, all the way up to Evanston. They are living up there because the people moved out from those places to go to the suburbs, and now you can see just as many blacks in a lot of these suburban towns that are adjacent to the city. They're living almost everywhere, and when you go down to the Northwestern Station, or any of the stations, you will see blacks coming back into the city because now some of them work for those big corporations and are making very good money.

April 8, 1992

IDA MAE CRESS

SCHOOLTEACHER AND ACTIVIST

Ida Mae Cress was ninety-two years old when we had our conversation, but her memories were still vivid and precise. Mrs. Cress was a member of the well-known and distinguished Griffin family. Her grandfather was born in Virginia but moved to Canada, where his German-born mother and African-American father had taken refuge to escape the tyranny of slavery and racial prejudice.

Mrs. Cress was born in 1903 in Chicago's Hyde Park neighborhood. She graduated from Hyde Park High School at a time when very few blacks attended that school or even lived in the neighborhood. While she was still quite young, her family bought a large single-family home near Thirty-first and Lake Park in the Douglas community. Her family remained in residence there until the New York Life Insurance Company, through eminent domain instituted by political leadership in the city, bought up all the property between Thirty-fifth Street on the south and Thirty-first Street on the north and between South Park on the west and Lake Park on the east. This meant that all of the residents of that area, including the Griffin family, were forced to move out regardless of their history, their present income, the quality of their maintenance of their property, or any other personal or public factor. This expulsion was accomplished under the rhetoric of "slum" clearance and urban renewal, and very soon the Lake Meadows housing development and shopping center grew out of these displacements. Fewer than 10 percent of the displaced families ever moved back into the neighborhood. Many of them moved into East Woodlawn, where the former restrictive covenants had been recently abolished by legal decree. It was during this period that I first met Ida Mae Cress as well as her physician husband and their three daughters.

Ida Mae Cress was a longtime public schoolteacher and is still a vigorous community activist. She helped to initiate and activate the Woodlawn Organization, which was organized by Saul Alinsky. The story of her life provides an important perspective on the continuing struggle of black people on the South Side of Chicago to preserve their community and its values from the very beginning of the twentieth century until the present era.

TB: Your grandfather was in the Civil War?

IC: Yes, my father's father, Charles Griffin, fought for the Union.

TB: And he lived in Chicago, didn't he?

IC: Well, let me see. He was born in Virginia, and when the Civil War was over, he went up to Canada, where he married Lorraine Cook, who was of mixed heritage. One of her parents had come to New York from Germany, and in New York she was working as a seamstress when she met this handsome brown-skinned man who had served in the Civil War. They moved to Canada because they were uncertain about their living together being accepted in New York at that time.

TB: And how old was your granddad when he married this pretty lady?

IC: Well, he'd been in the army.

TB: So he must have been at least seventeen, eighteen, nineteen, twenty years old.

IC: Yes, I would suppose he was probably in his early twenties when the war was over.

TB: So, in terms of his birth, that would take him back to about 1835.

IC: Yes.

TB: Did you ever have the opportunity to know him?

IC: Oh, yes, I can remember when we moved from Hyde Park back to Thirty-first and Ellis—that was in 1910—and my younger brother Charles was the first of my mother's children to be born there. Charles was born, I guess, in 1914, and Grandpa was living in the Soldiers' Home in Milwaukee by this time, but Charles was his grandson, and so he came down to Chicago to see him. Charles was named after Grandpa, but his middle name was Steven from my dad's name. And then a couple of years later Mom had another boy, and they named him Ernest.

TB: Had your grandfather or any of his family ever been enslaved?

IC: No, not that I know of.

TB: There were quite a few black people in Virginia and in Maryland who never were slaves, and so it seems that your grandfather must have been a free man who had volunteered for the Union army.

IC: Yes, and that's the reason why my brother, Ernest, feels so strongly about the location of the funeral home he owns. The reason is that back then, at that time, there was a place called Camp Douglas there where the funeral home is now located, and Camp Douglas was where my grandpa, Charles Griffin, volunteered for Civil War service!

TB: Oh, that's wonderful.

IC: And what's more, you see, we all went to *Douglas* School as well.

TB: Yes, that was because at one time Stephen Douglas had owned almost all of the land around there.

IC: Yes, and the park at Thirty-fifth and the lake is still called Douglas Park.

TB: And it sits there with almost no one who lives around there knowing anything about the connection with Stephen A. Douglas—or even knowing that what was then the old Illinois Central Railroad, all of that, was part of Stephen Douglas's enterprise. He wanted that railroad of his to become the major railroad that industry and commerce would use to go from north to south and from south to north. But he lost, and, of course, the South never gave up its hostility toward the North, and eventually all the major railroads went from east to west instead! [*Laughter.*]

IC: Most of us, we don't know our own history. Not our real history.

TB: And people forget the pioneers that black people have been in the development of this part of the city.

IC: That is certainly true.

TB: When your family first came to Chicago sometime around 1893, at that time there couldn't have been more than ten thousand of us living here in this city—and so they had to make their own way in order to survive and raise a family.

IC: Well, the fact is that the churches also had a pretty strong influence in those early days. The church was where people met and came together. Not many of them had been able to bring many things from their homes in the South to the city, and the church was really what brought them together. They continued to have a common church—whether it was a Methodist or a Baptist!

TB: And which church did your own family attend?

IC: Well, I would say in those earliest days, the churches that we attended were Bethel and Olivet.

TB: At that time, Bethel used to be at Thirtieth Street, just west of State Street.

IC: Yes, and the people who attended those churches, as a whole, they all lived in that area, all the way down to Thirty-ninth Street.

TB: And then you had another patch of black families that lived in southwest Woodlawn.

IC: Yes, that's right. Southwest Woodlawn. I still remember there was a family that lived next to us, down at Thirty-first and Ellis, and they moved from there out to Rhodes Avenue in the 6400 block.

TB: But they didn't live north of Sixty-third Street. They lived south.

IC: Yes, south of Sixty-third Street.

TB: And then you started to have black families living in Morgan Park as well.

IC: Yes, I remember because Helen Green, who was a friend of mine who had gone with me to Hyde Park High School, her family moved out to Morgan Park, and when I went to have lunch with her, that was my first experience going such a long way on the Halsted Street car.

[*Laughter.*]

TB: And what about the North Side and the West Side of that period?

IC: I don't recall ever having occasion to visit anybody on either the North Side or the West Side.

TB: Well, in that period of time around 1920, were there any black folk living, say, from Thirty-ninth and Michigan over to what was then called Grand Boulevard or south as far as Fifty-first Street?

IC: I don't recall, but I don't believe that anybody that I knew lived along Grand Boulevard.

TB: Well, when our family moved from Forty-ninth and Vincennes down to Fiftieth and Calumet—in 1924, I believe—that was considered a great *big* jump!

[*Laughter.*]

IC: And who were your new neighbors?

TB: They were white. All white.

IC: That's what I was going to say!

TB: And what happened when we moved in, in about a week or so, somebody bombed a building which had formerly been a synagogue but had just become Bethesda Church.

IC: Yes, I remember that happening because the Baptist minister there was also connected to Olivet Church. Was that one of those fires that happen "accidentally" on purpose?

TB: I really don't know. I was so little that I can't remember, but I know my daddy always thought that the white folks had bombed it because they thought that black folks were moving too fast.

IC: Yes.

TB: See, we were expanding and moving further south, and, as a matter of fact, at that time it became prestigious to live further south on either Michigan or Grand Boulevard—but not somewhere in between.

IC: Not in between?

TB: No, definitely *not* in between—but, even if you were living in a kitchenette, *if* you were living on Michigan or Grand Boulevard, you were considered to have a somewhat higher status than somebody who had to live on Prairie or Calumet! [*Laughter.*] But you said that you yourself didn't know anyone who lived that far south at that time.

IC: Well, there were some people that lived next door to us on Ellis Avenue, the Upshaw family, and they moved from, I guess, it would have been 3151 Ellis Avenue out to Sixty-fourth and Rhodes. That was quite a distance!

TB: Way out south! [*Laughter.*] Now, the movement south, aside from those little communities that we've been discussing, continued to be very interesting because it went further south block by block by block.

IC: Yes, it did.

TB: And then came the kitchenettes! [*Laughter.*]

IC: Oh, I can recall that some people felt sort of squeamish about those kitchenette apartments because, I guess, they tended to be overcrowded.

TB: And they were! Our family lived in a nice, large apartment, but we were forced to move out of it so they could cut it up and make smaller kitchenettes out of it, and that also made it harder for people like us to find a regular-sized apartment because the landlords could make so much more money by renting out all those smaller units.

IC: And they definitely made a lot of money!

TB: And one of the people who made good money on that type of housing was a man by the name of Carl Hansberry.

IC: But he wasn't the only one.

TB: No, but he made it possible for the others, and all this time black folk were still busy moving. They were creeping south, and they jumped across Wabash onto Michigan Avenue.

IC: Oh, yes, surely, because I can still remember that we would always walk home down Michigan Avenue from Olivet when it was at Twenty-seventh and Dearborn. And when I was in elementary school—at Douglas School—there was a family by the name of Kern. I don't know if they were Jewish or what, but the boy's name was Jacob and his sister's name was Cedre, and they were kids who were often brought to school in a little electric car. Do you remember those little electric cars that we used to see a long while ago?

TB: Yes, I remember.

IC: Their family was, you know, pretty well-to-do, and they lived at, I think, 2945 South Michigan. Their mother was quite generous, and she would do things to help the school where her kids were. I can remember at holidays she would give her children candy to bring to school, and they also brought their storybooks to school.

TB: Do you remember what kind of books they brought to your school?

IC: Yes, for example, the Oz storybooks were brought to school by Cedre and Jacob, and our teacher read those Oz stories to all of us.

TB: And this was at Douglas School?

IC: Yes, and when I started at kindergarten in 1910 at Douglas School, there was a little girl named Geneva Nettles, and she was the only other little brown person in the kindergarten. Then a few months later there were a few more of us that came in, and by the time I graduated from Douglas in 1920, the class was fifteen and fifteen—fifteen whites and fifteen blacks.

TB: Douglas was still very mixed. Where did you go to high school?

IC: Well, I had been born in Hyde Park, and my father had a good friend—George Garner—and one of George's brothers was going to Phillips, and he had been sort of goofing off like kids will do—so, anyway, Dad decided that he wanted me to go to Hyde Park High School in the neighborhood where I had been born.

TB: So, when you went to Hyde Park High School in 1920, about how many black students were there?

IC: When I started, because I was living north of Fifty-fifth Street, and I was using the old address in the neighborhood where I lived at Fifty-second and Lake Park, I was the only brown-skinned person in my division room. The class that year entering Hyde Park was larger than the main building could easily accommodate, so all the students who were living north of Fifty-fifth Street—for their freshman year—went to the branch, and they opened one of the old schools that had been closed that was on Fifty-fifth Street—around about Fifty-fifth and Kimbark. That school was reopened and renovated for the first-year class of 1923, but then we went over to the main building at the beginning of our second year. Leon Despres, who was well known in the Hyde Park area, was in my division room that first year.

TB: Your father opened a music store about this time, didn't he?

IC: Well, first he had a candy store at Thirty-fifth and State. Do you know where the State Theater used to be?

TB: Yes, I do.

IC: Well, his candy store was right next door to the State Theater, and my dad's sister, Aunt Martha, managed the store for him most of the time, and one day one of the local musicians—his father was the Episcopal minister at St. Thomas Church—came into the store, and he asked Dad or maybe it was Aunt Martha if he could put up a piece of his sheet music in the window so that people walking by would notice it and come in and ask about it, and that's just what happened! He sold a bunch of copies, and pretty soon several other people also came in and asked about displaying or putting their music in a position where people would see it and want to buy it, and that's when Dad decided, "Well, I guess I might as well open a music store!" So then he moved down to 3637 South State and started what was called the Griffin House of Music. A little later, by the time I hit eighth grade, I used to go over to the store after school and work. I can remember they had a couple of boys who delivered records and player piano rolls, and sometimes the boys would be sent downtown to pick up music or records that were a special request, so they would sometimes send me to make their deliveries. You know, people would call up and say, "Could you send me four or five records?" or "Would you send me certain player rolls?" They always want the current popular songs, and so I often went to deliver music to those places I had never been before, and that gave me a view of life that I was not familiar with—not with my father being a deacon and my mother a strict religious person. I had an opportunity to go to homes that were not quite so religious or so strict.

[*Laughter.*]

So I would deliver this music, and I would sit there while the person played the roll or the record and decided if they wanted it or not. Then they would pay me, and I would take that money back to the music store at 3637 State Street. That gave me a different kind of an education. I felt that I knew more than some of my friends knew!

TB: At least the ones who were girls!

[*Laughter.*]

Now, after you graduated from high school, where did you go to college?

IC: To Chicago Normal. When I graduated from high school, I wanted to be a doctor, but my father said, "There are two more coming after you. You had better go to a teachers' college." In those days most of the people I knew who continued their educations went to teachers' colleges.

TB: That was a two-year program, wasn't it?

IC: Yes, and so I went to the University of Chicago because they had the Loop Program where, if you were taking a major, you went to class twice a week, and if you were taking a minor, that was a class that met once a week. When I think about the tuition, I'm sure I paid twenty-five dollars for a class that met twice a week, and fifteen dollars for a class that met once a week!

[*Laughter.*]

And I was interested in sociology and human relations and things like that—so I majored in sociology.

TB: And so, after you left college, you went into teaching.

IC: Yes, I had been working for the Board of Education, but then the Depression came, and I was laid off. It was then that I started to work for the WPA, helping with the nursery school. Those teachers who had been laid off by the Board of Education because of the shortage of funds were glad to get the chance to work somewhere or other, and when the city developed a nursery school program, because I had been a kindergarten teacher, I was hired to work in that nursery school program. It turned out that Mrs. Rose Alschuler, who was Leon Despres's mother-in-law, was very active in developing the city's program for the WPA nursery school.

TB: So that was a forerunner of what we have now called Head Start programs.

IC: That's right. Very truly so. In fact, just today, I was reading something that I received in the mail from New York about a place called Hale House, where they have a program that's been developed by a Mrs. Hale for helping preschoolers whose parents in many cases have been on drugs and some of them may also have AIDS. And when I read this, I was struck by the fact that I'm very, very sure that the young woman who started this program is Dr. Lorraine Hale, who was one of my nursery school pupils here in Chicago! She sent out a letter telling about this Hale House program for preschoolers and at the top of her letter was a picture of my nursery school class and she is one of the children—more than likely—sitting on the floor by my feet.

TB: Oh!

IC: That was a class picture that was taken, I would say, during the Depression in the early thirties or a little bit later—possibly in the mid-thirties—and now she is using this picture of my nursery school class sitting on the floor by my feet to tell people about this new program that has been started to take care of young preschoolers whose parents need help!

TB: And you were already doing that sort of thing back during the thirties?

IC: During the thirties, yes.

TB: So you stayed with the nursery school program until how long?

IC: Well, in the meantime, because I had married in 1931, I proceeded to become a mother. Lorne, my oldest daughter, was born in 1934. And Frances, my second daughter, was born the next year—1935.

TB: She's a doctor now, isn't she?

IC: Yes, Frances is a psychiatrist. And then Barbara, my third child, was born in 1938.

TB: And Barbara was married to Robert Lawrence, who was the first black astronaut.

IC: Yes, but unfortunately he lost his life in a plane crash.

TB: So all of your children were born pretty close together.

IC: The two older girls were born very close together, and based on my own experience with my children, I started doing human relations work about the usefulness of planning the family, and I took groups of young mothers several times down to Planned Parenthood because from my own experience I think it is a good thing if women learn how to plan the size of their family and even plan the proper amount of space between their children.

TB: As I remember that period, young women at that time, when they got to the city, they just didn't have a lot of children.

IC: That is true. First of all, there was the problem of housing—accommodations for large families were almost impossible to find. And then, I think, when people lived in rural areas, they had farms and gardens, and they could raise enough food to feed a large family. Raising a family was a little more difficult in a crowded place like Chicago.

TB: Yes, well, it certainly was difficult for my mother. She just didn't have any more children after me. Maybe I just spoiled the whole thing!
[*Laughter.*]

IC: After Barbara, my third child, was born, then I went back to work at the Board of Education.

TB: What year was this?

IC: I guess after 1938. That's when I went back to District 11 and taught kindergarten and first grade at Drake School.

TB: And you stayed at Drake?

IC: Yes, I stayed at Drake until in 1962, when our district superintendent came to me one day and said, "How would you like to come out of the classroom?" Well, I had enjoyed my little kids, but I saw how nice it would be to do other work for the Board of Education, and because I had been interested in parenting, I was able to come out of the classroom and do parenting education. Many of our parents were people who had come to Chicago and did not know the city and all of the city services and facilities that were available. Because of various things that are part of the life of a lot of our African-Americans, they just did not have the knowledge of the city facilities that they needed to have. So I brought them down to Planned Parenthood, where the workers in that office were able to explain to them about using medical care and spacing the size of their family.

TB: Now, to go back a little bit, when you got married, where were you living?

IC: Where was I living? When I first married, the first six months that I was married, I lived on Fiftieth Place near Cottage Grove—714 East Fiftieth Place. My mother and father had been living at Thirty-first and Ellis from the time we moved from Hyde Park, but now he was moving over to Thirty-second and

Michigan near to where they had the funeral home, and he didn't want to sell or rent to strangers, and so he asked Henry and me if we would move back down to the house at Thirty-first and Ellis. So I moved back there in June—I had married in December.

TB: Your daddy was an undertaker too?

IC: No, he was not himself an undertaker, but I can explain a little bit about how he got into the funeral business. He was chairman of the Deacon's Board of our church, and in that position, before the days of welfare and assistance to people who were hard-pressed, Dad and some of the other deacons often had the responsibility of getting enough money to bury older people who did not have enough insurance. Maybe some of them didn't have any, and so they often had to go into their own pockets to help bury some of these elderly people, and that is why they formed what was called the Bell Funeral Home, and they kept it under that name for a number of years. Then, when the other men, one by one, because of their health or their age dropped out of the business, my dad asked my brother, Ernest, after he graduated from high school, to go and study the funeral business, and so then when Ernest took over the operation of the funeral home, they changed its name to the Griffin Funeral Home.

TB: So, during this period, you had moved back into the old family house.

IC: Yes, we moved back to the old family house at 3149 Ellis and stayed there until 1953, at which time New York Life started buying up all the property in the neighborhood. One by one, people were forced to sell their homes. We formed a neighborhood organization with the other property owners who lived in that area to try to fight and to hold on to our community.

TB: Now, at that time, there were still quite a few property owners in that neighborhood.

IC: There were quite a number of us, yes. The people who lived on Lake Park, on Ellis, on Cottage Grove Road—all of us were fighting to hold on to our property. We felt that since we were near the Loop, we were near the lake, we had the Illinois Central, we even had the Outer Drive—it was a desirable community, but, even so, one by one, the people were coerced into selling their property, and, as a matter of fact, we were one of the last families to move away from Thirty-first and Ellis.

TB: And so this invasion, promoted primarily by dollars from New York Life, destroyed the unity of the neighborhood and scattered the people who had been living there for so many years. What kind of means did the New York Life people use to convince people that they should sell their houses?

IC: Well, in some cases, they would approach a person whose children had grown up and moved out of the area, and they would say, "If you don't sell now, you won't get as much for your property." It was as though all the money they had to buy up the area was already beginning to run out. "And so you'd better sell right now and take advantage of the fact we still have some money." I can't really say what kind of prices those people were getting for their property. The organization that we formed was called the Property Conservation Commission, and we met at the home of Ollie Turner, who lived in the Thirty-second block of Ellis, down near Thirty-third Street. We met in her basement.

TB: This was from 1948 to 1953.

IC: Yes, right, and I was one of the last people to move from Ellis Avenue.

TB: That site and those sites became what is now Lake Meadows.

IC: That's right. That's where Lake Meadows is now.

TB: Prairie Shores came in about that same time and for the same reasons.

IC: Yes, you see, Michael Reese Hospital was in that area, and they also had their own desires for expansion.

TB: So, now, on the east you have Michael Reese and New York Life, and on the west you have IIT [Illinois Institute of Technology] encroaching—that was a whole lot of power to be up against.

IC: And I'm looking right now at the neighborhood where we live today, and I see that same pattern starting to develop once again. When we moved here in 1953, there wasn't a single vacant lot in the area, but then, around 1971 or 1972, we started having fires in the neighborhood. My husband and I used to get up at night because of what we had experienced with the fires that were set on Thirty-first Street. I remember one night we got up around eleven-thirty or twelve, and over here between Sixty-first and Sixty-second on University, I counted twenty-one firemen standing around with their hands behind their backs while there was just a teaspoon of water being put on the building where the fire was. The purpose was to let the building burn so that it would have to be remodeled, and I am looking right now across the street here where there used to be a complete block with no vacant lots. Now we already have two vacant lots.

TB: Yes, I noticed that.

IC: And when you see Sixty-third Street today, you want to cry because Sixty-third Street, when I was going to high school, looked like the Loop with all kinds of shops and stores, but today Sixty-third Street is just a tragic eyesore, and the condition of those few buildings that are left between Cottage Grove and Stony Island is a sad thing. But at least there is some effort now to improve that area.

TB: Where is that initiative coming from?

IC: Well, the Woodlawn Organization has had a lot to do with trying to hold on to this area for the people who are the current residents, but I had heard in recent months that the University of Chicago has been saying that they need additional housing facilities for their students and their faculty, so there is a question as to what will happen.

TB: Is it your impression that TWO is more powerful than the University of Chicago? I personally think that there is a quiet working relationship which is beginning to develop between them. In fact, just about ten days ago, TWO had a meeting, and there was a representative from the University of Chicago there, but then, of course, there are also a number of other people now who are beginning to realize that we have a very, very valuable part of the city.

IC: That's right. And so there is every reason for people to want this area, and for the people who already have it to value it and fight and work for it. I've already had the experience of having lived in an area that was taken away from the people who lived there.

TB: Yes, you've got that experience behind you.

IC: That's right.

TB: But the lesson that you learned from your experience in the old Douglas neighborhood is that certain forces are now trying to move in and cheapen your property and destroy its inherent value.

IC: Yes, definitely.

TB: And one way or the other, your family has lived in this same area since 1910.

IC: Yes, that is when we first moved here.

TB: These neighborhoods which your family and my family moved into were some of the most desirable areas of the city, and the pressure that is now being exerted to destabilize these neighborhoods is clearly racist as well as economic in its origins.

IC: Yes, definitely, and there's another thing that's very frightening and disturbing today. In the newspapers and radio and television, all you hear about this community is how many people have been shot and killed—and I feel there's almost like a silent, wicked, underhanded program encouraging us to kill each other and reduce our numbers.

TB: Sometimes it seems that way.

IC: And also just think of the kind of impression that all of that violence makes on our young people. They think that our history is how we have killed each other in the past and how now we're still doing the same kind of thing today—and that just isn't true!

TB: That's why we need to reach back and reclaim our own history and its heritage. When you reach back into what you have experienced in the past, then you can begin to see if that kind of experience fits in with and clarifies the needs and problems of the present.

IC: Yes.

TB: Now, going back to the school experience, you stayed in education for how long?

IC: I retired in 1971.

TB: So, altogether you were teaching in the school system for almost fifty years.

IC: Yes, from 1926 until 1971.

TB: And your daughters? One is in communications.

IC: Yes, that's Lorne. During the civil rights period she was very active in voter registration education, and now during the last few years she has been producing radio programs.

TB: And Dr. Weltsen, what is she doing now?

IC: Frances is still doing writing and lecturing. She went into psychiatry.

TB: In private practice?

IC: Yes, but she also travels quite a bit, giving talks and things of that sort.

TB: And Barbara?

IC: Barbara is in employment and training for the city of Chicago.

TB: You've done a remarkable job, and thanks so much for all the time you've given me.

IC: Well, you've helped my memory, and I'd like to thank you too!

August 7, 1992

ERNEST GRIFFIN

———

FUNERAL DIRECTOR AND CIVIL WAR HISTORIAN

Having a two-hour conversation with Mr. Ernest Griffin was indeed an enriching experience. First of all, he had lived in the Douglas area all of his life. Second, the Griffin Funeral Home in the thirty-two-hundred block of Martin Luther King Drive (formerly South Park Way and also once called Grand Boulevard) is located on the site where his paternal grandfather was inducted as a volunteer into the Union army in 1864, on land that at that time belonged to Illinois U.S. Senator Stephen A. Douglas, of the Lincoln-Douglas debate fame. As if that part of his background were not already interesting enough, one of his nieces, Barbara Lawrence, is the widow of America's first black astronaut, Major Robert Lawrence, who was killed in a airplane crash in the 1960s just before he was to take off into space. In addition, one of his sisters, Ida Mae Cress, was one of the first black people to move into southeast Woodlawn after the Shelley v. Kramer *Supreme Court decision of 1948 broke down the enforcement of restrictive covenants anywhere in the United States. The late Mrs. Cress was also one of the founders of the Woodlawn Organization, which was organized as a coordinated effort to save the neighborhood in which they had both been raised.*

There is so much more that I could and would like to say about Mr. Griffin and his family in this brief introduction, but I would rather let Mr. Griffin speak for himself and let you listen to what he has to say. In this way I can share with you what was for me a wonderful opportunity to learn more about more than a century of black South Side Chicagoans' experiences.

———

TB: I'll start right off at the beginning. Ernest, when were you born?

EG: I was born here in Chicago, Illinois, on February 20, 1912. At that time the street where I was born was known as Groveland Avenue. Later, in 1915, Groveland was changed to Ellis Avenue. As a matter of politics, they named Ellis Avenue after Samuel Ellis, who was active in one of the political parties and who also had a considerable real estate interest here in this city.

TB: Oh, is that right? When did your family first come to Chicago?

EG: My father, Stephen A. Griffin, came to Chicago in 1893. He was a native of Dresden, Ontario, Canada, and he was working on the railroad. He came down to Chicago in 1893 seeking employment during the World's Columbian Exposition. That's what lured him from the railroad to relocate here in Chicago.

TB: How did he get up to Dresden?

EG: Well, that's another very interesting story. We actually have a copy of the family Bible of the Griffin clan as far back as 1804, and we have been able to track down where our various ancestors came from. We've been able to check it all, and to the best of our knowledge they were originally a Negro slave family from Virginia. Their moving from place to place was undoubtedly by means of the Underground Railroad from Virginia to Ohio, and from Ohio on to Dresden, Ontario, Canada. Grandfather Griffin, my father's father, he was born in Cleveland, Ohio, on February 25, 1846, and like many Negroes, that movement carried them from the South through various channels of the Underground Railroad on up into Canada.

TB: Was he emancipated or was he still in slavery?

EG: No, when he was in Cleveland, he was a free man.

TB: What about the rest of your family?

EG: Let me read this to you. That Bible is very interesting as to how the Griffin clan and the Cook clan originally got together. We have a page in that family Bible that tells us our great-grandmother, Maria Sofia Pegou, was a German girl. She was born in 1829, in Pforzheim, Baden-Baden, Germany. This Bible was brought by her to New York, in 1847, after arriving in New York from Baden-Baden, Germany. She, along with a sister and brother, had sailed across the Atlantic Ocean in a small oceangoing craft. In New York she met and married a Negro named Daniel Cook. As I said, her maiden name was Maria Sofia Pegou, and they left New York shortly after marriage because her relatives threatened to kill her husband, and then they settled in Canada, Dresden, Kent County, Tenth Concession, Chatham Township. I don't have a copy of my father's birth certificate, but I do have the record of his birth in the family Bible. My father, the son of Charles H. Griffin, was born September 12, 1869, in Dresden, Ontario, Canada, and he often said that he was born on the Tenth Concession, Chatham Township.

TB: What does "Concession" mean?

EG: A "Concession" is a division area, the way the land is divided off in Canada. You were either born in maybe the First Concession, or Second Concession, or that sort of thing. Actually, it is a district.

TB: Like a parish? How did you do this research?

EG: As fate would have it, a cousin of mine has the family Bible in his possession. He is a first cousin to my dad, and it was his grandmother's Bible. So, he made a copy for me.

TB: My mother also kept a family Bible, and when she passed, I think my brother left it at the old house in the trunk, among all her other things. We were just so distraught, and I have often regretted not going back to get that trunk and the possessions that were in there. Of course, she was a faithful record keeper. My dad would say, "Mattie, where is—?" and she could go and look in the Bible and get that information about the family that we needed.

EG: I have an enlarged copy of one of the other pages. It shows in her own penmanship that Maria Sofia Pegou was born the twenty-fifth day of June, 1829.

TB: So your heritage is both African and German.

EG: Yes, that is correct.

TB: No Native American?

EG: No. On my father's side, the brother of Daniel Cook was named George William Cook. Just here a few months ago, the information came through that George William Cook died in 1931 in Philadelphia, and that he was a professor at Howard University. So I wrote to Philadelphia where we traced down the matters of burial and death certificates and obtained the information that his burial took place actually in Washington, D.C. That is to say, he died in Philly, but he was actually buried in Washington, D.C.

TB: There still is a famous Cook family living there in Washington, isn't there?

EG: Yes, and we are trying to track down if there is any relationship. This George William Cook headed the English department at Howard University at one time, but his death occurred before he had the opportunity to fulfill any other offices there on the staff of Howard University.

TB: There is a long-standing—what we loosely call an "aristocratic"—Cook family with a long heritage in Washington, D.C., and I wouldn't be surprised of a relationship because they were all members of the professorial category of our people. When you finish your research, you will have most of those details—so keep on doing it! One of the things that we suffer from is the lack of understanding about our historical background.

EG: That is because of the lack of actual written records.

TB: Very, very little was written, and what has happened is the white scholars have picked up everything they can find and, of course, have placed it in the archives of the various universities where most people don't have easy access to it—and, as a result, very few young blacks, Negroes, African-Americans can go back past two generations to understand anything about their historical background. That's why I always say to them, when I'm teaching, go talk with your grandma and your grandpa and find out how they survived.

EG: Well, this is my admonition to all those kids, all these young folks that we encounter. Do the best you can to catch the senior members of your family, talk with them, and if possible, one day when you can get them in a good frame of mind, and when their mind is clear and their memory pretty sharp, just let them tell you as much information about their past as they can glean from their fading memories.

TB: What about your mother's side of the family?

EG: On her side of the family, unfortunately, very little is known. All we know is that they were natives of Summit Pike County, Mississippi. Beyond that, all that we know is that on my mother's side of the family, one of our slave ancestors, rather than take the name of the slave master's family, decided to take the name of Clay, naming himself after the clay of the earth, and so in the family Bible record, the oldest member on my mother's side of the family is Robert Clay.

TB: Now, your granddad, from what I see on television and have heard on the radio, was quite an illustrious person.

EG: Yes, my grandfather Griffin was quite an interesting personality. Knowing that his wife's father's life had been threatened is what prompted him to come down to Chicago from Dresden, Ontario, Canada, and enlist for Civil War responsibilities. Now, we are told by the researchers and whatnot and those who are familiar with the enlistment of Negro men in Civil War service that at that period of time, Grandfather Griffin actually enlisted for his Civil War responsibilities here in Chicago, Illinois, on January 5, 1864. In that era of time, they did not have satellite locations for a man to go in to sign up for Civil War enlistment. If a man wanted to sign up for Civil War service, he was sent directly to the camp. And that is how and why grandfather Charles H. Griffin enlisted for Civil War service right here in Chicago, Illinois, on January 5, 1864, at Camp Douglas, precisely where you and I, Tim Black, are seated at this time—on the site of that same former Civil War camp.

TB: Oh, my gracious, how proud I am. That's great!

EG: His enlistment records show that he was mustered into Company B, Twenty-ninth Regiment of the United States Infantry. A number of the Negro men who were placed in that unit were sent right down to Quincy, Illinois, and that unit was officially mustered in there in Quincy, and then probably they were put on

board a train, and that particular unit was one of the first Negro units to participate and receive actual military fire action in the state of Virginia.

TB: Was that the forerunner of what later became the very famous Eighth Regiment?

EG: No, that would not be correct to say. The Eighth Regiment was actually composed of units of Negro men who were either drafted or enlisted for service in
World War I right here in Chicago, Illinois.

TB: But the Twenty-ninth Regiment was the original unit?

EG: Yes, the Twenty-ninth was the original unit.

TB: And it was composed of young men from where?

EG: They came from many areas, and they came right here to Camp Douglas and
were assembled and then sent by train down to Quincy, where their official mus-
tering in is recorded.

TB: Were there some whites in that unit?

EG: All the officers were white, yes. Did you by chance see the saber that we have?
Now, that's a very interesting factor of my history and of Grandfather Griffin's history. After my affiliation with the Civil War Roundtable men, I became very
closely affiliated with GAR Post 20, which is in Aurora, Illinois, and was invited
by them to participate in some of their activities. On October twenty-first of 1991,
I was invited out to Aurora, Illinois, to share with them in a memorial service.

TB: A memorial service for members of the Grand Army of the Republic.

EG: Yes, and after they concluded that particular military service on the twenty-first
day of October, we all were invited into their memorial hall to see the artifacts
and memorabilia that they have there. One of the men said to me, "Griffin, we
have something here in our memorabilia we feel that should be down at your location." I said, "What is that?" And they went into their case there and took out a
saber, and that saber that they pulled out was the saber that was issued to Captain
W. W. Flint, Company E, Twenty-ninth Regiment, United States Colored
Troops. I almost dropped that saber when I saw it. I just couldn't believe it. Here I
am holding a saber issued by the United States government to Captain William
W. Flint, of the same military unit as my grandfather, the only difference being
that Captain Flint was a captain of Company E, and Grandfather Griffin was a
private in Company B.

TB: Back then the Negro soldiers could rise in the noncommissioned ranks as high
as was possible.

EG: Yes, but according to the material that I have, one or two of them finally made
captain.

TB: And got into the commissioned officers' rank?

EG: Yes, they got into the commissioned officers' rank!

TB: But ordinarily, that was not the case.

EG: No, and it was not a rapid rise.

TB: In that war there were, I think, nineteen Congressional Medal of Honor winners who were black soldiers.

EG: That's correct, yes, and while we are on that subject, speaking of the Congressional Medal of Honor, have you ever heard about Sergeant William Carney? Well, I can fill you in on that. Sergeant William H. Carney was one of the men of the Massachusetts Fifty-fourth that stormed Fort Wagner, and the actual record is somewhat unclear, but I have a little book on the Negro soldier in my Civil War material, and I'm going to loan it to you.

TB: I'd appreciate it.

EG: I learned of him on one trip I made to Gettysburg. A dealer in memorabilia who has a store known as the Iron Horse there in Gettysburg put me in touch with a man up in Connecticut. I finally had a chance to meet him in person a year ago when I attended a ten-day seminar at the Gettysburg College. Bill Gladstone is his name.

TB: Bill Gladstone. Now, Milton Olive [II] was also there. His cousin is a neighbor of mine. [His son, Milton Olive III, won the Congressional Medal of Honor for jumping on a grenade to save the lives of four of his buddies. A lakefront park is named after him.]

EG: Milton Olive [III]'s father and I developed quite a nice relationship, and some years ago when he was living in Englewood, we served his family. Then he moved from Englewood out here to Chatham. So I guess he was living there in Chatham at the time of the son's death. So, through the years, quite frequently, we would encounter one another, and whenever we would run across material that we thought was of mutual interest, we would pass it on to one another. And so, three weeks ago now, when Milton Olive [II] died, we were the recipient of the service. But all through the years that I knew Mr. Olive, after the death of his son, I always felt and observed him to be a man who was still grieving over his son's death. Rarely ever did you see that man smile or did he ever exhibit a warm expression, and that is why I always had the feeling he was yet grieving over the death of his son.

TB: Yes, he grieved. That was his only child. Every time I saw him he'd ask if I wanted to go out to where his cousin had accumulated some of his son's personal memorabilia.

EG: That boy's mother died just four hours after he was born.

TB: Yes, I thought you might have known about that.

EG: Antoinette and Milton Olive were married for forty-two years. So that tells you it was a short period of time after the son's death that he remarried. One of the highlights that I felt that we were privileged to invoke in his funeral service was that knowing both of them I always had the impression they were still carrying this pent-up burden within themselves, and so on the day of the funeral service I was privileged to choose the musical portion of the service, and I chose to have our staff render a musical selection that you no doubt are familiar with. I venture to say, Tim Black, that you have heard it, and your folks have sung it many times. It was the old spiritual that has the phrase in it, "I'm going to lay down this burden and study war no more."

TB: "Down by the Riverside."

EG: So, we had our staff sing that song as part of the funeral service for Milton Olive, and they sang both verses. "I'm going to lay this burden down, down by the riverside, and study war no more, study war no more. I'm going to lay down my sword and shield, down by the riverside, and study war no more." To me that was one of the highlights of the service, and folks who attended the service just relished that. That just went over tremendously with them. Now, just for the benefit of your tape, I'm going to say this as well. Here, just this week, we had the services for a man who is one of the first Negro baseball players, a man who played for the American Negro Giants. His name was Jimmy Crutchfield. Did you know him?

TB: Yes, but I missed his service. When I was a little boy, we used to walk from Fifty-first and Prairie—my group, my crowd and I—to Thirty-seventh and Wentworth to the old American Giants Park to see him play ball.

EG: Yes, there was an old wood fence around there, wasn't there?

TB: Jimmy Crutchfield and Willie Wells, all of that group—I had a chance to see them. They were heroes to me. When I saw the notice the other day, I realized I had missed the service. What I'm trying to do is to recapture some of our history. If I missed the chance to interview a person, I always try to catch the service, so I can get at least a snippet of what that person was all about.

EG: And then you also have the opportunity, perhaps, of meeting a few of the other old-timers that are left on the scene from whom you can still learn considerable history. For example, at Mr. Crutchfield's service, there was one of his teammates who is now ninety-three years of age. At the funeral service, we were able to inject a little of what we consider embellishment to the service, and so, as we rolled the casket out, we placed a box of Cracker Jack and a bag of peanuts on top of his casket. Then I gave the cue to our musicians to start the selection, "Take Me Out to the Ball Game," and I asked the audience to softly join in and sing as we rolled Mr. Crutchfield out. "Take me out to the ball game. Take me out to the park. Buy me some peanuts and Cracker Jack. I don't care if I never come back!" and you got the implication as we were taking him out that he really doesn't care if he never comes back!

TB: Tell me a little more about your granddad. When he was in the Twenty-ninth Regiment during the Civil War, how long did he stay in service?

EG: He was in for a year and nine months.

TB: And a good part of that was in combat?

EG: Yes, other than the time he was in combat, he was out on sick leave. When their unit left Virginia, they sent him down to Texas. According to the information that we were able to run down, they put him on a ship from New Orleans to go to Texas, but they sat out on the water for seemingly a period of about a month, and while he was out there, he developed scurvy, and so he was mustered out down there in Texas.

TB: Then he did what?

EG: Then he went back to Canada and stayed there for a period of time until his children were grown. Then, one of his daughters moved to Grand Rapids, and he went from California to Grand Rapids and stayed there in Grand Rapids, Michigan, until that daughter died. Then he left there and came back this way, stayed here briefly and then went on back to San Diego. His health was poor after he came out of the service, and he stayed in San Diego for a period of time during which his health seemed to be improving, but then when his health began to break down again, he went into the Soldiers' Home and spent the balance of his time in the Soldiers' Home there in San Diego. Actually it wasn't in San Diego, it was more in a place on the outskirts of Los Angeles—and that's where his death occurred in 1926.

TB: Meanwhile, your dad?

EG: My dad remained here in Chicago.

TB: He was born in Chicago?

EG: No, my dad was born in Dresden, Ontario. He came to Chicago in 1893 seeking employment. He was working on the Canadian Pacific, and he finally worked up to where he was in charge of the buffet car, and, coming through Kansas, due to the laws there, they were not permitted to sell any liquor on Sunday. Well, Dad sold some whiskey out of the club car to a man who was a railroad spotter, and that man told him, "I'm going to write you up. When we get to Chicago, you turn in your keys." Well, when they arrived in Chicago, Dad told me, "I got off that train, and I just kept going." What he meant was that he didn't go about turning in his keys or anything else—and that's how he came to stay here in Chicago.

TB: Did he have any relatives?

EG: No, he had no relatives here at that time. All his sisters and brothers remained in Canada.

TB: So he was here completely on his own.

EG: Yes, he was here on his own, but he didn't mind waiting tables.

TB: Oh, that's right, he was an experienced waiter.

EG: So he waited tables, and he worked down at the Union Station for a period of time. He was one who was able to mix quite well with all sorts of people. While he was working there, he met a man who was opening the Lexington Hotel down on South Michigan Avenue.

TB: At Twenty-second Street.

EG: Yes, and so he also waited tables there for a period of time, and then he met another man who was opening up the old Chicago Beach Hotel. That man made him an offer that he would make twice the money he was making if he would go with him—so he went over to the Chicago Beach Hotel.

TB: Which was located at?

EG: It was located at Fifty-first and Hyde Park Boulevard. The hotel was built by a man named Mr. Hagly. Dad started working there for him the first of May in 1900, and he stayed there from 1900 until 1923, when they built the new building which later on was turned into the Fifth Army Headquarters, and he stayed there until 1939.

TB: By that time he was in charge of the staff?

EG: Yes, by that period of time he was made head porter of the entire staff there. As head porter, he hired all the bellboys there at the hotel and all the porters as well.

TB: And he met all of the famous people?

EG: That's exactly correct.

TB: Did he ever talk about some of the people that he hired?

EG: Yes, of course, but a great number of those men in that area and time were students, and they would come to Chicago or write to my father here when they got his address, and they would ask him if he would be able to employ them when they would come to Chicago over the summer vacation period. And so that's how many of those men earned their college tuition. They would come to Chicago, and they would work for Dad as a bellhop or as a porter at the hotel. The one that made the greatest strides and went to the highest height in the legal field after they had obtained the educational background that enabled them to pass the bar was Bill Dawson. He and his brother, Dr. Julian Dawson, both earned their tuition money working over their summer vacation periods. Bill first. Then, when he graduated from Fisk University, he made way for his brother, Julian. Julian followed through in his own educational attainment and obtained his M.D. degree. Then Bill and Julian even put their sister through school on the monies that they earned working at the Chicago Beach Hotel. As a result of all this, Bill Dawson became like a foster son to my parents and lived in our home with them for a period of time at 5215 Lake Avenue, which later became Lake Park Avenue.

TB: Were you living with them at that time?

EG: No, no. Mom and Dad had already moved from 5215 Lake Avenue, and incidentally, while they lived there, they had a delicatessen. They were the first Negroes that had a delicatessen in Hyde Park. But then in 1908, my dad bought this little piece of property down at 3149 Groveland. That's where my brother Charles was born, and I was also born at 3149 Groveland, but my sisters, Ida Mae and Helen, were born in Hyde Park back at 5215 Lake Avenue.

TB: I kind of grew up with young Julian when they were living at Fifty-second and Michigan.

EG: Do you see the way that property is so run-down today? By the way, Tim, where are you living now?

TB: I'm living on the edge of Kenwood—at Forty-ninth and Drexel.

EG: Well, then, when you leave here, you go over to Prairie Avenue, go south on Prairie Avenue at least to Fifty-first or to Fifty-fifth. Better still, go south on Prairie to Sixtieth Street, and then come over to King Drive and come on back down and then go back on home, and what we have seen—

TB: It makes you want to cry.

EG: Yes, you want to cry, brother. You will weep, you will weep! Now, yesterday Jimmy and I, we were going out to Kennedy-King, and to dodge some of the traffic, we went up Prairie. I had no idea of the plight of the property beginning at Thirty-ninth Street and Prairie and all the way down to Sixtieth Street. You just won't believe what you see, and it will set you to wondering what is going to become of that area. We'll say from King Drive on over to Michigan, that entire corridor down through there—you're going to wonder what will happen to it in the future.

TB: Land like that is too valuable for it to continue to lay fallow. You can see the creeping development that's starting to move south, and some of us have enough information to know it is very, very difficult to buy parcels of that land in there even now. Woodlawn is already being patched up a little bit by some developers, and before long you'll find that the next big thing will be new "gentrified" developments available for sale right there in West and East Woodlawn.

EG: Yes, for sale to those who happen to have enough money!

April 8, 1993

ETTA MOTEN BARNETT

VOCALIST ON STAGE AND SCREEN

Lauded the world over, this vocalist extraordinaire has performed for President Franklin Roosevelt and his wife, Eleanor, at the White House as well as for the thousands who saw her as Bess in the famed 1942 revival of Gershwin's Porgy and Bess. *Moten's singing and acting career was highlighted in three motion pictures, which remarkably were all filmed within a single year. In 1933, Etta Moten initiated her film career by dubbing the singing of "My Imaginary Sweetheart" for Ginger Rogers in* Professional Sweetheart. *Her other RKO film roles of that same year included an unforgettable performance of "The Carioca" in* Flying Down to Rio *and the dubbing of "Remember My Forgotten Man" for Joan Blondell in* Gold Diggers of 1933. *Etta Moten married Claude Barnett in 1934, during the time when Barnett was nurturing the classic Associated Negro Press news bureau, which he had founded in 1919. She has continued to be a pillar of Chicago's cultural life and a tremendous source of inspiration to all who have been fortunate enough to know her.*

TB: Where were you born?

EMB: In Weimar, Texas.

TB: How long did you live in Texas?

EMB: Well, I lived there with my parents, Ida and Reverend Freeman Moten. My father was an African Methodist Episcopal minister. This denomination came out of the Methodist Episcopal church, and my father was a minister who graduated from the theological seminary at Paul Quinn College in Waco, Texas. As a matter of fact, he had just graduated when he first met a widow named Sister Octavia Norman, who was my mother's mother. She was involved with the church, and she had two daughters, one of whom was named Sarah and the other Ida. I am the child of Ida.

TB: Now, Octavia Norman, was she born in servitude?

EMB: Somehow I don't believe that she was ever a slave.

TB: So she would have been born a free black in the South?

EMB: Yes, at least that's the way that I remember it. I know I never heard anyone say anything at all about her ever having been a slave. She had a brother, and I never heard them speak about him having been a slave either.

TB: Do you remember her?

EMB: Oh, yes, I remember Grandma Norman, but she lived in Waco, and soon after he married Ida, my father was assigned to his first church. It was in Weimar, which is where I was born. Weimar was a mostly German-speaking town, and that's why he was sent there. It was because he could speak German.

TB: Did you learn to speak German from your father?

EMB: No, I learned to speak German in college.

TB: When your father was growing up in Texas, did he learn to speak German because there were so many Germans in the community where he lived?

EMB: No, he learned Greek, Latin, and German when he was in college.

TB: Do you remember the name of your father's church in Weimar?

EMB: Probably it was called the Bethel AME Church. Paul Quinn was the name of the bishop in that diocese. At that time each of the AME dioceses had a school of its own, and most of them were named after the bishop of that diocese. So, if we had twelve bishops, we also had twelve colleges, but Papa graduated from the main AME seminary, which happened to be in Waco, Texas. The first of those towns that we lived in that I can really remember was Palestine, Texas, where we lived in the church parsonage. I still remember this little town because it was the first time that I ever saw men digging in the ground and coming up with water. They called what they were doing "digging a well," and that was the first time that I had ever seen anything like that. I also remember my birthday party while we were living there. I was sitting up in my high chair so that means that I must have been at least two or three years old. Well, I was sitting up there in that high chair, and I can still remember this great sea of milk with egg white on it. It was just eggnog, of course, but there was a whole sea of it, and it looked so big to me. I also saw my first grand piano in this little town. The other towns where we lived in Texas were places called Oakwood and Glidden and Columbus, and I still hear the names of some of those towns every now and then on the radio. That's because I listen to the radio much more than I listen to television.

TB: Well, that's probably wise.

EMB: My mother's sister also had only one child, and her name was Odale. We were reared like sisters. Odale eventually went to Paul Quinn, and so did I. She grew up to be a very fashionable young woman, and she lived in Beaumont, Texas, as a grown lady. As you probably know, Beaumont is near Houston.

TB: When your family was living in those small Texas towns, do you remember if your father had much interaction with German-speaking people?

EMB: Well, I remember hearing my father speak German because my father had a two-seated buggy with a lovely French umbrella mounted on it. It was sort of the Cadillac of its day, and sometimes I would ride around with him in this horse and buggy in this same town where I saw the eggnog, and the German men would sometimes be sitting out on their porches in front of their stores, and he would speak to them in German, and they would speak back to him in the same language.

TB: Do you remember if you or your father ever encountered any racial prejudice or discrimination?

EMB: Well, I don't remember ever being not allowed to go anyplace. Only in those stores, of course, you just didn't go behind the counter. You had to stay on the other side of the counter.

TB: So you didn't experience any of the hostility associated with Jim Crow or any form of segregation?

EMB: No, I really didn't know anything about that sort of thing, and I never heard my parents talk about things like that either.

TB: And you never heard about lynchings or anything like that?

EMB: No, I didn't know about those until later when I could read, and when I read about things like that happening, it usually wasn't in Texas. It was generally in those other southern states. In fact, I can also remember reading that Texas almost didn't want to come into the Union on account of things like that. That's one of the reasons that Texans feel that they're quite special people, and people down there really feel that you have to live up to something of value when you are a Texan. So that is the kind of Texans that the Motens were, and my grandpa had a farm, and all of his sons went to college. Papa's oldest brother was a lawyer and a graduate of Howard, and the whole family believed in the importance of education. As a matter of fact, it was because of the value they placed on education that at the age of ten I was sent away to boarding school.

TB: Where was the boarding school?

EMB: The place they sent me to was a boarding school associated with Paul Quinn College back in Waco.

TB: So it was part of the same seminary where your father had gone for his own education?

EMB: Yes, and the reason they had a boarding school like that was so that college students training to be teachers could do their practice teaching on the children like me who were there. During that time, my father was assigned to a different church every two or three years. You know, if a church needed to improve its membership he would be sent there to help them because he was quite an evangelical person, and he was a great speaker. I know that, even as a little child, I always used to like to hear my father preach because he spoke so well. Sometimes they would want somebody to come and help raise funds for building a new church, and then they would send him there to start organizing that sort of thing as well. Often the bishop of his diocese would come around and want to tour the area, and so he would take Papa along with him to point out the different things he needed to see and that sort of thing. So those are the reasons that he sent me on to Paul Quinn. It was because he was involved in so many activities, and he did not want my education to be interfered with.

TB: Did you miss your family while you were there?

EMB: Oh, no, I never missed my family while I was there because—well, I really don't know. I just never did, but I suppose the reason is that there was so much for me to do. I was in the choir, and that's when I learned how to sing and read music.

TB: Would this have been your first musical training?

EMB: Yes, that was my first real musical training, and I was this little girl that had this voice that they kept in training all the time. Mrs. Maggie Roberts was the music teacher, and she taught us to sing in parts. I was generally an alto in that choir, and we had to learn Latin by rote because some of the songs we sang were in that language. Well, anyway, while I was there at that boarding school, my parents moved to Kansas, and from there they went to Los Angeles, and I joined them while they were out there in California.

TB: Now, how old were you when you joined them in California?

EMB: I think that I must have been about fourteen or fifteen.

TB: Where did you live when you were in Los Angeles?

EMB: Papa was the pastor of a church in a Spanish neighborhood, and we lived in the parsonage.

TB: Do you remember the name of the neighborhood you were living in?

EMB: No, but I remember that it was a mixed neighborhood.

TB: Do you happen to remember the name of your father's church?

EMB: No, but it was the church where the Los Angeles chapter of the NAACP was first organized. I happen to remember that because I once had an occasion to report something to them that I thought that they should know about. At that time, in my class at the junior high school, there were only two of us who were not white, and our teacher, he spoke to our class about the fact that not everybody kept their yards clean and looking nice because it was becoming a mixed neighborhood, and, well, I didn't think that our teacher should have said something like that to our class, especially because it wasn't even true!

TB: So was your father involved with the NAACP there in Los Angeles?

EMB: Oh, yes, yes, yes, the Los Angeles chapter of the NAACP was established right there in the back of my father's church. He let them have their meetings in the church. He always made it available to them. The lady who was one of the organizers, I still remember her because she was the editor of a Negro newspaper called the *California Eagle*, and she was quite a remarkable person.

TB: Was your father ever an officer in that chapter?

EMB: No, he was a minister, and he didn't have time for things like that. Besides that, very soon my father became a presiding elder in the church, and my parents moved to Kansas City, Missouri, and I went to school in Quindaro, Kansas, which is just across the river from Kansas City. I went to high school at another church school which was associated with Western University, and one of the AME bishops who had a home there on the campus, Bishop Vernon, his signature was on the United States money, and that was the first time I had ever seen anything like that, and I was proud of it. I also remember being very impressed by a beautiful statue of John Brown, the famous abolitionist, that was there on that very same campus. Well, anyway, it was during my senior year that this sharp young officer who had just become first lieutenant came to campus in his new uniform and became the head of the school's business department.

TB: What was his name?

EMB: His name was Curtis Brooks, and because he was the head of the business department, one day I was told to go to his office so that he could look at my books, and, of course, we looked at each other as well, and, well, we fell in love because we were attracted to each other. But then, after his first year there, he decided he had to leave and go to Oklahoma. The reason for that was because his brother was married to a woman who was a native of Oklahoma and who owned about eighty-five acres of land which had oil on it, and so they needed Curtis to come and help them with their business. But by then we had become secretly and privately attached to each other as the result of my frequent visits to have him look at my books, and so he told me that he was going and that he would like to take me with him, and I told him that I had promised my father that I would never elope with anyone, and so we asked Papa's permission, and he said yes. At that time Curtis was twenty-six years old.

TB: Do you remember about what year this was?

EMB: It was 1919, and we went to, let me see, Okmulgee, Oklahoma, and that's where he established the Brooks Brothers General Store. It had mainly groceries and a meat market and so forth and so on, but it also had shoes and clothing, and it took care of most of the needs of the people who would come in from out in the country, and so he became very prosperous.

TB: In what part of Oklahoma was this?

EMB: Well, it was not too far from Tulsa, and, even though there was great prosperity, I soon learned that my husband was a philanderer. He always promised me that he would try to change, but he never did. There was never any improvement whatsoever, and he was always getting into trouble with one married woman after another. He just never changed, but he was a good father, and he loved his children—we had three little girls while we were down there—but, well, after three children and still no improvement, I decided that it was time to leave with my children and join my parents in Kansas City.

TB: That must have been a very difficult thing for you to do.

EMB: Yes, it was, and it had taken me a good long while to make up my mind, but when my mind was made up, then it wasn't very hard at all because I knew that I had been insulted. I was always true to him and continued to get pregnant, trying to make a little boy for him because he said he wanted one, but now I was glad I didn't make one for him. I've always been loyal like that. Scorpios are that way, you know?

TB: Did you maintain contact with him after you left?

EMB: Yes, but I never made any demands on him for alimony or anything like that because I was just through with him and that entire situation once and for all! So, anyway, my parents offered to keep my children, and my papa insisted, "You go on now and finish your education, and we will take care of your children for you." So that's what I did. I went to the University of Kansas just to try it out because I had been washing diapers for seven years by then, and now I wasn't sure if I could still do this kind of thing or not. But I did.

TB: Diapers are a lot harder than school.

[*Laughter.*]

So now you were living in Lawrence, and your children were back in Kansas City with your folks.

EMB: Yes, I was staying there in Lawrence during the week, but Kansas City was only about forty miles away, and I went back home most weekends to see my children and also because I had a choir at one of the churches in Kansas City. During the summer, our choir traveled with the Jackson Jubilee Singers. The leader of that group was a man named R. G. Jackson, and he invested all the money that I earned for me so that I never had to worry about paying for my tuition or anything like that. So, anyway, I graduated from the University of Kansas in 1931 with a major in voice and a minor in speech and drama. I had been in several plays at the university, and I also had a radio program with a singing quartet backing me up. I sang some of those Jackson Jubilee songs, and it turned out that people in all those adjoining states were also listening to these broadcasts, and so when I gave my graduating recital, it wasn't in their regular small auditorium but in the large one where they usually gave concerts, and over twenty-five hundred people were there at my recital! Well, Dean Donald M. Swarthout, who was the uncle of the opera singer Gladys Swarthout, told me, "You know after graduating you really should go to New York and try your luck at singing and acting." So I took him at his word and prepared myself to go.

TB: After graduating, you went directly to New York?

EMB: No, you see, after my graduating recital, the local newspaper wrote an article about how unusual it was and so forth and so on, and then somebody sent a clipping of that article to the Associated Negro Press office in Chicago. So, on my way to New York, I decided to stop off in Chicago because I had been invited to a reception. Claude Barnett was there, and he already knew all about my recital and who I was.

TB: And this was in 1931?

EMB: Yes, and I stopped off in Chicago on my way to New York.

TB: And this is when you first met your future husband?

EMB: Yes, because when I came here, he had been invited to the same reception, and he had already seen the newspaper clipping, and now he wanted to know what made me think that I would be able to do so well in New York. Well, I told him that the reason that I would do well is because I was really very good at what I do, and so he made me promise that I would write him letters and let him know what I was doing, and when I left him to go to New York, I had a handful of letters of introduction that he had written to various people on my behalf.

TB: Did you continue to keep in touch with him after you arrived in New York?

EMB: Yes, because I had promised to write to him and let him know my opinion of all that had happened to me, and so those letters sort of kept us in touch with each other, and they also provided him with materials he could use to write about me in the black newspapers such as the *Pittsburgh Courier* and the *Atlanta World*. You see, at that time the Associated Negro Press was very much like the Associated Press, and all the black newspapers received their news from Claude's organization. So that was all to my advantage.

TB: So you were almost a kind of correspondent in a sense for the ANP?

EMB: Exactly, and that was a great help to me at that point in my career.

TB: When you got to New York, where did you live?

EMB: At the YWCA.

TB: On 137th Street?

EMB: On 137th Street, yes.

TB: What was it like to live there?

EMB: It was all right. People like Ethel Waters used to come there to use the swimming pool. Mrs. Mary Bethune also used to come there, and so I was able to meet a lot of interesting people.

TB: Now, you were also very close to the Abyssinian Baptist Church, weren't you?

EMB: Well, as a matter of fact, it was right next door. I think that Paul Robeson's brother was a pastor at Abyssinian at that time.

TB: I believe that Adam Clayton Powell Sr. was also there at about that same time.

EMB: Yes, he was.

TB: Did you ever go to Abyssinian for services?

EMB: No, but I do remember being inside there. Anyway, here I was in New York, and Claude had given me these letters of introduction, and one of them was to Eva Jessye, and she was giving a concert with her group, and so she asked me to be with her on her program. Now, some people think that I actually joined her group, but I didn't. I just sang as a part of her program.

TB: Tell us who Eva Jessye is.

EMB: Eva Jessye was a woman who was a music person who had graduated from the Harvard Graduate School that I went to before I went to Kansas, and she was an alumni of that school, Western University Church School, that I had my high school work with.

TB: And then, from that appearance with Eva Jessye, you ended up appearing in several Broadway productions, didn't you?

EMB: Yes, somebody asked Eva Jessye if she knew someone who could sing the kind of popular songs that everybody was singing back then, and she said, "Oh, yes, I've got a friend from way out west who has just come here." Now, it's strange, but my career has always been like that practically all my life — somebody saying the right thing and putting me in the right place at the right time! I guess it must just be a matter of luck and friendship and that sort of thing. So I have had a good life, and I have had a number of things happen to me that I didn't even realize at the time were a "first" or anything at all like that. It was only later that I learned that I had done something that hadn't been done before. For example, singing at the White House. Everybody can get invited to the White House, but in those days I just didn't realize how unusual it was to have a personal invitation from the president's wife herself to come to the White House, but, of course, I was singing "Remember My Forgotten Man" and her husband liked that song. So, anyway, at that time I was appearing with a showing of that film I was in at a Negro theater called the Lincoln Theater when they told me that they wanted me to come to the White House and sing for the president because it was his birthday, and so I said, "That will be fine. I'd love to do that." So, after my performance at the Lincoln Theater, Mrs. Roosevelt sent a car for me, and I went directly to the White House. The secretary of agriculture was also there.

TB: Henry Wallace.

EMB: Yes, exactly, and also Gutzon Borglum, the sculptor who carved the presidents' faces on Mount Rushmore. Anna Roosevelt, the president's daughter, was there as well, but I don't think anyone else was there.

TB: It appears that there is some confusion, controversy, and inconsistency in the various accounts that have been written concerning the role you played in the creation of the character of Bess in Gershwin's opera *Porgy and Bess*, and I've read newspaper articles that make the claim either you or Anne Wiggins Brown was the original model for that character. Both of you, it seems, at different times came to Gershwin's apartment to work on the part with Gershwin while he was, I assume, playing the music on his piano.

EMB: Yes, well, that is true to a certain extent, but, in the first place, however, by that time the opera was already written, and Anne Brown had already auditioned with him. I had just made two pictures in Hollywood and was on my way to South America to appear in *Flying Down to Rio* when it opened down there when someone told me that they were casting for a new Gershwin opera. So I went there, and I sat down on the piano bench with him and heard his version of some of the songs that he had written for Bess to sing, and I said, "Oh, that's too high. You've written it all above the staff, and I'm not a soprano. I'm a mezzo and on the contralto side." Then he said, "Yeah, but you look like the Bess I want. I want Bess to look like you." Now, Anne Brown was a soprano, and she had the right kind of voice, but Gershwin wanted Bess to look like me, and I couldn't sing the part the way it was written because it was too high. So that is the way it really happened, but some overanxious publicity people are the ones who decided to say that the part of Bess was originally written for me, but that isn't true. What is true is that Anne Brown had a light-skinned face, but she had the right kind of voice. I had the right kind of face but the wrong kind of voice, and she got the part in the original production.

TB: What else did you do back in Kansas that helped lay the groundwork for your career?

EMB: I traveled in the summer and paid my money and went on to finish my school. During schooltime, I had already been singing in my father's church. I got a job at Lincoln University, at Jefferson City, where Parsons went later. Judge James Parsons was there in music later—much later. I had my contract with me and I had three girls to be sending money back to my parents. There again, we had a family tradition, the extended family thing was very prevalent in our history. When you wanted to do something, the least we can do, Papa would say to me, is to let you leave your children here with us and you go ahead and make it on your own. We can take care of the children for you. They did just that, and I went through, as I said, at the school on the campus of the University of Kansas. I had a good little reputation there as a performer and a singer. Of course, part of my making the extra money was that I had a radio show there in Lawrence, Kansas. I did this, I went there, met Eva Jessye, the singer Hall Johnson—remember the Hall Johnson Singers? I wrote back to this fine man that I had met as I had come through here because an Italian girl in my Italian class said, "You know my father's name is Helson and he knows when my people come. I told my father about this." I had a letter from her father that he had read about her reviews from the Lawrence papers about my concerts and my graduation concert. "When you come through, by all means let us know," he said. I happened to give him a call, and he took me to meet Claude Barnett. And not only that, this girl's father, Helson, was the fundraiser for Provident Hospital. Claude Barnett was on that Board of Trustees.

TB: Now, was Provident then at Fifty-first Street already or . . .

EMB: Yes, it was already at Fifty-first Street. It was a school, one of two schools for medicine. We had another one in St. Louis.

TB: Homer Phillips. If I can interrupt you—that's why your husband's contribution is so important. It was at a time that almost every black doctor that graduated from any medical school, and most of them graduated from Meharry Medical College, did his internship at Provident.

EMB: That's right, exactly. That's why they called it a teaching hospital. It also had a mixed trustee board. They also had people who had a connection with the University of Chicago that lasted quite some time. And that never was broken off until after Claude later became the first black chairman of that board. Then Wendell Green was the second one, Judge Green. And most people, as you said, did internships there, and residencies. It was a prestigious hospital. That's how I met him and went on to New York.

TB: You were impressed?

EMB: Absolutely, and of course, challenged. Because he said, "What makes you think you can be successful in New York?" I knew I could be successful and I knew if I couldn't, I could go back home to a job. Anyway, he helped me with lovely letters of introduction after I got there. And Eva Jessye, who had been a

Kansan. Eva Jessye had gone on and made good for herself and was the head of the Dixie Jubilee Singers. This choir made the music for *Hallelujah!*—the first all-Negro picture I had ever seen in my life.

TB: Was Richard B. Harrison in the picture?

EMB: Richard B. Harrison? No, he was not. It was my second or third year, second year there that I saw Richard B. Harrison come there. Richard B. Harrison was on Broadway when I got there in 1931. Richard Harrison was the "Lawd" in *Green Pastures*. Also, in *Green Pastures*—the play, not the movie—the person who had charge of the music was Hall Johnson. I was sort of impressed by him as a man and as a conductor and as the choir, the way they sang. I wrote to Claude about him, and he would make an article out of it. Of course, I remember eventually after I was in the picture *Flying Down to Rio* and came back here with the play and ended up in Hollywood and got in the pictures out there because of the letters he wrote to Clarence Muse. Clarence took me around to the studios. After *Flying Down to Rio*, I was invited to come to Rio de Janeiro, so when I went there I wrote back. From him I learned that the Associated Negro Press began from what he thought about when he went down to visit his mother who was in California at the time, to say good-bye just before he was supposed to go to war. Richard Perry said, "You are too important to be going to the war. You are needed here."

TB: He got a deferment?

EMB: Yes. Richard Perry said, "You are too important here for communication." So on the way there he found the lack of communication between our different communities. He stopped in Kansas City. It was such a great gap between Missouri and, say, Los Angeles. Several states in between—it was those people who had newspapers and had no connections with each other; they didn't know what was happening. Because, he said, there was an unwritten agreement among whites that there would be nothing about Negro people except with pictures, unless somebody robbed somebody. It wasn't even as liberal as it was in sports. That was the most liberal part, was sports. For example, in 1936, when I was out there in California, and Jesse Owens and Walker, the jumping man, and all of them were getting ready for the Olympics, it was the Negro papers that gave accounts of those men's work. And back when Jack Johnson knocked out Jeffries and all that stuff in 1910, when I was a little girl, well, that was an unusual thing. And you knew when he went to Mexico, and you knew whenever he fought. But I'll never forget when Jack Johnson was going to fight when I was a little girl—we were in Texas—Papa had the Union Picnic of Churches and paid twenty-five cents for little white boys to bring the telegram from the Western Union to the picnic grounds between the rounds. Papa went up to get up on the rock and he would read who won that round. I'll never forget that it was white boys and not little black boys that were in Western Union. And they came on bicycles. That kind of thing was the breakthrough of a black man getting into the white papers. But even the theater people didn't unless they were on the black circuit. Bill Robinson would be Bojangles, Bill, or Williams, and Walker, they weren't played up quite as big as the others; Ethel Waters not until later. I'm talking about early, early. And even Ethel laughed when she was in *As Thousands Cheer* and had been up in Harlem and been coming around to all the Negro theaters for years with her own company, and then Irving Berlin said he was going to do this thing and had it that he had discovered her. That was the greatest laugh in the world. So when you want these different surges of migration from different places, what they did after they got here, or what they did after they went to Los Angeles, or what they did after they went to Cleveland and to Detroit where the work was, if you can get at it, you'll find most of the rich materials about those days in the archives of the Negro press. This is the kind of thing that made the Associated Negro Press and the Negro press important to the history of our people.

TB: The archives are not there.

EMB: Claude's archives are there. And I hope that you can find some over at the *Defender*.

TB: Their archives have been transferred to the Chicago Public Library, I think.

EMB: Really, the *Defender* should have had it.

TB: It is hard to find material in terms of research.

EMB: If you can find some of the releases from the *Courier* from 1919 and from the *Defender*. The year 1919 was also I think—either 1919 or 1921—was one of your race riots here.

TB: That was 1919.

EMB: Is that when it was? That was when he started the Associated Negro Press. Also there were the Scott papers of Atlanta, the *Atlanta World*. Also try the *Cleveland Plainview*, the Negro paper. The *Kansas City Call* is Lucille Bluford. She has inherited that. She's a journalist and she owns it now. You see, the *Kansas City Call* was not as much in the theater thing, because they didn't go to Kansas City all that much and yet they might have because there were a lot of packinghouses.

TB: They were the first black daily. My concentration is more or less in Chicago; that's the reason for getting a look at his materials from the Chicago Historical Society. What Chicago will be is kind of what typifies this whole migration. One of the most dramatic examples. Because it's here through Claude and the agitators, general agitators, that we began to get the first black empowerment. Where was Claude from originally?

EMB: He was born in Florida. His mother was from a large family of girls—seven sisters. They were all from North Carolina originally. They ended up in Indiana, in a place called North Creek, Indiana. There was a whole county of blacks who were freed from slavery—free Negroes, as they called them. His family was part of that group. His grandfather and his mother later settled in Mattoon, Illinois, where he was reared until one of the aunts moved here, married, and lived back there on Vernon for years and years until she died, and they tore it down and made this housing thing back here.

TB: Do you know when she moved into this area?

EMB: Probably about 1910 or 1909, because this was Grand Boulevard—now King Drive—over here. This is as far south as the blacks were, and then they stopped, I think, at Thirty-eighth Street and Vernon and Rhodes and on over to the lake. But this area very quickly filled, so Claude said. Then the Supreme Life Building was built. Then from Thirty-fifth back that way, whites were moving out and leaving these old mansions. Bishop Carey lived down at Thirty-fourth Street. Doolittle School was there and Michael Reese, the main hospital, was on the other side of Thirty-first and on up to Thirty-fourth and Thirty-fifth. Those were solid streets that had the lovely homes on them, with people like Carey, who pastored our biggest church down there.

TB: Quinn Chapel at Twenty-sixth and Wabash, according to history, was one of the stops on the Underground Railroad.

EMB: That's right, named after one of our AME bishops. Claude's mother was in service. One of these bachelors that she kept house for here had told her that she should send her child to a place that knew more about Negro people. She sent him to Tuskegee and that was the turning point in Claude's life. Claude grew up to be a man and a confidant of Booker T. Washington, Dr. Robert Moton of Tuskegee, and Fred Patterson, Dr. Moton's son-in-law—Dr. Moton and Fred Patterson were both noted presidents of Washington's Tuskegee Institute. It was during our marriage that I got to know his association with Dr. Moton; Booker Washington had already died when we married in 1934.

TB: With two such busy lives, how did you and Claude decide to get married?

EMB: Claude and I kept up with each other through the correspondence, and every time he would go down to Tuskegee, I was in New York, and I would say, "Come by here to go to Tuskegee," and we would meet each other. Then Claude and I began to talk marriage and what was going to happen then. When we did marry, it happened after I had been to Hollywood. I came back after the picture and was in the New York area and the Washington area, as a matter of truth. He called on one of the Roosevelts' birthdays. Duke Ellington was downtown. A Jewish man had four Negro theaters that *Flying Down to Rio* showed in, and so I went there to do a personal appearance. You know, they didn't have television and radio then, to go around to talk about your picture, which was at the Lincoln Theater in

Washington. All the people that were in the city were doing something about the President's Ball. I think it was Halloween; the thirty-first of October was his birthday. Everybody got somewhere to perform. Duke Ellington came to the theater, a downtown theater, it happened to be. I went from my theater, someone went from the Howard, whoever was there. I think it might have been Sissle and Lena Horne, as a dancer, in front of the band. I went with my accompanist. I didn't need my accompanist because Duke played for everybody. There was a black Negro manager at the Lincoln Theater who said, "Miss Moten, I know that you have your own pianist, but I have hired a band to come and play your music, if you don't mind. It's a young man that we are interested in here because he is just starting out. He's very nice-looking and he will make a nice showing. If you don't mind, I'd like for him to play your music for you."

TB: Are you talking about Billy Eckstine? He was originally from Baltimore.

EMB: It was Billy Eckstine, who got to be very famous. It was also then that I went to some of my friends, invited them to come on and go to the ball. "They have a Negro on up here and one downtown, so when you get through come on and go to the dance, the Birthday Ball." At the ball I met a lady they introduced me to whose name was Mrs. McDuffy. She said, "You know, I'm at the White House and my husband is the valet to the president. I know that one of the favorite pictures that he likes to see when they want Mac to take him down, wheel him down to the projection room is your picture." She said, "I think it would be just wonderful if the president knew you were here." I want you to know that the very next day I had a note from the White House; it was from Mrs. Roosevelt. "Do please accept our invitation to come to the White House after your performance this evening. We will send a White House car for you." That is the way I got to be the first Negro that had been invited to sing at the White House. There was the one of Marian Anderson after that, in 1939. Hers was set up at the Steinway House, up in New York. Mine came from Mrs. McDuffy, who told Mrs. Roosevelt that I was there.

TB: Now, Mrs. McDuffy is black.

EMB: Yes. It is amazing how it happened. We went upstairs to their rooms, not as large as my living room, and there was a piano there. He came in with his pince-nez and blinking his eyes, and "How are you and what are you going to sing?" I sang several songs from Eva Jessye's book, *My Spirituals*. And I talked to them about it. I sang "Remember My Forgotten Man." That was his subject, you know. Those guys were complaining that they had not much recognition, those returning soldiers.

TB: From World War I.

EMB: Yes, and they had the pencils selling.

TB: "Brother, Can You Spare a Dime" days.

EMB: Same thing, same period. That's how that happened. Most of the things that happened to me and my career, including the meeting of Claude Barnett, was an accident, being at the right place at the right time. After *Flying Down to Rio*, the agents booked me two months in Rio de Janeiro appearing with the picture and two months in Buenos Aires, Argentina, and I had a radio program there. This man who owned the Lincoln Theater also owned one in Richmond and in Norfolk. He wanted me to open the picture in each of those places. So he sent me down there with my accompanist. In Norfolk Claude Barnett was over in Dr. Robert R. Moton's summer home, which was in Capahosic, Virginia. They called and invited me over there. Now, I have always been told that Dr. Moton and I were related. Dr. Moton had told an uncle of mine that our histories were the same. There were two African brothers who came here and my father was a descendant of one and Dr. Moton of the other. So, sure enough, when I met his daughters, he had one who looked more like me than she did her own sister! Anyway, we, Claude and I, were to talk about marriage. We wanted to talk about marriage in August. On June 23 we went and bought the license. Dr. Moton had taken us out fishing. He said, "You are both grown and you've already made up your minds. Why do you want to wait?" I said I hadn't told my family. He said, "Tell them later." So he gave me away and we were married on the lawn. His place was on the New York River and all the servants came out. The big dog was part of the scenery, a great, big, white hound. The photograph was very nice. The place is now used as the Moton Center for conferences. I have a brochure with the picture on it. I saw my tree under which I married. This was 1934, the year Claude and I got married, but we had met in '31. All those years . . .

TB: As one would have said, it didn't take long!

EMB: We had a very interesting life in that he was most supportive of my career. In his papers there's almost as much stuff out there about me and my career as it is about his Associated Negro Press. You will find lots and lots of material about Chicago and Chicago organizations. Now, Claude and I didn't see each other all that often, and that made our marriage lovely. I was on the road and he traveled and we'd meet. It was a continuous love affair. We'd meet places, interesting hotels and interesting restaurants and interesting cities. Certainly, when I was traveling with *Porgy and Bess* and he was with the Agricultural Department with Patterson and they would be in some place and I would be in Portland, and they would come to Portland. Our situation was really perfect, and we enjoyed each other that way because you just never got tired of each other. I think it's kind of nice.

TB: The public record speaks well of your success as Bess in Berlin's revival of *Porgy and Bess* back out in 1942. Tell us about Africa. You were something of an emissary along with Claude, weren't you?

EMB: That was after *Porgy and Bess*, about 1947. Claude was a member of the Phelps Stokes Corporation, and they had work in Africa. Every trustee was given a trip to Africa to see how the program was. So it happened that I was free to go when his time came to go in 1947.

TB: That was early. The British Empire and the French were still there. They were still in control.

EMB: But the Africans were talking about freedom. Claude knew a number of people there because he had been writing to them. The school was in Liberia that Phelps funded. We went by plane. There weren't jets then. We went from here to London and then went down from London on a small plane to Liberia, where we met the governor-general. They were always very eager to please. The British were polite; as President Tubman of Liberia used to say, they were good colonialists because they built up things for themselves. At home they might not have been the big shots that they were down there. They built roads as the French did not do, and when independence came, the Africans inherited all of this, the things that they had built, the water systems, good education. They sent the African leaders off to school to Cambridge and to Oxford and sometimes to other countries for education and trained them. They were good businesspeople. They were good clerks and knew how to run government. When freedom came, they were less chaotic. The French and the Belgians were very bad. The Belgians had no interest in education. They had a couple of people—there were two baccalaureate-degreed people in high places when the Congo went independent away from the Belgians. The British were here all the way down the map. Then there were the French. All the changes we were able to see because when we first went, in 1947, Africa was under the colonial rule. Then we went back to Liberia in 1950 for Dr. Tubman's inauguration. He stayed there as long as he lived as president.

TB: Was Dick Jones our representative then?

EMB: Dick Jones was there, yes. But our first representative was Dudley. Then Dick Jones came. Dick was a political appointment; he didn't know the diplomatic things. I guess he learned that later. We went back every time Tubman was inaugurated, about three or four times, over about twelve years. And every time we went, Claude had a staff of stringers. It was very interesting to see the growth and to see the independence. Seeing one of these first British independence celebrations was an absolutely most thrilling thing. We also went to Jamaica's and a number of others.

TB: Did you go to Nigeria?

EMB: We went back to Nigeria in 1960. But Ghana was first, and it was so thrilling how political the Africans themselves were. Over the years from when they were little boys and girls they all had been looking forward to the independence. Everybody was political and knew what was going on. They were mad at all the Americans who were there. But they knew Claude, and they had such respect for him they'd get over it. The young people would know what was happening worldwide because of, first, the broadcast that was over there, the Voice of America, and the British Reuters newspaper service. The British ran the African newspapers.

TB: You had a pipeline through Claude's paper. So they had some insight into black America.

EMB: Exactly, that was the only way that they had it.

TB: Did you get to the east coast?

EMB: Oh, yes, and southern Africa. Not to South Africa, but to southern Africa. And I've been to the east coast, Zimbabwe and Tanzania, Malawi and Ethiopia. I met Haile Selassie. Haile Selassie was very interesting. He was a king on his throne with a red carpet that you walked down to be accepted by him.

TB: And Etta Moten Barnett, you are a queen. I thank you for the time spent!

September 25, 1991

ALONZO PARHAM

PIONEER AND TRUE UNSUNG HERO

In 1928 or 1929 while I was still in fifth or sixth grade at Edmund Burke School in Chicago, I read in the Chicago Defender *and also heard my parents talk about the appointment of a Wendell Phillips High School honor student to the United States Military Academy at West Point. His name was Alonzo Parham. I had already been overwhelmed and overjoyed by the recent victory of Oscar DePriest as the U.S. representative from the First Congressional District of Illinois, and now his appointment of Alonzo Parham made my chest swell even more with pride. My mother and dad had always taught us that we could do anything we wanted if we only tried hard enough, and now we had an immediate example of how the seemingly impossible had been accomplished. What excuse could I possibly have for not also doing just as well in my own life?*

It came as quite a shock when we learned a year later that Cadet Parham had been dismissed for not meeting the "high standards" of West Point. I felt no less pride about him than I did before. The reason for this was because I was quite certain that he was dismissed not because he was in any way incompetent but because he was a "Negro," and history has revealed that my earlier suspicions were entirely correct.

Here, at age eighty-five, Parham briefly recounts some of the highlights of life, including the many accomplishments he has made by "playing against the odds." It was a refreshing and rewarding pleasure for me to have this opportunity of speaking with him.

TB: When were you born, Alonzo?

AP: I was born in 1911 in Fulton County, Georgia. That's where my father was born, and my mother was also from Georgia.

TB: And when did you come to Chicago?

AP: I came to Chicago in 1923. My father's mother and father were slaves. But my mother's mother I don't think was ever a slave. If she was, I don't know about it.

TB: When you first came to Chicago, did your mother and dad come with you?

AP: My father came first. He was here for maybe a month or two, and then my brother came. He was a year and eight months older than I. Then came my mother and my sister and myself. That was in 1923.

TB: Why did they come? Did they ever talk about it?

AP: Well, the farm situation in the South was pretty rough at that time. Boll weevils were eating practically all of the cotton, and it was sort of a one-crop economy down there. So my father decided that he would go someplace else. He went first to Virginia to a little town called Collins Creek, Virginia, and started working in the coal mines. Later on, he got a job out of the ground in the coke yards. That's when he wrote for my mother and my sister and I to come there. But my mother checked the place out, and when she discovered that there were no schools there beyond what we had already, she said that she wouldn't go there, and since my father had a brother in Chicago, he came here. I think his first job was in the packinghouse of Armour & Company.

TB: Were there many people from your home region already here?

AP: I think we were the first Chicagoans from that particular area in Georgia. There were others who came later.

TB: When you came to Chicago, where did you live?

AP: I was twelve then, and we lived on Roosevelt Road.

TB: How far west?

AP: You know where the Dan Ryan highway crosses Roosevelt Road now? That's where we lived.

TB: Was that a settlement of black people?

AP: No, only a few black people were there, but there were none living in the particular area where we were. Our address was on Roosevelt Road, but actually we lived in the back of a firm that had a business facing Roosevelt Road. You would go in from the front and go up these stairs and then go down the stairs at the back. Otherwise, you could come in from the alley to enter our house there on the ground floor.

TB: Did you go to church in those days?

AP: Well, my father's brother was a member of St. Mary's AME church.

TB: It's still there. My mother and dad also belonged to that church at one time. Reverend Thomas was the minister then. Where did you start school?

AP: There was a school at Thirteenth Street and O'Brien—the Foster School. The building itself may still be there. That's where I started school.

TB: Most of the students were black or white?

AP: There was a majority of white children there. They were Jewish, Polish, and Italian.

TB: Did you finish grade school there?

AP: I had already finished seventh grade when I came here to Chicago, and I had my promotion slip to eighth grade when I went to Foster School. When I went there, they asked me what grade I was in and I told them that I should be in the eighth grade and that I had my promotion slip. But then they questioned me as to where I had come from and said that I didn't qualify for eighth grade in Chicago because the schools in the South were pretty lousy schools. So they put me in the sixth grade—a year below the level I had finished. They had B and A classes. When you first went into sixth grade you were in B, and then at the end of the semester you were promoted to 6A, and then you went into 7B and so on. So they put me into 6B. This was my first experience of going to school with white people. I stayed in sixth grade exactly one week.

TB: One week? What happened?

AP: Well, the teacher said, "I think you can do 6A work," and she put me on the other side of the room with the kids who were doing 6A work. You see, the classrooms were divided in those days, and so I stayed there a week, and then she said, "I think you can do seventh-grade work." So she took me to the seventh-grade teacher, and the seventh-grade teacher put me in 7B, and I stayed there another week before she decided I probably could do the work that the 7A class was doing—so she moved me to the other side of the room, and I stayed there for another week, and then she said to me, "You know, I think you can do eighth-grade work," and I said to her, "I told you when you were admitting me that I had been promoted to the eighth grade!"—so she took me down to the first floor to the eighth-grade teacher, and the eighth-grade teacher said, "Well, maybe he could do eighth-grade work, but we've been working for a month, and he'll never be able to catch up." So I had to repeat 7A. I think there were only two or three black boys in that seventh grade, but I got along well because I had already done all of this work. The teacher was Irish: "And don't you forget it." Her last name was O'Donoghue, and her face was like a lemon, but she gave me a chance to shine in that class.

TB: She was a good teacher. She wasn't concerned about the fact that you happened to be Negro. You were a good student and that's what she respected.

AP: In Foster School at that time, most of the fellows in my class were white. The Negro boys were all from the sixth grade down, but they were kind of cool toward me because I ran with these white boys, and I think that they thought that I thought that I was better than them, but I was only with those white boys because they befriended me when I went into their room. So when I went outside, the white kids would play with me, but those black kids kind of ignored me. There was a little brother of a Jewish fellow in my class by the name of Benny Goldblatt, and Benny was a wrestler. There wasn't a boy in the school that could either throw or pin Benny, no matter what his weight was. Benny weighed only sixty or sixty-five pounds, but he was like an eagle. I've seen him stand up with his hands on knees—baseball fashion—and have these fellows try to put a headlock on him, and he'd slip out every time. Benny befriended me, and he had a book about wrestling written by Tom Jenkins, and Benny gave me a copy of that book. That's how I learned wrestling. I stayed in that school only about six or seven months, I think, but when I left, Benny was the only kid there that could throw me! [*Laughter.*]

TB: You learned his lessons very well—almost!

AP: Then we moved to the South Side. To 4862 Federal Street.

TB: This is 1924? Were there many blacks in that neighborhood?

AP: Yes, there were some black people living down on the Forty-seventh and Forty-sixth Street blocks. At that time my father was working at the stockyards.

TB: And your mother was a housewife?

AP: My mother could sew. She made dresses, and she could also dress hair. A woman had come through my mother's area in the South, and she had taught her the straightening and pressing of hair. My mother learned that. So when she came here she could do hair and also sew. But I think her first job was probably in a canning factory. Most of the women who came from the South worked in the canning factory.

TB: So, you're in the forty-eighth block on Federal, and the people who lived on the forty-seventh and forty-sixth block were mostly black people?

AP: Yes, and the children went to Coleman School or to the Catholic schools if they were Catholic. There was a majority of black students at Coleman School and just a sprinkling of white students. At Coleman I had about two months to finish in seventh grade before I went on to eighth grade, and a relative, my father's brother's wife, said, "The people here are tough. They're going to beat you up when you go to that school." Well, I had never thought about getting beaten up in a school. So I went there expecting those boys to jump on me, but when I got to school nobody bothered me. At recess time I went out, and still nobody bothered me. But then at lunchtime I went out on the school grounds, and I looked and saw a boy walking from side to side with the visor of his cap turned over his head, and he said to me, "You're new here, ain't you?" And I said yes. And he said, "You're the new boy." And I said yes. And he said, "What school do you come from?" I said, "Foster School." And he said, "That's on the West Side, ain't it?" And I said yeah! And he said, "You one of them bad niggers from the West Side, ain't you?" And I said, "No, I ain't bad."

[*Laughter.*]

And he said, "Yes, you is." And he started coming toward me, and I started backing away until finally I was backed up against the wall of the school, and there was no place to get away to, and he reached up and grabbed me and started to pull my jacket. That's when I discovered that the boys from the South Side were not wrestlers. They were boxers, and when this guy grabbed me, I grabbed his hand and we started to tussle. I sidestepped him and when he went past me, I hit his feet with my foot, upset him, and he hit the cement. Then he jumped back up and rushed me again, but this time I got a headlock on him — Benny had taught me how to slip on a headlock when a person's back was turned — so I got him by the waist and threw him up in the air and then let go, and he landed flat on his back. Then he got up and tried to go after me again, but another fellow came up and said, "Let him alone. He's already thrown you down three times."

[*Laughter.*]

So the next day I got to school and another boy came up to me and said, "Hey, new boy!" Then someone else said, "You'd better let that boy alone," and nobody bothered me the rest of the time I was in that school!

TB: What do you remember about the academic side of things?

AP: You know, they warned how tough it was going to be in the eighth grade, but I discovered that the arithmetic that was too hard for these kids was chiefly square root, and we had already had square root in seventh grade where I came from in Georgia. So square root was nothing to me — it was just something for them, and I didn't have to study at all! I just indulged myself. I studied manual training — we hadn't had that — and then I graduated from Coleman School.

TB: Well, that brings us up to about 1925. Did you go to Wendell Phillips from there?

AP: Yes.

TB: What was that experience like? Was Phillips mixed then?

AP: Well, we had a pretty good sprinkling of white kids then, but I would say it was about 80 percent black. We lived at Fifty-second and Dearborn Street. A black man owned the house we lived in. I don't know what his name was. I used to go to the Owl Theater on State Street on Saturdays and holidays, and they had these amateur contests on Saturdays. All of the kids that were in the school that danced would go up and get in the contest. The Charleston was very popular at that time, and I could do the Charleston better than almost anyone, but I wouldn't dare go on that stage because if I won a prize and took it home, my mother would skin me! [*Laughter.*]

Dancing was considered a sin at the time we came here.

TB: Yes, that kind of dancing!

AP: Any kind of dancing! Dancing itself was a sin. Even playing cards was a sin. So I wouldn't be caught dead on the stage in a contest. But when we were out in the alley, I danced circles around the rest of them!

[*Laughter.*]

Well, so I went to Phillips High School, and I discovered that the work there in history, English, grammar, physiology was all work that I had already done in the seventh grade back in the South where I came from. And the only thing that I had to study when I went to Phillips High School was algebra because we hadn't had algebra. So I had to study algebra and I also had to study French because I had never had French. But those are the only two things that I had to study. I didn't have to study anything else in high school until around the top of my second year or the first of my third year.

TB: Who were some of the teachers you remember from Phillips from that period?

AP: Annabelle Prescott was a teacher that I remember very well.

TB: She was the daughter of Bishop Carey and the sister of the late Archibald Carey, who became a judge and was an alderman. Was Archibald in your group?

AP: Yes, Archibald was at Phillips when I went there. I started there in February 1925, but he was getting ready to graduate.

TB: His sister was considerably older than Arch, I believe.

AP: And Mrs. Maudelle Bousfield was another teacher that I remember.

TB: Yes, Mrs. Bousfield was the first African-American teacher in the Chicago public schools. She later became a principal. Her husband was chief medical officer at Fort Huachuca during World War II.

AP: And there was a teacher named Pierce. I have forgotten his first name, but he taught science.

TB: Yes, I remember he was still at Phillips when I got there, and I have forgotten his first name too, but he was highly respected.

AP: Very, very highly respected. I remember if an athlete failed a subject or fell behind in a subject and they were giving him an F or a D or low grade, the coach would always come around to the teachers to try to get that low grade "fixed up." Well, Pierce taught physics, and when the coach would come in and talk to him, Pierce wouldn't change the grade!

[*Laughter.*]

TB: Yes, and when I got to Phillips, the coach would always advise you not to take Mr. Pierce's classes if you were on the team because they wanted to be able to "fix" your grade, and with Mr. Pierce that just wasn't possible.

AP: That's right.

TB: How many black teachers, proportionally, were at Phillips by then?

AP: I really don't know. It could have been about half and half. No more than that.

TB: There were some young black men playing some great basketball there at that time, weren't there?

AP: Yes, a lot of those fellows were my classmates. Let's see, who was on that team? Lawson Miller played center. Theodore Perry and Albert Pullins played forward. Ravel Harper played guard.

TB: Later they called him "Ghost" because he was supposed to be so elusive. And Pullins became known as "Runt."

AP: Well, he was already called "Runt" even then. He only weighed somewhere around 125 or 130 pounds. But that guy could play basketball! I don't think I have ever seen a better basketball player play line forward—unless maybe Michael Jordan, but then they changed one of the rules of basketball. You see, Pullins used to go down close to the floor with his hand behind the ball, and then they made a rule against that type of dribble. But at that time "Runt" would grab that ball and run into the floor and in just five or six bounces he would be all the way down at the other end of the floor!

TB: Yes, he was a brilliant basketball player.

AP: And in 1928 that team won the city championship in lightweight basketball.

TB: Yes, and later, according to what I have been told, Harper and Miller went down to the University of Illinois on scholarships.

AP: Yes, but both Miller and Harper were cut from their team, and Harper went to Loyola, but I don't know what happened to him after his first year there.

TB: My understanding is that they ganged up on him on the floor and broke his knee. At least that's what I heard.

AP: Well, anyway, Miller stayed at the University of Illinois, and he graduated from there.

TB: What happened to Pullins?

AP: Pullins didn't go to college. He may have gone south someplace and played for a year or so, something like that, but he didn't go on to graduate from college. He went into basketball. Somehow or other he got hooked up with the Harlem Globetrotters. They had two teams. One team played the western area of the United States and one team played the eastern area, and Pullins played with the western team.

TB: What was the political scene like, as you remember it, around that time? Were you becoming politically aware at all?

AP: Well, at that time all black people were Republicans. If anybody was a Democrat, we thought there was something wrong with them.

TB: What about Ed Wright? Does that name ring a bell?

AP: He was a criminal lawyer, wasn't he?

TB: Yes, but he was also a politician.

AP: That's right. If you got into trouble, you wanted to get Ed Wright as your lawyer. At about that same time—or was it later?—he became a member of the state legislature, and I heard it said that Ed Wright could get a person off of any criminal charge because he knew the law. He wrote the criminal law, and the way he wrote it was so that there were certain escapes, and he knew exactly where they were! But back then, in that era, Oscar DePriest, he was *the* politician in Chicago.

TB: How did you get to know DePriest?

AP: Well, when I first heard his name, I thought he was "Oscar the Priest."
[*Laughter.*]
Then when DePriest was elected to Congress—that was in 1928—he said that if he ever got into Congress the one thing that he was going to do was to appoint Negro boys to West Point and Annapolis, and so one day I was called down to the school's office, and the assistant principal—a guy named Harry Mendelson— came down and said, "How would you like to go to West Point?" So, just as a joke, I put my name on the list as a candidate, and then they gave several preliminary examinations to pick the fellows that they thought would be best academically able to handle the West Point routine. Well, when we found out the results of that first round of examinations, it turned out that I was among those that were kept in. Each time they gave another examination, I was always somewhere in that top group, and so I kept on moving up, and then when it got to be just a few fellows like eighteen or twenty—I was still in! So by this time it was a shame not to go on, and when it finally came down to the number one question in those examinations, I was still in there!

TB: Well, that was quite an achievement. What about the West Point experience? Your acceptance there made you the first African-American cadet to be admitted to West Point after Reconstruction. What was it like?

AP: Well, I only stayed about a half year there, and then I went to the University of Illinois for a year. When I was down there, I was pledged to the Kappa fraternity, and the Kappas had a basketball team that could beat the University of Illinois freshman team.

TB: And yet they couldn't play on the varsity!

AP: No. They wouldn't let them qualify.

TB: How many blacks were there at the University of Illinois then?

AP: I don't know, but there were three black fraternities. There were two sororities, but the University of Illinois was awful at that time. They would have been as racist as West Point if they had had the same degree of authority. You couldn't live in a dormitory. You couldn't even eat on the campus at that time. You had to find some place in either Champaign or Urbana where you could live.

TB: And that was usually with a black family?

AP: That was *always* with a black family.

TB: Well, you survived it.

AP: Yes, I stayed there for a year, but the following year I didn't have enough money to support me for a whole year in school, so I decided I would work at a job until I got enough money to spend another whole year in school, and the only jobs you could get in those days were shoeshine, barbershop, dishwasher . . .

TB: Regardless of the fact that you had been to college?

AP: Yes, you could only get work as a dishwasher or whatever in one of the white frat houses. Most of the other black fellows worked in these places. As a matter of fact, the only way many of them were able to get through school was because they could get their food at the house where they worked. I remember the fellows who worked at the white sorority and fraternity houses used to bring food over to the house where I lived, and that was a thing that really helped me out a lot. Even so, I decided I'd better go back to Chicago and work until I saved enough money. But then I lost my job, and my money dwindled and dwindled until I no longer had enough money to get down there. You see, at that time, in the early thirties, even after I had reached the age of twenty-one, when I worked and got paid, I had to take my paycheck home to my father and give it to him, but my mother managed the money, and with the money going away so fast for expenses I couldn't get enough money to go to school until I was, I guess, in my middle twenties. It was about that time that I became interested in women, and I wound up getting married. I think I got married when I was around twenty-six years old. I still thought that I might get back to school, but I was never able to. I never went back.

TB: So in order to make a living you got into civil service?

AP: No, the first job I had was as a delivery boy for a sign painter. He had worked for the Walgreen Company, and, as a matter of fact, he was one of the best that Walgreens had, but he left them and set up his own shop. It used to be in the fifty-sixth block of State Street.

TB: What was his name?

AP: Winters, and I went to work for him as a delivery boy. I think he paid me something like seven or eight dollars a week.

[*Laughter.*]

He told me, "You can't keep busy all day delivering signs. There's not that much work. If you want to, when you're not working, you can go back there in the back room and practice making letters." Well, I had learned in high school geometry how to copy things. I learned how to copy polygons, circles, squares, and whatnot by making a line that is parallel to the line that is already there. And I discovered that you could copy any drawing by simply following that same routine, and when Winters discovered that I could copy drawings, he said, "Well, next time we need to have a picture painted, you do it, and I'll pay you." So, if somebody wanted a picture of an ice-cream cone, well, I would get a picture of an ice-cream cone and copy it.

TB: And this was the beginning of your interest in art?

AP: No, I wasn't interested in art. I was interested in just simply copying things in order to make some money. So I copied a few things, and then he wanted to know, "What do you want for it?" And I said, "Whatever you think it's worth," and he said, "Well, it's worth ten cents to me," and he gave me a dime. And that's when I learned that you have to price and place the proper value on what you do yourself and not let someone else do it for you. Well, anyway, eventually I learned to make letters well enough to do some of the work that came in, and I learned how to make letters so well that I could have gone into business for myself, but, instead of that, I got a job working for the Illinois Occupational Survey. They did a survey of all of the people in Chicago that were on welfare. They were interviewed to find out what training or what profession they had, and then they were classified in terms of that information. Then, when the WPA came, they used these records to direct people to various jobs. So I worked on that occupational survey and learned the skill of interviewing and stuff like that. You know the book *Black Metropolis*?

TB: Yes, by St. Clair Drake and Horace Cayton.

AP: Yes, I worked on that project, and I interviewed chiefly young people because they had a youth division in the building. These were kids who were going through the Civilian Conservation Corps, where they were learning all kinds of skills: electrical wiring, telephone stringing.

TB: Those guys did very well when they were later drafted into the army. They did very well because they came in with skills.

AP: So I used to interview these young people and write those interviews up and turn them in to the project. Incidentally, it was then that I met Anna Langford's son. He was a draftsman for that project, and he used to make all the maps and the statistical charts. Then I got a job on the Works Progress Administration, but they had put on a ruling that anybody who had worked eighteen months on WPA would have to be recertified, and when I went down to the WPA for recertification, they couldn't find me a job in the writer's project or even a clerical job of any kind, and they told me if I were to take a labor job it would be easier to get me transferred to the writer's project than it would be to wait around for a job to show up. So, as I said, I had this family and that was a big responsibility for me, and I never liked to ask anybody for help. So I took the labor job, and I guess I was there from about March of 1938 until March of 1939. I don't remember the exact dates. By that time I already had two kids, and I was only getting sixty-five dollars a month. But they were paying anywhere from sixty-five up to ninety-five dollars a month on these writing projects — so I kept trying to get placed. In order to get transferred, though, they had to put in a requisition for you. Finally the supervisor informed me he wouldn't transfer me. Well, I went in and questioned the supervisor and I discovered that the requisition had never been sent! You see, the supervisor didn't like black people, and he thought that all black folks ought to be working on downscale labor jobs, and that was what I was doing, and that was where he wanted me to stay. So I decided in May of that year that I would go out to where they process the applications, and I would take a baseball bat, and I would find that supervisor, and he wouldn't be a supervisor anymore. I figured it wouldn't even matter very much whether or not I went to jail. On the salary I was getting the state could take care of my family just as well as I could. So I told my wife about my decision, and she said, "Well, don't do that because —" and I said, "No, this guy needs an education, and I'm going to give him one." This happened on the twenty-seventh or the twenty-eighth of May. So we had a holiday on the thirtieth of May, which I think was on a Thursday or a Friday. We had the whole weekend off and we were not to come back to work until Monday. Well, Monday I scheduled myself to give this guy a good whipping. He was white, of course. And I think it was on Saturday following the thirtieth of May that I got a telegram offering me a job on the courts from the Department of Labor in Springfield at one hundred dollars a month!

[*Laughter.*]

But I didn't have transportation to Springfield, so I went to my friend who had a car, and he knew a woman who worked as an elevator operator. He told this woman that I needed a place to stay. Well, this woman's husband owned a house in Springfield where his mother lived, and so I went down there and lived in that house. They served me food, and his mother said, "I'll do your laundry." At first she wouldn't tell me what I had to pay, but finally she told me that they would charge thirty dollars a month to stay at their house, and the woman charged me something like two or three dollars extra to do my laundry. That meant that I could maintain myself there as well as maintain my family up here in Chicago with that hundred dollars and still be able to save a little money too.

TB: As well as your self-esteem—and your safety!

AP: Yes, and I was starting to think about moving to Springfield and even looking for a house down there.

TB: Now, your son and your daughter, did they continue to live in Chicago?

AP: No, when my son graduated from Hyde Park High School, he was an up-and-coming track man. He was a hurdler. I think in his third year in high school he was the champion of the medium- and low-hurdle meet that took place in the city. My kid had just turned sixteen in February and I figured he could be an ace track man—so I had the idea then of sending him to Drake University in Des Moines because of his track potential. Well, he went out for track at Drake, but in his second year he told me he didn't want to go out for track anymore. It was too much work, and he was getting nothing out of it, and he didn't want to waste all of that time. One day he called me up and told me that he had changed his major, and two years later he graduated with a degree in nuclear physics. He came back here to Chicago but couldn't get a job. This was 1959 or 1960, and they wouldn't give him a job because as soon as you get your degree you are classified 1A, and you're likely to get drafted and have to do two or three years in the service. So, he told me that if he went one more time to an employer and they told him they couldn't give him a job because he was 1A that he was going to volunteer and do the service and come back and then get a job. So he enlisted and went to Air Force Officers School, and in no time he had a position as a second lieutenant. Then, when he had served his three years like he was supposed to as a second lieutenant, they gave him a promotion to first lieutenant, and when he was near the top of that, they gave him a promotion to captain. As a captain they sent him to Madrid, Spain, and gave him a tour of duty over there. Then he was sent to Vietnam, where they put him in communications. While he was in communications he got involved with computers and all of that stuff that goes with them, and he really liked what he was doing. So that's the way he went. He went through the service as a communications officer.

TB: All within the framework of the Air Force?

AP: Yes. I think he was a major, I guess, when they assigned him as a squadron commander and sent him back to California, where he was assigned to tracking those big bombers, the 52s, for the Strategic Air Command. He took us over to the place where he worked at Christmastime, and they had a screen over there that must have been about at least two or three stories tall, and he told my wife to watch that screen, and she watched the screen, and in about four minutes a missile came on the screen, and it said, "Merry Christmas, Mother."

TB: Oh, how beautiful! What a wonderful thing for him to do.

AP: So, he went on with that work, and he eventually got a degree in space management. He got that degree from the University of California. We went down to his graduation, he later on was assigned to Germany, and by then he was a lieutenant colonel. Then he came back here and was assigned to Fort Meade and was promoted to a full colonel and that's how he wound up. He retired in 1986.

TB: And he's still a young man.

AP: Yes, he's fifty-three now. He retired when he was forty-eight or forty-nine, something like that, after twenty-eight years of service, and now he works for a private defense contractor as an analyst.

TB: No wonder you're so proud of him, and I'm sure he's just as proud of you!

October 4, 1996

GWENDOLYN DAVIS

MUSICIAN

I first remember Gwen Davis as a shy but friendly little girl at Edmund Burke School, which was located at Fifty-fourth and South Park Way. I was in third grade, and she was in second grade. I knew her primarily through her sister Vivian, who was in the same classroom that I was. It was apparent that Gwen had talent in music, both vocal and instrumental, even when we were in grammar school. A little later she and Vivian pursued those talents successfully at DuSable High School under the disciplined musical directorship of the famed Captain Walter Henri Dyett.

Her family was a close-knit unit headed by a single mother. Her three brothers were known throughout the school and the neighborhood as tough guys, particularly in terms of their protection of their two beautiful and very smart "little" sisters. Eventually Gwen got married and had a daughter. Later on, she and her husband were among the first blacks to open a tavern on East Seventy-first Street after the "color bar" had been broken in the Park Manor community.

Throughout the years we have continued to be friends and have always managed to keep in touch with one another. It was indeed a pleasure for me to have this recorded conversation with Gwen about her public and private life. Because we have shared so many common experiences, our conversation brought back many memories to me, which I will always cherish, whether they were good or even not so good, because it was people like her who helped me so much in the process of "growing up," which made all these memories possible for both of us.

TB: I am talking to Gwendolyn Davis, who is one of my best and earliest friends. We attended Burke Elementary School together in the 1920s and 1930s. This is going to be a good conversation because we've known each other for so long.

GD: When we were coming up, things were so much different, weren't they? People were so much closer. To give you an idea about that, one night quite recently I was sitting at the end of the couch, and I saw this smoke. Well, my daughter gets up so early that she needs to go to bed early, and so I knew she was probably asleep. My grandson was in his room and still awake, and so I called to him and told him to go down to see what was causing all this smoke. Well, he couldn't see anything, and so he came back up and told his mother. Then she got up and told him to call the fire department or 911—I don't know which of them it was—which is what he did. Then she had me put on my coat and go out and sit in her car, but you know something? Nobody from even next door came over to see if anything was wrong or if there was anything they could do to help—and *that* is something I'll never be able to understand because our neighborhood used to be so different.

TB: It sure was. We were raised in a different time, under different circumstances, but I miss it—I really miss it.

GD: It was so much better, Tim.

TB: Yes, but now let's talk some about your life, if you don't mind.

GD: No, I don't mind. How far do you want me to go back?

TB: Where were you born?

GD: I was born here in Chicago, and I was the youngest of five. Mama had more children than that, but she lost a couple, and I was the youngest of those that survived. We lived on Fifty-third Street at 211 on the second floor. You know, child, that same building is still standing there.

TB: Before the war came along, we used to be around each other a lot more, but then, after the war, everybody began to move around, and we lost touch with each other for a while, didn't we?

GD: Yes, and during that time, I got married, and I had my first job. I was so proud of myself, Tim, because I was making eleven dollars a week.

TB: Was this with the liquor store?

GD: Yes. Do you remember when they had a chain of United Liquor stores?

TB: Yes, I remember those. I also remember that some of the Globetrotters used to work for them in the summertime with their delivery cars.

GD: Well, I got out of that business as soon as I could because I never really liked what I was doing. I quit because I got married, and that's also how I got involved with the carpeting business on Seventy-first Street. Do you know where Harvey Collins has that barbecue restaurant? That's where it was.

TB: Did you ever learn to drive?

GD: No, I never learned to drive.

TB: Oh, you didn't? Well, I know a number of people that don't drive. I don't drive that well myself.

GD: Well, it would be nice if I drove just enough to get myself around. As it is, I have to depend so much on somebody else, and I hate that. I really do.

TB: So were you still living with your family on Fifty-third when you first started to work?

GD: Yes.

TB: What about your mom and dad? Were they from Chicago?

GD: No, my mother and dad were both from Memphis, Tennessee, but they met here in Chicago.

TB: What are some of your earliest memories of your experiences here in Chicago?

GD: Well, I remember one time when Mama bawled out a policeman because of the way he was treating my brother Louis. Something had happened, and my sister Serena had made Louis so mad that he slapped her, and this policeman was coming to arrest Louis for doing that, and Mama wouldn't let them. How she managed to do that I don't know, but she did. The reason, I suppose, is that she was southern born and raised, Tim, and the women ran the house where she came up. The men didn't learn nothing about things like cooking and sewing, and consequently they never insisted on her handling situations like this, although they should have!

TB: Now, you and your sister Vivian were very different from your brothers Louis and Bill. At least that's the way it seemed to me.

GD: Didn't you know my other brother Beanie?

TB: I never knew Beanie all that well. He worked in the post office, didn't he?

GD: Yes, he worked there until he retired. You know, Beanie was the only one of my brothers that had to go into the service because Bill was crippled and Louis had that impediment—so they didn't have to go into the Second World War, but they put Beanie in the navy. That was in about '41 or '42, but before he went into the navy, he used to tend bar. You remember that place called Brownie's on Sixty-first Street? Well, that's where he learned about tending bar. He left there and went to work at Elliot Rouse's on Fifty-eighth and then at Speedy's on Fifty-fifth. When he'd served his time in the navy, he came back and worked at Speedy's again, and then he got his job at the post office.

TB: I never met your father. Were your mom and dad separated or did you lose your dad?

GD: Oh, no, they were separated when I was three years old, and that's something else that's always bothered me. My mother was such a gentle woman that I don't understand how she could have up and left this man with five children and another one on the way unless—it came to me then and it comes to me now—he must have been abusive to her.

TB: I met your mother. She was a fine person, and she probably just couldn't take it anymore.

GD: I guess she couldn't, and one of her favorite tales was about how he went to the corner and got on the streetcar, and that's the last we ever saw of him. We had to get a moving van to come and move us all out to my grandmother's apartment at 50 East Fiftieth. My grandmother's name was Hanna, and we lived with her until they put all of us out of there because they were going to turn all those large apartments into kitchenettes, and when we left there, we went to 231 East Fifty-first Street. That's where we all were until we became grown and started branching out.

TB: And that's where I remember you the most, over there on Fifty-first Street.

GD: Yeah, when we lived on Fifty-first, you can ask anybody, but I don't think that our door was ever locked. It was always open, and we were always able to bring our friends home with us, and our friends had the run of the house. But, of course, some of the other little children, their mothers wouldn't let kids beyond their kitchen door.

TB: Bill and Louis were gone most of the time, as I remember it.

GD: Bill was the first one to leave.

TB: No, I didn't mean gone away. I meant most of the time they were just out having fun. Those of us who were younger than them, we looked at Louis and Bill and said, "Their sisters are so different!" That's because they really protected you and Vivian.

GD: Yeah, they sure were there—Beanie especially—if anybody picked on me or if anything went wrong. I remember once some fellow got smart with me, and I came home for lunch and told Louis, and he said, "OK, I'll be there," and so we went back to school, and when the last bell had rung, we were waiting there outside the boys' playground, and the first guy that comes out is a guy named Homer. Well, Louis grabs Homer and says, "Is this the one?" I say, "Naw, naw" and point out a guy named Chris Smith who was the one, and Chris was just frozen to the spot where he was standing. Lord, Louis scared him, and he never did bother me anymore.

TB: So now you went to Burke. What do you remember about your days at Burke School?

GD: I remember Miss Kelly.

TB: "Miss Kelly with the big fat belly?"

GD: Yeah, Miss Kelly was really something—and then there was Mr. Schrock.

TB: Clarence Schrock.

GD: And I had one of my teachers who really liked me: Miss Burns.

TB: Margaret Burns.

GD: But you know what was really pitiful? We didn't have a ceremony at our graduation, and we had to go up to the classroom to get our diplomas.

TB: Was that for the entire class?

GD: Yeah, for the whole system.

TB: I didn't know about that, but in '32 when we had our graduation, it was very nice, and, in fact, we had a lot of parties after the ceremony.

GD: Well, not in '33, and I came out in '33.

TB: That's sad because young people look forward to things like that.

GD: Well, Mama did the best she could. My graduation dress cost ninety-eight cents!

TB: Well, ninety-eight cents was considered to be a lot back then.

GD: And that dress was on sale because it was more or less out of season by then. The season was changing, and that's also when I got my first pair of heels. Shoes like that cost either a dollar ninety-nine or two ninety-nine.

TB: And the boys' shoes were usually Thom McCanns.

GD: Back then the El fare was ten cents, and that's why we had to transfer to DuSable. We could walk to DuSable, but to go to Englewood it would cost twenty cents a day for me and twenty cents a day for Vivian plus our lunch money, and Mama just didn't have that much money. So that's why we had to transfer schools.

TB: When you went to Englewood, how long did you stay there?

GD: Only two years because, as soon as DuSable opened up, we had to transfer there.

TB: Well, I also had to transfer from Englewood, but it was under pressure because I had gotten into a little trouble with Virgis Eiland. We were cutting classes, and I got caught. Well, actually we both got caught, and when the officer asked us our names, I gave him my right name, but Virge gave him a wrong one, and so he got away.

GD: And didn't have to transfer?

TB: No, he didn't have to transfer.

[*Laughter.*]

March 13 and 20, 1995

IRMA CLARK

―――

LIBRARIAN, TEACHER, INSPIRATION

My earliest memory of Mrs. Irma Clark was at Wendell Phillips High School in Chicago, when she first arrived as librarian in the fall semester of 1934. From the very beginning she was noticeably gracious, patient, and very helpful to students carrying out assignments that required the full resources of the library. When we moved in 1935 into the new building at Forty-ninth and Wabash, which was originally named New Wendell Phillips High School but later changed, because of community demands, to DuSable High School, she very quickly and efficiently organized an extremely chaotic situation so that we students could have immediate use of the library. She did this task quietly and without any fanfare, but what she accomplished so efficiently was a very great and necessary service to both the students and the faculty at DuSable, who were operating in what was otherwise a very overcrowded and somewhat disorganized situation.

After I graduated in January of 1937, because we both lived in the same general neighborhood, I would still see her occasionally, and she and I would always have pleasant conversations about our memories of DuSable. Just before I was drafted into the army in 1943, Mrs. Clark and Ms. Mary Herrick attempted to bring former students of DuSable into an alumni group in order to give additional support to DuSable and its various educational, athletic, and cultural programs. Because of the intervention of the war, her immediate efforts toward accomplishing this worthy cause were not particularly successful. Immediately after the war was over and we returned home, however, she tried once again, and this time she was met with much greater success.

Then in 1954 I returned to DuSable as a practice teacher under the direct supervision of Miss Herrick. At that time we had a great basketball team as well as many students who demonstrated great skills academically. Mrs. Clark was still there to enhance the success of those students through her teaching and also the quality of the library that she had developed and maintained. I left DuSable once again after my student teaching assignment was completed and began to teach at a school in Gary, Indiana. When I left that job, I returned to DuSable in the fall of 1956, teaching Miss Herrick's classes at her request while she was on a two-year leave. During that time, Mrs. Clark was just as helpful and inspiring to me as she had always been, and she was able to create space within the library for the purpose of student meetings and projects and speaker forums for persons of note to speak to our classes. When I left DuSable again for other assignments at Farragut and Hyde Park high schools, Mrs. Clark continued her usual consistent and persistent work to make those of us who were graduates serve, organize, and continue to be proud of our alma mater. This interview offered me the rare opportunity to speak with her and to briefly review her life in terms of her experiences, her feelings, and her impressions. It was a real honor for me to be able to have a conversation like this, and, when you read the words she said, remember that she was over ninety years old at the time of this particular conversation.

TB: I am very happy to have this chance to chat with you. Tell me, when did you first come to Chicago?

IC: I came here sometime between 1926 and 1929.

TB: Where did you come from?

IC: I was born in Montgomery, Alabama, but we left there when I was two years old. Where I grew up and went to kindergarten and elementary school and high school was in Kansas City, Missouri. My father said he did not want to live in the South anymore, and so that's why we came to live in Kansas City.

TB: Where were your mother and dad born?

IC: My father was born in Talladega, Alabama, and my mother and my grandmother were both born in Montgomery, but I never lived there when I was growing up, and I only went back there much later on because my godparents and some of my mother's old friends were still living there.

TB: So your earliest memories are of your experiences in Kansas.

IC: Yes, in Kansas City, and, as you know, there are two cities there right across the river from each other: When you leave Kansas City, Missouri, all you have to do is to cross the river, and then you are in Kansas City, Kansas. The river is all that separates them. Back then there were some of the Oscar DePriest family living out there right across the river from us.

TB: Etta Moten is also from Kansas. Her father was an AME minister, and she went to school in Quindaro, where his church had a school. What did your dad do?

IC: My father had a business down near the railroad station. It was pretty successful because, back in those days, the trains were the only commercial travel business that anyone had, but I really don't know that much about all of that because I was only two years old.

TB: And your mother was with you?

IC: Oh, sure, we were all there together.

TB: How many brothers and sisters did you have?

IC: I did not have any brothers. I only had one sister, and I was four years older than her.

TB: How large was what might be called the "Negro" population in Kansas City back then?

IC: I can't tell you exactly, but there were quite a few. You see, that part of Missouri was never under slavery, and when we first went there, there were quite a few Negroes who had never been slaves nor had their ancestors.

TB: They were frontiersmen, and some of them were going on even further west.

IC: Yes, but quite a few of them stayed right there, and then later on a lot of others came and settled down as well. After we first came there, a good number of young doctors graduating from places like Meharry Medical College also settled down and started their lives in Kansas City. When he first went there, of course, my father did not yet have a house, but as soon as he got one, he sent for me and my mother, and I grew up there from kindergarten through elementary and high school. After that, I went to the University of Kansas for my first degree, but back then, although it was a big university, there were only a small group of Negroes, and there were prejudices. Well, they were nice to you and all that, but you didn't live there on the campus with the white folks, and things stayed like that until my final year when we tried to have a sorority house of our own in a house that was owned by a black family.

TB: Which sorority did you belong to?

IC: Alpha Kappa Alpha.

TB: Do you still keep in touch with any of your sorority sisters?

IC: Oh, yes, I do keep in touch, but I am not going to this thing that they are having this Saturday night. I am not going to that, but I was a national officer for three different positions in the past, and at least Lorraine Green and I still keep in touch.

TB: Yes, Mrs. Green. I understand that she is in good health and still driving.

IC: Well, she's my dear, dear friend. When she was a young lady, she also went to the University of Kansas, and she taught one or two years in one of the elementary schools in Kansas City. I went to the same church that she did.

TB: And what denomination was that?

IC: Episcopal, and, as someone who was older than us once said, "Lorraine has done everything here except get up and preach." You see, even as a young woman, she was very active, and so she organized all the young girls there in the church and formed a club. Some of those girls didn't even go to our church because there was also an AME church in the neighborhood, but all of them were about the same age, and so she organized this group which were called the Passion Flowers.

TB: The Passion Flowers?

IC: Yes, well, the other kids would sometimes tease us a little about the name, but it was religious significance, and we kept that name. So, when she got married, she asked the Passion Flowers to sing for her wedding. Her husband had taken a job on the railroad because that kind of job paid well in those days, and after they were married, he built a house for his mother and also one for them, but they decided to sell their home, and they came here to Chicago. They moved in with a "colored" lady that lived over there near the University of Chicago named Julia Brown, and, believe me, Mrs. Brown, she used to almost see red when I used that word "colored" around her. She would say to me, "Why do you use that word 'colored'? We're black!"

TB: Apparently Mrs. Brown was ahead of her time.

IC: Yes, well, at that time we were beginning to talk about being "black," but we weren't accepting it altogether. At least not yet.

TB: So then did your friend and her husband come here to Chicago before you?

IC: Oh, yes.

TB: Didn't you say that you went on further in your schooling?

IC: After I went to the University of Kansas, then I went for one summer to the University of Wisconsin, but I got my degree in library science at the University of Illinois.

TB: I don't believe that there were very many of us there at that time.

IC: Oh, no, there were actually lots of us who were there back then, but I didn't go there right away. You see I had been teaching at a school in Kansas City, and, at the end of my fourth year of teaching there, I got married, and then I subbed for another year. My husband had a job with a social agency in Kansas City, but then he was offered a job in Lexington, Kentucky, and then we moved there. We only stayed there nine months because someone shot at him for being so outspoken. That's when he decided he was going to go to law school!

TB: So that's why you came to Chicago.

IC: Yes.

TB: And when you came here, you already had some experience in teaching. Did you go right into teaching after you got here?

IC: No, I didn't because at that time you had to have some political pull in order to get a job like that, and we didn't know the right people.

TB: And, therefore, you didn't have enough what they later called "clout."

IC: That's right, but, even so, I went on in and took the examination. In fact, I took several civil service exams in library science, and so pretty soon I was able to get a job, and, well, here I am!

TB: When you and your husband first came to Chicago, where did you live?

IC: My father had died a long time before we moved here, and my mother was already living here. As a matter of fact, one of the reasons why we decided to come here was that my mother had already started buying a house on Forty-eighth.

TB: So your mother provided a place for you all to come, and you came and stayed with her.

IC: I stayed with her there until she died.

TB: Well, many families lived together like that back then, as I remember, and so that kind of thing was not at all unusual.

IC: No, it wasn't.

TB: Now, when you all moved in on Forty-eighth Street, the Regal and the Savoy, they hadn't yet been built, had they?

IC: No, but that's when they were starting to build those places. At that time Forty-seventh Street was the center for all our activity. There was a Walgreens on the corner and a bank across the street, and lots of people used to just come down there to do nothing more than to see people that they might have wanted to see.

TB: People got really dressed up when they went out there. Forty-seventh Street and South Park, which was then called Grand Boulevard, that was the hub of the neighborhood. Sinai Temple was still very active, but at one time it had been one of the richest and most prestigious Jewish synagogues in the entire country.

IC: Yes, it was still a synagogue when we first moved here.

TB: Their rabbi was a man named Louis Mann, and he was a very liberal person. Now, do you remember Poro College?

IC: Yes, it was in one of those old castle-like buildings.

TB: And there was another house right across the street from it that later on became the Met.

IC: Yes, that place was located just halfway through the block between Forty-seventh and Forty-eighth Streets.

TB: Now, when did you start teaching once again?

IC: Well, like I said, I took an examination, and then I got a job at Fenger High School.

TB: The students and faculty at Fenger were mostly white, weren't they?

IC: Yes, and, you see, I had always gone to black schools except, of course, when I went to college, and, even there, you had your little groups that stuck together. We had all our little activities together, and so I really didn't have a lot of contact with white kids or their parents until I got to Fenger, but, as it turned out, they were wonderful to me. You see, it was back in those days when we still had some of the original Dutch people living there as well as quite a few Polish, and Irish, and Jewish, and German—and that meant that, during the holiday seasons, I would always go home loaded down with all kinds of different ethnic things that the students would give me.

TB: Were their families first or second generation?

IC: Some were first, and some were second.

TB: It sounds like it must have been very pleasant for you to be there.

IC: Yes, it was wonderful.

TB: And you didn't encounter any form of prejudice.

IC: No, the children hadn't been trained that way. Some of those kids when they'd come into the library, sometimes they didn't know my name, and they would say, "You know who I mean: the lady in the library, the darker one." But what they were referring to was to color and not to race.

TB: What about your relations with the other teachers?

IC: Well, when I got to the place where I had a car of my own, I used to drive to Fenger every day, and since several of the teachers who were white lived over east of Cottage Grove, I would always pick them up in the morning, and they would ride with me to school.

TB: So you had a very good experience at Fenger.

IC: I had a beautiful experience. I was there for seven years, but then when the New Phillips High School was built and ready to open, they tapped me on the shoulder and said that I could be in charge over there.

TB: They said you could be in charge of the library.

IC: Yes, I became the head librarian.

TB: And then they changed the name of that high school from New Phillips to Du-Sable.

IC: That's right, but now look what's happened. You've made me spend my whole afternoon just reminiscing.

TB: Yes, but these are happy memories, aren't they?

IC: And those were happy days.

TB: You know, one of the things that I remember about you and some of the other teachers I had at DuSable is that, it seems to me, most of you really liked what you were doing.

IC: Well, I looked forward to going there each day. I really did.

TB: And it showed. That made a big difference to those of us who were students. We knew that you were always honest and sincere.

IC: I really liked what I was doing, and so I was always looking for things that might prove to be of interest and help to the students, and—boy!—did I look for things in those days! I couldn't help doing things like that because I like to be encouraging in every way I could. By the way, did you ever know Mrs. Frances Berry? She was a clerk at our library in DuSable.

TB: She was there later on when I taught at DuSable, and I remember that she was very nice, and I could always depend on her to take good care of the students that I sent to the library for special assignments. You know, I hated to leave that school when I did, but the principal at that time and I didn't get along so well.

IC: Who was the principal then?

TB: Mrs. Stack, and I understand that she and Mary Herrick, they didn't get along so well either.

IC: Do you remember Mrs. Helen Springer?

TB: Yes, she was from downstate Indiana. She became one of the moving spirits in the AARP, didn't she?

IC: Yes, Mrs. Springer was one of the conceivers, shakers, and rollers in getting that organization all together, and I must say that I am very glad she did because I am now one of the recipients of some of the benefits that they provide. Whenever they have something worthwhile to offer, they always send me some insurance papers to look at and see if I think it's worth doing, but I don't want to take out any more insurance if it isn't worthwhile. As a matter of fact, I think I already have enough coverage to take care of me if something happens—so I don't think I am going to take out any more, but you know they keep on sending me more information about new legislation or something and how that means that I should increase my coverage.

TB: Well, they are a *business* organization, aren't they? But now, getting back to your experiences at DuSable, how long were you there?

IC: From 1935 until 1968.

TB: So you were there for about thirty-three years. When you retired, did they add on those seven years you spent at Fenger?

IC: Yes, they did.

TB: So you were in the Chicago Public Schools system for forty years or more.

IC: Yes, and to prove it, they gave me a little forty-year pin for me to wear, but I don't even know where it is right now. I must be getting old and forgetful.

TB: Well, we all aren't getting any younger, and so we have our little problems. After I leave here today, I have to go over and make a call on the podiatrist.

IC: Well, lately I've been going to a new masseuse, but I think I'm going to quit.

TB: You go to a masseuse?

IC: Yes, but I don't care very much for her. I don't think she does me any good, and so I think I'll quit. The best podiatrist I ever had was Dr. Frederick Doyle.

TB: Was Dr. Doyle located here in the neighborhood?

IC: No, he was out south in that medical center they have at Seventy-fifth Street, not far off of Michigan Avenue. After he retired, I went to Dr. Burroughs, but then he died on me.

TB: All of a sudden?

IC: Yes, and that was right when I was getting ready to go to Egypt, and I needed to have some work done on me so I would be comfortable walking through all that hot sand, but he was gone, and so then I found this other doctor on Seventy-ninth Street, but something also must have happened to him because when I called there his phone was disconnected, and anytime a business phone is disconnected that means that they have gone out of business or something. So I just looked in the phone book and found another podiatrist right here in the Hyde Park Bank Building who is named Overton, and I thought that maybe he was related to the Overton family of Chicago fame, but he wasn't. He is from North Carolina, but I guess I'll have to go and see him anyway.

TB: You haven't been to see him ever before?

IC: No, and so I'm just going to have to take a risk.

Spring 1991

WAYMAN HANCOCK

HERBIE HANCOCK'S FATHER

Wayman Hancock, the father of the world-famous pianist and bandleader Herbie Hancock, lived in the same building as I before he decided to move to a senior citizens retirement center because of his wife's health. He later became ill and passed, and his wife is now in a nursing home. Herbie lives in California and travels professionally all over the world. He visits Chicago quite often, and his brother, Wayman Jr., is able to be with their mother daily.

Wayman Hancock Sr. was a very serious, contemplative man who told me during our conversation that before leaving the South he dreamed of Chicago as being "the Promised Land, the Land of Hope." When he came here, he found that conditions in some ways were better, but there was still discrimination, segregation, and racial prejudice in housing, jobs, and most of the other important aspects of daily life. However, he was a tough man and was determined to overcome these obstacles, if not for himself, then at least for his children. He talked with great pride about pushing his children through elementary school and then high school and college. Very early he and his wife detected the musical talent of their son Herbie, and they sent him to the best musical schools and instructors that were available in Chicago. They were not so much concerned with the cost but with the quality of training that could be obtained for their gifted son. Mr. Hancock told me in great detail about his exultation the night that Herbie performed as a young pianist with the Chicago Symphony Orchestra, and how he then went on with more worlds to conquer. Obvi-

ously, Herbie has lived up to and beyond his parents' hopes but, perhaps, not their dreams . . .

Wayman Hancock's story is an outstanding example of the ongoing struggle of an oppressed people for the survival and improvement not only for themselves but also in order to stake out and claim a better future for their children. Our conversation was an extremely moving experience for me.

––––––––

TB: Tell me, Wayman, where were you born?

WH: I was born in Albany, Georgia.

TB: When?

WH: December 25, 1910, and then after that my family moved to Macon and then to Atlanta and finally from Atlanta here to Chicago.

TB: When did your family arrive in Chicago?

WH: In 1920, yes, 1920.

TB: What caused the family to leave Georgia and come to Chicago?

WH: I think the stockyard strike was the cause of it. See, before then, not many blacks were working in the stockyards, not until they had a strike in the stockyards—that is what my grandfather told me about it. All the companies— Armour, Wilson, Swift . . .

TB: Cudahy?

WH: Yes, Cudahy—that's right. They all went south and started to recruit blacks, and some of us came up here in freight cars, and some didn't even have a place to stay and so they stayed out in the freight cars out in the yard—that's when the yards had trains running into them.

TB: Yes.

WH: And my grandfather was one of those who came up here, and later he sent for the rest of the family.

TB: And your mother and father, were they born in Albany?

WH: Both of them came from Georgia.

TB: When was your father born? Do you know?

WH: I really don't know.

TB: Your mother?

WH: She told me she was born the year of the world's fair in Chicago.

TB: In 1893.

WH: Yes, something like that.

TB: Were any of your grandparents born into slavery—or do you know?

WH: I remember I used to hear my grandfather talk about how things used to be when he was a boy, and I believe it was soon after slavery.

TB: How many brothers and sisters do you have?

WH: I've got three brothers and two sisters, but one sister's dead and one brother is dead. They were all born here in Chicago.

TB: And you were the only one born in Albany. That makes you the oldest.

WH: Yeah, I'm the oldest.

TB: So your family came to Chicago to work in the South Side stockyards.

WH: Yes, they were strikebreakers.

TB: I know the story because my dad did exactly the same thing!

WH: Up here there were better opportunities.

TB: Now, at the time when you were born, Albany was already a pretty sizable town. Do you remember anything about it?

WH: Yes, but only a little. I was too young to remember very much.

TB: Do you remember anything about Atlanta?

WH: Well, there in Atlanta there was a part called Pittsburgh, and that's the part we lived in.

TB: Mostly all black?

WH: All black.

TB: Was that close to the campuses?

WH: Well, I don't know which one it was, but I know it was near a campus.

TB: One of the black campuses?

WH: Yes.

TB: So when you came to Chicago, do you remember where your family settled first?

WH: The first place we lived was over on Browning Street—Thirty-sixth and Browning—that's the part that's over near Cottage Grove, and later we moved to Thirty-fifth and Wentworth, which was then an Italian neighborhood.

TB: Were there many black folk in that area?

WH: They were all mixed in together.

TB: And at that time, where was the black population, as you remember it, concentrated?

WH: Between the tracks all the way up to South Park, and from Thirty-first Street south all the way out to almost Sixty-third Street.

TB: Yes, and where you were living was close to work for your dad and your granddad.

WH: Yes.

TB: You had already gone to school in Georgia.

WH: Yeah, I started school there.

TB: And when you came here you went to which school?

WH: I started in Horace Mann School here in Chicago.

TB: Where was that?

WH: Thirty-sixth and Princeton.

TB: You were really over there in the heart of an Italian neighborhood, and so that was a mixed school, mostly white and mostly Italian.

WH: Yes, that's right.

TB: And about how many blacks were there? Ten percent? Fifteen percent? Do you remember?

WH: I would say maybe 25 percent.

TB: That much?

WH: I believe so because a lot of them were living from Thirty-third Street back to Thirty-ninth Street. See, there was no Dan Ryan at that time. There were streets there then.

TB: How'd you folks get along?

WH: We got along. We had some little fights, but just kids' fights.

TB: It wasn't a racial thing.

WH: No, the only racial thing we had was that sometimes the black kids and the Italian kids would go down to Twenty-ninth Street and fight the Chinks!
[*Laughter.*]
I'm sorry, but that's what we called them.

TB: Yes, yes.

WH: We would go down there to fight them.

TB: Did you get together and do it?

WH: Yes!
[*Laughter.*]

WH: In fact, we would fight the black guys who lived on the other side of the tracks because they were different from us, see!

TB: Yes, because they were from the other side of the tracks!

WH: Yeah! And what kind of fighting was it? We were throwing rocks! Or we'd catch one of them and beat him, or we'd get beat ourselves, but there was no killing.

TB: That was just not something that any of us even thought about.

WH: Yeah, we just wanted to fight. Sometimes it was over baseball or something else like that.

TB: Did you ever go to White Sox Park?

WH: Sure, sure, we went to White Sox Park, and we used to go to the American Giants Park too.

TB: Where was the American Giants Park?

WH: On Thirty-ninth Street west of Wentworth—around Thirty-ninth and Princeton, right in there. That was the old White Sox Park, and then when the White Sox built the one here in 1910, and moved over there, then the American Giants had that.

TB: The American Giants, which was a black team that was started by Rube Foster.

WH: You know, it's a funny thing—it's not funny either—but I was at the post office a couple of weeks ago, and I was buying some stamps, and the man ahead of me—an elderly man like me—was talking to the clerk behind the counter, and I heard him say something like, as I recall some of the conversation, "Yeah, I was up to Cooperstown . . ."

TB: Cooperstown, New York?

WH: Yes, and he says, "And they told me that, maybe this year they would put me in the Hall of Fame, and I need to be there because I'm worth it," and I said to myself, "I wonder who this guy is." So when he got through, I said, "You're going to go in the Hall of Fame?" And he said, "Yeah, I hope to." And I said, "Well, who are you?" And he said, "I'm Double Duty Radcliffe."

TB: Oh, my gracious!

WH: And I said, "Double Duty Radcliffe?" And he said, "You ever hear of me?" And I said, "Yeah, you've got a brother named Elliot and one named Sonny, and you've got a sister named Portia"—and I started naming all his family! And he said, "Where'd you hear of me?" And I said, "You and your family used to eat in my mother's restaurant there at Thirty-fifth and La Salle Street!"

[*Laughter.*]

I hadn't seen him in years.

TB: Where is he living now?

WH: He's living just down here—kind of around Forty-first and King Drive.

TB: He lives in that home right across from the church.

WH: Yes, yes, that home.

TB: Double Duty Radcliffe! Man, that's a name! So you went to the American Giants Park quite a bit?

WH: Well, I used to go there with my grandfather. He would go there. He hardly ever went to the White Sox Park, but he would always go to see the American Giants. If he didn't go there, he'd go out in the park and watch Negro ballplayers.

TB: Down in Washington Park?

WH: Yeah, yeah. We used to have what you'd call a little feud going on. I was telling him how good these white ballplayers were over there. I was bragging about them, and he was telling me, "They can't do nothin'. They don't play like these boys that I go see." But I was brainwashed, and I didn't think we could do anything as well as the white people did.

TB: But now times have changed.

WH: Yeah, it took me a long time to find out, but I found out. Given the same opportunity, we *always* excel.

TB: We almost have to in order to get recognized!

[*Laughter.*]

WH: We have to because we're good!

TB: And you have living proof in your own family!

[*Laughter.*]

And then, later on, the old American Giants Park was replaced by that housing development—Wentworth Gardens—because they had a fire, I think, during World War II, and it burned them down.

TB: Now, when you were going to elementary school, did you graduate from Horace Mann?

WH: Oh, no. My folks were moving.

TB: Well, where'd you move to?

WH: Fifty-seventh and Princeton.

TB: So you were moving farther south?

WH: Yeah, and then I went to Raymond Branch School—that was on Root Street and Federal. Then I went to Englewood High School.

TB: When did you go to Englewood?

WH: In '27, '28.

TB: Did you like that school or didn't like it?

WH: Well, I liked it, but I quit, and I went to work.

TB: Where were you working?

WH: At Lorraine's Cafeteria downtown as a busboy.

TB: Well, that was the job. Were there many blacks working downtown?

WH: Yeah, some were down there working as busboys, and some as waiters.

TB: Where was this place located?

WH: Between Van Buren and the next street going north on Wabash. I worked there for a while. Before that, I had been working all the time I was going to school in a grocery store for a fellow by the name of Newman.

TB: Where was that?

WH: First store he had was on Thirty-fifth and Federal Street for years. I was raised up right there. In fact, at one time, my family was living in the same apartment building because this apartment was divided up into two parts—a rear part and a front part—and a Jewish family lived in the front part, and we lived in the back, and they had an entrance from the side. I worked downstairs in the grocery.

TB: The people who lived in front of you, were they the owners of the store?

WH: Yes, they were the owners of the store.

TB: That was a sort of a "mom and pop" grocery store.

WH: Yes.

TB: But they had help. Boys who carried the groceries and bagged the stuff up, and—

WH: Yeah, that's right . . .

TB: What years were those?

WH: That was when I was in grammar school, but when I left Englewood, I started working downtown at this cafeteria and went from there to work in the fortieth block on Federal Street for that same fellow, Newman.

TB: Wayman, what kind of memories do you have about the people in the neighborhood and the kind of customers that Newman had coming and going? As you remember it, was the neighborhood crowded?

WH: Well, you know, at that time there were no projects over there on Fortieth and Federal.

TB: No.

WH: One of the families that lived over there was the Cole family—Nat Cole's folks—and they lived in the Thirty-ninth block on Dearborn. Eddie Cole went to school with me.

TB: That was Nat's older brother?

WH: Yes, he played bass, and he left school and went with Noble Sissle.

TB: Noble Sissle had a great band!

WH: But, before that, Eddie Cole and I, we used to be in the basement all the time playing with the piano they had.

TB: Did you play?

WH: Well, I played around a little with the piano. I mean, I had some lessons, but I didn't do much—but, anyhow, one of the things I do remember: We were playing around with the piano, trying to play pieces, and little Nat Cole, he'd come up there to the piano—he was just a little, bitty fellow—but he would always come there, and he would work them fingers of his just like you saw him whenever he played. Did you ever see him do with those two fingers like that?

TB: Yes, uh-huh.

WH: That's the way he'd do it, and we would always run him away because he was bothering us! We wanted to play, and we thought he just wanted to hit on the piano, you know?

[Laughter.]

During those times, we were moving all around in Chicago.

TB: Yes, every first of May used to be moving day!

WH: Yeah, yeah.

TB: And sometimes we moved in between!

[Laughter.]

WH: That's right, that's right, that's right.

TB: So then you moved way out—"way out south," as they used to call it.

WH: Yes, to Fifty-sixth and Lafayette.

TB: That was "way out south" in those days. What kind of neighborhood was that?

WH: Nice neighborhood, nice neighborhood. I wanted to go to Carter School because Carter School had a big gym and a swimming pool.

TB: Yes.

WH: The white kids went to Carter School. There were just a few blacks that went over there. So I gave a bogus address so I could be transferred over, but I wasn't over there for but a month or two. They found out that I didn't live there, so they sent me back to—

TB: Carter School—at Fifty-eighth and Michigan?

WH: Yes, that's right!

[Laughter.]

TB: And you wound up at Englewood.

WH: Yes, that's right.

TB: So what did you young guys do for recreation besides music?

WH: Well, like I said, I worked after school. I worked all the time from when I got out of school at three, three-thirty, till six-thirty, seven, sometimes eight—I forget, but I worked all the time.

TB: Every day?

WH: Part-time every day on school days, but on Saturday I worked the whole day.

TB: Which was from what to what?

WH: Eight to closing, which was six or something like that. That's where I learned how to butcher. I started out picking chickens and learned how to sell and also learned how to butcher.

TB: So that was like an apprenticeship to the butchers' union. When did you join the butchers' union?

WH: I joined the butchers' union years later. I was in the clerks' union before that. Clerks' union was J. Levert Kelly.

TB: J. Levert Kelly—St. Louis Kelly.

WH: Yes, St. Louis Kelly.

TB: What made you join the union?

WH: Well, see, when I was a clerk, we didn't make no money hardly, but when Roosevelt got in, they had to start giving us at least thirteen dollars a week.

TB: So they upped the minimum wage.

WH: Yeah, but when they upped the minimum wage, I got fired because the man couldn't pay me that much.

TB: Couldn't or wouldn't?

WH: He said "couldn't."

TB: So what happened?

WH: Well, I finally got another job with another Jewish fella at Fifty-first and Calumet, on the southeast corner. It was called Harold's Market.

TB: Did you butcher there?

WH: I did everything.

[*Laughter.*]

TB: That was right across from a drugstore called Mirsky's. What was that neighborhood like in those days?

WH: It was all right. It really hasn't changed much. It was just about what it is now. That neighborhood has not changed. The girls I see walking down the street look just about the same—only they looked better then!

[*Laughter.*]

TB: Across the street was another grocery, Bloom's. Was that there then?

WH: Yeah, Bloom's. Yes, it was.

TB: Abe Bloom. My brother worked for Abe Bloom. We lived right around the corner at Fifty-first and Michigan. There was a candy store in the middle of the block between Indiana and Prairie, and then there was a hardware store right across the street from that.

WH: It's still there.

TB: It's still there, yeah. In many ways, Fifty-first Street was kind of my "growing-up" street.

WH: Yeah, then later I started working with Joseph Pritz at his grocery store.

TB: Yeah, I remember Pritz very well. Do you remember Pete Chandler?

WH: Pete worked with me in Pritz's store.

TB: Pete was very important in helping to organize the union. In fact, he was kind of a catalyst because he had had experience working in a grocery store.

WH: That's right. After he left, I kept on working there. In fact, I had the keys to Pritz's store, and I used to open it up for him. This was years after his father died. I just did all his work for him because all he wanted to do was play poker! And they used to "take" him all the time. The problem for me was, he didn't want to give me any more money. He never gave me any kind of a raise or anything, and I didn't want to steal from him—I didn't want to take anything from him—and finally, I had to leave because I knew if I stayed there I was going to have to take from him.

TB: Yes.

WH: So I left him and got a job somewhere else. In fact, the job I got when I left him was working in the railroad as a stevedore unloading freight cars.

TB: How long did you stay there?

WH: Not very long because I was working as an "extra" down there, but then their policy changed, and they had to give you all the benefits of the regular men, or they must let you go. So they gave me a physical examination, and they said my tonsils needed to come out, and that I wasn't fit for work. That was the way they weeded me out—my tonsils!

TB: By this time you were how old?

WH: A grown man!

[*Bitter laughter.*]

TB: You were still in your twenties.

WH: Oh, yes, that was 1937, and I was married.

TB: Did you go into the army?

WH: No.

TB: Because you had a family?

WH: Well, due to the fact that I had a family, and I also had a defense job.

TB: Oh, you were in defense work?

WH: Yes, building O'Hare Field.

TB: Oh, is that right?

WH: Yes, you know, before that it was Douglas Airport.

TB: No, I didn't know that.

WH: Well, that's what it was. That's where they were building the B-29s.

TB: You were doing work that was important to the defense industry.

WH: Yeah, but after that I was drafted anyway. You know, after I got drafted, my daddy told me, "If you want to get in the army, don't tell them you want the army. Tell them you want the navy. And if you want to get into the navy, tell them you want the army." So that's what I did! When they passed me, they said, "What do you want?" I said, "I want to be a Marine." Well, I don't think they had any black Marines back then or at least not many, and they told me I had thirty to sixty days to close up my store—see, I also had a grocery store at that time.

TB: You had a grocery store at the same time you were working in defense?

WH: I was working there at night.

TB: And running the grocery store in the daytime?

WH: Yeah, my wife was actually running the grocery store.

TB: Where was the grocery store?

WH: At Forty-fifth and South Park on the west side of the street.

TB: So, when you were drafted, you just closed the store?

WH: Yes, and I sold my refrigerator cases to one of the Jones brothers.

TB: The guys that were running Policy?

WH: Yes, you know, later on I told Quincy about all of that. Quincy is a nephew of the Jones brothers.

TB: Quincy Jones is a nephew of Mac and George and Ed! I didn't know that.

WH: Quincy was over at the house with Herbie one time, and he told me about that. He said he was here visiting Thirty-fifth and Prairie, which was where he was raised, and that's where the Jones brothers lived.

TB: So you sold your refrigerator to them and closed the store. That store of yours was across the street from the Chicago Met, which was then the Metropolitan Funeral System.

WH: Yes.

TB: And I'd like for you to know that when I was working for the Metropolitan Funeral System, I used to drop into your store every once in a while to buy a candy bar or something!

WH: Well, soon after that I went to work for them too. I also worked over there at Chicago Met.

TB: When was that?

WH: Well, that would have to be—Herbie was born then—I had the store from '39 to '44—had to be '45 or '46.

TB: Where was your territory?

WH: St. Lawrence, Champlain from Sixty-first to Sixty-third.

TB: In the Woodlawn area. That was still pretty new in terms of black folks in that area.

WH: Yes, it was.

TB: Were you still living in that same building that wrapped around the corner?

WH: That's right. We had just about everything in that apartment building! We had some good people in there, and we had some characters in there as well, but they all were people. I treated them right, and I never had no trouble with them. My wife would treat those kids in the building just like one of her own—take them in, clean them up, feed them.

TB: Yes, there were all kinds—a wide variety of people—and down the street from there was Oscar DePriest's home.

WH: Yes, Oscar DePriest's.

TB: And that building is now a landmark, you know, but nobody does anything with it. I don't know why. And there was a garage in the back of the Met, wasn't there?

WH: Right.

TB: It's my understanding that garage was where they trained mechanics to be able to repair airplanes.

WH: Well, I wouldn't know about that. I don't remember anything about that. There was a garage back there, but it was mostly used by the Metropolitan and some of the office force. They had a big office force over there.

TB: Yeah.

WH: And some of the people in the neighborhood kept their cars there, but I didn't. If I had a car, it was on the street!

[*Laughter.*]

TB: So, well, then, you worked for Chicago Met for a while. Herbie was born in 1940—

WH: Right, 1940.

TB: When did you discover he could play the piano?

WH: When he was a baby, when he was crying, if we played music, he'd stop crying. He liked music. You could tell—from when he was just a baby. When he was a little youngster someone gave him a bugle, but you know you have to blow hard on a bugle to get any sound at all. Well, Herbie tried and tried to blow something on that bugle! And he couldn't blow nothing on that bugle!

[*Laughter.*]

But he was crazy about music. He always liked music. If he was crying or if something was bothering him, music would stop him. We could tell that right from the very first.

TB: How did he learn to develop this early interest in music?

WH: Well, my wife, she played music at church, and she recognized that Herbie was musically inclined.

TB: And she encouraged him to do it.

WH: Yes.

TB: Did he take formal lessons early?

WH: He was seven years old when he started.

TB: Did he start on piano or some other instrument?

WH: He started on piano. I found a guy who sold me a piano. What happened was that I was a meat peddler back then. I was selling meat out of an old truck. That truck was insulated, and I had a barrel in it that I used to fill up with ice to keep the meat cold, and I would buy meat from the Yards, and sell it to stores and restaurants. Well, one day I went by this church and this fellow who at that time was the bass fiddler with Nat King Cole—

TB: When Nat had the trio?

WH: Yes, anyway, that guy, he sold me a piano for twenty-five dollars. It came out of his father's church, or something like that.

[*Laughter.*]

TB: It was an upright?

WH: Yes, an upright, and I paid some guys a couple of dollars apiece, and we all moved it over to our apartment.

TB: Herbie said he wanted a piano, and he got one!

WH: He was only seven years old! And when he was eleven—after four years—he won a contest given by the Chicago Symphony Orchestra. The prize was to appear with the Chicago Symphony Orchestra, and that's what he did. He appeared with them, and he played Mozart's "Coronation Concerto."

TB: And you were as proud as you could be!

WH: Well, I was in the hospital when he played.

TB: Oh!

WH: I was in the hospital with undulant fever. At that time I had started working as a federal meat inspector for the Department of Agriculture at the stockyards, and I had contracted undulant fever. In man, it's called undulant fever. In animals, it's called brucellosis. It's something like Bang's disease. And there I was in the hospital, and I had to be in there five or six weeks while they gave me streptomycin and all those sorts of drugs. I had been in there for about two or three weeks, but they let me out to go to that concert, and Herbie played with that hundred-piece orchestra. The lights went down and when they came up, he was standing there by the piano.

TB: Well, I know that must have been a great night for you and your wife and the rest of your family. Was that in Orchestra Hall?

WH: Orchestra Hall, yes.

TB: And from that point, I guess, his musical career was kind of launched and on its way.

WH: Yes.

TB: Now, before Herbie really went "big time," which schools did he go to?

WH: Forrestville all the way through eighth grade.

TB: Then he went to Hyde Park High School, didn't he?

WH: Yes, he went there when he was twelve years old and graduated when he was sixteen. Then he went to Grinnell College.

TB: On a scholarship?

WH: Yes, and he got a degree from Grinnell and then went to Howard.

TB: And all this time that he is pursuing his education, he is also continuing to play music professionally.

WH: He was playing all the time. All the time getting more recognition for his music.

TB: But, then, when did you move into Hyde Park?

WH: It was 1968.

TB: You came from where?

WH: From 8229 South Park.

TB: So you were out in Chatham.

WH: Yes, I guess that's Chatham. I was out there for five years. And five years before that, I was living in French's building—Avery French, who used to teach at DuSable. He was the assistant principal.

TB: Yes, yes, Avery French. He lived at Evans and Sixty-second Street. In fact, I think he's still there. He still goes out to play a little tennis. A remarkable man. I had him when he was teaching at Phillips. I had him again when I went up to DuSable, and even now, whenever we meet, we always exchange pleasantries. He was a favorite guy of the students. Students liked him very much. So you were at Sixty-second and Evans, almost right across the street from the old Evans Hotel.

WH: The Evans Hotel was at Sixty-first Street, and I was at Sixty-second.

TB: Sixty-first, that's right. Down the street. And Lydia DePriest lived in that block. I don't know whether you knew her or not—Oscar DePriest's sister-in-law. Then you moved out south.

WH: Yes, to Eighty-seventh Street.

TB: Now, did you own these houses?

WH: No, we were renting. I had a grocery store there on Sixty-second Street.

TB: You have always had an interest in business.

WH: Yes.

TB: You were kind of an "entrepreneur," as they call it these days! Jobs were not just what you wanted to do. You wanted to be your own boss.

WH: Yeah, that's right. Well, do you remember how I was in the hospital when Herbie gave his first public performance? After that, I was in the hospital three times in two years.

TB: Oh, my!

WH: During the time that I was working for the Agriculture Department, and every time I'd get out of the hospital and go back to work, I'd get sick again, so I asked them to take me off of the killing floor—that's where I was working, and they wouldn't do it. If you were black, you worked on the killing floor, and that was as far as you could go. Whites had all the other jobs that were done in the processing of meat. They didn't have any blacks in those positions like they have now. They had one or two light-skinned guys who got that kind of job, but they didn't know that they were black until after they were hired. Anyhow, after being in the hospital three times in two years, and every time I was in there I didn't get paid—you only got two-thirds of your salary—and you didn't get it until *after* you got out of the hospital, so the family had to chip in and help to keep things going—my brothers, and my mother and father—so I quit!

TB: Uh-huh. Which packinghouse was this?

WH: It was not a packinghouse. I was working for the U.S. government. I was going to Swift, Armour, and any of them.

TB: But whichever one you'd go to, you'd always be on the killing floor.

WH: Yeah, the killing floor. So I asked them if I couldn't get off, and they said "No," and I said, "Well, I'm not going back." So they said, "Well, if you're not going back, you have to quit," and I said, "But I'm not going to quit." So, well, to make a long story short, to keep from being fired—and my wife's behind me all this time—she's helping me on this—we wrote a letter and sent copies to the surgeon general, to the boss of meat inspection here, and to the Civil Service Commission telling them about this whole thing, telling them that the reason I was resigning was because it was detrimental to me to go back on the killing floor.

TB: And that you'd been unable to get a transfer.

WH: That's right, and I told them why. Years later, in 1965—meantime I had gotten a job at the post office delivering mail on the North Side, and I met a couple of fellows that had been working for the government, and they said, "Come on back in, man. We're getting good jobs now." So I went back in and went right back to work on the killing floor!

[Bitter laughter.]

I did that for four years, but I finally got off of it and I got into processing. Better job. More money.

TB: Did you have to be in the union?

WH: Well, I didn't have to be.

TB: But you were in it because you were committed to the union movement.

WH: Always was. In fact, I might go up to a union meeting this Friday night even though I'm retired now.

TB: Now, you've been retired for how long?

WH: I retired in '84. July 1, '84. I retired after twenty-nine years.

TB: Twenty-nine years of service!

WH: Yes, and then in '88 they called me and asked me if I would come back as a temp—temporary—not in the same department I had been in but in the import division, just working with meat that was imported.

TB: From Argentina and places like that.

WH: Argentina, Australia . . .

TB: What does an inspector do?

WH: The main purpose is to ensure the quality of the meat, to make sure that it's wholesome.

TB: That's quite an important job. You were protecting the health of the entire community.

WH: Of course, and I enjoyed it.

TB: After you retired for a second time, did they increase your pension benefits?

WH: No, no, not at all, because they don't take any pension out when you come back to work as a temp—so the work I did when I came back didn't have any positive effect on my pension at all.

TB: Well, it is hard to deal with a person like you and not also deal with the accomplishments of your son and also your wife. You tell her I'm going to be calling her and ask to borrow a little of her time.

WH: I'm sure she'll be glad to speak with you, Tim.

September 17, 1991

JIMMY ELLIS

SAXOPHONIST AND TEACHER

I first met Jimmy Ellis while riding on the El on my way to downtown Chicago in about 1970. He was very concerned about the rumored merger of the powerful all-black musicians' local with the larger, even-more-powerful local that had historically been all white. I had seen him and heard him play his "very sweet" alto saxophone many times, of course, but I had never had any lengthy conversations with him before. He told me he believed that such a merger would prove to be a takeover of the black local, placing black musicians at a distinct disadvantage. Unfortunately, subsequent events proved that he was absolutely correct.

Jimmy's family is made up of successful professionals and businesspeople. One of his older brothers, Morris, is one of the most successful bandleaders in the Chicago area, but, despite his talent and love of music, Morris treats what he does as primarily a business. For Jimmy, the music always comes first.

Today Jimmy is constantly in demand as a musician and as a teacher. He reads a lot (about many things), thinks a lot (and not just about music), and speaks his mind (about everything). It was a real pleasure having this opportunity to speak informally with him.

TB: When were you born, Jimmy?

JE: On July 17, 1930. I'll be sixty-five on July 17. I was born at 5712 Michigan Avenue, right here in Chicago.

TB: And what about your mother and dad?

JE: Well, they were from Anniston, Alabama.

TB: Anniston?

JE: That's near Birmingham. But my father's mother was from Canada.

TB: Oh, really?

JE: I guess that must have been an Underground thing.

TB: Yes. Did you even meet her?

JE: I wish I had. The only person I can remember is my mother's father—George Wright was his name.

TB: And where was he from?

JE: Actually, he came from Alabama. There's so much history there. He made charcoal. He sold vegetables. He had a home in the hills and one in the valley. He had about nineteen children, and every one of them survived.

TB: When did your mother and dad come to Chicago? Did they marry here or did they marry in Alabama?

JE: They married here. My mother was brought here by Booker T. Washington's granddaughter.

TB: Oh, really?

JE: I've forgotten her name. She came here a few times when I was a child. She brought my mother here from Alabama. I was born in 1930, and my oldest brother, Fred, was born in 1925, after they were already here.

TB: And all of your brothers and sisters were born here?

JE: Yes. And my mother and father both came here as teenagers.

TB: Do you know when they were born?

JE: My father was born about 1903. And my mother was, maybe, 1907. He was a little older.

TB: And so when they came here, did you ever hear where they lived?

JE: Oh, yes. I can remember where from the time I was born. I remember for a short spell we lived at Forty-fifth and King Drive, where the Metropolitan Funeral Home is right now. There was a sculptor living right there where what used to be the Parkway Ballroom. He was a black man. He did some beautiful artwork. Others might be able to remember his name. But, anyway, that was around 1933. We stayed there for a short spell. It was a beautiful neighborhood because I used to hear Louis Armstrong and all the music. They used to have a little place across the street where they played all the jazz. Then we moved to Forty-ninth and Champlain.

TB: How old were you then?

JE: I was probably three and a half.

TB: So you don't remember much.

JE: No, but I still remember being there.

TB: Did Louis live around there?

JE: He lived at something like Forty-fourth and somewhere between King Drive and St. Lawrence—somewhere in that area.

TB: Earl Hines lived around there too, didn't he?

JE: Yes, somewhere in that area, because I've got Louis Armstrong's book that he wrote about his stay here in Chicago. And, really, it's an interesting book because Earl Hines and all of the other musicians used to congregate in this area. That's what a lot of people fail to realize. People talk about New York, but, hey, man, jazz started in Chicago. I mean, maybe not really started here, but . . .

TB: Yes, here is where it matured.

JE: When jazz came up the Mississippi, it didn't go directly to New York. This was the hotbed of jazz—right here in Chicago. This was the environment that was conducive to the development of jazz. Even Louis had to come *back* to Chicago. He had gone to New York for a while, but it was more like home here because Chicago has that proper type of atmosphere.

TB: Oh, yes! I remember when I went to New York for the first time there was no grass! Just cement.

JE: "Hey, I can't wait to get back! I need some *air!*"
[*Laughter.*]

TB: Did you know Louis's second wife, Lil?

JE: Not at all, but I had the opportunity of working opposite Louis, and if you remember Harry Gray, the president of Chicago 208, which is our local—we were the most powerful union in this country. Did you know it was about 1903 that blacks started their own musicians' union?

TB: Yes.

JE: Black folks put their own money into developing the first black local in the history of America. That local had more acts than any other local ever had, and they had power because of the cross section of talent they represented, but all that was lost through integration.

TB: Yes, that's when they merged. I remember being on the El one day with you, and you weren't certain which way they should be going—that is when the merger was being discussed.

JE: But, like I always said, I don't want to be a part of nothing you've got if I can't run it. If I've got to be *under* you, I'd rather not be *with* you. Be under me sometime! So, I never was for the merger, because I knew what was going to happen. Now we have *no* power. I've been a delegate to the convention of the American Federation of Musicians twice—once in Salt Lake City and once in Phoenix, Arizona—so I've been on the inside, and I've seen the whole mechanism of the

American Federation of Musicians in this part of the country and in Canada, and, believe me, blacks have no power in it. You see, when we were separate, when we went to conventions, blacks came from Detroit, from Philadelphia—then we had a voice to vote. But once we merged, we lost all of that.

TB: By the way, this brings me back some memories because a schoolmate of mine at Burke School, Buddy Smith, who played drums . . .

JE: I met Buddy.

TB: He was very active, I think, in the local. You guys spent so much time up there on Thirty-ninth Street, I thought that it was a nightclub!

JE: That's right! And I knew all the people who came through that local—Eddie South, Stuff Smith, Billie Holiday—all of those kinds of people—I knew them personally. There was a lot of *power*, and it was passed on. I'd go to the Regal Theater, and I *saw* these people and worked with a lot of them.

TB: You know, the first time I saw Lena Horne was over on Forty-seventh Street. She was walking down the street with—guess who?

JE: Who?

TB: Roy Wood.

[*Laughter.*]

JE: That's my man. I've known Roy almost all of my life. He's known my whole family.

TB: Well, the first time I saw Lena, we went up to the Brass Rail, and I said, "This is the prettiest woman I've ever seen." And I saw Ella Fitzgerald up on Forty-seventh Street coming out of the Regal. She had just become famous with "A-Tisket, A-Tasket," and I saw Billie Holiday—because I got to know both of them later as people that I really knew. But they were right here. They were in the neighborhood. They came to the neighborhood. Of course, later on things expanded so they could make more money doing other things. But, you know, I was in Pittsburgh the other day, and there was a little club there where they still have little jam sessions. So, in some places at least, some of that old flavor has been retained, and I don't care who lives where—we *all* used to have those cultural centers. Literary, musical, athletic. You know, if a guy wanted to learn how to be a boxer, there were lots of clubs where he could learn how to be a boxer. If he wanted to learn how to play tennis, there was a place out there on Fifty-seventh Street, and there used to be a little place down on Thirty-fifth Street where the women had a tennis club. So you had all of that around to draw from.

JE: Yes, I used to go by the Palm Tavern just to see all the stars, to see everybody looking good.

TB: Acting like they had some money!

[*Laughter.*]

JE: No one was ever too big. I introduced my mother to Nat King Cole after he had done "Mona Lisa." She came to see one of his shows, and I said, "This is my mother," and he came right over and talked to my mother. You see, there was real camaraderie.

TB: Nat was a beautiful guy. And he was just like that when I met him when I went to Phillips High School. Of course he wasn't singing then—he was just playing the piano and experimenting a lot because he was trying to play like Earl Hines. And if you listen to his earlier stuff, you'll hear he's got a lot from Hines, but he already had his big band around the neighborhood—even before he went to California.

JE: That's what I was always told about because that was before my time. He played at Warwick Hall, didn't he?

TB: Yes, they would have a battle of jazz there, and Nat had such a group—most of them were from DuSable—that we'd go up there cheering for the schools almost, even though some of us were already out of school. And Nat would play, man. He would really play. And, of course, he had to learn to sing—well, he didn't learn, he just started singing!

JE: Well, if you want to make some money, they always say, "Can you sing?"

TB: Yes, and so he went on and started singing and, of course, the trio got lost. I understand that one of the guys in the trio still lives in Chicago.

JE: Yes, Oscar Moore was the guitarist. He would be in his eighties now.

TB: Yes, but in the days of your years—and mine, of course—guys like you would have never had to leave the neighborhood if they didn't want to because there were so many places to perform. We used to have people come to town, and I would say, "Do you want to go out?" and when we were living at Fifty-sixth and Calumet, we'd just walk right around the corner to the 'Boogie, or walk down the street to the DeLisa, or go upstairs to the Golden Lily. And I knew a few people that made me feel important because, even though I wasn't a musician, I knew all those guys that were in my generation. Ray Nance might come up, Eddie Johnson might come up.

JE: That's right. Do you remember Natty Dominique? He came to Chicago from New Orleans. I used to talk to him. You talk to the elderly people like him and that's where you get the knowledge. I also used to talk to George Dixon. George was a good talker, and he would start smiling and telling me things, and I learned so much from him. I would sit like a student at his feet. And I would say, "Whatever you want to tell me, you talk about it."

TB: He used to live over there on Forty-seventh and Evans, but he left the band after he got married. He would play up at that place on the corner or Sixtieth and Cottage Grove. Fletcher Henderson's brother Horace also used to play there.

George told me he would take his horn up to that place on the streetcar—streetcars were still running then—and then when the gig was over at three or four in the morning, he would take his horn and get back on the streetcar and go back home, and he wasn't ever even thinking about anything happening, you know, and nothing did. And yet, just before he passed—about two or three months before that—he was just standing on the corner of Forty-seventh and Cottage Grove and two young guys ran up and mugged him.

JE: Yes, the times have changed.

TB: They certainly have. Now, when you went to school, where did you go first, Jimmy?

JE: I went to Willard.

TB: Old Willard. Frances E. Willard.

JE: Yes, and you went to Willard too, didn't you?

TB: Well, first I went to Fuller, then Forrestville, and *then* Willard. Then we jumped across the Boulevard, and I went to Burke. That's where I wound up, but we knew each other back then because of the softball teams. That's where I met Turk and Blackburn and all those guys.

JE: I still see Turk every now and then. He's a very nice person.

TB: Yes, he's one of those bright guys that didn't go to school. And he always talks about why he didn't go to school—because he was so busy playing ball.

JE: Well, in my family, it was mandatory that you go to school. Mandatory. I don't care where—somewhere.

TB: There was *no* way to get out of going!

JE: If you were out of work and you wanted to be a stick-up man, you'd have to go to stick-up-man school!

[*Laughter.*]

TB: Well, education was always important. School was the thing!

JE: Well, my family supported wherever I wanted to go to school. "You want to be a musician—whatever you want to be—well, OK, we'll support that, and we'll deny ourselves certain things we might want just to make sure that our children carry on."

TB: That was a tradition you just can't escape. You know, I still don't know how to not go to school!

[*Laughter.*]

JE: When I grew up, from my back window I could see Willard School, and in that neighborhood we had three pharmacies. We had Dr. Shaw on Fiftieth and Champlain, we had Dr. Smith on Forty-ninth and St. Lawrence, and we had Dr. Dawkins, the pharmacist, right nearby.

TB: Yes, you could walk around the neighborhood and get whatever you wanted.

JE: And my brothers would get flowers from Mr. McElmore back in the thirties and forties, and they made money selling those flowers over on Fifty-fifth Street, and at the Rhumboogie and the Harlem Club and the Club DeLisa. I have never even known any kind of poverty myself. I never wanted for food.

TB: Yes, the basics.

JE: My mother used to go to the market, and we would get food not only to feed our own family but to feed other people. My mother had such a beautiful nature that she would go to State Street, and she would always buy enough food to feed us and also some of the other people that we knew over at Bethel AME Church. So I didn't know what poor was and didn't even want to know. We never wanted for food. We may not have had Brooks Brothers suits, but we were clean. And not only that, if you wanted to buy drugs and things like that, you went to Calumet City. You didn't go next door. You know, you didn't buy it downstairs. There was a district for that kind of thing, and Two-Gun Pete knew it was there, but it was all on one spot. I'm not saying it was a wonderful thing, but if that's what you wanted, that was where you were going to have to go to get it. You didn't get it next door.

TB: And that's what's happening now. That's one of the changes.

JE: Back then it was different. There was always a baseball game. In the evening somebody was always doing something. There was always something to keep you interested.

TB: What were the ages of your brothers and sisters?

JE: Well, I'm the youngest. There's a year and something difference between me and Morris. And Curtis may be a year and something older, because now Curtis must be about sixty-eight.

TB: How time passes!

JE: And Martha's older. She's about seventy-one.

TB: Well, you're all pretty close together. Willard School was very busy during that period, and the playground was always active. We used to go out there and play together.

JE: Do you remember Ralph Johnson? He was an only child. He used to ride his bike backward. He'd try anything!

[*Laughter.*]

In that neighborhood around Forty-ninth and Champlain, everybody lived together. I knew Erskine Tate's mother. They lived across the street from me.

TB: Somebody talked with me today about Erskine Tate's wife, who is still living.

JE: She is?

TB: Yes, she still lives out there in Chatham Village.

JE: Well, I knew his mother because she taught music in the front of the building, and Erskine Tate would come by to see his mother. So many productive people lived around there!

TB: Did you know John Levy?

JE: Yes. I knew John Levy. Not very well, though.

TB: He went to Willard, but he was older than I was.

JE: Well, I didn't know he had gone to Willard, but I knew him. And John Nealy was a friend of mine.

TB: John Levy said he came back to do some writing, and he said he looked at the old neighborhood, and he started crying.

JE: I don't know any neighborhood that was more productive. I just think about my exposure to people that I could see. I remember David Dees. He didn't live in Chicago, but he came to Chicago. I remember so many other productive people. I remember Johnny Hartman. I remember Joe Louis. I remember Kelly's Stable, which was at Fiftieth Street near Forrestville. Jack Blackburn used to live down the street.

TB: Jack Blackburn was Joe Louis's trainer.

JE: Yes, he was up there near what they used to call Grand Boulevard. Remember those double-decker green buses they used to have?

TB: Yes, we used to climb up all those double decks and ride downtown. So, that neighborhood, that school, all those people that you had relationships with—for the most part it was a very pleasant experience.

JE: Oh, of course!

TB: And what did the neighborhood look like?

JE: What did it look like? It looked green because there was grass. Of course, there'd be some places where we'd play ball and in *those* places there might not be any grass. But it's really the people that made it what it was. There was a woman in my neighborhood called Miss Mason. You couldn't do nothin' without her seeing you. She would say, "What you doin', boy?" and she would report you like she was the police. So, everybody took care of each other. It was automatic. You didn't think about doing it. My father was there, and he'd say, "Get your hands out of your pockets. Stand up straight! What's wrong with you? Don't give me no slang—I don't want to hear it. Get out of that bed! Get off the corner! What you doin' on the corner?"

TB: And don't step on the grass!

JE: That's right. Hey, but when I grew up, people started talking about drugs, and now I've lived long enough to be sixty-five years old, but by the time I was in my forties half of my friends had already died from overdoses of drugs. I'm talking about before white folks ever even got involved. The kids I grew up with, every day I'd go up to the swimming pool, and there you'd hear that some guy went and got an overdose of whatever, and all these guys—these kids in high school and grammar school—very excellent musicians—they got messed up with that stuff.

TB: There was a tenor player that used to go to DuSable, and I used to see him down on Thirty-ninth Street.

JE: What did he look like?

TB: He looked something like you, but he was heavier. I forget his name, but while you were talking, I was thinking about him because he had so much talent.

JE: Well, you had to have so much talent! You had guys like Marion Price, who was a track star at DuSable High School. I knew him very well. Johnny Griffin, who lived right in that area. I knew him at DuSable. My brother Curtis and he graduated together.

TB: Now, at that time, when they graduated from DuSable, they were already good musicians.

JE: I think that's because Walter Dyett, the music teacher there at DuSable, had the awareness to know that, "Hey, I don't care if you don't like me. If you want to play the horn, then you've got to practice and do just what I say." So he wasn't soft. Total discipline was required.

TB: I know that.

JE: And you've got not only to be able to play the music—it's also how you looked, how you dressed—everything. "Whatever you're doing, if it's not in order, get out of here."

TB: I remember coming down the hall one day, and I said to myself, "Gee, how can everybody stay in that man's class?" But guys would be begging to get back in after he had put them out!

JE: And he only had one eye. The other eye was a glass eye, so a person wasn't always sure if he was talking to them. He'd say, "Get out of here!" and they'd say, "You talking to me?" and he'd say, "Yeah!"
[*Laughter.*]

TB: Oh, Cap [Dyett] was something else!

JE: Yes, but Walter Dyett was never a person who would stand off. Even during his lunch he would come over and talk to you. He was always a part of what you were doing. He was very strict, but he was not the type of person to pass by you and not talk to you or whatever.

TB: He was always friendly, but I just knew he was strict, and I used to wonder, "How does everybody take what he's putting down?"

JE: Well, if you don't learn that kind of discipline, they run over you.

TB: Getting ready for "Hi-Jinks" at DuSable was really an event, wasn't it?

JE: Well, Captain would teach school during the day, and then he would have to come back at night to rehearse for "Hi-Jinks." You've got the stage crew, the manager, the costumes—he put that whole thing together. And everybody learned something through it. It wasn't just the band. It was the whole production. Do you remember Johnny Hauser?

TB: Yes.

JE: Well, he was my private teacher. He was beautiful. And as a matter of fact, I did my practice teaching with him, but if it hadn't been for Walter Dyett, I don't know where I'd be today.

TB: We need to make a special fund for him—like we did for Miss Herrick. You remember Miss Mary Herrick?

JE: Yes, of course, I remember Miss Herrick.

TB: Now, we make contributions to the school in her name, and they provide for some small scholarships. Every year. The same thing should apply to those of you who knew Dyett.

JE: That's right.

TB: But you guys got some of your "uppances" from this man.

JE: That's right! And he understood the power of the mind. Cap was always strong with positive thinking. He was always telling us that we could do it! He radiated that to us.

TB: Was Miss Jones there when you were there?

JE: Yes, she was there. She taught my mother. My mother always talked about her music teacher, Miss Jones.

TB: She was a little lady who commanded respect. Never raised her voice above a whisper. In the choral area she was a little different than Walter Dyett, but she was just as demanding. When you entered DuSable, Bill Cousins and guys like that were still there, weren't they?

JE: Yes, Cousins and my brother Curtis were in class together.

TB: World War II was over when you graduated from high school, wasn't it?

JE: Oh, yes, but in that way I was really blessed, Tim, because when the GIs came back from the war—Buddy Smith and all of those other musicians—they all started bands, and you could always find someplace to play, and there were a lot of bands that young musicians could learn from. They had a lot of rehearsals. Those guys went to school on GI Bills and took arranging, and then they formed bands, and they kept passing music on to younger people.

TB: Oliver Coleman and all that group.

JE: Yes, and now we've lost all that. Now that's all gone.

TB: Yes, but I still remember when guys used to go down on Sunday morning and have jam sessions down on Thirty-ninth Street.

JE: Yes, at the Rhumboogie they had jam sessions in the morning and also at the Beige Room. The Beige Room was in the Pershing Hotel. Then the Pershing changed its name to Birdland and then to Budland because there was a suit against it because there was already a nightclub called that in New York.

TB: Yes, and the Club DeLisa used to have a "Blue Monday."

JE: You could jump out of one club right into another.

TB: That's right. Remember the Propeller Lounge?

JE: Yes, and you had Bay Street, the Cotton Club, and all kinds of other places.

TB: So when you left DuSable, you already had your union card?

JE: Oh, yes, I had already joined the musicians' union. At that same time—it was during the Korean War, 1951. I also became a Jehovah's Witness because I didn't want to go to that war, and they put me in jail, and I became very militant. I met a lot of people out there in Washington Park that reinforced exactly what I felt.

TB: Well, by then some of us had returned to talk about how we had been treated as black soldiers in the last war.

JE: Oh, yes, but I will tell you, and I will tell anybody, I won't accept that kind of treatment. I wasn't raised that way. I don't care if you don't like it, you're not going to make me poor. I'm not going to be dependent on white people. I don't care who it is—Gingrich, any of them—I don't care what any of those people do in this country. My sources are not white people.

TB: Are you still a Jehovah's Witness?

JE: No, I practice a form of mental science. I don't like any kind of organized religion because I don't like limitations.

TB: But you did go to Korea, didn't you?

JE: Well, you know, Tim, I finally had to go to Korea because all this had such a negative impact on my mother. When I got there, I worked as a medic, and that's when I began to read Gandhi's philosophy. This was back in 1956, when King was beginning what he was about, but, you know, I don't see things the same way. I don't need a ride on your bus. I'll buy my own bus. I don't ask you to let me ride on your bus. I want to have a bus of my own. That's the mistake the civil rights movement made. Look what happened. We built this part of the city, but then when the civil rights came through we were dispersed, and we lost the power that we had. Look, when the blacks got out of slavery, they knew how to do basically everything that needed to be done. We raised white people, and did all the work, and then we started our own schools. All of the time we were talking about education. That's how all of those schools like Wilberforce got started. It was because we wanted to help our own. We didn't ever have a lot of money.

TB: But we had a lot of creativity.

JE: My father's given name was Frederick Douglass. His parents named him that because Frederick Douglass was a powerful man at the time. They wanted to name their son after him, and I see *nothing* wrong with that. As a matter of fact, I'm proud of my father's name: Frederick Douglass Ellis. My wife's grandfather's name was Hannibal. These people were smart, and that was the environment I grew up in. Tim, your father left the South? He probably would have been hung if he hadn't left.

TB: Yes, it was time for him to go.

JE: Well, what I always think, Tim, I think it's in your blood. You cannot kill an idea. You can't *kill* the idea.

TB: No, it will stick.

JE: Because you are what your ancestors are.

TB: Because it's right—and also because it's survival.

JE: Yes, that's how we've survived.

TB: So when you began to really get serious about your music, were you playing full-time or part-time?

JE: I was full-time because, you know, I started as a teenager and I had no other responsibilities. Well, I was still going to school—the Chicago Conservatory—at the same time. I had been given a scholarship to Florida A&M, which I wish I had taken to this day, but I wanted to play, and so I went to the Conservatory and played on the side.

TB: So you went to the Chicago Conservatory?

JE: Yes, because I wanted to be on the road with the cats. But it worked out anyway because I still went to school.

TB: Who were some of the earlier groups that you played with?

JE: Well, a lot of musicians will not carry a full band all over the country. Like when they come to Chicago, they don't have to pay for air flight for the whole band—they just pick up musicians here in Chicago. This is the place where you can usually pick up musicians that can read the music and handle all the arrangements, and that's how I got to meet Earl Hines.

TB: What kind of guy was he?

JE: A nice guy, but—and I forgive him—he didn't want to fight the system. You know, I've never felt inferior to anyone. At that time his band was part of the Harlem Globetrotters touring show, and that show had people from all around the world in it—the Tung Brothers from China, the Lorano Brothers from Italy—but they didn't allow us to eat with the troupe in the South. They let those Italians eat there and those Chinese, but the blacks couldn't eat there with everyone else.

TB: It that right?

JE: Yes, and Earl Hines accepted it. Well, maybe that's OK for him, but I never did accept that type of treatment. I'd rather go out and get my own food—so I'd go up to the store and buy it for myself. But Earl Hines, he accepted that kind of policy at certain times, and I'm not going to blame him for it, but I think it was a very bad example. This was a traveling show with people from all around the world in it, and the first time we went south, he said, "Keep your mouth closed, boy. Don't you say nothing to these white people." He probably thought he was trying to save my life!

[*Laughter.*]

Because he thought that the white people were going to get mad. I understood that, but I won't take that. It was very easy to do what Earl did, but I didn't think it was right. They wouldn't serve us, and we were the band! You have to serve us along with everybody else! You see, we should have all gotten together and bought our own food, even if it was only cold cuts. You're not going to go and take and put me somewhere off to the side and then take my money and go back in the kitchen and fix my food. I don't want you to fix me *nothing* to eat. I'll get my own. I'm not going to eat your food. You go to a white restaurant and try to get them to serve us, and you know how it is when you walk in the door, and they don't want you in there. Well, "I don't want you to give me any of your eggs and bacon. Give me a donut and a cup of coffee someplace else." I'll just suffer!

[*Laughter.*]

So when you see that sweet roll of theirs, just suffer, but don't go to the back and eat where they tell you!

[*Laughter.*]

TB: One of the things I admire about Duke Ellington was that Duke felt so sensitive to things like that that he bought that railroad car—so that his guys would not have to endure those kinds of insults. And, Joe Louis, whatever people may have felt about his language, was a hero and a dignified person. But even someone like Sugar Ray Robinson couldn't take it, you know, when he was in the army, Sugar Ray just said, "No, I can't take this."

JE: Yes, I remember that.

TB: But Joe Louis was not a patsy, and I remember Louis Armstrong—was it 1956, 1957?—was in Cuba, I believe, playing, and the kids in Little Rock were going to school, and he told the president, "Go call out the military," and then somebody asked him a question, and he said, "If they can't save those kids, or do something for those kids in Little Rock, then to hell with the United States!" The papers had it all over, and his manager, Joe Glaser, asked him, "You didn't say that, did you, Louis?" And he said, "The hell I didn't!" Folks didn't realize that this man's been carrying that feeling. He could take it, but he was not going to let his children, you know, be abused in that public situation. That's when they needed to call out the troops. And they did.

JE: And don't forget Jackie Robinson. He took a whole lot of insults, you know, but he made things possible for many other people.

TB: Yes, he opened the doors. He wasn't even the best baseball player, but he was able to take it until he didn't have to anymore. One day somebody hit him on top of the head as he was sliding in, and he jumped up and poked the person in the nose. I mean a real poke. Jackie Robinson was a middleweight champion of the Pacific Coast League.

JE: He was very athletic, wasn't he?

TB: Oh, he played football, basketball, track—and his whole family was like that. One of his brothers, Mack Robinson, had been in the Olympics. He had to take it until he had proven himself. And that takes a *lot* of strength. I don't have it. I've never had that kind of strength. So when I would get mistreated, I would react right away.

JE: Well, you see, you came to interview me, but now I want to interview you! [*Laughter.*]
There's so much you know. That history, it's so important.

TB: When you became a pro, who were you with, or were you just freelancing?

JE: When I became a pro, I was still working with Captain Dyett. You know, he used to have a summer orchestra. We gave summer concerts in Washington Park. Usually we gave ten or twelve concerts a year, and even right out of high school I played with his dance bands. We worked at the Parkway Ballroom. I did a lot of jobs for him because he was giving me an opportunity to develop my talent. So I got into this business early. I worked for Lil Green when I was under twenty years old.

TB: How was Lil?

JE: Oh, I love her. She's sweet, and I also worked with Tampa Red and all of the old blues people back on Thirty-fifth Street here. Butterbeans and Susie "Peg Leg" Bates.

TB: About that same time you opened a bookstore, didn't you?

JE: Yes, I opened a bookstore in 1955.

TB: Where was the store?

JE: At 831 East Sixty-first Street—right across the street from the Woodlawn Hospital. It was called the Center Rail Bookstore. That's what I called it.

TB: How did you happen to get that idea?

JE: Well, you know, books have always been in my family. I've always loved books. My mother would sit at the table, man, and recite Paul Laurence Dunbar. So that was my basic interest because that's what I was around.

TB: Yes, and another thing that was true is not only did you have access to the books and the tradition of your family, but very often you saw the people that had done these things. You could stand on Forty-seventh and South Park—formerly it was Grand Boulevard—and you would see all of these luminaries at one point or another, whether they were writers or they were in music, or art, or athletics. You would see them there in the flesh.

JE: That's right.

TB: And most of the time they were friendly enough to say, "Hello," so your examples of accomplishment were standing there right in front of you.

JE: And then, I used to work for the Central Bookstore on Clark Street. It was that bookstore that had the books out front. So later on, I just got this idea that blacks didn't know enough about their own history, and so I said, "Well, I'm going to open a bookstore because I want the people to read," you know what I mean? The idea was not to make money, but, of course, you've got to make money to survive. But people weren't quite ready for what I was talking about, so you've got to put out some little pockets of novels to attract their attention, because my idea was really ahead of the times. As a matter of fact, people told me I was a damned fool at the time I opened up that bookstore. They said, "Blacks don't want to read nothin'." With a business like that, you had to be there every day, and it took me away from my music, but, you know, I've still got some of those first editions.

TB: Why don't you give them to Margaret Burroughs at the DuSable Museum?

JE: Well, I wanted to let Margaret use them, but I've got children myself. I would like for them to have those books. But what people should be able to do, I guess, is take my first edition of *The Life and Times of Frederick Douglass*, for instance, and put it on a display and say, "This is loaned by Jimmy Ellis." Hey, this is *my* book. I mean, I don't mind giving it to you if I'm dead and gone. Then it ain't going to mean nothing to me. But I'm not going to give it to you if you're not going to do with it what *I* want you to do with it. Sure, I'd like you to have it, but you have to have it under my terms. And I've let people use my library as a resource if they wanted to write, you know, because I've got some literature here that you never will find anywhere else. I can't take it nowhere with me, but I'm not going to abuse it.

TB: Well, those books are, indeed, precious.

JE: Well, I spend my time keeping stuff like this. Not for myself, but for others, and I know Margaret well. She was my only black teacher in high school, but Margaret's just too strict for me.

[*Laughter.*]

TB: I know. I know!

JE: Hey, I told Margaret to her *face*—when she asked me to play for those alumni— I said, "How much are you going to pay me?" And she said, "Well, we don't have any money." So I said, "Well then, you're not talking to me! I'm a musician. You can't call me in to play for free. You wouldn't go call the plumber and tell him to fix your sink for free!"

[*Laughter.*]

If your mama dies, you wouldn't tell the undertaker, "I ain't got no money."

[*Laughter.*]

Listen, I'm serious about this.

TB: I understand.

JE: You see, I may live to be a hundred—whatever—or I might die tomorrow, but, when you live to be a certain age, you have to shoulder your responsibilities. Now, if I'm sixty-five years old, I have the responsibility to leave something behind. You know, I have a workshop down on the campus of the University of Chicago. It's a good environment. You have to use all the forces around you, and I've been doing this for years. We have Eddie Johnson and all of these guys—the ones that are still around.

TB: Now young people are beginning to be interested in the music, and I see that people like Wynton Marsalis are trying to revive some of the spirit of jazz, but most of the musicians that I see now that are playing jazz and blues are nonblack. They're white.

JE: Well, I've been doing clinics, in South Bend, Indiana, at the high school and at the Notre Dame University Jazz Band, and they've got some fine young musicians there. They've got some blacks there—but only very few, and that's not enough. That's our responsibility. You've got a lot of teachers who've got degrees and haven't got jobs. Well, OK, give them a job. Teach the children and keep the money circulating within our own backyard.

TB: Well, you have made a contribution, a substantial contribution, and the people that you knew when you were first coming up inspired you to make that kind of contribution.

JE: That's right. Couldn't have ever done it without them! We have so many good people here—people that have been born here and have spent most of their lives here—these are the people who made you what you are. You didn't make yourself. Somebody helped you. You know, I saw this program on Arthur Ashe, the tennis player. He said the only thing he's sorry about is that he had to spend so much time wading through garbage to try to prove that "I'm OK," and yet he still achieved all those honors. That's why I have so much respect for Frederick Douglass. Can you imagine what he went through that you and I have never had to experience?

Being a child and maybe seeing your mother only three times. And this man was to become an orator! And his speeches, what power!

TB: Yes, he changed the history of America. It was Douglass who insisted that Lincoln induct black troops who were waiting to fight the good fight against slavery. He and a few others insisted that, if the Union army was going to win, they had to take those black guys and let them fight! But our own history in so many various areas—medicine, music, athletics—has not yet been written from the true source. It's still being written from outside. But you know the truth in terms of jazz music because it's a truth that comes from *inside* your own experience.

JE: Yes, even Duke Ellington, half of his music was published under the name of Irving Mills, a white guy who was his manager. All that music has Mills's name on it. Back then, in order to get your music published and sometimes even recorded, you had to go through these white people.

TB: Yes, but even so, youngsters of today's generation, it seems to me, miss some of the advantages we had.

JE: That's our fault. It's not their fault. If we don't get it to them, how are they going to know? If you can't pass it on, you can't blame them because they only know what they're exposed to. I teach privately, and I have my students sit down and listen to Sidney Bechet and Art Tatum because they have to be able to listen to really appreciate this kind of music. You can't just take a book. You've got to hear it and be in an environment with it. You have to pass that on to these children.

TB: And what are their reactions when they hear it?

JE: They're very fond of it, but I'm very strict when it comes to dealing with this music because that's the way it was given to me. And even though I've taught many students with all kinds of problems, I wade through all of that because I remember that once somebody *gave it to me*, and it's still in my mind. If you don't want it, I'll leave you alone. I'm not going to bother you. But if I see you want it, instead of a half-hour lesson, I'll give you an hour and a half, and you can come back tomorrow—if I think you're getting it. Because that is what it's for. It was given to me that way. Someone gave it to me. So it's not mine just to keep for myself.

TB: And the same is true about your books.

JE: It's just as true about the books as about the music.

TB: You are the keeper and the purveyor.

JE: I am the purveyor of the music and the keeper of these books!

January 9, 1995

MORRIS ELLIS

—

MUSICIAN AND BUSINESSMAN

I have known Morris Ellis as a musician for more than forty years. I have known Morris Ellis as a jazz bandleader and as a psychological social caseworker for at least thirty years. Likewise, I have known his brother, alto-saxophonist and clarinetist and bandleader Jimmy, and his other brother, Curtis, who is a pioneering black bookstore owner, as well as his sister, Martha, who has been an excellent educator for about those same thirty years. For me, knowing members of this wonderful family has been both an honor and a pleasure. Though each of them has a unique personality and style, one readily recognizes each of them being a member of the Ellis clan.

As we were recording this conversation in Morris Ellis's lovely home in the Beverly neighborhood of Chicago, the phone was constantly ringing as people from all over the Chicago area were requesting his musical services. He was always polite and extremely professional in quoting his fees and negotiating the specific arrangements. In all these conversations Morris Ellis was always a businessman first and a musician later, after all the practical business details had been ironed out. Surrounding him throughout his home are the beautiful memorabilia of his past and present musical life. Having this particular conversation with him was for me an extremely memorable pleasure.

—

TB: Morris, where were you born?

ME: I was born right here in Chicago at 5712 South Michigan. Mom didn't make it to the hospital!

TB: You had home delivery!

ME: Yes, home delivery!

TB: Where were your mother and dad born?

ME: My father and mother were born in small towns in Alabama. My mom was from a little place called Anniston, Alabama.

TB: That's just outside of Birmingham, isn't it?

ME: Yes. Later my parents both went to Wendell Phillips High School here in Chicago, and they both also attended Tuskegee. In fact, that's where they met.

TB: Is that right? Tuskegee had a special program for smart young men and women.

ME: Dad came to Chicago ahead of Mom, and Mom used to come to Chicago every summer to work with Booker T. Washington's daughter at Poro College. And the last summer before my parents got married, my grandfather said to my mother, "Well, you can't go back to Chicago anymore. You've got to stay here in Alabama." And Mom said she saved her pennies up and all of her seventeen brothers and sisters helped her to run away from home . . .
[*Laughter.*]
. . . to come to Chicago to be with my father, and when my grandfather saw my mother again, she had a two-year-old son in her arms—my oldest brother, Fred—named after my father.

TB: Did you know your granddad?

ME: Yes. He used to come up from Alabama to Chicago to visit every year. He was a big man, a tall man. He lived in a town called Hobson City, and in Hobson City, he was the minister, and he owned a bowling alley and had a big farm—you know, that's why he was able to have so many kids. He had seventeen kids from seven wives. He buried six of his wives, and the seventh buried him!
[*Laughter.*]

TB: Oh, that's quite a story!

ME: Mom took up playing the piano in Alabama when she was still at an early school age, and she used to always tell the story about how Grandfather would not allow a certain type of music to be played, but whenever he went to town—and they could see him go over the hill in the chuck wagon with the horse—she would jump on the piano. All of her brothers and sisters would come in, and they would dance to "Oh, You Beautiful Doll" and other songs like that. But she said one day my grandfather doubled back.

TB: He suspected something!

ME: Yes, and all this music was going on, and all the kids were dancing and having a heck of a time, and everybody saw my grandfather come back in but Mom!
[*Laughter.*]

All of her brothers and sisters quickly disappeared, and there she was still working out on the piano with "Oh, You Beautiful Doll"! So, anyway, Grandpa had a habit that whenever one of the kids had to be chastised, he would start singing a song. Whichever kid it was that had to be chastised, he would say to them, "You've got to help me sing this song. I can't quite get this melody together." My mother's nickname was Susabell, and so he said, "Come on, Susabell, and sing this song," and she said, "Oh, Papa, we didn't know that you would come back so soon!" But, anyway, that gives you an idea of the sort of background I came from. It was musical. My father played the clarinet. Mama played the piano, and, of course, my older sister, Martha, was going to be a classical pianist. She took lessons for years and years and years.

TB: Is Martha still at Chicago State?

ME: Yes, she officially retired in June, but I think she's busier now than she was before! She's always on the road, and she's got so much energy.

TB: Well, coming back to your life, Morris, you were born here in Chicago at Fifty-seventh Street and Michigan Avenue. That part of what we might loosely call "black Chicago" had just begun to be populated by people of color at that time, I believe.

ME: Well, we grew up at Forty-ninth and Champlain, right behind Willard School, so I went to Willard School for eight years.

TB: That was the old Grand Boulevard neighborhood.

ME: Yes, and the area we lived in was called "The Valley." It sort of had a slope downwards, and then, after graduating from Willard School, I went to DuSable High School for four years.

TB: What was that neighborhood like when you were growing up?

ME: It was a real community. A community where everybody knew everybody else. Everybody *cared* about everybody, and there was no such thing as "you belong to somebody else." It was, "You belong to *me*." Every adult on that block knew me and knew my family, plus my mother had an open-house policy anyway. If any of the adults in the whole community saw Morris Ellis doing something wrong, they had the right to chastise him — mentally, physically, whatever. And they would tell my folks! They'd call them up and take me back home! So, it was one of those situations where I didn't get into too much trouble. I was too busy trying to learn how to play my little horn. I started playing the horn when I was in grammar school, even though I don't think I really mastered it until I was at DuSable.

TB: Now at Willard, at that time, it seems to me, they had already developed a tradition of two things. One was pretty good athletes, and the other was fine musicians — because everybody played something!

ME: Yes. Well, everybody on the block played something. The way we got into it—my brother Jimmy and me—was that there was a guy named McKinley Thomas who at that time lived around the corner on Fiftieth Street. He was the head of the Elks' band in Chicago, and he used to have rehearsals down at Thirty-ninth and Indiana.

TB: Was that where the union headquarters was?

ME: Yes, up on the second floor. On Sundays he would rehearse the Elks' band, and he had all these extra instruments—so he would bring all the kids over and say, "Pick an instrument, and I'll teach you how to play it." I wanted to play the trumpet, but somebody else had already picked the one trumpet that he had—so he said, "Here, take this euphonium. It's got the three keys on it, and you play it just like a trumpet. The only difference is the mouthpiece. It's just a little larger, and when we get another trumpet, you can just switch right on over. You won't have lost anything." My brother Jimmy took the saxophone and started playing, and I took the euphonium, which is sometimes called a baritone. Well, anyway, by the time I got to DuSable High School, I was on the way to knowing what I was doing with that euphonium. I walked into the band room on my very first day there and asked Captain Walter Dyett if I could be in the band. Now, you have the same kind of mouthpiece on a baritone that you have on the trombone, and Captain Dyett needed some trombone players in the jazz band, and so he gave me a trombone and said, "Take this home. You've got a week to learn it." And it wasn't easy because there are two different clefs—a bass clef and a treble clef, but I worked and worked and worked and worked, and I taught myself to play the trombone! He told me what the seven positions were and said, "Here's the book," and I went on from there, and I played in the concert band at DuSable for four years. I played in the jazz band for four years, but my greatest experience was playing in the "Hi-Jinks," DuSable's musical revue, for four solid years. Cap taught us—in fact, he prepared us—to be ready to go out into the professional music world. He gave us the classical end of it. He gave us the theory, and he gave us the harmony. When the guys left DuSable, they were ready to go out into the world and play professionally, and I don't mean just still learn. But, even with the training I got from Dyett at DuSable, at that time I thought, "Well, maybe I don't want to be a musician." It was then I decided to go to Howard University. You see I wanted to become a dentist, and I had letters of recommendation from Dr. Clayborne—the dentist down at Forty-third Street. When I got on the train to go to Howard, my dad gave me ten dollars and said, "I don't know when I'll be able to send you some more money," and I said, "Well, take five of this back and send me my horn"—and sure enough, he wrapped up that horn and sent it to me, and when that horn got to Howard . . . well, I played my way all the way through that school!

[*Laughter.*]

TB: There was a place up on Forty-seventh Street and Fortune called Warwick Hall, which had a teacher named Erskine Tate. Did you ever hear of him?

ME: Erskine Tate lived right across the street from me on Forty-ninth and Champlain.

TB: Is that right?

ME: His mother, Mrs. Benson, taught all of the people in the neighborhood how to play the piano. She was *the* piano teacher. My mother knew Erskine Tate very well, but I never did know him professionally. I just knew *of* him. He would come to see his mother, and we would wander across the street and say, "There's Mr. Tate!"

TB: He was kind of legendary among my generation. If you were good enough, you went to Tate to learn the basics because you were afraid of the competition over at DuSable. And when you got to DuSable, you could then feel that you might be able to get somewhere because of your work with Tate. He had a dance band of his own during that period. He was older than Ray Nance. Did you know Ray?

ME: No, I didn't know Ray Nance.

TB: Well, he lived at Fifty-seventh and Michigan. He went to Phillips with Ziggy Joe Johnson a little after Milt Hinton. The Globetrotters had just started at that time. You see, I was still going to Burke School—but I kept up with what was what, although at the time I never dreamed I would be going to Phillips. But coming back to your DuSable experience, what were your impressions of that period of time and some of the people you knew that you can remember?

ME: Well, at DuSable, it was such a tradition for musicians to come in and train under Captain Dyett. There were so many great names, even at that time, and I'm talking about 1943 to 1947, who had been under Dyett and who were starting to go out into the world. We're talking about Gene Ammons, Benny Green, Johnny Griffin—people like that.

TB: Now, Benny later played with Duke Ellington for a while, didn't he?

ME: He played with Earl Hines, basically, but he did also play with Duke for a while.

TB: He played trombone too, didn't he?

ME: Yes, Benny Green was *the* trombone player for a time, and I wanted to be like him.

TB: And what about Johnny Griffin?

ME: Well, Johnny Griffin was a year ahead of me at DuSable.

TB: Is that right? Now, he left when he was about seventeen or so to go to Lionel Hampton's band, didn't he?

ME: No, he graduated, because his mother insisted.

TB: Yes, that's right. He had a tough family. I later had his kids in my classes at Hyde Park. He still comes back to see them once a year when he gets home.

ME: Well, you know, he started off playing the alto saxophone throughout high school. Then, when he graduated, Lionel Hampton took him in the band and switched him over to tenor so he could play on that famous "Flying Home."

TB: Well, he had a real challenge coming in after Arnett Cobb.

ME: Yes, it would be a big challenge for *anybody* to follow Arnett Cobb!

TB: You mentioned Benny Green. Who were some of the other people that you remember?

ME: Richard Davis was one of the great bassists. Milt Hinton was his idol. Richard should have been a classical bassist. Captain Dyett took some extra time with Richard Davis, and Richard turned out to be one of the finest bass players.

TB: And you had already met Dorothy Donegan, who had hit the top quite early on.

ME: Yes, and we could name guys who came out of DuSable who were able to go into show bands, but, even so, those guys were always kept out of the pit bands downtown because of the unions.

TB: At that time the unions were separate?

ME: Yes, there was Local 10 downtown and Local 208 on the South Side. There was an agreement that black musicians couldn't play north of Twelfth Street, and the white musicians wouldn't come south. It was unwritten, but still it was always in effect.

TB: Unless the bands came from out of town.

ME: Yes, that was different. They knew the out-of-town bands wouldn't stay around, so they didn't have to worry about them taking up the jobs.

TB: Now, on the academic side at DuSable, can you remember any of the academic or athletic stars?

ME: Well, you know, in high school to me everybody was equal. They hadn't yet had a chance to make a name for themselves.

TB: You mentioned the Hines brothers.

ME: Yes, there was Charles Hines, who was captain of the Sea Horses, the swimming team. And he's been in charge of the natatorium program for the city of Chicago for years. Once in a while, when I'm coming down the Outer Drive, I see him coming out of the Administration Building. But did you know Charles Hines was also a good drummer? He played all the drums. He was a player in the concert band, and he played in the jazz band at DuSable. His brother went on to Meharry Medical College and became a doctor, and the last I heard he was the head of Meharry.

TB: He still is, unless he has retired. He was quite a scholar. And Bill Cousins.

ME: Yes, Bill Cousins—Judge Cousins—a student who was a real scholar.

TB: Academically, as well as musically and otherwise, it was a good school. That was an age of such great talent in all kinds of fields, particularly in music and in athletics. Everybody was boxing when I was there, and between music and boxing and running track and doing everything else, it was exciting. The other day a guy called me from the BBC and said, "What was it like growing up on the South Side?" And I said, "Man, you missed it!" It was different from Harlem, in my opinion, because Harlem didn't have the space we had to move around in.

ME: Or the parks! But DuSable was such a fantastic school because all the teachers at DuSable took an interest in their students.

TB: Yes, whether they were black or white.

ME: Yes, it didn't matter, and I think one of our great teachers was Mary Herrick. Now we have that scholarship fund in her name. You know, she amazed me one day. I was in her class during the war, and she knew *every* student that came to her room by name, and she remembered them all. All the guys that went away to the service would write her, and she would write back to them. She was an unusual person.

TB: Yes, she was. She and Captain Dyett, in their own individual ways, were rivals. You know, she said to me once, "Well, one of the things I don't like in particular is them taking all that time doing 'Hi-Jinks,' but I guess at least he teaches them something."

ME: Well, one thing that was kind of nice was that there was no such thing as "time" for Captain Dyett, and I don't know how he did all the things he did. He would get to school early and open the doors because he was also assistant principal at that time. He would handle the Beginners' Band, the Intermediate Band, the Concert Band—which was the top band—the Jazz Band, the majorettes, and also put together the "Hi-Jinks" show, which was just as good as anything you would see on Broadway.

TB: Yes, it was. Tell us a little about the "Hi-Jinks" show.

ME: Well, I guess "Hi-Jinks" was Cap's idea. It was a student production that was a yearly event. They had two shows a day at DuSable High School, and it was always sold out in advance. He would write the script—I don't know whether he *always* wrote the script or not—but there would be a script and a theme, and he had all the students participating. It was the same thing you would see if you went to a big Broadway show, and he insisted on the same excellence. A lot of good stars came out of that.

TB: I understand that scouts used to come to sit in on the performances.

ME: Yes, and a lot of times Cap would bring back some of the top guys who had graduated from to DuSable to sit alongside us in the band pit. That was one of the most amazing things that could ever happen! Once we had Benny Green sitting beside us and we'd say, "Wow! This is really something!" And do you know another thing Captain used to do? When any big names came to Chicago, they would also come to DuSable because he would go over to the Regal Theater and get them! I've got a picture in my yearbook of Cap bringing in Duke Ellington to DuSable to do an assembly! I mean, nobody came through Chicago that Cap did not go and bring to his students. It was to show us that this is the way we were headed. That's when I got to meet Lawrence Brown, the greatest trombone player, I think, of all the times. Cap brought him over to DuSable. I remember looking at his horn. He had a horn that was so beat up I don't know how a note ever came out of it!

[*Laughter.*]

But he played the *prettiest* trombone you'd ever want to hear—"My Little Brown Book."

TB: Yes. I've got recordings of all that wonderful music.

ME: Right after Duke Ellington died, I was doing a jazz show on WBMX—it was a brand new station at that time out of Oak Park—and I had a show called *The Jazz Zone.*

TB: Yes, I remember.

ME: So I interviewed Mercer Ellington, and it was at that time that Mercer told me that he had donated all of his father's jazz manuscripts and original music to Yale University, and I said, "What? Why Yale? What's wrong with Morehouse and Howard and Johnson C. Smith, and on down the line?" And he said, "Well, they were going to build a special building just to house all of it." And I said, "Come on, Mercer, why give all that Duke wrote and struggled for to one of those white universities?"

TB: Yes, they'll study it, and then they will decide that they have become the *real* experts on his music.

ME: Oh, I was hurt. I was *really* hurt.

TB: Yes, and they've got another collection like that over at the University of Southern California.

ME: Well, it wasn't necessary, you know? My daughter graduated from Yale, but still you know what I mean? It was Duke's thing. White folks don't need it. *We* are the ones who need it.

TB: Yes. Well, that's why I'm doing what I'm doing. The original materials of these narratives will be concentrated at the Chicago Historical Society, but I have made a promise that they will also be available to students at DuSable, Phillips, and the DuSable Museum.

ME: Well, I think that's great, Tim.

TB: Well, that's what it's for. Folks can come to *us* and learn. That's the reason people like you have got to write your history. It's crucially important. Nobody writes your history like you do! They can play around with it, but they can't get it right. How would they know? Now, you went to Howard University from DuSable High School. What happened there, musically?

ME: Well, musically, as I think I mentioned to you, I was pretty busy because I had my father send me my horn. At that time I was in the premed course—I wanted to be a dentist. But the very first week after that horn came, I was able to join the Howard Swing Masters, and that band was loaded with guys who became stars later on. They had a lot of veterans just coming out of service. People like Benny Golson, who wrote "Killer Joe," were in that band. We had guys that came through the band like Frank West and Bill Chusis, a trombone player who's *still* with the Basie band. In other words, we had a very good, solid jazz band—I'm talking about 1947, 1948, 1949—and at that time they used to have a national contest for colleges with the best musicians to play in competition against a top jazz band, and so we played opposite the Basie band. Now, at that time Count Basie's band had gone down to just eight pieces because they just couldn't afford more. Well, we played opposite that Basie band at the old Knickerbocker in Washington, D.C., and we made Basie's band sound *so* bad—and that is the truth! Later on—as a matter of fact, the next day!—Basie came up to our campus and just about recruited the whole band!

[*Laughter.*]

Eddie Jones was also in our band at that time, and he went with Basie right then and played with him for ten or twelve years. Bill Dewes also came out of our band, but, anyway, it was from that point on that Basie went back into his full band.

TB: Was this before Joe Williams?

ME: Yes, this was before Joe Williams. Joe Williams didn't get into the band until around about 1954. At that time, musically, I was able to play Wednesdays through Saturdays, and that extra money really helped because we simply didn't have enough to send me to school.

TB: Yes, I know. It's a funny thing. If the parents have decided you are going to go to college, you didn't have much choice even though you didn't have the money!

[*Laughter.*]

ME: That's true!

TB: Like you said, your dad gave you only ten dollars.

ME: Yes, he said, "I'll send you some more," but I didn't know when that "more" would come, and so I played my way through the whole four years I was at Howard. We played the Howard Theater there—it was somewhat similar to the Regal Theater.

TB: Yes, I know. I had a lot of friends at Howard.

ME: Andy Young was in my class.

TB: Andrew Young, the former U.S. ambassador to the United Nations?

ME: Yes, Andy and I were great friends. We came to Howard at the same time, and he was a very young guy at the time. I think he was only about fifteen years old. His father, a dentist, brought him to Howard, and he told us to look after him because he was still a young boy, and he lived there in the dorm with us, and he was the most mischievous boy you would ever want to see!

TB: Really?

ME: Yes. We called him the "Water Brigade" because he poured water on the other kids while they were sleeping! But this is getting off the subject! At that time I always had the music in case my premed and dentistry didn't work out, and I found out in my third year that dentistry wasn't right for me, and so I switched over to psychology, and I got my degree in psychology, but all the time I still had music on the side. Then I came back to Chicago in 1951 and joined Red Saunders at the Club DeLisa, and I played with him at the Club DeLisa until it closed in 1954, and that's when I decided, "Well, I've got to do something." Nobody calls trombone players until after they've got everybody else in line! You've got your piano player, your bass player, your drummer, your trumpet player, your saxophone player, your guitar—so then "*if we need it*, we'll call in a trombone player." That's why I said, "Now, wait a minute. That doesn't seem quite right to me!"—and so I started my own band in 1955.

TB: And you've been in the business ever since then as well as continuing playing?

ME: Yes, ever since then.

TB: What kind of a guy was Red Saunders?

ME: His reputation was that he was the best showman in the country. He was easygoing, but he was also a good leader—a very good leader. He called me when one of his trombone players had an accident and couldn't perform, and I went in with the band. The band was full of guys who were top-notch. It was a good show band. We worked six nights and did a breakfast show on Monday morning. And that was another story—that breakfast show! Six o'clock on Monday morning you would see people lined up all the way around the corner at Fifty-fifth Street and State up to Michigan Avenue. I never could believe it. At the time I was working a day job as a caseworker in the Department of Welfare and then playing with the band at night—which meant that I would have to be there on Monday morning to play that show. We would play all night Sunday night, and then we would have about two or three hours in between before the breakfast show started at six o'clock in the morning—so we would sleep right there at the club, you know, on a table or whatever! And at eight o'clock I'd have to run out of there to go home, take a shower, and get to my eight-thirty job!

[*Laughter.*]

TB: You were really moving!

ME: I did that for about a year and a half, and it was definitely an experience. The Club DeLisa is another whole story that you've *got* to cover. That band at Club DeLisa! We had good musicians there in that club, and they had a good chorus line—not the prettiest girls in the world, but they could really dance, and when you put those lights down . . .

[*Laughter.*]

TB: And, like you say, Red was a fantastic leader. Your own band did stage shows at the Regal at one time, didn't you?

ME: Yes, in fact, Red Saunders came in after me at the Regal. I was there for about four months, and then Red came in. I think they wanted somebody who had a bigger reputation, and he was one of the big stars of the time. Al Benson was the guy who was doing all of the booking of the bands at that time.

TB: Al Benson—the disk jockey? He broke the union's grip on live music, didn't he?

ME: He sure did!

TB: His daughter went to DuSable, I believe.

ME: Yes, and unfortunately, she OD'd. But I always like to talk, Tim, about the time that we did the week with Dinah Washington at the Regal. Dinah was a great cook. She would come in and do a week at the Regal and on the last night of the show, to close down, she would put a spread downstairs in the band room for the musicians, and she cooked *every* dish herself. She was crazy about the musicians, and yet they all claimed she was so evil!

TB: Dinah was my friend, so I have no problem with anything you want to say about her!

[*Laughter.*]

ME: I loved her, but we were getting ready to rehearse one Friday morning for Dinah's show, and they told everybody, "Be in your seats at seven o'clock. Dinah's going to be on time." Well, it was seven o'clock, and the band was all seated on the stage, and then in came Dinah dragging her mink, and she looked up, and she recognized one of the guys in the band named Hobart Dotson, a trumpet player, and she said, "Hobart, how's yo' mammy?"

[*Laughter.*]

And Hobart took his horn and said, "'Miss Jones,' I'll kick your ass!" And she said, "That's right. Just treat me like a woman!"

[*Laughter.*]

Did you know they had gone to Phillips together?

TB: Yes, yes! By the way, did you even get to the Warwick Hall?

ME: No, I never went to the Warwick, but I understand that's where Nat Cole used to have his big band.

TB: Oh, man, at that time he was playing like Hines. Then later he developed his own style, but we didn't know that Nat could sing. We did *not* know he could sing!

ME: *Nat* didn't know he could sing—till he was forced to!

[*Laughter.*]

TB: Now, tell me, you've been describing all these appearances with important, famous musicians. What caused you to get into the business end of music? Most black musicians just play, enjoy it, get their money, and then go home. What impelled you to go into the business end?

ME: Well, I always knew there was a business end of music, but I didn't know what it was, and what really got me into the business end of music was an experience that happened to my brother, Jimmy. He had been playing with Earl Hines, and he decided to leave that band and come back to Chicago. On his way back to Chicago, he met a man on the train from Crystal Lake who said, "Jimmy, I want you to bring a band up to Crystal Lake on New Year's Eve," and Jimmy said OK. They talked again later on the phone, but there was no real contract—so on New Year's Eve, Jimmy and me—I was piano—and a drummer named Cecil Bolger and bass player Richard Davis—we all got on the train and went up to Crystal Lake. Well, we got up there with all the snow and all, and when we got to the station, the guy who was supposed to pick up the band and take us to wherever the ballroom was didn't show up—so Jimmy got him on the phone, and that guy said, "Oh, we canceled it." And I said, "Well, do we still get paid?" And Jimmy said, "I didn't have a written contract." So we got back to Chicago about four o'clock that morning hungry, cold, wet, and broke, and I said, "Now, *wait* a minute! There's got to be a better way to do this thing." So I decided I was going to become more involved in the business side of music. I knew I would have to be a businessman first and a musician second. And that's the way I have stuck with it from that point on, and that was back in 1955.

TB: There's only one other guy that I know—but I'm sure there are others—that looked at it the way you just expressed it, and that was John Levy.

ME: Yes, John has made a really fabulous career out of it, you know? And he doesn't handle a whole lot of artists. Joe Williams, Nancy Wilson, and maybe one or two others. That has been his entire managerial career, and he has managed those folks with an iron fist, believe me. If I had to go *through* John Levy to hire both of those artists, it would be a real experience. He has been a real businessman, and this business of music is a real business that we *need* to know about. For years—

and still even now—Jewish businessmen have made the money off of us. We are still not making the money out of this business that we should. I insist that you always should just say, "This is my price, and this is where it's going to stay *if* you want my services." A person can tell you how well you played for his daughter's wedding—that you really made the party a success and all of that. "Well, then, all right then, pay me, and when you pay me, you're going to pay me right!"

TB: If you're going to deliver the services, you deserve the pay.

ME: Oh, yes. "I'm going to make your party one of the best parties you ever had, but you're also going to pay for it—and you're going to sign a contract with me, and you're going to give me a big deposit, and *then* we are in business." All of that comes first. All of that comes before I take that band out there to Wilmette or wherever it is. I've been doing more stuff on the North Shore now than ever before, but there's another side of the story you need to know. I have given up on the musicians' union. I gave up on the musicians' union when Bill Berry asked me to play for Harold Washington's inauguration, and I had to hire forty-three musicians, and the musicians' union here gave me flak because they wanted to tell me *who* to hire. I would not let the musicians' union dictate to me, and when I went down before the board—because they called me down—I looked at the board, and there were all these white folks sitting around, and I said, "Who represents *me* around here?" "We represent you," they said. "No, no, no, I don't see any black faces around this board. There's no one here who speaks for me, if I don't speak for myself." And they said, "Well, you're the kind we'd like to have sitting on the board." And I said, "What kind am I?" That is when I decided that the union could do nothing for me, and so I gave up the union, and that's been a good thirteen years ago now.

TB: My understanding is that when the merger came, it was a disadvantage to the black musicians.

ME: Very, very much so. We were forced into that merger. And again, it was done by someone that I used to have respect for, and that was Red Saunders. The true picture behind Red Saunders and that merger was that he had been kicked out of the black union because he had refused to pay a fine. You know, he was the fair-haired boy for the black union for years. They let him get away with all kinds of stuff at Club DeLisa. I made seventy-three dollars a week playing six nights and a breakfast show, and he was always allowed to get away with this. But this time when he did something wrong, the board finally said, "Well, we're going to have to discipline you, Red."

TB: But more than money was lost in that merger.

ME: Yes, and you know what? We brought something to the table at that merger. We had a musicians' union building there at Fifty-second Street and Drexel which had something like forty-seven apartments in it. Musicians lived there. You know, they weren't making big money, but at least they always had a place to live that the black union had bought for them, and we had to throw all of that into the pot when we went into the merger.

TB: Is that right?

ME: All of it, and the musicians' union finally sold that building about three or four years ago. That's only one of the things that we lost, and I hate to be a negative person, and I'm not a negative person, but I believe the musicians' union has out-lived its usefulness. At one time I had to belong to the union because I did a lot of recording, and all recording contracts had to come through the union. I recorded with just about everybody you can think of. You just name someone, and I'll show you the albums! Jerry Butler, you name it. Donny Hathaway came to me, and I did a lot for him. But my biggest concern has always been that there are no blacks in the Chicago Symphony! Not *one* black in that entire Chicago Symphony Orchestra! And every year the unions go to war and call a strike to get the Symphony Orchestra its money, but in all of these years, there's not one black musician in that Chicago Symphony Orchestra. They make good money, and they get all kinds of benefits, but that's not my point. All of the other big cities have got blacks in their symphony orchestras, but not Chicago. This is still the most segregated city in the world.

TB: Who took over from James Petrillo [the musicians' union boss]?

ME: We had a guy named Bernie Richards in after Petrillo. Then after him was a guy named Nicky Bliss, and after Nicky Bliss was Hal Deseque. Currently it's a guy named Johnny Blusey.

TB: Have they ever had a black person on the board?

ME: Well, we had one black on the board of directors, but that was only because when the merger was forced they said we had to have one, and that was Frank Derrick. And Frank Derrick stayed on the board for a couple of years and then said, "Hey, I can't take this anymore," and he moved to New York. But he was the only black that we've ever had on the board of directors of the musicians' union—since the merger—and to me, that's a joke. A bad joke.

TB: Now, on the business end—where the big money, I suspect, is—has there been any sort of breakthrough in terms of the management?

ME: No, we're really just the tip of the iceberg when it comes to managing. You mentioned John Levy. John Levy could have been much bigger than he is now.

TB: Is that right?

ME: He decided he wasn't going to stretch himself out too far. He was going to enjoy his life. He was just going to get three or four top artists that he could manage.

TB: He was in New York for a long time. I think he managed George Shearing for a while.

ME: Well, he also *played* with Shearing for a while. So, anyway, I gave up the union, and people said, "Hey, you can't make it unless you belong to a union," but that's not true. I have worked *more* since giving up the union. I've made more money than I've ever made in my life since giving up the union. You don't *have* to belong to the union. Not anymore. There was a time when the unions all banded together, so if you didn't belong to a union, they could turn off your electricity, or they wouldn't deliver the whiskey, or whatever. But those days are gone. Unions have outlived themselves. They've outpriced themselves from the market.

TB: And sometimes they've been purely corrupt or doing what you've just indicated—shutting people out so you don't have access—and you've got to eat. You've still got to live.

ME: That's right, but you've always got the Right to Work Law, and you can't stop anybody from working. About six years ago I was playing at a party for Cecil Partee in the Empire Room of the Palmer House. Well, this guy came in from the union and said, "That's not a union band," and Cecil ran him out of the place! He told me about it later that night. So I called the union the next day, and I said, "The next time you send someone on my job to interfere with my making money and doing my business, I'll see you in federal court." I've had no problem with them since then. So now when they say to me, "Why don't you come back in?" I say, "What for? Why don't you see that some blacks get into the symphony orchestra? See that some blacks are on your board of directors?" And still there's not a one sitting on their board, and there are still no blacks in the Chicago Symphony Orchestra.

TB: I know what you're saying!

ME: You've got a couple of blacks in the Civic Orchestra, which is supposed to be the feeder for the Chicago Symphony Orchestra, but they wipe them out at the audition. It's supposed to be a blind audition with you behind the door playing and all, but I don't buy that. I don't buy it at all! Until the union has signed that it's going to be a fair and equal opportunity union, I don't even want to see it. I'll even go over on another street before I'll walk past their office on Washington! [*Laughter.*]
And I like to tease my brother about things like that.

TB: Is he still in the union?

ME: Yes, he's still in the union, and I say to him, "What *do* they do for you? Nothing. You pay your dues, and they make *sure* that you file your contract so that they can get their 6 percent off the top of your contract, and what services do you get for it?" I had an engagement once when I was in the union where a guy came through here, hired my band, wrote me a check for three thousand dollars that didn't clear, and he just disappeared—so I went and filed my claim with the union, and you know what they told me down there? They said, "Well, we'll put him on the defaulters list. He can't hire any more musicians." I said, "But what about my three thousand dollars?" And they said, "That's all we can do." So I said to them, "If that's all you can do—good-bye. I don't need you." I sometimes get wound up like that!

TB: Yes, yes, and with good reason! But now, since you have been what we might say "on your own" in all kinds of ways, where do you work mostly?

ME: Locally. I play all the country clubs, and all the hotels downtown. I play anywhere people call me, and there's hardly a place I have not played. I've played in some of the most exclusive clubs like the Racquet Club. You name them—I've played them all. And it has nothing to do with affiliation with unions. Now I get all my calls directly, and I don't even have to seek these jobs out. They seek me out because right now I have a reputation going. They want us.

TB: Well, they know you're good. As my generation gets older—and maybe your generation as well—what about the young people in the black community?

ME: A lot of our older clubs are dying off because they didn't bring in young folks to perpetuate the music, and some of the clubs that I have played in for twenty-five years or more have all of a sudden disappeared. The reason that has happened is mainly because they didn't plan properly for the future, and, of course, I still have some places like the Assembly, the Druids, and the Snakes where I can play every year, but you can just tell they aren't bringing in enough younger people, and when that happens, the place dies. So, once again, I've moved into a new area, and I thank God I did. I played for a club last month called the Chicago Presidents Club at Exmoor Country Club. To qualify to be in this club—it's the presidents of companies that are doing business in public relations—an organization will have to have done a hundred million dollars' worth of business. Tim Birch and Ed McCaskey were there—those kinds of people—and I'm still getting calls from people who were there inviting us to play for their own events. They said they really enjoyed it. "You made the evening for us." So, again, I don't have to belong to the union. All I've got to do is make sure we take care of the business, and that's what we're doing! Play good music, take care of the business, be on time, and then get the hell out of there!

TB: All of that requires a lot of discipline.

ME: All of it does.

TB: Some of which you learned at DuSable.

ME: Between my father and my teachers, I learned it all. You know, I think of Captain Dyett—my band teacher—every day and how he would say, "You are what you think you are." And also the way my father used to say, "No, I won't give you any time. Get up off your ass and get out there and hustle!" That's what he told all of us. When we were growing up, we had the guidance of a mother, a father, and the whole faculty at DuSable, and with all of them I just couldn't miss!

TB: And also with a stable community to support your aspirations.

ME: Yes, a *real* community, and that's just what we're missing nowadays. I feel so sorry for my kids. They don't have a real community like we did.

TB: You had a piece of the past, the present, and somebody made you dream about the future. I guess that was it.

ME: That's right, and now, if we don't get this drug problem under control, it'll kill the entire country.

TB: Yes, and it's both a white and black problem. You know, the drug dealers bring these drugs in and give them to these poor kids who don't have anything, and then to make money these kids become couriers and take those drugs on up to Wilmette, Winnetka, and all these other places because, in terms of the higher-priced drugs like cocaine, there are more white users than black—and so, in addition to the basic problem, this creates a further degree of separation based on race as well as class.

ME: Well, my experience being black, coming from a community that cared, coming from a school like DuSable that cared, and going to a university—our university—that cared, these are the things that have made me what I am—whatever I am—and, believe me, I don't think I'm anything extraordinary because I know that all those who came up with me during that time got the same kind of support and encouragement.

TB: Many success stories?

ME: Oh, many!

TB: Success was the norm.

ME: It was expected. In fact, it was demanded of us, and we accomplished *exactly* what we were supposed to. You yourself are living proof of it!

TB: Well, we all are. "We hoped and dreamed," my mama would say, and my daddy would say, "You'd better do what your mama said" on the domestic things, and he told me another thing. "Don't spend all your money. Pay the bills first. They're certain things you've got to pay right now."

ME: Yes, money's important, but, well, believe it or not, I turn down more jobs than I accept. To some I have to say, "Sorry, but this is the price."

TB: But I look at some of the guys who have been around, played a lot, and then when they come to the end of the journey . . .

ME: They have to do benefits for them. That hurts, and it's not all their fault. They've been taken advantage of. They've been used.

TB: And now white guys—journalists—that hung around with Hines and Duke, they are the ones who write about our music and musicians. Now they are the "experts," and they're the ones who are writing and taping and putting it all into their books.

ME: Well, if they don't record these experiences, then we'll lose them.

TB: What I'm trying to do is to make our history and our experiences available, as we say, "in our own words" to whomever wants to listen to it, especially young people like the ones at DuSable High School, for instance, so they can hear what we have to say—and they *will* listen—because, believe me, these kids would like things to be different from what they have seen and different from what they have heard. They need to acquire a different kind of perspective on their lives.

ME: Yes, I think so too. These are things they need to hear.

TB: But they don't have the proper models, and many of the role models that they do have—the most aggressive of them—are their white teachers. In our period of time it didn't matter so much because we also had some black role models at home or out on the street, but for these young people the only positive models they may see are these white men and white women, and they need more than that at this period of their life. They need strong people, like yourself, to model themselves on. Morris, this has been a great pleasure. Thank you for giving me this time.

ME: Thank you, Tim.

January 9, 1995

JOHN LEVY

———

JAZZ BUSINESSMAN/JAZZ MUSICIAN

John Levy was one of the few black jazz musicians who recognized very early in his ca-reer the necessity for him to become a businessman as well as a talented musician. As a result, in addition to playing with them as an acoustic bassist (and sometimes pianist), John also managed the careers of such stars as George Shearing and many others. He was also the manager of the late great lyricist and jazz and blues singer Joe Williams. Even now, in his late eighties, John continues to manage Nancy Wilson and several other well-known singers. In fact, at the present time, he is better known for these managerial successes rather than for his own excellent musicianship.

I first met John in 1935 while I was still a student at DuSable High School. Back then, he owned and operated a dance hall at Fifty-first and South Michigan Avenue. It was a very nice, well-managed place where on weekends we youngsters could go and be sure of having a good time. Young bands just forming in Chicago at that time—such as those of Nat King Cole, Danny Williams, Tony Fambro, and Ray Nance among others—would play there, and we would go to dance, listen, and enjoy the mu-sic and the friendship that surrounded us. John always had high standards and stood for no foolishness from any of us. If you dared to violate any of his rules for his place, he would put you out and tell you to never return. No one ever wanted to be exiled from a place like that, and so we all learned to be quite well behaved and still have a wonderful time.

Because of these many memories, I was especially thrilled and pleased when John granted me this interview from which you, the reader, will get some sense of the struggle that blacks had and still have in this field of music that they themselves have created.

TB: Were you born in Chicago?

JL: No, I was born in New Orleans on April 11, 1912, so I'm eighty years old now. First the men in my family came up here to Chicago, and then the women and children came up. I came up around 1918 because I was living in Chicago when the race riots happened. I remember them very well. Although I was just very young, I can still remember them.

TB: It was a dangerous and dramatic time.

JL: Yeah, and we were living at 2934 Cottage Grove.

TB: So you were right down there where it all happened.

JL: Thirtieth and Thirty-first Street at the lake, that's where all the rioting started, and although I didn't see that much of the rioting because being that young kept me out of it, you know, I heard everyone talking about what was happening.

TB: And you were conscious of it.

JL: Oh, yeah, I was very conscious of what was going on—and also conscious about race. I sort of got conscious about race things because under us in this three-story apartment place where we were living on the street level there was a grocery store run by German people, and they had been boycotted because of World War I, and they had some real problems.

TB: For them the war wasn't yet quite over.

JL: No, it wasn't over for them, and, fortunately or unfortunately, however you might look at it, none of my people—like my uncles or my father or any of us— were involved in the war.

TB: How many brothers and sisters do you have?

JL: I have none.

TB: You were the only child, but the rest of the Levy family almost all of them migrated—

JL: No, the migration was the Hagans, which was my mother's family, because that's where we all lived. My father's family never migrated to the North. His family stayed down there in Louisiana.

TB: That sounds sort of familiar. My daddy was born in Jacksonville, Alabama, and moved to Birmingham. That was where he met my mother, but none of his people ever migrated, and *all* of my mother's people did!
[*Laughter.*]

JL: That's the way it happened. All my mother's people migrated to Chicago, but my father's family—he even had a couple of brothers—none of them ever left

New Orleans. I didn't really know my father's people too well because my grandmother only spoke patois, as they called it—this broken Creole French—and I never could understand what she was saying!

[*Laughter.*]

TB: Was she light-skinned or dark-skinned?

JL: Black as coal.

TB: But mixed.

JL: Yeah, you see, the funny thing about New Orleans, I never really realized anything about race and a lot of that stuff until later—except I knew starting out that we went to separate schools. That was because next door to me was an Italian family who lived in what they called "a half a house," and in the other half some Creole people were living, and they were so light that their children were going to white schools. They could pass in those days. But I really didn't know anything about race back then.

TB: You had no strong feelings.

JL: No strong feelings about anything, you know. I didn't even think about it too much. We were in each other's houses and played and everything. The first time, I think, as a child that I first started realizing anything about race was on a streetcar. My godfather was a Creole, and he was white, and he liked to play jokes on me, you know, which was cruel, but anyway we'd get on a streetcar, and he'd say, "I'm going up front with the motorman, but you can't go up there. You've got to stay back here behind this sign"—you know, that sort of thing—and that was my first hint, but nobody ever talked about any racial conflict or anything. You see, in a place like New Orleans you had a real mixture.

TB: You've got Spanish. You've got French, Caribbean—

JL: Yes, you've got everything. My first realizing anything about race was when I came up to Chicago.

TB: Then it was clear.

JL: Then it was bad.

TB: Yes, the race riot.

JL: Well, the race riot dramatized the basic situation. Then, when I got further along in school, I began to understand what was going on.

TB: You went to Englewood, didn't you?

JL: Yes, I went to Englewood, and I went to Hyde Park.

TB: What grammar school did you go to?

JL: Willard.

TB: You know, Willard's still there, but the neighborhood's changed.

JL: Yeah, the school yard is all concrete now.

TB: You went to Willard all eight years?

JL: No, before that, I lived on Twenty-ninth and Cottage Grove, and I went to Drake. Drake was the first school I went to.

TB: That's at Twenty-sixth and Calumet.

JL: Yes, and then we moved into a building where the Royal Gardens was. It was the nightclub where King Oliver played. This has got to be 1920, '21.

TB: Jazz was just coming to town, coming north. Louis wasn't here yet, was he?

JL: No, Louis wasn't there yet, but he joined them later on.

TB: Well, then, the place you were living was around Thirty-first and State?

JL: Yes, in that area. I went to Douglas School while I was living there, and then we moved farther south. The first place we lived was on St. Lawrence, and we stayed in that neighborhood for the rest of my childhood in Chicago.

TB: That neighborhood was about Forty-seventh Street to Fifty-first.

JL: And Cottage Grove to State Street!

[*Laughter.*]

TB: To us that was the world!

[*Laughter.*]

JL: I worked, you know, in the drugstore — Sissle's Drugstore — on Fiftieth Place and Cottage Grove, and I delivered prescriptions. That's when I first learned to drive a car. Although I was too young, they weren't as strict then as they are now about who drove, and they had a little old car, and so I did that for them.

TB: So you went to high school at both Englewood *and* Hyde Park.

JL: Yes.

TB: How did that happen?

JL: Well, I went to Hyde Park first, but I transferred to Englewood because I knew a couple of people there. There were already a few blacks in Englewood.

TB: Yes.

JL: But not too many blacks in Hyde Park.

TB: Now, you're talking about the middle to late twenties. At that time there weren't a whole lot of blacks at Englewood either.

JL: No, not many.

TB: The experience for me at Englewood when I came there later was too hot for me, and I had to leave. At that time, blacks couldn't even use the swimming pool —

JL: You couldn't do nothing!

[*Laughter.*]

You were just going there, and that was about it unless you could play basketball or something.

TB: The only guy I knew at Hyde Park was Harold "Killer" Johnson. I don't know whether you —

JL: Yeah, Killer was there. Well, Killer and I were very close friends. In fact, we went to grammar school together.

TB: So he was about the same age as you.

JL: Yeah, oh, yeah.

TB: And Killer went on to be great with the Globetrotters.

JL: Yeah, that's right.

TB: Did you know George Easter?

JL: Yes.

TB: Well, George also grew up in that neighborhood. George was kind of like a cousin of mine, and he also went with the 'Trotters. When did you get into music?

JL: Oh, I had started music in New Orleans as a child. I started studying violin, and I used to follow those street bands. You know, I used to go out there when they had their parades and listen to that music. That's how I really got started. All my family, everybody was, you know, in the church playing or in the choir at St. Mark's Church, there at Fiftieth and Wabash.

TB: Reverend William Redman?

JL: Reverend Redman married me. He was one of them Mardi Gras types, like my grandmother and all those people! Beautiful hair and black as coal, you know.

TB: He was smart.

JL: He was smart, oh, yes!

TB: That was a great church.

JL: My uncle was in the choir there. A guy named Gossett was the musical director, and I studied a little piano, but I never really got into that because I wouldn't study. That was my problem. You know, I always had some kind of a deal going on. I mean, I was an entrepreneur—if there ever was one—from a child up until the present!

[*Laughter.*]

TB: To reinforce that, you were the first black guy that I knew that could play something who was also looking at the business end of things and not just the music.

JL: Yes, that's the way I was right from the very beginning! I remember every Sunday I had those dances and Nat Cole would come up there, and he'd be imitating Duke because he wore this same kind of white outfit, but it would be greasy because he couldn't afford to get it cleaned, you know, and it had white tails—

[*Laughter.*]

And, well, he tried to do everything just like Duke, and so when he sat down, he flipped his tails!

[*Laughter.*]

So, anyway, I was thinking about business all the time—always hustling!—and my friends and the people that I grew up with, they always said to me, "You know what, why can't you stick to one thing? Why don't you just settle on something?" But for me it was always something else. I was always doing something else. I worked in the post office at that time. I became a special-delivery messenger—it had to be 1930 or '31—because I had a '31 Ford. My mother died in '29, and from that my grandmother got some money, and they let me buy a car. It was one of those '31 Fords.

TB: I remember that car, and another thing I remember from that period is when you said that the piano wasn't your forte.

JL: Yes, but I did play piano!

TB: I know you did.

JL: Yeah, I played piano and tried to sing.

TB: I know. I'll never forget one Sunday, wherever it was, and you were playing and singing "A Hundred Years from Today."
[*Laughter.*]

JL: That was my song! I could sing and play a few other songs as well, but I didn't really get into music until I started playing bass, which was in '38, '39. I only really started playing bass then, and that was late for a person to be starting, but I'd been working at the post office, and then my aunt and my mother—well, my aunt more than my mother—they were maids at the Eastgate Hotel on the North Side of Chicago, and they got me a job there as a porter, houseman, all of that, but that happened because I got married very young. I was only eighteen years old when I got married.

TB: Well, a lot of guys and gals were getting married early in those days.

JL: Yeah, I got married very young. And, you know, pretty soon I had a family starting—my oldest son is now fifty-four.

TB: You had how many children by the first marriage?

JL: Three. Two boys and a girl. The girl was the youngest one. And now she's forty. Time passes! My youngest son worked in the business with me. I had an office in New York at 119 West Fifty-seventh Street, and then I came out here to Los Angeles and opened up an office—that's when I was married to Gail Fisher, the girl who was on the *Mannix* television series—and I have two children by her, one adopted and one that she already had.

TB: How long did you stay around Chicago?

JL: Until 1944. I worked around Chicago, you know, playing with different bands—

TB: Tony Fambro?

JL: Yes, Tony Fambro.

TB: Floyd Campbell, and all those guys.

JL: Yeah, yeah, well, I worked with my buddies, but I guess Fambro was the one that I worked with longer than anybody, and that's where I met Jimmy Jones when Stuff Smith came into town in 1943.

TB: Well, so you left Chicago in 1943?

JL: Yes, I left Chicago with Stuff Smith and Jimmy Jones. I opened on Fifty-second Street in August of 1944—at the Onyx Building on Fifty-second Street, and I stayed there a year at the Onyx Club. Then we broke up, but Jimmy stayed on after I left.

TB: Jimmy Jones, was he a Chicagoan?

JL: Yes, from Chicago. When I first heard him, he was playing piano with Fambro. He'd come back here from Kentucky State—that's where he'd graduated with a degree in music. Before that, he had been working in a small group with Eddie Johnson, who is still in Chicago, and another guy—I can't remember his name—but they had a trio together as kids, you know, and Jimmy Jones played the guitar. Then Eddie went on the guitar, and he went from there to sax. He had a hell of an ear.

TB: Eddie and I went to grammar school together.

JL: Oh, all right. You know Jimmy Jones then.

TB: Yes. But so, after that, then you moved to New York.

JL: Yeah, I moved to New York after that stint. I stayed in New York and recorded with a lot of different people. I worked with Phil Moore of the Phil Moore Four. I recorded with Erroll Garner, and in 1948 I got to work with Billie Holiday, and I worked with her for about a year, I guess, but I couldn't get along with John Levy, my mentor, my namesake, who was Billie Holiday's "old" man, and so I left that, and then I started, really, getting into the other end of the business—because that's what I was already doing with her, and so pretty soon that's what I was doing with everybody. With Phil Moore I was always the road manager. At that time I was living in Brooklyn across the street from Jimmy Jones, and one day I got a call to come downtown—to come down to Birdland on Fifty-second Street, you know, down on Broadway—and I went down there to work with Buddy Rich, and in working with Buddy Rich I met George Shearing, who was on the same bill. In those days they had the big band—Buddy Rich's band—and then there was George Shearing with a small group, and then there was Sarah Vaughan with her group. Jimmy Jones was working with Sarah Vaughan then, and at Birdland they had all these groups, and they performed right behind each other. That's how I met George, and when he left there, he asked me to record with him—so we started out together. As road manager, I was doing all the business for him and so finally he asked me if I would just take over all of it, which I did, and that's how I got into this end of it.

TB: Yes.

JL: But I was always doing all this anyway!

[*Laughter.*]

That's how I first went to New York with Stuff Smith. It was because Harry Gray wouldn't let Stuff work in Chicago without somebody being there to take care of business for him. So he called me one day and said, "Would you go and work with this fool?" And I went down there and worked with him and Raymond Waldu, who was playing piano, and, well, they both would stay drunk so much that nothing much was happening. You know, conversations like this bring out a lot of memories if somebody knows who you're talking about.

TB: Oliver Coleman was around, wasn't he?

JL: Yeah, sure, I remember Oliver Coleman.

TB: And there was another guy that played named Eustis "Hokum" Moore.

JL: Yeah, Hokum worked with me, and John Young played the piano.

TB: What about Johnny Letman?

JL: I worked with him later on with Phil Moore in New York after that period.

TB: Now, you guys left us here in Chicago high and dry when you brought all that talent to New York!

[*Laughter.*]

JL: Then in 1955 I moved to Teaneck, New Jersey, and there was a whole bunch of people from Chicago out there—there was Van Jones and his family, then finally they had to leave, and they moved out west.

TB: Yes, from what I understand, there was a group of you Chicago musicians who lived fairly close to one another. Almost like you had a little colony, more or less, but from the time you went with Shearing and split up with Billie Holiday, you started to concentrate on the business end of things.

JL: Yes, from '51 on.

TB: And right now you are the manager for—

JL: Just Nancy Wilson, Joe Williams, and Nina Frelau. That's all I want, because I don't want a lot of people. Nina is young and new, and I really got into working with her, you know, because I met her, and I liked her, and I respect what she's doing—she's a family person, and there's not a lot of headaches. I mean, she knows what she wants and everything. All the people I work with are nice, real nice people, to deal with. Other than that, I wouldn't even bother with anyone else because I've managed them all at one time or another.

TB: Who are some of the others you've managed?

JL: Well, Sarah Vaughan—almost *all* of the women that came up at that time, except for Ella Fitzgerald. I managed them all at some period in their careers because they came to me after I really started going. You know, you start doing things, and you set up publishing firms and all of that, and you know, I didn't even realize just how much *power* I had in the industry.

TB: Yes, that's another important question, I think, that I would like to probe you on, and that is, how many black "John Levys" are there out there who handle the same kind of big-time talent that you've been able to work with?

JL: Well, at that time, not too many.

TB: And now?

JL: A lot of them now, but they're young and inexperienced people—most of them, but even so, they are handling very high-powered acts—I mean, acts that are making a lot of money. But I'm not in that field. I don't, you know, do rap and all that kind of stuff. I don't deal with that. I wouldn't, at my age, try to do all that stuff.

[*Laughter.*]

TB: You're going to be true just to those people that you've already chosen to handle?

JL: Well, yes, that's what I'm doing.

TB: When you first started in '51, '52 to get into the real business end of music, were there many blacks active in that area?

JL: None.

TB: None? You're a pioneer.

JL: Yes, I'm a pioneer, but that's because people like George Shearing stood behind me. I mean, other people tried to sabotage me in so many different ways, but George stood behind me pretty good and wouldn't allow nothing like that to happen to me.

TB: He was always fair.

JL: Oh, yeah, yeah, and he is there for me now right until today, you know? That relationship still exists.

TB: I'm sure there must have been a lot of black people who were eager to have a black manager or spokesperson.

JL: Well, in those days, a lot of people didn't even have managers. They didn't have spokespersons. What they did was to sign up with an agency. They just went to their agents, you know?

TB: Such as William Morris.

JL: Well, William Morris came up later. I mean William Morris was there but not too many blacks were going through there at that time. Most of the time it was Moe Gale—the Gale Agency—where Ella Fitzgerald and all those people were, and then there was the Shaw Agency, which had Ray Charles, Fats Domino, and all the other black acts like that. They had them locked up.

TB: But not Louis.

JL: No, Louis Armstrong was with Joe Glaser at Associated Booking. Glaser had him, had Dizzy, had Roy, had all the trumpet players—Red Allen, and Higginbotham, and all those people—and Billie Holiday, Dinah Washington, and all of those people like that as well. When I came along, he helped me too because he remembered me from Stuff Smith. He was doing the booking for Stuff Smith. That's how I first met him. He didn't even know me, you know, but I handled the business and sent his commissions to him—so when we got ready to go to New York, he really sponsored me the whole way—and anything I did after that, he sponsored it. He tried to get me to go and work with Louis Armstrong playing bass, but I didn't want to play bass. I was looking for a job in the agency, but he wouldn't give me the job. He offered to give me work with Louis at a very good price at that time, but instead Milt Hinton went with Louis. Milt went to Phillips, didn't he?

TB: Yes, Wendell Phillips High School.

JL: Well, Milt's the one that started me out on the bass fiddle.

TB: You know, Milt is still as busy as a young person would be. He's got a schedule like a young man would.

JL: Oh, that's right, that's right. That's what keeps him going!

TB: But Milt is older than you, isn't he?

JL: Yes, he is.

TB: But coming back to the managing end, you were saying that Joe Glaser had been helpful to you.

JL: Yes, when I got into management and really started working at it, Joe Glaser was helpful because he handled a lot of talent that I had. In fact, at one time he handled everything I had except Nancy Wilson. Nancy didn't like him personally, and so she went to William Morris, but also, we were going in a different direction, you know? We were going for the Waldorfs and trying to establish a Lena Horne kind of thing, you know, with Nancy Wilson. That's what happened. She went that direction. She went on to Las Vegas and worked with Sammy Davis and all of that.

TB: I met Nancy Wilson during the civil rights days.

JL: Yes, she was very active, and, you know, she's still doing it. In fact, we just did something for the Thurgood Marshall Foundation.

TB: Is that right? What about Joe Williams? Joe has been a pro since back at Englewood.

JL: That's right. Right after high school, he started singing around Chicago in those clubs with bands like Jimmie Noone and then with Basie and finally on his own.

TB: When did you move out here to California?

JL: I came to California in the sixties because things were beginning to happen out here, and I set up the office out here.

TB: The industry was moving this way.

JL: A lot of interesting things were happening out this way, you know? There were a lot of recordings being made at Capitol Records.

TB: And you have a lot of people that recorded on Capitol?

JL: On Capitol, yes!

TB: Nat Cole was very important to Capitol.

JL: Oh, yes. That's how that deal came up with Nat Cole and George Shearing recording together. It happened because we were all on the same label. I was instrumental in getting black secretaries hired by Capitol. When I first went up there, there wasn't a single black person in the tower—not one.

TB: About when was that?

JL: Oh, it has to be in the sixties.

TB: That's relatively recent.

JL: Yeah.

TB: And Nat Cole was already their biggest star!

JL: Yeah!

[*Laughter.*]

So, I just went straight to the top of Capitol, and I asked Dave Cavanaugh why he didn't hire more black people on the business side of the operation, and Dave said, "Well, funny thing you mentioned it, but I just interviewed a black girl," and he said, "I'm thinking about hiring her." And, you know, I said, "Fine!" So, sure enough, about two or three weeks later he hired the first black secretary at Capitol Records—and that was Burgie, who became my secretary after that, and then she finally married Freddie Hubbard, who I was also managing at that time.

TB: About how many other black people were employed in that category of office help at Capitol Records at that time?

JL: I didn't know of any. And also I got the first black people to do promotion. Sydney Miller, who became pretty big in the industry, was hired because I spoke up and said, "We haven't got any black promotion people. When we go out on the road, it's always all these white guys who take us around." And that's the way it was in those days. So, finally, they broke it down and separated—which I still hate—the black music from the white. That's the way they let the blacks in, finally, into different departments and all that, and now, of course, they have all kinds of executive positions.

TB: If something happens in the industry—say, a recession or depression or something of that sort—will those guys and gals be expendable or will they hang on?

JL: Well, I guess, when it goes down, everybody is expendable, but I suppose it all depends on what stature you have attained within the industry.

TB: And now there's more opportunity.

JL: Oh, yes.

TB: And part of the reason for that you would say—and I would agree with you, is because you not only became a pioneer in the business end but also became, in your own way, a sort of spokesperson for those who were still outside the system.

JL: Right. Nancy was in the forefront of that, you know, but Nat Cole, he wasn't a part of that push, not directly.

TB: So you've been out here in California more than twenty years.

JL: Yeah.

TB: Do you live in Hollywood?

JL: Oh, no, I live close to my office here. I live right in what they call the Hancock Park area—nothing but the Jewish. All rabbis—I got rabbis on both sides of me, and rabbis across the street!

[*Laughter.*]

TB: So at least now you're probably going to go to heaven and meet the Messiah!

[*Laughter.*]

JL: Well, now I live in Hancock Park, but I've also lived in Beverly Hills, and in the Hollywood Hills, and all over the place.

TB: Now, you have a span of almost all your life in the music field. From that perspective, what do you think will be happening in the future to our music and the people that play it?

JL: Well, today the industry really is interested only in those black kids out there who play the rap music that is making all this money for them—

TB: Making the money for *them.*

JL: Yeah, and, you know, to me that's very unfortunate, but, that's their mentality, and you can't do anything about that.

TB: And what's happening with jazz is that experts like you and Joe and Nancy and all those other jazz musicians are becoming "artists in residence" somewhere.

JL: Well, I guess we've trained a lot of the young kids, but believe it or not, most of them are white!

TB: Yes, that's just the point I was making! There is also a kind of a renaissance, and now, it seems to me that the black youngsters are getting a little more excited about jazz because of what people like Wynton Marsalis are doing.

JL: Oh, yeah, yeah, that whole family has helped jazz a lot. They're well trained, well schooled, you know, and that's what you almost have to be today.

TB: The competition's very keen.

JL: Unless you're in a rap group, and then it doesn't make any difference.

TB: Just open your mouth and cuss!

[*Laughter.*]

Last point. I'm doing some work now with some people at the Field Museum and they asked me to give them background information indicating that there was an artistic renaissance in Chicago that in some ways was similar to the Harlem Renaissance in New York. What, roughly, would you say was the period that would be equal to that?

JL: Oh, sure, there was a time back in the thirties when you had black orchestras playing in every theater. You not only had a pit band but also a band on the stage like at the Regal. To me, that was the renaissance in the Chicago area.

TB: On State Street there was the Vendome.

JL: Yeah, you also had the Vendome. In fact, it started with Erskine Tate at the Vendome.

TB: And the Metropolitan Theater.

JL: That's where Sammy Stewart was.

TB: And they used to have something going on down at the Willard on Fifty-first Street.

JL: Yes, and on Forty-seventh Street as well!

TB: So there really was a parallel period.

JL: Oh, yes, yes. Sure, I would say so.

TB: Well, what would you say to a young guy or a young girl who was interested in maintaining the tradition and contributing to the future of the music that you grew up with and have made a living with, both in performing and in the managerial aspects? Where would a guy like you get started today? Where would a gal get started?

JL: Oh, well, today it's very difficult for young people. We no longer have the big bands where singers can get their training out there and then move on like Billie Holiday or Sarah did. You know, there was a training ground then, and there is no longer a training ground like that anymore.

TB: They go on to the big leagues right away.

JL: Right away! They have to jump right in with both feet and then it's sink or swim! There's no club circuit where you can learn. You're thrown right into the lion's den, and you've got to make it or break it—just like this girl I've got now, Nina. But she's fortunate, though, and we're taking it very slowly, step-by-step, and not trying to jump in there and do so many things at once. Fortunately, she's got a Philip Morris tour leaving on the first week in October, and she won't be back until the middle of December. By then, she'll have been all over the world. She's going to the Far East, London, Australia, you name it—all over the world!

TB: You've done a lot of traveling yourself, haven't you?

JL: Oh, yeah, I've been all over the world. I've been to Australia this year with Nancy and Lou Rawls, but I've cut back. I used to go to Japan every year. Around my birthday, April 11, I was in Japan for five years straight, every year.

TB: They enjoy our music.

JL: Oh, yes, they enjoy it, but they also appreciate it, and they even understand it. You know, back here most people don't understand it.

TB: Most people around here don't even know it!

JL: Then they don't know what they're missing.

August 12, 1992

EDDIE JOHNSON

CHICAGO JAZZ ICON

I first met Eddie Johnson in 1929 when we both were students at Edmund Burke School, which is located at Fifty-fourth and South Park Way (now Martin Luther King Drive). As is indicated in his narrative, when restrictive covenants started to loosen a little, his family moved farther south, and Eddie transferred to Carter Elementary School at Fifty-eighth and Michigan Boulevard. Even so, we always somehow managed to keep in touch. As a matter of fact, his older brother, Fred, and my older brother, Walt, remained close friends throughout their entire lifetime.

After graduating from Carter in 1933, Eddie went on to Englewood High School, where he was a star basketball and softball player, but by his classmates he is best remembered for his outstanding performances as a young tenor saxophonist in the high school jazz band, which was led by the late Danny Williams and had as its pianist the legendary writer-composer Jimmy Jones. That band was so good that all of its players were given full scholarships by Kentucky State College (now University). As a result, their band toured the South and taught jazz to other young black college students. Eddie returned home before graduation, however, and soon began playing professionally on the South Side. Devoted to his wife and young son, Eddie turned down an opportunity to play with Duke Ellington because of Duke's rigorous travel schedule.

He still plays beautiful music today, and his distinctive tone on tenor, as well as his gentle, caring style as a person, will live forever with those of us who have been fortunate enough to have known him and/or heard him play. His narrative helps us to understand the social and cultural environment of black musicians during the early

period of Chicago's jazz history—not only the struggles but also the fun and joy expe-
rienced by those young aspirants and pioneers of this creative music we still call jazz.

———————

TB: Eddie, where were you born?

EJ: I was born in Napoleonville, Louisiana, on December 11, 1920. My mother brought us—my older brother, Freddie, and me—here. We came to Chicago when I was two years old in 1922, and we stayed somewhere around Forty-ninth and Indiana. Then we moved near to Fifty-third Street, and that's where all my earliest recollections come from—5232 Indiana, I still remember that address—and my first recollection of school is when I was in first grade at Edmund Burke School.

TB: When you started at Burke, back then, in 1924 or '25, as you remember it, was it all black?

EJ: No, it was mostly black, but there were a few whites there as well. You know, in looking back, I just think I had a really tremendous education in both grammar school and high school.

TB: Yes, later on you went to Englewood High, didn't you?

EJ: Well, after I left Burke, I went to Carter. I graduated from Carter, and then we left Fifty-second and Indiana and moved over to Fifty-third and Wabash, and, after that, we moved to Fifty-eighth Street. That's when I went to Englewood.

TB: That's right. I remember that you used to live near Fifty-third and Wabash when you went to Carter.

EJ: Now, there you are talking about education! Tim, I still remember so many things that happened in the seventh, eighth grades there at Carter. One of my best friends was a young Jewish kid whose parents had a cleaning business over at Fifty-eighth and Prairie. Education-wise, I remember just as distinctly a time in seventh or eighth grade when we were being taught by an elderly Jewish teacher—we were having music appreciation or something—and we were listening to "Finlandia," the national anthem of Finland, and even today that's still one of my favorite classical tunes. At the time I just thought it was one of the prettiest things I'd ever heard, and it has stayed with me all these many years.

TB: It is gorgeous. I heard Eugene Ormandy do it once.

EJ: Well, you can just imagine what an impression that had on me at that early age!

TB: While you were at Carter, you probably met a number of people who went on to become quite notable, didn't you?

EJ: Sure. During that time at Carter School, there was a group of guys called the Camel Boosters. They were a group of young guys from around Fifty-eighth Street, and all of them were really good athletes. Do you remember that group? Joe Bowles and those guys?

TB: Yes, of course. Bowles was a great athlete in high school, and Joe went on to become outstanding in college in both basketball and track. He was quite a guy, but, yeah, Fifty-eighth Street was definitely the street where you young guys were operating at that time! Tell me what the neighborhood was like back then. Up and down the strip on Fifty-eighth Street, what type of people owned the businesses?

EJ: Well, the neighborhood had changed. A few whites, but probably 99 percent black, and the majority of the businesses were white. It was a mixture of blacks and whites, and the neighborhood was really very nice. Nobody had anything of substance when you speak of worldly things, but we were rich in family, and everybody got along.

TB: These were the Depression years, the thirties. As I remember, I was still living on the north end, and my folks had nothing, but they gave their children hope that "it's gonna be better" even though we were living in the midst of the Depression. "Things will get better if you just work hard and go to school." That's quite a contrast to those kids I saw this morning over at Twenty-sixth and California, at the county courthouse and jail. For them today, during our so-called booming economy, everything seems to be completely hopeless. That's a big difference.

EJ: It certainly is.

TB: Well, anyway, when you first went to Englewood, what year was that?

EJ: It was '34. I came out in '38, in February of that year.

TB: What was Englewood like during those years?

EJ: Well, at that time, Englewood was predominantly white. There were some problems, but everybody got along, although mostly, I guess, we did stay to ourselves, and once again I must say I think I got a hell of an education. I remember distinctly a chemistry teacher—a guy named Moretti—and we didn't know for sure whether he was just a weird dude or whether it was prejudice, but sometimes he would just leave the class and turn his back and go off into a little room of his as if to say, "What the heck? The hell with you!" But, you know, later on, thinking it over, I think what it was was that he went back in there and smoked some of his cigarettes.

[*Laughter.*]

TB: At that time Englewood had a good band and had a good chorus, a really excellent music program.

EJ: Yes, they did. I started playing around my sophomore year, but I was not in the band. My uncle was a musician: Joe Posten. He used to play with a famous piano player, and he'd show me the fingering—so that's how I started, but I ended up more or less being self-taught, and, of course, at that time we were also singing. Did you ever know Roy Winbush or Jimmy Jones?

TB: Yes, Jimmy Jones was an arranger and also a piano player. He went to Englewood at the same time as you?

EJ: Yes, and we had a singing trio called the Melody Mixers at that time. We were just kids, but we got hired to sing over at the world's fair from '33 to '34. I must have been about thirteen or somewhere around there. We even had a commercial that we sang for Hoover vacuum cleaners that they played on WCFL.

TB: Is this about the same time as when the Cats and the Fiddle had their little show?

EJ: Yes, I certainly remember the Cats and the Fiddle, but the Mills Brothers were the ones who were the idols! They were the big boys of the quartets, and the ones we most admired. I still remember Jimmy and me, we would be shooting marbles or playing ball or something, and Roy—he was the oldest—he would have the damnedest time trying to get us to clean up and go someplace and sing. What did we know about making a commercial? We just wanted to stay there and play baseball.

TB: Sure, or shoot marbles, play mumblety-peg, root-the-peg—do some things that were real. Was Roy already starting to paint by then?

EJ: He was just dabbling in art, drawing caricatures and the like, but nothing really serious. Jimmy was the one who was the brains behind the trio. He was playing piano and guitar, and he would teach us the parts and everything.

TB: Back then, it seemed like everybody that I knew could sing, dance, or play an instrument—everybody except me. I couldn't do it!
[*Laughter.*]
Remember Mary and Sadie Bruce, Sammy Dyer, and all those others? Everybody was always running up to Erskine Tate or someone and trying to learn a new note on the piano or something. Talent was really encouraged in that setting, as I remember it.

EJ: Yes, and everybody could dance!

TB: Well, like I said, except me!
[*Laughter.*]
When you guys had your trio, there were a lot of places where you could experiment and perfect your sound, weren't there?

EJ: Well, not so much for the vocal stuff, but, well, at that time you take, say, Fifty-fifth Street, Garfield Boulevard from South Park to just west of the Elevated, and in just that stretch of half a block there were something like thirty or more musicians working. Just imagine that! You had the Hurricane, remember that? That was Jesse Miller's place, and they had a five- or six-piece band there. There was the Rhumboogie, and they had a ten-piece band over there. That was underneath the El. Goon Gardner had four pieces over at the LaRue's, which was just a little tavern on Fifty-fifth Place, and I was upstairs playing with Coleman Hawkins, and we had ten pieces up there! So you can see there was a lot that was happening in just that little half a block.

TB: Half a block, and thirty or more talented musicians! And in the same neighborhood there were also a lot of places to practice and where they held auditions.

EJ: Yeah, but, well, "sitting in" as they called it, there wasn't too much of that at places like the Rhumboogie because they had a set format for their shows, but at places like the Hurricane the idea was just to get up on stage with your instrument and get a chance to play—but you had better be good!

TB: Now, going back to Englewood, there was also a band there, wasn't there? Danny Williams, I think.

EJ: Yeah, that's right. Danny Williams came out of Englewood, and I went to Kentucky State with that band.

TB: That whole band went over there? All of them?

EJ: Yeah, well, you see, at that time the Alabama State Collegians were really a terrific band—that's where Erskine Hawkins's band came out of—so somehow or other the people from Kentucky State heard about our band, and they offered all of us a full scholarship with room and board if we would come down there and on weekends go out to various little cities around Frankfort and do things to promote the school.

TB: That entire band—because of the quality as it was perceived and actually existed—went on from Englewood to Kentucky State with a full scholarship for everyone!

EJ: Yes, Danny Williams was the leader, and he took his dad's bus—his dad had managed the Williams Singers—and they went all over the world in that old bus. We called it the Ark. I mean, it was vintage!

[*Laughter.*]

And so we took that bus down there to transport us around. The guy that used to do the driving for us was a student there, and he would also help us with the setting up and all that, but you know what? In later life he became a vice president of Pepsi-Cola!

TB: What kind of campus was it like back then? How did you guys feel about your experience?

EJ: Oh, the school was terrific, but some of us, to be honest with you, didn't realize just how well off we were. I mean they treated us fine. Everything was peaceful, really nice, but then we got the itch. You know what I mean? We wanted to play, and so we got an itch in the soul. Most of us did, and, well, I stayed there about six or maybe eight months, I think, and then I came on back to Chicago. Hell, I had to get back here and blow, you know?

TB: So, now, you are seriously involved in the music. When did you meet Joe Williams?

EJ: I had already known Joe for a long time. When we were kids, a lot of us were playing ball around the neighborhood. Joe, he was from around Sixty-first, and I'm from around Fifty-eighth Street—so sometimes his team would play our team, and that's how we met. In fact, I think we met over at the Carter School playground, and that's when I struck up a friendship with Joe. Right then! And I knew when I first met Joe that he was going to make it because he had so much faith in himself. He was a terrific athlete, but, even then, he was always singing. I mean, he was playing center field or left field, but he was out there singing to himself, always singing!

TB: The first time I heard him, I remember he was singing "sweet" rather than the blues.

EJ: Yeah, that was his forte to begin with. At first he wanted to be known as a balladeer, but then in later life the blues made it possible for him to come back around and do it again.

TB: Carter School was also very much alive at that time. You know, I was listening to some stuff by Duke tonight, and Ray was on it. Back then Ray Nance lived over at Fifty-eighth and Michigan, and Ray used to come out in the playground—well, he couldn't play basketball, but he would try, and his mama would say, "Raymond!" and he would have to go back in and start practicing, and that's another thing to remember. You guys had some serious discipline about your profession. In terms of music you didn't just pick up your horn and say, "I think I'll blow."

EJ: You're right about that!

TB: So what happened after you came back to Chicago?

EJ: Well, I went to Wilson for a year and a half, and that's when I came in contact with Marl Young. He already had his law degree, but he didn't want to practice law—he wanted to play the piano! Marl had a band there at Wilson, and they would let us rehearse there. We weren't actually taking any classes, but they would let us use the music room, and we could go in there and play. At that time we also had a little dance act we did, Jimmy Bowman and myself and another very good friend, Jules Scullpy, so we would put on a show for them that was something similar to DuSable's "Hi-Jinks" show, but, of course, this was in a junior college, and Marl would stage the musical for us.

TB: Yes, Marl was very talented at all kinds of levels. He was even secretary of the musicians' union in California for a while, but what I remember best is when he used to write stuff for Little Miss Cornshucks when she was so popular.

EJ: He was really quite a guy. You know, he was the musical director for the *I Love Lucy* show for ten or twelve years, and sometimes we would go out to see him there on the Paramount lot. He was very talented but kind of strange, somewhat abrasive sometimes.

TB: Did you happen to know Lurlean Hunter? Boy, she had a beautiful voice, and I always wondered why she didn't go on the road. Good-looking woman!

EJ: And very talented! I knew her very well, but she passed while she was living up in Michigan.

TB: Did you know Nat Cole?

EJ: Not personally, but I used to sneak up to the Alvin at Fifty-first and Michigan and listen to him rehearse his band.

TB: He was one of the first persons that I met at Phillips, and he and I were also in the same homeroom at DuSable, and, even then, he played all the time, just like you said Joe sang all the time, right from the beginning—but, anyway, now, at this time, you are in your twenties, and now you're back in Chicago playing your kind of music.

EJ: Well, I was playing with a lot of different groups, and then I got with Coleman Hawkins and did some traveling around.

TB: What kind of guy was Coleman?

EJ: Very private person, difficult to know, you know? Very, very quiet. You would really have to pull things out of him. He never volunteered anything. He had already been to Europe and made his fame and all, and then he came back over here. He had recorded "Body and Soul" three or four years before this—I'm talking about '42, '43—and now he came back and made Chicago his base, so we would go out to different places but always come back here to Chicago.

TB: But, even on the road, it was always just "come to work and do your job."

EJ: That's it. Sometimes it would be no more than just "hello"—and that's all the words that would be spoken during the whole night! Hey, but what the hell, that Hawk could blow!

TB: So by now the war has come. What are some of the clubs that you remember from this period? As I remember it, we had the DeLisa on the north end of the track, and there used to be a little place around on Fifty-fifth Street at Wabash, the El Rado.

EJ: That was on the north side of Fifty-fifth Street, and it didn't last very long, but it was a beautiful place. It had a motif like the *Arabian Nights*. Then I also remember the Blue Heaven on Forty-seventh Street.

TB: Yes, and around Thirty-ninth Street and Oakwood Boulevard on Cottage Grove there used to be a little guy who played great tenor, but I think he died.

EJ: Well, that was also Gene Ammons's area, and Tom Archer played over there back then.

TB: Tom Archer, yes, he was very good, and then from about Sixtieth on up there were a lot of other places. Remember the Pershing?

EJ: The Pershing Lounge, yeah, and the Strand, and at Sixty-third the Pelican Lounge. You know, the thing I remember most about that place was the mermaid. They actually had a live "mermaid" swimming there behind the bar!

TB: Sixth-third Street was really alive. Remember Joe's Deluxe Club?

EJ: On Sixty-third and what's now King Drive!

TB: Did you ever play there?

EJ: Yeah, I worked there, and right on the next corner there was another place where all the youngsters used to hang out, the Avenue Lounge.

TB: They didn't have live music though, did they? Just a jukebox, but all the young guys and girls who knew each other or wanted to know each other, they would make it over to the Avenue.

EJ: That's right. They'd go there after the dances and also over to Hilliard's on Sixty-first.

TB: After you left Coleman Hawkins's band, what did you do?

EJ: Well, I traveled for a while with Cootie Williams. As a matter of fact, both me and Danny Williams went with Cootie for about a year. This was during the period when Cootie left Duke for a short while.

TB: There were several of them who decided to leave Duke about that same time. Hodges left Duke. Ray left Duke for a little while, but they all came back. They didn't sound as good away from Duke as they did when they were with him! At least that's what the general perception was.

EJ: And so they didn't get the bookings, and that's when they decided to go back! [*Laughter.*]

TB: Yes, well, now the war has come, and we all get those little notices in the mail. I registered over at Carter School.

EJ: I did also.

TB: Did you go into the service?

EJ: No, I wasn't in the service. I had a cavity on my lung, and, rather than go into a sanatorium, I opted for surgery, and that made me 4F!

TB: That was a blessing in disguise.

EJ: Yes, I considered myself to be blessed! [*Laughter.*]

TB: Did you have a family by this time?

EJ: Yeah, I married in '41, and we already had a son.

TB: And the girl you married was from DuSable?

EJ: Yes, Clara. She passed in '79, and you know I have nothing but good memories. Beautiful memories. That's why I just stayed here. I had such beautiful memories here with Clara, and besides, where else could I come home at two or maybe three in the morning and blow my horn if I wanted to and not be bothered by nobody?

TB: You have always impressed me as a person, and I'm just speculating, of course, but it's my guess that you never got into any of the bad habits that so many do.

EJ: No, I was fortunate. When I came along, some of the older musicians put their arms around me, especially the guys within the Johnny Long band. Guys like Warren Smith, and a lot of those guys said, "Look, you've got talent, kid. Don't mess it up. Go home and practice." So I guess I was very fortunate. After all, I had all the opportunity in the world to do something wrong.

TB: And don't forget that you also come from a strong family.

EJ: Well, that certainly had something to do with it. I mean, I knew how to say "no" and that was important, yes! And I'm certain, Tim, that the way I was brought up and all of that helped to steer me toward this particular group of musicians to hang out with rather than those other ones over there, the bad ones. You know what I mean?

TB: How did you get together with the famous Louis Jordan?

EJ: I was with Louis, I guess, around '45. When I went with him, I also had an offer from Duke, but Duke just wasn't paying the kind of money that Louis was paying at that time.

TB: And he's hot copy at this point. All over everywhere. I was overseas, and I said, "Oh, one of my friends is playing with Louis Jordan," and the cats would say— most of them were down-home boys—"You crazy," and then we'd hear Nat Cole on the radio or something, and I'd say, "Oh, yeah, we were in school together," and they wouldn't believe that either!

[*Laughter.*]

How long did you stay with Louis Jordan?

EJ: I was with Louis for about a year, maybe a year and a half. We made a lot of those big hits with him: "Choo Choo Ch'Boogie," "Ain't That Just Like a Woman," "Beware, Brother, Beware," "Barnyard Boogie," "Early in the Morning"—all those hits.

TB: Louis lived near Chicago, didn't he? Southwest, near Harvey?

EJ: Yeah, Harvey or Robbins, somewhere up in there. I think Louis passed in 1975, but if he had still been living today, that man would have been a billionaire because what they are doing now was what he was doing then.

TB: He was not only a musician. He was also a great entertainer.

EJ: And a strict disciplinarian. He furnished everything, clothing and all that, but when you get out there on that stage, your shoes had better be shined, and you don't ever do anything to distract from Louis Jordan. Yes, of course, we all had our little thing that we did. I mean, it was, as you might say, "choreographed," and we could rock our bodies or clap our hands or something, but go no further than that. He'd tell you, and, rightfully so, "People come here to see Louis

Jordan. They don't come here to see you." And since he's paying you such nice bucks, well, you just stood up there and played your part, and that was it.

TB: So, by now, you have been getting a lot of experience and confidence, and you are probably listening closely to a whole lot of different people because I can begin to hear a little bit of Webster and Hawk when I listen to you play.

EJ: That's right. I stole from all of them!

[*Laughter.*]

But at that time I was saying, "Pres [Lester Young] is my man," and I still think that all saxophone players should thank Pres for giving them something to shoot at. As a person, I didn't know Pres too well. He was also somewhat of a private person, and not many people really got to know him, but he was quite an individual! That's all I can say.

TB: The army seemed to have affected him very negatively. He used to spend time with a young lady that I knew, Clotele, a very pretty girl from Florida. She lived in the same building where I was, and when he would come to town, he would call her up, and we all would go out together sometimes, but, anyway, what happened to you after you left the Louis Jordan band?

EJ: Well, after I left Louis, I just stayed here in Chicago and jobbed around with different bands, and in between I'd sometimes take a little day job. See, I was never the "dedicated" musician. I tell this to people all the time. You take some of the guys that have really left their mark. Music was their entire life. That was it, and they weren't going to do anything else, but I wasn't that way. I couldn't see risking my wife or putting my kid in need or anything like that, so when nothing much was happening in the music business, I would go to a place where I could work whenever I wanted, and that was a shoe store over on Forty-seventh and Prairie. A Jewish guy—I'm sorry, but I can't think of his name right now—owned that place, and I would go there and sell shoes or whatever, and then, when the gigs got good again, I'd leave, but I could always go back.

TB: You had to make a living, and it had to be continuous.

EJ: Yeah, it was a way to make ends meet, more or less, and then I also started to get involved with insurance as well. I was with Golden State for a while.

TB: Did you know Jack Isbell?

EJ: Yeah, I used to work with Jack.

TB: You know what Jack told me? He said, "Tim, for fifty years I made a good living between Forty-fifth and Forty-seventh on South Park."

EJ: I saw him on TV just recently. He lives over near Eighty-ninth now, I guess, where they had a killing or something, and he was making a statement as to the current condition of the neighborhood.

TB: Yes, things have really changed. There have been some serious changes since that period that we've been talking about. You know, I was talking to George Dixon the other day, and he said that when he was playing at that place on Sixty-third and Cottage Grove, he would take his horn after work and walk home to where he was living at Forty-eighth and Evans and not ever have to worry about anything. Can you conceive of him doing that now?

EJ: Are you kidding? But, you know, at the Rhumboogie, after we played on Saturday night, we would go and lay down and go to sleep in the park and then go back to play for the Breakfast Dance, and there never were any problems. You know what I mean?

TB: You were also working for the government for a while, weren't you?

EJ: Yes, around '55, '56, I started working for the Veterans Administration, and there is where I first got interested in data processing. At that time the VA had an EAM.

TB: What was that?

EJ: An electrical accounting machine. They didn't have computers yet, but, anyway, I got interested. I started out working there as a clerk. You see, I wanted to take something easy so I could still play nights, and so I took an exam and got the clerk's job, but, doing my work, I was always passing these machines, and, like I said, I got interested. I met the boss of that section, and sometimes I'd stay over and help him. It was really fascinating. He would show me how to wire those things, and I finally got to the point where I got to be pretty good at it. Then, when the next exam came up from the city for trainees on EAM equipment, I took it and passed it, and that's how I got to work for the city! But let me tell you something. I have yet to see any entertainer or musician go to work for the public or private sector and not be able to make it. Never. It just doesn't happen. Any musician or singer that I know that left the music business and went in like I did, they have all gone all the way up to the top, and they have stayed there just as long as they have wanted to stay.

TB: Why is that? What's the reason?

EJ: I think that it is because in the music business you meet all kinds of people, and you get a little bit of psychology, and you also get a little bit of sociology, and I think that this makes a better person of you—so that then, when you go into the public or private sector, man, I mean, now the sky's the limit! The reason I say that, Tim, is that when I'm talking to somebody who is not in the entertainment field, a person like that could just say two or three words to me, and I would be able to know his entire life's history. You know what I mean? Just open your mouth and say something, and I can always tell exactly where you're coming from. This is all intuitive, of course, but this is so important in business because someone can just come up and I can tell right away—OK, I *know*—who he is and what he wants to talk about.

TB: So it seems that your life's experiences and your educational background have enabled you to move on and become extremely successful in an entirely different field of endeavor.

EJ: Right, and then with the advent of computers I finally got into management, and I just put the horn down. I might have practiced only once a week or something like that, oh, for maybe ten or fifteen years because all my time was taken up. I was like a workaholic, and so I rose. I went right to the top, and my next step would have been systems manager, which I didn't want, and so that was it.

TB: And it's about this time that you are also getting close to retirement.

EJ: Yes, I spent twenty-three years working there for the city, and during that time my son had passed and my wife had passed, and so I woke up one morning, and I said, "What the hell am I doing here? What do I need to work for? What the hell do I need with this? Let me out! I'm gone!" So that's how I retired.
[*Laughter.*]

TB: Looking back and summing up, what would you say about your life experience growing up in Chicago?

EJ: What would I say about it? Well, I don't remember ever being hungry. I suppose I came up as normal as one could, if there really is such a thing as "normal." All in all, I've had a good life.

TB: Well, I don't ever remember seeing you looking particularly ragged.

EJ: Tim, my mother was a seamstress. She could take a napkin and do wonders!
[*Laughter.*]

TB: What about that period during the Depression when about twenty-five million men were out of work, both black and white?

EJ: Even in those days, I didn't know anything about being hungry. What I had at home, even if it was nothing but potatoes and gravy, there was always enough of it.

TB: You didn't go to the NYA or the CCC?

EJ: No.

TB: I didn't either.

EJ: But let me tell you something. I did learn a lot of music from the people over at the Works Progress Administration. I remember the Jubilee Temple over there at Fifty-ninth Street, and once a week or so somebody would come by who knew something about music and would teach violin or whatever you were interested in, and every week I'd be right back there with my horn.

TB: They had a similar kind of center down at Bethesda on Fifty-third, right behind where you all used to live, so that kind of opportunity was available to everybody.

Life on the streets was comfortable and safe. It was a neighborhood where all the people knew each other, and there were hopes and dreams for the future.

EJ: Definitely.

TB: Now, in the music business, as you have played and experienced the development of what is called "jazz," do you agree with my perception that jazz is not necessarily dying but instead is shifting in its style and composition and also in its audience? I understand that at the present time jazz musicians usually play to bigger white audiences than they do to black. Is that true?

EJ: Oh, definitely. The jazz audience today is primarily "ofay." Yes, of course, you still continue to have a steady audience of blacks, more or less in my peer group, as well as all those younger whites who are listening and becoming influenced by what they hear, but our younger blacks, as I see it, they are going off on another tangent. I mean, they've been going off on this rap bit and whatever the hell you want to call it, and, Tim, it seems to me that they've just turned their backs on jazz. You know something? I really hate that word "jazz." I hate to identify what we're talking about—our kind of music—with a word like that, but I've got no better word, and I must confess, Tim, some of those things that I hear on records now that they are calling jazz just turn me off. You know, by now, I think I probably know a little bit about jazz, and if this kind of stuff does that to me, what does it do to the young guy out there listening to what he thinks is jazz for the first time? I mean, some of these soloists I hear playing on those horns are making the very same sounds that I made when I took my second lesson, except that now they have polished it up a little and are calling it "harmonics" or some such thing, and so I must say that, in my opinion, this so-called new music, or avant-garde, as they call it, may have something to do with turning our people away from our kind of music. Why that stuff doesn't turn the "ofays" away as well, I just don't know. I really don't.

TB: Maybe they have reconstructed our kind of music until it has become something that is more acceptable to them.

EJ: But not to us.

TB: So, the result of this is that young blacks aspiring to the field of music today have put jazz off to the side, and it is not being practiced or listened to as much as it once was.

EJ: Yes, and we don't even have many places to practice our craft anymore.

TB: Do you also attribute any of this to the market, that is to say, the economics of the present situation? After all, we can't afford to have the big bands anymore.

EJ: That's got nothing to do with it. It's the quality of the music that counts.

TB: That's true. You know, when I was at Joe Segal's down on Rush, I remember noticing a very dignified-looking woman, not young anymore, and she had her daughters with her, and Ahmad Jamal was playing, and he was in good form, and those young girls were sitting there, and they said, "Oh, mama!"—they were just screaming, boy!—and their mama was sitting there and looking very wise, and she said, "Oh, well, he's awfully old, isn't he?"

[*Laughter.*]

EJ: I wish I could see more scenes like that. Drag them there—and that will save them!

TB: Yes, because, when I went back there the next several times, I would see those same young women, but now they're with their boyfriends!

EJ: And they are discovering what's happening.

TB: Yes, and so I'm convinced that if these young people hear the right kind of music and absorb it fully, they will always carry it around with them in their heads and hearts. The music won't ever get lost if you can just get them to hear it a few times, but, even so, you've got to wonder why is it that our young people of today are not hearing the kind of music that means so much to us? What is your prediction about our music for the future?

EJ: Well, unfortunately, I'm not very optimistic about it.

TB: Perhaps there has to be some kind of a revival or something.

EJ: Yes, that would certainly help. As you know, Geraldine DeHaas and her group, they already have had groups going around to the schools playing for the kids, so that at least is a start. In fact, that is definitely a must, but that kind of thing has to be expanded. You know, in the white schools they've got "music appreciation," and they have live music in their grammar schools and high schools and colleges. We must find a way to expose our own kids to our music before their hearing gets messed up.

September 18, 1992

JUANITA TUCKER

TEACHER AND PRINCIPAL

Juanita Tucker was one of the most quietly passionate and determined persons I have ever known. Quiet because she never had to raise her voice to get attention in even the most noisy and chaotic situations. Determined because she set and maintained high goals and aspirations for not only herself but also for all of those around her, especially students. Passionate because of the energy and commitment that she put into everything that she was trying to achieve. She was also always compassionate toward those who did not or could not accomplish all that they would have liked to achieve because she realized that only a very few people are able to become what they might have been in this much-less-than-perfect society.

Her father came to Chicago from the South in the late twenties seeking a better life for himself and his family. As soon as he was able to obtain employment, he sent for the rest of his family, and, of course, Juanita was part of that northbound entourage. By working hard, her father was able to acquire property so that his family could have decent, comfortable housing. Juanita must have caught some of that undaunted strength and determination from her father because she went directly from her public school education, after graduating from Wendell Phillips, to Northwestern University's School of Music. At that time there were no rooms for blacks on campus, and so it was necessary for her to commute daily back to her home on the South Side or to her off-campus apartment.

During that same period, she also worked part-time in apparel shops as well as playing the organ and piano at Pilgrim Baptist Church, the original home of gospel music. Her primary interest and involvement, however, has always been education, and she spent over forty years of her life as a teacher and administrator in the neighborhood where she grew up and in the schools that she attended. Despite her husband's plea that she take a well-deserved retirement, she died while she was still active as the principal of her alma mater, Wendell Phillips High School. At no time during our conversation did she ever express even the slightest regret for that decision. She insisted that I record our conversation and was constantly cheerful, enthusiastic, and informative. She passed just two weeks later.

———

TB: This is May 24, 1996, and I'm talking with Ms. Juanita Tucker, lifetime resident of Chicago, lifetime resident of the neighborhood in which she now lives on the Thirty-sixth block of King Drive. She lives a couple of doors away from one of the most politically famous areas that existed anywhere in the United States for African-Americans—the Appomattox Club. Do you remember the Appomattox Club?

JT: Absolutely.

TB: That was the gathering place for black politicians in the early years. Ms. Tucker was principal of Wendell Phillips High School, which is one of the more famous African-American high schools in the United States. I think you also went to Wendell Phillips, did you not?

JT: Yes, I certainly did, but before we leave the discussion of the Appomattox Club, I certainly do remember it and the beautiful, beautiful building that housed it— graceful, elegant, prestigious. A lot of grand affairs were held in that building since the time that we moved into this 3600 block on King Drive. But even beyond that, we are right next door to where Dr. Daniel Hale Williams lived. He was just to the north of us, and the Ida B. Wells mansion is practically next door to that, and then we are right across the street from the home of Etta Moten Barnett, the famous dancer and singer. That is just a sample of what this area used to consist of. Right now, I am happy to say that Lu Palmer [noted political activist] lives right on the corner here. Most of the homes that are here are being pretty well maintained. Many of them have been purchased and are currently being rehabbed. So we are looking at a return to interest in and appreciation for the history of this area and the quality of the architecture, construction, and workmanship that went into these old homes.

TB: These buildings are works of art.

JT: Yes, these are definitely works of art.

TB: Around the corner is the home of the famous Eighth Infantry Regiment.

JT: Yes, and I just hope that one day they will restore it as well. There is just so much history there. It was the first home of the only African-American regiment in the country.

TB: It was the only African-American regiment that was *all* African-American, including the officers. There were others—the Twenty-fourth and the Twenty-fifth—in Texas, but they had white officers for the most part. The Eighth and Ninth Cavalry also had white officers, but the Eighth Regiment here was the first that had all African-American officers as well as enlisted personnel. It was a glorious part of World War I and World War II history. In World War I, General Pershing refused to accept these black combat soldiers, and they had to be taken into the French army as combat soldiers—not as service soldiers. Those troops of black soldiers spent more time during World War I on the front lines in France—in the Argonne Forest and other places—than any other Allied troops. They returned here at the end of the war, of course, as heroes. You are too young to know, and even I'm a little too young to know—but my parents' friends told us that as these troops paraded down these streets, the soldiers and the civilians both wept. Some members of the regiment had been lost, and so the monument, which is there on the corner of Thirty-fifth Street, is dedicated to those who fell in World War I. Some of my father's friends were among those who fell in battle. But then, after the troops returned, the famous race riot of 1919 took place very close to this same area that we are now talking about.

JT: Yes, that is correct. I know you have studied the Civil War era, so you probably know that a hospital was right there where the Griffin Funeral Home is now located. This whole area is so rich in history, it is just amazing.

TB: It is a moving experience every time I visit this area. Not far away from here was the home base for Louis Armstrong and Joe "King" Oliver. Jazz matured right here on Thirty-fifth Street. You know, as a kid growing up, I saw Benny Goodman play at the Armory, and for the first time two now-famous black musicians were in his band—Teddy Wilson and Lionel Hampton. And that same night, Joe Louis won the world heavyweight boxing championship and walked from Comiskey Park over to the Armory. The streets were full of people, and I was there! But now I'm telling you my age! This was 1937 or 1938, and we were so proud of these two black musicians who were already stars in their own right. The place was absolutely jam-packed—the whole street was jammed. You know, jitneys were in, but you couldn't catch a jitney. You had to walk to where you were going. South Park was full of people, full of life. They had a little ditty that they sang, "Joe Louis knocked Jim Braddock down, Jim Braddock got right up, and then Joe Louis knocked him down again. It makes no difference what you say, the champion is a nigger"—and without shame! All of that without shame—with pride, you see? It was a great moment of experience, and because we saw him so personally, Joe was even more beloved in our community than the present star of the Chicago Bulls could ever be.

JT: Yes, because he was right here. You could touch him. You could relate to him directly.

TB: Yes, so this area, as you indicated, is an area that needs to be retained, revived, and modernized, of course, but only to the extent that is absolutely necessary.

JT: But it must be preserved as much as possible.

TB: Preserved, yes. Of course, this is also home for me. I have a sense of pride about it. It was a place that was sterling and it can be that way again. Now, getting back to you, Juanita, where were you born?

JT: I was born in northern Louisiana, near Shreveport. My dad initially came to Chicago in 1942 and got a job here. The reason he came to Chicago is because my parents had such a great respect for education. Even though we were not destitute—my father was a farmer and he farmed three hundred acres of land that was in the family—but they knew they did not have the money to send their children to college, so my dad came to Chicago in 1942 with the idea that the rest of the family would follow as soon as he got a job and got settled. This was during the war, and he got a job working as a cook on the railroad. My mother, my other two sisters, and I followed in 1943. It was my first time coming to the big city, and I will never forget just how amazed I was! Of course, I didn't know the word "architecture" at that time! My dad and my uncle were renting rooms near Forty-fifth and Vincennes, so the very first church we went to—because we were church people at heart—was the Ebenezer Baptist Church at Forty-fifth and Vincennes. I was so impressed with that beautiful building I wrote back to my friends in Louisiana about how beautiful the churches were here in Chicago.

TB: How old were you then?

JT: I was thirteen when we came up from the South. Then we got an apartment on the second floor at 3020 Michigan Avenue. Across the street, at Thirty-first and Michigan, was a big hotel whose name I have forgotten. At that time Thirty-first Street was a thriving metropolis—all kinds of businesses were there. You could get anything you wanted. I never will forget Sunday afternoons. We would just walk around in the neighborhood. It was safe to walk around like that in those days. We walked to the Thirty-first Street Beach. Do you remember the OK Candy Shop that was around the corner on Cottage Grove? Oh, they had any kind of candy imaginable! So we would stop and get our candy and just walk and have a good time on Sunday. About this time, in 1943, I was enrolled in the seventh grade at Douglas Elementary School, and I wound up being the smartest little girl in the class! I guess at first I was a little afraid because I had heard all of those stories about coming to the big city of Chicago from down south and being put back in your grade level. Well, for whatever it is worth, what they were learning here in seventh grade I had already had in fourth and fifth grades in the South! The teachers down in Louisiana may have taught four or five grades together, but they made us learn! So I wound up being a very smart little girl, and I wound up as class president the next year when we graduated in 1944—*and* I wound up playing a piano solo! I guess I was always gifted in music, and I played Rachmaninoff's piano concerto for the eighth-grade graduation. I will never forget that, and I was thrilled that we were able to go on to Phillips High School. I have two sisters, and one of them also went to Phillips.

TB: Douglas had a lot of students at that time. The neighborhood was bulging.

JT: Yes, Douglas was the largest elementary school in the city. We had kitchenette apartments, rooming houses. People at that time lived together without animosity—at least not to any great extent.

TB: Yes, even if someone came into the building whom you didn't know, you treated them like family.

JT: That's right, you took them in and treated them like family. Those were the days, weren't they?

TB: Oh, my gracious, yes! Now the Grand Terrace was there, wasn't it?

JT: Yes, the Grand Terrace was still there at Thirty-fifth Street. But we spent most of our time in church because when we moved to Thirtieth and Michigan, we joined the Pilgrim Baptist Church.

TB: With the Reverend J. C. Austin?

JT: Yes, my mom and dad and my sisters and I joined that church and became very active, especially in the music department. We attended Sunday school and joined the chorus. I played for the junior church. The churches at that time—Pilgrim and Olivet, all of them—were bulging with people, and since I would be downstairs playing for the junior church, my sisters had to hold me a seat in the balcony at Pilgrim because it was always so crowded. There were people sitting on the steps, next to the walls. Of course, Reverend Austin was a great pulpiteer. We loved Pilgrim, and most of our extracurricular activities and socialization took place in that church. We went to rehearsal two or three times a week, and we sang at different churches as well. We were part of the Bethlehem Association and also the Baptist Association. So we did a lot of visiting the other churches in the neighborhood. It was, again, an era in which we could travel about and not have to worry about being safe. We knew we could get the streetcar home without any problem at all.

TB: There were also a lot of athletic activities for young men: baseball teams, basketball teams.

JT: Yes, and one thing I remember in particular was that Reverend Austin always talked a lot about Africa, and Pilgrim supported a mission in Africa. There was even a couple there at Pilgrim that eventually moved to Africa. That man's name was J. K. Moore, and he was in the choir—a deep bass singer. He and his wife moved to Africa. He was a printer, and I think he may have had a printing business here. I remember the church kept a map of West Africa on the wall. Their mission was located in West Africa, I believe.

TB: You know, Pilgrim is now designated as a landmark—Pilgrim and also Ebenezer as well—your two churches! Both of them were formerly synagogues.

JT: Yes, Adler and Sullivan built them.

TB: Now, at this time Thirty-fifth and Thirty-first Streets and, I guess, Thirty-ninth Street were flourishing business streets. Were many of those businesses owned and operated by African-Americans?

JT: Not so many. It was dominated by the other race, if I recall correctly. There were all kinds of businesses: jewelry stores, grocery stores, drugstores, shoe stores. I worked up on Forty-seventh Street for just about most of my entire high school career—at the Savoy Hosiery Shop near King Drive. There were a lot of businesses, but I believe that most of them were owned by whites at that time.

TB: They had a kind of organized conspiracy.

JT: Yes, to keep us in our place!

TB: Maybe Thirty-fifth and Thirty-first Streets were different, but on Forty-seventh Street, because it was such a thriving business area, the only thing that blacks could have were barbershops, taverns, and things of that sort. All of those clothing stores and jewelry shops were mostly Jewish-owned. It was only after the war when the neighborhood began to shift that blacks began to have a chance. Now, Scotty Piper, of course, was a tailor there back then, but he always worked for somebody else.

JT: And on Thirty-first Street, I. W. Brown had his casket company, but I really can't think of any other African-American businesses. They had doctors and dentists up and down Thirty-first Street, but they were all, of course, white. I remember we may have had a couple of restaurants, but I'm just not sure.

TB: Yes, there was one that we now call a "soul food" place on Thirty-first Street. I have forgotten the name of the lady that owned it. Then, of course, on Thirty-fifth Street—where IIT [Illinois Institute of Technology] is now—there was another nice soul food place. But they were very few and far between. There were also a number of small black-owned businesses because they still had some of the remnants of the old neighborhood before things began to move farther south. Ernest Griffin's father had a business at Thirty-first and State Street—a record and photography business—before he went into the funeral business. And when

I was a kid, there were a number of "high rollers," gambling types, who had businesses around there as well.

JT: I really don't remember any of those.

TB: So, after you graduated from Douglas, you went on to Phillips. What was that school like and who was the principal at that time?

JT: Well, it was very exciting. Maudelle B. Bousfield was the principal at that time. I understand that she was the first African-American principal in the city. She was a very strong person. The school was very crowded. I worked at Michael Reese Hospital every morning before I went to school, and I had to be at work at six-thirty in the morning. In our family we just always wanted to work. We didn't have to do it, but we were just very ambitious, and so I would leave home every morning from 3020 Michigan, take the Thirty-first Street streetcar over to Ellis Avenue and walk on over to Michael Reese Hospital, where I started peeling potatoes for the day! I worked from 6:30 A.M. until, I guess, about 9:30 A.M., and then I went on from there to school. Phillips must have had three or four thousand students at that time!

TB: The feeder schools were Douglas, Doolittle . . .

JT: Abbott and Drake—but they came from just about everywhere. People really wanted to come to Phillips. It was a joy to come to this high school.

TB: Buddy Young, the famous football player, graduated from Phillips in 1943 or 1944, before he went into the service. He was a great track star as well as a fine football player. One of the things that Mrs. Bousfield innovated was that she asked that the sports stars participate in the cooking and sewing classes. They did, and that attracted a lot more boys into these areas. Mrs. Bousfield's husband, Dr. Midian Bousfield, was the chief health officer at Fort Huachuca, which was the training ground for the Ninety-third and the Ninety-second Divisions that later went to Italy and the South Pacific. Who were some of the people that you remember from those days?

JT: Well, in my class we had Judge Albert Porter. Sam Cooke was also in my class.

TB: Sam Cooke, "Darling, ooh, ooh, ooh!"

JT: That's the one! And then there was Jacoby Dickens, who is now president of Seaway National Bank. Loretta Reed—the wife of Dr. Wilford Reed, the minister of Grant Memorial Church—was also in my class. Several people who later became school principals were in my class, including Genevieve Leonard. It was a class of achievers. I don't know, though, that we were any different from any other students in the city because at that time African-American students were highly motivated. Our parents put a lot of emphasis on education, and again, I say, that's the reason my people came from the South to Chicago—to get a good education for their children. We were blessed, just blessed. Back in Louisiana, we never had to walk to school. My dad would stop his plowing in the morning to see that we got to school. I had a cousin who was a teacher at the school and, of course, teachers were highly respected in those days. Sometimes we would ride to school with her and her husband in the morning, and at the end of the day, my dad would stop plowing or whatever kind of work he was doing and come to the school to pick up his cousin and us girls. So we were very privileged, and, of course, we were very active in the church down there in the South. My people were very staunch Baptists. That was all we knew, so it's been a blessing throughout my life.

TB: It's carried you through the hard times.

JT: Yes, it's carried me through, especially during the time we had the problem with the preservation of Phillips High School. We just depend on the Lord. We learn to do that at an early age. But, getting back to Phillips, we graduated in June of 1948, and I played Chopin's "Fantasie-Impromptu" at the graduation ceremony. And, of course, during the graduations in those times you could hear a pin drop from the moment the graduation started until it was over. There was no hint of an outcry or disorder. It was a very, very solemn, dignified occasion.

TB: Now, most of the families at Phillips at that time—though, I suspect, many of them lived in Ida B. Wells—were two-parent families, weren't they?

JT: Yes, they were, and they were proud to live in Ida B. Wells. It was a privilege because they admitted only highly screened families. I don't think they had any kind of disorder at all in Ida B. Wells or the offender would be put out of there in a minute. Oscar Brown Sr., I believe, was managing Ida B. Wells at that time. He was also a deacon at Pilgrim Baptist Church.

TB: That's right. I attended his funeral service there.

JT: And I played for it.

TB: The whole family was there. Oscar Brown Jr. and I are very good friends.

JT: Oscar Sr. was also the lawyer for the church, and I don't think he ever charged the church a dime for his services. He was quite a man. He also taught a Sunday school class for years.

TB: Now, going back for a moment to Pilgrim Baptist Church, I missed one of the most illustrious parts of Pilgrim's history—Thomas Dorsey, the creator of gospel music for the whole world! Were you there when he was associated with the church?

JT: Yes, I was.

TB: I remember he had his music studio on Oakwood Boulevard, near the bank. I was a young insurance agent for the Chicago Metropolitan at that time. Requests for copies of his music would be coming in from all over the world, particularly "Precious Lord."

JT: Oh, yes, "It's My Desire," "Peace in the Valley," so many of his songs. Yes, in church when I got off that organ bench or piano bench, my seat was right next to his. He was a legend. He directed our gospel chorus back then when gospel music was something that was new. It had a beat, and, of course, there were some that resisted that beat, but he did it with such style and such verve. You know he had a habit of pointing his finger in a particular way when he was directing? Well, we all used to mimic him and that finger! That was Thomas A. Dorsey and the way that I still remember him. We also had a senior choir that sang the most difficult kinds of classical music. We sang Handel's *Messiah*. We sang *Elijah* and so many other oratorios and requiems.

TB: Your own musical training was formal, wasn't it?

JT: Yes, I am a music major from Northwestern University. In those days the young people in the churches and the Sunday schools did operettas, concerts, and it was all classical music. I also did a lot of playing in high school. I played for the choir and for the modern dance group. They had a terrific modern dance group, and I remember one of the pieces that they danced to was Beethoven's "Moonlight Sonata." So there was a high degree of classical music throughout everything that we did. As I think of some of the songs that we did in the Sunday school chorus, it was most difficult music—"He Is Watching Over Israel," for instance. Gospel music took a little time to catch hold. We did spirituals and hymns, but as far as gospel music goes, we pretty much stuck with the classical music. We had learned to read music very well, and we did a great job of singing that classical music. As young people, we really loved singing that classical music!

TB: Now, after you graduated from Phillips in 1948, what happened then?

JT: At that time there were three junior colleges in the city: Wilson, which is now Kennedy-King; Herzl, which is where I went and which became Malcolm X; and Wright. I spent a semester at Herzl, and in 1949 I went on to Northwestern University. I didn't have a scholarship or any kind of financial assistance. My dad paid every penny of tuition! He worked on that railroad washing those dishes, cooking . . .

TB: Yes, I tell the younger generation about how hard their parents and grandparents worked. Last night I was at the CRS [Community Renewal Society] meeting, and we didn't see a single black face serving anything. Al Johnson looked over and said to me, "Tim, I don't see no dark faces!" This was at the Hilton Hotel—the old Stevens Hotel—and he said, "Tim, why is that?" And I said, "You go to the Palmer House, and it's the same thing." My guess is that today's young men and young women do not know what success stories came out of that kind of service.

JT: It was that kind of work that educated families and also paid the rent!

TB: Right. These are the kinds of jobs that I grew up with. You could go to work broke and come back with some money in your pocket.

JT: You took pride in whatever you did, and you worked any kind of honorable job. And even now, when we have our prom, I have so far been able to hold out in terms of sending our students downtown to those hotels because doing that is not good for our community. It would take their money out of the community in which they live.

TB: Where did your high school graduates go?

JT: To the Parkway Ballroom at Forty-fifth and South Park Way, and it was beautiful.

TB: So you went on to Northwestern University. About how many African-Americans were there at Northwestern at that time?

JT: I must have been on campus a whole month before I saw another African-American face. There may have been one or two other African-Americans in the school of music, but we could not even live on campus at that time. There was one little frame house somewhere on campus where they let African-Americans live, but it was pretty much taken up with those who were from out of town. We rented rooms in Evanston. We survived. I was so busy with church engagements that I was coming into Chicago every night anyway for some kind of rehearsal.

TB: And you felt safe, coming all the way from Evanston?

JT: Yes, all the way from Evanston, and then I went back out there after rehearsal, got off that El at Davis Street, and would either walk home or take the bus feeling perfectly safe.

TB: I'm sure the experience at Northwestern must have been academically challenging, but socially and culturally, what was it like? Of course, you were not on campus very much, were you?

JT: No, I was back and forth from home to campus and from the city to campus. On weekends I was home. Of course, being in the School of Music, you had to practice four or five hours a day, so you didn't really have any problem socially because you were there strictly for business. It never would occur to me to fail a class, you know—not with my dad working as hard as he was to pay my tuition.

TB: Was your mother a housewife?

JT: Yes, Mother was a housewife. Mother always wanted to work, but my dad would not let her work. You know about that—he just would *not* let her work!

TB: My mother was in the same position.

JT: Daddy was from the old school.

TB: Well, my father wanted her to be home when he got back from work, and he wanted her to be able to take care of the children.

JT: Yes, that was my mother's job as well. My dad bought a house at Thirty-fourth and Prairie in 1945. Now, of course, at that time it was very unusual for African-

Americans to own homes, but we purchased that little two-flat house, and I remember that the first thing that went into that house was the piano. We had been in the new house for only a week and my dad went out and bought the piano for me! He and I took the bus and bought a Stark piano. I still have it! I would get up in the morning around 4:30 or 5 A.M. and practice for an hour and a half or two hours before I left for school. The piano was right next to the bedroom, and the house was quite small with little, bitty rooms, but never once did my parents ever complain or talk about losing sleep or anything. They just loved us and loved giving us opportunities to achieve. So I would leave home, I guess, at about 6:30 A.M. and have to be at school at 8 A.M. I had classes all day, and then in the evening, if I wasn't staying in Evanston, I came back home.

TB: What happened after you left Northwestern?

JT: I graduated in 1952—a little early because I went to summer school—and then I started teaching school. At that time, even after I had a degree in music, it was hard to get a job in music in Chicago. So I went to Chicago Teachers College, took kindergarten and primary-school courses, and began teaching, mostly at Doolittle Elementary School.

TB: That school has a rich history too. Now, when you were at Doolittle, had Lake Meadows and Prairie Shores been built?

JT: Lake Meadows had been built, but not Prairie Shores. Then in 1955, I was assigned to Grant School on the West Side. It was located at 2400 West Wilcox, just a block or so off Western Avenue. Grant was on a double shift then, as I recall.

TB: Was the neighborhood mixed?

JT: It was mostly white and there was a lot of racism. I remember the students making all kinds of ugly remarks. Then a little later I came back to Doolittle again in 1955 and taught first grade. At that time most of the principals in the city were white. The principal of Doolittle at that time was Mr. Beavers. He was eventually the principal of Pershing School, which they built at Thirty-first and Rhodes. I was at Doolittle until 1963.

TB: You got married in 1955. Where did you live then?

JT: We stayed with our parents for a year or so, and then, for a little less than two years, we got an apartment on Fifty-second and Drexel. Except for that year and a half or so, that is the only time I have ever not been living here in this neighborhood.

TB: This is home to you.

JT: Yes, this is home. In 1957 my grandmother became ill and my father and mother made plans to move back to Louisiana. My husband and I came back and took over our family home at Thirty-fourth and Prairie and lived there from 1957 until 1963, when we purchased this house I am in now. We have been here for thirty-three years. Back at the time we first moved in, it had been cut up into all kinds of small rooms, little apartments, kitchenettes, and so forth. It was really a shambles.

TB: Oh, yes. We were still crowded, and every available piece of space was utilized to the fullest.

JT: I can still remember an old man coming in to look at the house and saying, "This place ain't good for nothing but to be torn down." Of course, that wasn't too far from my idea either! But we have been here a long time. It has been a great place to raise the children.

TB: How many children do you have?

JT: We have three children. Their ages are forty, thirty-five, and thirty.

TB: All this space!

JT: Yes, and we just opened the house up to our children's friends. I never will forget one incident. One day, when my daughter and I were both walking out there on the sidewalk, one of her classmates said to her, "Hey, Linda!"—that's my oldest child—"what floor do you live on, first or second?" But, of course, Linda didn't understand, and she said, "Well, we live on both of them," and the boy walked away saying, "Humpf, how could that be!" I thought that was so cute.

TB: Were the Duster family in any of your classes?

JT: Yes, one of them. Ida B. Wells's grandson, Charles.

TB: He just passed quite recently.

JT: And you know, another person in my class was one of S. B. Fuller's daughters. He had a thriving cosmetics business.

TB: Yes, and out of that business came Johnson Products. Was George Johnson at Phillips then?

JT: No, not when I was there.

TB: How long did you stay in the elementary school system?

JT: From 1952 until they transferred me to Phillips in 1963. I took the high school music exam. I loved everything that I was doing at elementary school and didn't have any intentions of leaving Doolittle. I remember that the principal, Dr. Kathleen Cooney, kept running up telling me, "I am working on it. They are not going to transfer you." They eventually put me into the seventh- and eighth-grade music—they called it "departmental"—so all I did was teach music all day. We did great things. One of the greatest things we did was to teach the "Hallelujah" chorus to ten or twelve classrooms. We would then combine the classes in the auditorium, and you are talking about a beautiful sound—elementary school students singing the "Hallelujah" chorus.

TB: An honest sound, not contrived.

JT: Yes, not contrived. Teachers—old, hardened teachers—had tears streaming down their faces. And it became a challenge to the kids to see which ones would get the solo parts. I enjoyed what I was doing and we did beautiful concertos. Doolittle, at that time, had a yearly extravaganza where the talent of the school was showcased. During the time that I taught music, we celebrated every holiday, including Negro History Week, of course.

TB: Were your students still coming from Ida B. Wells?

JT: Yes, and some of them were also coming from Lake Meadows. Reverend Brazier's children were there. As you know, he was the pastor of the Apostolic Church of God, and also one of the founders of the Woodlawn Organization. Then they moved me to Phillips in 1963, and I taught music there until 1968. I had a young male chorus at Phillips, and I didn't know it at the time, but they were putting all their problem young men in my male chorus. Well, when we had our first opportunity to sing, the whole school almost fell out because there were some of the most difficult boys in the school up there singing their hearts out! That was just fine with me. I didn't even know they were *supposed* to have been "problem" students! They loved it, especially when we sang "Stout Hearted Men"!

TB: That's what education is all about.

JT: Yes, and we did spirituals—"Soon I Will Be Done." We did Christmas music, Easter music. We did "The Holy City." I see the young people even now in the neighborhood that are still singing "Stout Hearted Men"! They loved it! We even won a competition with "Soon I Will Be Done With the Trouble." Back in those days it was a big thing for the choirs all over the city to go to the annual competition. So I took them to the competition one year and they just brought the house down. They absolutely brought the house down. So, I guess, as a result of that, they asked me to come into the counseling department. They let me keep the male chorus for a year after that, and at that time Phillips had one of the strongest choirs in the city. They went all over the country singing. Of course, it was all classical music and spirituals. They went to Germany—they went everywhere.

TB: Now, during the time when you were at Phillips, was Henry Springs in the administration?

JT: When I went there in 1963, Henry was the assistant principal. And by the way, he still keeps in touch with me. We grew up together. Henry produced some outstanding athletes at Phillips.

TB: Yes, he did. So you then went into the counseling office. What was that like?

JT: Oh, I loved it. At that time, around 1968, there was a big push to get African-American students into colleges. Do you happen to know Joyce Clark?

TB: Absolutely. She's a friend of mine.

JT: Well, there was a department at Central Office called the Higher Education Guidance Center. Joyce headed the center, and we prepared students for admission into colleges all over the country. She is a beautiful person and a hard worker. I worked with Joyce, and she and I even worked together during the summer. I think that the Higher Education Guidance Center was one of the best things we had in the high school, and it was one of the worst things that happened when they stopped that big push to get African-American students into U.S. colleges.

TB: Well, outside we had been agitating on that very level.

JT: OK, then, that's what it took! Somebody had to agitate. The rest have to be there to pick up the apples. We sent out graduates all over the country, and they have done well. We still hear from them.

TB: Now when did you become principal of Phillips High School?

JT: I became principal in 1990. I had become assistant principal in 1986 when one of the assistant principals left the school to go to the Division Office to work with Henry Springs.

TB: That's right. He was a district superintendent. Give me a succession of the principals of Phillips after Mrs. Bousfield, if you can remember.

JT: Yes, I remember them. After Mrs. Bousfield, there was Virginia B. Louis, a great principal. When I came back in 1963, her husband, Robert E. Louis, was principal. After Robert came Alonzo Crim.

TB: He later became superintendent of schools in Atlanta.

JT: Then after Dr. Crim, I believe Dr. William Finch came in in 1968. He was there from 1968 until 1971. He also is, by the way, a great supporter and mentor. Then there was Dr. Saddler, who had also graduated from Phillips. He wound up being the deputy superintendent of education. A great, great man. So Dr. Finch left in 1971, and then they brought in Mr. Daniel Caldwell, and after that Mrs. Ernestine Curry in January 1975. I succeeded her in 1990.

TB: Now, both in terms of the neighborhood and the school, what are some of the things that you have seen during this time that stand out in your memory? I mean by this the social climate, social change, the economic conditions—how have these things changed?

JT: I think that perhaps the most detrimental thing that happened in the neighborhood was the deterioration of the family in the housing developments, which meant that the entire student body was affected. Kids are good, parents are good, but the social evils crept in. The student attendance was affected. Even back in the seventies, we still had three and four thousand students at Phillips High School, but they were all well behaved. Then came the period in our nation that was the period of unrest, and we began to have problems.

TB: This change, I suspect, was somewhat sudden and dramatic. You were probably beginning to see it almost immediately—the reduction of standards in the selection of tenants to go into public housing, the losing of respect for relationships within the frame of the family . . .

JT: Right.

TB: Also, the welfare system injected itself into some of these problems by restricting the relationships between children and their fathers.

JT: Right, creating situations where the father was almost banned from living in his own home.

TB: All this is happening, and then you get jobs moving away.

JT: Yes, the war was over and jobs were moving away.

TB: And then a new element creeps in which is also dramatic in terms of its immediate effect—narcotics.

JT: Right, narcotics and the rise of gangs in the neighborhood.

TB: And the accompanying violence.

JT: Yes, and so all of that has certainly taken its toll, but, in spite of all that, I must say that the children, many of them, have remained steadfast and remained dedicated to their work and their community.

TB: And that's just remarkable. It is a tribute to the human spirit.

JT: Yes, it is a tribute to the human sprit.

TB: You, yourself, would call it God's hand.

JT: Yes, I would.

TB: I'll go along with that!

JT: The children that we have now made it through, and all during the eighties we worked with them very, very carefully. Now we were trying to regain what we had—the human spirit. As the renovation and rehab of this area take place, we are constantly telling the students that the change in the neighborhood is for them. Even in regard to the rehab of Phillips High School, my words to them almost every day are, "This is for you."

TB: Will the rehab be internal as well as external?

JT: Yes, and we are so happy about that. I became principal in 1990, and in 1991, before I had even been there a year, the first salvo was cast as far as closing Phillips High School—and since then, there have been I don't know how many more. So, since I have been principal, that's been primarily what I have been preoccupied with—trying to save the school. With the help of the Lord, we have by now, I think, reached the turning point.

TB: I know for a while there was a relatively active Alumni Association. Are they still active and generous with donations?

JT: Yes, very active, but just to tell you how things work, when I became principal, in November of that year, Dr. Saddler organized the alumni. You know, there were already several class organizations, but now we just put them all under one umbrella. And so we called the first meeting at Seaway National Bank—Jacoby Dickens let us use a room of his there—and we talked about organizing the alumni. Who would have guessed that in less than four months they would be ready to talk about closing Phillips down? So when that happened, the alumni were ready. That I attribute to the good Lord. We were ready. The alumni were there and already well organized, and they fought every step of the way. In addition, we were able to organize the ministers. There was a small group of ministers that were trying to help the schools. I remember going to the first meeting that they held down at the St. James Catholic Church. I believe that three schools had been invited, and I think I was the only principal that showed up. Before I knew it, we had an organization at Phillips called PAUL—Pastors Allied Under the Lord—and they were coming into Phillips every week! The point is that the Lord knew all this was coming before we did. That's why we had the alumni in place, had the ministers, had the churches already in place. We were able to work with the community organizations, and, of course, Lu Palmer was a very active member of the Local School Council, so when the attacks came there was plenty of support. I never will forget one night a representative from Channel 11 television came in and interviewed me. At that time Robert Starks was on the show, and he talked about the fact that Phillips was endangered because of its location. "It's in the way," he said. "It is sitting between the Dan Ryan and Lake Shore Drive—ten minutes from downtown and the lake," and the developers wanted the building. We knew it was political—and we were thankful that, in spite of everything that happened, we were able to garner the support needed to save Wendell Phillips High School. We went to the Board of Education three or four times—just hordes of us. People came from all over the country, Tim, to save Phillips. The alumni were getting ready to shut the Dan Ryan down, shut Lake Shore Drive down. Alumni came from California, from Philadelphia, from New York, and from Florida to save the school that they had once attended.

TB: You know, Phillips is home to me too. I graduated from DuSable—but both of them are home. Phillips saved my life. I was at Englewood High School, and I couldn't handle the racism that existed there. There were several levels of prejudice at that school. There was one of poverty, and we were poor. My daddy worked at the stockyards and had just lost his job. I was too dark for my middle-class colleagues who had finished at Burke School. And there was inherent racism in the faculty. On top of all this, there was my little daddy who didn't like white folks anyhow, and he had the audacity to talk back strongly when he felt the situation warranted it. So I said to myself, "I think I had better transfer without my mother's permission and knowledge!"

JT: You got an honorary transfer?

TB: Yes, I was the first person to receive one, and Phillips was a great experience for me. So many wonderful people!

JT: Students?

TB: Students and teachers! Now, today, given what you are doing already, what at the academic and social level would you like to infuse into what you already have in order to improve things?

JT: And make a difference!

TB: Yes, and make a difference! How many students come in as freshmen here at Phillips?

JT: We get about four hundred freshmen.

TB: How are they broken down in terms of male and female?

JT: About half and half.

TB: And then four years later . . .

JT: Well, you see, it is hard to get a handle on that breakdown in terms of any sort of accurate percentage because there is so much transferring in and out, and out and in. The neighborhood problems will necessitate the parents pulling them out to go to another school or even moving the entire family out of the neighborhood. Whatever it takes, whatever it is they can do to save that child's life, they do. We usually graduate about 150 to 155 students. Most of the problems, academically speaking, can be attributed to lack of attendance. If they come, we will teach them. We've got some excellent teachers here at Phillips High School. Now, Barbara Sizemore came back to Chicago about three or four years ago, and we latched right on to her and to her program at DePaul University. So we expect when the Illinois Goals Assessment Program scores come out that our students will be shown to do excellent work. We have worked very hard with teaching reading, math, social studies—and also how to take facts that they need from the written page. The IGAP is very uniquely constructed. Many of the answers are indirect, and the questions have more than one right answer. Barbara Sizemore has worked with us on developing test-taking skills, so we have gotten on an academic track here that we intend to keep on until all our students get an ACT score of 28 or above. We are going to work hard. *They* are working hard. I talked with a girl just last night, and, even though the IGAP and the other test are over, they are still working. We are giving them an opportunity to do portfolios and different kinds of assessments now, and they have worked very hard. The teachers have gone through a lot of training. We are working very closely with St. Ignatius and with Dr. Sokoni Karanja, who, as you know, heads the Centers for New Horizons and has done a lot of very positive things for the school. We expect to be the top school in the city in very short order. Mr. Harris has formed a Phillips Foundation that, in addition to the alumni group which we already have, we hope will provide a lot of advantages for the students above and beyond what Central Office will do. We have renovated the chemistry and physics labs. We are steadily on the lookout for good teachers. We got a teacher in this September when they closed down one of the Catholic schools—St. Martin De Porres—an excellent physics, chemistry, and math teacher. Those are the kinds of teachers that we are trying to get into Phillips. Our summer schedule for 1996 has very extensive training sessions for the staff so that when September comes, we will be able to all be on the same page and hit the ground running academically. There are thirteen people working in the settlement office there—alumni that are working just to get funds and resources into the school. The Phillips Foundation that Mr. Harris started is planning to close the school down for the summer and get in there and do the painting, plastering, and get a lot of rehab done. The school has been totally neglected. Nothing has been done since 1974.

TB: The thought having been that the school would soon be torn down?

JT: Yes, after they'd even fixed the roof—might have been in 1991 or 1992—they still hadn't given up plans for tearing it down! I must say that Mr. Paul Vallas, who has been CEO of Central Office, has just been marvelous. We invited him to come out and visit Phillips the very first day of school. We were at DePaul University with Barbara Sizemore's workshop this summer, and he was the main speaker at that event. I immediately went up to him and said, "Mr. Vallas, please feel free to come to Phillips. We would like you to come the first day of school." Well, I couldn't believe he came! And he was so gracious and so appreciative of the history of that school. He sat there at the window at the north end of the building, and he said, "I am going to give you an athletic field between Phillips and Mayo school." Mayo is the new elementary school, and Phillips, as you know, was at one time an elementary school too, but, I believe it was in 1964 or 1965, it became so overcrowded that they had to build the Mayo school at Thirty-seventh Street as a replacement for Phillips.

TB: They had a great principal.

JT: Oh, yes, indeed. Kids didn't come in their door without a book, as I understand it.

TB: Now, if you had the power to change things here at Phillips, what would you do?

JT: First, I would put pressure on the parents to send their students to school every day. No matter how well prepared we are, how anxious we are to teach well, without regular attendance on the part of the pupils, the teachers have got to go back and keep spinning their wheels, going over and over the same material. In math, for instance, they have got to be there every single day. We have got to move rapidly in those areas, and we can do it if the students will only just come to school every day.

TB: Why would the parents not send their kids to school or, in some cases, not allow them to come to school? Is it the fear of violence?

JT: I think it is just a breakdown of the family. When you are up late, or when so many of the kids work and don't get home until twelve or one o'clock, it's hard for them to get up and be at school at 7:30 A.M.

TB: But you used to do it.

JT: I sure did!

TB: So what do you think is happening to this generation?

JT: I don't know, I just don't know. But there is that lack of . . .

TB: Well, your daddy and mama were always there to say, "Get up!"

JT: That's right. And then, of course, there was the advent of television. They look at television too many hours a day.

TB: Yes, they turn it on in the morning and sometimes it doesn't go off even after they've gone to sleep.

JT: That's right. We knew we had to do our homework. It was quiet time, and you had to do your homework before you were allowed to go out and play.

TB: So there is a discipline that needs to be injected into the home life.

JT: Yes.

TB: The values of education have to be put in such a way that they transcend the values of looking at that TV box.

JT: Right!

TB: Particularly the kind of programs they look at! Now, when it's time to go to school and they have to go out into the street, what do you do about that? What about the kids who proclaim that they are frightened—particularly boy children—going between home and school?

JT: Those are real fears. We do know that they have difficulty coming to school. We find that now they all come to school kind of in droves. Many of them come here together from the same building. I don't know whether they gather and come together for the sake of safety or what. There are so many angles that this problem of success in school needs to be attacked from. They must do their homework; they must be in bed at a reasonable hour, with the television off; they must get up in the morning and get a good, hot breakfast. They can even get a good, hot breakfast at school, but it all really goes back to the parents!

TB: Now, many of your youngsters come from single-parent households, don't they?

JT: Many, many of them do.

TB: Do you have any idea how many?

JT: Oh, a large percentage of them. It is almost the exception to have a two-parent household.

TB: How many of the youngsters come from homes where that one parent or two parents graduated from high school?

JT: I don't have any hard data on that, but it's not very high. Many of them come from the Phillips family. You know the parents were themselves Phillips students, but the point is that the parents have lost the direct control of their children in so many cases.

TB: And now the children are making their own decisions.

JT: Many times the parents have to go to work, and they get the child up and dressed or at least wake the child up, but they are not there when it's time to make the child go to school. Plus that drive must really come from both without and within. The element that keeps the young men out also has a direct effect on them going to school. But, even if they do get to school, getting them here with their books and papers is an additional problem. To solve that kind of problem, we purchased book bags for all of our students so they could keep their things together more easily.

TB: Yes, I saw your students carrying them.

JT: Well, we had difficulty with getting them to use them in the beginning, but now they carry them pretty regularly.

TB: All the students that I see have them.

JT: But when I first got them, they wouldn't carry them. I never will forget one day I just stood at the door and wouldn't let anybody out without their taking a textbook with them. Oh, they had a time with me! "A book, Ms. Tucker, what you mean 'a book!'" We have been able to turn around a lot of attitudes like that. We must if we expect to get academically back on track. Until they get to that 28 ACT—which is what DePaul wants, which is what Loyola wants, which is what Roosevelt wants—then we are going to keep it up because we are convinced that they have the capacity to do it.

TB: The creative ability is there, the academic ability is there.

JT: Yes, it's there. You know what I tell them, Tim? I tell them this continually, and the first thing they hear from me when school opens is, "Good morning. I love you!" We say that all day, over and over. As I walk up and down the hall, I say, "I love you," and they will say it back. Now, when I first started saying it, it kind of shocked them. But I tell them that they are the smartest students that God ever put on the Earth. I go into this every chance I get. When they brought us over in the holds of ships from Africa and we were chained down like logs—like so many rows of logs—those who were less strong perished—and those who survived are the stock that we come from! Strong. Strong of mind, strong of body!

TB: How could anyone who was not strong like that be able to survive that two-hundred-year period of slavery? Only the strongest! First, there was the selection process in Africa itself. I ask my students, "If you were the slave traders and you went to get slaves, which ones would you choose?"

JT: Yes, in the first place, they always took the best, the strongest, and the ones who survived the voyage—

TB: There you've got the cream of the crop!

JT: Yes, so I tell my students, "You come from the cream of the crop."

TB: It is important that they understand that.

JT: Well, they hear if from me so often!

TB: As Howard Thurman says, "Oh! What it must have been like!" You know when I went to Goree Island in Senegal and looked out at that ocean and remembered that one day my ancestors had been imprisoned in one of those slave houses and then were taken forcibly in chains to a boat—not even knowing where they were going—that's when I said to myself, "My Lord, I have a responsibility. They did that for me. They could have just died, and it would all have been over! But they survived—and now I owe them something!"

JT: They could have died, and so many of them did, but those that survived—those who, in spite of everything, survived—my goodness, we owe it to them to do our best.

May 24, 1996

MILDRED BOWDEN
AND HERMENE HARTMAN

MOTHER AND DAUGHTER—TWO GENERATIONS

This conversation with Mildred Bowden was a lively, entertaining one, interrupted with only a few occasional requests for cutoffs on the tape recorder. Her daughter, Hermene Hartman, who is editor in chief and publisher of N'Digo, was standing close by, helping to assist her mother's memory, which seemed to me to be very good and extremely accurate. I think Hermene by instinct and training is a perfectionist, and, as a result, she helped fill in some important points and contributed a perspective that is representative of her own generation.

Ms. Bowden first came to Chicago from North Carolina as an infant, and as a young woman, she found it to be a very exciting and interesting place, particularly in terms of the nightlife. Her employment in various capacities in nightclubs on the South Side brought her into close contact with some of the most famous people in show business, such as Sarah Vaughan, Billie Holiday, Ella Fitzgerald, Ray Nance, Earl "Fatha" Hines as well as many others. Of course, her kinship with renowned jazz singer Johnny Hartman and the businessmen who were his brothers gave her an even broader range of experience.

It seems that almost all of Mildred Bowden's life has been spent on the South Side, as was also true of most South Side blacks of that same period. Despite gentle cautioning by Hermene, she clearly indicated that although there were nice people on the West Side, they all knew that they would have to come to the South Side if they really wanted to have the highest quality of entertainment and social events—and in my experience, most West Siders of that period would have been inclined to agree with her.

TB: Where were you born, Mildred?

MB: I was born in Apex, North Carolina, but I have been here since I was one year old.

TB: Oh, you are like me. I am from Birmingham.

MB: I am doing a genealogy study at the present time. There is a lot of information that I need to help me trace my family history.

TB: Your mother and dad, where were they born?

MB: They were born in North Carolina, but really I am almost an orphan.

TB: Didn't you know them?

MB: Not really. My father moved to Chicago after my mother died. He remarried, and my stepmother was my mother.

HH: Your mother died at what age?

MB: She was just nineteen.

TB: Oh, she was nineteen! Did you know any of your grandparents?

MB: No, but I have found some names, and I am working on it. I've found some names on my father's side, but I hit a bump on my mother's side.

TB: You will be able to trace it, but it takes patience.

MB: Oh yeah, it takes patience, but I'll be able to do it. I know that.

TB: I haven't gotten really far myself because I just don't have the patience right now, but one day sometime soon I'm going to go back to Birmingham. My mother was born in Florence, which is W. C. Handy's and Oscar DePriest's home. My dad was born in Jacksonville, but Birmingham is where they met. You said you were raised by your stepmother. Was that here in Chicago?

MB: Yes, in Chicago. We lived in a beautiful house at Thirty-first and Giles. We had a beautiful home. I was brought up in a well-to-do area.

TB: That's known as the Douglas area.

MB: I had a beautiful childhood until my stepmother died. She died when I was eleven. My father died when I was only five or six years old. She had another daughter who was my sister.

TB: Do you remember any of the people who lived around that neighborhood?

MB: What's so interesting is that I went on a tour this summer to Hot Springs, Arkansas, with a group called the Senior Friends that I belong to. There were two women that were there, and I walked up to one of them and asked, "Did you go to Douglas School?" and they both said yeah! So I said, "What are your names?" and it turns out that I remembered one of them.

HH: Tell him what you remembered.

MB: We remembered that we were in the first grade together!

[*Laughter.*]

Yes, we had been in first grade together. They lived in the same area I lived in, on Thirty-first Street. In those days, we could walk from my house to the Thirty-first Street Beach.

TB: If you don't mind, when were you born?

MB: Who, me? In 1921. No problem, I'm proud to tell my age. A lot of these young people today haven't ever seen anybody my age that's still walking.

[*Laughter.*]

And I'm still walking!

[*Continued laughter.*]

And I'm doing everything. I go to all the plays. I do everything I want to do, and I am so happy to be able to do it. Anyway, I met those women two months ago, and then we got together again. We went back over to Thirty-first Street, and we were talking about it like this, "The Franklin Theatre was right there at Thirty-first and Giles," "The A&P was the big food mart at that time," "We had a candy store over there," "We had a Chinese restaurant right next to it," "We had Florsheim's Shoes across the street," "Remember that dress shop?" Well, as a matter of fact, we had all kinds of stores and businesses. We were even laughing about the chicken market where we went and bought live chickens. The man would put that chicken down and that chicken would flutter all around and scare you half to death! So we would stand outside while that chicken was still fluttering all around. These kids today have never seen live chickens, but that's the way you bought them in those days. You went to the chicken market. You went to the meat market. My mother always sent me. I didn't have to cross but one street. She used to say I was her legs.

TB: Now there is a store on Fifty-third Street called Mr. G's, and the owner's grandfather had a store right on the corner of Thirty-first and South Park—you know that big building that used to be at Thirty-first Street?

MB: Oh, yeah, but like I said, we could walk to the beach, and there were a lot of homes. I'll tell you another one of the things I remember is that they widened South Park at that time—when I was a little girl. Automobiles and buses! These kids now cannot imagine that, but South Park was once a narrow street, and that's why they were widening it. I remember when they put the first buses out there. They were double-decked and that was a big deal for kids my age at the time, to ride on that double-decked bus. That was all you wanted to do.

TB: That was fun.

MB: It *was* fun! That was the first bus they put out on South Park. My mother was always fussing about the taxes, and I remember the time a policeman ran me off the grass, and she said, "Get his number! Get his number! I'm paying taxes for them to widen that street, and they better let you play over there!"

[*Laughter.*]

TB: Was the Memorial Statue there at Thirty-fifth Street?

MB: I don't remember that. I can't remember that because most of my activities were on Thirty-first Street. My mother would not let me venture very far away. We lived in the middle of the block at 3125 Giles, and I could walk to the corner, and then I would be right there on Thirty-first. Everything I knew about was what was up and down on Thirty-first Street.

TB: What kind of businesses do you remember?

MB: All kinds of businesses. Tailor shops. Lots of places.

TB: Of course, you were too young to participate, but you may remember there were also some nightspots.

MB: Well, they were past South Park. The Royal Gardens was on Thirty-first Street.

TB: That's where Louis Armstrong used to play.

MB: Right. This was past South Park going east, over in that area, and do you re-member the Grand Theater?

TB: The great Erskine Tate!

MB: Louis Armstrong was with him, I think.

TB: That's right.

MB: Erskine Tate! Now, my sister, she was an usher there. She was ten years old, I think, at the time, and she was an usher at the Grand Theater, but my mother did not let me go that far by myself.

TB: Do you remember anything about the Mecca Building?

MB: Yes! I lived in the Mecca Building at one time after my mother died. Well, when it was really fine, that was before my time. When I got to the Mecca Build-ing, it was not what it once was, but I'll tell you what it was equal to when it was built. What did you have there at Forty-seventh and Michigan?

TB: The Rosenwald?

MB: It was equal to the Rosenwald when it was built. Well, but, later on, you know, it went down to a tenement.

TB: Yeah, in the later years.

MB: Well, when I was there, it hadn't gone down quite to being a tenement, but it still was not the elite building that it once had been.

TB: Did your folks ever take you far enough to see the old Vincennes Hotel?

MB: No, but I'll tell you what I do remember, though. Sometimes they let me go up to see the show at the Regal Theater. My mother was sickly, and so I had to do things on my own, but she would figure out what I could and could not do, and so she put me on that bus I told you about on South Park, and I could ride to Forty-seventh — me and my little friend — get off and go to the Regal Theater. Then we would catch the bus and go back to Thirty-first and be right back home. So she had it all planned out to the last detail! But I never could go to State Street and over that way by myself.

TB: So the first school you went to was probably Douglas?

MB: Douglas School, yes. Douglas School was only half a block from my house, and that's why they had a little family joke about me. You see, when I went to kindergarten the first day, I came home for lunch and said, "I quit. I don't want to go back." Well, some of the teachers also came down Thirty-first Street for lunch, and so this teacher passed my house, and when she saw that I was outside playing, she said, "Mildred, where have you been? You haven't been to school?" I said, "I wanted to learn how to read and write, and we don't do nothing at that school but just play." So she said, "You come back to school, and we will see what we can do about that!"

[*Laughter.*]

TB: Did they have any black teachers there?

MB: I remember one black teacher that I had, and she was a good teacher, but that's the only black teacher I can remember off the top of my head.

TB: So you went to Douglas all eight years?

MB: Douglas used to go up to the eighth-grade level, but when I came out of Douglas, I went to Phillips because Phillips started at the junior high level, and then we graduated from eighth grade at Phillips. That was the first time that that had ever happened.

TB: Yeah, yeah.

MB: Before that, Douglas used to go to the eighth grade.

TB: I was there in that same period, and I also went to Wendell Phillips.

MB: I had two black teachers at Wendell Phillips. I know everybody remembers Mr. French.

TB: Absolutely!

MB: But he left Phillips and went to DuSable. Then Mrs. Bousfield came in as principal.

TB: And Mrs. Bousfield stayed at Phillips.

MB: I used to laugh at her. She wore glasses, but when she went to read, she would take them off.

[*Laughter.*]

Don't you remember her? She was tall, stately, and she wore those glasses right on the tip of her nose.

TB: Yeah, a pince-nez.

MB: Yeah, a pince-nez, and then she would take them off.

[*Laughter.*]

TB: She couldn't see, so she had to take them off!

[*Laughter.*]

Who are some of your classmates that you still remember? Was Nat Cole in your class? Do you remember him from junior high?

MB: Yeah, Nat Cole used to play at all our little dances. They had the Forum Hall on Forty-third where they had what they called "spotlight dancing" for younger kids like us. They had those dances early Sunday afternoons.

TB: "Matinee dancing."

MB: Yeah, and I certainly remember Nat Cole from those days.

TB: Ray Nance, was he there?

MB: Yeah, Ray Nance, Nat Cole, I think Redd Foxx—

TB: No, Redd Foxx was at DuSable.

MB: Oh, but I'll tell you who was in my music class. Ms. Mildred Bryant-Jones was my music teacher, and Dorothy Donegan was one of my classmates! She also taught a program over at my church.

TB: What church was that?

MB: Christ Universal Temple—Johnnie Colemon's church. Later on, when she was already a star, she was performing someplace, and I went over to Dorothy, and I said, "Dorothy, how are you doing?" She said hi, and I said, "I remember you from school. Do you remember Ms. Mildred Bryant-Jones?" and she said, "Shut up!"

[*Laughter.*]

That woman was the first person I ever knew who hyphenated her name, Bryant-Jones. When we would finish our class early, she would look up and see that we would have another ten minutes, and so she would let Dorothy play for the class. In those days, Dorothy would imitate Fats Waller. She could imitate Fats Waller in high school! That's how good she was.

TB: Now, when did you start at DuSable?

MB: I guess about '35 or '36.

TB: Somewhere in there.

MB: Are you older than I am?

TB: Yeah.

MB: I thought we were about the same. It was '35 or '36. It has been so long, but it was in that area. It was probably '35.

TB: What are your memories of DuSable in terms of academic as well as social and cultural matters?

MB: Well, one reason why everybody wanted to go to DuSable was that we were the first school I can remember to have typewriters and a typing class. We also had a swimming pool, and I don't think any of the other schools had that. The best school here was Hyde Park, but only the top students went to Hyde Park. Anybody who went to Hyde Park in those days had really high scores. But everybody wanted to go to DuSable anyway because it had that new swimming pool, and we had those new typewriters. We were taught shorthand, as well as typing. It was a complete business course, and you could leave DuSable after taking that business course in those days and work in any office. That's how qualified you were. That kind of qualification now would almost have to come from a college person.

TB: What about sports?

MB: Well, we had a basketball team.

TB: Yes, we sure did!

MB: Oh, we had a tough basketball team. We also had a nice new auditorium for the stage plays and the musical "Hi-Jinks." When they put that on, that was it! That was a big show, and a lot of big stars came out of it. We also had a big band. Captain Dyett's band was very popular. It hurts you to see what is happening now because back then it was really the top school on the South Side, but back then all the schools were good. Englewood was also a good school, but everybody had to live in their district and they got very strict. They tightened the rules down, and they would make you bring a telephone bill, a gas bill, or an electric bill to show that you really lived there before they would transfer you into another school. Now these kids of today probably haven't heard of anything like that.

TB: DuSable became so crowded that they also remade Phillips into a high school, and when they did, Maudelle Bousfield became principal.

MB: After DuSable had such an influx, that's when they started trying to send them out. They districted it off because kids were coming from everywhere to go to DuSable. You know, that's something else that I just don't understand. We had geography when I came along, and before you could pass or graduate, you had to know every state in the union and the capital of every state in the union. I know you remember that! I bet you these kids today don't even know the capital of Illinois.

[*Laughter.*]

TB: I think you are probably right.

MB: I'll tell you something else we had. We had spelling bees.

TB: Uh-huh. Uh-huh.

MB: We had a half hour or so for spelling every day, and on Friday we had a spelling test or spelling bee from the words that we had every day that week. We might have had five or six new words every single day. That's why we are so far ahead of these kids today.

TB: So you went on and graduated from DuSable?

MB: Yeah.

TB: Who were some of the people there at that time?

MB: Dempsey Travis was there. Harold Washington.

TB: Johnny Hartman went to DuSable at about that time.

MB: Yes, he went to DuSable. He was one of the big stars in "Hi-Jinks." There was also the saxophone player, Gene Ammons.

TB: Was he there when you were there?

MB: Uh-huh. And I'll tell you who else, John Johnson. Let me tell you what I did for him. Now, he was ahead of me, and he was publisher of the newspaper, the *Phillips Cite*. Do you remember that?

TB: Sure, sure.

MB: Well, the *Phillips Cite* did not change its name. It went right on over to Du-Sable and kept the same name.

TB: That's right.

MB: So, through the years, I had saved some of these newspapers where it was mentioned that I had made the honor roll, and I was going through all this stuff because I had to throw away some things. Well, Hermene was going down to see Mr. Johnson [co-owner and publisher of *Ebony* magazine] about something she was doing, and I got this paper out and his picture was on the front of the paper. I told Hermene, "Take this to Mr. Johnson and tell him this is wearing out from age, and if he wants this, he can have it." So she went down there and she said, "My mother sent you something, Mr. Johnson," and he looked at that picture, and he said, "Where am I at on here?" I told Hermene I know that he doesn't look *that* much different, and I'm sure that he can find himself if he just tries a little harder!" [*Laughter.*]

But he took that picture I sent to him, and I bet you he had it framed.

TB: Did you continue to live at Thirty-first Street?

MB: Oh, no, no, no! I went to Alfred Tennyson for one year. That was on the West Side. Then I came back to the South Side, and I lived at Fiftieth and St. Lawrence. That was a very nice neighborhood.

TB: Sure was. It was close to Willard School.

MB: Right.

TB: What was that neighborhood like then?

MB: We were living at Fiftieth and St. Lawrence, and it was a fine, fine neighborhood. Working people. We lived in that big courtyard building there. It is torn down now.

TB: Yes, it is. Things like that really make you want to cry because there are so many memories to these old buildings.

MB: That was a fine neighborhood. Over there in that area, everybody went to Fiftieth Street because Fiftieth Street was your business area back then, if you can remember that.

TB: Yeah, I remember that.

MB: See, Fifty-first Street at that time was a park, and you had all your big stores on Fiftieth. We had Jacobs Clothing where the ladies used to buy all their stockings. Did you know Scotty Piper?

TB: Scotty, yeah.

MB: Well, Scotty Piper lived up over me in the same building I lived in.

TB: Scotty was a tailor.

MB: He made the clothes for all the show people.

TB: Yeah, Duke, Basie . . .

MB: Now, I'll tell you another thing. We haven't mentioned the Warwick and the Forum Hall, but those places on Forty-seventh to Forty-third were where we had all of our proms.

TB: And also at Bacon's?

MB: Yes, at Bacon's Casino at Forty-ninth and Wabash. That's where all the schools had their proms, especially DuSable. We had all our big proms there.

TB: It was classic.

MB: Oh, yeah!

TB: Very classic! That place later became the USO.

MB: Oh, yes, Mayor Kelly's wife came out and made it a center that was used for the soldiers.

TB: Is that right? See, I was in the army overseas so I didn't get a chance to go there.

MB: Oh, yeah! Well, they really had it going, and all of the young women would volunteer to come in there and serve the soldiers and dance with them.

TB: The soldiers really enjoyed coming to Chicago.

MB: Ooh, yeah, we laid the red carpet out for them!

TB: They said, "We liked to come to Chicago because folks treated us so nice."

MB: Now, back in those days, Joe Louis became a champion too, and I was working at the Rhumboogie.

TB: Oh, did you work at the 'Boogie?

MB: Yes, I worked there from the day it opened until the day it closed. I was a cashier.

TB: So you know Little Joe from Chicago?

MB: Oh, yes. Joe Jacobson Johnson was the producer of the shows, and he really laid the carpet out for the soldiers.

TB: At the 'Boogie?

MB: Yeah, that's why they used to love to come here.

TB: Did you know Herb Jefferies? His brother used to hang around the 'Boogie a lot.

MB: I knew all of them.

TB: Who were some of the musicians that you remember from back then?

MB: T-Bone Walker. Arnett Cobb.

TB: Wasn't he with Jay McShann or somebody?

MB: When Arnett first came here from Texas, Charlie Glenn owned the 'Boogie then. Charlie went down south and found Arnett and brought his whole band up here. When they got here, they had never been out of the South before, and they didn't know nothing, and they didn't have nothing.

[*Laughter.*]

But he really went on to make it pretty big.

TB: Yeah, he was a great saxophone player.

MB: Moms Mabley, she was at the Rhumboogie. Bill "Bojangles" Robinson, he always came to the Rhumboogie when he came to town.

TB: Were you there when Coleman Hawkins came through town?

MB: I was there when everybody came! Now, I'll tell you who used to wash the dishes, and Charlie never would let him get on the stage. That was George Kirby!

[*Laughter.*]

George Kirby was working in the kitchen, and he would imitate everybody, and he used to tell Charlie, "Let me do it one night. Only one night! Just let me get out there," he used to tell Charlie. "Let me do it one night. Only one night! Just let me get out there one night, and let me do it!" But Charlie would never let him do it. So George went over to the DeLisa, and they let him do it!

TB: And then he became famous.

MB: And then he became very famous. I'll tell you who else I remember. Joe Williams, I remember him when he couldn't even get a job!

TB: Eckstine, was he still around?

MB: No, no, Eckstine was doing good in those days. He was a little bit too big for us.

TB: Were you at the 'Boogie when Sarah came there? Sarah Vaughan.

MB: Oh, yeah, but she was pretty big even then, and we couldn't afford those who were real big even though Charlie had made a lot of them stars.

TB: Do you know where the Pioneer Lounge used to be? That's where Austin Powell and the Cats and the Fiddle used to play.

MB: Oh sure, and don't leave out the DuSable Hotel.

TB: Oh, my gracious, yes!

MB: And don't leave out the Pershing Hotel! Do you remember the Beige Room?

TB: Where was it?

MB: In the Pershing Hotel.

TB: Oh, yes, yes, yes! That's where Earl Hines had his band.

MB: That was upstairs. The Beige Room was in the basement. When you wanted to take your girl out, that's where you went. Now, the DuSable Hotel, that's where you went for breakfast. Do you remember Kai's?

TB: Yeah.

MB: Everybody left the nightclubs and went over to Kai's for breakfast, and he was noted for his biscuits. That's where you went and got bacon and eggs, grits and biscuits.

[*Laughter.*]

Yes, the DuSable Hotel was really noted for their breakfast.

TB: And that's where a lot of out-of-town show people used to stay.

MB: Oh, that's where they all stayed, either at the DuSable or the Pershing. Those were our two big hotels, and that's where they all stayed because, as you know, we did not go downtown in those days.

TB: No, and we really didn't have to.

MB: That's right. We didn't have to, and I think I resent that today. I don't mind going downtown. It's fine, but I feel like I shouldn't have to, and the reason why I feel like that is because we had such fine places to go to right here. Remember on Sunday afternoons we used to go to the Brass Rail at Forty-seventh?

TB: Oh, yeah, yeah, what was the name of that band?

MB: Nelson Sykes and the Brass Rails, and on Sunday afternoons it was nothing to see all those big cars sitting out there at Calumet and Forty-seventh. Everybody went in there for cocktails.

TB: Might even be Lena Horne . . .

MB: Yeah, anybody who came to Chicago! I went to all those places, and I always had a good time! It was like you said. We didn't ever have to go downtown, for clothes, for nothing!

TB: In fact, back then, folks were coming here to have a great time!

MB: Oh yes! The DeLisa had their breakfast stand on Saturday night, Sunday morning. Rhumboogie had their breakfast stand Sunday night, Monday morning, and that's when they came in from the North Side and all over.

[*Laughter.*]

TB: So after the war, what happened?

MB: Now, during the war, that's when women started working in the war industries, Ford and—

TB: Chrysler.

MB: At all the big plants, and that's when people really began to have money, and they started buying property, and it was affluent here on the South Side.

TB: What about the newcomers who came during the war from the South?

MB: Those people came here to work. They were not looking for welfare. When people come to work, they have a different perspective than people that were coming in here in the later years just to get on welfare. Those are the people, in my idea, who never made the adjustment to living in the city.

HH: Let me ask you something. During the first migration, is it a possibility that the first wave, if you will, were an upper class of folks who came here for work purposes — and then after them came the sharecroppers who were another wave and another class of people. Black folks, we never divide ourselves up into class, but we have to realize that from day one out of Africa, we have always had our own class system. White folks made us think of ourselves as monolithic, but we have always been divided among ourselves. "You work inside the house, I work in the fields," therefore, even then, that was a class division. "You were the Pullman porter, I worked in the stockyards." That was another class thing, and it seems to me that the first wave who came here, they came with a different attitude, but they were also a different class, and they came here for work. Whereas, when the sharecroppers came, it wasn't that they weren't looking for work, but they had a dependent attitude because down there you just worked for the white man, and he gave you what he wanted you to have. But that wasn't that first generation. That was the second and third generation who came up north.

TB: Well, you are right about the first wave. When your mother and I came to Chicago as infants, our parents were people who voluntarily just picked up and left the South. They did not like the conditions they were living under. Whether they had money or didn't have money, they came north because they were running away from that Jim Crow system.

MB: Right.

HH: Right.

TB: And then, when they got here, they wanted their children to go to school. They were tickled to death for us to get through high school.

HH: Well, that's what I am saying. It's like you both say. You both have been here since you were one year old, and you became really the first generation of the northern experience. Your parents were really pioneers and true entrepreneurial types.

MB: Right!

HH: It's like if you listen to what Michael Jackson's father said. He said something that I think is reflective of what I am trying to capture. He was a steel mill worker, and when he had his kids singing and dancing on Saturdays after work, he said he had only one goal, "They will not know the steel mill. They will not have that experience. They will never know the steel mill." Your parents were saying, "My children, they ain't gonna know cotton! They ain't gonna know the tobacco picking! They are not going to know sharecropping!"

TB: My father actually did not go back south unless a brother or somebody died!

HH: My father too.

MB: About ten or twelve years ago, her father said to her, "I want to go to New Orleans."

HH: He wanted to take me and my cousin Diane to see where he came from. He felt that it was important. Before then, he had never had any desire to go back. He had no desire to let me see it or, for all practical purposes, to even talk about it. Whenever he talked about his past, he always called it "the Great Escape." Those were his words!

TB: So that makes your point about the reason people left at different periods of time. Now, there was also an in-between group of relatively young people who left when the war industries opened up. When Mr. Randolph made the demand that blacks be included in the war industry, a large number of young black folks left the South and came to the North. So this is between 1941 and 1945. Now comes 1945, and the war is over, and the war industry is shutting down, but some of that group are entrenched up here, and so now you have a whole new group as a result of the war. The cotton industry is literally kaput! And the sharecroppers and all those who worked on the plantations now have no place to go. Most of them are from Arkansas, Mississippi, from rural agricultural communities with almost no urban experience . . .

HH: And no labor skills.

TB: Yes, with no labor skills, which is quite different from that first migration, and even different from that interim migration!

HH: So then this group comes here and maybe went into the stockyards?

TB: Only temporarily, because the stockyards are beginning to close down.

HH: The steel mills?

TB: They also began to close down.

MB: Yes, the stockyards closed down in '56 or '57.

TB: Somewhere around there.

HH: So they got the tail wind of that.

TB: They also got the tail wind of McCormick, but all of those industries were beginning to leave the city or else close down altogether, and these are folks who came here primarily to work. They ain't talking about school now.

HH: Right!

TB: They wanted their children to work because that's what they were accustomed to in the rural agricultural areas. School was not important. Working was important. So now you are beginning to see a change in the kind of people in our community.

MB: Let me say this: There has always been a division between West Side people and South Side people. Always has been and there still is. That has not changed. When people from the West Side came over here, they felt that they were stepping up. And when we went over to the West Side, we were stepping down. Now, we didn't just go anywhere. When we went over to the West Side, we had reserved tables, and they laid the red carpet out for us, but even so, all the time we were there we felt like we were slumming.

TB: Many of that group of people were never able to make the move to the next level because all the opportunities had left.

HH: Well, what about city jobs, county jobs?

TB: The South Siders had already gobbled all those up. Of course, there were a few people like [John] Stroger. Stroger [now Cook County board president] snuck in.

HH: But I'm not talking at that level. I'm talking about patronage.

MB: Let me tell you what my experience with the patronage was. They gave us jobs, but the jobs they gave were the kind of jobs that our people did not want. The jobs they gave us were maintenance jobs, which most of our people did not want because we were very well educated.

TB: You are talking about South Siders.

MB: Yeah, but on the South Side at least some of us were able to get clerical jobs in the census office.

TB: But you had to have an education.

MB: Yeah, that's right! And we didn't have many jobs like that, but I'll tell you who got a lot of bailiff jobs: the whites.

TB: The Irish, Polish, Italians . . .

MB: And during the war, they hired some black policemen. They hired them, but they did not call them "policemen." They called them "temporaries." They had temporary policemen on the police force. Some of them were made regulars afterward and some of them were not, but all of those jobs were patronage. You had to know somebody to get one of those jobs. The post office, the police force . . .

TB: The fire department.

MB: And we still don't have that many firemen. The fire department was always one of the toughest places for black people to get jobs. Then, after the war, Ford and all those other kinds of plants started hiring and paying halfway decent wages, and black people began buying property.

TB: Where were they buying property?

MB: Woodlawn was great. I'll tell you an area that is going down now which was fine back then: Englewood. We were buying homes in that area over there. We had a fine shopping area over there.

TB: The Sixty-third Street shopping district.

MB: Sears Roebuck and many other stores like that.

TB: They had just about everything.

MB: It's too bad to see Englewood go down like it has because it used to be so nice.

TB: It was really very nice, and another thing that happened about that same time was that some black families from the South Side moved out west to Douglas Park for a little while.

MB: That's when Garfield Park and Douglas Park also became nice places to live.

TB: But then after a while some of them moved back because of the culture clash.

MB: That's right.

TB: There is also a little area of black people who had been living on the West Side just about as long as black people have been here on the South Side, but when that new wave of people came in, they were just like the folks on the South Side in their attitude toward the newcomers.

MB: Yeah, they had a little class thing of their own going on, but even with that little class thing that they had going, they still had a special feeling about the people on the South Side. It has never left. I worked with one of them, and I was shocked when I heard her on the phone one day. Her son got married, and he moved over here. He lived somewhere in Hyde Park, and I heard her on the phone saying, "Now, don't you forget now that you are over on that South Side, and don't you ever forget you are over on the South Side!" I couldn't believe that she was saying something like that because of her own family's prominent background on that West Side, but that just goes to show you that the class thing still exists!

TB: How long have you been living here in this house?

MB: We have been in here for twenty years.

TB: So where were you before?

MB: Lake Meadows. Hermene was raised in Lake Meadows.

TB: You still have an apartment down there?

MB: No.

TB: But your name is still in the phone book.

HH: That's my father's apartment.

MB: That's Herman's apartment. Yeah, his second wife is still there.

TB: Oh, I see.

MB: When Hermene was a baby, we lived at Sixtieth and Indiana, and then we moved to Lake Meadows, and we were in Lake Meadows for twenty-two years.

TB: Lake Meadows was pretty new then.

HH: Then, when I got married, we lived in South Shore at 7428 South Chapel. We stayed there for about two or three years, and then we moved here.

TB: What are some of the most important changes you have experienced or seen since the time that you came to Chicago in 1922 or '23?

MB: Some of the most drastic changes have been in housing, education, and schooling. We also used to have one of the finest health systems in the country here. All our schools had nurses. If you got sick in school, you went to the nurse, and the nurse would decide whether you go home or call your mother, but all that has changed. I never saw that anymore even when Hermene went to school. I don't remember that they even had a school nurse. Getting back to politics, Dawson, when he was in Congress, he thought he was doing something for his people when he built those projects. Those places were built at the same time as Lake Meadows. Some of the same cabinets they had in those projects were exactly the same things they had in Lake Meadows. Now, I have never been in Robert Taylor and neither has my daughter, but Ida B. Wells was the first one they built, and at first it was fine. You had to know somebody to get in there. Now, of course, it has gone down and become tenements, but that was not that man's dream or intentions. That generation that you just got through talking about never learned how to live in a place like that! Lake Meadows itself would be one of the biggest tenements in the city if it wasn't for the type of people who live there. The people there keep up their apartments, but where they live wouldn't be anything more than any other high-rise building if it wasn't for the class of people that live there. I lived in Lake Meadows twenty-two years, and I lived on the tenth floor.

TB: In which building?

MB: In 3440.

TB: That's one of the first buildings.

MB: It was Building Four. When you live down there, they don't call your address. They say you live in Building Four or some other building. I walked up only one time in twenty-two years to that tenth floor. During that time when the elevator was broken, I was working at night, and since it was at night when I came back, the guard walked up with me and then walked back down. By the next morning, the elevator was working again. That was an elevator building, and we could have had some of the same problems they have in the projects, but in Lake Meadows if your child was reported three times, they called you into the office and asked you to move because they said you were just not suited to live there. The kids in Lake Meadows didn't get on the elevator and punch every single floor! Children raised in those buildings lived just as if they were raised in a home. When you got tall enough to punch the elevator, you punched your own floor. You didn't get on there and punch every floor.

TB: They didn't play around with it.

MB: That's right. They had playgrounds, and you played in the playground.

TB: Did they screen you before you got in there?

MB: Oh yeah, they wanted to know what school you went to when I moved in there, and they had a nice class of people there. If you came out of apartments or homes and did not know how to live there, they taught you, and you were open and re-

MILDRED BOWDEN AND HERMENE HARTMAN   257

ceptive to having a nice place to live, and so you learned what you had to do to keep it nice. But then came the influx of people that you talked about, and they did not even try to learn how to use those elevators and all the other things that they needed to know.

HH: Mother, don't say that! Don't say they didn't try. They might have had some conditions and some restraints and some other conditional things that did not allow them to establish the right kind of standards.

TB: Yes, when you look at Ida B. Wells now, there is a great difference between then and now.

HH: That's right.

TB: I think what your mother is saying essentially is that the difference today in the folks that live there is in regard to their discipline and training. My cousin lived in Ida B. Wells when Oscar Brown's father was a manager, and it was hard to get in there.

MB: Everybody had their own lawn, and everybody took care of their own little yard.

TB: But if you pass there now, you don't see much of that. But, even today, there is still a difference between a place like that and places like the Robert Taylor Homes.

MB: I think it has definitely separated us because, I mean, you just don't know anybody who lives in Robert Taylor, and I don't want to know anybody. I never was the kind of person who felt uppity or biggity or better than anybody, but I don't have no reason to go over there, and there is no reason for them to come over here, and so we are absolutely—

TB: Separated!

MB: We are like foreigners to each other. We are absolutely foreigners.

TB: But you and Hermene are more fortunate than they are.

MB: Well, maybe so.

[*Laughter.*]

TB: Maybe we all are!

July 29, 1995

LOUIS CALDWELL

ACTIVIST AND FORMER STATE REPRESENTATIVE

Louis Caldwell was in the truest sense an activist. He was a very active husband, father, grandfather, and friend (of which he had many). He was active in education, business, religion, and other community affairs. And he was active in politics.

I first heard of "Louie" Caldwell just before I was inducted into the army in World War II, in 1943. As an active board member of the Chicago Urban League, he had started an organization named the Negro Chamber of Commerce. Its purpose was to encourage the development and support of black businesses on the black South Side of Chicago. It was to counteract the near-monopoly of small businesses in the black community by whites, particularly the prosperous Forty-seventh Street. The white businesspeople had an organization named the Forty-seventh Street Businessmen's Association that denied blacks membership in it and, because of white land owner-ship, restricted black leases to only certain kinds of businesses, such as barbershops, taverns, restaurants. These restrictions severely reduced the control of money spent by blacks. The one big exception was Policy—"the numbers"—which was illegal but was blinked at by city officials and tolerated (until later) by the organized mobsters.

Mr. Caldwell in the 1940s wrote his master's thesis on this particular activity and its importance in the black community as a wealth and job generator. His thesis re-search revealed that during the period researched, this Policy business grossed more than ten million dollars per year and created hundreds of well-paying jobs for resi-dents in the community. When the mobsters learned of this flow of money through a conversation with Ed Jones while he was imprisoned for tax evasion, they were amazed and decided to take over the Policy business.

During this period, Senator Estes Kefauver of Tennessee, an aspirant for the Democratic presidential nomination, accused Illinois Congressman William Dawson of condoning and harboring these illegal activities. As a result, the control of this business and income to the black community drastically diminished. However, this did not diminish Caldwell's activism or dedication to the social, cultural, political, and economic well-being of his community, Policy being just one of his interests.

In the 1970s he ran for state representative and won. He served three two-year terms. In addition to other liberal bills that he introduced or supported, he introduced one that would legalize Policy as a lottery game. The profits to be gained by this legislation were to be used for public schools. The bill won, and now what used to be illegal is legal. Unfortunately, the legal lottery has not resulted in better education funding by the state.

Mr. Caldwell has since died, but his legacy lives on. He was one of black Chicago's most dedicated heroes. It was indeed enlightening and a delightful pleasure to have this conversation with him.

TB: I remember a little bit myself about a fellow by the name of Jack McGruder, who operated what they called little "sub-stations" of the Policy operation. There were a lot of people — but most of them were women — who would go and put their numbers in at one of Jack's sub-stations, which were all over the South Side. Jack didn't own the wheel, but he had those sub-stations where you could go any time of the day or night. You didn't have to wait for your runner to come. You could just go put your number in right there.

LC: Well, of course, this is during the Depression, and you've got women sitting around all day with nothing to do, and they're bored as hell and just trying to figure out something to do to keep them from going stir crazy. So Policy really became very popular with them.

TB: As a social outlet?

LC: Yeah, social, but also —

TB: Well, there was also the potential for them to make a little money.

LC: That's right.

TB: Now, at that time, the greatest upsurge of activity was on Forty-seventh Street, of course.

LC: Yeah, back then, I would say — other than Harlem — that was the capital of black America!

TB: Well, when my family first came to Chicago, we moved to a place at Forty-ninth and St. Lawrence, and we always used to go to Thirty-fifth Street for entertainment. As a matter of fact, most of my daddy's friends were living somewhere around Thirty-fifth Street, and sometimes he would take us there. Two of the places that I remember going to are the Mecca Building and also the Vincennes Hotel because he had friends who were living there.

LC: The Vincennes Hotel! I used to go there with Hattie when I was in high school. Later on, she married Ulysses Keyes.

TB: Ulysses Keyes the lawyer?

LC: Yeah, and she trained him because in those days he couldn't speak correctly, and used to split verbs and things like that. He was working for the post office, and that's how he worked his way through law school. Later on, he ended up being the editorial writer for the *Bee*. That was Old Man Overton's newspaper.

TB: That was Mr. Overton of Overton Hygiene, wasn't it?

LC: That's right.

TB: And he also owned a bank, didn't he?

LC: Yes, the Overton National Bank at Thirty-sixth and State. He built that building, and that's also where he had the offices for that newspaper. You see Mr. Overton originally started the *Bee* as a public relations vehicle to promote his business activities, which were the Overton National Bank, the Overton Hygiene Company, and the Victory Life Insurance Company.

TB: I understand that he also helped to organize the Supreme Life Insurance Company.

LC: No, he didn't. That was T. K. Gibson, a guy who looked like he was white. Gibson came here from Columbus, Ohio, where he had a music shop and also his own little insurance company. Well, Gibson, Harry Pace, and Jefferson Ish, who was from Nashville, they all got together, and they organized and combined four small black insurance companies. That's how they started Supreme Life, and I still remember how much it impressed me at that time that these Negroes had sense enough to pool their resources like that. That was my theme song then—and it still is now!

TB: In what year did that merger occur?

LC: In 1920, and that building where they were located was where a white bank had been, you know?

TB: Yes, at Thirty-fifth and what is now King Drive.

LC: Yeah, and there was another bank like that at Forty-seventh and State, and another one was at Forty-third and Cottage Grove. You can still see the buildings where those banks were, but they all went down during the Depression and never opened again.

TB: Don't forget Jesse Binga's bank.

LC: Yeah, the Binga State Bank. He was also in the real estate business, and he lived in that building on the corner of Sixtieth and King Drive.

TB: So, what you're saying is that back then there was a thriving business community here, as well as entertainment, which attracted people and investment to come into the community.

LC: Yeah, but, even back then, all the entertainment was controlled by the whites. We had little bands that played at our own private dances, and the Jews and all the other white folks seemed to like those swing bands we had. I guess down in New Orleans they didn't mind our kind of music too much either, because that's where Louis Armstrong originated. Then, of course, he came up here, and that's when the white folks would come to the Negro community not just to listen to our music but also to learn how to play it. So young guys like Benny Goodman would come here from the West Side and places like that, and they got so good at playing it that at night after hours they would jam in private with our guys. But the places where those guys were playing *publicly* were places like the Aragon and the Trianon ballrooms, which was owned by Andrew Kartis (a Greek), and that's when the Jews began to take control. They realized that they had been losing out by not having black musicians. Black music had an altogether different sound with different tunes and different everything, and it attracted white people just as much as black people, and so they started hiring black musicians in those places where they'd only had white musicians before. But before they could really get it going for them, a lot of those niggers they were hiring went to Europe on tours, and they never came back!

TB: They began to feel a sense of freedom over there.

LC: Yeah, that's right. It was so different from the way things were in this country.

TB: Going back to what you were saying, there was a community of black jazz musicians here in Chicago that allowed young white guys like Benny Goodman and Dave Tough and Eddie Condon to come in and learn how to play our kind of music.

LC: Yeah, and those guys didn't really know exactly what they were doing except that it felt better to them when they were doing it, and that's what they kept on doing and getting paid for doing.

TB: Do you remember the Grand Terrace?

LC: Oh, man, the Grand Terrace was at King Drive and the Elevated! But the important thing to remember is that, once the white folks took it over, Negroes couldn't go to places like that anymore because they were not accepted. White folks would come here from the suburbs and from all the other parts of town for entertainment, but Negroes couldn't even attend those places and hear their own kind of music!

TB: But, coming back now to the developing cohesion within our own business community, a major contribution to this was initiated by you when you established the Negro Chamber of Commerce. What was it that sparked your interest in doing something like that?

LC: I wasn't trying to make no history or anything. I was just doing what comes naturally and also trying to give a little thought to what I was trying to do—and so I started doing a little research, and I found out what was really going on and what still needed doing. But, as a matter of fact, I got my greatest business training back when I was selling ice cream for Old Man Baldwin. You see, what I saw was that he didn't know what the hell he was doing, and I knew he had something I could grab hold of and make something out of.

TB: He really didn't know what a gold mine he had.

LC: No, and he was so intent on being the "boss" that he didn't even know if he had a gold mine or not! So I said to him, "Listen, you told me a year after I was first here that the doctors had told you to get out of Chicago for the winter, and, no matter what the situation here is, you want to stay alive, don't you?" So Old Man Baldwin thought it over and called me at home and said, "Caldwell, you're right. I'm going to do what the doctors said. I'm going to take Lettie and get out of here, and I want you to take charge of the business." I said, "Hold it! That's all very flattering, but before you go, we better have a meeting, not only with you and your doctor, but with you and your family, and also with you and your lawyer because I don't want that kind of responsibility unless I also have the authority to back it up. Responsibility without authority just won't work!" So, anyway, to make a long story short, I made him call a family meeting, and I explained to them what the problem was, and finally he said, "Well, all right, you're right. I'll leave, and you can be in charge." So then in about a week he left, but the nigger didn't tell me he was going to take all the company's cash with him!

[*Laughter.*]

At that time we took in eight or ten thousand dollars on a weekend, and that nigger took every damned cent. I mean, if you're going to steal some money, at least *please* leave enough so we can do a little business!

[*Laughter.*]

Well, on that Monday morning when I came in, his sister, she was looking kind of sheepish, and so I said, "What's the problem?" She said, "Mr. Caldwell, Mr. Baldwin took all the money we took in, and he owes this and owes that—and how are we going to pay all these bills?" So I said, "Well, let's see now. Can you sign checks?" She said, "Yeah," and I said, "Who else can sign?" "Well, I don't know," and so I said, "Well, let me tell you something. Cornelius"—that's Old Man Baldwin's son, his only son—"he's also been stealing money from the cash register and lying about it and trying to cheat the guys who work out in the plant, and now is the time when this kind of thing has got to stop!" So now this woman I'm talking to is Baldwin's sister, and this is an intelligent woman, but she hasn't had much experience in administration, and the reason why she doesn't have any experience like that is because Old Man Baldwin never gave her any authority. So I said to her, "Well, here's the situation," and we talked it over and decided to just wait it out. Well, Mr. Baldwin was gone three months out there in California, and by the time he got back, I'd changed the whole operation and made a real business out of it. That's when I learned a lot of the stuff that I never would have learned anyplace else, and I don't care how many degrees you have. It's experience like that that counts.

TB: What about your relations with Mr. Baldwin when he came back and saw what you had done?

LC: The only thing Old Man Baldwin ever got upset about was when somebody would come in, and I'd give them one of our half gallons of ice cream for free, and I would say, "Give your friends some of this and have yourselves a little party!" You see, Mr. Baldwin, he wouldn't spend no money for advertising, and that's how I was getting some free advertising for us. So then I tried doing the same sort of thing and arranged to give out samples in the grocery stores, and I would keep records of how much they sold the week before and the week following. Those records showed that my strategy worked, and pretty soon all the white companies, they wanted to buy into what we were doing.

TB: Where were you located?

LC: At Fifty-third and State. When I first started working there, I really didn't know a damned thing about the dairy business—so I went to school to find out, and I even joined the Dairymen's Association. As a matter of fact, when they had their national convention two or three years later, I was the only Negro on their organizing committee. So for ten years I stayed with Baldwin, and it wasn't easy because every time I'd take a day off that's when Old Man Baldwin did his devilment.

TB: I remember seeing those trucks of yours delivering ice cream to all the stores in the neighborhood.

LC: Well, as a matter of fact, we had only two delivery trucks of our own. Everything else was handled by vendors that bought a route from us, but people thought that Baldwin had nearly a dozen delivery trucks of its own because the company paid a fee to other independently owned trucks for carrying our name on their sides, and all those pimps driving them rode all around here every day. That's why people thought Baldwin had nearly a dozen trucks.

TB: And that was your way of getting more publicity.

LC: Yeah, and establishing an image of success, because if you are successful enough, then they don't care who you are or what color you are. They only see green.

September 10, 20, and 21, 1991

ALVIN "AL" BOUTTE

BUSINESSMAN AND BANKER

If there is a single individual who could claim credit for the continuous search for in-dependent "black power" through the combination of business and politics, that per-son would be Alvin Boutte. There are many others, such as automobile sales magnate Al Johnson, who were also constant and consistent in their support, but Al Boutte, starting out from a clearly defined political-economic position, was the one who was most responsible for the success of so many politicians and small African-American businesses in Chicago.

Though he was raised in Louisiana and went to school there all the way through Xavier University, he came directly to Chicago after his term of service in Korea as an army captain. He immediately adopted Chicago as his permanent home, and black Chicago adopted him likewise. In his early career, Boutte started a chain of black-owned and-staffed drugstores, and, because of his difficulties in obtaining financing for his business ventures, he joined with successful hair products entrepreneur George Johnson to establish the Independence Bank at Seventy-ninth and Cottage Grove to encourage the successful development of small black community-based businesses.

His active participation in the politics of the Third Ward aided the rise of the late Congressman Ralph Metcalfe to a position of political power in Chicago. Later on, he joined with Ed Gardner, Al Johnson, and publisher John H. Johnson to organize the black business community in supporting and financing the mayoral campaign of Harold Washington in 1982 and 1983. (White money shied away from Harold at that time despite the efforts and pleas of Edwin "Bill" Berry.)

Al Boutte is one of the many unsung heroes of black Chicago and of the nation as well. He tells his story well, and it is important that we listen carefully to what he has to say.

———

TB: Let's talk a little bit about your family.

AB: Well, I was born on October 10, 1929. My mother's maiden name was Darrenceburg. She came from a family of what you might say were Creoles or mulattos. They were primarily plasterers and people who worked in construction.

TB: So they were employed in the skilled trades area.

AB: Yes, and in those days blacks dominated that industry in Louisiana. My dad was from a little town called Reserve, Louisiana, and although his family was a very fine family, they were not considered to be at quite the same social level as my mother's.

TB: You first came to Chicago in about 1956, didn't you?

AB: A little before that. The year '53 or maybe '54.

TB: And then, when you got here, you operated at the maximum, and very soon you had seven pharmacies.

AB: That was my training.

TB: And then you were on the school board.

AB: That was in the late sixties.

TB: And you also went into the banking business.

AB: Yes, in 1964.

TB: The reason for that was there was no viable financial institution in the black community that was controlled by black people at that time. Where did you get your training?

AB: I got my training from Ted Roberts, who was at Harris Trust. He was formerly president of the Federal Reserve Bank of St. Louis, and he was also chief executive officer of Talman at one time.

TB: You were in good fortune to have someone like that to show you the ropes. How long did it take you to work with him before you felt comfortable enough to go off on your own?

AB: Two years.

TB: You already had some experience handling finances, didn't you?

AB: Sure, I had run businesses before.

TB: Your first business was where?

AB: Forty-seventh Street and Lake Park.

TB: What was the composition of the neighborhood like back then?

AB: It was almost all white.

TB: And the business you bought had formerly been owned by whites?

AB: Yes, it was a drugstore that had been owned by a man named Tom McCorley, and when I bought it, what I did was considered to be very controversial in those days because there weren't any blacks in that neighborhood.

TB: Much less in businesses that they owned!

AB: The first year or two, very few people even knew that I owned that store. They thought I just worked there. McCorley's son kept working for me, and that was my first venture.

TB: And then you expanded that venture to seven more. In the meanwhile, you became interested in civic life in Chicago, didn't you?

AB: Yes, my first taste of political life was in Ralph Metcalfe's office over at Forty-seventh Street.

TB: And that's where you first met a young man by the name of Harold Washington.

AB: And also Kenneth Wilson. I don't know if you remember Kenneth Wilson.

TB: Oh, yes, he became a judge. He was a county commissioner.

AB: And Cecil Partee.

TB: Who later became the city treasurer.

AB: We all used to hang out there in Metcalfe's office.

TB: Did you ever go down the street and eat any of Mack's chili?

AB: Sure!

TB: The Walgreens drugstore was still there.

AB: And the Palm was there in those days. Remember the Palm?

TB: The Palm Tavern? Yes, of course.

AB: Oh, it was a thriving street in those days. That's before all the department stores left, Tim. The Sutherland Hotel was there, and in those days—I'm talking about the 1950s—black musicians were limited as to where they could play.

TB: Not only where they could play, but also where they could live.

AB: Yes, also where they could live, and the Sutherland had some of the best entertainment in the country. It was just incredible!

TB: Greats like Dizzy Gillespie and Miles Davis.

AB: The first time I ever heard Aretha Franklin was at the Sutherland. The first time I ever saw Redd Foxx was at the Sutherland. They had some of the greatest black entertainers in the world!

TB: Such as the late Hazel Scott.

AB: Right, and Billie Holiday! The last time I saw Billie Holiday—this was just before she died—was there.

TB: So at that time the whole area from the lake all the way to State Street on Forty-seventh Street was alive.

AB: Yes, but not only alive musically. They also had black financial institutions there in those days. That's where Service Payroll was. Illinois Federal was on Forty-seventh Street in those days.

TB: That was in the Rosenwald, wasn't it?

AB: Right. The Rosenwald was a big deal because it was the first housing development for blacks. It was a cooperative. In fact, it was the first black cooperative in the United States.

TB: That's right.

AB: Julius Rosenwald had funded that and subsidized it on the basis of an idea which was given to him by the man that the Robert Taylor Homes on State Street is named after. But in those days there were no blacks on Seventy-ninth Street. There were no blacks on Eighty-seventh Street. I mean, we just hadn't come out here that far at that time. Fifty-fifth Street was the place that was developing, and it was where the old nightclubs were.

TB: The Rhumboogie and the DeLisa!

AB: Yes, but Forty-seventh Street was *the* street!

TB: But now, of course, things have changed a great deal.

AB: And when we examine those changes in our community—and we can go into education, into economic development, into business, into entertainment—if you track where we were prior to the civil rights movement and then track what has happened since, in every case you will find a process going on which has required the development of a different sort of individual with a different type of skills and training than those that were developed during the civil rights movement.

TB: Yes, you can't rerun saying, "Up against the wall!" Now you have to come into the corporate room, and you have got to come in with the same intent but with a different language, as well as certain other factors.

AB: Yes, and that process is still going on. If you will track the institutions of America and contrast what we have been with what we now have, you will see that we are still so far from where we want to be. It is pitiful. But, if you look at history, history will tell you what we now need to do to improve this situation. For example, colonialism—and I am now talking about mainly the history of Africa—has made a great impact on us here. You know the first African country to get its freedom was Ghana, and that's only been fifty years ago, Tim. So you are talking about an extremely short span of history.

TB: It was 1956!

AB: That's right, Tim. You know, in many ways segregation had a stabilizing effect on the community. Here was where all of the blacks with talent and education lived. They were part of the community. Now they're not. That's one of the tragedies of desegregation!

TB: We are beginning to find that out.

AB: Bill Dawson was the most powerful black politician in those days. Ralph Metcalfe was one of Bill Dawson's protégés.

TB: And around him were people like Kenneth Wilson and Harold Washington. There must have been some exciting discussions up in there!

AB: What we all talked about was watching the development of the black community and the fact that some day an independent political movement would have to be formed. This is where Gus Savage comes in. Gus was one of the first guys in the independent movement.

TB: That's right. He ran as an independent candidate.

AB: He was fearless, because at that time and in that context Daley was so difficult to deal with. Daley would only do business with one or two blacks, no matter what. I mean, first he would call Dawson, and later on, after Dawson died, he got involved with Metcalfe. Then the whole thing changed, but back in those days you only had one or two blacks that Daley would even talk to. He wouldn't discuss anything with anybody else.

TB: But around Dawson there were a lot of competent people.

AB: Oh, very competent, but do you realize that even today there are only six blacks in the Business Hall of Fame in Chicago? One of them is a guy named Earl Dickerson.

TB: Yes, Earl B. Dickerson!

AB: Absolutely, and in those days he was a very powerful independent politician. He and Dawson were friends, but Earl Dickerson became an independent because he was a businessman. He had an independent source of livelihood. He ran Supreme Life. Johnny Johnson also came out of that.

TB: Of the Johnson Publishing Company!

AB: Yes, but this was before Johnson Publishing Company. Earl Dickerson, God bless him!

TB: He died when he was ninety-three or ninety-four, and I had the honor to be called "professor" by him. I thought that was quite an honor coming from this guy because he was one of my heroes. In terms of that particular generation, he and Arch Carey were two guys that I really admired.

AB: Arch Carey was an independent too. Very independent!

TB: They both had an independent background.

AB: But they had the wherewithal to do it, Tim! I mean, that's the difference.

TB: And now you are also being inducted into Chicago's Business Hall of Fame.

AB: Well, I am not in it yet. I am being inducted with Donald Jacobs, the dean of the business school at Northwestern University, and five or six others.

TB: Yes, Charles Lake of R. R. Donnelley; Andrew McKenna of the Schwarz Paper Company; Donald Perkins from Jewel—you have some distinguished company there.

AB: Well, I am very honored to be a part of it.

TB: They should be honored to have you as part of it, I am telling you. Through the years I have learned of your activities and watched them, and I'm sure the rich experiences that you had here in Chicago could hardly have been available to you or a young man like you in Louisiana at that early period of your life.

AB: That's why I left. I had no relatives here and never have had any. I came here because I wanted to live in an area where they had a large number of blacks and where the opportunity was greater than what I knew it to be in Louisiana.

TB: Particularly given your experience then and your education.

AB: Right, I could have chosen New York or someplace in California, but for some reason I just happened to pick Chicago, even though I didn't know a single soul that was living here!

TB: You didn't know anyone here at all?

AB: Well, the only one I knew at all here in Chicago was Ralph Metcalfe because he had been the track coach at Xavier University in New Orleans.

TB: You didn't know the Blackburn brothers back then, did you?

AB: No, I didn't know them at that time.

TB: Henry also went to Xavier.

AB: And Leo went to DePaul, but at that time I didn't know them. The person that I looked up when I came to Chicago was Ralph Metcalfe. He was the one that I depended on. He was the one who was really my sponsor.

TB: Fantastic man. He and my brother went to the same high school, Tilden, and then he went to Marquette. Did you know I went to Xavier in '37, '38? I went down there with Blackburn and Lucius Thomas and that group playing basketball. But I left very early.

AB: Well, Xavier has always been a hotbed for Chicago basketball players. Some of the greatest black basketball players of that era came from Chicago. In terms of basketball, Xavier was a national power in those days!

TB: It really was.

AB: Sweetwater Clifton went to Xavier. I don't know if he played in the NBA in those days.

TB: They would not allow him to play at that time, but later on, of course, he did play in the NBA. In fact, he was one of the first blacks in the NBA. He played with New York.

AB: They had a wealth of athletic talent that came from Chicago—and all of that emanates from you know who? Ralph Metcalfe! Metcalfe was a tremendous recruiter for Xavier. He sent a lot of guys down there, including Jeremy White and Willie Black Braxton.

TB: I know them.

AB: And Warner Saunders. I mean all of these guys were athletes. Xavier had, I think, more athletes from Chicago than any other place.

TB: Well, at that time there was a fairly sizable black Catholic middle-class population in Chicago.

AB: Very much so.

TB: And, of course, here in Chicago we received a number of people from New Orleans and from Xavier, so there was a reciprocity that was involved.

AB: Well, I came here mainly because of Ralph Metcalfe.

TB: So then you obviously became associated with his organization, the Third Ward.

AB: Yes, I was in his organization, and when I needed some guidance or needed something done, he was the man I always went to. He was the one that first introduced me to Mayor Daley. In those days, Tim, blacks did things, even business things, through politics.

TB: Well, not just in those days. It is probably just as true today.

AB: No, it's not quite as true today.

TB: Now they are able to operate more independently?

AB: Oh, much more independently! The first line of credit I ever got to sell liquor in some of my drugstores, I had to go to Ralph because in those days they wouldn't give blacks any credit—so I had to go to Ralph, and Ralph went to Dawson, and Dawson called the wholesale liquor company, and that's how I got a thirty-day line of credit. That's what you did with politics in those days. I mean, politics back then was not just electing someone. It was an essential part of accomplishing the day-to-day things that you needed to get done. That's what politics was!

TB: So about that same time you met a young man by the name of Harold Washington.

AB: Yes, and Harold Washington had an independent streak ever since I've been there. He was always the guy that got up and was making some statement that could get him in trouble. His father used to try to calm him down. His father was also very active, as I'm sure you know, but Harold Washington had a strong independent streak even in those days!

TB: Eventually you sold your businesses, didn't you?

AB: Yes, I sold my businesses to Steinway Ford Hopkins. Remember them?

TB: Yes, I do.

AB: They are not in business any longer. They eventually sold out to Walgreens.

TB: Is that what happened to them? They had stores all over the South Side. So you sold to them? And then you moved into banking. Did you do that right away?

AB: No, in those days, Tim, I had made what I call a "colored" fortune. By that I mean that I had four or five hundred thousand dollars, which was an enormous amount of money in those days, and, frankly, I just rested for two years. I didn't do anything. But in those days if you made thirty or forty thousand dollars a year, that was plenty. Four or five hundred thousand dollars was really a lot of money in those days, and I didn't know exactly what I wanted to do.

TB: What drew you to the bank?

AB: The bank was failing.

TB: This was the Independence Bank?

AB: Yes, and it was failing. When it first started, no one really knew the business, and so George Johnson called me one day. Even though he and I both were associated with the bank, we were not working in it, and he said, "Al, either we are going to have to do something with that bank or get out of it," because our reputations were at stake, and so he and I decided to recapitalize it. That's when I asked Ted Roberts to teach me the business.

TB: What was the original capitalization?

AB: The original capitalization was eight hundred thousand dollars, but when I got here it was down to sixty-nine thousand dollars.

TB: Oh, my Lord! You couldn't meet payroll.

AB: No, but today capitalization is twenty-five million dollars with assets of about three hundred million dollars.

TB: So you are really going to sell it?

AB: We have already signed for about thirty-eight million dollars.

TB: All right! Well, you have done a yeoman service to the community.

AB: Well, Tim, I have got to be very honest with you. This company is worth a lot more than thirty-eight million dollars, but we wanted to sell it to blacks. We bought it black. We sold it black, but the new owner, he's not from Chicago. He's from Columbus.

TB: He did have some experience in Detroit, didn't he?

AB: Yes, he owns a small bank in Detroit. But his main business is that he owns a cable company in five states. He was the first African-American to own a cable company in the United States.

TB: How old are you now?

AB: I am sixty-four.

TB: And George is sixty-seven.

AB: And we both want to retire. I am not well, and now it has got to be the next generation to do whatever needs to be done.

TB: And this young man that has bought the bank is how old?

AB: He is forty-one.

TB: So he is just a little older than you were when you first came into this bank, and now you are passing it over to the next generation.

AB: We bought the bank in '68, but I didn't start working in the bank until '69.

TB: So you were still in your early forties. So this new guy has got some catching up to do. Is he familiar with Chicago?

AB: He is.

TB: Is he going to move here?

AB: He is going to move here. What I have done is taken him around, and now I have shown him just about everything I can.

TB: You and George both can also tell him your own experiences. So the future of the institution continues even though some of the players are leaving.

AB: And I think it will even be stronger.

TB: You really think so?

AB: Yes, because instead of having the two banks which we own now, he now owns three banks, and his vision is to have a series of banks throughout the Midwest.

TB: What is your opinion about Cole Taylor and First National coming up into the Woodlawn area?

AB: I don't have any problem with that, Tim, but I remember the time when there wasn't one black-owned business in downtown Chicago. There wasn't a single one. There was a law firm, but there was not one business.

TB: My brother was in that law firm.

AB: Was he?

TB: Yes, Walter Black.

AB: OK, then you know what I'm talking about! But now, of course, things have changed to some degree. As an example, many of the fast-food businesses in downtown Chicago are owned by blacks.

TB: That's revealing. What about that guy Cirilo McSween?

AB: Oh, Cirilo owns six of them downtown. He owns the one at the Museum of Science and Industry. He owns one at the Art Institute. He owns one at the Field Museum. He owns one at Jackson and Wabash. He just opened a new one in O'Hare Airport.

TB: And he's got one on State Street!

AB: Yes, he's got one on State Street! He also owns one in the Sears Tower.

TB: And there are other guys besides him.

AB: Oh, sure. He's not the only one. He's got the most, but there's blacks all over downtown. There are black advertising agencies, and every one of those black advertising agencies—there are nine of them, the big ones—all of them are downtown. Most of the black public relations firms are downtown. Most of the black law firms are downtown now. Not just McCoy, Ming, and Leighton.

TB: This evolution you're talking about from the South Side or the West Side to the central city, how may that have affected the black coalition and its effect on the politics of the city?

AB: Well, I think it has caused a greater independence among blacks, especially from a political standpoint. That's why you are going to find that it is becoming more and more difficult to get a coalition of blacks, because their interests are so different now. Blacks are moving to the suburbs, Tim. They don't live in Chicago. They want to live in the suburbs.

TB: Sad but true.

AB: Listen, Tim, between all of our companies, we have got a lot of employees. We have about forty officers, but, shit! At least thirty of them live in the suburbs! It's going to get harder and harder to keep the impact of this kind of coalition ticket because blacks are spreading out all over.

TB: Yes, but from another point of view that might mean that, therefore, they will be able to have a greater impact on the political and economic life in more places.

AB: Yes, and it's happening all over America! I just did a bond admission in Louisiana. We have a company there that underwrites bonds, and the people that do this for me went to Louisiana to negotiate this four-hundred-million-dollar bond issue, and the chairman of their finance committee is black! So, it's a new world.

TB: Yes, but it's still a hard world for many younger people who are not properly educated.

AB: Yes, that's true.

TB: I am wondering what you see as the future of the old South Side neighborhood. It still seems to me, strategically and aesthetically, one of the most desirable parts of any American city that one could possibly have.

AB: Yes, you're right. The desirability of the South Side and its accessibility to so much makes it too good for it to ever become nothing. It will turn around sooner or later, but when it does, it may not be all black.

TB: Why is that?

AB: Tim, if you work downtown and try to drive to Schaumburg at four-thirty in the afternoon, just see how long it will take you to get there! I mean, these people are going to get tired of that. It's changing even now!

TB: Yes, I am beginning to see a number of young blacks moving back into this area we were talking about. Those are irreplaceable structures along King Drive and Michigan and back over to Lake Park where your first business was located. You can't ever hope to duplicate buildings like that.

AB: Exactly. One of the great things I do when I travel is I ask a lot of questions, and I love Italy. I have been there six or seven times through the years. In a place like that because of their long history and traditions they make it much harder for you to tear an old building down than to go on some vacant land and build a new building. In order to tear a building down in Italy you almost need an act of Congress, and that is because of what you just said. I mean, they recognize the fact that those old buildings are irreplaceable. When you look at some of that architecture, some of these old buildings, you say, my God, who could possibly build anything like that today!

TB: Well, here on the South Side there are many similarities. As in Italy.

AB: Yes, but on a much smaller scale.

TB: Well, I would claim that old Grand Boulevard has some of that "European" grandeur.

AB: And it will come back, but it is not going to be all black. It's going to be a new constituency.

TB: Al, you were discussing the fact that lots of young black people and some older ones as well now do business from downtown, but we still have small businesses in places like Eighty-seventh Street, Seventy-ninth Street, even Seventy-fifth Street, although Seventy-fifth Street is in deterioration to some extent, and those small businesses are the greatest employer of people.

AB: Yes, by far!

TB: How do we get some piece of that action?

AB: Well, we are getting a piece of that, but what we are not getting is what the blacks consider the visible businesses. But you must remember that the visible businesses change with the needs of the people. There was a time my mother used to make extra money for our family by sewing, and so she purchased a sewing machine. In those days, Tim, I am guessing that seven out of every ten households most likely had a sewing machine, and that is why at that time the Singer Sewing Machine Company was one of the top ten companies.

TB: We had one of those old pedal machines.

AB: But I can tell you this, if you go around to one hundred houses today you probably won't find a single sewing machine. Times have changed and so, therefore, business has also changed. One of our biggest problems is that we are very reluctant to change as a people and to recognize the need for that change. That's why the entry into Woodlawn of Cole Taylor and First National would not bother me. Business is still there. There are still opportunities. Let's take grocery stores. Thirty years ago, do you know the largest grocery store chain in Chicago was A&P? A&P was the first large discount grocery chain, but, even so, you still had an enormous number of small groceries. Every community had at least five or ten grocery stores.

TB: "Ma and pa" groceries.

AB: But now you have five major chains, and the need for a "ma and pa" grocery store no longer exists in today's market. Same thing happened in the business that I was in, and that is why I got out of it. At one time in the city of Chicago, we had seventy-eight black-owned drugstores. Now you have only about fifteen or so.

TB: I don't even know where they are! But I know where yours were, and I still remember where Doxie's were!

AB: Yes, but today the independent drugstore is over. White, black, it doesn't matter now. It's over. So what we have to do is to find new kinds of businesses, and our young people understand this. They are not sitting still and saying we can't do anything. There is a lot of hope. But you can't live back in the 1950s. Today it's the small businesses that have the greatest growth. The number of small businesses today is enormous compared to the Ralph Metcalfe era that you and I have been talking about. But the difference is they aren't all on one street anymore. They are downtown. Every one of these fast-food franchises that Cirilo owns does a million dollars a year. Under our business rules, that means that the owner ought to make 10 percent. So you should be able to make a hundred thousand dollars, and that's why schoolteachers stop teaching and say, "I am going to open my own business." And when you say, "Well, it is too bad Gladys's is closed," what you are forgetting is that the McDonald's down the street is now owned by blacks. The one on Eighty-seventh Street is owned by blacks. In fact, in this neighborhood all the places like that are now owned by blacks.

TB: But does the capital that derives from these places get back into the black community?

AB: Oh, sure. But the black community is not defined anymore as you are describing it. It's way spread out. It's all over the place. Bob Beavers lives in Hinsdale. You have never heard of Bob Beavers?

TB: I have heard the name.

AB: Well, Bob Beavers is the most senior executive in McDonald's, and he is black.

TB: I didn't know that.

AB: And the only time Bob Beavers has ever been to the South Side is when I make him come in and have lunch with me once a year. Now here is a man that went to Harvard. He is from St. Paul, Minnesota, and when he moved to Chicago, he bought a home in Hinsdale.

TB: So now we have this growing middle class of blacks, college graduates for the most part, either integrated into the existing corporate structure or utilizing their skills for their own private businesses, and somewhere in the middle you have guys like I was—professionals, semiprofessionals, teachers, social workers—and, of course, we are getting on up in age. The members of our generation are retiring, dying, whatever nature makes us do, and now our children are relatively well educated and they probably will make it about as good as we or even better. But then you also have this vast number of what some people like to call "the underclass," for the want of a better descriptive term. What happens to them in your theoretical opinion?

AB: Well, I'll tell you what happens to them. Let's go back to Ralph Metcalfe. There are three areas of employment in a society. One is public employment, two is personal and private employment, and three is corporate employment. Back in the Ralph Metcalfe era, if you take the city, the county, the state, which are the three municipalities, my guess is that all of them combined probably employed no more than two or three blacks per hundred. But today the workforce of the city, the county, and all the local municipalities is at least about 30 percent African-Americans. We have already talked about the bad things that integration did for us by spreading us out, but in terms of public employment on a local level it is now at the 30 percent level. That's where it is, and during that same period, federal employment for blacks working at places like the Federal Courthouse was literally zero.

TB: No judges. No clerks.

AB: Forget that. I am also talking about the guys that handle supplies. That was then, but now we have an enormous number of African-Americans in the Chicago area that work for the federal government, and the best way for me to demonstrate this is to tell you I don't want you to go to but one agency. Just go to Social Security. When the first black in Chicago was hired by the Social Security agency, it made the headlines in the *Chicago Defender* and his name was George Stamps. I don't know if you remember him.

TB: Sure, I do. He used to live on Forty-seventh Street.

AB: Well, Social Security has eighteen offices in the Chicago area. You ought to go and visit them. African-Americans are all over the place. That's the bottom line. But it's not just Social Security. Take the Veterans Administration. Go into VA hospitals. The head of the Veterans Administration in the United States today is an African-American. But back in the 1950s, the Veterans hospital did not have one black nurse. Did you know that? Now Jesse Jackson won't admit it, but Jesse knows about all of this, and he won't admit it because to do so he believes would reduce his usefulness, and yet in terms of public employment clearly the numbers are there. They are there by federal edict.

TB: What about the private sector?

AB: Well, I am getting to that. The next section is corporate America. The first black that I ever knew to work for a big company, being other than a janitor or something like that, was a guy from Xavier, Eugene Saffold, and he was a Budweiser salesman. He was one of the first, and today his son works for Merrill Lynch as an investment banker. But the point is, in corporate America there was never a federal law in those days until Richard Nixon, when he was promoting this idea of black capitalism, said that if you are going to have a contract with the federal government you have to be fair with employment and so forth. So then, starting from zero, Sears and Marshall Field's and First National bank started to hire blacks, and remember—it was only just a few years before that when Bill Berry was picketing the First National bank because he was trying to get them to hire a teller and not a vice president! I mean a teller, Tim, because at that time there were none. There were no blacks anywhere in corporate America, and today there are still not enough, but the numbers have increased.

TB: Yes, at least they have increased from zero!

AB: So in terms of corporate America we have made enormous strides as far as employment. The third one is the one that you mentioned earlier: the small businesses and those who are self-employed. Well, for example, I will give you the names of five successful companies and won't have to go any further than that: Johnson Publishing, Soft Sheen, Seaway, Independence, and Luster Products. None of these companies existed in the Ralph Metcalfe era. Not one, and now the number of blacks who own businesses that employ other blacks has increased dramatically. What has not increased, what we have lost in this change, are our places of entertainment. At one time it was a very viable thing to have a theater in this neighborhood, and, as a matter of fact, every neighborhood, black or white, had its own theaters. We had the Rhodes here, for instance, but the habits of people always change, and blacks do not want to go to a theater in the neighborhood today. So all of those types of businesses were lost. All of the theater business was lost. All of the ballroom business was lost by integration. But, well, Jesus Christ, Tim, now they are going to the Hyatt! So it changes. It is not worse. In fact, now it is better, but it most certainly is different.

September 21, 1993

JAMES "JACK" ISBELL

BRONZEVILLE INSURANCE BUSINESSMAN

I first met Jack Isbell in about 1929 when we were both fourth-grade students at Edmund Burke Elementary School located on Fifty-fourth Street and what was then South Park (now Martin Luther King Drive). He was always well dressed, well mannered, studious, and politely aggressive. When we were in the sixth grade, his family moved farther south—in those days we moved quite often, for both more space and reasons of prestige—and Jack and his brother Bob transferred to Carter Elementary School at Fifty-eighth Street and Michigan Avenue. (This was the school that James T. Farrell of Studs Lonigan *fame attended in his grade school days.)*

We were still in the same general neighborhood, however, and Jack and I still met frequently on the basketball courts and softball fields at Carter School and in Washington Park. Also we were both "alley hustlers," selling vegetables off wagons and trucks in the alleys of the South Side. After graduating from Englewood High School, he married and went into the insurance business, first as an agent and then later as a manager and executive.

As an interesting highlight of our lengthy conversation, he revealed that in those capacities he has two nice homes (one in the city and one in Michigan), has sent his daughter to the University of California at Los Angeles, and has always been able to make that kind of a good living in the insurance business for more than fifty years from Bronzeville, with offices from Forty-fifth Street and South Park to Forty-seventh Street and South Park. But when I asked if that kind of career would be possible today, he quickly replied, "No!"

TB: You were born in Pittsburgh, weren't you?

JI: Yeah, born in Pittsburgh. It is just amazing how we moved here to Chicago from Pittsburgh. Mother came first in the last part of '28, and then my two brothers and I, we came in January of '29.

TB: Where were you living then?

JI: We lived at 5441 Prairie. I think it was a room and a half kitchenette.

TB: Yes, these were the kitchenette years. As I remember, even if you could afford a big apartment, you couldn't find one to rent. The landlords cut up all the larger apartments and converted them into smaller units so they could make a lot more money. We lived in one of those huge apartments at 5000 Grand Boulevard. It was owned by a man named Mulvihill, but we had to move. Mr. Mulvihill was egged on by his agent—who, by the way, was named Hansberry—to convert those large old apartments into kitchenettes.

JI: Hansberry was that guy's agent?

TB: Yes. Mr. Mulvihill was never there.

JI: I can relate to that because that's what happened to us. We moved thirteen times from 1929 to 1932. Thirteen times, this is the way we moved. I used to make a long wagon out of this "coaster wagon" that I had. Do you remember those little coaster wagons we would pump around on the street? Well, I would take the wheels off that wagon and make me a long one, and my brothers and I put everything we owned on this wagon and pushed it down the street to the next place where we were going to live! We always moved on May Day. That was moving day, and every time on May 1 when the rent came due, my mother would say, "Let's go, boys!" After we lived at 5441 Prairie, the next move was to 5529 Michigan. Then we moved to 5636 South Park Way. From there we started getting into apartments. First there was 365 East Fifty-sixth Street, and then we lived at 211 East Fifty-eighth Street. Then we moved to 248 East Fifty-eighth Street, and from there to 367 East Fifty-eighth. As a matter of fact, during those years, we were all up and down Fifty-eighth Street!

[*Laughter.*]

TB: When you and your brothers first came to Chicago, you went to Burke School, didn't you?

JI: Yes, but we moved, and we transferred to Carter.

TB: What were those school days at Carter like?

JI: First of all, we had all white teachers. There weren't any black teachers.

TB: Was that good or bad?

JI: At the moment I would say that it was good in one sense, but, of course, I really don't know what it would have been like if we had black teachers.

TB: You don't have the comparison.

JI: All I know is that they made you work, and you had to hustle in order to pass. You didn't pass by just being whoever you were. You had to get the grades. That was the thing I like about our generation—your generation and mine—was that we had to study. We had to know how to read and how to write.

TB: Was your mother working at this time?

JI: Mother worked out from home for a private family. She would go across Washington Park and work for the white folks in Hyde Park. Tim, my mother went to work with cardboard in her shoes! Then she would come home in the evening, and she used to do laundry for the people around our neighborhood. Men who were single would bring their shirts and things over to her. She also baked pies—apricot pies, dried peaches, whatever—and sell them for a dime. I tell you, she did everything in the world to make a living and to raise her boys in the right way. Our schooling was very important to her.

TB: How far did she go in school?

JI: I don't think she even finished high school.

TB: So she was not necessarily well schooled, but she was an intelligent, literate person who was concerned about your education.

JI: Yes, but Mother didn't have time to go to school. If there was any kind of problem or anything happened at Carter School, I was the one who had to go up there and get it settled.

TB: And that was the role that you had to play in your family. Almost like a father to your brothers.

JI: Well, it's that my mother had to work—so, if you don't mind my saying it, I was always aggressive. See, when I was a young man, twelve years old, I already had a paper route, The *Chicago Defender*. I used to sell more *Defenders* than most people sold. Brother, I could hustle! Tim, I used to get up in the morning on a Sunday and sell the *Chicago Herald Examiner*, the *Chicago Tribune*. Yelling down the alley as you went down, waking people up at six o'clock in the morning. You could do that at that time. I built these wagons that I was talking to you about earlier. I could take these wagons with my brothers off at Seventy-first Street where they had a farmers' market out there. And at this farmers' market I would buy cabbage or some sweet potatoes or whatever else they had and pull that wagon back to Sixty-seventh and South Park Way where the white people lived. Then I'd go down those alleys and start calling, "Sweet corn, cabbage, and cabbage sprouts, cabbage six for a dime and twenty cents a dozen." Boy, I was something special! And by the time I got to Fifty-sixth Street, I sold everything I had!
[*Laughter.*]

TB: My brother was doing the same thing over on Garfield!

[*Laughter.*]

How far south were you living then?

JI: As far south as I have *ever* lived, Fifty-eighth Street.

TB: Where were white people living at that time?

JI: They had to be living south of about Sixty-first Street.

TB: How much further east and west?

JI: At that time, back in those days, I would say probably as far east as you could go and also as far west.

TB: Now, there was also an enclave of blacks south of Sixty-third in Woodlawn at that time. Did you ever have anything to do with any of those black folks who lived there?

JI: No, I didn't. The only time I had anything at all to do with them was much later on when somebody gave me a prospect to go write up some insurance.

TB: But in your school days—

JI: In my school days, I had nothing to do with them. When I was in school, I would get on the El and go out to Englewood High School, which was Sixty-second Street and Stewart. Sometimes I used to run all the way to Englewood High School. Probably you heard the name, Fred Morgan. Later on, Fred became a fireman. Well, Fred and I used to run all the way to school. That was our exercise.

TB: So you went to Englewood and also took care of the family while your mother worked.

JI: Yes, and I was working on Friday, and Saturday, and Sunday.

TB: While your mother was taking care of the economic necessities, you were also giving some support in that area as well as giving supervision to your brothers while she was away. How did your brothers respond to that?

JI: Well, Bob, he sort of resented it at the time. He'd listen to me, but I always had to argue with him *before* he would listen. Mother would always say, "Now you listen to Jack!" She wanted me to be the number one son to take care of the other two boys.

TB: Now, in those Englewood years, the time around 1936 or so, what are some of the important things that you remember?

JI: You mean the people?

TB: Yes. Was Joe Bowles in that class?

JI: Oh, yeah, Joe was a great basketball player.

TB: Who were some of the other guys that you remember?

JI: The Edwards brothers. I think they were sons of a doctor who lived on Michigan Boulevard. They were light-complexion boys. Back in those days you didn't dare call a black man "black," and, well, one day one of those Edwards brothers got mad at James McCoy and called him "black," and then the next thing you know this Edwards boy was picking himself up off the ground. McCoy had hit him that quick! You didn't call *anybody* "black" in those days.

TB: Even if a guy was black you didn't call him "black" unless you knew him really well.

JI: That's right.

TB: Were you there at Englewood at the same time as Ed Johnson?

JI: Yeah, the saxophone player.

TB: And Joe Williams?

JI: Yeah, Joe Williams, the singer. Joe was with me at Englewood, but I went to school with Joe at Carter as well.

TB: While he was there at Englewood, did he ever do any singing?

JI: Well, I never knew he could sing, not at that time. I didn't even know Joe Williams was able to sing until one day I heard him with Count Basie. Then later—well, let me tell you one thing that happened. I took a cruise here a couple of years ago. It was what they called the "Jazz Festival" cruise, and Joe was one of the entertainers on that ship. Now, I hadn't seen Joe in twenty years or more, I guess, so one night he was sitting down listening to some of the other musicians, and I walked up to him and said, "Hey, Joe, how are you doing? You probably don't remember me, but we went to school together." And Joe said to me, "Oh, yeah, of course, I remember you. You are Jack Isbell!" Well, I was just knocked out that Joe could still remember me, and that night, the night that he performed on the ship, when Joe came on the stage, the first thing he said was, "Ladies and gentlemen, I want you all to know that I've got a friend out there in the audience that I went to high school with. His name is Jack Isbell. Jack, won't you please stand up?" I was just dumbfounded. It was such a nice thing for him to do.

TB: Were you ever involved in music yourself?

JI: When I went to Englewood in 1932, the first thing I did was to join the orchestra. See, I used to play the violin—so I joined the orchestra the first chance I got. The man over the orchestra was Dr. Burton, and I stayed in that orchestra for four years. My high school days were also very memorable in that was when Bob, my twin, and I started with what was known as the Golden Gloves. I used to box, and we put on exhibition matches at Englewood on the stage in the auditorium. I don't know if you will remember this or not.

TB: No, I don't remember any of that because I didn't stay there long.

JI: Well, I used to love to fight, and I was also on the track team. I liked to play hardball, but I didn't make the team. Before this, in '32, I had been in ROTC, but in 1934 they cut out ROTC, and that's why I had to take up gym.

TB: Back in those Englewood years, what was the relationship between blacks and whites like back then?

JI: Very good. I'm glad you asked that question, Tim. I can show you my class book, and you'll see I've got as many signed remarks by whites as I got from blacks. In fact, I got more from whites because the ratio of blacks to whites in that school was about one to five.

TB: Only about 20 percent black.

JI: Yes, and I don't ever remember a fight in all the years that I was at Englewood High School. I don't remember anything in terms of being black or white, and I got along just beautifully. In fact, I still remember that when this white guy ran for class president, I was the one who managed his campaign, and he won! I was also voted among the best dressed at Englewood. All these things are there in my book.

TB: And to be voted those kinds of honors you needed to obtain the support of a majority of the white students.

JI: Yes, so you can see that it was really quite an honor when you consider that you had 80 percent whites going there at that time.

TB: Now, I heard that although on that level things were good, on another level they had two separate proms, and I don't believe that blacks were allowed to use the swimming pool. When did you graduate from Englewood?

JI: I graduated in '36. Let me tell you about my graduation. I was in my last semester and getting ready to graduate in February. I always got good grades in school, but, you see, I had a temper, and this one teacher I had for geography or history or something like that, this teacher got me angry, and I told her off—and, Tim, she failed me! So I became what is known as a "nine-semester man." That meant I would be going to school from February to June taking just one subject, and, as a result, I didn't get my E for music. I didn't get my boxing E or my track E, and I was a very hurt young man. After that, I just stopped playing the violin.

TB: Yes, I can understand that. As you recall it, what was the general mood of things in the black community at that time? What did people do and how did they relate to one another? For example, what kinds of recreation did you do to pass away your leisure time?

JI: That's very simple to answer because many of us wanted to be some kind of an athlete. We liked playing ball: hardball, softball, football. Some of us even played basketball, but I was not one of them.

TB: So there were activities, particularly among the young men, which were physical in nature: basketball, baseball, softball, football, track—and all of that took up a lot of time, didn't it?

JI: It *improved* time. We didn't have enough time to ever worry about being poor. It was never on our mind that we lived in any way unlike anybody else.

TB: You did not feel that you were poor.

JI: No, because we had—well, listen, I'll tell you what we had. We had salt pork for our bacon, and we didn't have cow's liver. Hog liver was our liver. Hog liver and tripe.

TB: So, it seems to me, that during this period which is historically what they call the Great Depression, you and many of your friends were not depressed and did not feel deprived.

JI: Well, I guess within our own hearts, we knew we were deprived. We knew that we didn't have some of the things that some other people had, but we were all basically the same as anyone else in our peer group, and it was only later on when I remembered seeing Mother trying to climb the steps in this apartment and that apartment and so forth that I began to realize how things really were there where we were living.

TB: Back then, at the time when you graduated, how did you feel about the future?

JI: About the future? Well, you see, when I went to Englewood High School, I had already set lofty goals for myself. My motto was to do well. To excel! So, when I graduated, I had made a decision for myself that, "Jack, whatever you do always give it your all!" But I couldn't go to college. It was too expensive to even try to go, especially with two brothers and a mother who needed my help. So I decided the best thing for me to do was to wait for a while before going to college, and so, after graduating from high school, I decided to earn some money by going to work for a man named Bruce selling vegetables from a truck. Bill Bruce was a very likable person. He ran the vegetable truck, and his father ran a grocery store over on Thirty-fifth Street. I'd get up in the morning and go over to Thirty-fifth and State, where there was a little hash joint, and get something to eat.

TB: Do you remember the name of the hash joint?

JI: No, but whatever its name was, in the morning that's where we started out. From there we would get in the truck and go down the alley, and I would call out my wares—you know, "Sweet corn—big sale today," whatever it was we really wanted to push, and we usually sold out everything we had. Like I said, Mr. Bruce was a very fine person. Whatever we earned, we shared. We didn't have any kind of problem there. As a matter of fact, that's how I met my wife. Well, what I mean to say is this is how I got back with her. See, I used to go with Ann when she was still in high school, and so when she heard me call out my wares, she recognized my voice. She would come over to her window, wave at me, and I'd blow her a kiss. That was it!

[*Laughter.*]

So, anyway, this truck ran until November selling vegetables. In November it got cold as a wet hen. This was '36, and I'd never seen so much snow. There was so much snow they didn't have any automobiles out there in the streets. I got some belly sacks—you know what belly sacks are?—and wrapped them around my feet to keep them warm. But then one day we had to stop the truck. There was too much snow, and here it is almost Christmas, and I'm out of work. I didn't want that to ever happen again.

TB: How did you get into the insurance business?

JI: Well, in a way, selling vegetables was also my entree into the insurance business! [*Laughter.*]

You see, Mr. Livingston, who was the president of the Jackson Funeral System, had heard me calling out my wares, and I guess he thought if I could sell vegetables, I ought to be able to sell insurance—so he called me down to his office one day. I went to his office in my purple-and-white Englewood sweater, and I thought I was looking pretty good, but the first thing he said to me was, "Don't wear that sweater!" [*Laughter.*]

"Wear a shirt and tie, and you can come to work." So the next day I put on a shirt and tie and went to work, and that was the beginning of my work in insurance.

TB: So your first job in insurance was with the Jackson Funeral System?

JI: Yes, actually at that time it was still a burial policy company. Later on they became Jackson Mutual and offered a whole line of burial insurance.

TB: Jack, now, you may not remember it, but you are the one who brought me into the insurance business. I was returning from a job I had in Milwaukee in 1941, and I bumped into you. I was kind of looking for another job, and I knew you were in the insurance business. You were the agency director or something of that sort. At least you had a staff.

JI: Yes, in 1941, I already had a staff at that time. In fact, I was probably the youngest superintendent in the state of Illinois! I was only just a little over twenty years old.

TB: When were you born?

JI: In 1918.

TB: Then you and I are the same age. I'm December!

JI: I'm delighted to hear this!

TB: You really turned my life around. There are certain events in my life that have made a substantial difference that I always remember, and that was one of them. When I first came back from Milwaukee, I was down in the dumps. I was really in low gear.

JI: You know, what makes me feel so good about this, Tim, is that so many people have said to me something similar to what you are talking about now. I don't even remember all the incidents that they're talking about, but when someone says something like this to you, you just have to feel that you've been able to be of at least some service to others.

TB: Now, just after the time we're talking about, I went into the army. You went in too, didn't you?

JI: Yes, I was in for two and a half years.

TB: Did you get out of the country?

JI: I was in the European theater of operations.

TB: What kind of unit?

JI: Truck company. We were inducted here in Chicago.

TB: We may have been inducted on the same day! Do you remember the day and year?

JI: It was January of 1944. Before that, I had tried to enlist, but they turned me down. I was terribly disappointed because I wanted to fly—so I said, "Oh, no, now I'll have to wait."

TB: Why did you want to fly?

JI: Well, I had some friends down in Tuskegee, and I wanted to go with them. One of my brothers was already in the service, and I just couldn't see him in the service by himself. My wife didn't know that I felt this way. I think she would have died if she knew that I really wanted to go into the service.

TB: She wouldn't have approved?

JI: She would probably have killed me!

[*Laughter.*]

But, anyhow, they finally said, "OK, we'll send you," and I said, "Oh, no, now wait a minute, I don't want to go into the navy. I want to fly." At that time, Tim, the only way you could fly was to be in the Army Air Corps. The navy wasn't taking *any* blacks in the Naval Air Corps—so, to make a long story short, they finally stamped my papers "Army," and I was sent up to Fort Sheridan. When I got there, they issued me a uniform and called me to come into the office and said, "Private, what would you like to do in this army?" I said, "I want to fly!" "Oh, you want to fly. Well, we can fix that in a hurry. We'll send you out to building so-and-so at zero eight hundred hours, and you can take the test." Now, Tim, as you know, I have a fairly decent IQ—one that would get me in as a noncommissioned officer or whatever else—and I had never failed a test in all my life. So I go over to such-and-such building, sit down—and I'm the only black in the room. The test they gave me has questions like "Identify this enemy aircraft." "What's the name of this aircraft?" "Is this a rotary or fixed-wing aircraft?"—and, of course, at that time I didn't know anything about those kinds of airplanes, so I bombed that test but good, and that was the end of my hopes for going to pilot training. I was hurt, but, I guess, in the long run it all worked out fairly well. I was able to get by, but then later on when I went to take the noncommissioned officer's test, the officer in charge wanted to know what had happened on the test I had failed, and eventually, Tim, I had to write to the captain of my company to tell him that I was being discriminated against. I had to do that because I knew I was as smart as any officer that he had in his company, and I wanted a fair chance to go to Officer Candidate School.

TB: What happened?

JI: Well, I had a first sergeant who was sort of like an Uncle Tom, and he never wanted me to see the captain, but, well, even so, I reached the rank of supply sergeant.

TB: Where were you stationed?

JI: Down south in between Camp Hope and Camp McCain.

TB: Where was your first sergeant from?

JI: He was also from the South.

TB: Black?

JI: Yes, everybody in our unit was black except the officers. We had white officers. No black officers and no white enlisted men. There were only three black sergeants, Tim, in this whole unit, and we all had IQs of 110 or better.

TB: You had to have 110 in order to qualify for Officer Candidate School.

JI: One day the captain said to us, "All of you who want to go to Officer Candidate School step out," and of the three of us, I was the only one who stepped out. Now, here we are in the boondocks, out there with tents and all that, and so nothing happened right away, but when we headed to Camp Hope, I said to the captain, "Sir, when am I going to take that test?" He said, "OK, we'll send you," and I went to take the test the next day. Then I waited and waited for the results. It must have been about a month, and finally I went back to find out the results from the captain. To do this meant going over the sergeant's head, which, of course, he didn't like, but, listen, Tim, I know I passed that test, and the captain says to me, "Oh, Sergeant, I forgot to tell you that your test was inconclusive." So I said, "Well, what do I do?" and he said, "You can take the test over again if you want," so I go and take the test over again, and this time he said, "Well, you passed it," but, Tim, about fifteen minutes later we had to be on the boat going to Europe. Everywhere we went, the orders always got there late, and so I didn't get to go to Officer Candidate School until I got back here to Chicago in 1946!

TB: When you were stationed at Camp McCain, which was in Mississippi, what was the situation down there like?

JI: Well, Tim, it may surprise you, but my primary problem at that time was that I didn't have any money. You see, I'd gambled away all my money back at Fort

Sheridan, and when I came to Camp McCain, I didn't have anything left. I had run out of money, and I wanted to go see a movie, and the movies there cost about thirty-five cents to get in—so there was this fellow there that looked like he always had some money named Bernstein, and so I say, "Hey, Bernstein, let me have thirty-five cents, and I'll give it back to you on payday." "Well, Jack," he says, "I don't have anything myself right now, but later on tonight I will, and you can get it from me then." I said to myself, "How in the hell is he going to get that cash tonight?" Anyhow, I found out pretty quickly because that night Bernstein came over with his blanket into the dayroom, unfolded that blanket on the table there, threw down a pair of dice, and one of the other fellows picked those dice up and said, "I shoot a quarter," and Bernstein says, "The man shoots a quarter!" And the next thing I know a game is under way! But I can't play with them because I still don't have any money, so the next morning I ask him, "Say, are you going to loan me that thirty-five cents?" And he does, but instead of going to the movie with it, I went down to the PX and bought me a pair of red-and-white dice. Then a little later when the guys were in line for lunch I threw the dice out on the ground, and right away a fellow picked them up and said, "I shoot a quarter," and from that moment on I was never out of money, so help me God! And I established what I called a "casino." I had a dice game going and also a poker game, and pretty soon—believe it or not—I was lending the *officers* money!

[*Laughter.*]

Now, at that time, we all had what was called a "currency control book" in which you're supposed to keep a record of all the money you have, and so I kept a record of my money in this currency control book, and from time to time I would send my wife a letter with some American Express checks, and I'd tell her that I got lucky last night and won a few dollars. But believe me when I tell you I was not gambling personally.

TB: You were in business.

JI: That's right. I was in business, but then one day, a colonel—an MP!—sent for me in my company and told me to come down and explain how in the world I could have this large amount of money in my currency control book, and when I get there, he says to me, "Sergeant Isbell, how the hell could you have this kind of money?" See, we were only supposed to be making a certain limited amount of money each month, and I say, "Well, I must admit that I do a lot of gambling, and I guess I'm just lucky." "Well, I don't understand this," he says and goes on like that for a while, so when he finishes, I say, "Are you finished, sir?" He says, "Yes," and I say, "Now, let me say this to you. In all of my years"—I'm looking right at him, Tim—"in *all* those years my integrity has never been questioned. This is the first and only time that anybody has *ever* questioned my integrity—so I think, sir, what you need to do is not to talk to me. What you really need to do is to talk to my company commander because *he* is the one that approves my currency control book." And all the time I'm saying this, I'm looking him dead in the eye. I'm fixed on him. Oh, I'm not going to let him move an inch—and, well, that's the last I heard of it. Not another word! But, let me tell you, I was angry! I mean, all I was doing was just *legally* getting hold of a couple of extra dollars.

TB: When you were sent to Europe, where were you stationed?

JI: We were in Germany. First in a place called Furth, and then in Hamburg. We were in the Headquarters Unit.

TB: What was the responsibility of your Headquarters Unit?

JI: The Headquarters Unit just stayed where it was and kept the peace. We really didn't do anything. The war was almost over. Now, the place where we were stationed, all of our men are on the first and second floors, and there's another unit on the third and fourth floors. Well, one day when all of my officers had gone to town, some of our guys got kind of loud about something, and this officer came down from his unit upstairs to complain. He was a black officer—the first black officer that I had seen with the unit upstairs—and he began knocking on our doors and talking loud, so I said to him, "Sir, you have no right to be here. This is a company run by Captain John Flynn, and I am John Flynn's first sergeant. Anything you want out of this unit, you see me. I'm the number one ranking noncommissioned officer here today!" He was going to bust into a lot of different rooms without permission, and I said, "Don't do that, sir. You cannot do that to this unit, and I am going to ask you to leave." See, I was a bad-ass boy, and I didn't care what he wanted to do. It didn't make any difference to me.

TB: And you were operating within your authority.

JI: Yes, but he said to me, "I'm going to have you court-martialed," and I said, "Well, that's up to you." So he put in a charge against me. Then when Captain Flynn came back the next day, I told him what had really happened. "Captain Flynn, I hate to say this to you, but I am ashamed of this man and what he was doing." That guy was black, but he was giving me a hard time, and what I said must have sort of touched Captain Flynn because that was the last I heard of that!

TB: The experiences of a black soldier in a segregated army don't always end quite that way.

JI: Yes, the stories we could tell.

TB: During those last six months or so that you spent overseas, what were the German people like? They had been defeated. What kind of demeanor did they have? What kind of attitude particularly in regard to *black* American soldiers?

JI: Tim, I must tell you their demeanor was beautiful. I never met any Germans who seemingly were unfriendly.

TB: They didn't pay any attention to your race?

JI: At that time they didn't pay any attention to my being black. All the women over there were white, and they attended the USO clubs and enjoyed themselves with us.

TB: So, being a member of the conquering forces, you were treated fairly and were not discriminated against.

JI: Not by the Germans. As a matter of fact, I think that the black soldiers got more respect than the white boys. The reason was because the white men tended to be arrogant. The white soldier thought that he was superior to any German, and I think he lost out on a lot because of that.

TB: Yes, I'm told that the white guys used a nickname like "kraut" or some other derogatory description, and seldom did they ever even try to learn the language, whereas the black soldier, regardless of what his previous schooling might have been, he plunged in immediately to try to learn how to speak directly and treat the people as human beings just like himself.

JI: Well, I was one of those who felt just like the way you are talking now. I felt that all my relationships ought to be good ones, and I respected these people for being what they were, and they respected me. Everywhere I went I was looked upon as "Sarge Isbell." I also learned the language. I even made up a little German-language dictionary. Some German friends of mine there would tell me what the words were for "love" and things like that, and I made up a kind of picture diary. Consequently, I was able to communicate a little better, and that way, along with a little sign language, I was able to get along very well, both in Germany and in France.

TB: And that was quite different from the way that you were accustomed to being treated in the United States.

JI: A lot different. But, you know, what I most remember about the last part of my service in Europe was learning how to play poker. I think I must have told you this before.

TB: Well, you told me about your being in "business" back at Camp McCain.

JI: Yes, I had that little "casino" of mine, but, you know, I never really learned to play poker. Not to any real extent. So, anyway, one day, there in Germany, wherever we were, some of the fellows came by and said, "Hi, Sarge, how are you doing?" And they sat down with me and started to deal some cards. Well, I didn't have but about twenty dollars in *German* money, and, as you know, German money at that time wasn't worth very much.

TB: It was devalued.

JI: Yes, devalued, so if you had twenty dollars in German money, you could just act like it's nothing, like it doesn't matter at all, and when they said, "Let's play poker," I said, "I don't know how." "Oh, you know enough about it. Let's play!" And, well, Tim, to make a long story short, I sat down there and won three hundred dollars!

[*Laughter.*]

And the reason I won those three hundred dollars was only because they thought that I didn't know how to play. If I said, "I raise you," they just knew that Sarge didn't know what the hell he was doing, and they let me keep on doing it.

[*Laughter.*]

TB: You mean you really didn't know how to play?

JI: No, I didn't, but eventually I got it right!

[*Laughter.*]

TB: Were you just putting them on?

JI: Well, to tell the truth, I had watched them play from time to time, but I really didn't know the sequence of going up from a pair of threes to a full house and all of that. I didn't know any of that at all, and I was just hoping I had a good hand of some kind or other!

[*Laughter.*]

TB: When did you finally come back to the States?

JI: Well, after the war was over, my unit was stationed in Marseilles, and from Marseilles we were supposed to go to Asia, but instead we got our orders to be shipped to the Pacific. Then those orders were changed, and we were turned around in Rouen, and from there to LeHavre and then back home!

TB: And coming back, where did you land?

JI: In New York at Camp Kilmer.

TB: How did it feel getting back here?

JI: When we saw the Statue of Liberty, I thought that that must be the most beautiful sight you'd ever see. Then after Camp Kilmer, we came into Chicago by train, and I was separated from my unit at Fort Sheridan.

TB: Then it was back into civilian life!

JI: Yes, back into civilian life, and glad to be back, although I must say that I enjoyed being in the army.

TB: Well, you must have because you decided to stay in the reserves, didn't you?

JI: Well, let me be honest about that now. I didn't join the National Guard because I really wanted to. I joined the National Guard because I was asked. After having been separated from the service, I was out of work, and Colonel Jones—Dick Jones—wanted me to join his outfit. That was the 178th Regimental Combat Team, and something inside me told me to go ahead and join, and I'm glad today that I did because you know that little check that comes in every month still looks pretty good.

TB: Dick Jones later became a brigadier general, didn't he? And later he became an envoy to Liberia.

JI: That's right. I really didn't know him as strongly as I should have, perhaps, being in his unit and all, but it was always a pleasure for me being around him because, for some reason or another, he just took a liking to me personally, and when I say personally, I'm speaking about my wife as well as myself. Whenever we would go to camp, for some reason or another, he would always try to find me and say, "Hello, how are you doing, lieutenant?" And so, although I didn't really want to join the National Guard, that was the beginning of a very wonderful relationship between the Guard and myself.

TB: By this time were all branches of the service integrated?

JI: Well, speaking of integration, I became the adjutant of one outfit in the Eighty-fifth Division. There I was this black man standing in front of thousands of white troops and telling them what to do. This, to me, shows proof that there was integration, that there was proven leadership on the part of the black soldier, because, believe me, I don't want you to think I was the only one.

TB: Do you remember the names of any of those other black officers?

JI: Of course. They were guys like Daniel Snipe, Harold Thomas, Fred Rice—

TB: Those guys became very prominent people in the Chicago Police Department.

JI: And Erskine Inowa and George Simms, who became a commander.

TB: So, the army and the National Guard could prepare people for other things than just being a soldier.

JI: Exactly.

TB: And now, at this time we're talking about, you have two parallel careers. You are now on a career ladder in the armed service, and you also have a profession as a successful executive in the insurance business. Let's deal with that insurance business. When you came back, you were with which company?

JI: I was superintendent of a staff of men at Jackson.

TB: You went back to work at Jackson, and this was in 1946?

JI: Late '46, probably around June.

TB: So you went right back to work.

JI: Yeah, I didn't lose any time. I had to make a living. I worked for Jackson until '49. By that time I had been elevated to a manager, but I became disenchanted, Tim.

TB: Why was that?

JI: It was a small company. Only the president and vice president were making a fairly decent living, and they didn't want the company to grow any larger.

TB: Also, at this time, history tells me that the white insurance companies were beginning to get hungry for some of this black business, and they forced the issue to take both Jackson and Chicago Metropolitan out of the funeral business and become mutual insurance companies.

JI: You are right. Until about 1950 Jackson was still a funeral system, and Chicago Metropolitan was also a funeral system, but Jackson was the first company to become an old-line legal reserve company. Then Chicago Met followed behind them.

TB: So, when you left Jackson, where did you go?

JI: I went over to Mammoth. Mammoth was a health and accident insurance company along with life insurance.

TB: Was Mammoth black-owned?

JI: Yes, black-owned. Their home office was in Louisville, Kentucky. What happened was, I got a call from a man named Holman who was the president of Mammoth Life, and he said, "I'm coming to Chicago, and I want to talk with you. I'll be at the Pershing Hotel." So I went there to see what was on his mind, and he asked me what I was making. I think it was five thousand dollars a year, which seemed like big money at that time, and he said, "I tell you what. I'll also give you six thousand dollars to come over to us, and I'll give you an additional seven hundred fifty dollars expense money, tax free!" Now, an increase of one thousand seven hundred fifty dollars, an increase like that would change anybody's diet. So I told Mr. Livingston, "Sir, I'm going to have to leave you," and I left and went over to Mammoth, did my thing and did it well. I really got things moving!

TB: What was your capacity?

JI: They had two districts, one on the South Side and one on the West. I was the manager of Chicago One, the South Side district, and I was doing very well, but then in April of '51 Mr. Livingston sent a delegation over to my office in the South Center Building, and they asked me if I would consider coming back. So I went over there to talk with him. Now, Mr. Livingston was the agency officer as well as the president of the company, and so I said, "Mr. Livingston, the only way I'd come back I'd have to be the agency officer." He said, "Oh, not right now, but I'll tell you what I will do. We'll see how things work out, and if they work out all right, I'll make you agency officer in six months." Well, I knew my ability to get things going, so I took him up on it. But then six months went by, and nothing happened. So one day I just went to the printer and had some cards made with my name and "agency officer" printed on them!

[*Laughter.*]

Well, what could he do? What could he say? He had to accept me as the agency officer or he was going to lose me again, and he didn't want that to happen. Then, well, to make a long story short once again, I stayed until 1955, and then I went to school at Fort Benning.

TB: That was infantry school?

JI: Yes, I chose to go to school because I wanted to be upgraded, and the only way you could get upgraded was to go to school in a place like that, and I went down to Fort Benning, Georgia, for four months, but before I left for Fort Benning, Melvin McNary, who was vice president of Chicago Metropolitan and their agency officer as well, asked me if I would come over and work for them after completing my training. Well, I was released from the army on February 9, 1956, and February 16 was my first day at Chicago Met. Now, Mac knew that I knew something about insurance and also that I had had management experience over the years. What's more, he knew that I was active in the National Negro Insurance Association. So he knew all of this and he wanted me, but when I came over, he said, "Jack, I don't know exactly what I'm going to do with you, but I do know you've got all this talent," and I said, "Don't worry. We'll find a way!"
[*Laughter.*]

Now, at this time, they had just opened an office up in Gary, and Mac said, "Let's send you out there to Gary. Just report to Mr. Boyd Jarrell and tell him you want to learn the business and help him collect the Chicago Met debts." So I went out there, and Jarrell said to me, "I want you to take this district from Burr Street to Washington, and I want you to get this debit paying." OK, so I went to work and lowered the arrears on the debit, and I did just fine. But then Jarrell told me, "I'm going to take these debits away from you now, Mr. Isbell. What we want you to do is to start dealing with the debits that have built up back here in Chicago on Madison from Fifteenth to Twenty-fifth Streets." Well, the first week of doing that, I must have earned no more than about twelve dollars, so he said, "I'll tell you what I'm going to do. I'm going to send an experienced salesman out with you to show you exactly how it's done." Now this guy, his name was Red, I was supposed to meet him the next day at Fifteenth and Madison, and we were going to start working there. Red said, "OK, Mr. Isbell, we are going to start right here!" So we go over to a house, knock on the door, and a lady comes to the door. She says she doesn't want any insurance. So he goes upstairs, knocks on the door, and another lady comes to the door, and she also doesn't want any insurance. That's when I said to him, "Listen, Red, I'll tell you what. Why don't you let me make the approach and see if I can change her mind?" And that's all I needed, Tim. Now I was on my way!

TB: Jack, from what I know, you have spent if not all then probably 99 percent of your working life there in the black community working for companies in which the management was black.

JI: Yeah, that's true.

TB: But today it seems to me that it would be very unlikely for a young black man—no matter how intelligent or highly motivated he might be—to have a similar sort of career because of the current economic conditions within our community. At the present time, a young, aspiring, hard-driving black person, male or female, would not be able to feel the same degree of confidence that he or she would be able to have a successful fifty-year career working inside the black community for a black owner-controlled institution. Am I right about this?

JI: Tim, as I see it, I don't think that the young black today has exactly what we had so far as the desire and commitment to build black business. As soon as we put a training program in, what happens is that, as soon as we send them out into the field to make a living, fifteen minutes after they get out there, bingo, they are gone!

TB: And this is after they have already received professional training as the result of your sponsorship.

JI: Yes, after we've done all the training! We've spent so much money in this company just training people for our company, and then, right away they move on out of the community, and that's a tragedy. It shouldn't happen.

TB: Would you care to name any examples?

JI: Well, Tim, I don't like to name names, but I'll never forget Leo Blackburn. Blackburn and I came into the agency department of Chicago Met at the same time. He went into the ordinary department, and I went in to run the industrial department. Well, after a bit, Leo thought it was time for him to move on, and that's what he did, but when he left, he took almost all the accounts that he had with Chicago Met over to this other company that he was joining.

TB: Which was?

JI: It was a white-owned company.

TB: Was Leo in your generation?

JI: Yes, Leo was in my generation.

TB: Then he must have been one of the first that was involved in that transfer of training and experience over to the white agencies.

JI: Yes, and about the same time I had another friend named Langford Spraggins who was already with Metropolitan Life—I think it was in 1957—and one day Spraggins says to me, "Jack, you know you've got to get out of that company as quick as you can because that company is not going to last very long," and that made me very, very angry with Spraggins. I practically cursed him out on the street for telling me to leave my company. But, well, that was thirty-four years ago, and, as you know, we've been here ever since!

[*Laughter.*]

I would say, as a matter of fact, we have done a pretty darn good job of surviving, but I've helped a lot of men who are no longer with this company, who left shortly after they got the knowledge and went to work for other companies and have been working for those other companies all these past years, and that hurts me because I am the one who gave them their training.

TB: Taking your experience in terms of how people who have been trained in our community leave the community, what would be your guess as to the impact that this transfer has as it relates to the insurance industry as well as other black-owned corporations?

JI: Well, what has happened in this regard is that once the white man finally decided that the green dollar that blacks have was just as good as that green dollar that the whites have, consequently, they said, "Oh, let's go out and get this market!" That's when they began to recruit black men and black women to work for their companies, and, as a direct result, a lot of the business that we would normally be getting, Tim, we have lost. You know, I've got a nephew who is doing very, very well in the insurance business, but when he went to the University of Illinois, as soon as he graduated, Prudential called him to come down and work for them in their underwriting department. Then they put him in their school for sales because he wanted to sell, and this boy has done big, big things, but just think what could have happened if he had put in that same amount of time with Chicago Met or some other black-owned company! How much more his talent would have enhanced that company!

TB: Yes, and it would have created not only more job opportunities for more blacks in the community but also would have contributed an important image of success, as well as the fact that at least some of the dollars generated by this success would probably have turned around right here inside the black community.

JI: That is the truth without a doubt.

TB: And what's more, I think, your example might also illustrate the story of what integration has done to the black community on several other different kinds of levels. We pushed for integration, and we got some integration, but let me ask you a question: Inside this concept of integration, from the standpoint of comparison, taking your knowledge of the insurance business as an example, in all the companies that you know, just how many of the young blacks, male or female, have moved up to the executive or managerial positions in those corporate insurance companies that are white-owned and -controlled?

JI: Not very many, but there are those who have moved up.

TB: I'm not talking about the money now.

JI: I know. You are talking about their positions within the company.

TB: Yes, if you went into the corporate office and went up to the top level, just how many of these very able young black people would you find?

JI: You wouldn't find too many.

TB: One percent? Less than 1 percent?

JI: Oh, you probably have maybe 2 percent.

TB: In top managerial positions?

JI: Two percent—that's the most.

TB: And would you make a guess, Jack, as to how many African-American dollars are put directly into these large white corporations?

JI: I really wish I could give you an honest answer on that, but I can't. All I can tell you is that African-Americans have put lots of dollars into those white companies. Let me try to answer your question another way. Here in Chicago, at one time before the war, Chicago Metropolitan Mutual Assurance Company was taking care of all the black-owned industrial business. But then, after World War II, the white insurance companies began to realize that those dollars were just as good in their own pocket as they were in the black pocket. So they began shooting actively for that market, and pretty soon Metropolitan Life, which, of course, was completely white-owned, was doing just as much business in their one district office at Forty-seventh and Wabash as we were doing totally in Chicago Metropolitan, so that might give you a comparison to think about! You see people just don't understand certain things about the insurance business that they really need to know. At a place like Chicago Metropolitan you have a chairman of the board, you have a president, you have a few additional vice presidents, you have district managers, and so forth. All of this creates a tremendous overhead, and so the result is that you don't get quite as much for the premium dollar from us as you would from the white companies because we have to pay for all those managers, presidents, and chairmen of the board, whereas Metropolitan Life down there at Forty-seventh and Wabash only had a district manager, maybe two clerks, and a couple of staff managers. That was their entire overhead, and, believe me, it made a big difference.

TB: Absolutely. That was due to the fact that the central management could take care of a lot of things and eliminate certain kinds of unnecessary expenses. Another important point to consider is that Chicago Met or the other companies that you have named which were black-controlled, almost by the very nature of their existence, if they were successful and had surpluses to invest, would be bound or at least strongly inclined to invest those surpluses back in the black community. Would that also be as true of the white companies?

JI: No, I don't think that too many of the white companies ever invested a lot of their money in the black community. Now, as an exception to this, take New York Life.

They put up Lake Meadows down here, but I don't really know offhand of anything else that the white companies have done to enhance the black community or to even try to help keep the community alive.

TB: Well, the Lake Meadows development was primarily an effort to gentrify or, more properly, "regentrify" part of the community. Originally they had hoped they would attract some middle-class blacks, but mostly middle-class whites were the ones who came in, so it was not with the intention of enhancing opportunities within the existing community. For them it was looked at as a means for providing an easy access and convenience to a middle-class community, much of which they knew would be white. So in no way was this an altruistic move on their part. It was a move that was designed to create for them a great opportunity for refurbishing that which had been destroyed and which had once been a viable black community. When you look at the structure of these corporations and you see the top of it, in terms of decision making — those who make the decisions about how everything is going to operate — in that area, as you have said, you will find almost no blacks, and, therefore, though there may be young blacks in these corporations who personally may be making lots of money for themselves, when we look at what the impact of these white-owned companies has been on the quality of life in the larger black communities, what we see around us is devastation. Will you comment on this in terms of your own experience? To start with, when you came to work here on Forty-seventh Street, describe the way this community looked to you back then.

JI: Well, it was black. Forty-seventh Street was entirely black, and all this area was nice. By that I mean I could go down Forty-seventh Street and feel proud about all the stores and things that we had on that street, and those places were available to us because they were black organizations created by black entrepreneurs, and, as I have said to you before, I have always continued to work in this area. Now, Tim, I'm sure you know, for my own personal financial sake, I could have left Jackson, I could have left Mammoth, I could even have left Chicago Metropolitan and gone over to some of those other companies that were white-owned, but I just did not want to lose my identity. I wanted to be black. That's what I always was, and I intended to stay that way.

TB: And part of that is pride, isn't it?

JI: Oh yeah, very definitely it was a matter of pride. Everything that I have ever done, every dime that I have ever made was made through working directly with black people just like myself, and I'm proud of that. Very proud, as a matter of fact!

TB: And now, looking back at this fifty years that you have been talking about — the fifty years that you worked selling insurance between Forty-fifth and Forty-seventh—those were probably the fifty most prosperous and opportune years for black folks in the history of this country.

JI: I would have to agree with you.

TB: When you go to Atlanta, Detroit, Cleveland, Cincinnati, Kansas City—in all those cities wherever you go, you see the extent to which urban decay has destroyed the black community. There's no money there. None coming in, and what little there is, all of it goes out. I've been told that the Chinese dollar turns around five and a half times in the Chinese community because it is contained within that community, so you find almost no Chinese unemployment. The Jewish dollar turns around at least three times before it leaves. The Hispanic dollar turns around at least two times in its own community.

JI: And ours?

TB: Ours doesn't even get in. At least most of it doesn't get in. It is spent before we get it. What has happened at this juncture is that we are operating almost like a Third World country inside a First World country. That is why the history of how we got to be this way here in Chicago is so important for all of us to understand. During the period when our parents first came here, Chicago was the most prosperous of all the big northern cities. It had the greatest diversity.

JI: It offered the greatest opportunities.

TB: But now all of that has changed.

JI: It is no more.

July 30 and August 1 and 19, 1991

DORSEY DAY

UNION LEADER AND ACTIVIST

I first met Dorsey in 1960 at an organizing convention for the formation of the Negro American Labor Council, which was to be headed by Mr. A. Philip Randolph, the national president of the Brotherhood of Sleeping Car Porters. The need for us to create an organization of this kind was sparked by a sarcastic and personally insulting question that was directed toward Mr. Randolph by the national president of the AFL-CIO at their national convention in 1960. Irked and irritated by Mr. Randolph's persistent, eloquent demands for racial fairness from the various unions associated with the railroad industry, that organization's current president shouted, "Who the hell picked you to be the spokesman for the Negro people?" Apparently he had forgotten or decided to ignore the fact that Mr. Randolph was already nationally known for his civil rights and civil liberties positions. As a matter of fact, in 1941 he had been responsible for creation of the Fair Employment Practices Committee when Executive Order 8802 was signed by President Franklin D. Roosevelt. He had also been an important part of the Progressive Party team that forced President Harry S Truman to issue and sign in 1948 the executive order that outlawed racial discrimination in the armed forces. Under his leadership, the Brotherhood also helped to support the rise of Dr. Martin Luther King Jr. into national prominence. So that is why we met and organized the NALC in Detroit in 1960. Our purpose was to illustrate through our various union and community leadership roles in all parts of the country that A. Philip Randolph was indeed a major national spokesman for the Negro people.

Dorsey Day was an integral part of that and many other efforts that were made to enlarge the civil rights movement. Back then, he was the president of one of the locals of the United Automobile Workers. He had already given time and service in the U.S. Army Air Corps during World War II, and now he was working vigorously on education, housing, and other related community issues. He was (and still is) a terrific organizer, working closely and diligently with the late Mayor Harold Washington in his two successful campaigns and then remaining as a leading member of the "inner circle" of his most trusted advisers.

———

TB: I'm here with Dorsey Day—longtime friend, labor activist, beautiful guy—who has grown up here in Chicago. Dorsey, where were you born?

DD: I was born in Tuscaloosa, Alabama, on January 24, 1921. When I was six months old, my parents and I moved from Tuscaloosa, Alabama, to Chicago Heights, Illinois. My first few years in grammar school were in Chicago Heights, and when I was age eight or so, we left Chicago Heights and moved to the city of Chicago.

TB: How did your parents happen to choose Chicago Heights?

DD: Because my father had a job there working at the American Manganese Steel Company. My uncle had moved to Chicago Heights earlier, and when he learned of a job opening at the steel company, my dad moved there also.

TB: Did you have any brothers and sisters?

DD: I had one brother who was left in Tuscaloosa, Alabama, but he died when he was about five years old. We went back to his funeral, but it's so vague I can't even remember him.

TB: Did you go back to Tuscaloosa very often?

DD: No, I did not. As a matter of fact, I only went back when I was five years old and again briefly after World War II.

TB: Were your mother and father born in Tuscaloosa?

DD: Well, my mother was born in Tuscaloosa, and my father was born in Bessemer. I believe that's where the steel mills are.

TB: Yes, it's a place near Birmingham. My dad also worked at the steel mills there. Do you remember your grandparents?

DD: I remember my grandmother on my mother's side because she moved up to the North along with my father and mother and I. The four of us lived together for quite some time. My grandmother passed away here in Chicago.

TB: Did she ever talk about her early life?

DD: Very little, Tim. My grandmother seems to have been very, very quiet—an introvert. She didn't do much talking about her past life except when she got ready to cook!

[*Laughter.*]

And she could really cook! As a matter of fact, she taught me a lot about cooking. I started cooking my own breakfasts, Tim, when I started grammar school in Chicago Heights. My father was working nights and my mother was working days. My father didn't get home until three o'clock in the morning, and if I did *not* prepare a breakfast for myself, I didn't eat. I wasn't going to wake *him* up, and my mother wasn't home!

TB: Do you have any idea where you lived when you first moved to Chicago?

DD: Yes, we lived at 6641 Rhodes Avenue, in west Woodlawn, I believe.

TB: What was Woodlawn like at that time?

DD: The thing I remember most about it was that there were boundaries. At that time, when you got north across Sixty-third Street, you were in dangerous territory. I know because I used to deliver newspapers in that neighborhood as a youngster!

TB: Dangerous? What do you mean?

DD: I'm talking about the situation between blacks and whites. And, as a youngster, if you went north past Sixty-third Street, you were in dangerous territory because there were gangs. They would take your newspapers and take your money. And you were certainly a "nigger" at all times—if you got up that way. I remember that very well. Sixty-third Street was definitely the northern boundary.

TB: What was the southern boundary?

DD: At that point in my life I very rarely got down past Sixty-seventh or Sixty-eighth Street, so I'm not exactly sure what the east-west boundary was. It seems to me it ran from South Park—as it was called then—over to Cottage Grove.

TB: The west side of Cottage Grove?

DD: Right, *definitely* to the west side of Cottage Grove! I used to go over there on the west side of Cottage Grove and shine shoes. I made myself a little shoeshine box and shined shoes right there on the corner of Sixty-third and Cottage Grove— the west side. There were a lot of whites that came over to get their shoes shined, and then they would go on back over to the east side of Cottage Grove.

TB: What was the quality of life in the neighborhood, as you remember it?

DD: Well, my father changed jobs after we moved from Chicago Heights to Chicago, and he started working in the Armour stockyards. When we were living in Chicago Heights, he fell off of a furnace and the door on the furnace fell on his foot and cut off two and a half of his toes.

TB: Oh!

DD: So he was unable to do the same job he was doing in the steel mills, and even though they offered him a lifetime job, that wasn't really an acceptable offer because they were working from sunup to sundown with no overtime—they didn't have unions at that time. So he ultimately changed jobs and started working at the Armour stockyards when we moved to Chicago. I remember the kids in the neighborhood very well. I mentioned earlier having to deliver papers right up to that dangerous north borderline—Sixty-third Street. Well, there were a few of us in that particular neighborhood who loved to fight. My friends Clifford, Harry Solins, and a guy we called Shorty, who was about fourteen or fifteen years old and built like a tank! Those guys would dispatch me across the borderline and be watching to see what was going to happen. And then, when the whites pounced on *me*, they pounced on *them*!

[*Laughter.*]

I was kind of a decoy, and we had a lot of fun doing that!

TB: You were fighting with fists?

DD: Oh, yes! And that is another thing. Back in those days it was just plain fists—that's all they would fight with. I never even saw a knife in those days, just fists. And we also played "kick the can," handball, and softball—those kinds of activities. Just good, clean fun.

TB: Most of the homes in that area were either single-family or two-family homes, as I remember it.

DD: That's right, Tim. At 6641 Rhodes Avenue, there was a two-flat apartment building and we moved into the first-floor apartment. Mabel Sanford, who, as you know, was a great pianist, owned the building. She and her daughter lived on the second floor. I became very attached to her daughter and we were very good friends until she passed. They sent her to Paris to study music, and when she came back, I really became interested in the piano because she played so beautifully. So it was a pretty fair neighborhood in those days, Tim.

TB: Were most of the people working?

DD: Yes, yes. During that period most people were working. The best jobs, of course, were with the post office because it was a job—in most instances—where you could keep clean.

TB: You know, when E. Franklin Frazier wrote about the Negro family in Chicago—in one of his essays, or maybe in the beginning of one of his books—he described Woodlawn as being one of the most middle-class black communities in the country. At that point, he himself couldn't live on campus at the University of Chicago, even though he was going to school there, so he lived in Woodlawn. My own recollection of Woodlawn was that you all were some sort of snooty Negroes who thought you were better than those of us who lived in Grand Boulevard!

DD: Right, right!

TB: It had that flavor.

DD: Yes, it did!

TB: But that style of living, as I remember it, was quite impressive because there was such a stability in the neighborhood and the people all knew each other.

DD: Yes, that's true, Tim. And also, as you will remember, back in those days there was a feeling among the people who lived further north that those who lived in Woodlawn were picked on justifiably because they were the "haves," and those that lived farther north were the "have-nots"—and that's why it was pretty dangerous for a young fellow who lived in Woodlawn to go north. I remember very well one day I decided I wanted some chili, and there was a Chili Mac's somewhere on Prairie.

TB: There was one in the Fifty-seventh block on Prairie.

DD: Right, right, right, and they were having what they called, "Fifty-eighth Street Day." So I decided to get up nerve enough to walk my girlfriend from Woodlawn down to the Chili Mac's to get some chili, but I was secretly scared to death until I saw Harry Solins coming *back* from that direction! My girlfriend and I were on one side of the street, and he was on the *other* side of the street, and, believe me, I was *so* happy to see him!

[*Laughter.*]

I knew nobody was going to bother *him*, because he was about the *baddest* boy in Woodlawn!

[*Laughter.*]

TB: You went to James McCosh Grammar School, didn't you? What was McCosh like?

DD: Well, when I entered McCosh, it was about 50 percent black and 50 percent white—about half and half. As the years went on, it became more black than white. And ultimately it became all black, period. When I say "black," there were also a few Orientals there. There was one fellow and his sister, but I can't remember his name. He became an "honorary" black!

[*Laughter.*]

TB: He was probably Chinese.

DD: Yes, he was Chinese.

TB: Now, the Tivoli and the Trianon theaters were located on the east side of Cottage Grove. As a young person, did you go to the Tivoli?

DD: I went to the Tivoli, but there was a time—when I was very, very young—that the Tivoli had segregated seating.

TB: Oh, really?

DD: Yes, and, of course, you didn't go to the Trianon at all, you know.

TB: Yes.

DD: And the Chicago Theatre also had segregated seating when I was coming up as a kid.

TB: Yes, I know. Guy Lombardo used to play at the Trianon.

DD: Right, right, right, and Wayne King used to play there. My mother wound up working for Wayne King, the "Waltz King"!

TB: Oh, is that right?

DD: Yes, and I ultimately taught his kids how to play table tennis. Do you know, Tim, Wayne King became sort of a mentor to me, because he helped me get into the branch of the service I wanted to get into. He became a major in the army, and he wrote a letter to the army on my behalf. As a matter of fact, Tim, once I had determined that I was going to have to go into the service anyway, I planned on going in as a specialist for inspecting tank shoes—the treads that they put on tanks. After I had started working at the steel mill myself, there was a white fellow there whose father was the president of the company, and this guy went into the army and became a warrant officer making six hundred sixty-six dollars a month inspecting tank shoes. Well, that possibility excited me, you know, because that's exactly what I was doing in the plant. So I figured there was no reason I couldn't volunteer to go into the service and do that kind of specialized work. Well, I got all my papers together and Wayne King wrote a letter for me, along with the president of the steel company and several other people. Those letters followed me all through my army career, but I *never* got to be a warrant officer—never even got the opportunity to go into that branch of the service! At least Wayne King had tried his best to help me in that regard.

TB: Well, he was a decent person.

DD: Oh, he was a very, very decent person. As a matter of fact, I remember when I was stationed in Oscoda, Michigan—after I got into the air corps but *before* we went to Tuskegee—Wayne King volunteered to come *through* Oscoda to pick me up and bring me home on leave.

TB: However, they still didn't allow you to go to the Tivoli!

[*Laughter.*]

DD: No, they certainly didn't! As a matter of fact, those letters didn't get me *any-where,* even in terms of the service, because the job I wanted to do—and was qualified to do—I was never given the opportunity to do. And, of course, later on in life, I found out they didn't have any black folks doing that kind of work at all.

TB: The color line was absolute, regardless of your sponsors. It was official policy.

DD: Yes, it certainly was, Tim. No doubt about it.

TB: Now, going back a bit, James McCosh Grammar School seemed to me to be a pretty close-knit school—in terms of the students, at least. It had a lot of activity. Which grades were you there, Dorsey?

DD: I went to McCosh from the third grade until I graduated, Tim. After that, in 1936, I went on to Tilden Tech, which was an all-boys school.

TB: Who and what do you remember about Tilden?

DD: Well, in those days, Tim, Tilden mastered *all* the sports. They were the top in everything. People don't realize it, but the coaches at Tilden had six *thousand* boys to pick from in football, basketball, and track. That's why we excelled in all the sports. I don't think they realized how off-balance it was in terms of the other schools having more limited choices of players. A school like Lindblom, for instance, had both girls and boys at that time, and they had nowhere close to six thousand students to pick from. So, it was quite a school, except there were only about 12 to 14 percent black students.

TB: Do you remember any of the students?

DD: Oh, I remember my friends very well. One of them, a Polish fellow, was a really good friend. I remember him protecting me. Even fighting with his brothers about me. When we had fistfights, his brothers "whupped" him too! And another time, when my friend's brother had called me a "nigger," my friend beat up his own brother! I remember him very, very well. There were others that became friends as well, and we would *walk* from Woodlawn all the way to Tilden every morning, and then back again. And, Tim, back in those days, the worst thing that youngsters used to do going back and forth to school was to hitch a ride on the back of a car! We would grab a fender and stand on the back of the bumper—because the driver couldn't see us, you know—and ride! I did that once or twice. I wasn't very good at it and I knew darn well if my father ever found out I was doing it, I'd get killed, so I only did it very, very rarely! It was just a matter of somebody calling you—well, the word wasn't "chicken" at that time, but we had similar words!

[*Laughter.*]

One of the youngsters that I ran with was Sammy Rayner's youngest brother, Johnny.

TB: Yes, Sammy had been there at Tilden Tech earlier with my brother, Walter. Sammy's family, they lived in Woodlawn, didn't they?

DD: Oh, yes. There were quite a few influential families who lived in Woodlawn.

TB: Yes, and at that time Tilden Tech was considered to be kind of elitist. Although it had a mixed population, there was a relatively small number of blacks. The students were mostly Irish, Polish, and Italian, and most of those students that went to Tilden, as I remember, were prepared to go on to college.

DD: Oh, yes, that's very, very true, Tim. Well, I graduated from Tilden Tech in 1940, and went immediately into Wilson Junior College. I also got a job as a junior draftsman with a little company. This job was under the auspices of the NYA, the National Youth Administration.

TB: The NYA was part of President Roosevelt's program for young people.

DD: Yes, and a very good friend of mine, John Ringle, who also went to Tilden, and I were the only two blacks involved in that program. Under the auspices of the NYA, there had been a drafting contest, Tim, and the person who won the contest would have an opportunity to go to Hawaii to work with the naval department as a junior draftsman. This was just prior to World War II, and John beat me out by three points! So he was the one who was chosen over all of those white boys to go to Hawaii!

TB: This was just before Pearl Harbor.

DD: Yes, and during this time, Tim, I felt the need to be earning more money, so I convinced my uncle to get me a job where he was working at the steel mills. My father tried his best to convince me not to go to work in the steel mills but to continue my education. However, I chose to go to work in the steel mills, and after I had been there for just a short while, World War II broke out. I was nineteen and figured I was going to ultimately be drafted. So, like I said, I decided to volunteer for the army because I just *knew* I was going to get that job as a tank shoe specialist! [*Laughter.*]

TB: You just knew that the prejudice wouldn't apply to you!

DD: Right. That's right! At the time, Tim, it hadn't really dawned on me what prejudice truly was. All my life I had gone to schools that were interracial—with blacks being the lowest group, however, in that environment. But it hadn't really dawned on me because I had had a lot of good friends who were young white fellows. There were only a few that were antagonistic toward blacks, and I just didn't associate with them. So, racism hadn't really dawned on me, Tim, until I got in the service and that's when it really, really hit me. When I was drafted in 1942, I was put into basic training in Jefferson Barracks, Missouri. Of course, we had no black noncommissioned officers at that time. Well, when that white sergeant would come in each morning to wake us up, as he entered the barracks he would say, "Ah've been up all night tryin' to think of ways to make it hard fer ya." I'll never forget that!
[*Laughter.*]
Now, I had gotten married, Tim, while I was working at the steel mill in Chicago, and my wife came down to see me in Jefferson Barracks. We attempted to go to the show, and when we found out we would have to sit upstairs in the balcony, I just refused to do it. So I took her back to her hotel in Jefferson City, and then I had to take a bus back to the barracks and, of course, there were civilians on the bus too. Well, I was sitting in one of those little seats right at the door, you know— just a single seat—and there were plenty of empty seats all over the bus. Then this

white guy gets on the bus and insists that I get up and give him my seat! And that's when racism really, really hit me. I don't know if this man was as drunk as he pretended to be, but he kept on insisting on having my seat and calling me names and all. There were a couple of sailors on the bus, an elderly black woman, a couple of white soldiers, and two or three other folks. This elderly black woman and I were the only two blacks on the bus, and she started rocking in her seat saying, "Oh, Lord! Oh, Lord!" And I said to myself, "Now what in the world is going on?" I could feel the tension rising in the bus, and this man was standing right up in front of me holding on to the post and saying to me, "Get up, nigger! Let me sit down." Now, having been on what we used to call "the short end" several times in my life, I had a knife in my pocket and knew how to use it. So I finally got up out of my seat and let him sit down, but then I opened my knife and sat right down in his lap!

[*Laughter.*]

Tears were rolling down my cheeks because I thought for sure I was going to die—but whatever happened I was determined to take him with me!

TB: Yes!

DD: And he just sat there shivering—I could feel him shaking all over—because I was crying. It was a nightmare I'll never forget. We just sat there until *I* got ready to get off the bus. The bus driver didn't say a thing—not a word—and we drove right on to the barracks, and he let me off. When the soldiers there saw what happened, they just grinned. They just laughed, and nobody said a word because, I guess, to them it was funny, but to me it was a life-and-death struggle.

TB: Yes, yes, I know. I know that feeling! The way you feel when you are suddenly and blatantly confronted with racial prejudice at its height.

DD: Yes, at its very height!

TB: And at times like that, the law is on the other side.

DD: Yes, that's exactly right. It was quite frightening to me. That was my first experience with racial prejudice, and it happened when I was at an age that I could appreciate it in all of its ugliness. Sure, we used to fight with white youngsters—even in Chicago Heights—on our way to school and all, but this was a different kind of thing to start with, and at that time in my life, I was old enough to realize what was really happening.

TB: And at this point you were prepared to go for broke!

DD: That's right!

TB: The humiliation and the unfairness of it all strikes you so deeply. And what's more, here you are in uniform as well!

DD: Absolutely, absolutely!

TB: That same kind of incident happened to me in Richmond, Virginia, when I was on my way to visit my brother Walter, who was stationed in North Carolina. I didn't even *think* about sitting in the back of the streetcar—I just got on and sat down, and this white man and his girlfriend got onto the streetcar, saw me sitting there, turned red with anger, and got up to tell the conductor. I had decided to just ignore his lip, and he was really furious!

[*Laughter.*]

The conductor tried to make a compromise, and he offered to give me my money back if I'd get off, but I said to him, "You think you're going to tell me that I have to sit in the *back* of this streetcar when I'm about to go overseas and risk my life for this person who is not even in the service? No, *no,* I won't do that!"

DD: Yes, yes—I know exactly what you went through.

TB: Well, Dorsey, how long were you in basic training?

DD: About three months. Then, when they found out that I had had ROTC training at Tilden Tech, they gave me a PFC stripe there to drill new people just coming in, and there was a young white colonel there. You know, now that I think about it, Tim, there's a good possibility that Wayne King may have had something to do with this happening because I didn't know this man at all. I had never even met him. Anyway, this colonel sent for me, and he asked me if I would like to join the air force. Well, when I mentioned that I had volunteered to go into the special skills branch of the service, he just sort of smiled and then said once again, "How would you like to go into the air force?"

[*Laughter.*]

And I said, "Well, that's a good option, so I guess I'll accept it," but I didn't really know anything about Benjamin O. Davis's Ninety-ninth Squadron at that time.

TB: To get into the air force, you had to have scored quite high on the AGCT [Army General Classification Test]. Whether you were going to be on the ground or in the air, to get into the air force was considered elitist even for a white person at that time, so I'm certain this opportunity was considered to be "super-elitist" for a black person back then.

DD: Yes, it was. So, I accepted the offer and I went to school to be trained as an engineering and operations clerk in the U.S. Air Force. I was a corporal when I finally got out. In the meantime, I was in school for six weeks or so and then I joined the rest of the group at Selfridge Field, Michigan. Benjamin O. Davis was there at that time. He had come back from Africa with his Ninety-ninth Squadron to pick up an entire group of four squadrons. By this time he was a colonel and his father was a brigadier general. I met his father at one point. But at any rate, after we had our training at Selfridge Field, Michigan, we had special training at Oscoda,

Michigan, and we then had additional special training at Tuskegee. From there we headed for overseas by transport, and we landed in Foggia, Italy. Those first few months in Italy were very, very tough, and during those first few months, we didn't even have planes. Then we moved from Foggia to Bari, where we picked up our planes. I had an opportunity of visiting other areas because I also became a crew chief.

TB: What were your duties in that capacity?

DD: Well, a crew chief is the person that oversees the airplane for the benefit of the pilot. He's the chief maintenance person for that particular airplane which he is assigned to, and he also gives basic instructions to new pilots. He and the pilot, of course, become very, very close. The pilot sees him as the person who has got his life in his hands! As a crew chief, you got special privileges. About every fourteen days or so we'd have a leave, which gave us an opportunity to do a lot of traveling. I also had some free time, and we always had down time whenever the weather was bad or after we had sent our plane up to fly. So I used to play table tennis a great deal, and another person who was a table tennis enthusiast was Colonel Davis. He and I had a couple of matches of table tennis, and he allowed us to form a little table tennis club. I was the captain of the club, and he gave me a team to play table tennis at various tournaments in Italy. I had some pretty interesting experiences as a result of that. I met a lot of people and got very, very good with the language.

TB: Race was not a problem?

DD: No, no. As a matter of fact, on the contrary. I was told by the Italians that white soldiers had lied to them and had told them that we blacks had tails—that kind of stuff, you know? And when they found out that they had been lied to, then, of course, they knew they couldn't trust the white soldiers, and so we black soldiers in Italy became sort of like honorary Italians, especially if we could speak their language very fluently. By that time I had become so familiar with the language, Tim, that I even remember translating from one Italian person to another! That was because the dialect was so different from one part of the country to another that they could barely understand each other if they were from different areas! [*Laughter.*]

TB: And because you had been doing so much traveling, you knew all of the dialects!

DD: Yes.

TB: The best way to learn a language is always to live with the folks that speak it. That way you pick up all of the nuances. Now, what were the German forces doing about this time? They were almost immobile, weren't they?

DD: No, as a matter of fact, we were still flying all kinds of missions, mostly reconnaissance and flying cover for the bombers. Sometimes those bombers couldn't get back to their own bases, and they had to land on our field. Well, the guys in our outfit were very mentally alert, and they welcomed an opportunity to have those whites who landed on our base understand that we were mentally superior to them. We *wanted* those stranded white guys to come into our tents, you know, and stay overnight and get a little change in their perspective!

[*Laughter.*]

I had a guy in my tent—Warren Jacobs—who was a mental giant. He had an IQ of 187, and he was one of the ones who really wanted the whites to come in and talk so he could show them how superior he was mentally. He'd gloat on this! That kind of thing happened in a lot of tents throughout our whole area. Whenever those bombers were stranded on our base, we were happy to have those white boys come to their tents so we could show them up intellectually!

TB: It was kind of fun!

DD: Yes, it was! At least it was something different to do!

TB: So, how long did you stay in Italy, Dorsey?

DD: When the war ended in Italy, I got transferred to a Signal Corps outfit, and that's an experience in itself. When I first got to the Signal Corps outfit, I was interviewed by the captain and, incidentally, Tim, it turned out to be someone that I had known in Chicago before the war. I didn't recognize him, but he recognized me! As a youngster, I used to go out on the pier fishing in Lake Michigan, and this guy would also be out there fishing. I didn't know his name, of course, but I remembered having talked to him frequently.

TB: What a coincidence! Was this a white guy?

DD: No, a black guy. He asked me what kind of work I could do, and I said, "Well, look, since you don't have any airplanes here for me to crew, right now I really can't do anything!

[*Laughter.*]

So he laughed a little and said to me, "Well, go on, sergeant, and work out in the gym." And that's what I did! I lost weight, and when I left that outfit I was as trim and fit as anybody you'd ever want to see! At any rate, when we were finally sent back to our original base, there was nothing for me to do there either, so for the rest of the time that I was in Italy, I was at the University of Florence furthering my education. Here, again, was an interesting experience in my life. The University of Florence was one of the leading schools in Italy. They graded on a curve, Tim, and it was tough—really tough. But I had some wonderful times there.

TB: Now, when did you get back home, Dorsey?

DD: In the later part of 1945 I got back to the States. And when I got back here I found that things were no better racially than they had been when I left to go to the war. I had thought that what I would like to do would be to become a private investigator or a detective, and I also wanted to work for Wayne King—he had been so good to me. He was ailing by this time, however, and I decided it would be easier for me to go back to work for my plant. And, of course, because of the law, they had to give you a job.

TB: Preference.

DD: Preference, right. So I went back into the plant and entered Chicago State at the same time. I went to Roosevelt University for a short while too, but, in the meantime, I still continued working.

TB: You were still married at this time, weren't you?

DD: Yes, I was married, but as soon as I got home, Tim, my wife and I became estranged, and we finally got a divorce. I started playing table tennis again and met my second wife, Nellie, at this time. We ultimately got married and had children.

TB: During this time you had become interested in the labor movement, hadn't you?

DD: Yes, I became interested in the labor movement, Tim, because of what I found after I got back here to the States after the war. I found that it was almost impossible to move up in the ranks even in my own plant. I had trained many whites in various jobs, and I thought that *I* should also have had an opportunity of getting a promotion. Those same people that I had been training became my bosses, and my own position remained just the same. Then one day a very interesting thing happened, and, I guess, that's what changed my life so that subsequently I became a labor organizer. One day a guy from Peak Engineering Company came into the company office. I was the group leader with five people working under me, and four of them were white. I happened to have been in the corner of the office going through some files when this guy from Peak Engineering Company came into the office. He looked at the foreman's desk and saw a pink slip there indicating that somebody was getting a raise, and he said, "Oh, I see somebody's getting a raise, and I'll just bet he's a goddamned nigger!" Well, I was standing in the corner all this time, and he didn't see me there, but one of the white youngsters that was working under me was in the room too, and you could have heard a pin drop. When that guy realized that I was there in the room and had heard him, he just turned around and walked out. Well, let me tell you, this particular incident really got to me. I had done a lot of things for that company by this time, Tim, to indicate to them that I had the ability to be upgraded, and they had not responded at all. They said that they respected me. I had all kinds of verbal respect from the bosses, the superintendent, the vice president, and even the president. Well, this time I went up to the office of one of the vice presidents and reminded him, first of all, about everything that I had done for the company. They had even given me awards, you know? One was a monetary award for something that I had invented that could really make a lot of money for the company. Then I told him what had been happening over the years—that the people whom I had trained had gone way up over me, and I said I just couldn't understand that. I then told him about the incident that had just happened, and he said, "Well, do you want him to apologize?" And I said, "No, I'm not interested in an apology. That wouldn't do me any good because he meant what he said, and his apology wouldn't mean a thing to me. I'm just talking about what I should be doing in this company rather than what I'm doing as of right now—based on the time that I've been here and my proven ability." So the vice president said to me, "Dorsey, let's have a meeting tomorrow. Call the foreman up here and the superintendent, and we'll sit down and talk about it." So we had this little meeting, and the superintendent kind of grinned and said, "Well, Dorsey, what do you think you're qualified to do?" That made me mad, and I said, "I think that in the course of the experiences I've had in this plant, there's *nothing* here that I can't do, including your job!"

[*Laughter.*]

So the vice president said, "Dorsey, let's think about this, and I guarantee you that within six months you'll have a job that suits you." So I said, "All right, I'll wait those six months." But while I was waiting those six months, Tim, during that time the plant was organized by the United Auto Workers, and they were already having meetings on a monthly basis. To be honest with you, in all reality, I very rarely attended those first UAW meetings because I was thinking that I would be in management sooner or later. But anyway, I finally decided, out of curiosity, to start going to those meetings, and they became quite interesting to me. Then, when they had the union election—during that six-month period that I was still waiting to hear *if* I would be given a suitable promotion by my company—I decided to run for recording secretary of the UAW, and I won, which meant that I would now be sitting at the bargaining table across from the officers of my own company!

[*Laughter.*]

TB: Quite an ironic situation!

DD: Yes, in a situation like that, the company *immediately* offered me an opportunity to go into management—but I refused. I said to myself, and to them publicly, that the time for that kind of opportunity had already passed and that I was not going to go in that direction now. Another reason that I had for refusing the company's offer is that if they took me out of the union and put me in management, they could fire me at any time they wanted, and then I'd be out of a job.

TB: And by that time you had a family.

DD: Right, right. I had a family coming along, and I wanted some security. So I grew in the union as a result of that, and then we *forced* the company—over the bargaining table—to put blacks in managerial positions. Incidentally, Tim, when I first went to the plant, they had segregated washrooms.

TB: Is that right?

DD: Yes, sir, they had segregated washrooms. All of the lounges and places in the neighborhood where we could go to eat—except one that I remember right around the corner on 115th Street and Cottage Grove—were highly reluctant to serve blacks in their establishments. This was true all around that community of Pullman, Roseland—right on the borderline with the state of Indiana. Well, one day Ralph Robinson and I went into one of those lounge/taverns—just to be refused—and we broke *that* up! That was another experience, of course. I also was given enough leverage by the chairman of Fair Employment Practices to break up the segregated washroom situation in my former plant and to make sure things were equalized there. So those were my early days in the union, and, of course, I ultimately became the president of that local UAW. The reason I ran for president was this: We had a white guy who was president, and he wasn't a *bad* guy, but he was afraid that I was going to run against him, and I would say to him, "John, I'm not going to run against you unless you do something that's going to *cause* me to run against you." Well, he fouled up one time. You know, there was this black guy there in the plant who wanted to become a machinist, and John just gave him the runaround. Well, that disturbed me, and at the following union meeting, I stood up and said to John, "You can expect me to run against you now!" And so I ran against him, and I won. After that, except for a short period of time, I continued to be president of the local union for fourteen years, and, of course, from there I went into the political realm because, as a union person, it's just automatic that you would get involved in the political end of things as well. That was because you needed to make sure that the people who were elected represented your interests. So that's how it all evolved.

TB: And in this process you met Willoughby Abner.

DD: Oh, yes. Willoughby Abner became one of my best friends, and someone that I could really go to when I had serious problems. Willoughby was just a staff rep, but he was *the* political person and an activist in the labor movement here in this region—taking in Illinois, Iowa, and Nebraska. Of course, Willoughby also became the president of the Chicago NAACP for a short while. He was the guy who *really* gave me the training that I felt I needed, so we were very close.

TB: He was a very, very interesting guy.

DD: Yes, he certainly was!

TB: Had he stayed in Chicago, we would not have heard of Jesse Jackson. There would have been no room!

DD: That's right! That's right! Those two would have been doing the same thing, but they got Willoughby out of Chicago by offering him a job in Detroit that he couldn't refuse. So then he went to Detroit and organized the organizers!

[*Laughter.*]

TB: He was gifted and very eloquent.

DD: Yes, he was! Yes, sir, he was! And Walter Reuther got him out of the UAW because he could see what was coming!

[*Laughter.*]

TB: Wil ran for state senator one time as an independent. I think he was involved in the Progressive Party movement.

DD: Incidentally, Tim, the UAW had a training center in Ottawa, Illinois, and he also taught those sessions there. He was beautiful—just so eloquent!

TB: A lot of leadership emanated from him, a lot of union leadership and a lot of political leadership. When he left here we missed him.

DD: Yes, indeed. Incidentally, when he passed, I was scheduled to go to his funeral along with another black local union president, but there was a FAPB meeting that was very important to blacks in the UAW throughout the entire region, so we opted to go to this meeting rather than go to the funeral. We canceled our plane reservations, but you know something? Had we made that flight, we would have both been killed. You remember that crash at Midway?

TB: Yes, Wil's mother and sister were on that plane. I worked with his sister—we both taught, you know. That was a real tragedy. Well, Dorsey, what do you see in the future?

DD: It's gloomy from one side of the picture, Tim, because our youngsters have gotten in a groove that will take them down the drain, with drugs, etc. But then from the other side of the picture, when I do my traveling, I discover some untold success stories about youngsters who are really starting to move into categories that we have never even dreamed that they'd be in, and if we could just visualize everything from that standpoint, you'd think we were in quite good shape.

TB: Yes, that's true.

DD: And hopefully, that is the side that will eventually win because it seems to me that at least three-quarters of our future generation are already completely lost— it's that sad and that simple. And, of course, there's that "in between" group who are leaning toward the bad end because they too are on drugs, even though they have the sophistication to know better, and there's a good possibility that they will also fall over to the bad side because of this. So, it's really up in the air right now, Tim, but, hopefully, something will come about to make some positive changes for our young people.

TB: Yes.

DD: And as far as I can see there's still a heavy contest going on out there—economically—with whites recognizing that if they relinquish their grip on us blacks, we're going to take over our own destinies, and they won't be able to make what they want to make off of us anymore. They are making sure that this doesn't happen because they've got kids of their own that are coming up in the world. So there's that threat out there because of the economic situation throughout all of our communities. This situation isn't unique to Chicago. Detroit is even worse than it is here in that regard, because most of the industries in Detroit are connected to the auto industry. Those blacks who are still working in the plants in the auto industry are middle-class folks. They make a good salary, but rather than moving up, they're partying with the money they're making, just having a good time rather than seeing to it that their children are going off in the right direction. So it still can go either way.

TB: Yes, Dorsey, it can.

DD: All we can do is pray that things will work out better for us, but in the present climate politically, Tim, it doesn't look good to me because, if things keep going the way they're going, even though whites will be affected as well, blacks will be affected a whole lot more. They will be without benefit of welfare and without the social programs that are available to them today. If the politicians keep going in the direction that they're going, these programs will not be available to us tomorrow—it's just that simple. *Jobs* are the key to solving this thing. One of the things I wanted to talk to your senator about is that we've got to concentrate on getting good-quality jobs for black folks. Right now they are just not available. Let me tell you, there's a young girl here in Chicago that I talked to just the other day in this same regard. She has a degree and cannot find a job. She has gone *everywhere* putting in applications—she has done *everything* she can do, and she said to me, "Dorsey, I've done *everything* right—everything! They told me to go to school and get an education. That's what I've done. Now I've got my degree, and I *know* that I'm good, but I just can't get a job!" And when you multiply that level of frustration by the hundreds of thousands of other young folks out there with the same kind of problem, you know, it's creating a dangerous situation.

TB: Yes, it is.

DD: So, *jobs* are the key to the future.

July 7, 1995

JACOBY DICKENS

BANKER AND ENTREPRENEUR

Jacoby Dickens is a classic example of the kind of people who decide early in their lives that an ordinary job working for someone else is only going to be a very temporary thing for them and that eventually they are going to go into business for themselves. After graduating from Wendell Phillips High School and attending college, he obtained what seemed like a good, solid job with the Chicago Board of Education, but he was already initiating his quest for personal independence and entrepreneurial exploration. The opportunity he was waiting for arose during the early 1960s when he and his good friend, radio personality Daddy-o Daylie, worked together to create a large and impressive bowling alley in Chicago's middle-class Chatham neighborhood. Since they could not find the necessary financing for their venture from any of the local banks, they turned for advice to a black friend of theirs named Roland Burris. At that time Roland Burris was not yet involved in politics but was a vice president of the Continental Bank of Chicago, and he was able to negotiate a loan for them. Their business took off almost immediately and quickly expanded even further. When more money was needed to finance this expansion, they pooled their financial, business, and political resources with several other successful black entrepreneurs in order to establish the Seaway National Bank, which is now one of the most successful minority-owned banks in the country. In recent years, Mr. Dickens has expanded the services offered by the Seaway National Bank to help and encourage community redevelopment. In addition, he has helped to raise funds for and give practical advice to important black political candidates, such as the late Mayor Harold Washington. It is impossible to imagine our community without the many contributions that he has made.

TB: Jacoby, where were you born?

JD: Panama City, Florida, in June 1931. I don't know what the population was back then, but today it's about fifty thousand. My mother and father were both born within a fifty-mile radius of Panama City. My father was born on a farm which was about forty miles away, and my mother was born about fifty miles away in the other direction on a farm ninety miles straight west of Pensacola, which was a navy base at the time. My grandparents on both sides were from that same area. Both were raised in farming communities and came to Panama City because there was industry there. There was a paper mill and a shipyard and things like that. So they left the country to come to the city for employment. I have five sisters. I'm the third child, and I'm the only boy. We moved from Panama City, Florida, to Chicago in 1946.

TB: Most of the people from that area went to New York.

JD: Absolutely. Floridians always went right up the coast. Most of them made it all the way to New York, but there were some that dropped off along the way. My parents decided to come here because my father had a younger sister who came here in 1942. She had a good job and was doing well and was always telling my father that, if he ever decided to leave Florida, Chicago was the place he ought to go. So he came here to Chicago a few months ahead of the family and got himself established, and then we followed a few months later.

TB: Where did you attend high school?

JD: Wendell Phillips, right after World War II. We lived at 4242 South Wentworth. There were only two black families on the west side of Wentworth. That was the dividing line. I had some cousins that lived in the same building, and I remember them telling me that they had problems going two blocks west to school because there was always that dividing line between the blacks and the whites.

TB: It seemed like the Maginot Line. I remember a family along there on the west side that had a grocery store at Forty-fifth Street, I think.

JD: I have been in that store many times in my life, the one that you're talking about.

TB: Yes, on the east end the dividing line was Cottage Grove.

JD: Oh, there's no question about it. There were some places on Cottage Grove where it wasn't totally black, but anything east of Cottage Grove was just about all white. It was mostly Japanese and Chinese from Forty-third and Drexel over to the lake. Most of the inhabitants in that area were Orientals and whites. At one

A THRIVING COMMUNITY

LOCAL BUSINESSES, WORKERS, AND ENTREPRENEURS

Nile Queen Costumes general office (*above*) and shipping room (*opposite*)

Pullman employees

"Become a PORO Dealer . . ."

Neighborhood grocery

ENTERTAINMENT AND NIGHTLIFE

Major Smith Opera Quartet

Sammy Davis Jr.

Louis Jordan

Club DeLisa

Jimmy Bowman

Joe Louis and Sarah Vaughan with friends

Billie Holiday

FAMILIAR FACES
FROM THE NEIGHBORHOOD

Congressman Oscar DePriest

370th Infantry officers

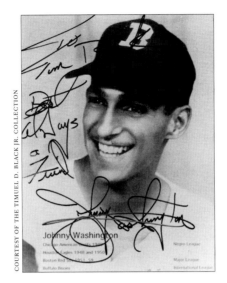

Johnny Washington of the Chicago American Giants, Negro League; Houston Eagles and Boston Red Sox, Major League; and Buffalo Browns, International League

HARLEM GLOBETROTTERS BASKETBALL TEAM - SEASON OF 1930-31
Left to right: (Standing) Abe Saperstein, Toots Wright, Byron Long, Inman Jackson, William Oliver, Seated: Al Pullins

Chicago's Harlem Globetrotters

The prominent Williams family: Morris, Annie, Morris Jr., Levi, and Willa

Edward Pryor and his daughter Elizabeth

Grade school graduation, June 1932, a day to celebrate: Timuel D. Black Jr.,
William T. Green, and Ms. Green

time I lived at 4140 Lake Park, and it was the same situation there. We were one black family out of a very few.

TB: What about the neighborhood you were living in? Tell me something about that.

JD: The neighborhood was very stable. You wouldn't recognize it today, but once it was a very proud neighborhood. After dark a lady could walk to the bus stop three or four blocks from her home without any fear of being harassed. Most of the people in the area knew each other, and it was a very warm kind of situation.

TB: Who were some of the people you remember from Phillips? Who was the principal when you were there?

JD: The principal was Maudelle Bousfield.

TB: A legendary person.

JD: She was the first black principal of a high school in the entire city of Chicago. Some of my classmates have gone on to be very successful. Sam Cooke, the singer, was in my class. Judge Porter, who just resigned as a judge in Chicago, was also in my class. Marla Gibbs, of *The Jeffersons*. Joan Johnson, George Johnson's ex-wife, was in the class ahead of me. The first black woman mayor in the state of California was a classmate. I have a lot of fond memories of my days at Wendell Phillips. I remember many of the teachers who had great influence on me. Yesterday I went to the Dixon School to talk to a group of kids because they are teaching the kids banking and those kinds of things. We were talking about success, and I told them I once had a teacher who taught Spanish. Her name was Mrs. Albert, and she said the problem with success is that it too often comes disguised as hard work, and that's why so many of us don't really accomplish many things. It's amazing how things like that penetrate your mind, and they just don't ever leave you. Mrs. Arven was my math teacher. Mr. Donner was the dean of boys, and he taught shop. There was Mr. Tortorelli, the basketball coach. Henry Springs came in sometime about my last year.

TB: Those were the special kind of teachers that students felt a personal kind of kinship to.

JD: Absolutely, and there was a great track team. Jim Golliday was one of the stars. He also broke a record in this country, but they disqualified it because of the wind factor. I think it was at Northwestern when he ran it. Jim also briefly played professional football. Buddy Young went on to do his thing at Illinois, and he became a professional football player and was one of the first executives with the National Football League. Earl Banks did well at Iowa and then became a coach at a college out in Baltimore. Another famous track person, Ira Murchison, was a little after me, but he was in that same group.

TB: That was a period of great things happening. Many people think it was just athletics, but there were some people there who were not in athletics and who also made a great contribution.

JD: Yes, and the present principal of Wendell Phillips was a classmate of mine, Juanita Tucker. We were in the same class. After Phillips, I went to Roosevelt College. At that time Roosevelt was just a college.

TB: You graduated from high school in 1948, so when you went to Roosevelt, it was almost in its infancy, and it had an open enrollment policy, which no other college in the country had at that time, in terms of enrolling blacks.

JD: It was groundbreaking. Roosevelt started out in a building over on Wabash, and then they moved to their present location. Then I went to George Williams, and I also spent some time at Florida A&M, but I never got a degree. I had 157 credit hours, which was more than enough to graduate, but I was going to school and working, and I was also already trying to be an entrepreneur. Every time I would find a deficiency of some kind in my education, of which at first there were many, I would go back to night school. I learned accounting and all of that stuff that I didn't get in day school. I went to school at the college level throughout the period from 1948 to 1978, thirty years, picking up those "need" and "functional" courses. Now I have at least three schools that are trying to get me to come and just sit down long enough to get my degree.

[*Laughter.*]

So I am going to finally accept a degree from Chicago State University. I think it's more meaningful for me to get it there, but I've had a similar offer from the University of Wisconsin and I don't even know how they got my name because I never went there. They probably just read somewhere something about what I've done.

TB: When you went to Florida A&M, did you go there because they had a great tradition?

JD: Well, they had a great marching band, but, no, I went because I still had a lot of relatives in Florida. I went back for two semesters. Incidentally, I now sit on the board at the School of Business at Florida A&M.

TB: Even then, you had some feelings about entrepreneurship.

JD: Well, the first job I ever had was back in Panama City. I must have been maybe nine or ten years old when I went to work for this Gilbert Grocery Store. Gilbert was a white entrepreneur, and I used to work for him after school Monday through Friday. I would also work all day Saturday, and half a day on Sunday, and I made one dollar and fifty cents a week. When school was out, I got an increase and made three dollars a week because by then I was working six and a half days a week full-time. But the most pointed thing about that was that I used to sit there, because he wanted me to stay, until he finished counting that day's receipts at night before we closed down, and I could see just how much money that this man was making! People would come in and get things on credit, and he would just write down what they bought but oftentimes the people were illiterate, and he would just put in there whatever he wanted to. Then, when they got paid, they would bring their check to him, and he would cash that check and take out what he claimed was his and give them back the difference. I said to myself, "My God!" Number one, he was not being fair, but, even if he had been fair, he could still make all the money he wanted to make, and I knew from that point on that I didn't want to work for anybody else. I wanted to work for myself.

TB: That was your goal.

JD: Yes, but it was more than a goal. It was a thirst!

TB: During your formative years in Chicago, you have described the neighborhood as being stable and safe. What kinds of recreational things did young people do in their spare time?

JD: I went to a Boys Club in the evening. It was in the 3800 block on Michigan. It's still there. Now it's called the Donnelly Center, but it used to be South Side Boys Club. The YMCA was active then, over at Thirty-seventh and Wabash, and there were the movies! There used to be a little theater on Thirty-fifth Street called the Louis and we had another movie house over at Forty-third and Wentworth. Those were the kinds of things that we did in those days. Every year on Bud Billiken Day, we used to go and follow the parade right on out of Washington Park. We never went home. As kids we used to stay out there all night. We slept on the grass, and nobody ever bothered us.

TB: Mama and Daddy weren't worried?

JD: Naw, they knew where we were, and they knew we were safe.

TB: Oh, boy, what a difference today! Now, getting back to adulthood, after you leave high school and become serious about making a living, and you now have a goal of becoming independent and working for yourself, how did you go about achieving those things? What were your experiences?

JD: Well, the first job I had out of high school was with Unity Mutual Life Insurance Company, which was originally the Unity Funeral Parlor. I worked for A. W. Williams. We were at 4719 South Indiana at the time. Earl B. Dickerson was the general counsel for the company. But I didn't do well in insurance. I made a living, and that was about all. So I left and went on to work at a Goldblatt's warehouse as a stock boy, but after a little while I also left that and went on because I had gone up the ladder just about as high as any black boy could in that organization. That just wasn't fulfilling enough for me, and so I moved on to work at the University of Illinois as a janitor at night. In the daytime I still had my Goldblatt's job. So I was working sixteen hours a day, and I did that for a period of five years. Then I worked as engineer for the Board of Education for the next ten or twelve years. My first school was Betsy Ross. My second school was Wendell Phillips, where I was an engineer for a couple of years. Then I went to Hyde Park. When I first started there, if someone didn't show up at another school, they would take one of the engineers out of our high school and send them over there to that other place.

TB: How many black engineers were there at that time?

JD: I was number six in the history of Chicago. Today that number is closer to a hundred. We used to hold classes in the boiler rooms at that time to teach aspiring blacks who wanted to become engineers like us.

TB: At that time there were only six black engineers employed in all the Chicago schools. How many schools were there?

JD: Seven hundred schools.

TB: And now you have almost a hundred out of approximately the same number of schools.

JD: Which means that we still haven't got there!

TB: Yes, we are still far away from home. How long did you stay in that area?

JD: Ten to twelve years, but at the same time while I was there I was getting involved in real estate. I bought my first building in the mid-fifties, and the person I bought it from was Dempsey Travis. He had an office at Forty-seventh off of King Drive. My first building was a four-flat at Seventieth and Wentworth. At the peak of my real estate adventures, I had 106 apartments, maybe as many as ten buildings at one time. Because I had been an engineer with the Board of Education, I knew how to do electrical and plumbing repairs, so we did all of our own maintenance. I had a crew of five guys, and we did all the repair and maintenance work in all those buildings.

TB: Are you still in real estate?

JD: No, I sold all my real estate off in the mid-sixties. When I first got in the business, people still had some respect for property. As time went on, with the advent of dope and all the things that infiltrated our neighborhoods, I just found it very difficult to operate in that kind of environment. You go to some place to collect your rent, and not only is the person not there, but they have moved everything out, including your fixtures, bathtub, and everything else! It really got to be bad. So I got out of that, and I went into the bowling business with Daddy-o Daylie in 1969. Dempsey Travis was also the broker for that deal.

TB: At one time that was the busiest bowling alley on the South Side.

JD: It was in the top 3 percent of the entire country.

TB: How did all this come about?

JD: Well, Daddy-o Daylie and I—

TB: You're talking about Daddy-o, the famous disc jockey?

JD: Right, at the time there was a bowling alley at Sixtieth and Stony Island called South Shore, and I went in there sometimes to bowl in the league. I just bowled at that place the first year, but the next year I became president of the league, and then Daddy-o asked me to help work with him to promote the leagues and that kind of thing. We did a marketing thing and were quite successful at it, but then the place burned down, and the gentleman who owned the Starlight asked us to come over there, and we started doing the same promotional thing for him. The neighborhood was changing from white to black, and after it got all black, the Jewish fellow there, Allen Luxembourg, said he wanted out of there. So Daddy-o and I went around looking for someone to buy this place, and it occurred to me one day, hell, why am I looking for someone to buy it? I already knew the business. I had learned it from the ground up. So we went back and started putting a package together. We were one of the first SBA loan recipients, but it was not easy to come by this. We went to at least eight downtown banks before we could get a loan. Finally after being rejected and turned down by seven of them, we went to Continental Bank. The loan officer that I spoke to there was Roland Burris, the present Illinois attorney general. After reviewing my package, he said, "Bar none, this is the finest package I have ever looked at. I don't need anything else from you." Well, what he didn't know at the time was that I had already been to seven other banks and had been turned down! So, by then, anything that any bank could possibly think to ask me, I had already put it into the package. Well, ten days after I sat there in front of Roland, they called and told me that I had the loan. On May 2 of 1969, Daddy-o and I purchased that place, and from that I went on to buy other bowling alleys.

TB: That entrepreneurship spirit never leaves you.

JD: Oh, no, even when I was a kid, I was the only guy in the neighborhood down in Florida that had a lemonade stand. As a matter of fact, I had three lemonade stands! I had two other kids working for me on other streets, not the street I was on. You see, I took care of my own street, and I had two franchises! After the cost of putting the ingredients of the lemonade together, they got 50 percent of the take. Back then, I guess I wasn't very much of a businessman, giving them 50 percent of the take, but after I took out the expenses, we split fifty-fifty on the money they made at these two other lemonade stands.

TB: Those bowling alleys were the beginning of your really moving into something that was substantially successful, and part of the reason for that success was the result of the exposure that Daddy-o had on the radio.

JD: Oh yeah, that was a great asset. That was in '69. After we were in there for about three years, we reached a point where we were in the top 3 percent in the entire country. That measurement is based on how many games were bowled in each lane, and we were open twenty-four hours a day. We drew from all of Chicago because we were one of the first black centers for bowling. Sonny Boswell was there before us, but he had passed away, and we were the largest—a twenty-four-lane house, when all the other houses were just sixteen-lane houses. You know, some of them are much bigger today, but the timing was right for us. Back then, it was a time when blacks could not get into the American Bowling Congress, which is the organization that governs bowling. I still have one bowling alley left over on Torrence which I've had since '75, and which my daughter still operates. It's very successful. If you spoke of the top houses on the South Side of Chicago, it would be in the top three.

TB: But you left the bowling business in terms of "hands-on."

JD: Yes. Ernie Collins, who was the second chairman of Seaway Bank, came to me back in the mid-seventies and said, "I'd like for you to buy some stock in the bank." I asked him, "Why?" And he said, "Well, I'm having a problem. Some of the stockholders are trying to move against me, and I want to take control, but I need somebody to come in with me and buy some stock. I'll buy 39 or 38 percent of the stock, but I want you to buy 13 percent, and then between the two of us we'll have 51 percent, and we can keep control of the bank." Well, after about seven months, all of that came to pass, and I came into the bank as a director, but in a few months I was appointed vice chairman, and Ernie Collins was still the chairman. It went on like that from '78 for the next four years, and then Ernie said, "I want to get out because I'm getting too old. Why don't you put together a team to buy me out?" And so for the next two years, he and I fought about what the proper price ought to be. Finally, we agreed in '86, and that's when I bought Ernie out and became the controlling interest. But I became chairman earlier than that. I became chairman in '84 while he was still there.

TB: Now, Ernie Collins was also a member of the Collins family which pioneered in the barbecue business. I remember the first place they had. It was on Sixty-first Street, and then they opened up a number of other places.

JD: Ernie was the most successful of all of the brothers—there were seven, I think—and they all were entrepreneurs or something. Most of them were in barbecue, but some were in groceries, and one of them had taverns.

TB: But Ernie is the one who seemed to have the most drive, and I wanted to get that on the record because a person like that who is driven for success, whatever he started with, his drive will always move him or her beyond what has already been accomplished to another, higher level of challenge. You and Ernie seem to always have had that urge to do something beyond what you've already done.

JD: You know, Tim, I never had the mentality of corporate America. You know what I mean? Just working and becoming a vice president of some already-successful corporation and having that be the ceiling for me. That just wasn't suited with my personality. I wanted to do something for myself, and I always wanted to do it with other black folks because I knew that if I had a business and my customers were black, white people couldn't just come and take those folks away from me. That's why every business that I've been involved with has been with other blacks, and I tell many people that I see in the bank today—those who want to go downtown and do all that kind of thing outside of this community—that we are sitting right here in the middle of the most successful black community in the world. The income per household here is the highest of any major black community in the world. By "major," I mean one hundred thousand people or more. You will not find any area in the world where black people live that's more successful and has more income per household than the Park Manor, Chatham, and the West Chesterfield areas that we're sitting in right here. I mean, in this country, in '91, black folks spent three hundred billion dollars for goods and services, and I'm told that in '92, that number is going to approach four hundred billion dollars! To make a long story short, if we were to compare that to the gross national product of all the countries around the world, we would be number two. Number two! Second only to the white money that's spent in this country. But, as it stands, only 6 percent of those monies get spent with companies that are owned by another black person. That means that we are exporting 94 percent of all these dollars out of our community, never to return again. That 6 percent that we spend with each other makes at least five and a half to six turns before it exits from the community. If we were able to double that number from 6 percent to 12 percent, it is estimated that across the country—and this is from data provided by the U.S. Census Bureau—it would mean three million jobs for black folks. We haven't ever seen that kind of economic boon in our lifetime, and now to make it happen all we have to do is make a concentrated effort to do our business with each other.

TB: Do we have enough black-owned businesses to absorb that kind of change?

JD: Oh, no, I don't see the existing businesses absorbing all this, but as a result of increased activity within our own communities, a lot of new black-owned businesses would be generated very quickly. You know, I can remember a time when there was hardly a single black merchant on Forty-seventh Street.

TB: Yes, except for poolrooms and barbershops and such.

JD: The first black business I remember that was of any significance was the Palm Tavern. The Jewish merchants had the rest of that street all locked up.

TB: Yes, and they would not permit blacks to rent stores there.

JD: I've been told that, but you are more in touch with that period than I am.

TB: Well, the facts were that at one time the Jones brothers owned a Ben Franklin store on the north side of Forty-seventh Street, right down from the Palm Tavern. They remained there for a while, but then when the Jones brothers decided to change residence, due to pressure, and they moved to Mexico, and then that all changed.

JD: The rest of the world is not going to have respect for our community until we can control our own community economically. That is absolutely a must. I'm not saying that we need to go out and picket or keep other folks from coming into our community. Let them come, but they can't stay here if we don't do business with them. We need to exercise every opportunity to do business with each other and stop making excuses for not doing it and going someplace else.

TB: At the present time, a large number of merchants in the business area from Sixty-seventh Street to Seventy-ninth Street are nonblack. They are mostly Asian. Do you get a substantial amount of their banking business here in this bank?

JD: Almost zero. Seaway Bank's the largest black bank in the country, but if we have five Asian merchants banking here, they are only tokens. The Korean merchants don't do anything in our community.

TB: We have two examples of relatively recent buyouts of established companies within the black community. Chicago Metropolitan is the first, and then you have Supreme, which has now been bought by United of America.

JD: Yes, a group is now negotiating for part of that property in order to put a Checker's hamburger branch in that area where Supreme was at Thirty-fifth Street. I've heard that the building is going to be torn down.

TB: That building also has its own history. It was Supreme Liberty Life. It had those three names because it made a merger within the community. Now, what happens when these small economic and financial institutions become managed from the outside, rather than from the inside?

JD: "He who has the gold makes the rules." If outside people own it, we are going to come up short, but the future's very unpredictable. Now they are talking about selling the Independence Bank, where Al Boutte is president, to South Shore, but South Shore is not a black bank. They put a lot of their money into investment in Poland because the owner is Polish. What's more, to tell you the truth about it, I want to buy the Independence Bank. I talked with them last year about both Drexel and Independence, but the number that they are looking for is just too damned high. I'm willing to pay a fair price. I don't want to steal it. I don't need to steal it. I think Seaway is the most viable buyer around, and at Seaway I have a controlling interest, and I don't ever want Seaway to be anything but what it is right now, and that is a black institution. I am presently working on restructuring my will so that the people who receive it after me won't be able to make any change away from that!

TB: Now, our Chicago-based black-owned business community years ago gave a lot of inspiration to young men like you. Once upon a time, it seemed to have the strength to become a community which could almost be self-contained and successful. When I grew up, from the first job I ever had until the time I went to college, my total means of making a living was right here in this black community. Not too long ago, I talked with Jack Isbell. We grew up together.

JD: No kidding? I've known Jack forever. I even knew his wife's mother, Mrs. Mc-Clerkins. She died at 103 or something like that, and I also knew her uncle, Leonard Livingston. See, in Florida, where Leonard came from, his mother was my godmother. We lived across the street from each other, and I would come home from school, and I would go in his mother's house to stay until my parents got home. Her name was Mrs. Simmons, and she was as grand and gracious a lady as you would ever want to meet. That little town was called Panama City, Florida, and Jack Isbell used to drive Leonard Livingston down there to see his mother when we were living across the street from her.

TB: Jack came to Chicago after I was here already. We went to grammar school together, Burke School. Anyway, Jack told me recently that all of his life he has worked here in the black community, starting as a peddler in the alley selling vegetables. Then, eventually, after he met his wife, Mr. Livingston gave him a job working for the Jackson Funeral System. Jack said that he had made his entire financial success from working with people in the area from Forty-fifth and what is now King Drive down to Forty-seventh and King Drive, just that two-block area! He had sent his daughter to school and did all the things that normal families were doing in that same area, but when I asked him, "Jack, could you ever do all that again?" He said, "No, that could not be." What I'm wondering is what we should say to young people after we send them to school and promise them that they will be the recipients of benefits from their perseverance? What can we offer them now right here in our community?

JD: We have got to be able to offer them opportunities to succeed. I get a ton of applications. I know I have at least four or five of them right now on my desk from M.B.A.s who are looking for jobs. We tell them to "go to school, get an education, so that you can prepare yourself for success in this capitalistic form of society that we have here," and now they're having problems finding a job, and I don't have an answer for them. I just know that we have to do things to create more businesses in our own community. That's why I admire the people who have started business institutions. It's not very often in a person's lifetime that they can start something and have it reach the magnitude of being the largest black-owned bank in the country with assets in excess of two hundred ten million dollars. It would be a travesty to allow that kind of institution to leave the community, but if we want to perpetuate the things we have already accomplished, we can't allow Seaway Bank to remain its present size. We have to keep on making this bank bigger. That's why my thoughts are, "I want Independence Bank, I want Drexel." But we must continue to control what we are doing so that we will continue to have some hand in development of the entire community. We just can't build it up and sell it to some outsiders just to make some money and think that we have made any kind of a lasting contribution to this community. When Harold Washington started to run for mayor of the city of Chicago, I never thought that he had a chance, but I gave Harold more money than I ever gave a politician in my life simply because I wanted him to look good in the race, even though I never thought he was going to win. On the election night, I still thought that the "machine" was going to find some way in which to take this victory away from us. You know, even if we actually won it, I thought they'd take it away from us, but history shows that I was wrong in that evaluation, and I was wrong for one simple reason. I did not recognize the fact that we had a candidate that was able to galvanize all segments of the community, and that's all that's missing today. If we could have one man like that today, we could do it again! But now they say, "Well, we need this and that. We need to have outside help." But we don't need help from anyone. We can do it by ourselves!

TB: That's right. When Harold and I talked about the election, he closed the door and smiled and said, "Tim, if everybody in our community came out to vote, we wouldn't need nobody else." I said that, "That's true," and he said, "But we can't make everybody come out—so let's go after all the others." But we still have the necessary leverage because we still have the numbers of registered voters. In your opinion, did Harold's tenure in office make a difference?

JD: It made a difference because it opened up a lot of things in this community. It opened up things business-wise, it opened up things socially, and it opened up areas that we had never been exposed to before. He opened some doors that could never be closed again. There are a lot of things that he had a big effect on, but he never got any proper credit for what he was able to accomplish.

TB: So, in your opinion, there is an intimate relationship between the nature of the economic and the political. The first successful campaign of Harold Washington was organized and financed by the people in the black community with black leadership at their forefront.

JD: Yes, and the media folks wouldn't give us a dime's worth of attention. We had to go down to ABC or NBC to get our commercials on. It was strictly grass roots. When I was designing what I wanted to do with my life, I never wanted to be in a situation where the people I was attempting to do business with were white. I always wanted to do business inside my own community. I didn't want anyone ever to come and take that away from me. I also knew if I didn't do it right the people here would simply not continue to do business with me, and that was fine with me, but I didn't ever want a situation where people would not do business with me because of my race or my color. So, everything that I have ever accomplished in my life has always been directed toward this community. I am comfortable here. This is my home. I feel good coming here every day.

TB: Yes, but our young people today, they don't have the thrill that I had growing up when I went to work for Chicago Met and watched people like Cole and Ewing, and all the rest of those entrepreneurs, as they functioned and made a decent living. That was a necessary form of inspiration for me. Now, as you have said, taking into consideration that no business or community can survive unless it has the ability to expand, what I was just thinking was that with all of this new talent frustrated and currently unable to find suitable jobs, what communities should do is to set aside a group of what DuBois called "the talented tenth" to do some thinking and create new kinds of possibilities.

JD: Create a think tank?

TB: Yes, has there ever been any thought among the leadership about trying to organize a cadre of young black men and women into a group like this?

JD: I don't know of any, but you're right. We need something like that desperately. We're going to have to move in those directions. We can't continue to allow all those bright young minds to go to waste, and we're successful enough now that we can afford to do something of that nature and make it work.

TB: We've got the legal minds. We've got the economic minds. We've got people like me who are getting old but can still give a little bit. We have a cadre of qualified people who can begin to develop the abilities of these young people so that they can expand on their own kind of genius. What I want is for our young black intellectuals to develop a sense of loyalty to the community which spawned them, and become an inspirational model for the young men and women who may not have been as privileged as they have been.

JD: We've got to put an organization like that together but not have it as a onetime thing. This thing has to go on into perpetuity.

TB: An idea like this is not new. I saw Eddie Williams over there at the Joint Center for Political and Economic Studies in Washington, D.C., and he has done some of what we're talking about, but he has expanded so much and so quickly that now he's got a lot of white money involved, and a lot of white "experts" determining policies. When I go there, I don't see blacks anymore, and I believe that is not what Eddie would want. I think that the reason he started the Joint Center was to not only dispense information but also to train young blacks, and now he's got white folks there who think they know more about black folks than black folks do themselves! Yet I can't reject my hope for the future. I still dream of a city like Chicago as an experimental kind of thing, as some kind of a "work in progress," as something that has still not reached anything like its true potential. Does that make any sense?

JD: It makes all the sense in the world, but we have to set the necessary things in motion that will enforce what you are saying. Now, we are not going to pick a merchant up who comes into our area from the outside and just throw him out, but we are going to have to make him understand what our own game plan is in regard to this community. "If you are going to be part of this community, and if you are going to stay here and be successful in this community, then this is what has got to happen. This is our plan." And if that person doesn't buy into the situation as we have defined it, then our enforcement has to come into play. In other words, we don't give him no business. That's all there is to it. We don't have to do anything else to him, and if nobody goes to his door, pretty soon he will be gone.

March 17, 1993

DOROTHY McCONNER

CHIEF MANAGING OFFICER

I first met Dorothy at a party in her lovely apartment in Hyde Park. She was introducing my cousin Stanley McConner to some of her closest friends. She had met him while she was on a business trip to Baltimore, where Stanley was a public school administrator. At that time she was a vice president and chief operating officer for Johnson Products, a hair care company headquartered in Chicago. Dorothy and Stan were so impressed with each other that they fell in love and were married soon thereafter. My cousin was extremely lucky to have married such a wonderful, caring person as Dorothy. Though they both had been married previously, they acted toward each other as if this were their first love. They always treated each other magnificently and with great mutual respect. In addition to cuddling Stan, she was very close to her aging parents. When for reasons of health her parents moved to Tucson, Arizona, she and Stan visited them there on many occasions.

In addition to her position of responsibility at Johnson Products, Dorothy was a volunteer for many worthy causes, including a term as secretary of the board of the Chicago Urban League. Later on, when she discovered that she had developed cancer, she resigned from her job, and Stan did likewise, and they moved to Tucson in 1985. Despite her own physical condition, she continued to spend a great deal of her time with her parents and doing voluntary civic work. Annually, we would have a McConner family reunion in various cities, and Dorothy was always one of the chief planners and arrangers for these much-anticipated affairs. To me she was just as much my cousin as Stan.

In 1997, realizing that her illness might prove to be terminal and knowing that her life story was unique and highly interesting, we taped our conversation while we were both attending our family reunion in Tucson. She passed in 2000, and I am lucky to have these words of hers to share with you.

TB: Dorothy, where were you born?

DM: I was born in Birmingham, Alabama.

TB: What was your maiden name?

DM: Hamilton.

TB: And you left Birmingham how long ago?

DM: I left Birmingham when I was about fourteen years old. When we moved away from Birmingham, I had just entered Parker High School, but years ago it was called Industrial High.

TB: That school has a great deal of fame attached to it. In fact, Angela Davis went to Parker Junior High School.

DM: My mother also went to Industrial High.

TB: As did all my cousins! So, now just as you are entering high school, you leave Birmingham. You and who?

DM: My grandmother. My mother was already here trying to better herself so that she could help us in the South. But then my grandmother became ill, and my mother thought it best that we come up north to Chicago. So we left in June of 1943.

TB: That was almost in the exact middle of World War II.

DM: Yes, that's when I started at Phillips, but I had really gotten a good education in the South, and I already had so many credits that I got out of high school in three and a half years instead of the usual four. Because of all those credits that I had when I came to Chicago from Birmingham, they put me in 10B instead of 10A.

TB: That's right. During that period of time, we had mid-semester promotions and graduations. Who are some of the people you remember from Phillips?

DM: The principal was Mrs. Maudelle Bousfield.

TB: And she was the first black principal at any level in the entire Chicago public school system. That seems kind of unbelievable, doesn't it? Only *one* black principal in a whole system of that magnitude!

DM: Her daughter is living here, and we are friends.

TB: Her daughter lives here?

DM: Yes, Maudelle B. Bousfield Evans. She is Leonard Evans's wife.

TB: Is that right?

DM: Leonard and Maudelle live about two blocks from us.

TB: This world is so small.

DM: Yes, it is.

TB: Well, so you come to Chicago and go to Phillips. What did you do after you graduated?

DM: I went to Hampton College in Maryland, but I did not graduate from there. I had to come back to Chicago because my mother was working two jobs to keep me in school. She didn't want me to work. She wanted me to just study. That's why she was working those two full-time jobs, but when I came back home and saw my mother and saw what physical effect those jobs were having upon her, I decided I should go to business school, and that's just what I did. I went to Peters Business College and learned some practical skills.

TB: Was that on Forty-seventh Street then?

DM: No, it was on Fifty-fifth. Then I went to Chicago State and got a bachelor's degree. Later on, I did graduate work at Northwestern.

TB: I'm sure you would have gone on and completed your graduate work if you hadn't married my cousin, but let me tell you, it was a beautiful experience for me to learn that you were going to marry him!

DM: Well, I will tell you it was the best thing that ever happened to me. Stan is the real source of joy in my life.

TB: Dorothy, you are now the retired executive president of Johnson Products, the worldwide famous hair care production firm that was founded by George Johnson. Tell me, how did you first get started in the hair care business?

DM: Well, Tim, before answering that question, before I really get started, just let me thank you for this opportunity to talk with you. You asked how did I get started in the hair care business? Well, first I went to Hampton Institute, and while I was there I became friends with two of Mr. Fuller's daughters—that's S. B. Fuller of the Fuller Products Company, which he started in Chicago back in 1935. I went to Hampton in 1945, and I was there for a couple of years. Then in 1950 I went to work for Mr. Fuller, who was manufacturing all kinds of beauty products for the black consumer market. I came by this position because, I have to admit, one of his daughters was my roommate back at Hampton Institute. Tim, I always wanted to work in an office like that. That desire goes all the way back to my days in Birmingham, Alabama, when I was still a little girl. My grandmother used to go to the rental office to pay our monthly rent, and all the ladies in the rental office had on such nice clothes. I will never forget that as long as I live. It left a lasting impression because both my grandmother and my mother, they used to always have to carry clothes with them to work. They would have to change into work clothes, and I said when I grow up I am going to have the kind of job that whatever I wear to work that's what I am also going to be working in. I am not taking any change of clothing! So, when this opportunity at Fuller Products presented itself, I went to work for Mr. Fuller and worked for him in one of his branches for ten years, as a secretary to the branch manager. Fuller Products was a door-to-door sales organization, and they had salespeople who would come into the office every day, and we would set specific sales goals for them. We were doing management by "objectives" back in 1950, which is a long time before that kind of concept became famous. Our salesmen would come in every day, and we would set up personal goals for them to reach in their sales for that day. We would tell them how much they had to sell every day to make a certain amount of money every week. So, if somebody wanted to buy a home, or if they wanted to buy a car, we would set these objectives for them, and then they would know exactly what they had to do on a day-to-day basis in order to reach those personal goals. That's why I have always said that working at Fuller Products Company gave me my basic understanding of how a business should be run and of how to motivate people so that a business can be run successfully.

TB: Where were they located then?

DM: Well, when I first went to work there, they were located at 2700 South Wabash, but during the time that I worked for him, Mr. Fuller bought another building at Twenty-sixth and Wabash. He had a three-story building there. So, after that, he had two plants in that area. I worked for him from 1950 until 1960—for ten years. But, even before that time, I already knew Mr. George Johnson and his wife, Joan, from my days back in high school. You know, they were Phillips High School students too.

TB: It was a great school—and it was in a great neighborhood at that time.

DM: That's right, it was. I lived just two blocks from Phillips at that time. We were living at Forty-first and Prairie. The kids in that neighborhood were a really very cohesive group, and we really enjoyed each other's company. You know, I still maintain relationships with some of those people from the old neighborhood. But, getting back to my going to work for Johnson Products Company, as I have said, I knew Mr. Johnson and Joan back from the time when we went to Phillips together, and now they came to me and said that they needed someone like me to come and help them—so I said to them, "Well, I really don't want to get too much involved in this business of yours because I've been here in this situation with Fuller Products where my job has become my whole soul, both mind and body!" You see, we worked there six days a week—even on Saturday nights—and then every second Sunday afternoon we would also have a big business meeting from about two until about five. What I'm saying is that Fuller Products had really become a total way of life for me, and so I told them, "Listen, I want to go to work for you, and I will be glad to give you a full day's work for a full day's pay, but that's it! I don't want to get into anything again that I am going to get all that much involved in." Well, so then I went to work for Johnson Products, and, of course, just the opposite happened!

[*Laughter.*]

TB: Now, Johnson himself had also formerly worked for Fuller, hadn't he?

DM: Yes, he had worked for Fuller for ten years, but I don't want to get into his story because I am sure at some point you will be talking with him, and I will let him tell his own story in his own kind of way. Well, when I started working in his office, I have always been the kind of person that whatever needs to be done, that's what I will do. It makes no difference to me what it is that needs doing. I have no problem with things like that. So the day that I started at Johnson Products Company, when I talked with them about coming to work for them, I told them exactly what I was earning at that time. This was in 1960, and I was earning about nine thousand dollars a year. That was pretty darn good for that time, and when I told them what I was earning, they never made any comment or raised any objection. But, Tim, I know I am going to get ahead of my story, but the first Friday that I got my paycheck—and please remember that I had been making one hundred fifty dollars a week—it was for only seventy-five dollars. Well, I almost died, and I said, "Oh, my God, what have I done? I didn't negotiate this deal properly. What have I done to myself? Well, at any rate, I know now what I have got to do. I have to prove to these folks that I am worth much more than this to them." So, anyway, I started working in their office, and, just as I have said, I did whatever needed to be done, and I learned how to do it. That's why I learned their accounting system before they put in their first automated billing machine.

TB: Where were they located then?

DM: They were located on Green Street—Fifty-eighth and Green. That's just west of Halsted Street. I joined them in 1960, but in 1964 a fire destroyed the building. That's when Mr. Johnson started looking for property, and we built the building on Eighty-sixth Street and the Dan Ryan.

TB: By this time the company had gone public?

DM: No, we didn't go public until 1969.

TB: By "public" this means you are now selling shares?

DM: Yes, we were the first major black company to be on the stock exchange. We started out on the American Stock Exchange, which really gave us a lot of prominence in the world. I am about to get in George's story again, but I guess his story is part of my own as well. See, when I first joined them, their annual sales were at only about four hundred thousand dollars, but during the next thirty years that I was there, sales went up to approaching fifty million dollars! I was fortunate enough to be a part of that tremendous growth in the company. I saw all the different stages of the company, and it really made an interesting career for me. I just considered myself fortunate to be a part of what happened, and, right from the first, I always considered myself to be an asset for Johnson Products. But on the very first day that I went to work there, Mr. Johnson, he didn't even tell me what he wanted me to do—and Mrs. Johnson, she didn't tell me either! [*Laughter.*]

So I went on out in the plant. I knew one of the girls that was working out there filling some orders that were what we called "*Ebony* orders." These were orders that would come in from a little coupon we had running in *Ebony* magazine. People would order our products through those ads in *Ebony*, and we would pack up one or two of those orders at a time and ship them out. So I went on out there and said, "Is there anything I can do?" You see, I thought that if they didn't know what they wanted me to do in the front office, probably there would be at least something useful that I could do out there, but then, well, Mr. Johnson came out, and he was all excited. "Oh, Dorothy, we didn't hire you to work in the plant," he said. And I said, "Then you all will have to take the time to tell me what you want me to do. Just let me work out here today and see how things are done." So I worked out there for about a half of the day, and then I came inside and started doing different things in their main office. Well, before too long, I became secretary to the president, and I think that came about because there were times when Mr. Johnson was traveling and when his mail would come in and start to pile up. At first I would just go and get the mail, and if it didn't say "personal," I would open it up, and categorize it. Then, when they came back in town, I would go over with them what had come in, and we would make decisions together about how everything was going to be taken care of. So, anyway, it got to the point that I always opened the mail whether they were there or not. Those things that I could handle I would handle, and I would leave those things that needed a decision from them for them to handle. As a result of that, I became Mr. Johnson's secretary. Then the office started growing, and I started hiring additional people to do additional things. That's when I became manager of the office and really started learning the business end of things. We continued to grow, and I was becoming involved in all the different departments and in all of the different phases of the business—sales, marketing, and all of those different areas—and naturally I grew too. We really only started to become departmentalized when we went public. That was because, at that time, the exchange people would tell you that you have got to have a "vice president of marketing," you've got to have a "vice president of sales," and you must have a "vice president of finance"—and we hadn't ever before had any of those kind of people in the company!

TB: So they were forcing a certain kind of discipline and structure on you.

DM: Yes, they did.

TB: And you are now on Eighty-seventh Street in a brand new building?

DM: We wanted a building in that location because it was quite visible from the Dan Ryan Expressway. It really became a landmark for black business to aspire to.

TB: Yes, it did.

DM: And we became a role model for other black businesses.

TB: Now, that building, as I remember it, had an apartment in it where Mr. Johnson could stay overnight.

DM: No, maybe Johnson *Publishing* might have had an apartment like that, but not Johnson Products. Let me try to remember. Adjacent to Mr. Johnson's office was a rest room where there was a little two-seater bench, and his office had two couches in it. Adjacent to his office was a conference room that seated twelve people, and next to that was a room that we made into a gym which we wanted our directors to use, but those guys never got there early enough to ever use it very much, and so we started using it as a storage space instead.

TB: And at this time your own responsibilities within the company were increasing, weren't they?

DM: Yes, and my first officer-level position was when I became "secretary of the corporation." In that position I maintained the company minutes. I would set up the meetings for our directors, and I kept the minutes for those board of directors meetings and kept them abreast of what was going on in the company. In addition, I also had some responsibilities to the American Stock Exchange in terms of reporting certain types of information.

TB: After you became public, how was your board of directors chosen?

DM: Well, it was chosen from people who had been associated with the company — like E. Ernest LaFontant, who was the company's attorney at the time. He became our general counsel.

TB: Wasn't he the late Jewel LaFontant's husband?

DM: Right. Then there was the guy who had been working with us as our accountant. He became vice president of finance. Shortly thereafter, Mr. Johnson's brother, who had been with Fuller Products Company, came in as our vice president of sales — when his brother John joined us, that's when we really jumped to sales in the millions of dollars. That was because now George Johnson did not have to run the business and also run the sales force as well. Now that he had somebody who concentrated solely on sales, he could concentrate on the business end of the company. While all that was happening, my own career was continuing to evolve, and I became vice president of administration because I was responsible for all the interworkings of the company, so to speak. Whatever went on inside that building was more or less my responsibility.

TB: And by now you have how many employees?

DM: When I first joined Johnson Products, there were only 13 employees. Then, after we went public, we had 200 to 250, including our plant workers. You could see the company growing each and every year. We were never unionized because we always tried to give our employees what a union would only promise to give them, and I always felt very good about that. Not that I have anything against unions because I know that unions have been good for the labor market, but their attempts to unionize Johnson Products a couple of times were not successful because everything that they asked for we were already giving to our employees.

TB: How would somebody like me—an outsider—get on your board? Buy into the stock?

DM: Well, now, of course, you would have to own stocks in order to be a board member, but that's not the way you would get on it unless you bought a certain large amount of stock and you forced your way in. We never had that kind of experience. All of the stock information when people bought stock and that kind of thing would come directly to the office of the secretary of the corporation, and so I would see for myself who was buying. Well, at one time I noticed there was a company out east that was buying up a lot of our stock. So when we had our next shareholders' meeting, we all were really wondering if they were going to be there, but they never showed, and we don't know to this day what their motives might have been.

TB: And all this time your company continued to prosper.

DM: Oh, yes, we paid a dividend every year.

TB: Rumor has it that at one time Revlon Products was going to try to take over Johnson Products.

DM: No, we never had any competitors like that on our board. As a matter of fact, we never had any hostile board members.

TB: And pretty soon, as a matter of fact, you were also on a lot of other boards, weren't you?

DM: Yes, someone said, "Let's bring Dorothy McConner on with us because she is doing such a good job over at Johnson Products," and so I was on the board of the Rehabilitation Center of Chicago. I was on the board of DePaul University. I was on the board of Metropolitan Mutual Assurance Company and the board of the Chicago Urban League. As a matter of fact, I served as their secretary for many years.

TB: Mr. Johnson was also very active on a lot of boards. At one time he even had a philanthropic foundation of his own.

DM: Yes, he had a foundation and personally contributed a million dollars to that foundation in order to provide scholarships for our black students pursuing a business career. He even had to hire a full-time administrator for that foundation.

TB: Yes, and Bill Berry, who had retired from the Urban League, was the first administrator, wasn't he?

DM: Yes, he and Sophie Beth managed those programs. I can't remember the number of students that benefited from it, but it was a considerable number.

TB: And you continued to work with the company until when?

DM: I continued to work for the company until my retirement in 1989. The company began to change somewhat when Mr. Johnson's elder son became president of the company toward the end of my tenure. I had really planned to retire at fifty-five, but I wasn't quite ready to quit at fifty-five, so I stayed on until I was sixty.

TB: In recent years I've noticed that there have been some dramatic changes in the marketing of black beauty and hair care products. I wonder if you would care to comment on what's been happening?

DM: Sure, I would. You know back at the beginning when I first started to get involved, the only competition for our products came from other black-owned companies, and what has happened is that Asian entrepreneurs and investors have now come in and bought up all those black-owned beauty supply companies. A company like Johnson Products used to sell directly to the retailers and to the beauticians in the little beauty shops, but now it seems as though those little beauty shops hardly exist anymore. Instead you have these big conglomerates getting together and housing themselves in big department stores, and, believe me, that kind of thing has caused a great loss of income for black businesses like ours.

TB: Yes, and those black-owned businesses were serving and giving back to the black community by making a social as well as an economic investment in the community where they made their money. For an example, Mr. Johnson told me recently that when he first went in to work with Mr. Fuller, at that time black-owned companies controlled about 60 percent of the African-American consumer market for hair care and beauty products, but now he said that their share is less than 7 percent of that market. I also understand that now that market has also substantially increased in terms of usage and that currently black folks spend in excess of *six* billion dollars each year for products of this kind, and so that kind of dramatic drop in percentage creates a severe economic loss to our entire community.

DM: Yes, especially when you think what that means when you translate that shift into dollars and cents!

TB: Dorothy, what other kind of changes, if there were any, can you remember about what Chicago was like when you first came here in 1943 and when you left in 1989? That's a period of about forty-six years. Was it just a matter of you growing up or were there some real changes, which you witnessed as well?

DM: You know, Tim, I am just going to say this. I hope that I am not getting way off base, but I just happen to feel that most of those changes were for the better, and I really believe that now all our problems about race relations can be solved on an individual basis. I know I have white friends, but I don't even think of them as "white" friends, and I don't think that they think of me as an "African-American" friend either. They just think of me as a friend, and we are all comfortable with each other. I think we still continue to have those same beliefs when we go to social functions together, even though on some of those occasions I might be the only African-American that is there. You just have to have the right kind of attitude and education, and I'll always remember that when we first got to Chicago, it was like coming to heaven for us because here at last we had the opportunity to earn some money and get a good education in order to better ourselves. I know that I was eager to start working right away while I was still in high school — in the afternoons after my classes were over.

TB: Back then there were jobs for young people that were available right here in the neighborhood near your school.

DM: Yes, there were a lot of jobs like that. There were jobs at places like the Wilcox Products bookstores where you just stored books and that kind of thing. They always made jobs available for high school kids. Then, after working there, I worked for a company that made knitted scarves, and there were always jobs for kids to get after school in places like that as well. I made about fifteen dollars a week, which was pretty good money for a kid back then, but you know, I don't think those kinds of jobs are available now. I don't know whether the jobs have moved out of the city or whether those jobs are just no longer there anywhere. It seems to me that today most of these kids are just sitting around and looking forward to getting a check from the government every month.

TB: Are you talking about welfare now?

DM: Yes, but, instead of collecting welfare, they should be out cutting somebody's grass or cleaning somebody's porch. I don't know where we lost all that.

TB: That kind of pride and incentive?

DM: Yes, I just don't know where that got lost or how it can ever be regained.

July 26, 1997

GEORGE JOHNSON

———

FROM RAGS TO RICHES

George Johnson epitomizes the talent, the drive, the tenacity, and the vision that a true entrepreneur starting out on his own must possess in order to become and remain successful. It was a real pleasure for me to listen to him relate his stories of how his mother brought him and his brother from Mississippi to Chicago and how she overcame the challenges of life in this large and often harsh urban environment. Her efforts inspired George and his brother to attain the American dream of success, although that "dream" has been and continues to be tainted by elements of racism, some of which were initiated or at least actively supported by government agencies and large corporations. Without rancor or bitterness, in his descriptions of his continuing quest to overcome these kind of obstacles, George Johnson provides a truly glowing example of what it takes for a black person to become successful in the United States as it has been and in many ways as it still is.

An early mentor for Mr. Johnson was Mr. S. B. Fuller, who was the founder of an extremely successful skin and hair care products company. Building on his experience with Mr. Fuller, George Johnson was soon on the road toward developing a company of his own that would eventually have an annual gross of over three hundred million dollars. His is a "rags to riches" story with a distinctly black scenario that reveals the struggles that are necessary for lasting success.

TB: George, where were you born?

GJ: Tim, I was born in Bridgeton, Mississippi, which is not too far from Laurel. I was born in 1927. June 16, as a matter of fact.

TB: And your mother and father?

GJ: My mother was born in Heidelberg, Mississippi. She is still living. She will be eighty-one years old next month. My father just died last year. He was eighty-three or eighty-four, I am not quite sure. He was born somewhere in Alabama, but his family moved over to Mississippi, and I think my mother and father met in Laurel.

TB: Do you know why your father's family moved to Mississippi?

GJ: I think it was for economic reasons. I knew my grandfather, but I wasn't old enough to be inquisitive. I didn't ever ask to find out anything about his background. But when I say I was not old enough, I might as well tell you also that I didn't even know my grandfather, nor my father, by sight until I was ten years old! You see, my mother brought me to Chicago when I was two years old!

TB: So your mother brought you to Chicago when you were two, which would be about 1929.

GJ: Yes, 1929, exactly! My youngest brother was about four or five months old at that time. My oldest brother was four, and I was two. My mother put all three of us on her hip and came north because she had a sister and two brothers that had already left Mississippi and had been writing to her constantly about the improvements in the quality of life for black people in Chicago. She had been, of course, trying to get my father to get interested, but my father had all this time been in Mississippi and had all his roots in Mississippi, and he wanted to remain there in Mississippi. Also, he told me some years ago that he had been victim of some of the rumors that the southern whites, especially employers, had put out about the dangers that lurked up north for black folks. In other words, they did this to discourage migration because that kind of migration was already in high gear in the twenties and thirties.

TB: At that time, immigration of Europeans had slowed down or stopped, and they needed labor up north, and the South was a major source of that labor supply.

GJ: My mother was—I got to tell you this, Tim—the reason that I love her so much is because I admire her courage. I didn't know it when I was a kid, but when I look back at what decisions my mother had to make at only eighteen years of age to take herself and her three children and come up here to Chicago—that took great courage! She had not ever before been a "working" wife but even so, when she came to Chicago in that August—I think she got here on a Saturday—she found a job and started working right away.

TB: This was the beginning of the Depression, and jobs were hard to find.

GJ: That's true, but she got a job within those first two weeks at Michael Reese Hospital, and she stayed there at Michael Reese Hospital for the next sixteen years.

TB: So, during that time, you all lived on the South Side?

GJ: Yes, but we lived in a lot of places on the South Side. We started out living at Twenty-ninth and Ellis. Believe it or not, I still remember that place. We didn't stay there very long, maybe less than a year, but I was so terrified by the darkness of the hall that I thought there must be a hole there in the middle of it, and I would always pass through that area almost hugging at the wall! This was in an apartment in a two-story, stone building, as I remember it, and it was all divided into rooms. We had a big room in the front on the second floor, and we all slept together in one bed.

TB: That was a very common practice in that period.

GJ: Right, and that's how we started. My mother kept that job all during the Depression. She already had two sisters and two brothers in Chicago before she got here, and she brought her younger sister along with her when she came.

TB: She had a lot of courage, but she also had some contacts.

GJ: Well, she did. Her oldest sister, Aunt Bessie, sent her the money and the encouragement to do it. But it must have been hard for an eighteen-year-old woman—with three children—to leave her husband like that. Not that there was any conflict between them, except that she wanted to leave the South—and I thank God that she did!

TB: Let me tell you, my daddy was working in the steel mills in Birmingham, and, to some extent, my mother had the same feelings that your mother had, but when my grandmother came here and became ill looking after another daughter—my mother's baby sister—my mother picked us up and brought us to Chicago, and then my daddy followed later on. But she was an older person than your mother. Mama must have been about twenty-two.

GJ: I mentioned to you that I did not know my father until I was ten, nor my grandfather, but that isn't quite true. I did not know my father by sight, but I knew who he was. To me, my father was a letter that my brothers and I got once a month with three one-dollar bills in that letter and a lot of loving words. He constantly told us how he missed us, how he loved us, and how he wished he could be with us. He constantly told us that. After my mother left, he went to Piney Woods School and organized a singing group called the Piney Woods Blind Boys, and they used to go singing all up throughout the country.

TB: So, somewhat early in your life there was an example of some entrepreneurship in your family.

GJ: Well, if you can call that kind of thing "entrepreneurship."

TB: Yes, but at least he had a little bit of functioning independently instead of just having an ordinary job. So, then you came to Chicago and lived on the Near South Side.

GJ: Right, actually between Twenty-ninth and Thirty-fifth Streets is where I grew up in this city.

TB: That was your world.

GJ: I think we moved from Twenty-ninth and Ellis to the 3100 block on Vernon, and then we lived on Thirty-second and Wabash, and then we moved to Thirty-fourth and Vernon.

TB: That was a neighborhood. I mean, the people there felt a kind of kinship. You know, I lived farther south, but I knew a lot of guys of my generation who lived in that area.

GJ: It was real community to me over there where we lived on the east side of South Park Way then. It was a little better than on the west side of South Park Way because I used to have to pick my way through that part of the neighborhood when I went to the Louis Theater. Do you remember the Louis Theater?

TB: On Thirty-fifth Street.

GJ: And the State Theater?

TB: Yes.

GJ: Well, I had to find a new route every weekend to avoid some of the boys.

TB: Those guys are always going to ask you to lend them a dime or a quarter or something.

GJ: Yes, yes. They'd catch up with you on the corner just before you could get to the movie theater and say, "Can you loan me a dime?" Well, it's three of them, and so how are you going to refuse?

TB: But the degree of fear of what these kids have to face today just wasn't there, not that kind of fear.

GJ: No, we could even be shrewd. I never will forget I had a system. If I was going to the State Theater, I would kind of wait and hide under the El tracks until I saw it getting a little busy on the corner because there was a drugstore on that corner. Then I would make it over to the drugstore, and then I would listen to people talk. Now, these were grown people, or at least bigger people, and I knew they were going to the Louis Theater—so, when they left that place, I would get right next to them and just walk right like I was with them and run into the Louis Theater!

TB: But you had to have a system.

GJ: Yes, you had to have a system!

TB: I used to run down the street on Prairie from Fiftieth to Forty-seventh Street to go to—I forget the name of the show that was there then—and I would have my money in my mouth, and I would run right up and put the money down.

GJ: Then, of course, you had to be well rested through the movie because you knew you were going to have to run home. I mean, it was a rare Sunday afternoon that I didn't have to run home.

TB: But the movie was so good that you wanted to go anyway. Was the Vendome still open when you were growing up?

GJ: It was down at Thirty-third Street, I think, wasn't it?

TB: Yes.

GJ: Oh, yes, it was open. They used to have a stage show. You know, I saw Ella Fitzgerald at the Vendome. I think when she first started it was with Chick Webb in 1936. That's when I heard "A-Tisket, A-Tasket."

TB: Yes, she was about sixteen or seventeen years old.

GJ: Maybe fourteen!

TB: She was a young woman. Just a girl.

GJ: She was his adopted daughter.

TB: Right, she was Chick Webb's adopted daughter. Because she was an orphan.

GJ: Yes, but Thirty-third Street was rough. It was really rough. I used to deliver newspapers. I had my own route when I was about ten, and my route used to take me all the way down to Thirty-first Street, but I was always very careful down there. Thirty-first and Cottage, especially over there by that Ellis building, you really better watch it because it was pretty rough back there in the thirties.

TB: These were the Depression years, and if you lived south of Thirty-first Street, at that time you considered yourself a little better than the folks who lived on Thirty-first Street.

GJ: That's true, because, if you remember, there was one block between Rhodes and Cottage Grove where really well-to-do people lived. In fact, the only middle-class blacks that I ever knew in my life as I was coming up lived between Rhodes and Cottage Grove on Thirty-fourth Street. Doctors, lawyers, ministers—and I played with the children of those people. William Simmons was the only black executive with Peoples Gas, and he ran that office at Thirty-ninth and Wabash. Do you remember that office?

TB: Yes, I do.

GJ: Well, I used to play with William Simmons Jr.—his son.

TB: So that block was an exclusive block

GJ: Yes, but the kids couldn't be exclusive.

TB: Or could they?

GJ: Let me tell you, that was a beautiful thing too because, you know, everybody wasn't having as tough a time as I was. As I told you, I had a paper route, and my paper route went all the way to Thirty-first Street, but I also took care of Thirty-fourth Street between Woodland and Groveland Park. There were no black folks over there. All those were white folks.

TB: Was the Vincennes Hotel in there?

GJ: Yes, Mrs. Barnett owned the Vincennes Hotel. And the branch offices for the newspaper were just across the street on Thirty-seventh.

TB: Which paper was that?

GJ: The *Herald Examiner,* which became the *Herald American* and then went out of business. It was a Hearst newspaper.

TB: Yes, part of the Hearst chain. Now, what elementary school did you go to?

GJ: Well, I made the rounds. I started at St. Elizabeth. Then I went to Douglas. Then I went to Doolittle, and when I graduated from Doolittle, then I went to Phillips.

TB: When did you graduate from Doolittle?

GJ: In 1941. It was a June graduation.

TB: So you were just going into high school about the same time that World War II started.

GJ: Yes, I remember that day, brother. I never will forget. I came out of the Louis Theater and heard the news, "Pearl Harbor was bombed. The nation is at war." I was walking home just scared to death. What does this mean? What does all this mean?

TB: Did you have any relatives old enough to go to the service?

GJ: My oldest brother, John, was two years older than me, so John became eligible, of course, for the draft before I did, but he was ultimately rejected, and ultimately so was I.

TB: Who are some of the people at Doolittle that you still remember?

GJ: Bill Henderson, the singer, went to school with me.

TB: When you were at Phillips—that was the period of Buddy Young and that great football team.

GJ: Right, he was a little bit ahead of me, but I was going to Phillips when he was still raising hell!

TB: Great team!

GJ: Absolutely. I remember Leonard Sachs, who was the coach.

TB: Yeah, Leonard Sachs.

GJ: I was not far from him when he dropped dead.

TB: Is that right? At school?

GJ: He dropped dead at school right there on the second floor.

TB: You also had a principal who was fairly well known.

GJ: You mean Mrs. Bousfield?

TB: Yes, she was the first black principal, I think, in Chicago. Her husband was a doctor.

GJ: You know, I never knew her husband.

TB: Well, just to give you a little background—just quickly—he was a colonel. He was also a doctor, and he was head of the medical resources at Fort Huachuca, Arizona, where the Ninety-second and the Ninety-third Divisions trained. They lived then in what we called the "big shot" neighborhood of West Chesterfield. But Mrs. Bousfield was an unusually brilliant, great woman. That school had a lot of spirit too.

GJ: Oh, my God, yes. There weren't but two high schools where blacks were welcome: DuSable and Phillips. I think during the war they created Dunbar.

TB: Yes, well, Dunbar was "special vocational," and, as I remember, it was part of Phillips originally, and Mr. Campbell—Clifford Campbell—wasn't he there at Phillips?

GJ: Sure, he was there at Phillips.

TB: Well, my understanding from some of my friends who were in school about that same time—and I am just citing this as an example of how precious and important Phillips was to our community—is that Mr. Campbell was concerned about the youngsters that were dropping out, and he believed that they would want to stay in school if they could be taught to do something useful with their hands, and that's when he started experimenting with some very innovative new programs. One of the programs that he started over there was called Airplane Mechanics. Who'd ever heard of something like that? But that's what he did! He was a very innovative guy, and he chose his staff from the best and most competent people rather than how many degrees they had. So some of his faculty did not necessarily have college degrees. Some of them went back later and got them, but they were hired because they were competent in their fields of carpentry, electricity, or whatever it might be. Then later, of course, they built upon the programs he developed at Phillips and created the new school that became Dunbar.

GJ: Campbell was a special kind of guy.

TB: Did you know him?

GJ: Oh, we knew him all right. He was a stern disciplinarian.

TB: They said he wasn't scared of anybody.

GJ: Yes, and we also had a policeman around there who used to kind of help keep everybody halfway straight.

TB: Two-Gun Pete [Sylvester Washington]?

GJ: Yes, and when things got a little rough, Two-Gun Pete would say, "I own this street!" I mean, he would walk up and down—just one man!

TB: Of course, at Phillips, during that period of time, there were a lot of guys, I guess, who became important. Some of them became judges. Gus was there—Gus Savage.

GJ: There were a lot of guys at Phillips that did very well.

TB: Some of them went into the professions. Of course, I am in the Hall of Fame—just like you are—at Phillips.

GJ: Is that right? You went to Phillips?

TB: Yeah, I was before you, though. I was there with Nat Cole.

GJ: Nat was ahead of me, and so was Dinah Washington.

TB: I knew Dinah. She was behind me, behind Nat, and before that, of course, there was Ray Nance and many, many others. People like Milt Hinton, the great bass player, were also there. So, then, when did you leave Phillips?

GJ: Actually, I dropped out of Phillips to go to work for Fuller Products.

TB: When was that?

GJ: Oh, I went to work for Fuller, I guess, in 1945, just before the end of the war.

TB: Who was Mr. Fuller?

GJ: Who was he? Let me tell you about him. My oldest brother, John, and I had an agreement that if John got a job someplace he would get me a job in that same place, and if I got a job someplace, then I would get him a job. So, wherever he worked or wherever I was, we were together all the time. During high school, before working for Fuller Products, I had a job down at the College Inn. Do you remember the College Inn?

TB: Oh, absolutely, at the Sherman Hotel. What were you doing there?

GJ: I was working at the College Inn as a busboy.

TB: Did you share the tips?

GJ: Oh, God. I worked with two or three waiters, and they were supposed to share the tips, but they only gave me what they wanted me to have. Even so, I made real nice money, and then when John graduated, he got involved with Fuller Products. So he told me, "George, you ought to come over here and go to the meeting with me on Saturday." So I went with him to a Saturday morning meeting at Thirty-fifth and Vernon. That was S. B. Fuller's headquarters, upstairs. I met him, and I said to John, "This man is really something!" I mean, he was a phenomenal person. In his presence you could just feel the energy coming from him. His impact on people was almost mystical, and he was a tremendously sincere person. When you heard him speak, he was very convincing, because he believed in what he was saying. He was telling you that you could take responsibility for yourself, and I credit him for giving me the confidence to do what I did. He said, "Just take what you have and make what you want of yourself." So I went to work for him.

TB: Now, at that time how old were you?

GJ: I was seventeen years old when I went to work for him. I hadn't as yet made my eighteenth birthday.

TB: This was in 1945.

GJ: Yes, that's when I started working for him and started selling with John. Selling door-to-door!

TB: What were you selling?

GJ: Fuller had hair products. He had bath products. He had perfume, cologne, creams, deodorant. I mean that bag I carried was heavy with products. You would even carry two bags if you could sell that much!

TB: Did he manufacture his own products?

GJ: Most of them. Most of those products he manufactured right upstairs. When I went to work for Fuller Products, it looked tremendously big to me, but actually he was only doing approximately four hundred thousand dollars a year.

TB: Which was big for a black business.

GJ: Yes, in 1945, there wasn't anything else going on in the black community like that.

TB: Except in insurance.

GJ: I don't even know how many insurance companies were really churning out that kind of money.

TB: I think Supreme was and maybe Chicago Met.

GJ: Well, I started out in sales with John, but I couldn't do what John could do. John could go out there and sell every day, but I had a hard time taking money away from people that I considered couldn't afford it. I really had a hard time. I had to be awfully, awfully broke, and I had to have something that I wanted awfully, awfully bad for me to go out, and, well, you know, I would walk into somebody's house, and I would open the case, and this woman would have one or two babies sitting there on the floor, nasty and dirty, and she would just be smelling all this stuff I had and really wanting to buy it, and, well, I would take her money, but I had a hard time taking it when I didn't really need it. I used to say to John it was a shame. Anyway, I was a cream puff when it came to real hard selling. I couldn't sell hard in those situations, but, of course, when I found somebody whom I considered *could* afford it, I could talk my butt off. And I would sell my butt off too! But, when I would go up and down Forty-seventh and Calumet, in that area, you know, and you started climbing those three-story apartments, and they were all living in these single rooms—kitchenettes—then it was difficult.

TB: Tell me, just for the record, during that period of time you could just knock on people's doors, and they would open the door for you?

GJ: Oh, yes, absolutely. During that time, we didn't need the precautions that we have today. People still had enough trust and enough faith in each other that they would open the door. They really would. I could knock on a door, and it was very seldom, if somebody was there, that I didn't get in. Now, sometimes people opened the door and saw what you were selling, and they would—bam!—close the door in your face. Certainly that happened a lot of times, but people always opened their doors, and you just walked right in and took up as much of their time as they would let you. My brother John was a great salesman, and he could always make a sale, and I could do it too when I had to, but sometimes I just couldn't do it. It would be my luck to always knock on a door where there were the other kind of folks who answered.

TB: What kind of money were salesmen making?

GJ: Let me tell you something, the ace salesmen at Fuller Products at that time were making more money than any of the professionals on the South Side because Fuller was smart. You see, Fuller had a competition going on between people all the time. He would challenge us. Fuller knew how to motivate people. He could get 150 percent out of people you wouldn't suspect could do anything at all. It was amazing. It was absolutely amazing, and at that time there were people who were making—do you believe?—three hundred dollars a week!

TB: In that period?

GJ: Yes, in that period! He had a woman—can't remember her name—who was one of his top salespeople. She used to have a lot of makeup on her eyes. I could never forget her. She tried to push her daughter off on me!

TB: But she couldn't sell that one!

GJ: No, she couldn't sell that one, but she was a hell of a salesperson. She had a romantic attachment to Fuller, and that's why she had such a drive. But she didn't get so far with him because Miss Thornton, who ultimately became Mrs. Fuller, was also there all the time. She was keeping the books for the company.

TB: So you stayed there for a while.

GJ: Let me tell you why I stopped selling. You see, I was really attracted to the manufacturing end of things, the reason being because in my chemistry classes at Phillips I was pretty good, and it was fascinating to me to mix those products. At that time Fuller had only one man working back there doing the mixing, so one day I went in to Fuller's office and told him I was really more interested in working on the inside. "Ain't no money inside," he said, and I said, "Well, even so, I would prefer to be inside. I really want to work in the lab."

TB: How many agents did Fuller have at that time?

GJ: Well, when I first went to work for him, he only had one branch, which was the one on Thirty-fifth Street, and he probably had about fifty-eight salesmen full-time, and maybe fifty or seventy-five part-time. And then he went out to 6245 Cottage Grove and leased a whole big three-story building. At that time there were no blacks in business on that side of Cottage Grove, but the thing about it was, he had the money, so we moved into there and that really started his growth, and our sales jumped like mad. Hell, you see this thing moving, and you say to yourself, "I am going to get on board!"

TB: Yes, people in the neighborhood began to hear that some of the guys over there are making some money, some real dough.

GJ: Yes, and they saw that these guys were driving cars, and I mean, Mr. Fuller had one of the first Buicks that came off the damned assembly line. You know during the war you didn't see many new cars like that.

TB: And by now he has expanded beyond Chicago.

GJ: Yes, he expanded to New York in 1946, in a branch that was established at 149th Street and Seventh Avenue. He had a nice big office there. Anyway, Fuller was expanding like mad and his products were moving like mad. I was learning, and by this time I had all the responsibilities for his full line of products. I was doing the compounding and also learning the research too. But I was doing this all on my own. Rick McGuire came to work at Fuller Products in 1947 while he was still going to IIT [Illinois Institute of Technology]. Now, Mr. Fuller already knew Rick's father, who owned a grocery store on the West Side. You see, back in 1945, Mr. Fuller couldn't go downtown or anywhere else to borrow any money. No financial institution was interested in loaning him any money, but he was very creative, and he certainly took some risks, and in order to do the things he wanted to do he was willing to pay people some very high interest. So he went to Rick's father, and he asked Mr. McGuire if he would loan him the money at an extremely high rate of interest. At that time interest rates were maybe 2.5 to 3 percent on your money or even less, but he was willing to pay 5, and later on 10 percent, in order to raise the money to do the things he wanted to do. Now, he had a damned good cash flow because the money was coming in, but ultimately you can overburden yourself with those big interest rates and a big debt like that.

TB: And now the United States government is also finding that out!

GJ: That's the truth. Anyway, that is how he financed that move and that's how he financed that acquisition. Do you remember Robinson Electric over on Sixty-first Street?

TB: Yes.

GJ: Well, he went by Robinson one night, and he saw the light was on and just knocked on the door. He didn't even know Robinson, but he just walked in there and told him who he was and told him that he had some things he was trying to do and that he needed money. "If you can loan me some money, I am willing to pay you 10 percent interest!"—and so he walked out of there with ten thousand dollars.

TB: But that meant that he would have to pay back one thousand dollars in interest!

GJ: Anyway, that's how he raised enough money to buy Boyer in about 1948, and we moved down there from Sixty-third Street. It was a seven-story building at 2900 South Wabash, which was large enough that it could hold everything.

TB: Tremendous floor space.

GJ: That's right. Anyway, we moved down there, and that was really the beginning. Fuller's vision was astounding for a man of his era. He was only doing three or four million, but he was already thinking about building a hundred-million-dollar business, and if he had just half the kind of treatment that the average white businessman is usually accorded, he would have succeeded in reaching that goal.

TB: Did any of his competitors recognize the market that he was beaming at?

GJ: Well, even if they did, they couldn't do anything about it. First of all, you don't need to advertise. Your advertisement is your product being placed in the hands of a consumer with a knowledgeable person right there to talk about that product in a positive way, and also to give you firsthand instruction as to how to get the best benefit out of that product. All you can do on television is just get people interested enough to ask for some information about the products, but this was coming right into your home.

TB: And you would personalize everything.

GJ: Yes, so you didn't have to worry about competitors, but believe me, door-to-door selling is a tough business, and, you know, things change. Certainly many things have changed here in our community.

TB: But back then Fuller was operating, as Adam Clayton Powell would say, "audaciously and bodaciously."

GJ: And courageously too! You know, Mr. Fuller never had a small thought. You see, Mr. Fuller could paint a picture that would really blow your mind. He said, "Reach for the stars," and he meant *literally* reach for those stars. Then, if you miss, don't worry about falling because it is very likely that you will fall on top of the mountain! Let me tell you something. I don't know anybody that has even done anything great by thinking small. You are going to have to think big, and that's exactly what Mr. Fuller did. After Fuller bought Boyer, he started laying plans to build an empire. He was going to have a dress factory, and his first step toward that was to buy the South Center. Then he bought the Regal Theater in about 1951. I don't know why in hell he bought the Regal Theater, but I guess when he bought that building he got the Regal Theater as well.

TB: Yes, it was just one big complex that was built back in 1926 or 1927.

GJ: Yes, it was all one complex, and I can remember the people who had the store on the corner, the little haberdasher, they were scared to death they were going to lose their lease, and he had to go out there and assure them that they would not lose their lease. He said, "Look, I am going to do my own thing. We won't be in competition." But you can't do everything by yourself, and there are only so many ways you can divide yourself, and though he had people who were faithful, they didn't have the necessary expertise in these areas. It is awfully hard to get into a business venture and learn after you buy something how to run it the right way, but, of course, what I'm saying now is hindsight. You can always be critical after the fact, and I am not trying to be critical.

TB: No, you are being analytical.

GJ: Well, at that time we all believed that he could make it work.

TB: Yes, but another thing that happened was that the neighborhood changed.

GJ: The entire marketplace changed tremendously and quickly because of all the changes that took place after the war, and that also gave him a problem. At first it gave him a boost because the income of blacks began to rise—they had more disposable income—and then it kept on rising, but even in the recession, Fuller Products went up. It was good times for him. When it was bad times for the country, it was good times for him. But then, later on, when it was good times for the country, it became bad times for him. The reason for this was because in good times like these people could just run out and get a job, and they knew they were going to get one hundred twenty dollars or one hundred twenty-five dollars every week, especially if they were in a union. But, anyway, at the time we are approaching now, my brother John opened a branch in Brooklyn. It was the biggest branch Fuller had on the East Coast, and he did a good job out there. So, anyway, one day in 1953, I was going down on the elevator, and this guy I didn't recognize got on the elevator, and he looked so unhappy that I just said, "Hey, what the heck is wrong with you?" There were a couple of other people in the elevator, but I just couldn't resist asking this guy what was wrong. So he said to me that he had come here and talked with Mr. Fuller because he thought he could get a black man to help him get some of his problems straightened out. So I said, "What are you looking for? What are you trying to do?" He said he had a product he wanted Fuller to make for him, and I said, "Well, I don't know what you are talking about, but I work in the lab and maybe Mr. Fuller didn't take enough time to fully understand what you are trying to do." So he gave me his card, and I said, "If I have some time in the future, I will try to come and see if maybe we can help you." So I put his card in my pocket, and I guess I laid it on my dresser or somewhere, but anyway I didn't come across that card for about a month, and when I saw it again, I said to my wife, "I think I'll take the streetcar and go over on Sixty-fourth and Cottage Grove and see what this guy is doing." So I went over there and walked in the door of this guy's barbershop, and I was just flabbergasted.

People were standing all around the wall waiting for their turn, and the jukebox was jumping, and I have never seen people working so fast in my life! Then I saw the guy who gave me the card, and I spoke to him. "What in the world is this?" I said, and he said, "Don't bother me now, baby. I'll be with you in a minute. Can't talk to you now!" He was combing so fast on this guy that he was working on that I just started breaking up. I broke out laughing. It was such a comical scene, but, anyway, he finally got some free time, and he showed me what he was doing. That was the first time I had ever seen anything like this going on. He was straightening hair! So I said, "Let me see that stuff you're doing that straightening with," and, well, that gallon jar was separated in about three different layers. They had a layer of pink stuff on top, then a cloudy layer that was oil, and water was on the bottom. So he would take a big stick and stir this gallon jar, and then he would put some of this mixture in a small jar. Then he would take a comb and take some of the stuff from the small jar and put it on the guy's head, but, as soon as he started working with the stuff, it started breaking down and that alkalinity that it contained was coming free, and I saw that—so I said, "Man, I don't know how you do this." And he said, "Well, I just do it!" So I said, "What else is there around here?"—because this stuff was really bad, but it turned out that there was nothing else he had that was commercially available, and so I said, "Well, give me the names of all of the ingredients that you put in that mixture, and I will pick some of that stuff up, and I'll take a look and see what we can do to improve and perfect it," and that is how my company got started!

TB: Johnson Products?

GJ: Yes, trying to solve this other guy's problem created an opportunity for me, and I gave him an opportunity to be a part of it. See, he was really the best guy to sell the product because people knew him all over the country. Everybody in the music business, all the stage people, plus all the pimps, all the hustlers, and everybody else, they all knew that he was the best in the business. Nobody could "finger wave" the way that this guy could finger wave. But to solve his problem took me about six months. This was about the middle of 1953, and we didn't finally get the problems all worked out until about January of 1954. So then I told him, "You know, now we can market this. We can go half and half," and he said, "Well, how much do you think it will take to get it started?" I knew I could borrow two hundred fifty dollars, but it would take at least five hundred dollars. So he wrote out a check for two hundred fifty dollars, and I went and got my two hundred fifty dollars, and that is how JPC got started! But the most significant thing about how Johnson Products got started was not the fact that we made a better product or anything like that, but it was the fact that I knew that I could succeed. This was a cinch, as far as I was concerned. In other words, my confidence level was so high that I had no doubt that I could do it! Never thought about failure. Never thought about that I wouldn't make it. I started in February of '54, and I rented space in the back of Leon Cooper's Beauty Supply Company at 517 East Sixty-third Street for thirty-five dollars a month and stayed there for maybe about a year.

TB: So, during that year, how many employees did you have?

GJ: Actually, I employed my youngest brother. My wife came in later, and my mother was doing part-time. See, my mother still worked for Fuller Products. My mother went to work for Fuller at the end of 1945, and in two years she was the supervisor. In just two years she was running the plant! That's where she had been until I retired her in 1965. In 1965, she left there, and, believe me, just like when I left he had a tough time replacing me, he also had a tough time replacing her. Maybe a tougher time because she was dealing with about sixty-five or seventy women, and trying to deal with that many women is not easy! She ran the whole production floor and did a very good job. My mother is a very unusual person. She really is. She is a strong woman. She is good. She is fair. She is decent. But she is strong, and she is the boss.

TB: And she doesn't have to flaunt it.

GJ: That's right.

TB: So at the beginning it was just the four of you. Did you do your own sales?

GJ: At first I was making it and also selling it, but then I taught my brother Robert how to make it, and I did all the selling and the marketing.

TB: Were you on the street?

GJ: I wasn't only on the street. I was all over this country! I was in wholesale sales as well.

TB: So now you are going for a mass-market sales operation.

GJ: No, not a mass sales operation. I am selling to barbers. You see, I can only sell to barbers through wholesalers if I can get those wholesalers to carry my line, and those wholesalers don't want to carry my line because they don't know anything about it. They never heard of it, and they haven't had any calls for it, so they are not interested. This means that I've got to go out and sell directly to all those barbers. I've got to go out and teach barbers who aren't even thinking about making this kind of money to buy some of these products from me. The first time I went to St. Louis I found out that nobody was doing any processing there, so I had to hire a barber, fly him down to St. Louis on their off days, which was a Monday, and he would hold an all-day clinic for these St. Louis barbers for free. That's when we taught them how to do what was called the "process" and the "finger wave." Now, at that time these guys were making forty dollars a week cutting hair for a dollar or for eighty-five cents, and we told them you can buy this product, and you can use this technique, and guys will come in here and ask for it, and you can charge them five bucks! That's how we turned those guys into making one hundred forty dollars a week. That's how it went. From forty dollars a week to one hundred forty dollars or one hundred fifty dollars a week, and when a shop was really getting hot, they were making two hundred dollars and three hundred dollars a week! Nelson, who was my partner to start with, didn't go out and sell because, instead of him going out and selling, people would come by and buy our products from him directly, and, believe me, when people heard about these products, they really started to come in, and he used to work really long hours. He would close at 2 A.M. and would be back there at 9 A.M. That's how it was going, but it wasn't going fast enough for me. It was too slow. He was going too slow, and so I told him one day, "We have got people calling us up from Cleveland. We have got people calling us up from Detroit. We have got people calling us up from Indianapolis. We have got a hundred places we can go, and I can't wait. I've got to handle this all by myself!" Anyway, I went and got some proper legal advice and when he heard what I had to say, the judge said to him, "You take half of what you came in with, and you go your own way." So he left, and I stayed right here!

TB: And now you are in the position to be the sole decision maker.

GJ: Well, I was already making all the decisions, but now I can go on and do what I really want to do. Now I was free to go out and hire other guys. I hired that barber to fly down to St. Louis, and then I sent him to Kansas City and from Kansas to Detroit. I sent him everywhere. Houston, New York, everywhere I went, I had him with me to demonstrate the product. All they had to do was to see it work, and my price was reasonable. See, I was charging them a dollar for a jar, twelve dollars for a case. But, then, when I got to New York, you know how rough those boys were? They thought they had New York already locked up because they already had their own brand of hair straightener. One of those guys was called Jaber, and one was called Posner. Both of them were Jewish guys, and they were selling that stuff of theirs at seventy-five cents a jar. Mine was actually worth more than a dollar a jar, but I tried to keep the price as close to them as I could possibly keep it. So I sold it for a dollar a jar and twelve dollars a case. Then, as soon as I left town, this guy Posner comes in, and he cuts his price from nine dollars to six dollars a case and bought back all my stuff by paying them what they paid me, and then they took all my stuff out. That way he gave them something they couldn't refuse. So I said I would leave New York alone, and I put New York on the back burner and went everywhere else in the country and built the business, and then later I attacked New York when I had some ammunition and could come in there in a big way. But we didn't come here to talk about Johnson Products. We came here to talk about Chicago.

TB: But that's also part of Chicago.

GJ: Yes, it is. You know I am not the only one that Mr. Fuller helped. Fuller mentored Johnny Johnson too, and I can tell you that I know that Mr. Fuller interceded for Johnny with the draft board, and Johnny never went into the army.

TB: They didn't have any children, but he and Eunice were married by then.

GJ: When he had done as much as he could do with *Negro Digest*, then he started *Ebony*, and Fuller was shipping copies of *Ebony* to every one of his branches with the instructions for his people to sell the magazines. "Get those magazines in circulation!" And Fuller was also supporting him with two or three pages of ads. I mean, nobody else was advertising in that magazine except Fuller!

TB: Just Fuller?

GJ: Yes, the white market didn't want him or his publications. They didn't pay him any attention. Fuller did the same thing for *Ebony* that I did for *Essence*. When *Essence* got started, *Essence* looked like it was never going to make it, so I gave them guaranteed forty-eight pages of advertising a year. I gave them four pages a month. I didn't really need four pages a month, but we needed another media outlet besides *Ebony*, and they were more upscale. I saw my thing going upscale, and Johnny kept his publication on a plane which has always stayed the same.

TB: No, it hasn't changed very much.

GJ: But *Essence* is contemporary, and it is more like the *Vogues* and the *Bazaars*. So I did all I could to sustain them until they got on their feet.

TB: How many employees do you have by this time?

GJ: I guess when I moved in there, I had maybe six employees, Tim. We were in that building from '58 until '64. We had a fire there in October of 1964, and by the time the fire hit, we must have had about thirty-eight or forty people.

TB: What was your volume of business?

GJ: I grossed a million dollars in '64. It was the first time we grossed a million dollars ever. It took ten years to reach a million dollars, but when the fire hit us in '64, we were literally out of business. Fortunately for me and for my employees, I had an excellent relationship with my former employers, and do you know what Mr. Fuller did? The next morning after the fire he called me up, and he said, "George, come down here. I want to talk to you." So I went down to Fuller Products Company, and you can imagine how I felt. I was really in a trance. It was so hard for me to believe that my business had burned down. That fire went all the way from the basement up to the roof, and all of my inventory, all of my raw materials, and a lot of my machinery were affected by that fire. So I was essentially out of business, and then, when I went to his office at about 11 A.M. on the next day, at first he quoted something from the Book of Job to me about how Job was able to get beyond his problems, and then for a time he was going on about how these are the kinds of things that can make us strong, these are the kinds of challenges and trials that really prove to you who you are. He told me, "You know, the same fire that melts the gold hardens the steel!" But I didn't really hear any of what he was saying until he said, "Well, you know Fuller Products Company hasn't been doing all that well lately, and our production isn't anything like what it used to be, and we probably have got a lot of unused room on our production floor, and anything that you can use here in this building is at your service. Now I snapped out of it, and I said, "What?" I said, "You mean I can come down here and bring my people and go to work?" He said, "Absolutely. You can do anything that is not conflicting or interfering." Anyway, at that time my mother, of course, was still supervising his production. She was his plant manager, and so I got together with my mother, and my brother John was also still working for him, and we planned how we would bring our people in. I leaned on my suppliers, and my suppliers went out to their customers and got immediately enough raw materials to get us going again. They were drawing from the various people who had the same kind of products and the same kind of raw materials, such as glass and whatnot that we used. Believe it or not, Tim, within one week we were back producing! All my competitors, especially Posner, who was my biggest nemesis at that time, were elated and chuckling because they thought that the fire had stopped me, but when they found out that my products weren't out of stock, and when they saw that new stocks kept coming in, they couldn't understand it. So, anyway, we operated down at Fuller Products Company for about four months, and then I was able to rent a temporary place out at 7700 South Chicago Avenue. As soon as I got production started out there, I went to look for a permanent place. I lived at 8412 Michigan at the time, and I knew about this big landfill that started around Eighty-fifth and ran all the way to Eighty-seventh, and I found out who owned that property. When we contacted them, they wanted a dollar a square foot, or something like that, which was a lot of money. So I went and talked to a guy named Harold Greenwald at the South Side Bank, and I said, "Listen, you got twelve acres out there that are being used as a dumping ground." The junk on that property was piled up twelve feet above the sidewalk in some places and in other places only about nine or ten feet, but all of it was full of broken-up pavement and concrete sidewalks and curbs that were excavated when they put new streets in, and I said, "Look, I want to purchase two acres on the corner at Eighty-fifth and Lafayette, and I will give you enough money so that you can get rid of all that stuff and have a sizable, salable piece of property, but ain't nobody going to buy it in the condition it is in now." What I told him was that he would not only have a salable piece of property but would also get rid of an eyesore in the community, and I said, "I am going to put up a beautiful new building here, and I don't want to see all this junk surrounding me." That's the way I sold him that idea, and he bought it! I think I gave him eighty-six thousand dollars cash for two acres. He had to add about another ten thousand dollars of his own in order to excavate all that ground down to sidewalk level. It took a while, but I immediately got the architects working, and we started building our new building, which was finally completed in about September 1966. Anyway, it was a hell of a period. But I think it was my greatest low period, personally.

TB: But now your market is all over the country.

GJ: Yes, our market then was all over the country where black people lived, and that is also true today as well, except that now we consider our market to be anywhere where black people live.

TB: All over the world?

GJ: Let me tell you something. I had ideas back in 1960 of going to Nigeria. I even had hotel and flight reservations to attend the ceremony of independence in Nigeria in October of 1960. But in August of 1960, they assassinated Patrice Lumumba, who was the great liberator and a leader of the reparation movement in the Congo, and that really frightened me, and I said, "My God, do I really want to go?" I mean, what happened to him was totally unexpected, and it was very discouraging. The Congo, of course, is not that far from Nigeria, so I decided maybe I had better wait and see how well the mantle of freedom will be worn by the Nigerians. Then, as you know, in 1966 they had their first coup, and their president was deposed and the military took over. When that happened, I said to myself, "You know, maybe I made the right decision." However, people kept coming looking for me, so I went over there in 1972 and started working on organizing a manufacturing installation. By 1972 Johnson Products Company was doing very, very well internationally.

TB: You had gone public by then?

GJ: We went public in 1969. As I said, it took us ten years to get to one million, but it took us only five years to get to ten million. So in 1969 with ten million in sales—actually about eleven million—we went public! But you know something? I can look back on that decision and if you were to ask me today, would I do it again? I think I would say, "No." Of course, you can never turn the clock back, and no matter what your experience teaches you, you know what is done is done. It was a decision that had its positive sides and its negative sides, but I guess I focused more on the positive side than I did on the negative side. I think today with what I have learned through experience I would definitely pay a lot more attention to those negative factors and then make a different kind of decision.

TB: By "going public" you opened the floodgates.

GJ: Yes, actually I didn't realize what a fishbowl I was getting into. I absolutely put this company and myself into a fishbowl, but there were some reasons—some good reasons—for doing it. I think there could have been some other avenues better explored that I didn't explore because the attractiveness of "going public" was so fascinating to me.

TB: Well, at least it was a way for you to attract new capital.

GJ: Yes, but I wasn't trying to raise capital. No, the real reason was that I had a serious estate problem and a potential IRS problem because, as you might remember, in 1969, you still had 71 percent personal income tax. We had a high rate of corporate tax, and, as an individual, I had personal income tax—but, although we paid our corporate taxes, everything I took out of the company, I had to pay personal taxes on! So, rather than having to go up against that 71 percent tax, for a long time I didn't pay myself a whole lot of money. I didn't take a lot of money out of the company, but then, as a result, the company had a lot of money.

TB: And so, when you went public, it meant that now folks could buy into your business and own a piece of the company.

GJ: Yes, but it also meant that from that day on I had to report to the public, and everybody thought they knew how to run my business, so that's why I said that if I had it all to do over again, I would think a lot harder than I thought about it at that time. But, well, as I said, I had a lot of personal reasons—especially the estate problem. If something had happened to me, it would have been a very disastrous thing for my family because anything that would have been taken out of the company for death taxes would have been taxed first at a corporate rate and then at the high death rate. In other words, my wife was in a position where she would have had to sell the company in order to pay the dadgum taxes! Well, I suppose insurance is one of the ways you can hedge against that, but it would have had to be a huge amount of insurance, and that kind of thing just wasn't attractive to me. I never have liked the idea. Why I carry all that insurance? It ain't really that appetizing! I don't know how you feel about it.

TB: Yes, I feel that same way too.

GJ: It is a necessary evil, as far as I am concerned. Anyway for me this was a hell of a period. As a matter of fact, personally, I think this was the greatest low period in my entire life because I was faced with so many challenges. I mean, it was just one after another, and then I was also growing personally in a lot of directions.

TB: Yes, about this time you also began to do a lot of public service.

GJ: Well, I always believed that I had a responsibility in that area. You know there is a verse in the Bible that says to whom more is given more is required, and I have always felt that was absolutely true, and that it applied to me. So the more I was given, the more it was required of me to give. I wanted people to work for me with their heart and soul and not just for wages. I wanted them to give the best that they could give, and the only way that people will work that way is when they want to do it, and the only way people will want to do it is when you make them feel that they are a part of what they are doing—that it is not just for you, but that it is for them as well as for you. Anyway, when we were employing twenty-seven people and had gross sales of six hundred twenty-seven thousand dollars, I started Johnson Products' company profit-sharing plan. This was in 1962, and I gave the full amount that I was allowed by Internal Revenue. Every year I gave 15 percent of the pretax profits to the profit-sharing plan, and between 1962 and 1980 the company put a lot of money into the profit-sharing program. Then in the middle eighties I had some very serious financial problems, and, as a result, I had to start reducing staff. That was something that I never, ever wanted to do. I had never had a layoff. We had gone through recessions, but we had never laid off anybody until 1985, and then it was a matter of saving this company for the benefit of those that it could still carry.

TB: By this time, at your peak, you had how many employees in sales and staff?

GJ: By 1985 there were over five hundred people. We had about eighty or ninety people out of the city, and all the rest of them were here, so when I had to start this reduction in staff, it was a real heartbreaker for me. The only thing that really helped me to accept it was that I had to do it for the benefit of the majority. We were top-heavy with high-salary people, but our main problem was that we were caught off-base during a good portion of the eighties because that is when the "curl" came in, and we couldn't jump right into the market for the "curl" because we already had such a major investment in the relaxer market. In 1979, I think our sales were close to forty million dollars, and all of that was either relaxers or Afro-Sheen hair spray for men. None of that was in curls. So in our best interests we couldn't promote the curl because if you use the curl you couldn't also use a relaxer, but we were watching the market very carefully and starting to develop new products to try to deal with it, and eventually we put out an excellent product. This was a product that would have been far better for the market had it succeeded. Those hairdressers had been using a cream relaxer from us for all these years now, so a cream curl product was something that would be very easy for them to adapt to, but we thought we had a product that was even better than the cream curl. It was a liquid. It took just a little bit longer to set than the cream, but it was a lot better for the hair, and we felt that we had a superior product, but, when we finally came out with the product, we couldn't get the hairdressers to make the switch from using a cream to a liquid. They clung to the cream, and, as a result, we were on the wrong side of the street, and we were really needing to find a way to recapture the market. We were already saturating *Ebony*, and I think they will tell you at *Essence* that our company was absolutely instrumental in keeping their publication afloat. I felt that we needed *Essence* because I saw that the format of *Ebony* did not reach our entire market, and so I supported *Essence*, and I gave them four pages every month with two years of the money up front. We gave them the money up front so that they could survive.

TB: They were based in New York.

GJ: Yeah, they were based in New York and, in fact, they did survive, but, by 1969, even *Essence* and *Ebony* and *Jet* were not really reaching all of the market, and we wanted to find a way to make the electronic media work for us, so—well, you might not remember this, but I hope I can bring it back to your memory—in 1969 we had a program that we put on in a limited market called *And Beautiful*. This was the first time that Redd Foxx was ever on a national television program. We had dancing. We had singing. Oh, we had great stars!

TB: Yes, it was excellent.

GJ: Sure, it was excellent. Anyway, we did it in 1969, and we did it again in 1970. In 1970 we called our program *And Beautiful Too*. *And Beautiful Too* was a visual history of black music. It started off with the ship coming from Africa across the Atlantic and so forth, and then we saw the growth of black music in America, and, believe me, that show cost us a lot of money!

TB: You were on prime time on Saturday.

GJ: Yes, we put that out in prime time in about twenty-something markets, and it showed me that we could be effective, but, even so, it was a failure because we couldn't convince the retailers to stock enough products to really make it pay off for us. What happened was that immediately after each of these shows the shelves in stores across the United States where we were distributed were just wiped out, but then they stayed out of stock until the next stocking cycle! Walgreens, for instance, would have a two-week cycle, and every two weeks they restocked the shelves. They used to carry additional stock in the back room which would be their reserve stock, but then they stopped doing that, and now at this time they were restocking their shelves only once every two weeks. So, if the shelves were stocked two or three days before the show, after the weekend—we showed on Friday or Saturday night—their shelves would be clean by Monday morning and then they would be out of stock until the next stocking cycle.

TB: But *And Beautiful* and *And Beautiful Too* were very successful in terms of entertainment and very successful in terms of the size of the audience that they generated, weren't they?

GJ: Yes, of course, the product impact was made, but the revenue from it didn't happen for us because, as I just told you, although we tried to presell and alert the retailers that this would have a high impact and that it was being scheduled for this certain day, they didn't respond to any of that. This is typical of the retail market. You know, "You got to show me," but you see, after we show them, then it's too late. The show is over, and what they needed to have was to have an overabundance of supplies there to keep feeding the demand as it walked in the store, and they weren't prepared for that. So, as it turned out, we didn't get the revenues out of those shows that we expected, and, believe me, those shows were really expensive to produce.

TB: I can imagine. After all, they were first-rate.

GJ: Well, as you know, I didn't do those shows alone. An advertising agency put those shows together for us, and the guy that was working for the advertising agency, Tom Kuhn, was a very creative guy, and Tom was friends with a good friend of Don Cornelius. They used to hang out and drink together.

TB: Here in Chicago?

GJ: Yes, here in Chicago. Now, Tom is a white boy, but Tom was really with it. He was very much involved in all black things. In fact, I think he had a black girlfriend. So, anyway, Tom and Don and I discussed *Soul Train*, which at that time in 1970 and '71 was a local program on Channel 26. It was being broadcast in black and white, and Tom thought that if *Soul Train* was in color we could get it played on stations all around the country, so I put up the money to make a pilot program for not a lot of money that was shot in color. I think the pilot was like thirty minutes, and *Soul Train*, of course, was always an hour show, but, anyway, when I saw the pilot I thought it was money well spent. So Don and I entered into an agreement, and I would own half of the show, and he would own half of the show. We would promote the show as *Don Cornelius's Soul Train*, and we would take this thing national! We went out to California to Metromedia and started producing *Soul Train* in color for the national market. I think the first time we showed *Don Cornelius's Soul Train* we had nine markets, and we went everywhere trying to get acts to come on for scale, but the only act we could get to come on for scale was Wilson Pickett!

TB: Is that right? When you say "scale," you mean the stars expected you to pay them above union scale for their performances.

GJ: Right. In other words, we didn't want to pay their usual professional fees for their work because they had something to gain from the exposure we were providing for them and this was an opportunity for them to play their latest number that they wanted to promote. We were just like the disc jockeys, but now we were going to put them on television, and if people see hot numbers on television, those people are going to buy that record! So Wilson Pickett understood that, and Wilson Pickett was willing to come on for scale, but I had to bring him and his band all the way from New York at my expense and put them up in a hotel, and that was a big cost, but at least I had a big name!

TB: The rest of the black artists would not do that for you?

GJ: Listen, we couldn't get them no matter how we begged. I never will forget going into Berry Gordy's office with Don and we couldn't get any Motown artists. Not a single one! It was a hell of a struggle in those first shows to get anybody to come on *Soul Train* at scale, but eventually it began to get better and better as we began to get more and more markets and as the show began to be talked about and written about. You know, I'd like to tell you a story. We started this thing in 1971, and we celebrated the twentieth anniversary of *Soul Train* here in Chicago in 1991. As I have said, Johnson Products was partners with Don at the beginning, and the way it worked for us was I had 50 percent of the advertising spots, and Don was selling the other 50 percent of the spots. Anyway, we made a lot of money, plus we were going through a recession about 1978, and during a recession like that the first thing that companies do is to cut back on advertising, and so we were saturating the program with the ads that we already had. Some of those ads were repeated at least twice in the same program. So, about 1978, I basically gave my share of the show to Don for the privilege of Don carrying us forward at no cost to our company. That was a good deal for him and a good deal for us as well. He kept us in that show at no cost for ten years after that!

TB: Is that right?

GJ: Anyway, that is how we finally did find a way to make the electronic media work for us. We did it by establishing the success of *Soul Train*.

TB: You were pioneers.

GJ: We proved it, brother!

TB: I remember that when things were going very well you moved into that gorgeous building near Eighty-seventh Street.

GJ: Let me tell you something about that building. Tim, that building has a lot of significance to me. Years earlier, Mr. Fuller had really embedded in my mind that we had a responsibility to be good role models. We had a responsibility to make it, to be visible and by our example to lead. That's why I wanted that property, because I had envisioned what kind of a building we were going to put there. It was going to be a building that would have to be noticed, and, as you know, that building sits right on top of the Dan Ryan Expressway and hundreds of thousands of cars pass by there, and I was determined that we would make a statement. All those things that we did to build what we built were designed to really prove and to help young black people and mature black people to believe in themselves and what they could accomplish. Because what Mr. Fuller always said—and I lived to see the truth of it—was that black people don't believe that they can do what white people do, but black people do believe they can do what they see other black people doing, and they absolutely believe that! So, if you are doing something that's good, let them know about it because, believe me, they will be motivated to try to do it for themselves, and that is absolutely true. Do you know how many competitors that I have now? Can you imagine how many blacks are in the hair care business? Would you have any idea how many companies are out there? Well, around the country you can count about thirty to thirty-five, and every one of them comes in because they know about the success of Johnson Products.

TB: They saw you succeed, and so now they believe they also can do it.

GJ: Yeah, that's right. That's the truth. Some black people don't believe that we can compete with white people. I believe we can. In fact, I know it, but generally we don't believe it. What we say is, "Hey, I can do what that nigger is doing! I know I can do what that nigger is doing." I mean, how many times have you heard that?

TB: A lot of times.

GJ: And that goes for something good as well as for something bad, but just let me tell you about myself. When I started Johnson Products Company, I never ever thought I would not make it. I knew I could make it because Fuller Products was making around three hundred thousand dollars a year when I went there, and when I left it was about five million. I saw that kind of growth, and Mr. Fuller always taught us that you can do anything that you want to do—so I never had any negative thoughts about whether or not I could make it. It was just how was I going to make it and when. Mr. Fuller taught me: Take what you have and make what you want—and don't go around here trying to alibi or make excuses because you don't have this or that. You just take what you have and make what you want!

TB: But that means you have to develop a real spirit of entrepreneurship.

GJ: Yeah, but you know, I didn't understand what an entrepreneur was until many years after I started my business. When somebody told me I was an entrepreneur, I had to go and look it up and find out what an entrepreneur was!

TB: Well, they are unusual people. I will tell you that. You know there are guys like me who can know the intricacies—technical, intellectual—but still would be scared to take the kind of chances and risk that you took.

GJ: Well, let me tell you something, I didn't have any choice. I had to be an entrepreneur. My mother was the one who was afraid, not me. I already had two children when I started this business. My youngest was just a year and one month, and my oldest boy was just a month shy of being two, and my mother knew that Fuller Products was a good place to work, and it was growing, and I was secure in a place like that—so she was concerned about me jeopardizing my future by leaving Fuller Products. But I told her that I wasn't worried about my future. That was one of the few times that I had to lift my mother's spirits because my mother has always been lifting mine, and I had to convince her that she did not need to worry because I had no doubt that I would succeed because we were making something that nobody else had ever made. Now, when I say "we," that's me and Dr. Herbert A. Martini—and with his genius and his knowledge of the market we were able to accomplish what we did. I did a lot of the actual work, but he trained me to be a chemist, and he understood what very few people knew about cosmetic chemistry. He was a genius. He was a natural-born German who had come here in the late thirties and so at the start of the war they rounded him up, and he was placed in detention.

TB: There was a lot of fear. Do you remember how they also put the Japanese in detention during the war?

GJ: Yes, and then, when he came out of detention and tried to get a job, no white companies would hire him because he was German.

TB: It was because of discrimination that those white companies wouldn't hire him.

GJ: Yes, but Fuller hired him, and that is when I met him. I was there long before he came, but he was the one who really taught me the business. By this time it was 1954, and most of the major cosmetic companies in Germany had been returned to their previous owners, and so he wrote to those companies in Europe and asked for samples of their raw materials, especially any of their emulsifiers, that might be the answer to this problem we were having, and, as a result, we must have tried forty or fifty different kind of emulsifiers before we found one that would tolerate the level of alkalinity that we would have to have for marketing our hair straightener. What we did that was unique in making Ultra Wave was in the way that we emulsified the product. That is what made it different from everything else because nothing that had sodium hydroxide in it was ever emulsified before, and we are the ones who did it!

TB: So you came on the market with something which was needed and, therefore, salable.

GJ: Let me tell you, I even tried to sell a variation of the basic idea to hairdressers when the "natural" came in. The middle sixties was a traumatic time, and a hell of a lot of hairdressers were sitting on their butts in their beauty salons not knowing what the hell to do with this desire to go "natural."

TB: Well, that desire accompanies the social movement of that time.

GJ: Right, and so I sold a program called the "Ultra Natural," in which you used Ultra Sheen relaxer to the point where you just gave the hair a brilliance but you didn't take all the curl out. In other words, it wasn't any longer in the natural tight or so-called kinky state. A woman with a lot of hair on her head couldn't put a normal comb through her hair. That's why they used to take those big-tooth shampoo combs and go through the "natural" with them, because anything smaller would break. But now they could take the relaxer and just put enough through the hair to give it a good shine because a real natural is really dull, but with this relaxer they would have a lot of highlights, and it would also be easy to comb through and also much more manageable. So that's how Ultra Sheen survived the natural. Then we jumped on the Afro Sheen bandwagon, and we dominated that market in the sixties. Then, later on, of course, it went back again to the relaxers. The relaxer is what really has the longevity.

TB: Now, apart from the business, I know at this time you were also with the Urban League.

GJ: Oh, yes. Bill Berry came to me in the early sixties, and the first day he came into my office I thought that I would not pay any attention to the Urban League because I was so busy trying to establish Johnson Products. But when he told me about the work he was doing, I committed to it right then. Yeah, I gave him some money right then, and he walked out with a check. I think a few months later he asked me to go on their board, and, in fact, I was president of the board in 1969 and 1970. Besides the Urban League board, I also got involved with Junior Achievement in the middle sixties, and today I am still involved with both Junior Achievement and the Urban League.

TB: I used to see your name whether it was on the board or as a contributor of some substance to a number of things that I would go to. You know, I get around to a lot of those places that a lot of us don't get to. I don't know if it was the aquarium or the planetarium, the Art Institute or any of those other places, but I have seen your name in prominence among almost all of them. That was unusual because you and John Johnson were the only two people of color that I was aware of who were doing that sort of thing. I was impressed by what you have been doing because it gives me the feeling of us moving beyond our own boundaries and extending our support beyond the so-called Black Belt or whatever else you might want to call it. You know, people often accuse us black folks of being recipients and seldom donors, and on occasion they will say, "You now have black millionaires and you have black rich people, but, well, when you want something, you come to us, and you never give anything back"—and so wherever I go I want to see if I can detect the name of one of us so that I can feel that we are growing beyond our own boundaries and sharing some of the civic responsibilities. But now looking back to the issue of the competition, George, eventually you decided to get into the white market as well.

GJ: Yes, I did decide to try. And why did I do this? In 1963 I tried to see if I could expand the distribution of Ultra Sheen, which was my flagship line, into the general market because we did some research in the white market, and the research said that white people did not respond to the name of Ultra Sheen as being a product exclusively for blacks. This is what the research showed and what it meant was we would be successful if we properly presented our products to the white consumer as well. So we developed an advertising program which involved print and broadcast media and point-of-sales materials. We had posters made. We did small twenty-second TV ads that showed two white United Airlines stewardesses and one black stewardess. The point-of-sale material had the same three people, two white United Airlines stewardesses with a black United Airlines stewardess in the middle, and really the ad looked like the black girl was trying to integrate. That's what it looked like. We used Chicago and Washington as the two markets to test it. Chicago, because we thought we had Walgreens here which had the best distribution, and after all, this is home for us. We could monitor it and do a really good job. We used Washington because Washington had a high level of black consumers. Well, anyway, we had an agreement with Walgreens that they were going to give us distribution in all of their stores on a much broader base than we had ever had. We even tagged all of our advertising to say "Get it at Walgreens," and Walgreens was supposed to give us this storewide distribution. We even had an incentive plan for the salespeople at the stores and for the people who serviced those stores where they could get premiums on a point basis. Our whole marketing approach turned on those ads, and we did everything we promised to do, but when we did our store checks, we found out that Walgreens never did what they should do. As a matter of fact, we had a better shake in Washington than we had in Chicago, but Washington wasn't enough, and Walgreens didn't want to expand our market beyond the black community, where it was already established.

TB: Good old Walgreens that started out at Forty-first and Cottage Grove!

GJ: But, listen, I understood what they were saying—so I dropped the idea, but, well, we tried it again in the mid-seventies. More or less in the mood of desperation, I decided to revive it. The desperation was caused by a series of events that had happened to the company by the mid-seventies. The competition wasn't really all that severe. Most of those products were helter-skelter, and they were available only behind the counter. You had to ask for them. We had moved our products out on the shelves with Ultra Wave and the companion products of Ultra Wave because we'd told them, "If you are going to sell these products, you are going to have to put them out where the people can see them," and they told us that one of the major reasons they wouldn't put the products out on the shelves was because they were afraid that black people would pilfer the products, and so we told them, "Look, when you see just how fast this stuff is selling you will also see that you will recoup whatever you might lose through pilferage. In fact, you are going to do more than just recoup because of your volume of sales, but, if you continue to keep these products behind the counter, you ain't going to have any volume, so now you had better decide exactly what you want to do." So that's when they started to put the products out there, and they didn't have anything in the store that moved out as fast as Ultra Wave. And then when we put the Ultra Sheen conditioner and its companion products out, and when they really started moving, those guys didn't know what the hell to do. They didn't know what to say. We were heroes, and that's how we established the "ethnic hair care" section. It got special attention from the retailers because they didn't move anything in their stores as fast as our stuff. The "Ultra Wave Hair Culture" was phenomenal, and from now on I am not going to have to worry about going back behind that counter ever again!

TB: They didn't give a damn about shrinkage because, if you got big enough volume, shrinkage is just part of doing business.

GJ: Yes, and you just figure it into the cost. The first real powerful bit of competition that I became aware of was from Revlon. Revlon really wanted to come into this market, and they sent some feelers out to me which I rebuffed. I just wasn't interested, and I let them know it. At that time I was in negotiation with a small company called Deluxal. I won't go into detail, but I was talking with the guy that owned Deluxal, and he was willing to sell. We had two or three lunches, and we were talking about the price, but then, all of a sudden, I don't get any more calls from him and I don't get my calls returned, and the next thing I know—I think a month and a half later—never having any further communication, is that he has sold to Revlon. Now, that really was a blow, but it didn't frighten me. What Revlon did was to take that company and use their muscle and their marketing and whatnot to pursue us, but they didn't do hardly any better with their products than that company they bought was doing already. So, after about two years of trying to push Deluxal, they put their own name on the Deluxal products, and they started making a relaxer to compete with Ultra Sheen, which they called Revlon Realistic Cream Relaxer, but they weren't getting anywhere with that either because we already had that market locked up. Then, when they couldn't move me that way, that is when I started having trouble with the FTC [Federal Trade Commission]. The FTC sent me a letter telling me that they had seen my ads, and they wanted me to substantiate certain claims that had been made. It seemed like a routine investigation, but I thought it strange that the letter came to me from Seattle, although I am in Chicago, and normally most of these cases would be handled out of their Washington, D.C., office. Anyway, we went out to Seattle and started discussing matters with the FTC in order to find out what they wanted us to do, and we were negotiating with them for the better part of a year. I told them right away at the first meeting that whatever they wanted us to do I did not mind doing as long as all of our competitors had to do the same thing. I just didn't want them putting me at a disadvantage, and they assured us from that very first meeting that that was not their intention, and I pointed out to them the fact that Revlon had been pursuing me and that Revlon was a giant company compared to ours and that they had done everything they could do to try to take over our market, and I did not want to be required to do anything that Revlon was not also required to do.

TB: Why do you think they had their Seattle office contact you?

GJ: Well, even George Birch, who is my lawyer and who is a specialist in food and drug law as well as Federal Trade Commission law, he was very hard put to understand why this was handled out of the Seattle office instead of Washington, D.C. I really can't tell you why except that Seattle was an out-of-the-way place, and I didn't have any contacts there. I knew some people in Washington, and, of course, we had the Black Caucus out there, but even Jesse Jackson couldn't find out the real reason from the chairman of the FTC, who gave him a completely blasé explanation, which never satisfied me in the slightest. He told Jesse that his people were thumbing through *Ebony* and saw from our ads that we were very prominent, and they thought that the time had come for the FTC to look into protecting the black consumer against misleading advertising, blah, blah, blah!

TB: What was the accusation?

GJ: I think in one of our ads we might have used the word "gentle"—that is, we said that our product was able to "gently" relax the hair, and they challenged that. They wanted us to substantiate our claim. They wanted us to admit that anything containing sodium hydroxide couldn't be gentle, and more blah, blah, blah! All of that was just a lame excuse!

TB: A decoy?

GJ: Yeah, a decoy, and when we got out there they told us that they had a bunch of horror stories about the effects of our product on people, but then they couldn't produce any of those horror stories. Not one. None at all, and we found out later on, of course, that they were flying all over the country trying to come up with some of those horror stories *after* the investigation had already gotten started. As I'm sure you know, an investigation of this type usually gets started *because* of horror stories that you've got documented, but this time they didn't have any real documentation, and so they were even advertising around to people who were doctors at various places and asking them, "Have you had any problems . . . blah, blah, blah!" Now, if this product of ours was really dangerous in any way, those doctors would have been calling all the health departments—but here the FTC was running out and trying to find some complaints!

TB: And why do you think they acted that way?

GJ: Well, Tim, they claimed they wanted to do something for black consumers, but I think it was all part of a scheme that was initiated by Revlon. You see, Revlon had previously made an out-of-the-way offer to me through a lawyer, and I told him, "No!" At that time he wouldn't tell me who the offer was really coming from, but I later learned that, in fact, it did come from Revlon. That's why I think that this so-called investigation was all a part of a scheme to try to stop us and to try to hurt us, so the only avenue that we had left to us was to sue the FTC, which is exactly what we did in early June of 1975!

TB: At this point, what was your gross revenue?

GJ: I think in June of 1975 our annual revenues were about thirty-six or thirty-seven million.

TB: And going up?

GJ: Yes, in '74 it was about thirty-three million, so we were jumping toward some pretty big numbers, but then for the fiscal year ending in 1976 there was only about a 5 percent increase in volume! In other words, they stopped us cold! Up till then we had 85 percent of the relaxer market among professionals, but that share of the market was cut in half within the next two years! Plus, as a matter of fact, this was also an assassination of the brand name, which had been a stalwart for us in establishing our company. Ultra Sheen had been one of the most trusted names in relaxers, and to this day it still has not recovered from what they tried to do. But, even so, no matter what, the company has survived, and the reason that this company has survived is that we were well financed and could weather the storm. Tim, let me tell you, it is a strange thing, but this so-called free enterprise system works in a lot of ways, some fair and some not, but at least when it comes to personal care products, it is not color-blind, and this "free enterprise system" is obviously not yet ready to accept a black-owned company entering the general market with personal care products. I don't know of any exceptions, but then take a look at my son. He owns Baldwin Ice Cream, and Baldwin Ice Cream is being sold in Dominick's, Jewel, Kroger, A&P—every place you look! And it is being sold to people everywhere who happen to like ice cream because there's no ethnic connotation to Baldwin Ice Cream. You'll also find Reggio's Pizza in Dominick's and the Jewel and a lot of other places as well.

TB: And Reggio's is also produced by a black-owned company.

GJ: Yeah, it's owned by John Clark. Reggio's Pizza is just a small company now, but it is growing, and it is growing because there is no ethnic or cultural connotation to it.

TB: According to my perception, at the present time all the black-owned companies combined still have only a relatively small portion of the sales for personal care products even within our own community.

GJ: They say that this is at least a two-billion-dollar market, and we've got less than half of that. We possibly have only just over one-third, and yet we are the ones who created and developed this market!

TB: In your opinion, what is the reason that black women, who are the greatest utilizers of these products, do not put their hard-earned dollars back into these black-owned companies which will create jobs and put money back into their own communities?

GJ: Well, if black-produced products are available and if they know that these products are produced by black companies, I definitely think that those are the products that would be purchased, but, of course, black women are just like all other consumers, and that means that they are susceptible to the impressions they receive from advertising, and if the impact of that advertising is such that it puts a certain brand on their mind, then that is the brand that they are going to pick up from off the shelf, and they are not necessarily going to remember or even care whether it's a black company or not. Now, if a person is from Chicago, they would probably know that a Johnson product is produced by a black company, but in a place like Birmingham, for instance, they very well might not.

TB: Is price a determining factor?

GJ: Well, sure, it's important, but, as a matter of fact, the other companies seem to be much higher priced than we are. So price doesn't really seem to be a determining factor. In a recession, however, price does become quite an issue, and the higher-priced products get the least amount of attention. At times like that, people will think, "Well, this is probably not as good as that, but it's cheaper, and I'm going to buy it because it will do almost the same thing," but then they wind up being surprised because what they bought just might be a whole lot better than that other, more expensive brand!

TB: At what point in your business career did you first get involved in banking?

GJ: Well, let me tell you, I have a very good reason for getting into the banking business.

TB: How long have you been in it?

GJ: This will be the twenty-ninth year. Johnson Products was started in 1954, and, along with six or seven other fellows, we started the Independence Bank in 1964.

TB: Would you mind saying who your partners were?

GJ: OK, Al Boutte and Morrie Polk were both founding directors. Marshall Bynum, who is now deceased, was also one of the founding directors. Charlie Pinkart, Phil Constater, Bob Bacon—anyway it was four blacks and, I guess, four whites.

TB: How did you decide to get into it?

GJ: Well, you see, I had been banking at Chatham Bank before that bank closed. In fact, when Chatham Bank closed, it closed with some of my money still in it! It was located at 7936 South Cottage Grove Avenue, and I'd started banking there because I lived in Chatham, and so I wanted to bank in Chatham, but one of the main reasons I got into banking on my own was because when my business was still very small, only about two years old, most of what I was doing I was doing by hand, and, believe me, mixing our Ultra Wave hair conditioner was a very tough job. It was a straining thing for me to take that stick when the cream started getting thick and to keep it stirring, It was very, very, very straining on me because at that time I was only 152 pounds, and I even injured myself doing all that stirring, and so I wanted to buy a machine that would do it for me. Now, since by that time I was banking at the South Side Bank, I went over to South Side, and I asked them if I could fill out an application for a business loan, and you know what? They laughed at me.

TB: Where was the South Side Bank located at that time?

GJ: At Forty-seventh and Cottage. I had some money in that bank and was never overdrawn, but when I told them what my business was and what I wanted the money for, like I just said, they just laughed at me!

TB: And there they were doing all of their business right in the heart of the black community!

GJ: Yes, and since they laughed at me, the very next day I took all my money out of that bank, and I got a little better break over at Chicago City Bank, and I was able to get a small mortgage, but I was never able to get any kind of a business loan out of that bank either. So, anyway, by then I knew just how difficult it was to get money when you needed money to help your business grow, and then when this bank also closed and the FDIC was operating there trying to collect their debts, I recognized that this was really going to be a terrible blot on the entire community because, as you know, a bank is the business center of any community, and when a bank goes under, then people begin to leave, and the community starts to go down and fall apart. So, when I learned that there was a group that had been formed to try to reopen this bank, I joined it immediately, and I started to bring in some other guys as well. Anyway, we ultimately did get that bank open, but it was like being under the shadow of a ghost, and not a very nice ghost at that! You see at this time we were only insured up to ten thousand dollars, and we had about forty thousand already invested in that bank. So, for all of us operating in that bank, it was just like having the shadow of a ghost hovering all around you, and it really slowed down our growth.

TB: When did your new bank open?

GJ: Our bank began as the Independence Bank, and we opened on the fifth of December, 1964.

TB: In that same building?

GJ: Yes, in that same old building, and then, only about three weeks later, the Seaway Bank opened down the street at eighty-five-something Cottage Grove, just about two blocks away from us. Now, when we were in the process of formation, we tried to get together with Seaway, and we had a meeting, and we would have come together with Seaway except for one thing. There was one person that Seaway under no conceivable circumstances would ever want to be involved with, and that was the same guy who had started organizing our group. Well, we were, I guess, loyal to a fault to Herbie, but those guys at Seaway were adamant about not including him, and that is why we did not get together. It would have been one strong bank out there, but, because of our unwillingness to sacrifice Herbie, we now have two separate banks.

TB: Are they both the same kind of banks?

GJ: Well, I think our bank is a lot different from Seaway. We are similar in many ways, of course, but we also go way beyond what they do, and I think we generate far more noninterest income than Seaway does. Seaway would be considered more of a traditional neighborhood bank, but we are a neighborhood bank *plus*. You might even say we are a hybrid because we have also been involved in investment banking. We have a corporate trust, and we can offer money management services. Just recently we signed a five-year contract with the city to process all of their credit cards, and our corporate partner in that is Sears Roebuck. So now if you want to pay your parking ticket with a credit card, if your car has been towed away and you want to pay the car-pound and towing charges, if you're out at the airport and you have been someplace for four or five days and when you come back you've got a forty-five-dollar parking ticket, now you can pay all of these charges with your credit card — and we are the ones who process all of that! We also own the foreign exchange facility out at O'Hare, and we are eventually going to get all the credit card business for the water department as well.

TB: You also do a lot of home mortgages, don't you?

GJ: Yes, we do. In fact, we just signed a contract with General Electric, and now we can offer mortgages at better rates than anybody else in town.

TB: Looking from the outside as objectively as possible, I have always been proud that we have had two what I consider to be extremely substantial banks right here in our neighborhood. I guess my feeling would be that two are always better than one because having two gives the prospective depositor or some person who might be looking for a small loan more than one place in which to do business. What about the South Shore Bank? How does that fit in?

GJ: Well, the South Shore is basically a community development bank, and their thing really is rehabbing and developing multi-unit buildings.

TB: In the South Shore area?

GJ: Yes, originally in the South Shore area, but now they are also dealing in the Austin area. They are even dealing in places out of the city like Upper Michigan and overseas in Poland, but their main thing is still redeveloping the local community.

TB: So now, with the combination of Johnson Products and the Independence Bank, you are—

GJ: No, they were never connected. The Independence Bank has always been a personal investment on my part. Johnson Products has never invested even a single dime in the Independence Bank, and I must tell you, Tim, that my interest when I came into my involvement with the Independence Bank was really to serve the local community. I thought that we had to have a bank here even if we had to have it in that old bank building with its bad reputation after its having been closed by the FDIC. It was better for the community to have that bank operating there than to have that building standing abandoned and encouraging further deterioration. Instead of that, I believed that we should encourage development, so it all started out as a social endeavor for me and remained that way for a number of years. During that time I ultimately had to put more of my own money into the bank because our capital had gotten to be dangerously low, and we were about to have some serious problems, and so that's the way I wound up becoming the principal shareholder.

TB: How did you guys get the necessary training?

GJ: At first we didn't have any training at all. We were completely dependent upon our corresponding bank to help us learn the ropes, and so the Harris Bank was supposedly shepherding us along and guiding us and helping us to put the bank together. At one point they even secured for us a very qualified president who had formerly been, I think, executive vice president at Southeast National over at Sixty-third and Woodlawn. Musak was his name, but they let him get away.

TB: Would you explain what you mean by a "corresponding" bank?

GJ: Well, all neighborhood banks have a larger bank, usually downtown, that they do their own banking with, and so we do our banking with Harris. The Seaway Bank, they bank with Continental, and that means that Continental assumes the responsibility of guiding them, just as Harris assumes the responsibility for guiding us. But the smart thing that Continental did for Seaway that Harris didn't duplicate for us was that they invested the money that had been raised, and that money, of course, started to earn dividends, and with those dividends from that money they were able to pay a full salary to the president they had selected, who was Hal Algot. But unfortunately, our folks weren't that sharp, and Musak only hung around our bank until he had a chance to go and earn a real living someplace else. He went and took a job, I think, at either the Northwest Bank or some other bank out north. Then, when he left, Harris gave us another guy, but he wasn't very strong, and he cost us a lot of money.

TB: So you guys really had to learn the banking business the hard way.

GJ: Absolutely. We needed some help and practical advice. When we first started the business, Al Boutte had a string of drugstores, but by this time we are already in the late sixties, and by now Al has decided that he was going to get out of the drugstore business, and so Al sold all his drugstores sometime about '69 and decided that he would like to go to work for Johnson Products. In fact, Al had already located a pharmaceutical company that was on the market, and we decided that we wanted to buy it. So we corresponded with the owners for a while, and then we said we wanted to come out and take a look, so we sent Al Boutte out to take a look at them, but when they took a look at Al and saw that Al was black, all of a sudden that company wasn't for sale anymore! Now, by this time, Al was also already involved with us in the bank, and after our third president kind of fizzled out, Al said, "To hell with all those guys! I don't think this thing is that complicated," and so we didn't try to hire anyone else from outside. We hired Al Boutte, and Al became president of the bank in 1970. After that, Al went to school to learn the fine points of banking, and very quickly Al became one of the best bankers in Chicago, bar none, and he is still one of the best!

TB: So, after a period of trial and error, you decided that you had the proper talent right there in your own organization, and, as a result, you came up doing a lot better in a relatively short period of time.

GJ: Yes, we came up doing a lot better, absolutely.

TB: George, you and Al and quite a few of the other people that I know and have known through the years, all of you, are in that tradition of going from selling apples on the street corner to creating a very successful business. How can young people — particularly young blacks — learn from your example and your experience? In other words, how can they obtain that spirit of entrepreneurship that came to so many in your generation?

GJ: Well, I suppose it all comes from contact, and I think that the only way that young blacks can get that kind of entrepreneurial spirit is through making some kind of contact with those who have already been successful. They have got to make contact with somebody like that either from a distance or from actual experience. I've already told you that I believe that we blacks only believe we can do what we see that other blacks are doing and have accomplished, and what this means is, even from a distance, when we get to learn about what black entrepreneurs have done and are doing, information like that is vital to them because that kind of thing captures their imagination. It motivates them, and somehow they start to zero in and read more and try to learn more about how they can get started, but the best way, of course, is through establishing some form of personal contact.

TB: Which is more difficult now than ever because of the drastic reduction in numbers of successful black-owned businesses in our community.

GJ: Yes, that certainly makes it much more difficult for them.

TB: For all of us. You know, I don't see the dollars even getting into our community anymore. It all stays downtown! Last night I was looking at a story about John Hope Franklin, and how when he grew up in this little subdivision of Tulsa, Oklahoma, for a period of time they had a great deal of prosperity brought on by the fact that they couldn't go too far out of that neighborhood to do business of any kind, and that form of segregated isolation forced them into a more creative mode of living.

GJ: Well, do you know what Mr. Fuller always used to say? He said, "Out of every disadvantage, there is an advantage, and you always have to look for some form of advantage in any disadvantage." Now, it is obviously a form of disadvantage to all be put together and segregated in one separate place, but, in fact, that can also be a kind of advantage! I saw that right away. As a matter of fact, I have often said that the segregation policy worked to my advantage in many ways because it cut my costs and reduced my time, and, as you know, I had to move fast because I didn't have a lot of money, and I certainly didn't have any time to waste! So I learned right from the beginning how to find and establish my market, and I could hit a town that I'd never been to before in my life and just get close to the downtown area, find the railroad track and follow that railroad track away from downtown, and what do you know? Pretty soon, before you get too far, there you are right in the heart of the ghetto! Then you just do your business and get the hell out of that town and go on to the next place. You don't ever have to cover the whole city. I mean, that city could cover two hundred square miles. You just have got to focus on that one little section, or maybe two at the most, and you can find them quickly, deal with them, and then move on.

TB: That's very interesting, but tell me how did the politics of those isolated communities fit into the economics of what you were doing?

GJ: Well, maybe politics has more relevance today to the black business community than it used to have, but back then, I didn't get any help from the politicians even though, as a matter of fact, I was in politics before I started Johnson Products. By the time I was eighteen years old, I was already Edison Love's assistant precinct captain in the Sixth Ward, and at that time I couldn't even vote!

TB: So for you there has always been a separation between business and politics.

GJ: Oh, yeah, from my own personal experience, I can't tell you where politics has ever helped me in my business. In fact, I really see politics as depending more on business than business depending on politics, and I've noticed that every time my business began to grow and get more visible I would also begin to get more frequent visits from the local politicians looking for my support.

TB: Well, I guess the reason I am asking is because the black business community has been very generous to some politicians, particularly the late Harold Washington.

GJ: Yes, well, as a matter of fact, I think that that was when Johnson Products probably got stronger into a political situation than at any other time in its history. Back then, Bill Berry, as you recall, was the executive director of the Urban League, and I was the president during the last two years of his directorship, and, well, we sort of just decided one day that we would leave together because he wanted to do other things, and, as it happened, I had some things that he could do. So, he resigned and came to work for Johnson Products Company as my special assistant. His title was assistant to the president, but, in fact, he was responsible for developing our social conscience, and naturally that was something that he did very, very well. We wanted to make certain that we were an exemplary corporate citizen, and, along with what I had already been doing and with what Bill developed, we wound up establishing two foundations. One of these was the Johnson Products Company Foundation. That's the one we call the George E. Johnson Foundation, but it was funded entirely by Johnson Products, and out of that fund we contributed to 181 community organizations! Then, in 1972, I gave one and a half million dollars of my own money to form another foundation which was called the George E. Johnson Educational Fund, and Bill was the top executive of that foundation. I had given him the kind of a format that I wanted him to follow in terms of the means for dispensing the existing funds of that foundation, and what I told him was that I expected him within ten years to exhaust those funds, and I restricted the recipients of those awards to kids from the ghettos and from out of the projects. We didn't want to take any responsibility off of any middle-class mama or papa who could afford to send their kids to college. You see, I only wanted to help kids who, unless somebody like me helped them, would have no chance at all of getting a college education. The only qualifications for them were, number one, that they had to have graduated from high school so that they could qualify to get into an accredited college or university, and, number two, I put in a restriction that they had to be interested in the sciences or business. Well, let me tell you, Bill did a very good job of determining whether or not the family income would have allowed anyone to go to the school they wanted. Bill took that responsibility, and then he hired a woman who was just unbelievable, Cloteel Best. Did you ever happen to know her?

TB: Yes, I think I did.

GJ: Well, anyway, Cloteel was the one who really ran the foundation because Bill was doing so many other things, and she qualified the kids. She corresponded with them. She knew all about each of them and also about exactly what to do to help them. Now, when I gave my money, I thought we were going to have to pay the whole tuition for each kid, but you know what Cloteel did? She found out if there was any Pell Grant money available, and, if there was, whatever that particular child was entitled to from the city or state, she got all of that money. She made the application for them, and when that funding was secured, then, and only then, she bridged the gap between those funds and the tuition, and whatever that was, that was what we paid, and because of that, she also had enough left in the budget for each of those kids to make two trips home each year. So what happened was that Bill and Cloteel were able to take that principal of one and a half million dollars, which I expected to last no more than ten years, and invest it for the benefit of the foundation.

TB: So that instead of becoming exhausted, the principal was now earning money.

GJ: That's right! Oh, my gosh, let me let you, that money was generating so much income that pretty soon we were only just slightly eating into the principal, and, as a result, we did not run out of money until about 1986. At that time I asked Bill to tell me how many kids we had helped, and he told me that sixteen hundred young people went through college on the G. E. Johnson scholarship fund!

TB: This is a major contribution because that represents sixteen hundred kids who would not otherwise have been able to complete their educations.

GJ: Yes, like I said, we only accepted a kid that didn't have the money to get into an accredited college. I never tried to get involved where anybody would feel obligated or whatever to me personally. I was just the fund, but, anyway, the best thing that ever happened to me was Cloteel Best getting involved because it wasn't just the money that helped those kids. She helped them in terms of counseling, and when we started out I didn't think we would ever come anywhere close to providing scholarships for sixteen hundred kids, and I've got to tell you, it was just the greatest thrill for me to discover that my projections were completely wrong!

TB: At this same time you and Bill Berry were also involved in politics, weren't you?

GJ: Well, in 1983, Bill and I were looking around at what was developing on the horizon, and we saw that what with Jane Byrne not being that strong in terms of her support as mayor, guys like you were starting to talk with Harold Washington, but at that time Harold still wasn't committed, and you guys were trying your best to encourage him to run. As I remember it, Renault Robinson was trying to raise some money, and the final decision on whether or not Harold was going to throw his hat in the ring was going to be based on how much money you guys were going to be able to raise.

TB: Yes, at that time I was one of those who were actively helping to encourage him.

GJ: OK, well, Bill and I were also watching Daley. The fifth of December was the deadline for him to withdraw from the race, but Daley decided that he was going to run, and so now you had both Jane Byrne and Daley in the race, and that is when Harold finally threw his own hat in and ran for mayor.

TB: Don't forget that his decision also came about because of the success of our voter registration drive.

GJ: Right, which Soft Sheen helped to support. What was that slogan? "Come Alive October 5!"

TB: Yes, and I was chairman of that as well. We put a lot more people out to vote.

GJ: Yes, the real secret to the whole thing at that time was the registration of people who were capable of voting. "Come Alive October 5" put over one hundred thousand people out to vote on the ballot, and that's when Harold decided to throw his hat in the race. But we still weren't entirely sure it was going to be a three-way race until the fifth of December. Then, when the fifth of December came and Daley did not withdraw, Bill and I were jumping up and down because now this was definitely a three-way race, and Harold had a real chance to win. It could really happen. But at that time very few white folks knew anything about Harold, and I already knew Harold very well because I had been his finance chairman in 1977. Back then, I had raised maybe twenty-five thousand dollars for his campaign. It wasn't a lot of money, and when Harold ran in the primary, he lost, and Bilandic went on to win that election for mayor, but now it's six years later, and it's a three-way race, and so now we decided to get really serious. This is when Bill got in touch with Renault Robinson, and, all of us, we sat down and talked with Harold, and the first thing that I said was that the reason we were getting involved was because we realized that Harold needed Bill's help in his campaign. Although Harold was a congressman, white folks in the city didn't know him and didn't trust him, but they knew Bill, and they trusted Bill. So we put a deal together that, if Renault got out of the picture, Bill would take over chairmanship of Harold's campaign, and we also gave him a bunch of people— Juanita Passmore, Grayson Mitchell, Dwayne Kyles—to help him out, plus we loaned him one hundred forty-five thousand dollars.

TB: Al Johnson was involved, wasn't he?

GJ: Not right away. Al was with Seaway, and they didn't flip. So the first serious money came from us, plus what's more, we decided to get Al Boutte involved to help clean up Harold's finances. Al paid off all his debts and sold his car and took care of everything like that because, as you know, Harold was a maverick, and he didn't take care of his business affairs the way he should have. Anyway, we had to get all these little things that were problems out of the way and try to put a cloak of respectability around him and make him somebody that could appeal to the white folks downtown so that, even if they didn't do a lot to help, at least they wouldn't go out of their way to hurt him, and that is when his campaign really started to take off, as you know very well, because you also were involved.

TB: Well, I had been asked to chair the voter registration drive, and we had a space down at 417 East Forty-seventh Street that sort of acted as the focal point for those who wanted materials and guidance. All the phone banks were in there, and every time "Come Alive October 5" would come up, all those phones would light up. It was great. It was just beautiful and thrilling, but, according to what you're saying, it was really the successful black business community coordinated by Bill and led by you and others like Al Boutte that really laid the groundwork for that first primary and enabled it to become successful for Harold. It certainly wasn't white money that caused that to happen.

GJ: I think that what Bill did was that Bill sort of "neutralized" white folks. They weren't giving money or support to Harold. They didn't give anything to Jane. They had to give to Daley, but now they didn't give a hell of a lot to Daley either, and you know what? I think that Harold himself probably made the biggest contribution of anybody to his own success. When they held those debates, Harold came off like an absolute scholar. Jane Byrne, she was nothing but a mouth. She's bright, but half the shit she said might not even be correct, and Daley couldn't even talk—so Harold came out looking very, very good.

TB: He was well prepared, and then he finessed it so that the others were shooting at each other. They were afraid to shoot at him because it might look like their attack was racist, and so they were locked into a position where they were forced to go into combat with each other.

GJ: Let me tell you something: We ended up putting a bunch of money into that campaign, but it didn't take as much money in '83 as it took in '87.

TB: No, not nearly as much.

GJ: But, anyway, I think that the first time Harold was elected, it was like a gift from God. It absolutely seemed like it was a gift from God because never in my wildest dream did I think I would live to see a black mayor of Chicago. Not at any time in my lifetime did I ever think it would really happen.

TB: It was a great moment. I got calls from all over the country, and people who had been away from Chicago for a long time came back just to be here and be a part of what was going on.

GJ: But the whole thing hinged on it being a three-way race. If it had been a "heads-up" type of situation, we would have never made it.

TB: Yes, and the same thing happened with Carol Moseley-Braun. If it had not been for it being a three-way race, she would not have won her election to the U.S. Senate.

GJ: Oh, yes, I know. Listen, my neighbor, Al Hofeld, spent four million dollars on his campaign. If it hadn't been for Hofeld, Dixon would have been an absolute shoo-in, but, by spending all that money, Hofeld split the vote and let all the black votes go to Carol. Even then, as you know, she only won by 3 percent.

TB: Now, bring us back to business here. When he got into office, Harold was able to help some black businesses. I don't mean your business. I mean small businesses that were just starting out.

GJ: That's true. Harold helped Baldwin Ice Cream. We got the foreign exchange service out at O'Hare in partnership with the First National bank because of Harold. You see, Harold made it very clear to them that what they were doing had to be done in partnership with a minority company, and that "minority" was us! Before Harold was elected, the people who were in his type of position weren't interested in giving us a piece of the pie, but now Harold was insisting that we get our own piece of that pie, and so he really helped a lot of black businesses. Harold helped our bank. Harold helped Seaway. Harold helped Lawndale.

TB: So there was a kind of reciprocity that was involved. You know the *real* reason that Reconstruction [1865–1878] failed was because at that time blacks did not have an economic cushion. They didn't have a solid enough economic base to continue to support themselves, particularly in North and South Carolina. They were able to win political positions, but they did not have the continuous level of economic support that was required to hold on to what they had acquired.

GJ: What you are saying is that they didn't have the economic entities that could continue to give them a solid base of support.

TB: Whereas, when Harold was elected here, guys like you had something already going that could continue to give him support. I want to emphasize how important that is because what I am trying to do is to provide an opportunity for young people to understand through the histories of George Johnson and others that, although life is always a struggle, nevertheless, it can be successful. The reason that this is so important now is because it's my guess that the days of the stockyards and the steel mills and all those other great, big places where people used to go when they first started to work, those days are over, and, therefore, young African-Americans just starting out will have to be looking toward the small business world in order to be able to survive. But at present they don't, and the way it is now, black college graduates who are not able to get a job with a large corporation usually don't see any practical alternative. In contrast to this, when I walk through our community and go over to Chinatown, I still see a lot of small businesses that are controlled by the people that live there.

GJ: Well, if you're going to make a comparison with Chinatown, you have to realize that over there you've got a condition that was created by a long-standing succession which has taken place through handing down those small businesses from one generation to another. They have managed to accomplish that sort of thing, but in our community we are still at a stage where our second generation is not yet stable enough to maintain and contribute to what has been handed down to them and then be able to pass that on, and that is why, as you know, we haven't got very many third-generation organizations. I mean, there have been a lot of successful businesses started here by black entrepreneurs, but then the second generation comes along and just pisses it away, and when that happens, usually some of what happens is the entrepreneur's own damned fault. Look at my own situation. I have four children now, and maybe our family will get past this kind of problem with the second generation and begin to establish a continuing tradition of our own.

TB: Like the Chinese and the Jewish communities have already done so successfully.

GJ: Yes, but the original entrepreneur in a community like our own still has a really formidable problem to overcome. Usually this type of person has had to struggle very hard and against all the odds to create out of his own imagination everything that he has built, and, having come out of some really deprived situations, it is difficult for him to have the discipline to subject his children to the type of things that gave him his own degree of strength. That is very difficult for him to do.

TB: Yes, you can try to help them get around some of those pitfalls, but you can only help them out so much. The rest of the way they have to go on their own.

GJ: And you also have to have a strong woman who sees the situation the same way you do because, if you don't, those children are never going to rise to your level. They are never going to have the kind of strength you have. You see, I know exactly what made me the way I am, and do you know what it was? It was the ability to handle responsibility, as well as the *willingness* to handle responsibility. For me this wasn't a planned thing. In fact, by no means was it planned or chosen. For me it was a necessity of life.

TB: And then it became part of your character.

GJ: Yes, I always remember my mother, when she was only eighteen years old, she already had three children, and she brought us to Chicago, and, the week after she got here she got a job in a kitchen. I mean, she had a very tough time. Fortunately, she had a sister that could watch after us to some extent, but, anyway, as we grew up with no father to guide us, my young mother made it very clear what was required from us, and I can tell you right now that I have not been without a job since I was six years old. She made it clear to me that if I wanted candy or to go to a show or whatever, I had better find a way to get those things on my own because all of the money that she made in that kitchen was just barely enough to keep a roof over our heads and some food on the table for us to share.

TB: Right from the beginning, you had to find a way of your own to get what you wanted, but, you know, I suspect that she also set a definite limit as to what you could do to obtain those things and that meant not getting into any kind of trouble.

GJ: Right.

TB: And, of course, that requires another kind of discipline.

GJ: That's true. She had to leave us alone a lot, but she always left us with the idea that if you want to have these little things that you see other kids with, you have got to find a way to get them that is proper and legitimate—and at the same time we also had the responsibility for the house. My mother expected when she got home that all the beds were made, that the dishes were cleaned, that the clothes were washed, and that they were ironed. I mean, I was washing and ironing clothes at a time when I just barely reached the ironing board. Of course, at first my oldest brother, John, was doing most of it, but it was responsibility of that kind that really formed, I think, the kind of character that we have. I didn't mind doing these things. I took a paper route when I was eight years old, and then I worked not only that paper route, but I also worked in the cleaners, and I stayed with that paper route until I started high school. Then I found out that I could make some better money downtown in a restaurant as a busboy, so I took a job downtown in the Sherman Hotel at the College Inn, and I did that as long as I stayed in high school. I did a whole lot of other things too, always knowing I had to do something to help out as much as I could. So, when my kids were coming up, I tried to give them that same sense of responsibility, and I used to tell the kids, "You are going to take the garbage out. You are going to make your own beds. You are going to do all these things that I tell you to do," but then, when I'd come home, I would say, "Did you make your bed?" "No, I didn't make my bed." "Did you take out the garbage?" "No, I didn't take out the garbage." "Well, why not?" "Well, Mom said we didn't have to," and so I would confront her and say, "I gave those kids some chores to do, and I expect them to do what I told them to do. What's wrong with that?" And she'd say, "But, George, what do you think I hired Glory for?" That's our maid!

TB: And so the real message didn't get through.

GJ: Let me tell you something. This is really funny. I was trying to make my kids understand about hard work and responsibility—at this time, I think, they were about nine and eleven—so I sat them down and said, "You guys have got to understand certain things. Let me tell you what I used to do." So I went through all the various things that I had to do when I was a kid even younger than them. I told them how I shined shoes, and how I used to go up and down the back stairs collecting bottles, boxes, paper—everything I could—and take it all over to the junk man and sell it just so I could get me three or four pennies and be able to buy my candy. I told them how I had to work the whole damned week in order to get just enough money to buy a ticket for the movie show! I told them all the kinds of things that I had to do just to make a little money and that at the same time I was expected to go to school, wash the clothes, clean up the house, and all those other things that I had to do, and you know what? My nine-year-old says, "Well, Dad, aren't you glad that you are living here with us now?"

[*Laughter.*]

And that let me know that my message didn't get over. I suppose when you are truly affluent it is very difficult to teach a real sense of responsibility to your kids. It is even hard for you to make yourself want to do it, but I always knew that it was necessary for my children to understand that they didn't just get all these things they've got because they are who they are, but that they had to do something in order to earn those things and not just take them for granted.

TB: I am afraid that today fewer kids, particularly in families where there has been even a modicum of success, are developing those attitudes of personal responsibility about which we have been speaking.

GJ: Yes, and let me tell you something. I did have my kids work summers at Johnson Products, and I paid them just like everybody else, so at least they had that kind of work experience, but, even so, they were there working for their father, and so they had sort of "invisible" privileges. I mean, who the hell is going to give them a hard time? They were treated as if they were something special, but, if they had been working for somebody else and having to conform to rules somewhere else, a place where if they violated those rules they would have to suffer the consequences, then it would have been a whole lot different for them!

December 18, 1992, and April 1 and 12, 1993

WALTER "BUDDY" BROWN

WELL-TRAVELED HUSTLER

I first met Walter "Buddy" Brown at Edmund Burke School. He was a bit older and in a grade or so beyond mine at Burke. Everyone knew Buddy as a thin, wiry, wily, tough guy. From the very beginning we all realized that he was a hustler and the kind of person who always liked to take chances. He liked to gamble and would not even shoot marbles with us "for free." We had at that time several other guys like that who lived around the neighborhood, guys like Lionel "Chinkie" Tyler and Virgil "Fess" Canty.

Not so very many years later, Buddy Boy took off for New York with another former schoolmate of mine, Mary White, who was a talented dancer. Their idea was for him to "hustle in the Big Apple" and for her to try to get a dancing job at the famous Cotton Club in Harlem or one of the other major nightclubs. She was a very pretty girl, but New York was already full of pretty girls, as well as hustlers who were much more experienced than Buddy. As a result, they broke up, and Buddy returned to Chicago, where he has always been able to make a good living by some form of hustling. In fact, he would always only take the kind of jobs in which he could hustle a little extra money on the side.

Because Buddy doesn't mind taking risks and has always been adventurous, he really likes to travel and has spent a large part of his adult life visiting many parts of the world including places in Europe, Asia, Africa, South America, and the Caribbean. He has worked as a doorman at one of the prestigious Near North residential high-rises, and every so often, according to some of the residents that I know, they'll bump into him in the Himalayas, Indonesia, or some other remote, unusual, and unexpected place.

As is indicated in our conversation, he continues to be a very interesting man. We meet each other at least once a year at the annual Fifty-eighth Street picnic, and he always has new stories to tell and photos to show of his latest travels and adventures.

TB: The period that we are talking about—the period that you and I grew up in Chicago—it's hard for young people to believe the kind of relationship that we had with one another all across the South Side. If you were to go from Forty-third to Sixty-third and from the Rock Island tracks over to Cottage Grove, there was just one big neighborhood where everybody knew each other.

BB: Yeah, wherever you went, you always knew somebody.

TB: And another thing about this neighborhood, there used to be so many places you could go to have fun. You could go anyplace you wanted, and you didn't have to worry, and you didn't have to go downtown. In fact, people came *here* from out of town just to enjoy themselves.

BB: Yeah, to come over here and go to places like the DeLisa and all those other joints. We had places like that all over the South Side. You didn't have to go nowhere else. You felt good, and you could walk around wherever you wanted at any time of the day or night. I remember when people used to sleep out in Washington Park, and you didn't ever have to worry about anyone doing nothing to you. You could even sleep safely right over there on Garfield Boulevard.

TB: Yes, right out there on the Midway! Whatever other guys were doing, that was their business, and if you left them alone, they wouldn't bother you at all.

BB: All the sporting life—all the hustlers, all the pimps—everything was over on Fifty-fifth Street. That was where the action was. All the better-known big-time pimps were there. Guys like Earl Walker. His name was even in a book by Dr. Reitman called *The Second Oldest Profession.*

TB: Yes, some of those guys lived upstairs over what later became the Rhumboogie.

BB: That's right, and that place up over the Rhumboogie is also where Roy Eldridge stayed when he first came to town, when he was playing down at the Three Deuces. Bob Redcross lived up there too. Bob lived in one apartment, and Roy Eldridge lived right next door. Bob moved to New York at the same time that Billy Eckstine did.

TB: Where did Eckstine stay while he was here in Chicago?

BB: He used to stay in the Savoy Hotel, but, you know, when he first came into town, he wasn't doing no good at all. In fact, he wasn't doing nothing, and he used to hang out with us at Tootie's. Remember Tootie's, underneath the El on the corner there on Fifty-fifth?

TB: Yes, I do.

BB: Tootie was a Jewish fellow. His real name was Julius Shapiro, but his nickname was Tootie. He used to be a hustler over on the West Side, and he and I got to be real tight. I always had a car at my disposal 'cause at that time I drove a cab, but I could also always go get Tootie's car and drive it around if I wanted to. Tootie and Gold, they were brothers-in-law. Gold's was over on Fifty-eighth Street, and when Tootie split up with him, Tootie opened his own place on Fifty-fifth Street.

TB: I seldom went to Tootie's or Gold's. I used to go across the street to Herb's. Do you remember Noble Thomas? He had some trouble right outside of Gold's.

BB: Sure, I remember Noble. He got out of jail and got killed the same day he got out. It happened up there at Fifty-eighth Street in that alley next to Gold's. He got in a fight and knocked somebody down or something, and that guy went home and got a pistol and came back there. When Noble saw him coming, he cut out, and that guy shot him in the alley right there by Gold's. Noble, he had a sister named Harriet, didn't he?

TB: Yes, that's right. I had almost forgotten about her. They lived, I think, at Fifty-sixth and South Park.

BB: Do you remember Shorty Rawlings?

TB: Yes, of course.

BB: Later on, he became my brother-in-law, but, before that, it was at Tootie's that he got cut. That's where he got that scar on his face. Do you remember Pretty Boy? He was out of Detroit originally, and we used to call him Pretty Boy 'cause he was a nice-looking kid—but very dangerous. Well, Shorty Rawlings and two other guys—there were three of them—they were all there at Tootie's, and they decided they were going to jump Pretty Boy! Well, now, I was tight with all of them, and so I was kind of like a peacemaker, and so I was at least able to stop the thing from happening inside the joint, see, because in Tootie's we policed the place ourselves, and when all this started, I tried to get them to talk to each other, and then, in order to get them all out of there, I took Pretty Boy outside. What I'm saying is that I broke it up inside and took them all outside, and that's when Pretty Boy went into action, and when he got through, all three of them was cut, including Shorty! All three of them was shanked, and so when Pretty Boy got through, there was nobody there but him. After that, Pretty Boy went on back to Detroit, and I haven't heard anything more about him since then.

TB: At that time around there, I suppose, almost everybody carried a shank.

BB: Yeah, that's true.

TB: And if you used it, you had better be fast.

BB: Well, I carried one, but I never cut anyone. Back then, we all used to carry these big, old fish knives that we used to steal up there at Woolworth's when Woolworth's was still on Fifty-fifth, right there on the corner of the alley. We'd go in there, and we'd shoplift two or three of them old fish knives that had a little hump on their back. Everyone carried one. At that time we used to wear them corduroy pants that had twin watch pockets, and you'd have a blade in each one of those pockets! But I never fooled around with knives too much because I was more of a pistol man. I guess I got that way from my dad. I never seen my dad when he didn't carry his pistol! Anyway, at that time, there were at least four, maybe five, different guys there at Tootie's that were dealing pot or coke or whatever, but there was never no conflict. Each one of them had their own customers, and the rule was you didn't cut in on nobody else's trade. There was no humbugs about anything like that. Like I said, we policed that place ourselves. Even Two-Gun Pete was not allowed in there. Any disturbances that came up, we took care of them ourselves.

TB: Two-Gun Pete—his real name was Sylvester Washington. Whenever he'd see me hanging out with those guys on Fifty-eighth Street, he'd always say, "Shorty, what are you doing over here?" And I'd say, "I don't know, Mr. Washington. Nothing much. I guess maybe I'd better be going on back home now." You see, I was always a little bit afraid of him. I mean that guy was really pretty tough. How did you keep him out of Tootie's?

BB: Well, I don't know, but he just didn't come in there. He must have kind of liked me because he was crazy about Miss Finley, and he knew that her son, Bobby, and I were tight. That's probably why he didn't mess with me. That's most likely the only reason I got a pass from him because at that time I was with everything and everybody, if you know what I mean. And he knew it! I mean, I'm sure he knew it. He even found out that they called me Little Cat Eye because—well, see, at that time I was dealing. By the way, do you remember Little Smokey?

TB: Yes.

BB: Well, Smokey and Two-Gun Pete were real tight, and one time Smokey had me bring a can of pot over to Cooper's. We used to sell it by the can back then—Prince Albert cans are what we used to stash it in—and so I went there, and I'll never forget what happened. We were sitting there in Cooper's, and I had this can of pot with me in my pocket. Now, at that time, I really didn't know anything about Two-Gun Pete other than his reputation, and I didn't have any kind of problems with him, but, well, here we were sitting in there, and Two-Gun Pete comes in, and he comes over to where we're sitting together and sits right down with us! Well, naturally, I'm scared to death, but then Smokey tells me he was getting what I got for Two-Gun—and so we did our little business with him, but, believe me, all that time my heart was still in my mouth!

TB: Back then most of the sporting life was concentrated on Fifty-fifth Street. Didn't some of those guys leave and go to Detroit for a while?

BB: Yeah, and from Detroit to New York! Shelton, Jock, Louie Hindon—they were the three major pimps, but I remember Jock was about the smoothest one of all of them. I mean he was the real thing. I don't know if you knew Jock, but he kind of adopted me because he felt that I had potential in terms of what they were doing, you understand? Jock used to tell me, "You can catch more flies with sugar than you can with salt," but back then I was just too crude to understand what he meant, and so one time I knocked one of those girls of his down. Well, before that, a whole lot of them girls had a kind of crush on me, but when they found out that I had knocked one of them down, they all sort of backed off and stayed away. At that time Jock had a girl we used to call "Mama." Later on, she ran a whore-house over in Ohio, but, anyway, Jock got busted, and he went to the joint, and when he came out, Louie Hindon, myself, and this girl called Mama, we all went down to pick him up from Stateville. All the time we were riding down there, Mama had with her one of those little luggage boxes like women used to carry, and then when we finally get there and Jock comes out of the joint, he gets in the car with us, and she gives him this luggage box, and he opens it, and it's full of money! It seems she'd been saving this money, and, you know, banking this money for him while he was in the joint, and so when he came out, she laid this thing on him! Well, at that time I had never seen so much money before. It had to be at least twenty or thirty thousand dollars, and I would imagine that it might have been even more!

TB: Did you know Ily Kelly?

BB: Sure, I knew Ily. The guy that killed him was Big Cat Eye. You see, back then, I was just a little boy, but, by me having eyes this color just like his, that guy, Big Cat Eye, he used to tell people I was his little brother. We weren't related, and I didn't know nothing about his family other than what I learned from just being on the street. Anyway, all of them, they used to gamble there in what used to be the Garfield Hotel, down in a place in the basement.

TB: That was at Fifty-fifth and Prairie.

BB: Right, and Duke Carone, the bass player, he also used to live in that hotel. He was married to a white girl, and they lived upstairs. Anyway, all of them, they used to gamble down there in the basement, but Big Cat Eye, he didn't want me in there. I was too young, you understand?

TB: The Belmont Hotel was across the street from the Garfield, wasn't it?

BB: No, the hotel across the street was the Spencer. They were on opposite corners. The Spencer was there on the northeast corner, and the Garfield was on the southwest corner.

TB: I used them both.

BB: I guess we all did, but where I remember you mostly from is down at Fifty-third across from Bethesda Church. They had a vacant lot there where they played sandlot basketball.

TB: They also played a lot of softball in that place.

BB: Yeah, and, speaking of Bethesda, I guess you were living in that area when that church got bombed.

TB: We were living at 5012 Calumet.

BB: And I was living at 5427 Indiana! That church had a side entrance over on Fifty-third Street, and that's where they threw a bomb and blew up all them steps. We heard the explosion from our house, but we didn't know right away what it was or what had happened.

TB: We had just moved there from Forty-ninth and Vincennes.

BB: Well, we'd already been living there for a while. In fact, when we first moved there, it was all Jews in that neighborhood, and that church was still a synagogue.

TB: Did you know Johnny Dove? He was Dr. Lillian Dove's son, and they lived over there at Fifty-fourth and Michigan.

BB: Sure, we all went to St. Mark's Church together. She made a lot of money in her practice, didn't she?

TB: She was supposed to be very good. Most of her clientele were white.

BB: Yes, she was tops, but her son, Johnny, he wound up in trouble.

TB: Is that what happened to Johnny? You know, at the time I never could figure what it was that broke him down.

BB: Another guy I remember from grammar school who turned out to be a pretty good gambler was Lionel Tyler. We used to call him Chinkie or sometimes Tight Eyes. You knew Chinkie, didn't you?

TB: Yes, and he had a brother named Ruben.

BB: And they all lived at Fifty-ninth and Prairie.

TB: Yes, but when I first knew them, they lived somewhere around Fifty-fourth and Calumet.

BB: And then a little bit later on they moved to Fifty-ninth Street, right next to the grocery store.

TB: Yes, I remember when Ruben died.

BB: Whatever happened to his wife? She was a very pretty girl.

TB: I never knew her.

BB: Chinkie also had a wife, but I never knew her.

TB: Well, she had a restaurant on Sixty-first Street, and I used to go up there and eat with him. Then he got sick, and she died about a year after Chink.

BB: Do you remember Fess Canty?

TB: His real name was Virgil, but everybody always called him Fess. His mother always tried to get him out of every kind of trouble that he got into!

BB: Yeah, his mother really spoiled him.

TB: But he was the kingpin of Fifty-eighth Street for a while.

BB: Everybody on Fifty-eighth Street knew Fess. Actually, my family helped integrate Fifty-eighth Street. It was mostly all white in that area, and we were the first black family to move in there on Sixtieth Street. We lived at 230 East Sixtieth Street. A little later the Lightfoots moved into the neighborhood. I used to go with the Lightfoot boy's sister, Elsie. In fact, Elsie and I are still tight. I was her first man, and she was my first love. We stay in touch even now.

TB: But back then, at that time, there were still very few blacks living in that neighborhood.

BB: Yeah, when I first came to Carter School, there were still a lot of white kids. As a matter of fact, Carter School and some other school up north were the only two public schools in all of Chicago that had any kind of a swimming pool.

TB: Carter also had a very good playground.

BB: Well, when I first came there, there was this old boy named "Dee Dee," and he was supposed to be the king of the yard at that time, but I knocked him down. At that time you fought with your fists. You wouldn't carry knives and things of that nature.

TB: The idea was that you always had to fight fair.

BB: Everybody didn't jump in. The rest of the guys would just stand around while we duked it out. You see, when those guys found out that I'd come from Thirty-first and State, which was known as a place where they had some pretty bad dudes, then I would be challenged, and if it was a challenge, then I would meet that challenge! I would never back off from nobody. I mean, I didn't look for nothing, but I also didn't back off, and I would fight in school, in church, anywhere. The fact that I would do that gave me a little respect, and pretty soon people just didn't jump on me anymore. Well, they might bristle up a little every now and then, but after we fought, the next day we were friends again or something like that.

TB: Later on, after you left school, you became friends with many of the famous entertainers of that period.

BB: Yeah, that's true.

TB: Did you know Baby Lawrence?

BB: Oh, sure, I knew him. He worked at Joe's Deluxe, at the Cabin Inn, and all those places.

TB: The Cabin Inn was down at Thirty-first Street, wasn't it?

BB: Well, the original one was at Thirty-fourth and State, but then later on they moved to the middle of the block at Thirty-fifth and State. But as for Baby Lawrence, of course, I remember him quite well. Sometimes we'd leave Joe's Deluxe together, and he'd dance all the way from Sixty-third down to Fifty-fifth Street, all up and down the street, up against all the buildings. He was the greatest dancer I've ever seen—absolutely fantastic!—and when it came down to doing that "sand" thing—well, the "Sand Man," that was him! If he had just been white, he would have been really famous.

TB: David "Baby" Lawrence died in London, but the last time I saw him was right here on Fifty-fifth Street. You also knew Billie Holiday, didn't you?

BB: Oh, yeah! When Billie came into town in those days, she would always stay with Julius Duffy. Now, at that time, Country was the bartender down at Tootie's, and he roomed in an apartment upstairs with Duffy. Well, the first time that he met Billie Holiday, he was sitting down up there, and Billie comes through on her way to the bathroom in the nude with just a towel on her arm! That's how Country first met Billie. She was standing there right in front of him completely in the nude, and so Duffy said, "I'd like you to meet Billie Holiday"—and, well, it just took his breath away!

TB: Yes, she was good-looking all right. Do you remember Clotele?

BB: Yeah, I still see Clotele quite a lot. She has a place over on Sixty-ninth Street. The kids are running it for her, but she's there on Mondays and Tuesdays. Her brother Bo is still a doorman over at Chestnut and Lake Shore Drive.

TB: The last time I saw Bo was in the office of Dr. Rogers, the dentist. He used to have his place over on Fifty-eighth Street, but he moved over on Calumet, and the last time I saw Bo it was there. I used to keep up with all those sorts of things, and Lester Reed tends to keep me posted, but—

BB: Now, Lester and I go way, way back. He is one of the few guys that still calls me Walter because he knew me before anyone started calling me Cat Eye or Buddy.

TB: You probably met Peter Brown at about that same time.

BB: I didn't know Lester then. Peter was one of the first ones I remember because we started together in kindergarten. See, that was shortly after Peter and his family came here from New Orleans. Peter and I had to be about five years old. Both of our families were living at Sixty-fourth and Champlain during the race riot period. That was in '22, wasn't it?

TB: No, it was in 1919, but they may have had another one a little later.

BB: When we were in grammar school, Pete used to go with a girl, Marie Bryant, who was a dancer and became a well-known choreographer out there in Hollywood sometime later on.

TB: Did you ever know Ollie Boris? He was also a dancer. He danced with Cab Calloway when Cab had his Cabineers. He and Oliver Benton, when they came out of the army, they had a place in Brooklyn that used to be some kind of a hang-out. I forget just where it was, but most of the guys from Chicago would go there when they were in town.

BB: Well, maybe you remember a guy named Rubie Blakely.

TB: He used to sing with Jimmie Lunceford for a while, didn't he?

BB: Yeah, well, he used to go with my older sister. His family, they lived directly across the street from us. They lived in that building on the north side of the street that ran all the way from the alley to State Street. We lived across the street at 9 East Fifty-first Street. That's where we lived when our house fell down.

TB: Your house fell down?

BB: Yeah, the houses we had at that time, they were frame houses, and they all had eight or ten of those big poles—you know, like the kind they used for telephone poles—and the house would sit there on top of those poles, but underneath it was vacant. Just a big hole, and, well, I guess, one day the ground must have gave way because our house all of a sudden started to lean on the house next door to it.

TB: My goodness!

BB: Yeah, our house just leaned over on the other one, and Rubell, who was in the Boy Scouts at that time, came over and helped my father bring down our house after it had started to collapse!

TB: You told me once that around this same time you also used to do a little "red lighting" over on Wabash Avenue.

BB: Oh, shoot, as a matter of fact, I used to do a whole lot of "red lighting" over there in that area back then. Remember those sorts of "tapestries" they used to have? They were like oil paintings on black velvet, and just about every house had one. I think they came from Mexico or someplace like that. Well, one time I stole a whole truckload of those things. I gave my mother one of them for Mother's Day, and the rest of them I sold all up and down the street. Me and two other guys, each of us must have made at least three, four, five hundred dollars, which was a whole lot of money in those days, but we were so hot that we had to get ourselves out of town for a little while. That's when we left here and did a little hoboing. We were just getting out of town for a while till things cooled down.

TB: Tell me about your experiences during the war. As I remember it, while you were in the army down in Georgia, you told me you wrote a letter to the president's wife.

BB: Yeah, I wrote a letter to Mrs. Roosevelt, and I told her about the problems we were having with discrimination on the base, and she turned my letter over to the attorney general.

TB: Were you in the infantry or the air force?

BB: Air force! I was in the 456 Aviation Squad stationed in Macon, Georgia. Actually it was more in Robins, Georgia, which was about eighteen miles outside of Macon. We used to have to ride at the back of the bus if we wanted to go from Robins over to the main PX, which was a *white* PX, up there in Macon, and they had those civilian white girls working there in that PX, and every time we'd drink a Coke or something, they'd take and break our glasses after we drank from them! Well, at that time I was gambling and winning a lot of money, and so I would take as many guys as would go with me up there to that PX in Macon, and we would make them little girls break them glasses until finally they had to put in paper cups!

[*Laughter.*]

We really went through some changes down there at that base—and so I sent a photo of this big hanging tree that was out in front of our camp, and I told Mrs. Roosevelt about the fact that we had to ride at the back of the bus and all the other things that we had to do, and she was the one that started the ball rolling to see that things like that would change.

TB: Did conditions get better?

BB: Well, after that, I got six months in the guardhouse for going AWOL, and, let me tell you, even the guardhouse was segregated! I mean, you had a black section, and you had a white section, but even though we had one of those chain-link fences between the white prisoners and us, we would play volleyball over the top of that fence until they finally stopped us even from doing that.

TB: Were you in the guardhouse for the entire six months?

BB: Well, they gave me six months at hard labor, but then, when they found my medical records, they stopped that hard labor and made me what was called a "bunkhouse orderly." Everybody had to clean up their own space, but every morning I was the one who had to see that the beds were correctly lined up and that there weren't any straws from the broom or strings from the mop left around on the floor when the officers came out for inspection—and so that's how I put in the rest of my time. I finally wound up doing four months and five days.

TB: When you were discharged, did any of that go against you?

BB: Oh, yeah, it's on my discharge paper. I got an honorable discharge, but I never got no disability. I never got nothing! Well, anyway, they sent us from Macon back to Atlanta, and that's where we were supposed to take the train to come back to Fort Sheridan for our discharge, but when we got to Atlanta, even though we had our papers and were supposed to have a compartment or a berth, they wouldn't give us any kind of berth until we got up north to Cincinnati because of the type of law they had down there.

TB: Yes, that was the kind of law that was still operative down there below the so-called Mason-Dixon line.

BB: Yeah, that's right, and, believe me, by the time we got to Cincinnati I didn't want no berth no how, you know? So, anyway, I came on back to Fort Sheridan and got my discharge. I was inducted at Fort Sheridan, and I was discharged at Fort Sheridan. I went in in '43 and came out on May 8, 1946!

TB: A lot of guys from Fifty-eighth Street got inducted at the same time I was inducted. I don't know if you were there when we went up there to Fort Sheridan and got separated out on the train. Remember that electric train they had that went up there?

BB: Yeah, well, Leo Anstell and I were inducted at the same time. At that time I didn't drink. I mean, I had completely quit drinking, and I didn't mess with no whiskey, but Leo and me, we had a fifth of whiskey and all we needed to play craps that we decided to take along with us—and so, once we got started, Leo started a little game on that electric train with everyone putting down just ten dollars apiece, and, by the time we got up there to Fort Sheridan, between us, Leo and me, we had about three or four hundred dollars, and the reason for that particular degree of success was because all the time we were feeding them other cats that whiskey while we were also sliding those dice at them! Then, when we got to Fort Sheridan, well, we spread the blanket out again, and, believe me, we never looked back! Then they shipped me out away from there. I mean, I was the first to go, and they shipped me to Greensboro, North Carolina. That's when I thought that I had lost my gambling partner, Leo, but then, lo and behold, a week or so later here comes Leo, and so we were back in business again, but that became the last I ever seen him, and, as a matter of fact, I haven't even heard anything from Leo ever since he joined the Jehovah's Witnesses and became a preacher, but, before then, let me tell you, Leo was the smoothest out of all the gamblers that I have ever run into and that I knew personally. He was the smoothest card dealer I had ever run across. I mean, this man could deal seconds on cards with just one hand! He was good with cards and I was good with the dice, so he would run the card game and I would run the dice game, and then at night we would split up whatever we had won, and pretty soon we were loaning money as well as winning money! [*Taking out a small stack of photos, he hands them one at a time to Timuel Black.*] Look at this! This was taken in the DeLisa. Remember that mirror as you came in the door? Well, there's my wife—the mother of my son—and that's me, and there's my mother. That was the first time my mother had been in a nightclub, and by me knowing everybody in the joint— Billy Mitchell and all the rest of them—they dedicated the show that night to my mother! That's when I was in my "heydays." I was really on my game back then, and here—look here at this one. That's also in the DeLisa. They used to have a professional photographer, and here's my wife, Lucille, again, and Shorty Charles Robertson, and there's Billie Holiday. You were asking about Billie— well, you can see for yourself that's how tight we were! [*Handing a small printed card to Timuel Black.*] Now, here's something else you might find interesting. When my son was born, this is the announcement I had printed up.

TB [*Reading aloud what is printed on the announcement.*]: "The Brown Production Company of 50 East Ninety-first Street, Chicago, proudly announces the release of its first new model. Walter 'Buddy' Brown: Chief Engineer and Designer, Lucille Brown: Production Manager, Doctor Bustermoney: Technical Adviser. The new release—Walter Michael Brown—will be available for public inspection at the DeLisa at eleven o'clock on March 2, 1951. Shipping weight: five pounds, twelve ounces. Special features and accessories include an ample supply of changeable seat covers to fit a fully outfitted streamlined chassis, and a ball-bearing engine with a standard water-cooled exhaust system."

BB: Well, that's my son. He'll be forty-three next month. He was here just this morning.

TB: It's good that you stay close and keep in touch.

BB: It hasn't always been easy raising him the right way, what with my wife being white. I mean, their ways of raising kids and doing things like that are so much different from ours. For one thing, ours is more strict. Now, of course, I don't believe in beatings and things like that, but, you know, if necessary, I would punish him, and my wife would not.

TB: So that created some problems for the both of you.

BB: Yeah, and also for my son, but my wife and me, we had another kind of problem even when we first got together. We weren't married yet, but we had been living together up in the Savoy Hotel for about two years, and I would probably talk to her mother over the telephone at least every other day, but at that time her mother still didn't know whether I was colored or white or whatever. Well, all of the phone calls at that place went through the hotel's switchboard, and one of the cats that was on the switchboard down there had been trying to hit on my woman, so one morning he told my future mother-in-law, "Did you know that your daughter is living here with a colored fellow?" And so that is when she first found out that I was colored! Anyway, I told her she'd better come over here and get acquainted, and so she and her husband came over to the hotel where we were living, and that's when we first got to know each other. They weren't rich people or nothing like that. They probably weren't even middle class. As a matter of fact, we were probably doing a little better than they were because by this time I was starting to get hold of some money on a regular basis. Anyway, the way it turned out, the old man was a prince, and he told his wife, "Listen, they've been living here this long together, and they seem to get along together pretty well, and they have a nice place here—so what's the difference?" But her mother still wasn't too much for it, and so Lucille said to her, "Well, you better accept things the way they are because this is the way it is going to be. I don't care what you think or what you say, you can't stop us because we are planning on getting married!" So that's when we decided to go out and get married. We got married in '48, and my son was born in '51. Now, when I first met them, her parents lived over on the 1400 block on North La Salle, but then they moved out to Summit, and then, after my son was born, pretty soon they moved to Forty-eighth Street over there by the Harding Museum.

TB: The Harding Museum used to be located at Forty-eighth and Lake Park.

BB: Yeah, that's right. They moved over there to where she could come by and have contact with us without any problems. When they were living in Summit, I would take my wife and son out there and drop them off. The neighbors out there, they would never see me because, like I said, I would just drop them off and go on my own way, but then, when my kid would be playing out there in the yard, those neighbors could see that he was starting to get a little bit darker, and so they started asking a bunch of questions.

TB: Your wife's parents were starting to get some static from their white neighbors?

BB: Yeah, but I mean, it was nothing physical or nothing like that. It was just words—kind of innuendoes—so my mother-in-law said, "Wherever I am at, my grandson is always going to be able to come and visit me whenever he wants, and so I am going to get us on out of here," and that's when they moved over on Forty-eighth. We were living in a place at Forty-eighth and St. Lawrence, and they leased a place right across the street from us—and, let me tell you, that's when our trouble started!

TB: In what way?

BB: Well, first of all, when this kid of ours came along, that woman, she turned around completely. I mean she started buying more black periodicals than I did: the *Defender, Ebony,* and all of that sort of thing.

TB: She became a real convert!

BB: Well, they were from a small town in Kansas, and if there was any colored at all in a place like that, well, there certainly weren't any too many, and so my mother-in-law's sisters, they all had that "anti" thing in them, but she would tell them before they would come over to visit, "Now, look, my son-in-law is colored, and I am not going to have no static from you in my house. If you come over here, you have got to accept him because he is always welcome in my house," and, well, I can't say for sure that they got converted, but from then on they at least had to go along with it if they wanted to come by and visit. That's the way it had to be, and it was this grandson of hers that turned her around. I mean, he is the one who really converted her.

TB: Well, look, after all, that little boy was her grandson!

BB: Yeah, and the fact that he was her grandson made her think he was supposed to have anything that he wanted—anything at all, and that spoiled him! That's what I was trying to tell her from the time when he was still just a little kid.

TB: But she didn't want to hear what you were saying.

BB: That's right, she didn't, but, well, later on, just before she passed away, as things started changing with him, as a matter of fact, she did tell me, "Now I can understand what you were saying, and I mean to tell you that I am really sorry," but by then the damage was already done. I mean, she remembered how I had warned her, "You are giving him too many things and taking all his independence away." Listen, as you know, I have always been a hustler, and that's why I knew just how important it was for him to get out and be on his own because we are not always going to be around here to back him up, and so I begged them, "Please don't do this to him," but they couldn't understand what I was saying. Not a word, and, let me tell you, I wasn't raised like that. I never had nobody give me nothing. Everything that I have accomplished I can truthfully say I got on my own. My people didn't have nothing to give me, and so everything I got I got out on the streets or by my wits. I never had nobody give me nothing. I had nothing that was ever willed to me—nothing! But, even so, I've always been able to take care of myself and do whatever it is I want to do and go wherever it is I want to go. Listen, I want to show you something. [Hands a photo album to Timuel Black.] This is my book on Europe. These photos are from my first trip there. Lucille and her daughter and me, we drove all through there for five weeks. Lucille's daughter was teaching school in Battenburg, Germany, and so she met us in Luxembourg. Well, what with her working for the military, they gave us everything we needed, so we did just like those students do during the summer. Part of the time we would live in a tent in those tourist camps, and sometimes we would stay in a hotel, and for those five weeks we just traveled all around. Nothing was planned. Now, all of these are photos of the places where we went: Germany, Austria, Belgium, Holland, France, Italy—we covered all of that in just those five weeks!

TB [Turning to another page in the album.]: And what about these photos?

BB: Those are from Dachau. It's a museum now, and I took these pictures there. They had big wall-size pictures of some of the atrocities and terrible things that happened there, and I took pictures of those pictures. This is a gas chamber.

Here's the incinerator. This place is just outside of Munich, and the people in that area still won't admit that these things happened. Most of the people in that area won't even talk about it.

TB: Where is Lucille's daughter now?

BB: Well, she came back to the States, and now she's living in Palo Alto. As a matter of fact, she's the superintendent of a school district out there.

TB: You must be very proud of her.

BB: Now that you mention it, yeah, I am.

February 4, 1994

COMMANDER
MILTON DEAS JR.

FORMER CHICAGO POLICE CAPTAIN

Police Captain Milton Deas has accumulated a long, distinguished history as a very good high school student (DuSable) and college student (University of Wisconsin, 1941), as a United States Army commissioned combat officer (first lieutenant) during World War II, and then as a Chicago police officer rising to the rank of captain before his retirement. His father before him had served in the U.S. Army in World War I in combat in France. When the war was over, the elder Milton Deas was able to join the small number of blacks on the Chicago Police Department, where eventually he rose to become the second African-American to become a station commander.

I first met Milton Jr. in 1933, when we were both students at Wendell Phillips High School in Chicago. As I recall, he was a member of the swimming team, and was a very well-disciplined student. We had a fire at Phillips, and the faculty and students were rushed off to a new building in progress that we know now as DuSable High School. He was in one of the first graduating classes at that school, which had been named New Wendell Phillips (1935–1936). After he graduated, he went to the University of Wisconsin and joined ROTC just as he had been an officer in ROTC at Phillips. He served with distinction in World War II and returned home to the police force in Chicago. An interesting part of his story is how he witnessed the beginnings of the growing illicit drug trade in the area around Thirty-ninth and Cottage Grove (which became known as "Dopeville, U.S.A.") and how he and other African-American officers were forbidden to intercede "because it was not in their district." That statement pushed me to recall similar admonitions made to black officers during the rise of the violent street gangs in Woodlawn during the 1960s.

———

TB: Were you an only child?

MD: Yes, I was an only child. No brothers, no sisters.

TB: Did your mom and dad have any brothers or sisters?

MD: My dad didn't have any sisters, but he had a brother named Carter, and Carter Deas had about eleven children!

TB: Did any of them live here in Chicago?

MD: The first of my cousins that came here was from Charleston, South Carolina. He was in the navy, and when he got out, Dad got him a job at the White Paper Company on Forty-ninth Street, and he came to live with us at Forty-fifth and Prairie. When I was in high school, I remember some mornings I would walk with him to up to the White Paper Company, and then I'd go on to DuSable on my own. He just passed about two years ago.

TB: Where and when were you born?

MD: Right here in Chicago, February 20, 1920, at Provident Hospital, when it was over around Thirty-second Street.

TB: That was the second time they moved it. Later on, of course, they moved out to Fifty-first Street.

MD: That's where they were when my mother was there on staff.

TB: My nephew was born there, and his doctor, Dr. Diggs, was just a young doctor there at that time. So your mother was there on staff. Where had she gotten her training?

MD: I really don't know. Her maiden name was Hernana Weatherall. When she first met Dad, he was already on the job.

TB: He was a police officer?

MD: Yes, and since he was a lead officer in that particular area, every now and then he got cut or something or he would have to come in or bring in a guy to the emergency room, and she'd be there and, as a result of that, that's how they got to know one another.

TB: Was your mother from Chicago too?

MD: No, she was from Savanna, Illinois.

TB: Did you know your grandparents?

MD: No, I didn't. In fact, I didn't even know my real mother. My mother died when I was six months old, so I never knew her.

TB: Your dad was from Chicago?

MD: No, Dad was from Charleston, South Carolina. About nine years after my mother passed, he married again, and I've always made it known that if my real mother had lived and was able to come back to me now and say, "How was your stepmother? Did she treat you well?" I could look her in the eye and say, "Had you lived, it could not have been better for me." You see, my stepmother was a beautiful person.

TB: Isn't that great? That is what Bill Davis also says about his stepmother. You know Bill Jr.? His real mother died while he was quite young, and he was very fortunate to have his father remarry because his father was on the go most of the time.

MD: I remember my dad was also gone quite a bit because he had to make sure he kept that job—his badge, you know—and when he married again it was not until 1929. In that interim period, it was hard for him trying to take care of his baby, but he said he definitely wasn't going to give me up for any adoption. He was going to keep me, and so a lady he had known for a long time by the name of Ella Dawson took good care of me for a long time. She had a son of her own.

TB: That wasn't the family of William Dawson, was it?

MD: No, they were not related to Congressman Dawson.

TB: Where were you all living at?

MD: When my mother passed away, we were on La Salle at Thirty-second. Then when I was five years old, I believe it was, we moved to 4533 Prairie. That was in 1925.

TB: Do you remember what the neighborhood was like?

MD: Yes, of course, I remember what the neighborhood was like. You see, I lived there from that time until I was twenty-seven years old. In fact, when I came out of service, the wife and I stayed there three or four months before we got us an apartment.

TB: Is that right? And all that time you were growing up you were living at Forty-fifth Street.

MD: Well, there was a short period when my dad had purchased a place at Thirty-seventh and Calumet, and I thought I was going to have to go to school there, but what happened was, the woman that had me all the time when I was a baby up until my dad married again, he let her move in that house, and then we went back to Prairie. That way I was able to go to Phillips, and I went there for a little while. Then it caught on fire, and I went over to DuSable.

TB: You were at Phillips in 1935 when they had the fire there. What grammar school did you go to?

MD: Forrestville, but I started out in kindergarten at Felsenthal down on Calumet.

TB: In the Forty-second block on Calumet? When I went to Forrestville, at that time it was the largest elementary school in the United States. I had gone to

Forrestville earlier. I went there before you. I went from Fuller to Forrestville to Willard and then to Burke. We were moving around quite a lot at that time, but Forrestville was a big school physically. Do you remember the horse trough that used to be there? When you went there, were they still ringing the old electric bell?

MD: The horse trough I don't remember, but they were still ringing that electric bell when I went there. They were also doing that same kind of thing at Felsenthal. I also remember how they used to play "pile on," and all of the guys would run and jump up on one kid. Well, one day they did that to me, and I had an uncle who was married to the sister of my stepmother—I only use the term "stepmother" for positive identification because normally I would say it was "mother"—and he was a policeman. He had a nickname, Jesse James, but his real name was James Howling—and so when he saw what was happening to me, he took his club, and he was whacking and pulling them off me, and when he finally got down to the bottom, there I was! Well, he just looked at me and said, "Boy, why did you let them jump on you like that? I'm going to kill you if you ever let that kind of thing happen again."

TB: "Pile on" was torturous but also kind of fun, and it wasn't really vicious, but, of course, you needed to be up on top sometimes.

[*Laughter.*]

MD: Sometimes, yes! We had our fights and everything like that and maybe somebody got hit with a stick, but guns? No way!

TB: If you pulled out more than that stick, you would be ostracized, and no one wanted to have anything else to do with you. They played games fair back then. Why don't you tell me a little more of what you remember about the neighborhood where you grew up?

MD: Well, as a child growing up in that neighborhood, there were only certain parts of it—like on State and Dearborn and La Salle where the projects are now—that were ever considered to be anything like a ghetto. Thirty-ninth Street east of State Street was the northern borderline for the Fifth District, and I think it went south out to Sixty-second or Sixty-third. You had a lot of big apartment buildings throughout that area, and all of them were well kept. They had janitors that took good care of them.

TB: And they had grass all over. Patches of green wherever you looked.

MD: Yes, you know, I remember that one of my first assignments on the force was watering the grass and painting the railings. A lot of the people around there were property owners, and there were only a few of those kitchenettes. I think that maybe you'd find one or two of those in every block, but you also had some of your finer people such as doctors living there as well, and in those buildings over on Michigan Avenue, if there were three, four, or five families living on a single floor, you wouldn't hardly know about it until you actually went inside, because the outside was so well kept.

TB: Yes, and the backyards were well kept up as well because people often used to come in and go out the back way.

MD: And if there were some vacant lots, those would be the only places where you'd ever see any broken glass. I can still remember how that broken glass in those vacant lots sometimes sparkled just like sequins!

TB: As I remember, back when I was living around Fifty-third, on "Clean Up Week" we'd all try to clean up those vacant lots because that's where we wanted to play softball.

MD: We'd do the same thing, but we played most of our softball at Washington Park. We also used to play over there where the Parkway Ballroom is now, and I remember they used to have some big boulders there, and sometimes we'd run and sometimes almost hit against those boulders trying to catch the ball. Wherever we found a flat surface we'd usually clean it up and smooth it out because we used to like to pitch horseshoes, and we loved to roller-skate.

TB: Those kind of activities kept most of us busy enough so that when time came for us to go home, we'd go in the house and go right to bed.

MD: But if you stayed out too long, then Mama or somebody would always call you to come in, and, of course, we didn't stray far away. At least I know I didn't, and most of them in my block, none of us strayed away from where we lived for our activities. The reason for that was, well, in the first place, I wasn't allowed after five o'clock to stay out in the front yard to play, and I had to go play out in the back, and then, after that, I always had to come in and clean up—but, after five, there was no playing out in the front because it might make the lawn look bad!

TB: And that front yard was considered to be "sacred" ground.

MD: Yes, and you know something? Even after I got to be a teenager and started to go courting, every Friday evening, my parents always knew exactly where they'd find me. I'd always be at the Public Theater on Forty-seventh Street looking to see the pictures and cartoons or something like that with a girl or maybe sometimes with just my cousin!

[*Laughter.*]

TB: But, of course, nearby there were other movie theaters such as the Metropolitan and the Regal.

MD: And you also had the Willard.

TB: That was on Fifty-first, wasn't it?

MD: Right on the corner.

TB: And then you had the Owl at Forty-seventh and State Street.

MD: And the Apollo over there in Forrestville.

TB: But the main thing is that there were a lot of places to go and things to do, and that sort of thing definitely made a great deal of difference and prevented young people in our generation from getting bored and into some kind of trouble.

MD: And Mama and Daddy and everybody else were right there looking around to see if everything was all right, and all of them, they had carte blanche to whip your butt if they saw that you were doing anything that was wrong. After that, then they'd go and report what you did to your family, and you'd get another dose when you got back home!

[*Laughter.*]

TB: Back then many of our teachers were also living in the neighborhood.

MD: That's right, and that's why I said I had no sense of ever living in what could be called a "ghetto." You couldn't call it anything like that because you had so many teachers and doctors and postal workers and firemen living right here next to you.

TB: Back then, if a girl got pregnant, she was almost ostracized, and, of course, the guy would always be expected to marry her, but now when I see some of these children who are living in this same neighborhood, I am certain for most of them there is no way for them even to know who their papa is!

MD: Who he is or *where* he is.

TB: But, back in those days when you were growing up, things were quite different.

MD: They most certainly were.

TB: Getting back to your own history, tell me, when did you graduate from Forrestville?

MD: Well, I didn't actually graduate from there. I went to kindergarten, and about half a semester of first grade there, and then I was transferred to Felsenthal. When I went to Wendell Phillips, they had a junior high, and my classroom was out in one of the portables. In the winter when you'd sit in the back, you'd freeze, and when you'd sit in the front, you'd burn up, and yet we accepted that. We didn't pay it any attention. It didn't get in the way of what we learned.

TB: So you went to junior high at Phillips?

MD: Yes, but I left there after the fire and went to the new building. That's when I went to DuSable.

TB: I believe Ray Nance was there at Phillips at that time. Did you know him?

MD: Yes, I knew Ray; but you see, I wasn't much of a social guy. I was sort of a loner.

TB: Still protected by your dad?

MD: I guess so, but everyone said I was going to become a drum major because I already looked like I was a drum major. It was somewhat apparent because Ray was bowlegged, and I was bowlegged. Ray was short, and I was short, but we both were dark-brown-skinned and had the same general physical characteristics. We both blew trumpet, and both of us were proteges of Walter Dyett. That meant that both of us had to learn from him exactly what we were supposed to do, and, believe me, it wasn't just a matter of walking down the street with the marching band and blowing the whistle. There were the right turns, the left turns, and all of that, and they had to be done correctly because every year we had to have a review. I don't know if you remember it or not, but all of the high school bands, we'd go to Soldier Field, and sometimes army officers came out there to review us. So the entire ROTC from all the high schools and all the bands would have to be out there to be reviewed. Well, there was a certain ceremony that goes along with all that, and so Dyett would take us out to the park to practice, and if anybody ever forgot what to do, Dyett would get very, very angry.

TB: Yes, I never was in his class, but I heard he was a stern disciplinarian.

MD: He was the only one of the Board of Education personnel at that time that was able to use words that we considered curse words and not be reprimanded or docked for doing it. He would say, "Goddamn it!" or "What the hell!" "Goddamn it, you big dummy, can't you do what you're supposed to do?" But me, I would always have studied what I was supposed to do and have it down to a T, and so one time when he twirled the baton and said, "Can anybody in this band do this, because I'm sick and tired of doing it all by myself," I said, "I think I can," and he said, "Well, all right, then come on, and let's see you do it." So I went on out there and did that thing just like it was nothing at all.

TB: Were you practicing a lot?

MD: Sure, I practiced. I got out in my backyard and practiced every day, so when Dyett told me to take the band on in, shucks, you should have seen me!

TB: That's right. I remember seeing you when you were the leader of DuSable's marching band!

MD: And I still remember one time, instead of going down to Forty-ninth Street, I brought the band over to Fifty-first Street. They still had horses and wagons then, and when I spotted the horses and wagons coming, I'd signal my drummers, and they'd stop and start hitting the rim—tick, tick, tick—instead of frightening the horses. Then, when we'd pass the horses, I'd give them the roll-off. You see, there were two of them in the band that lived on Fifty-first Street, and we went over there so their friends and family could see them! On later days when we went marching, I'd march them kids on down past my own house so my mother could see us. I'd tell her in the morning, mostly on Wednesdays, "We're going to march today." She'd say, "Are you going to bring them by?" And I'd say, "Yes, we're coming on by," and when we did, she'd hear us coming because by the time we got to Forty-sixth, I'd already have them making a whole lot of noise!

TB: When you were at DuSable, who were some of the other teachers you remember?

MD: Well, I remember Dyett best because of music. You see, I started playing the piano when I was about seven years old. As a matter of fact, I've still got the receipt from my first piano lesson. My teacher was Hattie Goldsby, and my dad had her come over to the house and give me lessons because I was still quite small. Then as I grew older, I went around to the Forty-fourth block on Michigan where Pauline Lee lived. She was my second piano teacher.

TB: Do you remember Mr. French? You know, I saw him just recently. He's been ill, but he's still moving along, just as sharp and nice as ever.

MD: I don't know if I would recognize him, but I remember his name, Avery French. The swimming teacher was named Mackey.

TB: Yes, Bill Mackey. What about the football coach?

MD: Ben Mosby, and there were two Wilsons teaching there. Mrs. Wilson and her daughter. One was the art teacher, and the other was in music—and speaking of music, Dorothy Donegan was in my class. But when we were students over at DuSable, she wasn't too good at counting, and Dyett used to get on her so hard that she would sometimes end up in tears, and I would feel sorry for her, so, as opposed to just sitting back and seeing her get it all the time, I would sit sometimes on the piano stool beside her, and I would count for her. I didn't think I was doing any big thing. It was just out of friendship for Dorothy. Well, a lot of the kids—you know how clannish DuSable was back then—they were ostracizing Dorothy because she was just not as affluent as some of them, and she didn't come to school as well dressed as they did and all of that sort of thing, but she had talent, and they didn't have the kind of talent that she had, and so I would sit there sometimes and talk to her, and that's how she got to know me. Later on, I remember one time my wife and I were in New York, and we went to a nightclub where she was playing and she automatically spotted me right away. She was such a sweet person.

TB: So when you left DuSable, what did you do?

MD: Well, because I admired my father so much, I always wanted to be a policeman, but, back in those days when I was coming along, parents who were police officers, they wanted their sons to be something that was quote "better" unquote than a policeman. Sometimes they'd even say, "Listen, I don't want you to be a police officer." And so it was a long time before I had the nerve to come to my father and tell him what I really wanted to do. That was because I was brought up with, "Now, listen, boy, you do what your dad tells you to do" or what your mother *and* dad tell you you have to do.

TB: That is the way that it was in our generation.

MD: Yes, and so you did what you were told without any questions. You might not always like it, but you did it, and so I didn't say anything when Dad sent me away to the University of Wisconsin, but, well, I only stayed up there for two semesters, and all the time that I'm there I'm running around following squad cars every chance I can get, and I wasn't studying as much as I should, you know? But I stayed there for a full year, and then Dad sent me to Howard University. I went to the music school they had there, and I learned to play the violin, the cello, the viola, even the bass fiddle, and a whole lot of other instruments as well, but I said to myself, "I'm only doing this to satisfy Mom and Dad," and so I also only stayed there for a year as well. After that, I came back to Chicago, and I went to Washburne to take typing and shorthand because at that time Dad was still in the police department. He had to write reports, and it fared better if you could type the reports, as opposed to writing them, because if your handwriting was not very legible, it would be a problem for the supervisor. So that's why I went to Washburne and started taking up typing, and after a while the teacher said, "You've gotten all the basics. There is no more that I can teach you. I suggest you go down to Cortez Peters Business College. That place was up over the Jones boys facility on Forty-seventh Street, and so that's where I went.

TB: At that time Cortez Peters had one of the best typing schools in the country, but he also made "remedies." Did you know that?

MD: All I knew was that he was the fastest typist I ever saw. He could even type with mittens on! Did you ever seen him do that?

TB: No, I never saw that.

MD: Of course, he was wearing not leather but soft mittens when he did that, and then another thing he could do was he could sit down and take a manuscript and type it out exactly correctly and at the same time recite some kind of poetry. He could do that and still be typing at the same time! So it was my ambition back then to type just like Cortez Peters, and I really worked at it, and I got to be pretty good.

TB: Then, when the new technology came before you retired, you were able to transfer that kind of skill right onto computers, weren't you?

MD: Oh, no, they didn't have computers yet. They were just getting computers there when I retired. They had some for the records and communications department down on Eleventh Street, but in the district station where I was, they were just beginning to get them in the detective division before I left.

TB: I imagine it would have been easier for you if they had had computers because you had the typing background and experience.

MD: Yes, and typing was really not a problem for me because I played the piano. Dad got me an old typewriter, and he used to bring me that yellow paper that they had an abundance of in the police department, and I'd practice. I would sit in the dining room, turn on the radio, and practice with the rhythm. I just practiced, practiced, practiced until I got real good at it, but then the first thing you know I said, "Dad, look, I've already been away from home for a long time, and I'm a grown man, and now I want to join the police." So I sat down with him, and I told him just how much I appreciated everything that he's done for me in regard to my getting a higher education. He listened for a while, and then he said, "It's just that I would like for you to be something better, but now I'll tell you what I want you to do. You know they have passed a law whereby you have to go and do one year in the military. It's mandatory for you to do that, so what I'd like for you to do is to go and do your military service and *then* come back here and join the force if you still want to. That way at least your career won't be interrupted by you having to go off into the service." So I said, "Well, sure, I'll do that." What else could I say?

TB: You had no choice.

MD: Not really, and, well, as it turned out, when I first went into the army, they needed as many typists as they could get because there were so many administrative forms that had to be made out on every individual. So I went in as a clerk typist. They grabbed me, and for seven days I was sent directly to a place down there at Thirty-fifth and Giles, I slept down there and everything, just getting these forms made out.

TB: After that, were you in the training unit at Fort Custer?

MD: I wouldn't say "training unit" because we were transferred directly into the 184th Field Artillery. I just packed up everything and went on up to Fort Custer. I was up there exactly eleven months to the date when the Japs bombed Pearl Harbor, and, needless to say, I didn't get out of the army after just one year. As a matter of fact, I didn't come back to Chicago, except on furloughs, until my terminal leave in 1947. I went away in 1940, and I didn't come back to stay until almost eight years later.

TB: That's a long period of time, especially for a young man.

MD: Yes, that was certainly something that I didn't expect.

TB: None of us did.

MD: But, anyway, when I first went up to Fort Custer, they had some officers from the regular army that came down and brought us heavy-duty guns—such as 155 howitzers—and we were training with them. I made corporal, then buck sergeant, then first sergeant, and then I went away to OCS at Fort Knox. When I got there, there were thirteen blacks out of a class that was about 130. So they put us in a one-room barrack, and that's where I stayed.

TB: All the 130 in that one room?

MD: No, just all the blacks. We were all what they called the "ninety-day wonders." You'd go there for three months and come out and get what they call a "shave tail." What they would do was to cut the tail off the shirt and make an epaulet for you.

TB: You were then about twenty?

MD: Let's see, that was in 1943, and so I was twenty-two and just about to become twenty-three. Well, like I said, there was thirteen of us who were black, and one week before we were going to graduate, just one week now, they shipped seven of us back to our units. I had been there for eighty-three out of ninety days, and then they kicked me out and claimed that I didn't have leadership ability, but they didn't send me back to my own unit at Fort Custer. Instead of that, they sent me to some other unit, and so when I got there, I sat down and I typed up a request for transfer back to my original unit. It necessitated thirteen endorsements through thirteen different channels for me to get back, and so I typed up all thirteen of those endorsements and carried them by hand to the proper channels, and they were approved, and so that's how I got sent back to my unit. When I got back there, at that time Theopolis Mann was the colonel, and he said to me, "Sit down, and let me tell you something. Don't let this reversal keep you from wanting to become an officer. If you didn't have the ability, I would not have sent you. Now, here is what I want you to do. There is a forty-five-day period that you must wait before you can reapply. You wait out this forty-five days, and then I'm going to send you again, but this time I'm going to send you to Fort Hood, Texas." So that's what happened, and there is where I got my commission. I was in the 795th Tankers Battalion when I was in Fort Custer, and then, after I went to Fort Hood and got my commission, I was in the 614th Tankers Battalion, and that's where I was when I went overseas.

TB: When did you go overseas?

MD: I went over in 1944, and, well, like I said, I never really did intend to be in the military, but I had promised my dad that I would keep my nose clean and stay out of trouble and come back home in one piece just like he wanted me to, so, well, I joined up again with my old unit over there in Normandy, and we went out onto Utah Beach and Omaha Beach. For what we did, the French awarded us with the Croix de Guerre with Palms, which, I guess, is pretty big stuff over there.

TB: It's their highest award for bravery under fire.

MD: Well, back in '44, something else happened. Here let me share this with you. This is going back to the police stuff now, but this is an important part of my dad's history and his experiences in the police department during the month of February 1941. This is what he wrote in his report:

During the month of February 1944, the Race Relations Committee held a series of four weekly conferences for the purpose of discussing race relations problems. These meetings were held in the City Council chambers at the City Hall. All the police captains in the city were ordered to attend by Commissioner James P. Augnon. The chairman of the committee was Mr. Edwin Embree, who is also the president of the Julius Rosenwald Fund. Mr. Embree made a motion that one of the captains be selected to say something on the subject of juvenile delinquency, and I had the honor of being chosen by the other captains to do the job.

I wanted to read this to you because I wanted you to hear an example that would show, even as far back as then, that a black man who was a captain on the police force was treated with respect and recognized as something, and what I'm trying to show you is that, even though Dad didn't have a high level of education, he had vision and foresight. Just let me read you this:

In my opinion, the prevention of delinquency requires the participation of many groups, including the home, the school, churches, and recreational agencies, as well as law enforcement agencies. However, a patrolman on the beat can play a very important and essential part in the prevention of juvenile delinquency by talking to the boys or girls in a firm but friendly manner. Patrolmen should particularly pay attention to the poolrooms, dance halls, and other places of recreation where juveniles gather. The patrolman should question them when they are found on the street late at night, but in questioning a boy or girl, a policeman must first try to gain their confidence. He must always treat a juvenile with consideration and be friendly, firm, and positive in order to try to discover their particular problem, because they have problems just the same as grown-ups. He should never resort to profanity or brand them as a thief, liar, or even a bad boy or girl. In conclusion, I would like to add that, as indicated in my own personal experience, I think that very often parents are too eager to place the blame on the police and on schoolteachers instead of accepting personal responsibilities in the way that they should.

That was what he said fifty years ago!

TB: And it was prophetic.

MD: But it is still what we are trying to get people to realize, and that is that there is not just one person or agency or group of people that is going to be able to face this problem and eradicate it. It's going to take correlation and coordination on many different levels in order to accomplish anything.

TB: And many of the parents are still looking for excuses not to live up to their own responsibilities.

MD: That's right.

TB: Back then there was so much trouble that I could have gotten into, but there were so many pressures on me that I couldn't. You know, I didn't really mean to stay out of trouble, but everywhere I turned there was always someone who was looking out for me. There were teachers, preachers, and neighbors that Mom and Dad could question as to what I might have been doing. That's the way it was for both of us back then, but, now getting back to your own history, after the war, what happened when you went to work for the police department?

MD: Well, when I first joined the force, there were only four other black detectives in my entire unit.

TB: And how big was that unit?

MD: I'd say about 102 men, and it was loaded with talent, both blacks and whites, just loaded with talent, but the top leadership demoralized everyone. The guy that was my predecessor told me that they had already gone through at least a hundred sergeants, but I was very fortunate, and we all worked together and did our best to overcome those internal kind of problems and get our real work done.

TB: As a person who was in police service for a long period of time, in terms of criminal activity, what were some of the most active districts or areas?

MD: Well, when I look back, as I was coming along, I remember that the "problem" areas were the old Fifth District at Forty-eighth and Wabash, and naturally we had the Maxwell Street area as well, and then the Sixth District over there in Hyde Park was starting to come up in terms of crime. You see, the Sixth District was beginning to have a lot of activity that was involved with dope. Now, if you can picture it in your mind, this area I'm talking about is this side of Drexel and this side south of Thirty-ninth Street all the way over to the lake. The area that was north of Thirty-ninth Street was the Fourth District, and that's where my dad's station was. It was at Thirty-fifth and Rhodes.

TB: Having boundaries like that, did that sort of thing ever hamper your police work?

MD: Well, to a certain extent, of course, it did. As a matter of fact, sometimes a guy would get cut or something, and we'd get a call, but by the time we'd get there to pick him up, he might have been dragged over into someone else's district.

TB: That's what they called "avoiding turf." What about stolen goods? How did you handle that type of situation?

MD: Well, we had all these people out on the street trying to sell "hot" stuff. Of course, a lot of what they were selling wasn't really "hot" at all, but they were putting the label of "hot" on something just to make it sell. So, for example, some guy thinks he's buying a "hot" TV set and getting it really cheap, but he ends up buying a box full of bricks! You see, some guy gets hold of an empty Zenith box and fills it with bricks, and then he seals it up real nice and tells you to notice that the box hasn't even been opened yet and that he just got off the train or truck or whatever. Then, when that person who bought it gets back home, he discovers that all he's got is a load of bricks, and that's when he calls us and says that he's been robbed! That means that now we're supposed to go out there and find the person that sold it to him, but by then, of course, that person is long gone.

TB: So, in your early years on the force, you were stationed in the Fifth District, and you witnessed that district become increasingly active in terms of criminal activity.

MD: Yes, it was becoming one of the most active areas in terms of crimes and misdemeanors.

TB: What were some of the most persistent and difficult offenses that occurred back then? Or don't those two categories belong together?

MD: Well, you had your homicides and your robberies, stabbings and shootings, even people getting hit on the head with baseball bats and things like that. Automobiles got stolen, and, as a matter of fact, in that district at one time or another you probably had just about any kind of crime you might want to name.

TB: But when somebody would get involved in any kind of serious difficulty, particularly if they weren't too far gone already, at least back then you had some well-equipped hospitals close by, such as Provident, to take them to, didn't you?

MD: Yes, most of them from the Fifth District went to Provident because that was the closest one. Later on they might have been transferred over to County, but that's the first place where we took people whenever there was an emergency.

TB: What about Woodlawn back then? Was that also another trouble spot?

MD: Woodlawn is around Sixty-third and Harper, and back then that was in the Seventh District. It was getting to be pretty crowded, and there were some problems, but Wabash Avenue down in the Fourth District was a problem area as well because that's where they had a lot of activity involving Policy. As I remember it, the Jones brothers used to live right there at Forty-seventh and Michigan.

TB: Policy is now called lottery, of course, but back then it was illegal, and "the numbers racket" is what the politicians liked to call it. What do you remember about the relationship between Policy, which was originally developed inside the black community, and organized crime?

MD: Well, I can certainly remember the time when a black guy named Ted Rowe, who was involved in Policy, got shot right there at Fifty-third and Michigan.

TB: From what I understand, he got shot because white gangsters wanted Rowe to get out so they could take over. By then those guys had already run the Jones brothers out of town.

MD: Yes, but in order to convince those Jones boys that they had to leave, they kidnapped one of them, and the night that they kidnapped him, my mother heard their car when it turned on Forty-sixth!

TB: That was near your house, but how did she know that what she heard was the kidnappers' car?

MD: Well, they'd turned onto Forty-sixth over near Prairie and Calumet, but I guess they weren't very familiar with the area, and so they thought they could drive right on through and get away that way, *but*, as you might remember, the 4600 block between Prairie and Calumet is a dead end, and you can't get through there with a car. Sure, you could walk through the cigar stand, but you couldn't drive any kind of a car through there. So, well, they shot on up there, and then they discovered they couldn't make it through, and so they turned right around and came on back. That's when my mother heard them!

TB: That happened in 1944 or '45, didn't it?

MD: No, I think it was earlier than that. Anyway, it was definitely after one of the Jones brothers took the heat for tax evasion, and one of the gangsters who was with him in the Indiana Federal Prison heard him talking about how much money was involved in his Policy operation. Prior to that, those white guys thought that Policy was just peanuts, but that's when they found out that those guys were millionaires, and they had yachts and homes in France. That's when organized crime started to force its way into our community.

TB: Yes, and when I returned from the army, I noticed right away that things were changing and that something very different was going on in the neighborhood that we're talking about. When I left to go into the army, there were a few of the guys I knew who used to smoke marijuana, and they hung out in places around Fifty-fifth, and there were some other guys like that over on Forty-seventh, but there were only a very few, and most of those guys were just trying to imitate entertainers. But, after the war, things changed a lot around Forty-seventh Street in terms of the use of narcotics. Oakwood and most of that area became a sort of hotbed of drug traffic.

MD: Yes, narcotics had already become much more popular by that time. Like you said, some of your entertainers used heroin, and a few used cocaine because they had enough money to afford it, but back then even the guy who just used marijuana, he was classified as a "junkie." I remember one time we arrested one of those guys that had just sold five thousand dollars' worth of that stuff, and when we grabbed him, he still had all that money with him in tens and twenties. As a matter of fact, he had so much money that we had to stop by the Drexel Bank to get money wrappers for it. Then we took him back to the station and counted out his money, but there was so much to count that, before we could finish, some of us just slumped down and started to fall asleep, and someone would have to say, "Hey, wake up! We're still counting this money." So, anyway, when we finally got finished counting, we found out that this guy had been carrying almost five thousand dollars, and, believe me, he knew exactly how much money he had! [*Laughter.*]

The ironic thing is that about two weeks later he was arrested again, and this time he was carrying even more money than before. So we let him take all that money with him into the cell and put it into a pillowcase. The news guys, they even had a picture of him in their paper with all his money there in that jail cell, but the reason that we did that was because, you see, the only safe that we had there at the station didn't have a lock on it, and so, just to be on the safe side, we put all the money in the lockup right along with the prisoner. Sometimes when you'd arrest someone like that, you wouldn't always have time to search them properly, and they would try to hide whatever they were carrying right there in the backseat of the squad car. They would try sticking their narcotics or whatever down in the seat because they didn't have nowhere else to hide them. So you had to tell a lot of the inexperienced policemen to be more careful and always check the backseat out because some guy might even have hidden a gun somewhere back there, and then, when you pick up some other hoodlum for a traffic violation or something, that guy might reach down in the seat and find that gun and try to do something with it!

TB: And for some people like that, the craving for narcotics gets to be so great that they will do anything, no matter how foolish it might be, to get out of a situation like that.

MD: Yes, and for that same reason some of the younger women were now going into prostitution, and some of the guys who were using were pimping for those prostitutes, but, of course, many of the others just started stealing or sticking people up.

TB: And so you began to get a substantial increase in violent crime.

MD: Yes, this is in the sixties, and people like you and I would be out there working hard all day long trying to make an honest living and take care of our families, and then one day—wham!—here comes this guy saying, "Give me your money, man," and, even though you might not have resisted, you still might get shot or cut up. Then, when the police come along, you give them a report if you're able, and that becomes another crime statistic, because the guy who did it is gone, and so you've got another unsolved crime out there. If someone actually gets caught and arrested, this also puts an additional strain on the police force because now the arresting officers have to go and make more visits to the courts. The way things were happening back then, I was going to court almost every single day. At least I was able to accomplish a few things because I had enough experience to know who was and who wasn't involved in drugs and things like that. By then I guess I knew all of those guys down there in Englewood, and, of course, they knew me too, but I really didn't get to do as much as I might have because that's when I got transferred. What was going on was no longer in my district, and there was nothing more I could do about that situation.

TB: That same sort of thing happened to certain well-respected and knowledgeable black police officers over in Woodlawn. They were transferred out, and after they left, the problems with drugs and violence very quickly got even worse.

MD: Yes, they certainly did, and during all those years, I was really working hard and never taking much of any kind of a break. In fact, it was only in 1978 when Sam and I were finally getting ourselves ready to go on a long vacation together—

TB: Do you mean Sam Nolan?

MD: Yes, he was deputy superintendent by then, and Sam asked me to make all the necessary arrangements, and I had it all set up so that Sam Nolan and I would take our wives and go together to Hong Kong. I had it all lined up, and we were going to go, say, like this next Saturday, but then on that Wednesday, I get a phone call. By then in my mind I'm already on my vacation, and, well, the call is to report to the superintendent's office. Now, this was the Wednesday morning that was just three days before we were supposed to go away, and so I said, "Is this really the superintendent's office?" They said yes, and so I said, "All right." But then I called back right away, and I said, "This is Lieutenant Deas, and I am calling to authenticate a telephone call I just received from this office," and they told me that they had, in fact, placed that call. So I just said, "Well, thank you very much," and hung up. You see, policemen can sometimes play some pretty rough jokes on each other, and I wanted to be absolutely sure what was going on before I told my wife anything. You see, she had already been getting a little discouraged about things because they had called me on several other occasions when I was on my day off to come back in and do something, and so she said, "Baby, they won't even let you have a vacation, gee whiz!" I said, "Well, there's nothing I can do about it. I guess I'll have to dust off my shoes and get my shirt and everything all together and be ready for tomorrow morning." So that next morning when I dropped her off at work, I said, "Well, I'll see you later, dear, but wish me luck!" Because in the meantime I'm going through my mind and taking inventories of all my activities, and I'm wondering what I might have done. Well, when I get down there, one of the other fellows comes in, and he's in uniform. Then another fellow comes in. He's also in uniform, and they both look at me, and then they say they are wondering just what this is all about. So, anyway, by me being in the detective division, I'm the only one there who isn't wearing a uniform, and they call me in first, and then they say to me, "Captain, we have called you in here today to tell you that you have been appointed station commander." Now, this came as a complete surprise, and, of course, this was a promotion above the rank of captain, and it was also a position which was civil service exempt. As a matter of fact, station commander was exactly the same position that my dad had held when he retired, and now they're giving it to me! Here I was all worried and upset, and now they're telling me something like this, and you know what? Well, I'm kind of emotional about things like that, and so I say, "Excuse me," because I have to walk away and be alone for a moment. Nimocks was there, and he said to me, "Don't cry," because he knew what I was feeling. You see, I was happy, but I was also sad. It was such a dramatic moment. If only somehow my dad could have been there to share this honor with me. Even now, I don't know how to put what I was feeling into the proper words.

TB: You just did. Thank you. Thank you very much.

July 9, 1993

DR. RUDY NIMOCKS

LAW ENFORCEMENT AND SECURITY OFFICER

In addition to a long and distinguished career in law enforcement, Dr. Rudy Nimocks is also a first-rate intellectual who is deeply concerned with contemporary social issues. At present he is the chief security officer for the campus and the area immediately surrounding the University of Chicago. His security force is composed of a hand-picked group of relatively young men and women who are multiracial and well trained for their job. Some of the older ones in this group are early retirees from the Chicago Police Department, as is also true for Dr. Nimocks. When he left the police department, he was chief of detectives for homicides, and there were many who believe that he should have been appointed superintendent.

After his retirement, he was offered the University of Chicago job because the school was looking for a person who was not only an experienced law enforcement officer but also had a solid academic background, and Dr. Nimocks more than filled those requirements. As the communities surrounding the University of Chicago went through changes that were economic, social, cultural, and political, they realized how important it was to have a person like him in a position of so much responsibility.

Nimocks grew up on the black South Side of Chicago during the forties and fifties, and so he knows the territory and the complexities of its history. He is a scholarly person who also is concerned about the contemporary community where he works and lives. He understands and appreciates civil rights and civil liberties. He also wants peace, but the peace he wants is one that is just and responsive to human needs.

TB: Commander Nimocks, I'd like to get a little insight into your ideas as a professional law enforcement officer. I've seen some police work in Chicago—as well as in other places throughout the world—and one of the things that I've noted is that some policemen, as individuals, and some police forces create more dislike and fear among the population than others. I would compliment you by saying that I believe that, generally speaking, the people that I know respect you as a professional police officer in the tradition of those who want to see law and order carried out with justice. I have talked to two other law enforcement officers—LeRoy O'Shield, who was a student of mine, and Howard Saffold, who was also a student of mine. You once said to me that you always knew that you were going to be a police officer despite all of the handicaps that existed against African-Americans in that field when you started in 1956. What exactly did you mean by that? I know that there were very few blacks on the Chicago police force at that time. And how, as a young man, did you come to the decision that you wanted to be a law enforcement officer?

RN: Well, I guess I just had a fascination for playing cops and robbers—to put it bluntly! On previous occasions, I had been an insurance man and also worked at a lot of other jobs. I had even thought about becoming a professional fighter when I was in high school. I drove a bus for five years, and I worked in the U.S. post office for a short period of time, but I just wasn't satisfied with those jobs, so I went to the fire department for one year. Then I came to the police department, and I have enjoyed policing from the day I started the job. I enjoy it as much now after almost forty years as I did when I first started. I think it's a most exciting enterprise in a democratic society—to say the least—but I think it's more difficult here than anywhere else that I can think of because of the way this country runs as a democracy.

TB: Yes, everybody has rights. We have to adhere to the Constitution.

RN: Yes, everybody has rights. The individual is supreme in this country. As a matter of fact, this is the best country in the world—for an individual—but sometimes the rights of the individual are tough on the group as a whole. Now, that may sound strange, but that's the way it is. For example, protecting the rights of individuals has something to do with our courts being clogged. The individual bonds and the appeal process slow things down. Our system has to show that every individual gets all of his or her rights, and that can be burdensome to a system that's overflowing with cases—but I wouldn't have it any other way, personally.

TB: There are those who say that the victim has rights as well, and that those rights are sometimes ignored.

RN: Well, the victim does have rights, but when you look at the Constitution, I think you will discover that the guarantees that are incorporated into the language of the Constitution have a lot to do with people who are being handled by the authorities—for want of a better way to put it—meaning an individual who is being accused or who is about to have something taken away from him. The language of the Constitution has to do with the way that the individual will be afforded his rights and his due processes.

TB: Well, what about the victim who may have been hit over the head or lost a relative by this system which protects the individual civil rights of the perpetrator?

RN: Well, the victim is cast in the unfortunate role of not being the accused. And all of the language in the Constitution that I allude to has to do with the accused, not with the victim. There is very little language in the Constitution that has to do with the victim—only with the person who has been accused or charged and is about to have something taken away from him.

TB: Yes, it comes under the old English Common Law. But in some countries—particularly in Europe—you have to prove innocence.

RN: Yes, you're guilty until proven innocent. Well, it's just the opposite here, and that's because the founding fathers wanted to make sure that some of the less fortunate were protected from the deprivation of rights they had suffered in the old country. They determined that those laws were not to be continued here. Search and seizure, the right to face your accuser, and the right to be tried by your peers—all of that sort of thing. Those rights were not afforded them before they came to this country.

TB: Yes, some of those laws have even been exemplified in later years by the *Miranda* case and other cases.

RN: Well, yes. They have been fine-tuned by *Miranda* and *Escobedo* and some of the other so-called landmark decisions.

TB: Your decision, then, to join the police force, was based on a personal need to find satisfaction on the job.

RN: That's right.

TB: Did stability have anything to do with it?

RN: Not really, because I never had any difficulty finding a job, and I always had the feeling that I could do about as well as anybody else if given the opportunity. I was never desperate for work. As a matter of fact, I don't think that I've been out of work since I came out of the service. I first started working when I was about six or seven years old, delivering groceries and picking chickens and all of that kind of thing in the neighborhood.

[*Laughter.*]

TB: Yes, I remember!

RN: So just getting a job wasn't anything. It never dawned on me that if I left one job that I wouldn't be able to get another one. I never had that fear.

TB: Would you elaborate on your observations of the evolution of the Chicago Police Department in terms of minorities?

RN: In the Chicago Police Department we have had to evolve from a state of affairs in which there was just a handful of black supervisors—at the *lower* level—in the entire department in 1956!

TB: By supervisors you mean the rank of sergeant and above?

RN: Yes, in 1956 there were no blacks above the rank of lieutenant. Two things happened later that were beyond belief at that time. One was that there would be a black mayor. The other was that there would be a black chief of police. Things like that were just unthinkable in that period of time. As a matter of fact—as I'm sure you've been told before—in some police stations, they only had certain automobiles that blacks could work in, and certain posts in districts where they were allowed to work, and certain posts where blacks were allowed to work in plain clothes. Just the opportunity to work in civilian dress was a very prestigious job back then for a black officer. If you got into the Detective Bureau as a black, that was considered a huge step. Even though they had black detectives in some districts, the detective division was all down at Eleventh and State, so if you got assigned down there it was a big thing.

TB: What kind of role did politics play in these assignments or promotions, if any?

RN: Well, I've heard people say that politics had a lot to do with it. It may have, but if it did, I don't have evidence of it. It's just a lot of talk. Now, I know that in certain districts you can get transferred from one district to another because of politics— possibly—but I'm not even sure of that. This is just something that I heard. Those are all things that I've never experienced personally because I didn't know any politicians to speak of. I wasn't politically oriented at all. There is always some rumor about, "This policeman is here because he knows so and so, or he is a personal friend of such and such," and this and that. I've heard that sort of thing, but I don't have any proof. Now, it may be true—I don't know. But personally I don't think that politics alone would get you promoted. I think that demonstrated performance over time is what really gets you recognition. Now, if you happen to know a politician in *addition* to that, well, certainly that would be to the good, as they say. But I've seen a lot of cases where the simple fact is that some people perform better than others. They get more recognition and better assignments, and they do better on promotional exams. For many, many years a lot of black police officers would say, "Why take the examination? If you don't have some clout—if you don't have somebody behind you—you'd just be wasting your three dollars." You know, at that time you had to pay three dollars and go down there and sign the book and all of that kind of thing! When I first came to the department, I believed that nonsense. At that time I was working with a guy named Wesley Jones. He was the guy who broke me into the detective division down at Eleventh Street. He had been down there for a couple of years, and I had just gotten there. He and another man down there named Wilber Allen were the two guys that broke me in. Well, the time came to give the examination—this was in 1960 or 1961—and Wilber said to me, "Why don't you take this exam?" This was the first time they had had an exam in several years—exams were few and far between—and I said, "Why should I? I don't know anybody. Nobody's going to recognize my name." And he said, "Well, if you don't take the exam, you're sure not going to pass!" So, he took the exam himself and he passed! He got promoted to sergeant back in 1961. And that was the largest group of black sergeants *ever* promoted up until then.

TB: Yes, I remember.

RN: Well, then I fooled around and didn't get promoted to sergeant until 1970—ten years later! To this day I believe that there was a ten-year difference in our promotional tracks simply because of the fact I did not take the exam, because I feel now that if I had taken the exam, I would have been able to pass, but I still had this negative opinion in the back of my mind. I had been listening too much to "If you don't have the clout you can't get promoted" and all of that negative feedback. What really astounds me is that at this late date there are still some police officers who believe this nonsense, so they don't take the examinations seriously. Of course, they won't ever get promoted.

TB: And then they blame it on the system.

RN: Yes, they blame it on the system, and I don't agree with that at all.

TB: Now, in terms of district assignments and such, it seemed to me, as I moved around the city, I almost never saw, as a youngster and even up until recently, black officers assigned in districts where there were predominantly white populations. What factors went into making those kinds of district assignments? Was my perception too limited, or was it correct?

RN: Well, I think your perception was accurate in the fact that most of the black police officers worked in black districts. But there are a couple of reasons for that. One is that most black police officers don't want to go all the way across the city to work in another district if they can get to work in fifteen minutes rather than forty-five. Years ago, before the police department in this city started to take on a more liberal view, it was also customary for black police officers to be assigned to black districts. Now, that was a combination of two very strong facts. Number one, often black police officers were not welcome in certain districts in Chicago, and that situation prevailed for a very long time. The people in this city just were not accustomed to being policed by blacks. They were, of course, accustomed to black people being policed by whites. But white people—say, from the North

Side or way west, around Western Avenue—weren't accustomed to having black officers in their areas. There weren't that many of them then, of course—very few, in fact. Even now, if you go way up on the Northwest Side, I don't think you're going to find a lot of black police officers there. But now, I think it's because they simply don't want to travel that far. Who wants to travel forty-five minutes when they can get to work in fifteen or twenty minutes?

TB: The system has opened up then?

RN: Oh, yes.

TB: I know that when I was working at Wright College, occasionally you would find black officers. And again, as you indicated, they would live relatively close to that area.

RN: Yes, that's considered a perk—that you get to live close to your own district. But for many, many years there was an ongoing policy saying that you would not be assigned to the district where you lived.

TB: Is that right?

RN: Yes, but that has gone by the boards now, and I don't know what the rationale for that was except that people didn't want to police their own neighbors. Of course, that's all changed now. It was a more conservative society then. Now, after the so-called Days of Rage, and the rebellion against authority in the 1960s, people don't feel the same way about that kind of authority. The president resigned, and the attorney general went to jail, and they sent governors and judges and many corrupt officials to jail, so there's a different attitude that prevails about authority now. People question authority more. They're more exacting as to what you're supposed to do. Just like in the old days giving up the corner—well, now the Supreme Court does say it's unconstitutional for you to run somebody off the public way if they're not doing any harm.

TB: Yes. Freedom of assembly—the First Amendment.

RN: That's right. But nobody even thought about anything like that back then—not to my knowledge anyway. And then you have the watchdog organizations like the American Civil Liberties Union who follow up on this sort of thing. So you just have a different attitude. Young people come up now with a much more questioning and demanding attitude.

TB: You've come through two generations of young people in your police work, Rudy. Do you think that the influence of the family and the church has waned in respect to these differences in behavior and attitude?

RN: Certainly, I think it has diminished considerably, especially the family because, as time has gone by, we have developed rapid communication and television, we've gone to the moon, and everything is instantaneous. You see world-shattering events almost instantly—just like Desert Storm, for instance. We were able to see the whole war on television. Well, you weren't able to do that thirty years ago! And in this country the young people are not so concerned with home anymore. They're more independent. They want to get out and do things—get away from the nest rather than stay in it. When you look at this country—as opposed to the Orient, for instance—young people don't seem to have the same respect for their elders that they do in the East. So I think that all of that has to do with the different role not only that the police must play but the different perception people have of the police. It's all part of the mix as far as I'm concerned.

TB: Going back to your theme about the evolution of the work of the police department, philosophically, when you started, how did you view the role of a policeman and the law enforcement agency as such?

RN: Well, you have to have some stabilizer in a complex and democratic society like we have here. You can't have all of these millions of people living together and interacting with each other every day and not have some rules. Otherwise there would be anarchy and people would do what they pretty well pleased. Of course, they're almost doing that now!

[*Laughter.*]

But at least there's some sanction. So I think the more complicated a society gets, the more need there is to have an authority to keep it stable so everybody can get along. Everybody needs to have a chance to do what they want to do. People need to be safe even though it's crowded and there's all sorts of weaponry floating around. And that's another thing I could talk about all day—this maniacal romance we have in this country with guns. But anyway, you have to have something to keep things in check or otherwise a city as large and as complex as Chicago couldn't exist. Everybody would have to go and barricade up some place! Let me elaborate on that point. When I first started as a policeman, I perceived my role to be very authoritarian. There was right and wrong—no gray. You did what you were supposed to do or you were going to jail. But as time has passed, that role has gotten less and less authoritarian, and now the policeman's role is almost laissez-faire—you are not there just to swing the big stick. You're there to interact and to compromise and to organize, and that sort of thing. So, to me, the role now is much different than is was in 1956.

TB: If that's so—and I agree—then the selection of officers has to be more discreet, or does it? What qualities that he or she didn't have to have then should he or she have now?

RN: Well, I go back to the fifties. I can't go back any further because that's when I started. But I think, even then, to be a successful police officer it did require a certain degree of talent—especially communication skills—and a certain degree of flexibility. For example, there's an old adage that a police officer has to be able to walk with kings and talk with beggars—that kind of thing. You have to be able to go from one spectrum to the other when it comes to communicating with people. I think that skill is needed more *now* than it was then. I don't agree that that kind of skill was not needed in the so-called "early" periods like the fifties or even any time earlier than that. I think a police officer should always have that skill. I think the need is more *apparent* now than is was then—much more apparent now because of the kind of things that they're talking about now. The so-called "policing alternatives" that are being tried as experiments around the country are a reflection of the fact that our society now requires a different type of attitude. A lot of policemen don't take to that idea. They think that's more like social work than it is law enforcement. A lot of old-time policemen—because they haven't been accustomed to doing it—don't like that kind of complication in their day-to-day work. They want it to be pretty much cut and dried. You know, just find out who did it, go out and arrest him and take him to jail and bring him before the court. To them all this talking about the lights on the streets and the noise in the neighborhood and all of these things that are not really violations of the law are "quality-of-life" issues rather than criminality. But now police officers are going to become more involved in the quality of life in the community whether they like it or not, because that's what people want, and police officers in this country, whether they realize it or not, eventually take on all the attributes that the public demands. Now, sometimes it takes a long time for those attributes to clearly present themselves, but once it becomes clear that this is what the public wants, police officers don't have *any* say about it because if they don't do what the public wants they're going to have to get out. The chief of police or the police superintendent will get fired. If he is told by the elected officials, "This is what we want. We want you to do this, this, this, and this," and if he can't do it—or won't do it—eventually he's going to get kicked out. The marching orders for him will come down from on high. So if the police executive wants his job, he's going to have to perform in the way that the elected officials *want* him to perform. We have to answer to the electorate. We are answerable to the public who elect the officials that we report to. Some writers would call that—as far as police administration goes—the "albatross" of police administration. That means you've got this political mandate around your neck and sometimes it does get to be an albatross. You can't get rid of it, and it's something that you think you ought not to be doing. Well, that could be true, but it also may not be true.

TB: What it might do is create a dilemma for the chief, which probably then filters down to the lower ranks in terms of how one carries out the job to maintain the degree of law and order that would allow the system to flow smoothly. You mentioned the hysteria about weaponry, and that we have almost as many weapons as we have citizens. We've got a traffic somewhere that brings these weapons into the community. We also have a traffic that brings the narcotics in. My guess is that most police officers have strong feelings about both of these problems in terms of doing their jobs.

RN: Yes, they have very strong feelings, but you do it the way the elected official wants you to do it or you just have to find something else to do. That's the dilemma. Now, when they say, "We've got all these thugs out there in that neighborhood. I want you to go out there and get them off the street. Restore peace to that neighborhood. I want all of these people to stop coming down to my office picketing and demonstrating and talking about they've been abandoned when it comes to law enforcement. You're superintendent of police. I pay you a lot of money. Go take care of it." And then, when you get out in the neighborhood, as a police official, you may find that the biggest complaint that folks have is just this: They've got all of these gangbangers standing around on the street, and people are afraid to come out of their houses, and they all want something to be done about it. So you go out, and you round up all the thugs, and you lock them up—and then a little while after that, you get a subpoena to appear in federal court as a defendant to explain why it is that you are violating these people's constitutional rights!

[*Laughter.*]

TB: And people like me are sitting on the board!

RN: Yes, and people say, "My son can't stand out on the corner? He wasn't doing anything." So that's a dilemma—yes, it is. And it's a dilemma when you go out and pick up some kid with a gun, and before the day is over he's right back out on the street again. He didn't post any bond. All he had to do was just sign a promissory note that he'd appear in court on such and such a date and at such and such a time. And do you know what? If he does not appear in court on such and such a date and at such and such a time, nobody's going to go out and look for him like they would have done in the old days. Years ago if you didn't appear in court, a warrant would be issued for your arrest, and that warrant would go to the district station, and some warrant officer from that station—and others—would be trying to find you. But that doesn't happen nowadays. If people don't show up in court, nobody looks for them unless it's a capital offense. Some interested police officer out of pride might say, "Well, I'm going to get you. You didn't show up for this homicide"—or whatever it was—"and I'm going to find you." That's about the only way the guilty person would get tracked down. But as a routine procedure, it doesn't happen anymore. They simply wait until you get arrested again for something else, and *then* they say, "We see the accused didn't show up in court." So you see now there's a big difference—a huge, huge difference, and that's a quandary and that's a real dilemma.

TB: The sweeps of the low-rental housing development as carried on by Vince Lane created a problem for both those who are antiviolent as well as those who are pro–civil liberties because—although I'm not on the board anymore, I'm still in an advisory capacity—I know that the kids were advised to contact the ACLU to protect their rights.

RN: Sure. I'm not surprised. The sweeps at Cabrini-Green and other places were done on an emergency basis. People were getting shot. They had to lay on the floor or get in the bathtub to keep from getting shot—all of that kind of thing. That's why the sweeps were done.

TB: Yes, I know.

RN: And that's why the ACLU backed off.

TB: Well, some of us were helping them back off. They wanted to go forward, but some of us said, "That's crazy."

RN: Yes. It *is*. It's ludicrous. You know, people were afraid to go to sleep at night and afraid to send their kids to school because the place was loaded with weapons, and they had people running around shooting all of the time. What else are you going to do? You've got to do something to protect those people!

TB: Yes, and that becomes a very difficult thing, I suspect, for a commanding officer because his heart is in one place and his head—

RN: Not really. It's not that difficult, and you know why it isn't difficult? Because the commanding officer—or whatever his title may be—only wants to know what the law is. He wants to know what he can do and what he can't do. Now, if there's a law that says we can't do that, then he's not going to do it, but if it says we can do it—if the legal counsel for the police department says we can do this even though we might get sued because what we're doing is the right thing to do—then boom! He's going to do it! No problem. It's that easy!

TB: Because that's your job.

RN: Yes, that's your job—to follow the law, whatever the law is. If you think you're following the law in good conscience and you know you're not violating the law, then that's what you should do and then be prepared to explain yourself in an inquiry, if that happens to become necessary.

TB: Now, coming back to another problem, it's not a problem for me, but how do you feel about gun control?

RN: Oh, I'm absolutely in favor of it. It's crazy not to have gun control.

TB: But how do you have gun control without violating the Second Amendment?

RN: Well, the Second Amendment was written in 1787. This country isn't a militia anymore where everybody might be called to arms and all of that. Those kinds of conditions prevailed in 1787, but they don't prevail *now*. We've got police departments, we've got the army, we've got the National Guard, we've got all kinds of federal law enforcement agencies and local law enforcement agencies. They didn't have all of that back in 1787.

TB: The Second Amendment has been defended by organizations like the National Rifle Association, which apparently has been quite successful in maintaining that position. I don't know what it is that they consider that they are protecting.

RN: I think it's the politics and then the money—very simply put. The National Rifle Association supports some candidates, and they attack others with all their might and all their money, and they have been able to do that successfully for a long time. They have the backing of some very conservative people who have money and resources, and they support them—to the hilt.

TB: Do you think that there is a segment of the society, a large segment, that believes in the Second Amendment as an expression of personal freedom guaranteed by the Constitution?

RN: Sure I do.

TB: They would say, for instance, "I need my hunting rifle."

RN: Well, you see, rifles and shotguns are not the real problem. The real problem is handguns. Now, I'm not only talking about assault rifles that can shoot thirty-five rounds in two seconds. I'm also talking about handguns—those nine-millimeter and thirty-caliber weapons. People can go out and buy them like candy. That's the problem.

TB: In the best of all possible worlds, as a law enforcement officer, how would you strike a balance in terms of the concept of the right to bear arms and the right of a community to be safe from the possession and use of firearms?

RN: Well, that's almost a contradiction, because if you would say we are going to allow citizens to have firearms—especially pistols—but we're also going to restrict their use, it's like saying "yes" and "no" in the same breath. In the first place, if you are allowed to own a firearm as a private citizen, all you are doing, in effect, is supplying weapons to the criminal because the criminal is going to break into your house and get your gun and take it away from you—or some scenario like that. People have this false sense of security if they own a gun, but that gun in their house is not going to make them any more safe.

TB: It may actually endanger them more.

RN: Yes, that's right, because criminals aren't stupid. They know when you're in the house and when you're out of the house. If they want to get to you badly enough, they'll get you coming in or going out, so to feel that nothing's going to happen to you because you've got a house full of guns is crazy.

TB: And then there's the danger of your own children getting hold of them.

RN: Yes. Children sneaking the guns out of the house and letting the gangbangers use them and then sneaking them back in, or letting some of their friends even know they have guns in their house. Those are also really serious problems.

TB: And their use in domestic quarrels, where, in the heat of the moment, someone decides they have to get rid of somebody they don't like—just then, that minute.

RN: That's right. I've sat across the table—just like I'm sitting across the table talking to you—talking to people who are chained to the wall. They have handcuffs on, you know, and they will be saying, "I really didn't know. Oh, I'm so sorry." And they go on crying and saying that they didn't mean to do it.

TB: But it's already been done. If the gun hadn't been there, the person would still be alive. They might have had a fight, but the victim wouldn't be dead. And people say, "Well, they could have killed them with a knife," but it's a lot more difficult to kill somebody with a knife than it is with a gun. And in addition to that, you don't see these kids accidentally killing themselves playing Russian roulette with a knife! For instance, the kids are out on the school lot and a drive-by car full of thugs comes along. They spray and kill innocent people—children, in this case. Most of the time they hit somebody they didn't even know.

RN: Yes, and you're going to tell me that guns should be available to anybody who wants to buy one? You know, this is the only country in the world where you can do that!

TB: Why haven't the police, as an organization that has influence on politicians, tried to do something about gun control?

RN: Well, the police have banded together. They have the National Association of Chiefs of Police. And the Illinois Association of Chiefs of Police has lobbied against these bills. They have gone to Washington, D.C., in support of the Brady Bill, but the NRA is more powerful because they have more money. They make contributions to some politicians, and they campaign *against* candidates that are in favor of gun control.

TB: I remember when Ab Mikva was congressman in this district, he introduced one of the first gun control bills at the national level, and the NRA went to work on him. Fortunately, he was in a fairly safe district, so he survived, but he had to water down the bill.

RN: Well, somebody watered it down. They always get it watered down. But you've just got a certain segment of elected officials who are cozy with the NRA, and that's a big problem.

TB: Where does all of that financial support come from?

RN: Oh, from contributions from millionaires, from the gun manufacturers—from all kinds of people, and also from private citizens who have the mistaken notion that they're bigger and badder and safer because they've got a gun.

TB: London is at least two times the size of Chicago, and aside from special assignments, the police don't carry guns.

RN: Yes, but now there's some talk over there of late in which, under certain circumstances, they want the police to carry a gun. What has happened over there
is that now some of the seeds that England sowed years and years ago are coming
to fruition. The people in some of the countries that England formerly ruled are
coming to England to live, and it's becoming a multicultural society. It's not so
homogeneous anymore, and with that you're starting to get more crime, more
friction, more violence. Narcotics are starting to proliferate to some greater degree over there, and all of these things working together have shaken the stability
in London and in other large cities. So the police—in self-defense, in many
cases—feel that they need to have guns in a broader range of circumstances than
they've ever had in the past, and they're looking to countries like America and
asking us questions. For instance, they're calling to ask how we set up our community relations division and questions of that nature.

TB: This situation is very new to them.

RN: Oh, yes.

TB: What about the proliferation of narcotics? There are some people—and I happen to be one of them—who feel that there is an ongoing, continuing danger to
the common good of a community and individuals within the community from
the widespread availability and use of narcotics.

RN: Yes, and also a danger to the entire country as well, for that matter.

TB: Yes, I think so too. I, personally, would opt for legalizing drugs. How would a police officer feel about that?

RN: I'm absolutely against the legalization of drugs.

TB: Against legalizing them?

RN: Yes, I am diametrically opposed to the legalization of drugs.

TB: I see. Would you share some of your reasons for that?

RN: Well, in the first place, it doesn't work. They tried legalization in Great Britain,
and it hasn't worked. It limits people to a certain amount of drugs and so forth,
but what people simply do is, for instance, if they want to get more than their five
grams or three grams—or whatever the amount is that they're given every
month—they go out and buy what they want under the counter. It's the same
thing all over again, and it creates another black market. So that doesn't work.
And on top of that, people who ingest narcotics in one form or another often engage in very bizarre, uncivil behavior, and if you made it legal, some of the people who might be sitting on the fence would hurry up and go out and buy some
drugs—and then they're hooked. So I just don't think it would work. I think we
have enough people acting badly under the present circumstances, and it would

amplify the problem even more by making drugs more readily available. I just don't see where it's going to help us.

TB: But by now illegal drugs are already the second largest growth industry in the United States. More than two hundred billion dollars goes into illegal narcotics every single year!

RN: Yes, I'm aware of that.

TB: Well, you want to take the profit out of that, don't you?

RN: But I don't think legalization is going to take the profit out of it. For example, some kid goes into the drugstore and buys marijuana to find out what marijuana does. It gives him a buzz, and he starts smoking it on a regular basis. Then he finds that once his body becomes accustomed to it, the buzz doesn't last as long. It takes more and more to keep him high. So the next step is, "Well, I'm going to try something else. This marijuana is getting to be old hat. Maybe, if I try something else, I can get a better high." So he goes in, and he buys heroin—or whatever else is legalized out there—and then he gets hooked. He becomes an addict. So you can't say it's going to take the profit out of it because people are never going to have enough. And if they can't get enough by going to the drugstore or the prescription house and getting it, then they're going to get it like they're getting it now—somebody is going to sell it to them.

TB: Well, how do you deal with that if this is a major cause of crime? I'm told by some people that recently—in the last twenty years—at least 50 percent of arrests and convictions are narcotics-related.

RN: It's higher than that. It may be 60 or 65, or maybe even more than that. If you go over to County Jail, where they've done some surveys, they've found that the percentages are even higher than that—75 and 80 percent. It's a huge, huge problem, and it requires something on an international scale to deal with it. For example, this country has some very conservative notions about how much intrusion you can exercise at our borders—at our ports of entry. Now they're increasing surveillance, and you know they're working on it because they have started putting metal detectors at airports. But there's too much concern about the individual and the individual's rights when we don't, in my opinion, take stringent enough measures to make sure that contraband like narcotics doesn't come into this country. I wouldn't have any objections to having *all* of the luggage being searched. You can look at my luggage anytime you feel like it! In detail! But the airlines say that it takes too much time and that it's going to cost them X number of dollars. So now we're talking about an international problem. The drugs that are grown in South America are processed in Mexico, France, and places like that. There's no way anybody's going to tell me that the enforcement agencies across the world don't know where these places are and who is engaged in these activities. It's just a matter of how strong an enforcement effort an individual country's going to take. Now, some countries are going to argue, "Well, this is a main industry for us. Our people don't have anything else to do. And it's *your* people who are the drug addicts. You stop your people from using the drugs, and then we won't have any need to be growing them." But you can use that argument forever and you never will get anywhere, because it's an argument that never will resolve itself. You're never going to get the people in this country to a state of affairs where most of them—or at least a satisfactory number of them—won't use drugs, because I don't think, psychologically, most human beings are that strong. Some people are just susceptible to that kind of temptation, and I don't care what you do, you're not going to get some of them to not use drugs or to quit using them. Now, it's harder for them to quit than it is for them not to use them in the first place—much harder. So you're right, if you can get people not to use drugs in the first place—if you can get to them before they go to grammar school—four, five, six years old—if you can get them psychologically oriented to the idea that the use of drugs is a bad thing, maybe you can do something about the problem. But it's not working that way, and it's not working that way most especially in very poor communities where you don't have the family support, you don't have the parental guidance, and you don't have a living environment where you can learn to resist these kinds of temptations. For example, in very, very poor neighborhoods you have a high proliferation of narcotics because everybody's doing it. The parents did it, and their parents before them did it, and now all of their little running buddies are doing it as well!

TB: Yes, you'd be out of place if you didn't do it. So, on the one end, you have the poor folks in places like Peru, Bolivia, and Colombia who grow the stuff, and then other poor folks who not only use it but act as couriers in places like the United States and Great Britain where rich people have got the money to buy those drugs.

RN: Yes, and we catch these couriers every once in a while as they come in from different countries. Several women came over from a country in Africa recently, and they had plastic bags in their stomachs full of drugs. A couple of them died. And now we're also getting drugs from places like Haiti. These are places where the people are in very poor circumstances, and that form of temptation represents a lot of money to them.

TB: And so they take risks.

RN: That's right. They take risks. It's an industry for the suppliers, but it's a job for them. They may not look at what they are doing as being a criminal act like police officers do or like you do, so it's an international problem. It is not a problem that can be solved *within* this country. You can't say, "We're going to solve this problem right here within our own borders." That's nonsense. It can never happen that way—at least I don't think so, anyway.

TB: Now, what happens, for example, when a policeman at Robert Taylor Homes or Cabrini-Green or on Forty-seventh Street has to make some decision on the spot when he or she is confronted with this chain of events like this?

RN: Well, it goes right back to what I told you about the basic principles of the law. It's really not that difficult. A good policeman doesn't rationalize all of this. For this policeman in your example, it wouldn't make any difference. It's way back in the dark recesses of his mind—these things I'm talking about. They're not things that he just learned the day before yesterday by reading a magazine. He's seen these problems evolve and get bigger and bigger, and he was aware of it, but if he caught somebody dealing drugs, or if he caught someone with possession of drugs, it would never dawn on him that he shouldn't arrest that person because of all of these "ifs, ands, buts, and wherefores." It is *simple*. The person is in violation of the law, and this is what the officer was hired to do. This is his mandate. This is what the law requires him to do.

TB: So you do your job.

RN: Yes, so I do my job. And sometimes when they are arrested and are brought into the police station, they get out so quickly, they beat me home! And so I go back, and I arrest them again tomorrow for the same thing. Most policemen will accept that. That's just part of the scenario here. From the time they walk into the academy, they have *some* idea that that's the way it works.

TB: And that's what you find where there are concentrations of poverty in places like public housing and in other places as well.

RN: Well, I wouldn't say all these places where these problems exist are impoverished, but most of them have very, very low income. I wouldn't call them impoverished because they do have some recourse to help—relief agencies and other organizations—but they are at the bottom of the socioeconomic spectrum. They're vulnerable.

TB: And they're heavily concentrated.

RN: Yes, they're all piled in there together.

TB: Sharing common—

RN: Common disasters. Right.

TB: How would you cope with them?

RN: Well, I would disperse them. I would put them out into all the neighborhoods and let every neighborhood have some subsidized housing. Of course, there are a lot of poor people in Chicago, but Chicago's a huge place. Why should you stack them seventeen stories high—all those people in the same unfortunate circumstance? All with just single-parent homes and all of that kind of thing? To me, it's ridiculous.

TB: Should we let other neighborhoods absorb some of this poverty?

RN: Why, of course. Then you don't have this massive negative impact on any one neighborhood. Otherwise you can be sure that the neighborhood that has these people in this stacked-up circumstance—this stacked-up, *poor*, unfortunate circumstance—you can bet that that neighborhood's going to have some really serious problems.

TB: The evidence that I'm aware of indicates that when you do move some folks from those unfortunate conditions that they were living in for a long time, that their behavior changes, their attitude changes, and that their children's behavior and attitudes change even more dramatically.

RN: Absolutely.

TB: The change is even more dramatic because they tend to want to fit into the new environment, and very often in only one generation they do better. And—who knows?—in the next generation they may have wiped out the biggest part of that negative past altogether, which, of course, would also help simplify police work.

RN: Oh, absolutely! Well, you know, human beings want to be liked. Everybody wants to fit in. You want to be accepted in your group. So if you go over to a new environment where nobody's playing the radio at three o'clock in the morning, where nobody's standing out on the street corner calling everybody a "motherfucker" and all of the dirty names, where you don't see people sitting around or staggering up and down the street drinking wine—if you found yourself in a neighborhood where they didn't have any of this type of behavior—then it's altogether different psychologically for you to choose to engage *yourself* in these kinds of behavior. You know, you feel there's a sanction against that kind of behavior there, and that this is not an accepted mode of bonding. So then the fence-sitters, I think, would hop over on the right side rather than fall on the wrong side. But, of course, there still will be some who just are completely lost.

TB: But those would be the exceptions.

RN: Yes, some of them may not be able to adapt, but I think that those would probably be few in number, especially when you're talking about young people.

TB: Yes, there would only be a very small residue. What role do the new forms of communication, such as television and the other media, play in this process? There are some that argue that they have no effect on the minds, attitudes, and behavior of people, and there are others who argue they do and who are now putting pressure on the major networks to regulate violence. In your opinion, does violence in the media have any impact on the violence we see in our neighborhoods?

RN: It has a *profound* impact on the behavior of young people. There's no way that I think it would not have, because young people are very impressionable. As police officers, you can see them try to emulate what they have seen on the media. They start to take on the facade, the body language—just like they see the entertainers, the rappers do. You notice what they're doing with their hands, and you see little kids—seven, eight, ten, twelve years old—take on all of those same mannerisms, and then they start talking about "killing the pigs" and all of that kind of talk. You see those little kids talking the same kind of stuff out in the street, so to say it doesn't have any impact on them, to my mind, you've got to be blind to believe that! But it's usually more of a copycat syndrome with young people, especially adolescents, than it is with older people.

TB: Yes, if it didn't have the intended effect, particularly in terms of increased ratings, then the networks wouldn't use so much violence.

RN: Well, it's scintillating. You know, people just seem to like to see violence. From the days of the Romans with the lions eating people in the arena, this is something that excites people. It's part of the human psyche, I guess. But I think it should be a recognized part and should be dealt with in a *positive* way. Accept the fact that there is a tendency that humans have to engage in violence and then try to channel that tendency in some less socially destructive way.

TB: And don't continue to stimulate and to copy violent behavior and act it out in the context of their own lives, which is precisely what television tends to do.

RN: Right, and have swift sanctions when people *do* engage in violence.

TB: It is becoming more and more complicated, as I see it, for police officers to do their duty. Do you believe that police officers should be better trained?

RN: Oh, they have to be. Today most police officers have at least high school diplomas, and there's some talk now that they're going to require two years of college or at least some number of college credits, like we have now in this department. You have to have a minimum of fifteen hours of law enforcement before you can work here.

TB: Where do they get their training?

RN: When we hire them, we give them ten weeks here, then we give them one year of probation, and after that we send them to the Chicago Police Academy for what you call the Metro Program.

TB: Do they get academic credit?

RN: Yes, the state of Illinois requires that in order to be a police officer you must have, I believe, at least 421 hours of their prescribed training. So, after they have ten weeks and one year probation, we send them to the Chicago Police Academy, where they get the 421-plus hours that they need.

TB: So they get a lot of theory as well as practice.

RN: Yes, and then they have to pass a certification exam.

TB: This is because they're dealing with a much more highly complex community?

RN: Yes, and a much better-informed community. Today people are much more conscious of their constitutional rights.

TB: And they are also much more activist, and that must create some really sophisticated conditions that police officers have to be prepared to deal with. By this time, Rudy, you have spent almost forty years in police work, haven't you?

RN: Yes, I had thirty-two years with the Chicago Police Department, and I've been here for four years, so that's thirty-six years.

TB: And you're still a young man!

RN: Yes, still going strong!

TB: Are your mother and dad both gone?

RN: My dad is. He died when he was seventy-three, but my mother will be one hundred years old on September 2.

TB: That's wonderful! Is she here in Chicago?

RN: Yes, she's in the same building with us.

TB: Well, Rudy, one of the things I'm happy and proud of is that so many of you younger folks have taken an optimistic view of life and inserted yourselves into the life of the city in order to help make it a better place to live. A subject which I didn't touch on earlier in our conversation is the subject of the two great migrations to Chicago from the South. The first migration was the one in which your dad came here right after the turn of the century and which continued up until World War II, and the second influx from the South came after World War II. In your opinion, are there differences between these two populations in terms of the social circumstances? How do you view these two migrations?

RN: Well, when the first migration came—the one that my father, my mother, and even my grandfather were involved in—there was white migration into the city too. The Irish, for example, and the Polish. But I think the Hispanic population is the fastest-growing minority in Chicago right now, and we even have people coming up here from South America. As a matter of fact, people are coming from *everywhere* more frequently now and in a greater *variety* than they did when my parents migrated here. They come because of the sophistication in transportation, for example, and the greater availability of information.

TB: What about opportunites—in the job market, for instance—for these newcomers?

RN: Well, I don't think opportunities for certain people are as prevalent as they once were. For example, if you come to a place like Chicago now, and if you don't have a skill, you can't get a job, but before World War II if you came here and didn't have a skill, you could always find work.

TB: A strong back was all you needed.

RN: Yes, that's right, but nowadays you have a problem finding work because those attributes are less and less in demand. You know, this is the age of robotics, where machinery is doing most of the work.

TB: Well, for your dad and my dad, and those that came before, a strong back was really all they needed, and if they had more than that, then they had a big advantage.

RN: Yes, the stockyards, the steel mills, the railroads were hiring—places like that where you didn't have to be a professional.

TB: You could work hard, raise your family, and send your children to college. Now, the second migration from Mississippi came during and after World War II. How, in your opinion, did it differ from the first migration?

RN: Well, many of the people that came here at that time, as far as I can determine, did not have a lot of skills, but many of them acquired skills after they got here, and they became teachers, entered government service, or became policemen.

TB: Yes, but what about those who were not able to get to that level because the steel mills and stockyards and most of the other labor opportunities had shut down?

RN: Well, that series of circumstances has directly contributed, I believe, to this huge public housing situation that we have and the kind of social depression that you find there now. That happened because these people couldn't assimilate themselves. They didn't pick up the skills or *couldn't* pick up the skills, and they went on relief because there really wasn't anything else for them to do. There were simply not as many opportunities for work as there had been in the past.

TB: So they were less fortunate. I often say, if my daddy had come to Chicago in 1947 or 1948 with what he brought from Birmingham, Alabama, his children could *not* have gone to college unless something unusual had happened. But, as it was back then, we just took it for granted that if we wanted to go to college— somehow—it was going to be possible. You know, my mother didn't work outside the home. Only my dad had a job. We didn't have much money, but even my brother and I could go and find little odd jobs. Like you were saying—picking chickens, delivering groceries . . .

RN: And working on the watermelon wagon!

TB: Yes, and now all of that's gone. So these youngsters, many of whom your colleagues encounter on the streets, do not have the same kind of opportunities that my generation—and to a lesser extent, your generation—have had. I could always say, "Here's something right here in this neighborhood that I can do to keep me busy, and I can find a little job and at least make enough money to go to the movies."

RN: To put it very succinctly, our society has become more and more competitive. You have to have more skills in order to successfully compete, as compared to the situation years and years ago.

TB: Yes, in places like Florida, if you're even going to survive there, particularly in Miami, you'd better be able to speak two languages.

RN: That's right, and in Europe that's a common thing. If you want to work in a hotel or on an airline, or even as a bellboy, you have to be bilingual. Over there, speaking two or three languages is very common because the countries are so close together, and they're so small that people are constantly running back and forth between them.

TB: Well, this is also becoming more and more common here. Even in places as large as California, if one is not bilingual, he or she may be shut out of opportunity.

RN: Yes, that's right. You know, I've got a son-in-law in the police department, and I've been encouraging him to learn Spanish.

TB: Yes, as we begin to look at the Chicago police force itself, we begin to find more and more Spanish officers as well as a larger Spanish community.

RN: That's right, but there's also more need for non-Spanish people to speak Spanish. If you're a police officer in Chicago, you're going to find yourself working at certain times in a district with a large Spanish population, and you're going to be at a very distinct disadvantage if you can't speak the language.

TB: Well, this is already happening in the public schools. Part of it's national pride. Farragut High School, where I taught some years ago, demanded to have a Hispanic principal. They're making that demand, and they have the political power to enforce that demand. Now when you walk down the halls at Farragut and hear the students talking to each other, you don't know whether they're talking about you or not because you don't understand the language! Rudy, thank you so much for sharing your time and your very valuable insights with us.

RN: Thank you, Tim. It's been my great pleasure to spend this time with you.

July 6, 1993

LeROY MARTIN

FORMER SUPERINTENDENT OF POLICE

I have only known LeRoy Martin, superintendent of the Chicago Police Department from 1987 to 1992, since he was first appointed to that position by the late Harold Washington, the first black mayor of Chicago. After his retirement from the Chicago Police Department, he became the chief security officer for the Chicago Housing Authority. However brief our infrequent contacts have been, they always are pleasant and productive.

His accounts of growing up on the racially and ethnically mixed West Side reveal the quality and dynamics of those complex relationships. Also, the stories he tells about his strong family ties are particularly memorable because they are told with so much humor and affection. His public elementary and high school memories also made for good conversation, as did his memories of his experiences in the army during the Korean War and his anecdotes about his early jobs in the post office and as a black pioneer working for the Chicago Transit Authority.

He said that though he is now "retired," he is not "tired." And so he continues in various public service agencies and donates a great deal of time as a volunteer to others. He is deeply concerned about the present plight of many black youth who have had or are having trouble with the law.

Superintendent Martin is a knowledgeable and intelligent man who is tough and fearless but always fair. He was a good superintendent with a vision for a better future for young people who are in trouble. He presses for prevention but does not tolerate violation of the law. He also believes in redemption and has positive hopes for the future.

TB: Superintendent, how long have you been in law enforcement?

LM: Thirty-seven years, Tim. I was twenty-four years old when I started back in 1955. I served thirty-seven years, and I came out at age sixty-one.

TB: LeRoy, where were you born?

LM: In Lawndale on the West Side of Chicago.

TB: And when were you born?

LM: In 1929.

TB: In terms of the West Side, you're an old-timer! What part of the West Side are you from?

LM: From the area of Roosevelt Road—right off of Ashland Avenue.

TB: Which school was this near?

LM: Well, near Smyth School and near Thomas Jefferson School. I attended Thomas Jefferson School. Now back then—not trying to be disparaging of any race—the area I was born in was called "Jew Town."

TB: Is that right?

LM: Yes, and the reason it was called "Jew Town" was because it was close to Maxwell Street, which is where many Jewish merchants had their shops.

TB: That is now being phased out, unfortunately.

LM: Right, so, if you hear the West Siders talk, they would say I was not really a West Sider. I was from "Jew Town."

[*Laughter.*]

TB: You were also close to the area called Little Italy.

LM: Yes, that was Taylor Street—just two blocks away. In fact, I can tell you a funny story about that. Smyth School, which was two blocks south of where I lived, was all black. Jefferson School, which was two blocks to the north, was almost all Italians. I lived on the north side of Roosevelt Road, and the school boundary was the middle of Roosevelt Road. All the kids that lived on the north side of the street had to go to Jefferson. All the kids on the south side went to Smyth School. Well, when I arrived at Jefferson, I was like a fly in a bottle of buttermilk! At that school you had to do one of two things—run fast or fight! And I did a combination because the welcome mat was not extended when I got there!

[*Laughter.*]

TB: Were all the teachers white?

LM: Yes, all the teachers were white. In fact, I did not have a black instructor until I attended Roosevelt University.

TB: Is that a fact?

LM: Yes, so I was full-grown before I studied under my first black teacher. I was born and raised in Chicago and never had a black teacher while I was growing up!

TB: What was the neighborhood like around Maxwell Street in the twenties and thirties?

LM: Well, in the thirties, Maxwell Street was inhabited by Jewish merchants. Some blacks may have worked over there, but no stores or peddler carts were owned or operated by blacks at that time. All we did there was shop. Just a half a block north of where I lived the people were all Italians. The north side of Roosevelt Road was partially black, and then south of Roosevelt Road going on down to maybe around Fifteenth Street was black. Now, this was before the Jane Addams, the ABLA [Addams, Brooks, Loomis, and Abbott] housing development, and the Robert Brooks facility were built. All that didn't exist then. They were built in the mid-thirties or early forties.

TB: What was the general socioeconomic status at that time?

LM: Well, you know, it was bad. Black people worked, but the good jobs for black people were as waiters on the railroad. A few fellows might have been lucky and had jobs in the stockyards. There were no black bus drivers and very, very few black postal workers. There were very, very few black police officers and no black firefighters at that time. Those jobs were held primarily by white men, and we blacks had service jobs. My mother used to clean and do day work, and my father was a porter for the Chicago, Milwaukee & St. Paul Railway so he used to travel a lot.

TB: Was he a member of the Brotherhood?

LM: Yes, he was. A. Philip Randolph organized the porters, of course. So those were the jobs that blacks held at that time. We didn't hold any civil service jobs to any extent.

TB: What was the neighborhood like then?

LM: Well, most of the people around the neighborhood were related to one another, because in those days, when people migrated up here from the South, they usually settled in the same general area as their relatives who had come up here earlier.

TB: How many brothers and sisters do you have, LeRoy?

LM: I have two brothers and two sisters. I'm right in the middle.

TB: Where did your mother and dad come from?

LM: They were from Helena, Mississippi. You see, a lot of black people came up from Helena and from Clarksdale, Mississippi. And what happened in those days is, there was more cohesiveness among us because those who had already come up to Chicago sent for those who were still trapped down there in the South. It wasn't unusual for a father to come up and leave his wife and children in the South and then send for them after he got kind of a toehold. Then what happened up here is that cousins, grandmothers—they all lived next door to each other or upstairs. Most of your relatives lived within, say, half a block of each other. That was because ones that were already in Chicago were busy finding housing for those that were coming up. That's why everybody lived in clusters. Either they were related or they already knew each other from back home. Also, it was common for a black man to bring another black man to a job and introduce him to the employer as his cousin and get him hired as his cousin.

TB: That was the network!

[*Laughter.*]

LM: Yes, so all our family that was here in Chicago lived within about a block of each other.

TB: If they hollered real loud, you could hear them!

LM: Yes, and it was nothing to go over to see your first cousin and stay over. Friends or relatives baby-sat while your mother and father went somewhere. At that time most of the housing on the West Side was coal-heated. You had that old pot-bellied stove in the living room, and people don't remember, Tim, but we had a galvanized tub to take baths in! And I tell my children about how we used to let the water run in the sink to keep it from freezing up in the winter!

TB: That's right!

LM: You see, moving water won't freeze, and that's the way we kept the pipes from busting by having a little bit of running water in the sink all night. I remember my father had an old 1936 Ford, and he used to drain the radiator at night because we didn't have permanent antifreeze back then—just alcohol—and it used to evaporate, so men used to drain the radiators at night and then refill them in the morning after they started their cars.

[*Laughter.*]

Yes, those were the old days, and to this day, if I had to, I could still make a fire so it wouldn't go out during the nighttime!

TB: Could you crank a car?

LM: Oh, yeah! But if you cranked it and pulled that handle back at the same time—and you were standing there—it would knock your arm off!

[*Laughter.*]

TB: That's right! So you had that harmony of the community and the harmony of the close relationships.

LM: Yes, and as blacks got jobs and stayed on them a little while, they began to move south, to around Thirty-fifth Street, where housing was better—steam-heated rooms and hot running water!

TB: You graduated from Jefferson in 1943, and World War II was in progress at that time.

LM: Yes, it had started in 1941.

TB: So you remember that period pretty well. After graduating from Thomas Jefferson, where did you go to school?

LM: I went to Crane Technical Institute, Tim, and when I got over there, the racial situation was just about the same as it had been at Thomas Jefferson. In fact, Tim, the only sport that they would allow blacks to participate in was track.

TB: Is that right?

LM: That's all. And at Thomas Jefferson they didn't permit blacks to become patrol boys at the traffic crossings. The most that we could do in a place like that was to become hallway monitors. We could not be patrol boys on the street at the traffic cross.

TB: Because that was high status?

LM: Yes, that was high status. And when I got to high school, the situation was almost as bad. Like I said, the only thing they had for blacks was running track, and the ironic part about it was that the athletic teams they had over there weren't any good! The basketball and the football team were no good, but they still wouldn't let us participate!

TB: What years were you at Crane, LeRoy?

LM: I went there in 1943 and graduated in January of 1947 — you know, we used to have two graduations. We had four thousand students at that time. It was huge, you know.

TB: Was Crane Junior College in existence back them?

LM: No, they didn't have the junior college back then. Well, after I left Crane, I went to Herzl Junior College — which was the old Crane — and then later Herzl became Malcolm X.

TB: Yes, yes. I was being considered for promotion to president of old Crane at one time — before it became Malcolm X. I knew when my nomination went to the board, though, that I wasn't going to be chosen because the board knew what the mayor *didn't* want in a president, and that was me!
[*Laughter.*]
They may not have known exactly what he *wanted*, but they certainly knew what he *didn't* want! And by that time I had made my little reputation, which wasn't in favor with the mayor! So what was the relationship like between the students and the faculty at Crane?

LM: It was good, but like I say, there was subtle racism — not overt or anything. The vast majority of the student population was white — a few Hispanics, a few blacks, but overwhelmingly white.

TB: What ethnic group were the whites?

LM: Mostly Italian with some Polish.

TB: Were you in a technical program at Crane?

LM: Yes, I was in a technical program, and I learned a lot of skills that I still use to-day. You know, I can still fix a fan and put an outlet in—all those things I learned at Crane. It was basically a vocational school for those who were going to go into a trade. After I graduated from Crane, I went on to Herzl, and I got what we now call an associate's degree. After I got those two degrees, I dropped out of school and went to work for the Chicago Transit Authority. I drove a streetcar—the old "big red"! They still had a few on the streets back then in 1950. In fact, the only streets that had the modern streetcars were State, Clark, and Madison. Every-thing else was a "big red." And, then, slowly they phased those out too.

TB: What line was that?

LM: Broadway-State and Clark-Wentworth. When I got hired, I was living at 1442 Roosevelt. You know where that station is? It's at Devon and Clark. That was 6400 north, and at that time I didn't have an automobile, and so I had to get up and take the streetcar to get up there and go to work!

[*Laughter.*]

But you know, back then, you did what you had to do, and at that time I thought it was a good job!

TB: Sure, and then in terms of hiring for blacks, they had just begun to be a part of that force. They hadn't been there that long.

LM: Yes, if it had not been for World War II, we might not have been on the force as soon as we were, but there was an acute shortage of men at that time and that opened up an opportunity. But I recall to this day one time I pulled up to a corner and a white lady was running for my streetcar from across the street, and she looked up, and when she saw it was me driving, she turned around and stepped back up on the curb!

[*Laughter.*]

TB: Yellow and Checker Cab companies were just beginning to hire black drivers around this same time, and they tried to confine them, of course, to the South Side, but that just wasn't possible for very long.

LM: And the police department put on a bunch of blacks during World War II as temporary police officers. They did not want to give them permanent status, with the intent that when the war ended and the white boys returned, the blacks would be laid off. But the blacks that had already got on the force—and some other people—put up such a holler and a stink about it that they had to make them permanent!

TB: Yeah, I remember some of the first guys who were conductors and motormen in the beginning of the forties. I was drafted in 1943, but I watched things change a little bit. Before I was drafted, I was working in Chicago with what was then the Metropolitan Funeral System—which later became the Chicago Met—on

Forty-fifth Street and South Park. Some of the guys, realizing that the pressure was on to take blacks onto the streetcars, left Met to drive a streetcar because that would give them a deferment, and when they would come driving a streetcar down Forty-seventh Street, everybody would turn around and say, "Look, that's Johnny Barnes. He's a big shot now!"

[*Laughter.*]

LM: It was a step up to have a good job like that at that time.

TB: Yes, it bypasses the stockyards and the steel mills!

LM: Back in the mid-fifties, just before I quit working for the CTA, Rudy Nimocks and I drove buses out of Thirty-ninth Street and Rockwell. That station is still there—the Archer Avenue bus station. Then Rudy went with Park District security, which later on merged with the city.

TB: Now, had the CTA merged when you were there? It had formerly been the Chicago Surface Lines, you know.

LM: Yes, it was the CTA already when I started there—it had already merged. Martin Kennelly was the mayor after Ed Kelly during the mid-fifties, and then in 1955, Daley came in. I remember so clearly because I got hired by the police department in August of 1955, and we were the first police officers that were hired under the new mayor, Richard J. Daley.

TB: Just as you were pioneering in public transportation—and by pioneering I mean you were in the first group of a sizable number of blacks that were hired—I would imagine that when you were hired into the police department that there were not a large number of blacks there at that time.

LM: Yes, when I came on the police department in 1955, out of sixteen thousand police officers in the city of Chicago, there were just five black sergeants and only one black lieutenant . . .

TB: One? Just one?

LM: One. Kinzey Bluett, and he was the acting captain of the Wabash Avenue Station on Forty-eighth Street. He wasn't a full captain, but he was the only black lieutenant in the city. The five sergeants were Bob Harness, McCall, Pointleroy, Carol Miles, and Carl Nelson, who had been Joe Louis's bodyguard.

TB: Carl was assigned to Joe Louis most of the time, wasn't he?

LM: No, I think he was through with that assignment, because by then he was at the Prairie Avenue Station as desk sergeant—that's why I always remember him. He was a very polite man—not grumpy like a lot of police officers were back then, and always very well dressed, you know, a diplomat.

TB: Yes.

[*Laughter.*]

So he was at the Prairie Avenue Station, which had just opened about then. Did that replace the old Staten Station?

LM: Yes, Staten was gone when I came there. In fact, that station at Twentieth Street and Prairie and the Wabash Avenue Station were the only two police stations out of thirty-eight police stations at that time that had black police officers working behind the desk.

TB: Is that right? Maxwell Street did not have them?

LM: No, not Maxwell Street or any other station. Maxwell had a few black officers working out of it, but all the desk officers were white.

TB: When I was a teenager, I understand that Sylvester Washington worked Maxwell Street for a little while.

LM: Yes, what I heard is that the Italians from Taylor Street had him sent back to the South Side.

[*Laughter.*]

TB: Yes, that's what I also heard. I was always scared of that guy, but I liked him! So when you came on the force there was one lieutenant, five sergeants, and no commanding officers.

LM: No, but I did run into one ex-police captain from that time who was black. I was standing on the corner of Sixty-third and Cottage Grove and the shine wasn't even off my uniform yet, and a fellow walked up to me, a very tall gentleman, and he told me that he was a former police officer. And I said, "Oh that's good. Are you retired?" And he said, "Yes. As a matter of fact, I was a captain. My name is Chester Scott."

TB: Oh, yes, he was there in the real early days.

LM: Right, and Milton Deas [Sr.]—they were also there in those early days. Those guys were all gone when I came on, but you know, I had heard their names.

TB: Well, Milton Jr. and I were in high school together.

LM: Yeah, well, you know, the station out on 103rd Street is named after his father.

TB: Is that right?

LM: Yes, and the Wentworth Avenue Station is named after Bob Harness—so they named two stations after black officers.

TB: Bob Harness is one of my favorite guys. We would be out on the playground shooting dice. Bob knew that we were out there and that we were supposed to be playing baseball or something like that, and when he came through everybody would run and drop their money!

[*Laughter.*]

We knew if Bob caught us we were going to get hurt!

LM: Oh, yeah! Yes, indeed!

TB: But he had a great deal of race pride.

LM: Tremendous. He was a tremendous example to the other police officers of how a man could endure a lot of things and still be a man.

TB: Yes. Now, how many detectives were on the force when you came on?

LM: I haven't got the count, but there weren't many, and the only places where a black detective was allowed to work was in burglary and robbery. They weren't working in homicide even though we had a lot of blacks killing blacks. Those investigations were all conducted by white detectives.

TB: By this time, narcotics were beginning to come into the city in fairly sizable quantities, weren't they?

LM: Right.

TB: I know there were two detectives—Brice and Simms—who worked out of narcotics at that time.

LM: Yes, they were two celebrated detectives.

TB: So, just as you are getting into the service, narcotics is becoming big stuff.

LM: Yes, it is beginning to come in in large quantities and is beginning to be peddled. I don't think that it got a real toehold back then compared to now because the economy was still good.

TB: Yes.

LM: You see, people were working, so the narcotic dealers weren't able to get distributors easily, like they have in times when the economy is very slow and they can find people who can't get real jobs to work for them. In those days any kind of use of dope was still kind of restricted to the fast crowd. Cocaine and heroin were just beginning to come into the South Side and the West Side, and some people were beginning to use it. But again, like I said, again, the steel mills and the stockyards were still going strong.

TB: Yes, and there was International Harvester and other places like that.

LM: Right, places where unskilled people could make a good living—so that kind of thing didn't get a real toehold in the working class.

TB: Yes, you're right, because before I went into the service, the big thing among the guys that I ran with was reefer.

LM: Yes, reefer—marijuana.

TB: And you know, a guy would pass me a reefer, and somebody would say, "No, he doesn't do that." And that was it!

LM: Yes, that was the big thing then.

TB: When I came *out* of the service, in the middle forties, heroin had begun to slip in, but it was used by *selected* people, like Billie Holiday and other musicians, people who had some money.

LM: Right—nightlife people, Policy people . . .

TB: And the guys who were peddling were in that life too.

[*Laughter.*]

So it wasn't down at the roots, as we call it.

LM: Exactly. So you didn't see then what you see now on every corner, even around playgrounds—you didn't see that then. In fact, you had to seek out the guy who was selling.

TB: Oh, yeah, you had to know what you were doing. The market was so tight that when Billie would come into town, the price would go up. The idea was she was going to buy more than she needed, you know, so the price would go up. The market was not a broad market then, and, of course, it had a high level of stigmatization in the community.

LM: And, you know, some of the police officers were doing business with Policy people and gamblers at that time, but drugs were a no-no. Everybody was afraid that drugs would ruin your life, and so nobody wanted to have anything to do with drug dealers. It would change over the years, of course, but at that time, it was kind of a despised type of activity that you wouldn't want to engage in.

TB: Yes. So where were you stationed at this period of time—when you began to move up?

LM: At the old Woodlawn Station at Sixty-fourth. I can still remember when the Blackstone Rangers was just a street gang—just a bunch of teenage punks standing on the corner. At that time, you know, they weren't into much of anything, but as time went on they began to get into criminal activity.

TB: Yes, in the late fifties they had not yet emerged as an organized violent street gang. When Jeff Fort, the leader of the Blackstone Rangers, was a student at Hyde Park High School, he was a tough, natural leader, but he respected me and other black teachers there at that time. However, the administration didn't want him at Hyde Park—it had a certain amount of snobbery. So first chance they got, they put him out. They did that while I was away in Washington, D.C., on business for the president's office. And I asked some of the guys like Fred Johnson, "Why didn't you go in and stop this?" and he said, "Well, the superintendent of police wouldn't let us."

LM: So that was O. W. Wilson?

TB: Yes, they said, "He won't let us." And that says to me, "Well, he was getting orders from somebody else." I have my own theory on this matter in regard to whom was actually responsible.

LM: Well, as the gang began to grow and become more violent, certain people like that fellow who inherited the fortune from the guy who invented the Bendix starter drive—he had set up a fund just to bail them out of jail. He did that in collaboration with Reverend John Fry and the Presbyterian Church. Remember that guy?

TB: Yes, John Fry. He tried to get me to come over and help him with what he called "The Nation." By this time it seems he had given them a new name!

LM: Well, you see, that's when I knew that it was more than just a bunch of kids. It was a plot. Because when a church minister hides weapons in a church for gang members, you know there's got to be a deeper purpose than just trying to help those kids. Then you're really trying to destroy a neighborhood—which is what they did.

TB: Yes, and the black officers that I knew, almost from the beginning, realized the socially destructive potential of allowing something like this to continue.

LM: Yes.

TB: And so they were prepared to stop it before it got to be too big.

LM: And don't forget that Blackstone Rangers was a prototype for what we have today all over the nation. Gangs didn't exist to that extent before that time. We had some gangs back in the thirties and forties, but there wasn't any killing.

TB: And most kids just grew out of it.

LM: Yeah, everybody grew out of it. They grew up and grew out of it.

TB: They went on to get a job, get married, and raise a family!

[*Laughter.*]

LM: Yes, and that was the end of their affiliation.

TB: You couldn't hang out on the corner anymore!

[*Laughter.*]

LM: Yes, and that's all it was—it was hanging out and playing ball, but it *never* was about moneymaking.

TB: Later on, it became a business, but at first those kids did not have that level of sophistication. They simply did not have that. That factor had to be brought in from the outside and carefully instilled, and that was what Reverend Fry and—I forget the name of that Catholic guy—they wanted me to do. They knew those kids would like me, and what they wanted was for me to legitimize what they were doing. I understood that very clearly, and I was not prepared to give them that advantage and to be used in that way. And then I tried to talk with the guys on the streets—and by this time they began to make a little money by shaking down people, shaking down the students and all—because by that time they had begun to feel that they were not wanted at Hyde Park High School, and that brought the members of the gang still closer together.

LM: Right.

TB: So I used to go around to the poolroom that was there on Sixty-third Street and shoot pool and try to get them to go back in school, but they wouldn't go back. Now, you worked in the Woodlawn Station about this time. What was the neighborhood like?

LM: Well, Woodlawn was jumping. You had the Crown Propeller Lounge up there on Sixty-third Street as well as the Tivoli. We also had Harry's Show Lounge where Leon Abbey was playing the violin and Lonnie Simmons was playing the organ. Ahmad Jamal was playing at the Pershing. Mickey Fitzhugh and Cadillac Bob had a joint called Toast of the Town right there off of Sixty-third Street on Cottage Grove. On a Saturday night you couldn't make it from one end of Sixty-third Street to the other! There were just too many jazz joints! The Surf, the Kit Kat Club—all those places were really jumping back then.

TB: We lived at Sixty-third and Vernon, and sometimes my wife and I would get up at one o'clock A.M. and say, "Let's go out!"

[*Laughter.*]

There was no kind of danger, and you could go out and listen to some music for a little while and then go back home and go to bed. The neighborhood was still stable.

LM: Oh, yes. There was no danger. People were sitting in the park all the time and sleeping on the fire escapes on a hot night.

TB: There were a lot of people on the street all the time and so there was a lot of safety in just the numbers of people.

LM: Yeah, and if you did become a victim of a crime—a stickup man was just that. He would stick you up and take what you had and leave. He didn't beat you, and he wouldn't dare shoot you. You didn't resist, and, you know, he just took your valuables and left!

TB: In fact, a pocketbook snatcher wasn't even supposed to have a weapon.

LM: That's right.

TB: He would just snatch your pocketbook and take his chances of getting caught!

LM: House burglars didn't carry weapons because they were thieves. They came in to steal, but they didn't come in to hurt anybody.

TB: I suppose there was a code of conduct even among the crooks.

LM: Yes, and in those days it was surprising for a woman to say she was robbed and molested because the guys didn't do that. The guy would take the money and go somewhere else and buy what he wanted, but he didn't do things like that.

TB: How long did you stay at Woodlawn, LeRoy?

LM: I stayed at Woodlawn about two years, Tim.

TB: What were the conditions like at Woodlawn?

LM: Well, Tim, when I was a young police officer at the old Woodlawn Station—to show you some of the things that we as African-Americans had to put up with—when they didn't have enough white police officers to put in the squad cars, they would put the cars in the garage.

TB: Put the cars in the garage?

LM: Yes, they would put the cars in the garage, and we had to walk. And this was in wintertime!

TB: And you had no recourse?

LM: No recourse.

TB: If you wanted to keep your job, you had no recourse. Did you have job security?

LM: No. There was no union—there was nothing. The closest thing to a union was the alderman or the ward committeeman, and if he didn't take up your battle—if you had one—your battle didn't get taken up. So your best bet was just to try to stay out of trouble, because that's the way things worked at that time, if you wanted to stay on the job.

TB: Yes, but, all things considered, it was considered to be a good job.

LM: Yes, and it was a good job. There were no layoffs. There was a steady paycheck every two weeks. It was the kind of job with which a man could make plans to buy a house and raise a family, but, Tim, when we blacks came on the force back then, we didn't come on this job looking for a career like the white boys did or even for any, say, promotions. We just came on just trying to get away from that "last to hire, first to fire" situation because, you know, that has always been the albatross around the black man's neck all of his life, and at least the police department and the post office offered some sort of security, and that's why most of us joined. Back then, if you were to talk to Rudy Nimocks, myself, Fred Rice, or George Sanders and ask, "What is your ambition by the time you retire from the police department?" our answers would have been, "We hope we would make detective—be out of uniform—before we retire," but the thought of becoming a lieutenant or a sergeant wasn't even in our thinking. It was just an impossible goal because there were too many political ties at that time, and blacks didn't have any voice in this town politically.

TB: And this was less than thirty-five years ago?

LM: Yes, you see, the real breakthrough for blacks didn't come until O. W. Wilson came in.

TB: Oh, yes. I liked him.

LM: Yes, I loved him. I loved him because most of us would not have made rank had it not been for him. He came here with a new kind of attitude.

TB: Well, that's when we were integrating Rainbow Beach.

LM: Yes, an incident early in my career happened there at Rainbow Beach. I have forgotten the exact date, but I have an article about it from the *Chicago Defender*. I was a patrol officer in the traffic division. Back then the traffic division's roll call was at three in the afternoon, and the district's roll call was at four. Well, we got a call about a disturbance at Rainbow Beach around three-thirty, and the only police officers on the street were traffic officers. All the regular police officers were coming off duty at the station, and those coming on duty hadn't gotten into their squad cars yet. So they sent all traffic cars out to Rainbow Beach. When I got out there, what I saw was that a black couple were entirely surrounded by a mob of angry white people.

TB: Oh, yes. Yes, that's right.

LM: Yes, and so they were really surprised when two or three of us black officers from the traffic division showed up in response to their call for help. Well, when I got out there and saw what was really happening—they were cursing at those black people and everything—and, well, I don't know, Tim, maybe I've always just been stubborn, but I said to myself, "If that's my job, I am going to do it." I can still remember right now that one of the spectators out there was taking pictures, and he said to me, "Say, nigger, come over here and get your black face in the picture," and so then I did something stupid, which I probably shouldn't have done. I ran into the crowd to get him, and I found that honky and brought him out of there, and when my colleagues saw me coming out with him, they opened the doors to the paddy wagon, and I tried to drive his head through that wall—because you did those sorts of things back then!

[*Laughter.*]

And when we came back to the station, the other police officers were just coming out of the station to relieve us, and they sent us on our way! But I have an article from the *Chicago Defender* recounting the incident, and the reporter said, "There was one arrest made that day by a Negro police officer by the name of LeRoy Martin."

[*Laughter.*]

TB: Yes, yes, we were out there during that same period at other incidents like that, and whenever we saw those black officers we felt much more comfortable because we knew that those black officers would do their job!

[*Laughter.*]

LM: But do you know where most of the black officers were during that time, Tim? Most of the black officers were out at Trumbull Park. Remember Trumbull Park was up in arms because they were moving blacks out there, and we had a permanent detail of police officers stationed out there. Actually what happened—with the exception of the black officers that worked in Wabash Avenue, Woodlawn, and Englewood—was they really didn't have that much for us to do in the other places. Some of us were in districts where they didn't have many blacks, and they didn't want us riding in the squad cars like the white people, but they had to try to find something for us to do, and so they sent a bunch of us out to Trumbull Park. Then they sent a bunch of us down into the subway. They were really just trying to find something for us to do to keep us out of doing real police work.

TB: Yes.

LM: You see, just a few guys were doing any kind of real police work—guys like Parson Simm, Sam Nolan. Sam, I think, was down in Gambling out at the commissioner's office. Sylvester Washington and those guys had all left by then. Guys out on Wabash were doing police work, but that was a black district. The rest of us—they just found things for us to do to keep us away from the station.

TB: But even so, so you were moving up now. You became a sergeant in 1965? Had you become a detective first?

LM: No, I didn't become a detective. Never wanted to become a detective, you know, because after Wilson came, things began to move for us. We began to get a little break, and so I made sergeant in 1965, and I spent most of my time in the youth division. Then in 1975 I made lieutenant.

TB: Tell me about your experiences in the youth division.

LM: We were handling juvenile offenders—you know, wayward kids getting themselves in trouble. These were kids that had committed crimes, but, you know, Tim, I'm very proud of one particular situation, a situation in which I had to be strong and in which I drew strength from examples of my colleagues over the years. I remember two black kids were in a vacant apartment, and someone called the police. When the police came, one kid ran in the closet and hid, and the other kid ran out the back door. Some officers had their guns out, and as they were walking through the flat, this kid bolted out of the closet, and a policeman shot him. Well, they caught the other kid, and he was unharmed. Now, juveniles are treated under a different statute than adults. Chapter Thirty-Eight is for adult criminals and Chapter Thirty-Seven is for children—juveniles. Well, they brought this juvenile to the old Fillmore Station and turned him over to the youth division—which was me. Now, the law says that once a child is turned over to the juvenile authorities, they are to act as a surrogate parent until that child is adjudicated. He is not to be handled by the regular police. So now the police were involved in a shooting, and the only witness was this kid, and so they came over from the detective division, and they wanted to take this kid back to the Maxwell Street Station to interrogate him about the shooting and clear the policeman. But I told them that they couldn't do that. Well, you know, they were white police officers, and they said, "You're supposed to be our brother . . ."

TB: In the same "fraternity" with them.

LM: Yes, in the same fraternity, and they said to me, "Turn this kid over to us so we can take him back over there and get a statement from him." And I said, "Well, by law I can't do that. When you had him, you should have kept him, but once you cross this threshold and turn him over to me, then he becomes mine and I can't let you have him back." Tim, about twenty minutes later, standing in the door was a chief. Now, a chief was the right hand of God when you're a sergeant down there in the trenches. Well, he came in and wanted to know who was the sergeant that was refusing to give up that kid. And I told him that I was. I said, "Chief, by law I can't turn him over. He was remanded to my custody." And so the chief said to me, "What if I give you an order?" And I said, "Well, look, you're the chief. I'm still a policeman. Now, if you want to give me an order and take him away from me, that way I'll release him, but I want you to know that I'm going to report it to downtown—that you came in and pulled rank on me, and took the kid." So he pulled rank on me and took the kid, and I reported it through downtown. You know, nothing ever happened to that kid, but I think back sometimes on the number of things I've done that could have eclipsed my career, and I guess somebody must watch over you. When you're doing right, you will prevail.

TB: Yes, when you go back and you think about Harness and those guys who laid some standards, you say to yourself, "What would Bob have done in this situation?"

LM: Yes, and then the answer is as clear as glass! In the long run, right always wins out. And you know what? I said that same thing to myself after I became superintendent of the police department, because twenty-five days after I got appointed Mayor Washington died.

TB: That's right.

LM: So then a new mayor was coming in, and anytime a new guy comes in he can bring his own superintendent with him. Well, Sawyer came in and he was there for a year and a half or so before he was defeated, and then in came Richard M. Daley!

TB: Yes.

LM: So again, I didn't know what my future was going to be. But you know, you think about those things, and I've thought about them, and I've also thought that one of these days I'm going to be an ex-policeman. I'm not always going to be a policeman—certainly not always going to be the superintendent—and the question I asked myself was, "Can you shave and look yourself in the face as the kind of man that you were, or are you going to be turned into some sort of lackey trying to keep a job?" And I said, "I'd rather be able to say I'm the ex-superintendent and didn't last but twenty-five days or didn't last but a year and a half, but I could shave in the morning and look myself in the face and say, 'Listen, you didn't become anybody's boy. You know, you were a man up to the end.'"

TB: Yes, that's so important. Now, when you got to be sergeant, you went to Fill-more?

LM: Yes. I went to Fillmore, and I stayed there about five years.

TB: Who was the commander there at that time?

LM: George Simms.

TB: George Simms—my wild friend!

[*Laughter.*]

And after five years you left there and became a lieutenant. What year was this?

LM: This was 1975. Simms was now deputy chief, but he was still on the West Side, so when I got the promotion I begged them to send me back to Fillmore. I liked working over there. They already had me scheduled on the West Side, but they sent me to Twenty-third and Damen, Marquette Station, and they didn't send me back over to Simms. So I worked over there at the Marquette Station until I got transferred downtown.

TB: What were you doing there?

LM: I became an inspector, and I stayed there about three years, and then I became a commanding officer in the detective division. I was a lieutenant then of the burglary division out at Fifty-first Street and Wentworth, up on the second floor. Richard Brzeczek was the superintendent then and Jane Byrne was the mayor, and I got promoted to commander and sent down to the narcotics section—a place that I never wanted to work—but I ended up commander of the section down there. And, you know, it worked out nicely working down there, and they kept me there a couple of years, and then they sent me out to the detective division at the new station out on 111th and Calumet Skyway. Then they promoted me to a deputy chief and sent me back to the West Side. They sent me back home because both he and I thought that this would be my last assignment, and I wanted to go back to the West Side. So, I stayed over there at Harrison and Kedzie for four years, and then I put in for the job of superintendent, and Harold Washington promoted me. Tim, I think that something that people should remember is that there have only been two black superintendents here in Chicago—Fred Rice and myself. Sam Nolan was the acting superintendent only.

TB: Yes, I remember.

LM: And the irony of the situation is that both of us were appointed by the same man—a black man. A black man had never been appointed superintendent of the police department before by a white man.

TB: Yes, yes, that is true.

LM: And I think that one of the greatest things that Harold Washington did was he gave so many younger blacks who had been trained in various skills an opportunity that they never would have had without him. The talent was there, but it was untapped talent.

TB: Yes, yes, I can see that. LeRoy, you have had somewhere around thirty-seven, thirty-eight years of service, and so you have a long view over time. Now, from your knowledge and experience, can you tell me what is police work really all about?

LM: Police work is basically just trying to contain the problems that occur in a geographical area, trying to make sure that the parts of the city that work continue to work, and in those parts that don't work trying to keep the level of violence down and under control. That's basically it, if you want to really boil it down. What police work does, all over the nation, is to try to protect the city's economic interests. Fred Rice and I were probably luckier than any other superintendents that ever have sat in that chair, and when I say "luckier," I mean we were fortunate to work for mayors that gave us latitude to try to do our jobs right. Now, O. W. Wilson had the latitude also, but that's because he came in on the heels of scandal.

TB: Yes, he did. It's people like that who set the example.

LM: That's right.

TB: But do the officer and his superiors see their jobs as part of a total community that has to be protected but also has to be respected? That must be a pretty sensitive balance to maintain.

LM: It is. That's a very tough order because the black community, traditionally, has been underemployed, and unemployed to a larger extent than any other part of the city, and, sociologically, we know that poverty breeds crime. We have had our share of crime in the black community, and the good people in that community are constantly asking the police or the system to protect them, but the justice system has not been very just to the black criminal, particularly in regards to trying to rehabilitate him or do something for him, other than just contain him. For too long a time, the black police officers were just used to contain the black community, not to help it, but just to contain it, and, as a result, unfortunately, too many black police officers saw opportunities for their careers to be advanced through victimizing their own people.

TB: Yes.

LM: And so the police department has not been as helpful in the black community as it could have been or even *should* have been, because it has been manipulated by the white power structure, and we didn't have any real power within that structure. So those officers on the lower rung, for the most part, were always trying to do what they thought the upper ranks wanted them to do, and that was to victimize their own people. And so we never got the kind of policemen that we really deserved— that were as helpful, you know, as they were in other neighborhoods. For example, in a white neighborhood they may know the police officer as a neighbor who *happens* to be a police officer, but, Tim, in our communities the policeman has been looked upon as being an oppressor. The police have never been liked in the black community because of the way that law enforcement was used for so many years.

TB: Yes, and that's the reason Harold Washington was such an important person in making appointments, because when Fred Rice was picked, there was a sigh of relief among a lot of black folk about the possibility of improvement in the delivery of justice.

LM: Yes.

TB: We just felt that some improvement might happen—at least symbolically—and the same thing happened when you were made superintendent. Symbolically, there was a more comfortable feeling and at this point in history—the law enforcement agencies being as important as they are to the welfare of a community—it's important that people begin to feel comfortable with them.

LM: Well, during the Washington years—and, I hope, during the time I was superintendent—ranking black officers had the feeling that they could go out and really be good police officers and not have to worry about retaliation from downtown because the way it used to be, downtown would say, "You're not keeping those people in line," and when they said "those people," they meant "those *black* people in line," and so that's what the black policeman thought his job was under the *white* administration—to keep those of us in the black community in line.

TB: Yes, yes.

LM: But, like I said, that wasn't Rice's or my motivation, because both of us knew that once our careers were over we were coming back here to live in the black community.

[*Laughter.*]

You know we weren't going to be downtown permanently. That was just temporary, and we wanted our conduct to be such that we'd be welcomed back home and respected.

TB: Yes, that's certainly true. Now, what is your work with the Chicago Housing Authority like, LeRoy, and how long have you been here?

LM: Tim, I've been here at the CHA about fifteen months now. I started here the day after I retired from the Chicago Police Department.

TB: How big is this assignment?

LM: Well, in this assignment I have approximately eleven hundred officers, including some contracted police offices from private security agencies, and I have over six hundred of my own officers working here at the CHA.

TB: Are they from the Chicago Police Department?

LM: Three hundred of the officers here were trained by the Chicago Police Department, and we have some officers who have retired from the Chicago Police Department, but the majority of them are officers who were trained by the Chicago Police Department in the Police Academy.

TB: And you have enforcement powers?

LM: Yes, we have the same powers as the Chicago Police Department. The only difference is that our officers work primarily here on CHA's property. The problem we had with the Chicago Police Department was that when we did have police officers working here, they would always apply for transfers, so we were in a constant state of flux and transition with no lasting stability.

TB: But now you've got a stable force.

LM: Now I've got a stable force of trained police officers and security officers—both men and women.

TB: And both black and white?

LM: Well, some white and some Hispanic, but primarily black.

TB: Most of your clients are black?

LM: That's correct. We're trying to do something about the crime within public housing, and I believe that one of the tinderboxes within the city of Chicago is public housing, because you have poor people living right on top of other poor people. So many have lost hope, and when a person loses hope or loses a dream, he becomes dangerous because he doesn't feel that he has anything to lose, and many of our young people over here feel just exactly that way. Hopefully, we can do something not only to stem the crime but also to set a positive example by our presence here. I took this on certainly not for money, because the city was generous enough to give me a good pension, but this is one of the few challenges that I've ever had where my own people were involved, and in which I have an opportunity to serve my own people almost exclusively as a trained police professional. I like it and I really look upon it almost as a gift—to have the opportunity to be in this situation and to serve, because so many times we, as black people, never get the services of the kind of professional person that we need and deserve. You know, the talented person is usually sent somewhere else, to another community, and we get the castoffs.

TB: Yes, that's often too true. I know when I was at Wright some of my former students said, "Mr. Black, what are you doing over there with all of those white folks when we need you over here?" I felt so bad—

[*Laughter.*]

—that I wound up coming back home where I would be much more useful, because if we don't do it who's going to do it?

LM: Exactly. Too many of us really don't feel an obligation to the black community, and we sort of defect from our communities and from making a contribution, but the real challenge is to make that contribution from downtown—or wherever we are.

TB: What are the major problems in a public housing concentration of this kind?

LM: The major problem that you have here is young people trying to earn money to buy material things through the selling of narcotics. That's our main problem over here, and what people don't understand or don't *want* to understand is this. You often hear people speaking about offering the young people an alternative. Well, now, I don't know what alternative there is for money in the materialistic society we have here in America today, and that materialism has filtered down to the least of us. It's ridiculous to rashly tell a young man out there to put that dope bag down because it's "wrong." He knew it was wrong when he picked it up. He will ask you, "Well, how can I buy the Michael Jordan shoes?" Or, "How can I get those gold chains? How can I get that automobile? And how can I get a pretty girl to go with the automobile?" The way our society's structured, you can only get that through acquiring money. You see, society has to realize what it has done to people to put them in this frame of mind. Today we're into the fast everything—the instant everything. The instant meal, the drive-in restaurants. And kids not only want fast food, they want fast money—they want fast wealth. The hardest challenge is trying to convince a young person like that to put all of his gratification off till he has finished school four or five years from now—to convince him that he'll get what he wants, but that he'll have to wait. Trying to get them in the frame of mind that "I'm willing to go to school, and I'm willing to wait five years before I get this" is really very difficult. Society thinks it can cure a lack of money with a basketball hoop or a baseball game, but when that kid gets through with all of those activities, he's still without the things that this society has told him he needs.

TB: It's more than what "he needs"—it's what he *has* to have in order to appear as a successful human being.

LM: Right, and you know, Tim, if you sit down and watch television you see so much wealth in those programs—the big limousines, the big fancy hotels, pretty people dressed nicely drinking champagne.

TB: Having fun.

LM: Yes, having fun, and the "fun" in this country has been equated with money. You can't have "fun" unless you've got money—so how can we be surprised at their behavior? The problem is, how can we deprogram these kids?

TB: Yes, particularly when so much that could correct that attitude is not available for many of these kids—like good schools.

LM: Yes.

TB: The schools are sympathetic to all of the things you were just talking about, and so they can say, "Listen, you're going to get all of that, and you're to have it for the rest of your life, but now you've got to wait a little while longer"—and meanwhile they can try to develop within them that necessary feeling of internal satisfaction. Even so, other factors complicate the situation. For example, approximately what percentage of families are single-parent families in your jurisdiction?

LM: Well, I would say a good 70 to 75 percent of our residents are single-parent families which are headed by females.

TB: And how many receive some form of governmental assistance?

LM: About 90 percent.

TB: So you have a concentration of poverty, a concentration of single-parent households, and institutions that are not able to deal with this problem in an acceptable fashion—that is, the religious, the educational, and the economic institutions—which means, then, that institutions that deal with criminal behavior have to take up the slack in many, many ways.

LM: Yes, society has undercut the support systems that used to exist to keep a family on track and to keep the young people on track. Unfortunately, in our society, when we in law enforcement started to run into budget problems, they started to cut services out of places where they would get the least amount of resistance, and the least amount of resistance that they receive is from poor people.

TB: Yes, because poor people are not organized, and they don't have time or resources to *get* organized.

LM: Yes, what have they done? They've cut the social workers. They've cut the truant officers out of the schools. They've cut probation officers out of the lives of those people who are being released from institutions and who now have nobody to help guide them or keep them on the right track. And these cuts are all in the poor neighborhoods. That's where they've cut teachers. Class sizes are larger now when, in fact, they should be smaller because they've got problem children who need more attention, not less. But, you see, these are all the places that society can cut, and it doesn't meet the same resistance that they would meet if they went into an organized community and tried to make these same kind of cuts.

TB: Yes, it makes a whole lot of difference. You were saying, when we first started talking, when you first went on the force there were something like sixteen thousand policemen?

LM: Yes, sixteen thousand policemen.

TB: The city was a bit larger then—maybe three million five, but now it's down to, what?

LM: Well, about three million, and now we're down to twelve thousand five hundred police officers.

TB: So that's a substantial reduction combined with an increase in problems, and now, as a result, the individual policeman has more work to do.

LM: He certainly has more work to do than he did back in my day.

TB: And the guy who is doing wrong has more skills!

LM: Far more!

[*Laughter.*]

TB: And in a concentration like this how many of these parents are still very young?

LM: Oh, the overwhelming majority, I would say. Around 80 percent of the parents here are under twenty-three years of age, and they have, on an average, two or three children. So by cutting out the social services, most of these youngsters have never been trained in parenting, you see. They started their families while they were still teenagers, while they still should have been in high school, so they never acquired the parenting skills.

TB: In some cases you have as many as three generations living here.

LM: Oh, there are a lot of three-generation families here and even a few four-generation families. There are a lot of grandmothers, daughters, and grand-daughters living here. We have great-grandmothers who are living here who are still in their forties! You know, that comes to me as a revelation! We think of people that are great-grandparents as being, you know, in their late sixties and seventies. But we have people here in their late forties that are great-grandmothers!

TB: Would it make sense to disperse this population?

LM: It would make sense to disperse it to some extent, because I think an established community taking in a number of inner-city residents could socialize them to conform to their own community's standards. But it may be hard because I do believe that violence has become normal for so many of these young kids. When you grow up with anything, that is what becomes the norm. The shootings and the abuse, the battery of young children by boyfriends seems normal to them because they have so much of it. But, if some of these people were moved into other communities, they would see a different light, and many of them would probably learn to conform to those other standards.

TB: Community pressure would make them change, because it's community pressure that makes them do what they do now.

LM: Exactly. Exactly.

TB: I'm told that when a girl gets to be fourteen or fifteen and she doesn't have a baby, she—

LM: She is almost ostracized, so that becomes the norm here—to have a baby at fourteen.

TB: And so dispersal might help.

LM: Yes, this kind of concentration isn't doing any good.

TB: Yes, but we know why the housing project was built like this. It was built to contain and control, at least partially for political reasons, a large bloc of black voters so that they would be available whenever they were needed.

LM: Yes, but it was built mainly to keep the blacks from going west—particularly into Bridgeport.

TB: Yes, yes. Or east into Hyde Park!

[*Laughter.*]

So, "liberals" are not so liberal when you get ready to act and really start to change things!

[*Laughter.*]

When Dr. King was in town, he said, "Let's start with our friends. Let's go to the North Shore suburbs." But those people who had been giving King all of that money said no.

LM: Yes.

TB: So, to solve a problem like this you're going to need a lot of help.

LM: Yes, they need a lot of help here—and not just police help. Trying to contain or suppress people into not committing crimes is only a short-term answer. You see, the long-term answer is to teach a better way of life and try to get these young people into something meaningful—then you won't need all the policemen.

TB: They become their own policemen.

LM: Yes, you see, a guy who's working doesn't have to steal, and African-Americans are not criminals by nature.

TB: No.

LM: But we've been put into this situation almost by necessity. Tim, both you and I remember when Policy was an underground economy in the black community, but had it not been for Policy—and as an ex-police officer I don't want to ever give a criminal credit for anything!—but a lot of people would have starved had it not been for Policy.

TB: Yes, it brought in a lot of jobs on the South Side and on the West Side as well.

LM: Yes, it was a way of pumping money into the economy.

TB: Big Jim Martin was a big man on the West Side, and the Jones brothers—

LM: They were on the South Side.

TB: And they were not forcing anybody to play the game.

LM: But they fed a lot of families because it was the Depression, and, as you and I both know, if white people were out of work, the black man would be even worse off. An unfortunate parallel to that situation is the fact that narcotics has become an underground economy in our own time.

TB: Yes, but one more important thing needs to be mentioned. When we were growing up, we had the strength of the community and our extended family was always close by, and now most of that no longer exists.

LM: Yes, that sort of network of support no longer exists.

TB: And also the immediate family was closer then.

LM: Much closer. And, you know, poor as people were back then—

TB: It wasn't just a matter of money.

LM: Right. See, everybody came home to have dinner at the same time. Even though we were poor, Daddy always sat at the head of the table, and the kids sat around, and we all had dinner together and shared some experiences at that time.

TB: We talked with each other.

LM: Yes, and today even our middle-class families are having problems with their children, and part of that is because Daddy's working two jobs and Mama's working two jobs. Almost everybody in the family eats at a different time, and when they're not eating, they're in different parts of the house watching television or doing different things, so even when the family is together in the same structure, the family isn't *really* together. Like the fellow down here that's dealing dope and chasing his dreams, the middle-class guy's chasing a dream too, but he's doing it with two jobs, and it takes him away from things that he should be attending to that he's not attending to. So now we have problems even in that type of situation.

TB: The malaise that we see in low-rental housing is a heightened, dramatic reflection of what's happening in the total society, in the larger society. There's a difference in intensity but not really any big difference in kind.

LM: Exactly, Tim.

TB: The larger society does act in a more subtle way, but *maybe* the guy who steals five million dollars from the stock market, maybe he is responsible for taking more lives than the guy that takes money violently on the street, but we look at that other guy differently, and we only call one of them a thief.

LM: Yes, that's the way it's been.

TB: LeRoy, it's been such a great pleasure talking to you. Thank you so much for your insight into these problems.

LM: It's been my pleasure, Tim.

June 30, 1993

JUDGE EARL STRAYHORN

—

ILLINOIS COUNTY COURT JUDGE

It's hard for me unless I am in a rather formal situation to address Earl Strayhorn as "Judge." You see, we have known each other as friends since 1927, when we were in the fourth grade together at Edmund Burke School on the South Side of Chicago. He went to summer school at the end of the regular school year, and that's when he got ahead of me by a half year, and he has kept that same lead ever since!

Earl and my late brother, Walter K. Black, went to Tilden Technical High School together, and then both of them went on scholarships to the University of Illinois at Urbana-Champaign, where they and the other few black students (fewer than one hundred out of a total enrollment of more than ten thousand) had to deal with the racism which existed at that time on all levels, both on campus and in the town. A person like Earl Strayhorn is a shining example of the efforts that were made and the level of success that was achieved by young black men of that generation despite the many obstacles, academic as well as social.

Like most of his black contemporaries at the University of Illinois, Earl became a member of the United States Army during World War II. Because of their academic successes, most of these young men became officers and were assigned to combat units in Europe and the Far East. Although they were fighting "to make the world safe for democracy," they discovered they had to deal on a daily basis with internal forms of racism.

After the war, Earl Strayhorn went to DePaul Law School, and, after graduating from there, he was appointed as an assistant to the State's Attorney's Office. After that, he went into private practice, and then he launched his successful campaign to become a judge. In that capacity he has had a long and distinguished career, and it is only in recent years that he has retired from public service.

Before going into the army, Earl had married, and he and his wife, Lygia, have two children, both of whom have now had successful careers. I am very proud to be able to call Judge Strayhorn "Earl" because he continues to be my friend.

———

TB: Where were you born, Judge?

ES: I was born in Columbus, Mississippi, on April 24, 1918, and my folks brought me up to Chicago in 1924 when I was six years old. My first home was on Thirty-fifth Street. I stayed there one year, and then we moved to Fiftieth and Prairie, and I entered Burke School, which was at Fifty-fourth and what was then South Park Way. My family consisted of my mother, my father, and my younger brother, who was also born in Mississippi. He was three years old when we came to Chicago. He later also went to Burke School.

TB: What was the racial composition of the school at that time?

ES: It was mixed. We had white children who were children of the custodians and the people that took care of the buildings that were owned by white people. And then there were children of merchants in the neighborhood. Almost 99 percent of the merchants were white and that 99 percent of them lived right there in the neighborhood.

TB: They were mostly Jewish, I imagine.

ES: They were a mixture.

TB: I see. And at the school itself were all the teachers white?

ES: Yes, all white. I never had a black teacher in elementary school or in high school.

TB: Yes, and it was very unlikely that you had one in college. So your entire educational experience came from dedicated teachers that happened to be white.

ES: Yes, that's true.

TB: What was the educational experience like at Burke School?

ES: It was no nonsense. The school was definitely in control. The students were there from families that supported the educational process and who were available to the teachers for any kind of disciplinary problems that the children exhibited, which were few and far between. They were mostly just mischievous, that's all. But, in so far as *disrupting* the process, we didn't have any of that. We didn't have any kids in there that were so big a problem that the teachers had to take substantial time out of their teaching day to be disciplinarians. All the teacher said was, "All right, class quiet." And then you could hear a pin drop.

TB: About how many students were there to a class?

ES: Oh, I would say that the class load was twenty-five to thirty or maybe less. In those days I wasn't, you know, really interested in knowing what the class size was, so I'm just guessing.

TB: Who were some of the teachers you remember?

ES: Well, I remember Clarence Schrock.

TB: Clarence Schrock: "B-U-R-K-E . . ."

ES: Yes, he wrote that song, and I can still remember it! And I remember Miss Holman, Miss Hornsby, and Miss Kelly. Miss Kelly was a *great* big woman with a big bust and real slender legs, and we gave her the nickname of "City Hall on Sticks"! Miss Murphy and Miss Mullin were young teachers.

TB: Where did the teachers live?

ES: I don't recall any of the teachers living in the immediate community.

TB: My impressions were that they didn't live very far away from the school. So the atmosphere of the school was one of learning. Do you remember any of the students that went to Burke that became somewhat outstanding later?

ES: Harold Murray became a chemist.

TB: Do you remember Charles White? The artist?

ES: Sure, I remember Charles White. Charles White went to Tilden Technical High School with me. I remember Carl Cotton. He became a taxidermist at the Field Museum. I remember Anita . . .

TB: Macabee?

ES: Yes, Macabee. She was the belle of the class!

[*Laughter.*]

TB: Now, in terms of that immediate neighborhood, how far south did blacks live by this time?

ES: Well, there were a lot of blacks in Carter School over on Michigan, and so blacks had gotten down as far as Sixty-first Street, I'm sure.

TB: Yes. Now, when did you graduate from Burke?

ES: I graduated in January of 1932.

TB: That was a period when there were graduations twice a year?

ES: Yes, but our class did not have a formal graduation exercise because we were so bad and mischievous! We defied Miss Kelly and Mr. Schrock, and they told us if we didn't straighten up our act we weren't going to get to participate in the graduation exercises. We would have eraser fights when Miss Kelly was out of the room, and then when she'd come back, the room would be up for grabs! So, as a consequence, we did not have a formal graduation. We were given our diplomas seated in our room!

[*Laughter.*]

TB: After you left Burke, you went to Tilden Technical High School. What was Tilden like then?

ES: Well, this was before DuSable was built, because when I went to Tilden, they were just building DuSable. In fact, we used to walk through the construction site there where DuSable was being built. As we walked to Tilden, we'd go from Fiftieth Street and Prairie down Fiftieth over to State and down State to Forty-seventh, and then we'd walk down Forty-seventh to Forty-eighth and Union. We would walk in order to save the three cents carfare so that we could use that money to buy us a bread and gravy lunch at Tilden!

TB: You walked from Fiftieth Street? You're talking about two miles!

ES: Yes, that's right.

TB: Who would do this walk with you?

ES: Wilbur and Harold Murray, and all of those boys in the neighborhood that went to Tilden, because Tilden was an all-boys school at that time.

TB: So all of the boys in the neighborhood went to Tilden?

ES: No, not all of the boys, just some of the boys. You had to have a certain grade point average in order to get admitted to Tilden at that time.

TB: I take it that at that time Tilden was a college prep school.

ES: Yes, I guess so.

TB: It seems to me they were preparing students for college-level technical and engineering programs.

ES: There were only three technical high schools in the city then. There were no vocational high schools. They had Tilden, Lindblom, and Lane—those were the only three.

TB: That's right, and they were all-boys schools.

ES: Yes, all boys, and Lucy Flower School in Garfield Park was an all-girls school.

TB: So you walked to school. What was it like going through a neighborhood that was not black?

ES: We didn't have any problems, really, until we got past the railroad tracks on Forty-seventh Street.

TB: That's the old Rock Island Railroad tracks, isn't it?

ES: Yes, and then when our family moved to Fifty-second Street and Michigan, our route was Fifty-second and Michigan, then down Fifty-first Street to Wallace, which was the end of the railroad tracks, and then on down along the railroad tracks to school. The railroad tracks were the buffer, so we didn't have any problems until we got out from under the railroad tracks, but then we'd have to fight from Fifty-first Street all the way back down to Forty-eighth Street to school! But the fighting was just fending off rocks and snowballs. There were no weapons.

TB: Or if somebody caused a fistfight.

ES: Or a fistfight—right!

TB: What kind of work did your dad do?

ES: My father worked at the Pullman Company in the paint department. He got lead poisoning when the lead built up in his system, and that threw him out on disability. He had worked there so long that they had to retire him on pension. He was only forty-seven years old or so. I was a sophomore in college at the time.

TB: Is that right? And did your mother work?

ES: Yes, my mother worked as a clerk at Consumer's Grocery Store, and when Consumer's was bought by the Kroger Company, it became Kroger-Consumer's. It was a corporate chain, like Jewel is today.

TB: Returning to your experiences at Tilden, how many black students were at Tilden at that time?

ES: Oh, there couldn't have been more than fifty.

TB: Out of how many?

ES: There were probably about five thousand students in all.

TB: Do you remember any of them?

ES: I remember the Springs brothers: Caleb and Henry. Caleb became a scientist, and when he retired, he was working at the University of Chicago nuclear processing facility. And Henry became a district superintendent here in the Chicago public school system.

TB: Henry, as I remember, coached some pretty famous track stars when he was at Wendell Phillips High School.

ES: Yes, he did.

TB: Now, didn't Ralph Metcalfe [a star of the 1936 Olympics] precede you at Tilden?

ES: Yes, he graduated a year before I got there.

TB: Well, what was your own experience like at Tilden?

ES: The black students and white students coexisted. We had some good friends who were white students there, and the other white students didn't really bother us. Once we got to school, you see, it was a safe haven. We might have to fight to get to school, but once we got in, there weren't big fights going on or anything like that.

TB: And how were the teachers?

ES: The teachers? Well, you do their work, and you got your grade. Although we did have a couple of teachers that didn't want us to be fully assimilated. Do you remember John Fewkes?

TB: Yes, he later became president of the teachers' union.

ES: Right. Well, he taught swimming at Tilden, and he did his damnedest to keep it segregated and keep the blacks out of the swimming pool. But we always managed to get in to do our swimming, which we had to do in order to graduate! But no black could try out for the swimming team. And in later years, when he became involved in the teachers' union and became prominent and I became prominent in politics here, he used to introduce me at events as being one of his "boys"—he was so proud of the achievements that I had made!

[*Laughter.*]

And I would laugh to myself because he hadn't helped me through a *damned* thing at Tilden! As a matter of fact, he had been one of the blackest marks in my existence there. He was a *stone* racist.

TB: Did you know Julian Dawson, whose uncle later became the Congressman William Levi Dawson?

ES: Yes, I did.

TB: And you got to know him rather well!

ES: Right!

[*Laughter.*]

TB: Well, now, you graduated from Tilden in 1936?

ES: Yes, I wanted to go to the University of Wisconsin, but I couldn't raise the money to pay the out-of-state tuition, which they required, and so I ended up going down to the University of Illinois at Urbana-Champaign, where the tuition was thirty-five dollars a semester!

[*Laughter.*]

I could pay that! And when I got down to Champaign, Tim, your brother, Walter Black, got me a job which took care of all of my meals—waiting tables at one of the white fraternity houses, Kappa Sigma. And I kept that job for four years. All I had to do was pay for my room at the Kappa house—after I moved into the Kappa house. During my first semester, I lived off campus in a private home.

TB: Now, this was in 1936. You were out of school for a while, weren't you?

ES: No, I wasn't just "out." I flunked out of my first semester because I wouldn't go to class, I wouldn't study, and I caroused all night!

[*Laughter.*]

TB: It was your first time away from home, wasn't it?

ES: Yes, my first time away from home! And at the end of the semester, I didn't pass one course—not even PE! The only course I passed was a two-hour hygiene course, and so they kicked my butt out! They sent me home! But they finally let me back the following September on a straight C probation. It took me four years after that to bring my grade point average up to a C, because I had gotten all those failing grades that first semester!

TB: Earl, how many black students were at the University of Illinois at that time?

ES: I would say about one hundred.

TB: Out of a population of how many students?

ES: Probably ten thousand.

TB: One hundred black students—both male and female?

ES: Yes, and we all knew one another. I met my future wife, Lygia, down there.

TB: Is that right?

ES: Yes, but she didn't come down as a freshman until I was a junior.

TB: You were in ROTC at the University of Illinois, weren't you?

ES: Illinois is a land-grant college, and so it was mandatory that every male student take two years of military training. So I did my two years, and then that was it. I wasn't concerned about the military at that point. I didn't become concerned about the military until after I had graduated in June of 1941, because at that time the brand new Selective Service Act was in effect, and so I had to register to go in for my year's duty. The Selective Service Act was enacted October 14, 1940, requiring all able-bodied American men aged eighteen years or over to register and serve one year in the United States military. At that time Mussolini, Hitler, and Tojo were spreading their seeds of hate and distrust across the world, and war was imminent.

TB: Had the Germans already attacked Poland?

ES: Yes, they attacked Poland in 1939, and they were just taking over Europe. France and England were procrastinating and Chamberlain had done his fold-up and let Hitler take over Poland.

TB: And Czechoslovakia.

ES: Yes, and Czechoslovakia.

TB: When did you get drafted?

ES: I got drafted on October 14, 1941, and I was married two months earlier. I had married on August 17 of 1941, less than a year after the enactment of the Selective Service Act, and just two or three months after my graduation from college, and then I went into the army to do my one year of service.

TB: And then came Pearl Harbor on December 7, 1941!

ES: Yes, and I had been in the service almost two months at that time down at Tuskegee air force base in Alabama. I was a guard—on top of the guard tower—and the sergeant came up and said, "The Japanese have just bombed Pearl Harbor." And I said, "Where's Pearl Harbor?" I didn't even know where it was! And, well, that kept me in for another five and a half years.

TB: So you were at Tuskegee?

ES: Yes.

TB: The Tuskegee Airmen were just beginning to develop at this time.

ES: Right, right, the War Department had put that unit together in response to black pressure to have black men that were in the air force up in the air. It was a segregated outfit, and I was down there as an enlisted man. I was the first sergeant of the Military Police unit on the base.

TB: You received several promotions, didn't you?

ES: Well, I went into the army as a private, and when I came off of active duty, I was a first lieutenant in the artillery. I had served in the ETO [European theater of operations] in the Italian campaign in the Ninety-second Division artillery under Mark Clark, who then headed the Fifth Army.

TB: When D Day came, where were you?

ES: When D Day came on June the sixth, 1944, I was in the middle of the Atlantic Ocean in a convoy on my way to Italy.

TB: And then when VE Day came, where were you?

ES: When VE Day came, I was in Italy somewhere just north of Milan. When we got there, we never retreated—we kept on advancing. Our unit had a very important function because we had the big guns that anchored the Fifth Army line.

TB: Among the black soldiers that you observed or had the responsibility of commanding, how was the morale?

ES: Well, being an artillery unit, we were generally at least two or three miles behind the actual front line. We were the support division, and the morale in our unit was always sky-high! We never had any morale problems at all. Our guys were good. They knew they were good, and they were well instructed and well led, so morale was not ever a problem for us.

TB: Because it was a well-coordinated, well-disciplined operation.

ES: Then, after VE Day, we were supposed to be transported back west through the Panama Canal to a staging area somewhere near Guadalcanal to prepare for what was going to be an attack on the island of Japan. But before we loaded onto the ship, the atomic bomb was dropped, and VJ Day came about, and that changed the plans for our going to the South Pacific, and we were then routed back to the United States to be discharged.

TB: When you came back, where did you go to live?

ES: I was living at 6737 South St. Lawrence Avenue.

TB: And so now you're out of the army—a long, grueling experience—and you've spent almost all of your previous life in school preparing for professional life, but you haven't started that yet because the army intervened.

ES: I call it now "a European vacation courtesy of Adolf Hitler."

TB: That's a humorous way to put it, to say the least, given what I saw at Buchenwald.

ES: While you were in the service, you were always thinking about what you'd do if you came out alive, so the plans that had solidified in my mind were to go to law school when I got back, and these plans were helped on, by the way, by the many, many night conversations that I had with Cyrus Colter. At that time Cyrus was already a lawyer, and it was Cyrus who really convinced me that I should go to law school.

TB: How did you meet him?

ES: Cyrus was part of my unit, and he was always pushing me to go into law school, and so my mind was set! It was so set that even before getting back to the United States, I had already filed applications with the University of Chicago, DePaul, and John Marshall, all of which were here in Chicago, for entry to their law schools. I was turned down by the University of Chicago and accepted by DePaul, and so that's where I decided I was going to go. At that time DePaul's law school was located at 64 East Lake Street, and I was a member of the first postwar class.

TB: You certainly didn't waste any time!

ES: No, the GI Bill was in effect at that time, so my tuition and books were paid for by the government, plus I got a monthly stipend which wasn't enough for me and my family, and so, therefore, I had to work as well as go to school. I began by working at the post office at the main branch, down at Van Buren and Canal Street, and I worked there after my classes from four o'clock in the afternoon until nine at night.

TB: That's what they called "short hours."

ES: Yes, but that job didn't make me enough money, so I went over to the Illinois Central Railroad station as a redcap. This was where I had already worked while I was in college, and I made much more money as a redcap than I did with "short hours" at the post office.

TB: So when did you graduate from law school?

ES: Well, when my class entered law school, we told our dean that since our class was composed of 99 percent returning veterans, we felt that we didn't have any time to waste, so we told him we didn't want any vacation time at all! We wanted to go straight through and go on out and pass the bar and get to work—and, in that way, by not taking any vacations, we did what would normally take three years in just two years.

TB: You cut it by an entire year!

ES: Yes, we cut it by a year! And I graduated in 1948. By then, my first child, Earl, had died, and I had another boy, Donald, and then my daughter, Earlene.

TB: At this time was your wife working?

ES: No, we made do with the stipend I was getting from the government and the money I was making doing the redcapping.

TB: So, now, you've graduated from law school. What did you do then?

ES: I graduated in June of 1948, and I took the bar exam shortly after graduation, and while I was waiting for receipt of my exam results, I went back to working full-time as a redcap.

TB: The redcap is the person who picks up the baggage, brings it back—

ES: Loads it on the train, takes it off—

TB: And then is at the mercy of the public giving some kind of money in return for the services rendered.

ES: Yes, except the funny thing is that the company found out that we were making so much money that they decided that they were going to get in on a good thing, so they began to take a percentage of what we made by making us pay them twenty-five cents a bag for every bag we handled!

[*Laughter.*]

TB: And for years there had been guys that, well, raised their families—

ES: And bought property, sent their kids to school, and they did it by being redcaps. A fine, fine group of men!

TB: So being a redcap for many of you was—

ES: A transition. A bridge!

TB: So when did you pass the bar, Earl?

ES: Back in those days, if you passed, the bar examiners, when they notified the successful applicant that he had passed, would include with their letter all the forms that had to be filled out and returned for the process to be completed. Each applicant had to get six people to write letters of recommendation—three from lawyers and three from nonlawyers—plus a lot of other personal information. So it turned out, if you passed, the notification would come in a pretty thick envelope and have extra postage on it. But, if you flunked, it would just come in a small-sized envelope with the regular postage, so I told my wife if I got a real thick envelope from the Board of Bar Examiners that would mean I passed, and she should call me at work, but if I got a thin envelope with just regular postage, don't bother calling!

[*Laughter.*]

So one day I was at work, and I was down on the platform meeting a train called the Wolverine that traveled between Chicago and Detroit, and I had told all the other redcaps that it was about time for the bar exam results to come out "so if my wife calls me, you let me know just as soon as she calls because she's going to call me if I pass," and then she called! She left the message with the guy out in front who was meeting all the cabs, and he sent her message down to the platform by word of mouth—"Earl passed the bar exam!" "Earl passed the bar exam!"—and finally it got all the way down to me on the platform where I was loading that Wolverine train. All of them, those men, they were as interested in my welfare as much as their own, and my passing the bar meant almost as much to them as it did to me.

They were so proud of me, and I was proud of myself too. I passed on the first try!

TB: At that time how many black lawyers were there here in the city?

ES: Less than one hundred.

TB: Out of about how many lawyers?

ES: Out of at least twelve or thirteen thousand.

TB: And all the way along, you had not only that kind of support but also that kind of expectation.

ES: Yes, you weren't looked upon with favor if you just did enough to get by. Your family, the people in the neighborhood, your friends, your church people, they all expected you to succeed at the upper level. The people in my neighborhood, they didn't have any opportunity to go to college down there in the South where most of them were from. So, when I was one of the people in our neighborhood that went to college, they expected me to do more than well. They expected me to excel!

TB: And they shared your success.

ES: Hey, of course, they shared my success, and they gave all of us a boost because we knew they'd kick us in our butt if we didn't succeed! And not just our folks—our parents and our families—but the people in the neighborhood as well. Even the old ladies would say, "Oh, you can do much better than that!" And you know that old lady who used to kick my butt when she saw me doing something in the neighborhood before my mama or papa got home? Well, that same old lady did the same thing when I grew older and went on to college!

TB: You were a part of her extended family.

ES: And she was part of mine, so I had to answer to all of these people.

TB: It seems you'd got yourself into a trap. You couldn't escape.

ES: No excuses!

TB: No excuses, no escape!

ES: No excuse—except: "You dead, boy!" That's the only acceptable excuse—you die!

[*Laughter.*]

TB: So, when you got the good news that you'd passed the bar, what happens then?

ES: I was sworn in down in Springfield on the twenty-first of June in 1948.

TB: Just two years after leaving the service!

ES: Well, two years and a little more had passed by then.

TB: So, you passed the bar and are sworn in. What happens next?

ES: Then came the step of trying to get a job, and at that time we didn't have any black law firms, but we did have black lawyers, and I wanted to work with Euclid Taylor.

TB: Who was he?

ES: Euclid Taylor was one of the most prominent black criminal lawyers in Chicago at that time, and I wanted to work in his office, and so I set up a daily vigil there in his office trying to get an appointment with him to see if I couldn't get a job.

TB: Where was his office located?

ES: He was located then where he was when he died over there at 188 West Randolph Street. He was one of the few black lawyers that was located downtown, and I think he was able to get downtown only because one of his partners who shared the space with him happened to look like a white man. But, anyhow, I kept on going down there and sitting for hours and hours on end, and he never came in, so after six days of experiences like this, I decided, "Well, the hell with it! I can't wait any longer," so instead I became associated with an old lawyer whom many at this point might consider a "rabble-rouser" because he had filed a suit against the city of Chicago representing a black person for discriminatory action that was done by a governmental agency, and he had won! His name was A. W. Williams, and he had his offices over there in the basement of his home at 3646 South Michigan Avenue, and he gave me a job of sorts. He would give me a stipend for handling some of his work, and I would get a percentage of whatever his fee was, and he also gave me an office to practice out of. Now, you've got to understand—a new lawyer in those days was of no benefit to anyone because he doesn't yet know his way around the courthouse. What's more, you don't even have any clients outside the members of your own family, and, of course, you can't charge them, so I was suffering from that "new lawyer syndrome" until I went in with Mr. Williams in July of 1948, and I was lucky because 1948 was a national election year!

TB: That was the Dewey-Truman year.

ES: And, on a local level, included in this election was the race for county state's attorney, and the Democratic candidate for this office was a man named John S. Boyle. One of the committees that he formed was a veterans' committee, and that particular committee happened to be chaired by a classmate of mine from DePaul, Denny O'Hara, and you know, one of the things that happened to us in law school was that, being returned veterans, we were a little older and more sophisticated than most, and for us race was not a consideration at all.

TB: Within the framework of the legal profession?

ES: No, within the framework of interpersonal relations. In that area race was of no consideration in my class.

TB: How big was your class?

ES: Oh, we had about eighty-eight.

TB: And how many of those were black?

ES: Only four, but for us race was no problem at all. We studied together. We worked together. We cried together. We cussed together. We drank together. All that we were interested in was "Can you do the work that is required?" and so when Denny came to me and asked me to work with him on the veterans' committee, I said, "Hell, yes!" Now, at this time, Tim, I had no experience at all with any political organization, Democratic or Republican. I had always voted every time the polls opened, but I had never had any form of involvement with any kind of candidate or political campaign, and now I became part of this committee, and once I came aboard, I came aboard fully, and I worked! I stuffed envelopes, I answered the phone, and I did everything for the campaign that I was asked to do and more. As a result, I was very visible in the campaign headquarters. So when I finally met the candidate, at that time in that place it looks like I'm like a fly in a bottle of buttermilk!

[*Laughter.*]

Now, let me tell you, this old Irishman, I can't say he wasn't prejudiced. All I can say is that he wasn't prejudiced against me. Or, maybe, what I can say is that I changed his innate prejudice against blacks. I really don't know, but he saw what I was doing, and so when he won, he called me into his office and said, "I want to thank you for your support and all the work you've done, and now that I've won, I want to ask you a question: What do you want?" And I said, "John, I want to go out on the West Side with you."

TB: And that meant the Criminal Courts Building?

ES: Yes, over at Twenty-sixth and California, and at that time there had never been a black assistant state's attorney assigned to the criminal trial division. They did have a fellow named McCoy who looked like a white man in the appeals division, and Euclid had already been there in the extradition department, where he had done a brilliant job because it was Euclid's work that resulted in the extradition from Turkey of that famous Chicago robber baron, Samuel Insull. It was Euclid's work that got him brought back, and then we had Richard Harewood, who had been in the municipal court division trying misdemeanor cases, but up to that time there had been no black ever assigned to the Criminal Court, so I said to Boyle, "John, I want to go out to the Criminal Court with you," and he said, "All right, what ward do you live in?" I said, "I live in the Twentieth Ward," because at that time we had moved back to a house that my wife's mother owned there at 5442 South Dearborn, and the ward committeeman there was a guy I knew named Kenneth Campbell. So Boyle said I should go get a letter of recommendation from him, and then "I'll give you a job as assistant state's attorney." Well, I already knew him because we'd been in service together, so I make an appointment and go in to see him in his office at Fifty-ninth and State, and I say to him, "Colonel"—because that's what we always called him—"Boyle has offered me a job, and he's asked me to get a letter of recommendation from you." He said, "All right," and I go out thinking it's going to be done without any problems, but then one week goes by. Two weeks go by.

[*Laughter.*]

Three weeks go by, and finally Boyle calls me and says, "Where the hell's that goddamned letter? You'd better go back and tell that guy that I'm waiting for that letter so I can put the papers through and get you on the payroll." So I go back, but when I go back, now I'm having trouble seeing him, and it takes another ten days before I finally get in to see him, and then he says to me, "Well, why should I give you a letter? I've got people who've worked here in this organization for years, and they're also lawyers, and they're much more deserving of my support than you are." So I said, "Well, are you going to give me a letter of recommendation or not?" And he said, "No, right now I've got somebody else that I'm pushing." Then I go back and tell all this to John, and John says, "all right"—expletive deleted!—"I will appoint you as my personal appointee, and I will reduce that guy's allotment by one!"

[*Laughter.*]

Because in those days each ward had its own specific number of patronage workers that they could hire, and when Campbell learned that I was going to be Boyle's personal appointee, then the letter came through.

TB: Pronto!

ES: Pronto, and Boyle said, "Now, listen, young man, you're going to have to join the political organization." So I joined the Thirtieth Ward Regular Democratic Organization, and that was the beginning of my political career.

TB: But, meanwhile, you are continuing your affiliation with the military, aren't you?

ES: Well, when I went into law school, I put my military career on hold, and it stayed on inactive status until I graduated, but once I had graduated, then I joined the Illinois National Guard and came aboard here at Thirty-fifth and Giles in the 184th Field Artillery division as an executive officer.

TB: So now you've joined the Regular Democratic Organization, and you're also back in the military, and you're moving ahead in both.

ES: Well, Boyle started me out in the Police Courts. In those days, above the police stations there were courtrooms where you heard misdemeanors, and that's where I started, but I told Boyle, "What I really want is to try cases and come over to the Criminal Court," and he said," Yes, that's fine, but first we're going to get your feet wet." So he started me out in the municipal division, and I worked over at Forty-eighth and Wabash, and the bailiff that was there in charge of taking care of that courtroom became a great friend to me and took me under his wing. Remember, back in those days corruption was wide open, and bribes were flowing freely all over the place.

TB: Who was the head of the Democratic Organization at this time?

ES: Jake Arvey.

TB: They had bail bondsmen back then, didn't they?

ES: Yes, and it was a highly lucrative business back in those days. The biggest bail bondsmen had their office right across the street from the court at Forty-eighth and Wabash. As a matter of fact, bail bondsmen's offices surrounded the police station, and they really ran the court system! Money was flowing, but before I took my oath of office as assistant state's attorney, I'll never forget that Boyle told me, "All I expect from you is honesty and integrity." Now, remember, at this time, there were only two black judges in the system.

TB: In the whole system?

ES: Yes, in the whole municipal system in Cook County. Only 2 out of 150! One was Wendell Green. The other was Henry Ferguson. Green was a real scholar—very, very serious—so I asked him for advice, and he said to me, "If there ever comes a point where you feel that you are not making enough from your salary, and you think you have to take additional money from other people for doing your job, then that is the day you quit and go into some other line of work, because in a position like the one you have you are going to be tested and tested severely." And that was the best advice that anyone ever gave me. So combining Boyle's statement about "honesty and integrity" with Green's advice about what to expect, plus adding in Fitzgerald's [the court bailiff] protection—he knew everything about all the corruption that was going on in the court system—after a certain time the word got out about me. "You can't buy him," and they began to deal around me. They knew they could not deal through me because they knew that I was not going to take any of their money. And the bail bondsmen liked that about me because it meant that they didn't have to worry anymore about the expense of paying off the state's attorney. As a consequence, when I left the State's Attorney's Office, the bail bondsmen became my best source of recommended revenue. In fact, they got me more clients than I would have ever gotten by myself because they knew that I was honest, and I also became the bail bondsmen's attorney for the purpose of getting their licenses renewed every year.

TB: How long did you stay in the Municipal Court?

ES: I stayed there about six months, and then I was transferred to Eleventh and State, where they had a Women's Court dealing primarily with prostitution and abuse to women, and then I worked at the Gun Court, and I stayed there for about six months before they transferred me over to Twenty-sixth and California, where they started me out in the auto theft unit. Then they transferred me to the fraud unit, and finally after two years of going around to various divisions of the State's Attorney's Office, Boyle called me in in July of 1950 and said, "On September 5 you are going to be assigned to the criminal trial division, and you are going to the courtroom of Judge William Touhy."

TB: Now, at this point, you would be the only black guy in a trial situation in the whole building.

ES: Well, it turned out that I was the second, because Boyle had already made an assignment of another black who came aboard two weeks before I did into the trial division, and that person's name was Archie Lescene.

TB: And later on he also became a judge.

ES: Yes, but, anyway, Judge Touhy was a former state's attorney of Cook County, and I was assigned to try as prosecutor every case that was assigned to William Touhy. Well, John S. Boyle made this transition easier for me by assigning Bob McDonald as my trial partner and by making our supervisor Leo Potter. Now, let me tell you a little about Leo Potter. When we were in office together, he had already been an assistant state's attorney for something like fifteen years. He had the most brilliant legal mind that I have ever run into. As a matter of fact, he was a genius in his ability to be able to read something and at some future time recall to mind precisely what it was that he had read: the volume number, the case name, the page number that he was quoting from, and the exact quote!
[*Laughter.*]

TB: That must have saved a lot of work!

ES: A fantastic, brilliant legal mind, but he had the personality of this chair!
[*Laughter.*]

TB: Like none at all?

ES: Yes, like none at all!

TB: How did you communicate?

ES: Well, as a result of this personality quirk, he could not be a good trial lawyer because he could not communicate with a jury.

TB: Yes, I imagine not. And in that court most of your cases were jury cases.

ES: Of course! You've got to be able to communicate with the judge and with the jury, so he couldn't be a good trial lawyer, but he was a brilliant lawyer, and he became our teacher. The best thing he ever did for us was that when he found out whom it was that he was going to have to teach, he called us into his office, and he said, "All right. You all want to be trial lawyers. Fine. I am not going to do your work for you. Don't any of you sons of bitches come to me for any help until you have exhausted every means that you can think of for solving your assigned problem. I'm not going to do your work." That was the best thing he could have said! That meant that before we went to Leo we had to have gone to the library. We had to have looked at every damned case we could think of to try to find the one that was most applicable, and then we would have to go out and investigate the facts. We had to have told the police, "You've got to get me this witness," because when we went to Leo and told him what evidence we had found, he would say,

"Well, what about the police? Have they brought this witness in?" And if we didn't say, "Yes," he said, "Well, get the hell out of my office. You haven't done your homework!" And then when we had done all of our homework, he would say, "Well, what's your theory?" Then we'd have to sit down and tell him what our theory was, and he'd usually take the goddamned theory apart. "Did you think about this? What about that? Why didn't you get that point?" And then after all of that had been done, he'd say, "Well, why don't you just go and look in 333 Illinois, page 500, line 6? Look it up, and that's where you'll find the answer there to your problem!"

[*Laughter.*]

But he made us lawyers!

TB: Yes, he certainly did!

ES: He wasn't going to carry us, he was going to support us. And he made us do our work. It was, "Do your homework before you come to me asking for any help."

TB: He gave you a sense of order, discipline, and organization.

ES: Oh, of course! And that's the first lesson for being a trial lawyer. In the first case he assigned me, he was testing me. He was Polish, and I don't say he was a racist, but he didn't give me any slack. He had never worked with blacks before. The first case we had to prepare in that courtroom was a murder case. It happened at a liquor store at Thirty-fifth and Giles where three men had gone in that store and killed the clerk.

TB: Was the clerk black or white?

ES: He was white. And the defense counsels in that case were Aaron Payne, Euclid Taylor, and Joe Clayton.

TB: Three good lawyers!

ES: That was my first case in the criminal trial division, and here I was going before Judge William Touhy and against three lawyers that would chew you up and spit you out in little, bitty pieces and then say, "Come on, son, let's go out and get a drink!" This was my first case, and Leo said, "You go on and prepare this case. You try him." Well, I tried that case and beat all three of them!

TB: Oh, you did?

ES: I sure did! I sure did! I got a conviction.

TB: Was it a jury trial?

ES: No, it was a bench trial, but I got a conviction, and they didn't give me any slack.

TB: Yes. Well, you're a tough guy.

ES: I know! So Leo demanded of us that we prepare our own cases, and he was the one that taught me how to be a lawyer and a prosecutor. He taught my partner, Bob McDonald, the same thing, except Bob had the Irish disease of letting booze take over, and he eventually went down the tube because the Outfit got a hold of him through his craze for drink and gambling. They got him in their pocket, and then they wouldn't let him out.

TB: Yes, yes.

ES: Eventually he wound up going to the penitentiary because he got involved with the Outfit, but, even so, he's still my friend.

TB: Yes, yes.

ES: So then I became an assistant in Touhy's court, and I began to try cases against the great criminal defense lawyers such as Charlie Bellows, Harry Bush, and George Crane, and I learned a lot from each one of them. I went from working for Judge Touhy to working with Judge "Black Jack" Dempsey and then on to Judge Abraham Lincoln Marovitz when he was on the state side—and I learned from each one of them too. I stayed in the office in the criminal trial division for two years until 1952, when Boyle fell out with the Democratic Party because of the Moretti case. The Democratic Party dumped him as the candidate for state's attorney of Cook County and selected instead a man by the name of John Gutknecht.

TB: Who was the chairman of the Cook County Democratic Party at this time?

ES: As far as I can remember, Jake Arvey was still chairman.

TB: Jake Arvey. Richard Daley had not taken over yet?

ES: No, Richard J. Daley had not taken over yet.

TB: Now, briefly, what was the Moretti case?

ES: Well, the Chicago Police Department had assigned certain Chicago policemen to the State's Attorney's Office—these policemen were going to be investigators for the State's Attorney's Office—and one of those investigators was a man by the name of Moretti. After Moretti had been assigned to the State's Attorney's Office, he got involved in some kind of a conflict on a night when he was out drinking or something like that. Anyway, there was a confrontation, and out of this confrontation somebody got killed. At that time, Moretti was on John Boyle's staff. Boyle was out of the city when this happened, but the people who were in charge of the actual day-to-day operations of his office decided that they were going to sweep this thing under the rug. They mishandled it and, in trying to whitewash it, it became a big, big political scandal, and Moretti, subsequently, was indicted, charged, and convicted of the murder of this individual. But all that dirt of the attempted fixing in that case fell off onto Boyle, and that was the real reason that the Democratic Party dumped him as a candidate for state's attorney.

TB: Boyle became the scapegoat—for right or wrong.

ES: Yes, and they backed Gutknecht instead. As a matter of fact, Boyle became a pariah for about six to eight years before he gradually worked his way back into the good graces of the Democratic Party. He eventually ended up as a judge, as he should have.

TB: Was Martin Kennelly the mayor at this time?

ES: Yes, Kelly was now out, and we had Martin Kennelly.

TB: Martin Kennelly—supposedly the reform mayor.

ES: Supposedly.

TB: So that would all fit in with the so-called cleaning-up operation of that time.

ES: Yes. So I stayed in the State's Attorney's Office throughout the entire term of John S. Boyle, and when the party decided not to retain him—when he went out in 1952—I went out as well. In fact, I resigned.

TB: By this time approximately how many cases had you tried?

ES: Oh, by this time I was an efficient trial attorney. In the two years since I'd been in the criminal trial division, I had tried, probably, forty jury cases and over three hundred bench trials. So now I was an accomplished trial attorney.

TB: What is the count on convictions, approximately?

ES: Ninety-two percent conviction rate.

TB: Ninety-two percent! So, at this point, then, it was clear to anyone looking at the record that you were now, as you've just indicated, an accomplished trial lawyer of high repute.

ES: Yes.

TB: So then you decided to leave office . . .

ES: Yes, I left the office with a good reputation, a reputation for being honest, a reputation for being a good trial lawyer, a reputation for being incorruptible, and I went out into private practice in 1952. During this time, my old friend John Rogers and I came back into close relationship with one another. Jack at that time had been practicing in the law firm of Howard Jeeter, and he was beginning to feel his oats and wanting to go out on his own. He and I were about thirty-four or thirty-five years old at that time. We had been childhood friends. We had gone to high school together, and we were compatible, so we decided that we were going to form our own firm and go into practice together. We had always liked one another.

TB: This is the Jack Rogers who is now a judge?

ES: Yes, John W. Rogers Sr.

TB: This is the father of John Rogers Jr. and former husband of Jewel Stradford Rogers LaFontant, who herself came out of a rather distinguished family.

ES: Yes, her father was Cornelius Stradford, a prominent black lawyer on the Republican side.

TB: She has not relented!

ES: Not relented one bit! She is her father's daughter. So Jack and I agreed that we were going into practice together as partners, and we set out trying to find office space. Now, at that time, it was hard for blacks to get good office space. Racism again. Every place we looked at—just as soon as they would see us—it all went down the drain! "The answer is no!"

TB: Now, this is in the downtown area?

ES: Yes, downtown—that's where we decided we wanted to start.

TB: How many black lawyers were downtown at that time?

ES: Oh, ten or fifteen.

TB: People like Carey?

ES: Yes, and Euclid and Prescott—they were still downtown. Jeeter and his partner were there.

TB: Was Westbrook down there?

ES: No, he was dead by this time.

TB: But Westbrook's successor, Claude Holman, his office was downtown too, wasn't it?

ES: Yes, but it was a hassle getting space downtown if you were black, even though by now I had advanced to the point where I was beginning to get some political recognition.

TB: Were you still in the Twentieth Ward?

ES: No, I was in the Second Ward—the mother ward! I was with William Levi Dawson—now I was in his ward!

TB: Had you moved to Lake Meadows by this time?

ES: Oh, yes.

TB: You were one of the first residents in Lake Meadows. It was a new development at that time.

ES: Yes, and by then I had a little name recognition, and Jack and I started to make some waves. We started getting publicity about the difficulty we were having getting a space in the Loop area because we were black, and we even got a couple of newspaper articles published in the *Chicago Daily News*, which is no longer being published, about the difficulty we were having, and then we finally got property at 64 West Randolph. But what they gave us was just a space with four walls. They must have thought that by giving us just the four walls that we were going to have to hire artisans to construct the interior walls of the office space. But what they didn't know was that Jack and I had gone to Tilden Technical High School, and I said, "The hell with that! We can do it ourselves!" So we sat down and planned what our offices would look like. We knew what our space was, and so we drew up a floor plan, and then we drew up a plan of what we wanted the office to look like, and we drew up what it was going to require in terms of workmanship, and then we went out and bought the lumber, bought the wallboards, bought the wallpaper, and bought the carpeting! And he and I, with our own hands, divided that four-wall bare space into a four-office suite with a hallway, a bay for the secretary, and a reception area—and we built it all ourselves!

TB: Saving yourself about how much money?

ES: Oh, in 1952, saving ourselves maybe at least twenty-five, thirty thousand dollars. We put up floor-to-ceiling walls, insulation, soundproofing. He and I did that all ourselves! And the white building manager never did believe we could do it. He'd come down there while we were working, and he'd look, and he'd shake his head, and then when we finished it, he came down and said, "I didn't really believe you could do it!"

TB: You may have reduced a little bit of racism right there!
[*Laughter.*]

ES: Well, I don't know, but he saw that we had used all of the top-of-the-line materials in our work. In our reception room we had something that hadn't been generally used in the United States before—we had Japanese grass cloth on our walls. It was a beautiful thing, and we hung it ourselves! We did everything! Jack and I would come in at night—after our work in our other jobs—and on weekends and work on constructing our office. And when it was finished, then we brought in a young man that had just graduated from the University of Chicago Law School—Ray Harth.

TB: Yes, he's still practicing, isn't he?

ES: Yes, he's still practicing. And then, of course, Jack at that time was still married to Jewel, and so we formed the law firm of Rogers, Rogers, Strayhorn, and Harth at 64 West Randolph Street—in 1952.

TB: And was that the genesis of your private practice?

ES: Yes, we stayed there, and we up built our practice. Ray became the domestic expert. Jack was the real estate expert. I was the criminal trial lawyer. Jewel was actually our "rainmaker" because she'd bring cases in, and then we'd just assign them out to whomever was the expert in that field. And that's where we started—right there! We stayed there until they began to take that property to build the Civic Center, around 1956. By this time, of course, Richard J. Daley was the mayor.

TB: Yes. Now, at this time you now have three different facets to your career in operation: You are a political person, you are a professional person—as a lawyer—and you are still also in the military. Let's take these one at a time. What rank are you in the military at about this time—say, around 1952 to 1960?

ES: Well, militarily, I was advancing up the ladder of promotion in the National Guard. I went from an executive officer in an artillery battery to a staff officer, and then on to become the commander of a military battery as a captain. Then I went on to become a major as an intelligence officer in the S2 on the battalion staff. Eventually I ended up as the executive officer of the battalion as a major, and then finally I became a lieutenant colonel.

TB: You retired as a lieutenant colonel?

ES: Yes, as a lieutenant colonel.

TB: And you were in the service how many years all together?

ES: All together twenty-seven years. I finally retired in 1969.

TB: By this time the site of your military activity had changed, hadn't it?

ES: Yes, it was changed from Eighth Regiment Armory at Thirty-fifth and Giles to the armory at Fifty-second and Cottage Grove.

TB: And was your battalion still having those beautiful military balls?

ES: Oh, yes.

TB: Now, when you moved to Fifty-second and Cottage Grove, what battalion did you replace—or was the armory that was there empty at that time?

ES: No, it wasn't empty. The 122nd Battalion had been staying there. We replaced them. They moved out the infantry that was white.

TB: Why did you have to leave the old armory on Thirty-fifth Street?

ES: They decided to close it down. After they built the Dan Ryan Expressway, they didn't think that the old armory was big enough because in building the Dan Ryan they had to destroy another armory which had been located at Thirty-third and Wentworth.

TB: So it was more the result of a political decision than a military one?

ES: Yes, and then after I retired in 1968, then there was a big fight within the army hierarchy that occurred during the years when Otto Kerner was governor. After I retired, the army was also starting to play certain kinds of games, and they tried to make a white person commander of the unit that I had commanded at Fifty-second and Cottage. The person that should have been the commander was a man by the name of LeRoy Stevens, who had been my executive officer, but he had been transferred and made a part of the Thirty-third Brigade, which was white-commanded and racist. Well, the reason for that was that the Thirty-third Brigade commander, a man by the name of Colonel Curtis Melon, decided that he was going to make a white person the commander over there at Fifty-second and Cottage Grove.

TB: And the soldiers over there were still predominantly black, were they?

ES: Yes, they were predominantly black because by then we had a ˈ̣ ᵢᵢ ᵢn to integrate the National Guard. Well, anyway, there was a great brouh. ᵢᵢᵢ ᵢcause this man had bypassed Stevens, whose bona fides were A-plus. And so there was a complaint filed concerning that situation, and Kerner called a summit conference, and in this conference it was proved that the brigade was racist and that the brigade had been manipulated so that a white commander could take over and force out Stevens. The situation before had always been that the black executive officer moved up and became the commander. But now they were trying to by-pass Stevens, and so there was a hearing in the governor's office, and when they found out that it was just as we said it was—that there was racism involved—they tried to change the situation. Kerner called me in because I had worked with him before, and he said, "Earl, you've got to help me out of this situation. Will you come out of retirement and resume command of the unit? We'll straighten this situation out, and after you leave, then Stevens will take over the unit." And I said, "Yes, but I'm only going to come back for a year, General"—I always called him "General."

TB: He was a brigadier, wasn't he?

ES: No, he was a major general. And so I was reactivated, and I took over the command of the unit for, oh, about fourteen months, and then I left, and Stevens came in.

TB: Now, you left in 1969—and that gave you twenty-seven years of service.

ES: Yes, and my unit was activated in every one of the civil disturbance situations that took place during that time—two Martin Luther King riots, the Democratic National Convention riot, the Cicero march—we were called out on all of those areas, and we served, and we never fired a single shot! Do you want to know something? As a result of the activity of my unit in all of these civil disturbances, the entire United States Army rewrote their field manual with reference to civil disturbances, and what they wrote was based upon the action and the action reports of my unit.

TB: That was because you had correctly managed these potentially explosive situations.

ES: Yes, as opposed to what had happened with the Ohio National Guard in their action in Kent, Ohio, where they killed all of those kids there at Kent State University.

TB: Yes, there were several instances like that. They also had one at Jackson State.

ES: Yes, and we had to put down riotous situations that were much more disturbing than anything that had happened at Kent State. People were burning down buildings in the situation that we were in, and we put it down without resorting to the use of weaponry. They rewrote the whole field manual as a result of what we did here in Chicago.

TB: So now, as I was saying, there are three simultaneous operations going for you. What about the political? You are now in the Second Ward, aren't you?

ES: Yes, by now I have transferred over to the Second Ward by virtue of moving my residence from 5442 South Dearborn, which was in the Twentieth Ward, to the new Lake Meadows area. As a matter of fact, my family was the first family to live in Lake Meadows. Now, as I mentioned previously, the Second Ward was under the control of the legendary William Levi Dawson. He was the ward committeeman, and I came under his control when I moved into this area. I became active in Dawson's organization and, as a lawyer, I was adviser to him in legal matters.

TB: Who was the alderman in the Second Ward at that time?

ES: The alderman at that time was Bill Barnett. So I became the legal adviser to Congressman Bill Dawson, and I was also placed in charge of organizing the ward on Election Day. On that day, I would be actually chief operator of the ward, and all of the decisions concerning what was going on in the ward and in the election on Election Day would be made by me. The Second Ward was the strongest ward in the Democratic Organization outside of the Twenty-fourth Ward—which, of course, was Arvey's own ward.

TB: But the Second Ward was the strongest of the black wards.

ES: Yes, it was tops.

TB: In the state as well as the city?

ES: Yes, and in the country as well.

TB: So that kind of political power supersedes even what Jones had in New York?

ES: Yes, of course. Dawson's ward was the strongest black political machine in the entire country.

TB: Yes, and he could always deliver what needed to be delivered!

ES: And he delivered not only the Second Ward, but by now he had consolidated the Third Ward, the Fourth Ward, all of the Fifth Ward, part of the Sixth Ward, the Seventh Ward, the Eighth Ward, and the Twentieth Ward! He had all of those mechanisms completely under his control.

TB: Would you say that more than any single individual in Chicago, Bill Dawson was responsible for the late Mayor Richard J. Daley becoming the mayor of the city of Chicago?

ES: Had it not been for Bill Dawson, Richard J. Daley would not have been the mayor of the city of Chicago when he became the mayor. I'm not saying he might not have eventually become the mayor, but that would have been eight, ten, twelve, or fourteen years down the line. Yes, but Dawson was definitely responsible for Richard J. Daley becoming the mayor of Chicago when he became mayor. Not only did he put Daley's name in front of the nation, but he was also responsible for Kennelly being told that he, Kennelly, was not going to be the Democratic candidate for mayor. In those days it was a tradition that if the current mayor was a Democrat, he would automatically be renominated as the Democratic candidate in the coming election, but, well, because of certain things that occurred during the Kennelly regime, Kennelly was the first Democratic mayor in many years who was not renominated. What caused the break between Kennelly and Dawson was that Kennelly claimed that he was attempting to drive gambling and horse racing and Policy out of Chicago. But this was really only a charade—just a way to get favorable publicity—and, in fact, all of the focus was directed toward the Policy operations, which, of course, were all black.

TB: And which were called by people like Kennelly the "numbers racket."

ES: Yes, and the horse racing and all the other gambling operations, they all were left entirely intact. Well, Dawson went in to talk with Kennelly concerning this imbalance, and Kennelly insulted him personally. Dawson said, "I can appreciate it, I can understand. I support your efforts to control the gambling operations in this city, but your police department is concentrating exclusively on black areas—and black people—and all the white gambling operations are being left untouched." That's when Kennelly insulted him and told him, "Listen, I'm running this operation. You don't tell me how to run my police department. They're doing what I have told them to do, and this is the way it's going to be." And so Dawson said, "Well, in that case, mayor, you will not see me in your office again during your term." And then, when it came time for Kennelly to go before the selection committee to be retained as mayor, he discovered that the committee was composed of all of those mustached political operators—the Nashes, the Arveys, the old Kelly Machine group—and Dawson himself! Well, even so, when it came time to announce the candidate for the Democratic nomination for mayor, Dawson happened to be in Washington, and Kennelly thought that it was going to be a done deal that he would automatically be the Democraic candidate. Well, when Arvey announced, "Congressman Dawson has instructed me to state that he cannot support and will not support Martin Kennelly for reelection as mayor of the city of Chicago," it was just like when they bombed Pearl Harbor! Because at that time Dawson had control of all of those organizations that I was just talking about, and without his support no Democrat could hope to be elected. Well, so they recessed the meeting in order to get Dawson back into town, and when he came back, Dawson told them once again, "No, I will not support Kennelly." You see, he recalled the insult that Kennelly had given to him three and a half years before, and so he said, "All of you can support the nominee if you will, but I will not support him." And all those old politicians knew that without the support of Dawson's wards—of his black political organization—they could not possibly win the election. So they dropped Kennelly flat and looked around desperately for a new candidate that Dawson would support, and that's when they came up with Richard J. Daley. That's the way Daley got nominated and elected and first came into office, and, being the smart and ambitious young man that he was, he consolidated all those areas that had not yet been consolidated! But, during all his time as mayor of the city of Chicago, William Levi Dawson was always one of the people who remained in Daley's inner circle, and the reason for that was that the first three elections Daley won, he won because of Dawson.

TB: Yes, it was because of the black vote that Daley won his first three elections—even against Adamowski, who had jumped ship and gone over to the Republican Party and taken almost all of the Polish community along with him. And then, of course, in 1963, the black vote was decisive in the election of John F. Kennedy as the president of the United States. It was the black vote here in Chicago that carried Kennedy into the president's office.

ES: And apparently it was also Dawson that brought Daley over to Kennedy.

TB: Oh, is that right?

ES: That's my belief based on the fact that Dawson had known Kennedy in Washington long before Kennedy ever got in contact with Daley.

TB: Dawson sold Kennedy to Daley?

ES: Dawson didn't have to sell Kennedy to Daley. Kennedy had so goddamned much money through his damned daddy and so much power of his own, and the political machine that he came out of was so well organized, that he was going to win that election no matter what! But Dawson was the "bridge" between Kennedy and the Democratic Organization of Cook County.

TB: Let me ask you another question. It is obvious that you have been a great success in your military, legal, and political careers. What do you think is the basic reason for all of your continuing achievements?

ES: All the advancement I made in the military, all the work that I did as a lawyer, my entire career as a judge—everything that I have ever achieved is a result of the basic values I learned from my family and friends and the solid educational experiences of my early years in school—and now that I'm getting older, I feel like it's payback time. It can be the way it was once again, and it must be for the sake of the future. I think I owe some payback to try to get the system back to that position where it was once again. I believe this can be done by traditional methods of good faith, sitting down, talking to one another, and coming to a conclusion and finding a solution that can be achieved without breaking apart the system. Everybody knows money for education is short, but the central school system has become bloated and has not only taken money that could have been used elsewhere but has also caused the slowness of achievement of school programs that are currently possible because they have so many layers of bureaucracy that they have to go through before they get down to the school level where the damned things can be carried out. I believe that an effective turnaround must be made within the elementary school system, because that's where the system has the greatest chance of having significant results in healing. It's easier to teach kids who don't already have their minds made up.

TB: It sounds good, but what about the politics of this?

ES: What about the politics? Listen, I know all the players, and nobody's got a ring in my nose. I'm strong enough to buck anybody because nobody can force me to go in any direction that I don't want because of some political agenda that they want to achieve. My political agenda is education for children. I know the political situation, and I believe in school reform. Nobody knows anything more about budgets—multimillion-dollar budgets—than I do. I worked for seven years in the sanitary district dealing with a budget clearly as large, if not larger, than that of the entire public school system!

TB: It will take a lot of money. Who's going to pay for all of this?

ES: It's going to have to be paid for by all of us.

TB: The taxpayers?

ES: Of course, we're going to benefit from it, and we ought to pay for it. It's not going to increase the money that we pay in taxes. In fact, it ought to reduce our taxes because of the benefits which we will gain in reducing the number of kids that end up going to the penitentiary.

TB: How much does it cost to keep a young man or woman in a penitentiary for a year?

ES: The current figures range between seventeen and twenty thousand dollars.

TB: That's a lot of money.

ES: And it's per each individual.

TB: In other words, it costs about as much as going to Harvard or Yale. What do we do with those young people who are now already in some kind of trouble?

ES: Those are ones that will have to be written off.

TB: Don't you think they can be rehabilitated?

ES: Listen, I don't believe in the word "rehabilitation" because there is no effective form of rehabilitation going on at the present time in any institution within the penal system anywhere in the United States. All the present penal system does is to act as a warehouse and incarcerate individuals for the duration of their term of imprisonment. It does not do anything to change their behavior for the better. At the present time there are not any kinds of programs that you or anyone else can point out to me that exist in any penal system in this country that result in the individuals within that system modifying their behavior for the future.

TB: So what you're saying is that our society is stratifying into two separate lines of development, one at the bottom of society and one at the top. But what are we going to do about a society like our own that disappoints even those that reach the top because there's nothing for them when they get there?

ES: We just have to keep working on that society to improve it. We have to keep facing up to racism and to sexism wherever they exist, and the target area for addressing all these problems is our educational system. If we can find a way to get our educational system back up to par, then a properly educated individual will always be prepared to fight sexism and racism because that individual will recognize those problems for what they are and find appropriate ways to eliminate these problems as they continue to arise.

TB: What you're saying is that we must not ever underestimate the importance of education.

ES: Yes, in my judgment, the key to all of our social problems is a high-grade educational system.

TB: In your opinion, are Chicago and Cook County in any way different from the conditions and problems in other jurisdictions elsewhere in the country? Are we typical or not?

ES: Well, typical or not typical, all I know is that I think that at the present time the southern part of our country has faced up to its racial problems more honestly and with greater effectiveness in terms of bringing all the races together than the northern part of our nation has achieved so far, and in many ways the South has become more advanced than we are up here in the North.

September 20, 1992, and March 1, 1993

JUSTICE WILLIAM COUSINS

———

ILLINOIS APPELLATE COURT JUSTICE

I first met Justice Cousins in 1956 when he and several other of his classmates from the DuSable High School class of 1946 were gathering to organize a celebration in honor of their tenth anniversary. I was very impressed with him then and have continued to be impressed with him ever since. His personal characteristics of intelligence, integrity, courage, and self-discipline continue to be a tremendous source of inspiration for me as well as for many others. He has an unwavering sense of what is morally right or wrong and has always been steadfast and fearless (and, I suspect, somewhat lonely) in his constant and consistent applications of these convictions.

I have witnessed him switch from a promising career in the Republican Party to one as an independent Democrat during the Goldwater campaign of 1964. I later had the pleasure of both watching and participating in his own campaigns as he ran for political office first as an independent alderman, then as a judge of the Circuit Court, and finally as a justice of the Appellate Court. It took the combined efforts of both the regular Republican and Democratic political machines to block his quest for a position on the Illinois Supreme Court, but, even then, the margin by which he was defeated by his carefully chosen black female opponent in the Democratic primary was extremely narrow.

What I did not discover until this conversation was the full extent of his academic and military accomplishments. To me, these aspects of his career are absolutely fascinating and provide a much deeper understanding of the experiences that clarified the vision and further strengthened the tenacity of this formidable man. It was an honor for me to have this unique opportunity of speaking with him.

TB: Bill, where were you born?

WC: I was born October 6, 1927, in Swiftown, Mississippi. Swiftown is about ninety miles due south of Memphis on the eastern side of the Mississippi River, but it is not on most maps. It's a plantation town in the Delta. I don't know that it even has—or even did have—five hundred people. It was a cotton-picking town and the biggest thing there was the cotton gin, so I am informed. It's right outside of Belzoni. I visited there for the first and only time since my parents left Swiftown on the occasion that I was going from Chicago to New Orleans for a National Bar Association convention.

TB: Were your mother and dad born there?

WC: No, they weren't. Dad was born July 8, 1903, in Jackson, Mississippi, and my mother was born in Little Rock, Arkansas, but Swiftown was where they settled down. My dad's name was William. My grandfather's name was also William.

TB: Did your family move to Chicago then?

WC: No. My family moved to Memphis from Swiftown when I was five years old. I started elementary school in Memphis and remained there until I was in the sixth grade, when my family moved here to Chicago. I was eleven years old at the time.

TB: Why do you think your family came to Chicago?

WC: It was because of my grandmother, Lula, who was really the matriarch of the family.

TB: Did you have any brothers or sisters?

WC: I had a sister, but she died very early, just before we left Swiftown, and under tragic circumstances. She was burned in a fire and expired on that account. I was old enough to remember that episode, you see, as I was with her in the fire. My family moved to Memphis shortly thereafter. I have no other brothers or sisters. My grandmother had eleven children by my grandfather.

TB: Was this on your mother's side or your father's side?

WC: On my father's side. My grandmother had relocated to Chicago a year or two before we moved here. Other members of the family moved here, for the most part, within the course of three years. We moved to 4735 South Langley Street. My grandmother's cousin, whose name was John Poole, was a postal worker living in Chicago at that time. He owned a building here and a large number of our family members were already living there by the time we moved to Chicago. It was a sort of communal living. I came here to Chicago twice before I finally came to stay. The first time I came alone with my uncle's wife. My uncle was a railroad man. He worked on the Illinois Central. I was in the sixth grade at the time. I went to Willard School in Chicago for about a month and a half or two, but then I went back to Memphis and finished the sixth grade there. After that year, my mother and my dad came up to Chicago permanently. My dad was already here when I first came to Chicago. He had come up a little earlier than my mother and myself.

TB: Did you come up on the Illinois Central Railroad?

WC: The first time, yes.

TB: Now, the fact that members of your family were already here means that your mom and dad had some assurance that there was a place to go if things got really rough.

WC: Yes. As I said, my grandmother's cousin was a postal employee and he seemed to be, by the standards that we observed, rather well-to-do. He was responsible, really, for causing my grandmother to come here, and the rest of the family followed her.

TB: What were the incentives that drew your family here?

WC: They were looking for a better way of life and an opportunity for employment.

TB: Better opportunities than in Memphis?

WC: Oh, yes. People in the South at that time felt that things were better up north. And, on balance, that was so. They were able to find regular work.

TB: Not cotton.

WC: No, not cotton anymore.

TB: The stockyards, steel mills, railroads—all were hiring.

WC: Yes. My dad worked at the stockyards for many years until they began to phase them out.

TB: Bill, you lived near Forty-seventh Street when your family first arrived in Chicago, didn't you?

WC: Yes, when I first came here. When we came back the second time, we moved in with an aunt who at that time lived close to Forrestville school, at about Forty-fourth Street and Champlain Avenue. At that time, in 1939, Forrestville was a good-sized grade school. There were a lot of kids there. I never had any problems adjusting and really never gave too much thought to the differences, for that matter. Let's say I integrated and blended in—kind of like moving from one house to another, but one big difference between the public school systems of Chicago and those in Memphis was that in Chicago we had half years. In other words, you could change grades at half year. I graduated from Forrestville in midyear and did the same thing at DuSable High School. They moved me up a half grade when I came here to Chicago. The students in Chicago were no more advanced than the students were in Memphis at the same grade level. In the South, we received a lot of instruction that was along the lines of what we now call black history, but that was because the schools were predominantly black. Everything was segregated in the South. The fact is, in Memphis I had to go from my house to an all-black school that was some distance away. Every day I passed the area where they had white schools, which we blacks could not attend. They talk about all of this busing business nowadays. Well, there was no busing business then—you just walked. And you got *cold*. It wasn't extremely cold in Memphis by comparison to Chicago, but I can remember some days when my fingers were just numb and aching. So this is what we went through. And I have a certificate for perfect attendance at school—never late, never absent. This was in grade school in Memphis. Here in Chicago we were on the half-year track, and I was moved from B section to A section and the result is that I graduated from Forrestville school in January of 1941.

TB: Do you remember any of the people who went to Forrestville?

WC: Well, one of my classmates was Johnny Hartman, the musician. And then a number of my classmates from DuSable were also from Forrestville. Herbert Almo was one in particular who has been my friend since grade school.

TB: Were there any black teachers at Forrestville at the time you were there?

WC: Yes, Nelson Woodley's wife, who was my math teacher there, made a big impression on me.

TB: Did anything about the social conditions cause your parents to feel more comfortable here than in Memphis?

WC: My parents never really were activists. Let me say their interest was in having a better opportunity for making a living. My mother worked as a domestic in Memphis, and she also worked as a domestic after she came here to Chicago. And even during the time I was in law school, my mother still worked as a domestic. She worked for a family called Schulemann. Their son, a contemporary of mine, became a lawyer also. Except for the war years, when she worked in a factory for a brief period of time, she was a domestic until she stopped working.

TB: After graduating from Forrestville in 1941, where did you then go to high school, Bill?

WC: I went to Wendell Phillips High School for one year because I was living on the corner of Forty-fourth Street and Evans. At that time the boundary line between DuSable High School and Phillips High School was about Forty-fifth Street, and so I went to Phillips. But after my first year at Phillips they changed the boundary line to Forty-third Street, and so then I went to DuSable.

TB: Do you remember anything about the Phillips experience?

WC: Oh, yes, surely I do. Willis Thomas and Leon Finney were there. There was a pretty good football team at that time. The football player Horace Chandler was a good friend of mine. Horace started playing football and running track after I left DuSable. When I went to DuSable, I was not a good trackman, but I went out for track—partly from a selfish point of view, so that I could improve my ability to move out fast, and that's a fact!

[*Laughter.*]

We had city meets on occasion, and during one of these I ran a relay on the mile relay team. Horace Chandler was a star then. He was a quarter-mile champion, and he looked upon me as a little brother. He later got into difficulties healthwise because he didn't take care of himself, but he was the star of the Phillips football team—after Buddy Young, of course.

TB: There was sort of an interchange between Phillips and DuSable, it seems to me, that was amiable, cordial.

WC: Well, it was cordial, but it was very competitive too. Of course, you went to DuSable, Tim.

TB: I went to both DuSable and Phillips High School.

WC: Well, relations were cordial at the time you were there because DuSable was really an outgrowth of Phillips, but by the time I was at DuSable, particularly by the time I was a junior or senior, there was rivalry.

TB: Who was the principal when you were at Phillips?

WC: I think it was Mrs. Maudelle Bousfield.

TB: She was the first black principal in the Chicago public schools. She came from Douglas or Doolittle School and became principal of Wendell Phillips. Did you have any immediate impressions about the differences between DuSable High School and Phillips High School?

WC: Not anything that was noteworthy. Again, it was like moving from one house to another. You left one set of friends and got another set of friends, retaining some of the friends you had had previously, and that's always been so with me.

TB: Were there students you had known from Forrestville at both Phillips and DuSable?

WC: Yes, and we also met up again later on in life.

TB: Now this was in 1941, at the beginning of World War II. What kind of impact did that have on DuSable, or the neighborhood?

WC: It definitely did have an impact on DuSable and the neighborhood. The war brought about a sense of uncertainty about the future and as to what would come after the war. In my senior year, some of the male students left school before they had graduated. They were eighteen, and they were called up by the Draft Board. Some also volunteered. I had turned seventeen at this time. I was in ROTC at DuSable for three years, and I continued my ROTC in college. I later went to the University of Illinois, which is a land-grant college, so you were required to be in ROTC there. I was among the graduates in the first Advanced ROTC group after the war at the University of Illinois.

TB: What do you remember of your DuSable experiences, academically and socially?

WC: Well, I was very active and I was also very studious. I read widely both in school and outside of school. I did not realize until later that I read much more widely than the average person. I belonged to the Book of the Month Club and during that time I read books like *Native Son, New World A-Coming,* and *A Tree Grows in Brooklyn.* I participated in a lot of different activities that were enriching like High YMCA. I went to various places around the county and even to places like Springfield in connection with these activities. I was the president of my class during my last year. I had gone to Tilden High School for a summer to take a course or two so that I could have even more freedom to participate in what you call extracurricular activities during my last year at DuSable. There are some students in my class who probably would say, "We got you started in politics!" And I continued on with my beginning experiences there. I was third in my class in terms of academic performance. And also, at that time, we high school students had a certain political awareness of things. I remember while I was at DuSable High School we had a "social room," and they didn't have Jean Baptiste DuSable's portrait in it. So our class conducted a campaign to have his portrait put in there. We were at loggerheads with the administration about that. So we had some social consciousness and awareness even back there at that time.

TB: Was that the case because our country was involved in the war, and some of your friends were already in the service?

WC: Yes, but aside from the war situation, this was a matter of social consciousness and an awareness, to some extent, of who we were. We had the Negro History Club, as we called it at that time. Also, in Memphis there had been a certain awareness in the grade schools of who we were, and one of the reasons was that in Memphis it was an all-black situation. In fact, this is one of the advantages of being in an all-black situation. At times they seek to make you aware of who you are and the importance of your being the best that you can be as a black person. So a difference in the two school systems was that in the schools here in Chicago, where we had mixed classes—predominantly white at times—there wasn't this same kind of emphasis. In fact, it may have been just the other way around!

TB: Yes, that is true, Bill. Tell me, what were the neighborhoods like back then?

WC: Well, the neighborhoods were comparatively safe. You could get from one place to another in short order, and often you could walk to where you were going. Of course, now things have changed. Now you don't freely go from one neighborhood to another. If you do, you're out of your zone, but that was not so back then. Oh, we had some people out there who were into some things they shouldn't have been doing, but they weren't shooting people. They might try to catch you and take something from you, but that was about the size of it. I don't recall having any fear about going anyplace.

TB: Yes, you could walk the streets day or night. What kind of recreation did young people involve themselves in at that time?

WC: Washington Park was the gathering park on weekends. Most weekends I found myself at Washington Park on a regular basis.

TB: There were places to go and things to do right in the neighborhood.

WC: That's right. And, of course, you didn't go to *some* places for your social life. I guess they had the war down on Forty-seventh Street. I hardly went down there. It was pretty rough. But there were other places to go. A lot of private places to attend. There was the Parkway Ballroom, for instance, which was put up when I was at Forrestville.

TB: Yes, the neighborhood had a certain unity and community. For fun and recreation there was the Savoy, the Regal, Washington Park, and many other places.

WC: Yes, we went to church on Sundays and after church, quite frequently, we went over to Washington Park and played softball or football, depending on the season. We had no big problem in finding a place to play. We would even play out in the street sometimes.

TB: And with the Savoy, the Regal, and the Michigan, there were places for a kid to go where he didn't feel uncomfortable. So you graduated from DuSable in January of 1945?

WC: Yes, and I went to the University of Illinois because DuSable had obtained a General Assembly scholarship from Representative Charles Skyles—which they, in turn, gave to me. I had never set foot at the University of Illinois before, and I would not have gone but for that scholarship. So with the scholarship, together with support from my family and arrangements to have a job during the summer, we had no problem taking care of the financial requirements at school. But if I hadn't had the General Assembly scholarship, I would have gone to a school like Roosevelt here in the city. No matter what, there was no question but that I was going on to college.

TB: Your mother and father fully supported you?

WC: Oh, fully. Whatever I needed, they provided. So I went to the University of Illinois down at Urbana-Champaign for three and a half years—from January of 1945 to June of 1948. Ordinarily it's a four-year program, but during my first year I got credit for the equivalent of twenty-one hours. I proficiencied out of one four-hour course and several courses were combined courses, so I got a lot of hours' credit. Actually, college was no more difficult for me than was high school. DuSable was a great help to me.

TB: Did many of the graduating seniors from your class go on to college?

WC: A number of my classmates graduated from college, either by virtue of going to college right out of high school or, in some instances, by returning to college later on. A number of them became teachers. My running buddy, Ed Cox, became a teacher and is an assistant principal. It seems to me, Tim, as though the young people in high school at that time were a little more mature than they are today. And I think it's more than just appearances. They were a little more mature for their age in terms of being serious. I don't mean they were more intelligent. I mean being serious about doing something with their lives.

TB: Well, many of those students had the benefits of parents who were also emotionally mature.

WC: Yes, that's true too. I think that the times also had something to do with it. These were times when people figured they had to work hard, and many young people thought it was important to work and strive to make the most of what they had the opportunity to do. Opportunity in those days did not come as easily as it comes today. Now there are all sorts of opportunities, and people are more choosy and selective and sometimes don't realize the need to really work and make the sacrifices necessary in order to attain the goals that they consider to be important.

TB: Were you still in ROTC at this time?

WC: I was in ROTC all the time I was at the University of Illinois. I didn't go to the service because I was too young—barely too young, but too young. I went to the University of Illinois at age seventeen, and the war ended in 1945. I graduated with my bachelor's degree in political science, with a minor in economics—with honors—and I was also awarded the distinction of being the outstanding graduate of the Advanced ROTC Corps because of my scholarship achievements.

TB: How many blacks were in the advanced military training at the University of Illinois at that time?

WC: There was only one other black.

TB: What was the total number of the Advanced group?

WC: Well, that was over one hundred, I would say. There were different components—engineers, artillery, and so on.

TB: What was your recollection about the African-American representation in the entire group?

WC: I only recall that there was one other black in my infantry program.

TB: All right. I just wanted to get some ratio not necessarily based on ability—although that certainly had something to do with it—but some other factors which were in operation that would also account for it. There just being two or three or even ten blacks in a public institution of probably three hundred is important to note. So you left the University of Illinois with a commission?

wc: Yes, I had a commission of second lieutenant. I did not go into service then but attended law school. At the beginning of my last year of law school, though, I received orders to report to the First Airborne Division at Fort Breckenridge, Kentucky, just after the beginning of the new year. It would have been in 1951 that I was due to report. Since my last year of law school started in September of 1950, I appealed from having to report, and the basis of my appeal was interesting. I had sought to affiliate with the Massachusetts Military District and participate as an active reservist, which I should have had the right to do. I was at Harvard University in Cambridge, Massachusetts, at the time. But, notwithstanding President Harry Truman's executive order to desegregate the armed forces, they did not allow blacks in that unit at that time, and so I was not allowed to participate. Now, what I did arrange to do was to participate with a group that was sort of lawyer-oriented. I had not yet become a lawyer, but it was a sort of a military-justice kind of a group, and I participated from time to time with them. But what happened is that when they called me to service, because I was unattached and unassigned, in effect, they called me as an individual—as an infantry officer. The policy was that if you were unassigned they called you as an individual; if you were with a unit, they didn't call you unless they called the entire unit. So I indicated that I was being penalized, in effect, because of discriminatory policies which resulted in my being excluded from this unit. They didn't call the unit and so, as a result, I was at large, and they called me individually. I also indicated that I was enrolled in my last year of law school and was scheduled to graduate the following June. I requested, therefore, that they rescind my orders at this time to allow me to complete my schooling. I withdrew from school, though, because I received no response immediately, and I came home. Then it just so happened that during the Christmas holiday, before January of the new year, I received orders from the army granting my request and rescinding those prior orders, therefore allowing me to graduate from Harvard Law School. I received an unusual kind of a directive, though, which was to report to the commandant of Fort Devens, Massachusetts, the day after my graduation.

tb: How many blacks were in law school at Harvard at that time?

wc: There were six blacks in my first-year class to start with. The classes were about five hundred. There were three of us who graduated out of a class of close to five hundred. And, by the way, Tim, I have a problem with people who get uptight when you talk about quotas. On the Circuit Court, at times, we had occasion to have this matter addressed. We were seeking to get more associate judges who were blacks, and you didn't talk about "quotas" but about "affirmative action" at that time. Chief Justice Conover told me there were a lot of people concerned about "affirmative action." To him, that was a problem—so I said, "Well, Chief, let's call it 'goals.'" But there's nothing wrong with quotas. And I can say that and will say that. The problem is the purpose for which they're used, and if they're used for wrongful purpose they're bad, but if they're not used for wrongful purpose there's nothing per se that says quotas are bad. Now, you have to dress that up in the proper language for these people who get uptight, and so you dress it up and call it something else like "goals" in order to be more inclusive. Back then we only had three black graduates in a class of almost five hundred people because of their restricting their quotas. Talk about the need to have things different than they were! After all, what's wrong with proportional representation? When I was in college, I was taught that this was the way to do it in this state in order to be sure that minorities had a voice. There is nothing wrong with that concept per se. The question is, how you're going to employ it? With all of these imbalances that we've had, there's no question but that we have to have something positive and something affirmative. In the climate and the circumstances we've had, and in the climate and circumstances that we still have, we can't just leave things out there without any affirmative efforts going on. So we have to have built-in efforts to ensure that we are not locked out, because otherwise others are not going to bring us in by virtue of their generosity and benevolence and good graces. It's against the grain for them to do that. Basically and fundamentally, people do not give up what they have without some struggle. If they have and you don't have, they're not going to give anything to you out of their generosity so that you can share part of what they have. They're not going to do that unless there is some mechanism of policy that results in their doing it. Otherwise, it will not happen, you see. And to say that it's otherwise is to ignore history and reality.

TB: Yes, that's certainly true. Well, after you reported to Fort Devens the day after your graduation, were you then ordered directly into the service, Bill?

WC: Yes. I didn't even come home. I graduated and the next day I reported to the commandant of Fort Devens, Massachusetts, which was not too far from Boston, maybe thirty-five or forty miles, and started my military career. Interestingly enough, at Fort Devens, Massachusetts, they had an infantry unit, but they did not assign me to the infantry. Instead, they assigned me to the quartermaster corps.

[*Laughter.*]

And, of course, I raised an issue about that. I advised the commanding officers that I was an infantry officer. I had nothing against the quartermaster corps—indeed, I performed my services as quartermaster—but I was an infantry officer and did not understand why I was not being assigned to an infantry unit. I remained at Fort Devens, Massachusetts, for about three months. Then I had orders, initially, to report to Fort Dix, which was at that time an infantry training base. I went there, and I was processed through there to Camp Kilmer, New Jersey, where I was assigned to courts and boards. All I did there for a few months was to participate in court-martials. I was generally the defense attorney, representing persons charged with offenses against the code of military justice.

TB: Bill, why did you stay in the infantry when you could have been in the quartermaster corps? A lot of guys would say, "Why would he change?"—the assumption being that the quartermaster corps would be more safe.

WC: Well, it was a rear-guard unit and so forth. You're not up front in the same sense as the infantry, but I did not think that way. My thinking was, "I'll do my duty," and I never gave that other matter any consideration at all. Indeed, if I had gone, initially I would have been in the 101st Airborne. I was a soldier. I was trained to be a soldier and had a profile as a soldier. You do what you're told to do, and you don't step back. I was an only son, but I never raised that issue. Anyway, then I got orders to go to the Far East Command, which meant that ultimately I would go to Korea.

TB: Had the conflict begun in Korea?

WC: Oh, yes. The Chinese had jumped across the Yalu River in 1950, before I had gotten my initial orders. It was now over a year later in the fall of 1951. The conflict was raging over there. I got orders to go to the Far East Command, but it was via Fort Benning, Georgia, where I was to spend almost four months in further training. I did this from the beginning of January of 1952 until the end of May of 1952. On one particular weekend I drove over to Montgomery. And I might say that although I was born in Swiftown, Mississippi, my parents left Swiftown when I was five years old and went to Memphis, where I started grade school and remained until they came to Chicago. I've been in Chicago ever since. But until I went to Fort Benning, Georgia, during the time I was in the service, I had never been back south. While I was still at Camp Kilmer, New Jersey, I purchased an automobile because I had no intention of having to be subjected to some of those things they were doing in the south. I had no intention of that.

TB: Of subjecting yourself to the indignities of public transportation?

WC: Yes. I had no intention of doing that, because my makeup was such and my mindset was such that I could not accept it. I would have had problems in the South, considering my nature and my disposition. My attitude was such that I never used the term "nigger," and nobody ever used it to me after I left the South. That was just something I didn't do. I didn't use it. And nobody used it to me. So I went everywhere in my car. I could even say at the University of Illinois when they wouldn't let blacks go to those local movie theaters, I never went to a movie theater where I had to sit in the balcony in Champaign. I didn't do that. Others went, but I didn't. Because as a youngster this was my orientation, you see. But anyway, on this highway I was just driving and talking. I was recently out of school, and I expressed myself more like a student coming out of an eastern school than I do now. It was very clear that I was from someplace else — not the South.

[*Laughter.*]

And this is what they took exception to and called me to task for. But at any rate, after they had dressed me down, you know, and called me "nigger" and told me to call them "sir" and so forth, they told me to go on down the road and not to look back. That was a hurtful experience.

TB: And you were an officer in the United States Army!

WC: Yes. But I was not in uniform; I was in civilian clothes like anybody else. But whether I was in uniform or not didn't really make any difference, because when I was assigned to Camp Kilmer, for instance, and I had occasion to go to Washington, D.C., they wouldn't serve me in restaurants even though I was in my dress uniform.

TB: In Washington, D.C., the capital of the United States?

WC: Yes, I raised Hades in there, you know. I was in my dress uniform. But that is the way things were in the fall of 1951.

TB: And Ralph Bunche was already known worldwide by that time as the secretary-general of the United Nations.

WC: Yes, but if you were black, you could not eat in a restaurant in Washington, D.C., in 1951. I can attest to that!

[*Laughter.*]

Yes. No matter who you were, that is the way things were. Now, we are sometimes shy about talking about the way things ought to be, but that's a lot of baloney because if you know how people have been, and you know how people are, you know basically that people act like they have to act. And if they aren't required by law to act in certain ways, then they will continue to act in a manner that does not demonstrate proper respect for the rights of others, you see?

TB: Yes, of course.

WC: After I left Fort Benning, I had thirty days' leave, and then I went to Japan in June of 1952 and was assigned, initially, to what was called a First Cavalry Division, where I underwent further training in the field. I was really trained razor-sharp by the time I got to Korea. I spent from June until October in Japan, and then I was sent to Korea, where I was assigned to the Second Infantry Division as an infantry platoon leader. Initially, I was a mortar platoon leader in a heavy-weapons company. Later I was assigned to an infantry unit. I had some travails in Korea and some very trying times that resulted because of what I considered to be the systematic shafting of blacks. I raised an issue here. You see, there was a high rate of personnel turnover in Korea, and the junior officers moved up fast. If you were second, you moved up to first, and the young white officers were moving up to become commanders, but they were systematically shafting the young black officers. For no good reason at all, they were moving some of the young black officers aside so they wouldn't move on up. I brought this to the attention of some people, and then the same sort of thing happened to me. You see, Tim, I had been in combat after I got there in October until in mid-December, when we were pulled off the front. We went to the island of Kedjudo, and when we got there, the company commander there indicated to me there that he was relieving me of my assignment. That's what it amounted to, because he was going to put me in charge of duties relating to mess, you see. So what did I do? I wrote a letter to the army, and that letter outlined what I viewed as a systematic shafting of blacks in Korea. I really had become the subject of this issue. Interestingly enough, after a while I received a communication from the commandant of my regiment, Joe Stilwell Jr. Washington had sent him my communication, and now he was contacting me to speak to me about it. I was piloted in a two-seater plane from Kedjudo to Kojudo so that I could meet with Joe Stilwell Jr. about this matter. Well, he heard me regarding these complaints. But one of the things this move on me was also calculated to do was to prevent me from getting my next promotion. This would do that, you see — at least, that's the way I looked at it. So, after we had talked for a while, he said to me, "You know, you don't have to remain in Korea very much longer because your rotation will be due soon anyway. But if you elect to remain, what I would do is I would transfer you from your battalion to another battalion and give you a different assignment, an assignment as an infantry platoon leader. Then I would make some decisions as a result of this. But," he said, "that's your choice." And I said to him, "I choose to remain." So as a result of that, I was transferred from that battalion to another battalion and given an infantry unit that would return to the front. And not too long after that, they had a ceremony in which I was cited as one of the two outstanding officers in that division for that month. I was a soldier, you see, and the general of the Second Division, General Fry, pinned my first lieutenant bars on me.

TB: The Second Division was one of the most decorated divisions in the Korean War.

WC: Yes, and as a result of my disclosure, the battalion commander of the battalion that I had been in lost his command, and the company commander was also relieved. Now, this is the mess I was dealing with in Korea. These were adverse circumstances, where, if they had gotten me pinned down, they could have done me in. But by some quirk of fate, I was able to slip that situation and avoid the anger of a man who was eager to become the commander, because the communications I sent forward went through certain channels, and he never did understand how and why they went through those channels instead of through him! [*Laughter.*]

TB: Now, wait a minute, Bill, before you leave this subject. There were a lot of soldiers who had been young people at the time of World War II who were now going back as officers. A lot of complaints were coming stateside about the treatment of black troops even after President Harry S Truman's executive order and the demands of the NAACP under the leadership of Thurgood Marshall. He went through Korea, and there was a sudden change in status of black soldiers. By the way, did you command both black and white soldiers, Bill?

WC: Surely. My platoons were mixed. I had one of the most all-American kind of units you'd ever find. It was comprised of whites, blacks, Koreans, and Filipinos. Now, during this time that I was overseas, Tim, I met my wife-to-be in Japan. When I was sent back to Korea, she and I continued to correspond, and we decided we would be married. You were entitled to a certain amount of "R&R" time, so I went back to Japan and made arrangements to marry. Then I returned to Korea, and when I had finished my tour of duty there, it was arranged that, rather than come directly to the States, I would go back to Japan and we would be married there. After my wife and I were married, then orders were cut returning me to the States, and my wife remained in Japan until a later date.

TB: So you returned to the States alone?

WC: Yes, in June of 1953. We'd been married in May of 1953. I was then processed through Camp Carson, Colorado, and I came on home to Chicago. What I did then for the next six weeks, for all practical purposes, was to become somewhat of a hermit. Why? Because I hadn't taken the bar as yet. I studied intensely to take the bar, which was given at the end of July. Immediately after taking the bar exam, I started to work for the Chicago Title and Trust Company as a lawyer—although I was not actually a lawyer until later, when I was sworn in.

TB: You still had rank and status in the military at that time, didn't you?

WC: Yes, I was a reservist. I came back from Korea a first lieutenant, then I was promoted from first lieutenant to captain, and in the later part of the sixties I was promoted to major. And you see, the way it is in the military is, when you're an officer, you remain an officer until you retire. You may go on inactive reserve, but if something happens, you are subject to call—as a lot of officers who had already served found out in the case of Korea. They had to go back and serve another tour of duty. But what I did is, after being out of active service for a year—at the end of 1954—I affiliated with the 178th Regimental Combat Team, the National Guard over here, as an officer. I stayed with the National Guard until about 1961, when I transferred into the reserve and changed my branch to JAG. I then became active as a JAG officer—an adjutant general's officer. Later I actually retired as a JAG officer in 1976. I had interesting experiences here too, relative to my reserve activities. I have been retired for more than twenty years now.

TB: What is your rank?

WC: I'm a light colonel.

TB: A "light colonel" is a lieutenant colonel.

WC: Yes, and I served in the reservists as a staff judge advocate of a transportation brigade—ultimately—then I retired. I had some problems in connection with my military career when I entered the Chicago political scene, though. I became an alderman of the Eighth Ward of the city of Chicago in 1967. I was active, and during the Vietnam conflict, I had views that that action overseas was misconceived. I expressed those views on some forums. I was absolutely certain that we were off base in several ways. For one thing, I had completed the commanding general staff course that is required for officers of the army in order for them to qualify to become a general. And as an officer, I had the fundamental training, and I understood the basic concepts of the rules of war and the like. So I could see that the Vietnam conflict was wrong on several bases. One was that there were certain moral problems about it. But aside from that, it was also an unwinnable situation. Now, when I say "moral," there are a lot of questions regarding the rightness or wrongness of how that situation in Vietnam came about. But you just can't win in a military situation if you don't know who the enemy is and where the enemy is. And in that particular situation, the enemy was all around and everywhere. It was a civil conflict in which you couldn't know where the enemy was, and so that made an impossible kind of situation. Now, much later, they've recognized that. But this was the view that I had regarding this conflict at the time, and I expressed it clearly. But while I was expressing this view I always said that I was still an officer and a soldier, and if I had been called to go over there to do my duty, I would have gone. I would have gone even though, in my opinion, it was a misconceived conflict. Now, was I right or was I wrong? Indeed, in 1968, during the Democratic National Convention, I was a candidate for delegate to the convention. Dr. Quentin Young was also a candidate for delegate. We ran on the Peace and Justice platform. We didn't win. We did get a lot of votes— more votes than anybody else in this state who lost running on a Democratic ticket at that time. I was not then a staff advocate. I was a major and was deputy staff advocate of a division here in this area. And when the election was over and I returned, I was called in and told that certain people in the army had tried to live with this conflict of opinion, but couldn't live with it anymore. I had to find another home. The problem was that some people didn't understand why I wished to be active in the military but at the same time hold the public positions that I did, which were considered to be inconsistent for an officer in the military. And I told them I separated the two positions. And they said that other people knew more about this than I did. But I said, "I have a right to have my opinion in a public capacity. I'm a citizen." However, some people didn't see that that could be done and told me that I should find another home. I said, "Well, how much time do I have?" And I was told to take whatever time I needed. This was the beginning of the summer, so they said I had till the beginning of the fall. So I discontinued my attendance with that unit. They had another detachment out here at a building in Hyde Park. I went out there, and I spoke to the JAG officer about affiliating, and he told me, "You have a reputation as a troublemaker. Did you know that?" I said, "No, I didn't know that." Well, the word had been put out by a high-ranking officer, you know, to block me from getting attached. So then for about two years I was in a limbo in which I did not have an assignment. I should have had an assignment, but I was being blocked. Then one day a judge approached me. He was an officer, a light colonel, and active in the reserves. He knew I was a JAG officer too, and he asked me when I was in his court if I was assigned. And I said, "No, I don't have an assignment." And he told me to go over to the headquarters that met around Harlem just south of Harrison and to speak to the commanding officer there because they had a position that was open for a JAG officer. So I did, and I spoke to this officer, a general, and after we had talked for a while, he said, "Welcome aboard." And so I began my duties as a staff judge advocate of that unit. About a year later, the general called me in and he said, "Bill, my God, what did you do to get people angry?" I said, "I didn't do anything to anyone." And he said, "Well, I had to process papers to have you promoted, maybe to light colonel, and then I got this communication from out of town . . ." Well, my records had been doctored up! In other words, that's what it boiled down to—inaccurate records. They had pulled an efficiency report that had been written about me during the time that I was the deputy. They had written a favorable report on me, but what they had inserted in my file was designed to do me in. The general who was in charge of my division—a wonderful officer, a West Pointer—saw things for what they were and recognized my officer qualifications. He sent me the efficiency report that had been made, and what they had put in there would forever bar me being promoted beyond my current rank. I had to then go to work and make submissions which included a copy of the report that had been processed—but had never been sent forward—together with some letters and communications from other officers who were mindful of my performance in the service. To this was added communications with some other individuals who could put to rest any doubts as to my loyalty to this country. This is what's involved, you see. So those old records were pulled and ultimately, when that was done, I was promoted.

TB: But this was some years later?

WC: Yes, the whole process took about two years.

TB: And during this time you were moving toward mandatory retirement?

WC: Yes, because I was commissioned an ROTC officer on the date I graduated from college. That was in 1948, and although I had not been active all that period of time, the way they determine when you're going to retire is by a twenty-eight-year span of service and by then you should be a colonel. So, in twenty-eight years, although I had not been active, when that time arrived, that was my time to be retired. At any rate, I was promoted then and finished out my career as an active reservist as a staff judge advocate of the 325th—of the Transportation Brigade, Eighty-fifth Division—a reserve division.

TB: But you had had a lot to deal with in repairing your damaged reputation, didn't you?

WC: Yes, all that fuss about my records. It just shows you the level to which certain people—some of whom are high and mighty—will stoop when they disagree with you. It's an awful thing to be subject to the whims of those who really have the power to do you in or not do you in. They can do some god-awful things.

TB: Yes, they can. But you had those records removed?

WC: Yes, I did.

TB: Bill, after you returned to Chicago from Korea in 1953 and studied for the bar exam, what direction did your career take then?

WC: Immediately after completing the bar exam, which was in late July of 1953, I went to look for a job. Interestingly enough, one of the first places I went to was the United States district attorney's office. They had a district attorney then by the name of Cheiken. I went to the office and up to the receptionist's desk and I asked her if I could see the district attorney. She asked me what about, and I said I was there to see about applying for a position as assistant United States district attorney. She asked if I had an appointment. I said, "No, I don't have an appointment," and she was probably a little surprised. She then went into Mr. Cheiken's office and told him that there was a young man who wanted to speak to him about applying for work in the United States district attorney's office, and he said, "Send him on in." He had a huge office. At least it seemed huge to me then. At any rate, we sat down, and I talked with him. I told him about my educational background and that I was recently out of the service and the like. We had a good conversation and at the end of that conversation he said something to me that I never forgot. He asked me a question. He said, "Who are your sponsors?" Well, I knew a number of prominent black lawyers. They were generally members of my fraternity—Kappa Alpha Psi. I knew Earl B. Dickerson—he was one of the leaders of our fraternity. I knew J. Ernest Wilkins—he was then the assistant secretary of labor. I knew Earl Neal's dad. I knew attorney Braden's dad, Edward Braden. I knew all these people. And then he said to me, "I'll tell you what you do. You go out and you get some sponsors." Now, what did that mean to me? That was my introduction to politics in Chicago. These were Republicans, and, of course, they were not quite in the same league with the Democrats in terms of their political machine. I didn't exactly know what was going on here, but I knew enough to know that what was going on wasn't right. It wasn't right the way that things were being run in this city. This was 1953. And, of course, on the Democratic side, things were even worse than that. The next thing I did was to go to the Chicago Title and Trust Company. I walked right in off the street and went up to the personnel office and said, "I'm here to apply for the position of attorney." I had not yet been sworn in, but I had taken the bar and you can become an attorney—a member of the bar—in certain offices even before you are actually sworn in. I was hired on the spot as a title examiner. I stayed there until 1957.

TB: How many blacks were at Chicago Title and Trust at that time?

WC: There were two black attorneys, Larry Carroll and Bill Boland. I was the third black they hired. Now, what they did, even though I was hired—because they had an arrangement with the Urban League to screen people whom they hired—is to have me go back to the Urban League office just so they would have me processed in accordance with their arrangement.

TB: Who was the executive director of the Urban League at that time?

WC: It wasn't Bill Berry. In fact, I don't think he was at the Urban League at that time. But he may have been.

TB: What was the total number of staff, in terms of the professional staff, that were blacks?

WC: Well, we three were the only black attorneys at the title company, but they had other blacks working there in different capacities. Carl McCormick was working there. He wasn't yet a lawyer. He was still in school at the time. He's now a justice here.

TB: But in terms of the legal staff, they only had three blacks?

WC: Yes, that was it.

TB: And what was the total staff?

WC: I would say it could very well have been a hundred. There were a lot of lawyers. Interestingly enough, one day one of those black officers said to me, "You know, we've come a long way, and we haven't reached the millennium yet." He went out of his way to tell me this. Now, I knew what he was saying to me. They had started to include blacks at Chicago Title and Trust, but things were not equal there yet. So what he was telling me was that if you have aspirations, even in this company, you must realize that we have come a long way, but that there is still a ceiling. And so it was. Then, when Adamowski was elected state's attorney in 1956, I was active as a Republican. I had become active as a Republican not because I had a Republican background, however. My parents had both been Democrats. My whole family had been Democrats. My first vote was when I was stationed in Korea in 1952, and I voted for Adlai Stevenson by absentee ballot. At that time I had become active with the local association of the National Lawyers Guild. They didn't accept any blacks in these other organizations. The first black admitted to the Chicago Bar Association in 1948 was Sidney Jones Jr. who is still living in the Chicago area. You simply couldn't get into any of these white organizations. They didn't admit us.

TB: They could pass Sidney Jones in even though Sidney Jones was a black man because, of course, a person would have to ask Sidney Jones, "Are you black?" [*Laughter.*]

WC: Yes, that was the situation. And the National Lawyers Guild did have a program to try to do something positive toward advancing the cause of blacks. Dickerson, I think, was the president of the National Lawyers Guild. This organization, though, was on Senator Joe McCarthy's list of suspicious organizations. You wouldn't exactly be disqualified for belonging to it, but they would take a close second look at you. So that was my background when I came home from the service. In this political climate it was quite easy to see that blacks were being exploited politically.

TB: Bill, you have had a very full political career here in Chicago. Would you share some of your experiences and reflections with us?

WC: Well, Tim, politically, to me, it's very fundamental and axiomatic that you have to have numbers of voters. It's one of the main ingredients of power. Our numbers here in the African-American community weren't in the past what they are now, but even then we had numbers, and yet we were being used, and we were not benefiting from our numbers, and that was quite obvious. I couldn't, in good conscience, align myself with such a situation. Instead, I felt that since the Republicans were not in office, if we worked with them on principles, maybe they would develop in the proper direction. That was my theory. Besides, I still remembered that district attorney Cheiken told me, "Get yourself some sponsors." So I was active as a Young Republican—very active. The fact is, I was voted the "Outstanding Young Republican" in Illinois in 1958, in terms of my activity around the state. At any rate, early in 1961, a prominent businessman and Republican named Jim Worthy organized the Republican Citizen's League, and they asked me to become a member of their board, which I did. And then one day in

March of 1961, the *Chicago Tribune* published an article about a new Republican Citizen's League and listed their directors. About two weeks later, at the beginning of March, they entered my division [of Chicago Title and Trust] to interview Blair Bonds, a fine fellow. At this time Blair called me in, and said, "Bill, why did you do it?" I said, "What do you mean, Blair? What did I do?" He said, "Why did you join this protest group, this 'League?'" Then he said, "Bill, I'm going to have to ask for your resignation." And I said, "Well, Blair, give me the date of the newspaper article." It was March 1. So you see, I was fired retroactively. But that was the way things worked. I shed no tears. I just went on out of the office. I was already meeting in the evenings with attorney Jim Lemon regarding some matters, and I began to build my practice full-time that way. So this is how I got started in practice—just got shoved on out there! Later I was involved in the formation of, and was one of the initiators of, a law practice with three other lawyers: attorneys R. A. S. Turner, Garland Watt, and Marvin Gavin. Marv is now an associate judge. I did this until about 1968, then I affiliated with LaFontant and her husband in their practice, and after that with Adolphus Rivers. I worked with Rivers for about two years before I became a rep of the Circuit Court. I then became a judge in the Circuit Court in 1977.

TB: In the meantime you had become an alderman, hadn't you?

WC: Yes, I had become an alderman in 1967, and I had also become very active in civil rights activities. I was well known, and in the area of the Eighth Ward I had tremendous support. In an election before the aldermanic election, there was a group of us who had gotten behind Charles Chew. He had been alderman, and we realized Charles was in difficulty as an alderman. The state senator position was available there, and so I initially was Charles Chew's campaign manager in 1966. In 1963 he had run against Spike Slight over in the Seventeenth Ward and had won there as an alderman. The next aldermanic election was coming up in 1967. Charlie was well known, but there was a view that Charlie was vulnerable at home.

TB: This was when he was being labeled Rolls Royce Charlie?

WC: Well, at any rate, he ran, and I was his campaign manager at that time. Our area was in the Eighth Ward. Gus Savage and Jim Montgomery were also involved in Charlie's campaign at that time.

TB: Jim Montgomery, by the way, had been in the Young Republicans with you at this time, hadn't he? And by this time you were already moving toward independence.

WC: Well, going back a little bit, you see, although I had been active as a Republican in 1962, when Goldwater emerged, I publicly left the Republican Party because I perceived quite clearly that Goldwater was taking over the party and others were yielding to him. His views were extreme, and I could not operate in that setting. I had been on the line, politically, in one sense. Since then, party-wise, I have been a Democrat, but I have not been active as a party person since 1962. At any rate, it was thought that after Chew won the election, I would be a candidate from the Eighth Ward. But what happened was that Jim Montgomery and Gus Savage both ran, and I did not have Chew's support. Chew really did an about-face. He did an about-face right away—I mean immediately.

TB: By this time he had moved into Pullman, to the Regular Democratic Organization.

WC: Yes. He was sworn in, you know, before officially announcing his change over to the Regular Democratic Organization.

TB: It was a dramatic turnaround.

WC: Yes, and I found out that Chew was on the other side as soon as I started my campaign!

TB: Who was alderman in the Eighth then?

WC: Condon was the alderman.

TB: Condon—who was a white guy?

WC: Yes, and the demographics of the situation were such that he should not have been able to win. The ward was a good 60 percent black. But, of course, that's not a super majority.

TB: It's enough, though, considering the quality of the people in that ward. Now, there had been a previous race against him, but there was more than one black candidate in the race.

WC: Well, there was not a serious campaign against him before.

TB: It that right?

WC: Yes. Not for blacks. There was a fellow named Kustner—something like that—who had been an alderman there during the 1950s vis-à-vis Condon. He was white, and so they tried to put Ernie Banks up as a Republican with his sponsors, but that just wasn't working. The situation was such that they did not want Condon to run. Instead, they designated Les Bland to run. He was a businessman. I knew him well, but I was surprised, and I think I asked him, "Les, what are you doing?" And he said, "I'm getting ready to become alderman." And I said, "All right, Les, you'd better move into that ward!" You see, he did not even live in the Eighth Ward, but that didn't seem to make any difference to him. The main reason that he lost was because he did not live in that ward. I knew where he lived. I had been to his house, you know. He lived in the Twenty-first Ward! So we presented this matter to the board, and they asked me to run, and I won in a runoff.

TB: Yes, it was a very exciting race.

WC: I held my own, as I've always been able to do in the black area, and matched the votes from that area as they came from other areas. Les and I went into a runoff, and the white candidate was eliminated. He had gotten the votes from the white area and only a couple of hundred votes separated him from Les. But Les ran in the runoff with me, and he got his votes from that area. Immediately after the election a reporter came by my house to talk to me, and this interview later appeared on the news. He asked me what the issues were, and I told them, "Race and space." I knew what I was talking about, because race has always been, is now, and will always be a consideration in decisions regarding the way things are done in this city—and it was particularly so then. And also at that time developers were trying to exploit the land and grab whatever they could—pure exploitation. So you had to guard against abuse and misuse of the land. At the time I became alderman, I took an inventory of every plot of vacant land of any size in the Eighth Ward and moved to preclude these developers from being able to do some things they had in mind. And as a result of that, we still don't have buildings there of a certain kind.

TB: Yes, there are no high-rises there!

WC: Yes, we took care of that, along with some other things. You see, these are matters which don't have to do specifically with civil rights, but which do have to do with the preservation of the quality of the area.

TB: Now, while this was happening on the South Side, on the West Side were there any independent black aldermen?

WC: Well, we had some black aldermen from the West Side at that time, but they were certainly not independent.

TB: Yes, they were all part of the regular organization. So that means that there were now three independent black aldermen, and you became the spokesperson for the community rather than Leon Despres.

WC: Well, we were sticking along with Leon, but we were speaking our own minds.

TB: Yes, you were speaking out for all of us, and that altered forever the idea that we had to necessarily depend on a white person to speak for the grievances of black people.

WC: Well, nobody can speak for black people like black people. There are just some things that can't be done by anybody else.

TB: Yes, that's certainly true, Bill. So now there are three black representatives who have taken on the idea of independence from the regular organization, and they are responding to the legitimate wishes of the community as much as they are able to. How did that operate? You were there for two terms?

WC: Yes, two terms and part of a third. I was elected three times. I was elected in 1967, in 1971, and again in 1975. Then I became a judge in 1976. My approach, you know, as a people's representative was that my role was to do just that—to represent the people. And there was no problem about what to do when there was a conflict, and there were constant conflicts at that time. I can say that there were hardly any occasions where I felt compelled to take positions that were in derogation of what the prevailing view was in my ward and, for that matter, in the city as a whole. When you represent a ward, sometimes you have the need to inform the people about the real issues. You see, they were often poorly advised about what was actually taking place.

TB: So you had started to have regular community forums.

WC: Oh, yes. It was an ongoing way to provide information. We used a newsletter, and, of course, just reading that newsletter from meeting to meeting helped keep them informed. I had people who told me they really liked this style of politics.

TB: What were the boundaries of the Eighth Ward at that time?

WC: The boundaries, initially, were from Seventy-third Street to 107th Street, in that area between Cottage Grove and Stony Island. And then it went off on two wings. The western wing went over to State Street, but it was only between Seventy-ninth and Eighty-third Streets, where there was a concentration of votes and where I initially had overwhelming strength. That was the Chatham area. Then the other wing went on the east side from Seventy-seventh Street and Ninetieth Street or something like that. We had ninety-six thousand people living in the ward when I first ran. The average size of a ward was determined to be about sixty-five thousand, so at that time we were way oversized. So when they had the redistricting, which took place after the 1970 census, it was understood that they would use this as an excuse to try to downsize our ward. Of course, they had no problem in deciding what they were going to take away, and that was that area of Chatham where I had most of my support.

[*Laughter.*]

And another time, in early 1972, what happened was that they gerrymandered, you know, drawing maps so as to dilute black strength and prevent us from electing black aldermen. There was some litigation that we had regarding that, and I was one of the principal plaintiffs in that suit. Actually, we could show they had been deliberately gerrymandered to minimize the opportunity for us to elect black representatives. A lot of the evidence came from the area of the Southeast Side. And what did they do? Judge McMillan in the District Court decided to strike the city map regarding the Eighth and the Seventh Wards, and then they redrew old boundaries shifting the wards. And, of course, the organization people considered that to be a victory for them because they thought they had me! But eventually, a year later, that went up on appeal to the Seventh Circuit Court of Appeals, and they overturned McMillan's decision and his finding. We then restored those wards to the way they had been before.

TB: Their intent was, therefore, to do damage to you.

WC: Yes, it was.

TB: You then ran for the judiciary in 1976, as an independent candidate?

WC: Yes, I ran in the Democratic primaries as an independent. I have never asked for party support for any office for which I have run, Tim. I may have indicated to you earlier that my initial race was for the state legislature in the Twenty-ninth Legislative District in 1962, when I ran as a Republican. When I launched my campaign I thought that I had a realistic chance of winning. I had taken a look at the previous returns for some period of time in the Twenty-ninth Legislative District. There was a representative there at that time named Schneider, who was getting up in age. I didn't think he was very well known, and I didn't think he was very active, you see? But I got a hard lesson about politics from that campaign. I carried the black wards that were in that district, but so far as its population was concerned, there were still probably more whites than blacks in that district, and at that time I didn't appreciate that the racial consideration in voting was as important as it was. I knew it was a factor, of course, but I really didn't know it was as strong as it was. What happened in that race was that I carried the predominantly black portions, even though I didn't have the support of the Republican committeemen. This was in 1962, and I figured that if I got more than half of the average votes that had come in for the Republicans in the past elections, I'd win. That's why I had accepted my campaign. But I didn't get that half. I didn't get even half of what had come in before. This is what happened. Let's say if the average vote per precinct in the predominantly white area in the Republican primary had been, for instance, one hundred votes before this time, well, it now jumped up to three hundred votes. And in many cases it was three hundred to nothing for me—so that was a lesson to me. And I said, "Now then, there's a reason for this, you see—and it's me." And it reinforced my view that the advisable course to take in electoral politics in this city and in this state is to take care of your home base. You cannot bank on the other bases. If something happens in your favor on the other bases, it is all well and good, but you can never bank on that happening.

TB: Yes, black voters will vote for a white candidate, but white voters are not likely to vote for a black candidate.

WC: And in particular, white folks will not vote for a black candidate if they perceive him as being militant. This is somewhat intimidating to them. And yet there are times when one has to be militant about certain things. If you look at blacks who really get a good deal of white support, generally they are not militant. Not ever.

They are usually conservative, or at the most centrist in their approach. This is a fact of life. And even in our state where we have some blacks doing well in public positions, they still shy away from certain issues.

TB: Yes, they have no desire to upset the status quo. When Dr. King came to Chicago, I am certain that you remember that there were many blacks in privileged positions that were opposed to him coming here.

WC: Yes, I do, and to pretend that it's otherwise is really just to deceive yourself.

TB: If you attempt to bring about social, economic, or political change, you're a threat to the status quo, whether it's in a neighborhood or wherever it might be.

WC: Yes. If it's different, then it's considered to be radical. And if you are radical and black, you can forget about it. That's the problem. And that's a problem we still have.

TB: That's an American problem.

WC: Yes. Blacks who are elected in predominantly white areas more frequently than not have to modify their positions. They have to conduct themselves in a way so that they aren't perceived by whites to be too black, because, if they were so perceived, the white majority would turn them out, and that's a fact of life. No question about it. No "ifs," "ands," or "buts" about it. In my personal experience, when you deal with a white who's been elected in an area that is large—generally statewide—you can deal with him on the QT, but if something comes up that is a controversial subject, they will make an immediate exit. They won't be identified, you know, if things get too black. This is the way it is. They won't carry the ball if it has a connotation of being identified as black. These are the facts of life. But people of color in this city have always responded in my elections, and I do not complain about diminished black vote. I never have complained about that. In any election in which I have run, the votes that I have received from the black community have been equivalent to those votes from outside—except when I was a Republican. As an independent, when I ran for alderman, there was a substantial white portion in that ward, but the votes that came from the area where I had my base were at least as strong. At least as strong or I would not have won! [Laughter.]

TB: When you ran for judge, however, you were running on a larger scale.

WC: Yes, and, of course, there are some wards in this city, particularly on the Southwest Side, where they get loops [get characterized racially]—I mean, they get loops!—and you really get cut out. It's happened right down the line. There's a pattern there, and it follows just the same whether I was running for judge, or whether Harold Washington was running for mayor, or whoever's running. It's just a question of how much white backlash you're going to get. And you're always going to get quite a bit of backlash.

TB: How long were you in the Circuit Court of Illinois, Bill?

WC: From 1976 until last year, 1992—sixteen years.

TB: What are your recollections of your experiences in that court? You were certainly a hardworking judge.

WC: As I look at everything that I have done, all except a few years of that time were spent in the criminal division. I was a felony trial court judge. As a Circuit Court judge, I was always a trial court judge. And I wanted to be assigned to the criminal division even though, as an attorney, I was primarily a civil lawyer. But I wanted to be there because of the magnitude of the problem that was there. That's where you can determine whether or not you're really giving justice—in those criminal areas. The problems there are matters of great magnitude, and in my own way I do feel that I had some impact. In the whole scheme of things, it was small, but I do feel that I had some personal impact. I visited the prison one time during the Christmas holidays, and the level of respect that the inmates accorded me indicated that at least they thought I had been fair, even though I have had to impose some severe penalties. Some of the people I tried will never get out of jail—never ever get out. But the nature of what they did and their mindset was such that that's the best way for them to go, for society's sake and for their sake. But, of course, I can't say that I would be considered to have been nice to them.

TB: Well, it was a question of fairness.

WC: Yes, and by and large, I believe that the defendants before me felt that they were receiving a fair trial and that they had been dealt with fairly. I had one instance where this fellow, a big fellow, had gone into a speakeasy and had lost all of his money. He went out and came back with a loaded gun. He then put everybody on the floor and took their money, and then he took the money from the cash register. There was a guard in there, and the guard drew his gun, and he shot the defendant, but it was not a fatal wound. Then the defendant shot the guard right between the eyes, saying, "I'll teach you!" The defendant then walked on out of the place, got caught and arrested. And, of course, he came up for trial, and he thought that under the circumstances he had a right to do what he had done. However, he got forty years, and he felt that the public defender had not handled his case well, and so he turned on the public defender in my courtroom! The state's attorney jumped back and went over toward the window away from the defendant! Then the defendant looked at me, and he said, "Yeah, you're all right, but not him!"—and he made a gesture with his hand toward the state's attorney!

[*Laughter.*]

Now, look at this portrait I have over here. It was drawn by a fellow who had been a defendant in my court. He had been given probation, and I had forgotten all about it. I didn't even recognize him when I saw him down in the lobby of the new Criminal Courts Building one day when I was passing through. He had what looked like a portrait in his hands. He was talking to one of my deputies, and I asked him what he had and if I could see it. It appeared to be a portrait of myself, and so I said, "What is this? What would this cost?" And he said to me, "Judge, nothing—for you. You're my hero," and he gave that to me! I have also received many communications from people who have been in my court, some of which would move you to tears, but I have also had some experiences which allow me to know for certain that there are some situations where I was able to salvage some people and turn them in the right direction. During the course of my time on the bench, I always tried to put something into the minds of the individuals that stood before me, and this has stayed with some of them, based on what they have brought to my attention later. This indicates to me that I was able to make a little bit of difference in some situations, and that gives one a sense of satisfaction.

TB: How heavy was the caseload when you went into that court?

WC: Oh, initially, very heavy. They added new judges or reduced the caseload to some extent, but the number of cases you still had to address constantly increased and is still increasing. And it is happening in large part because of the inundation of our courts with drug cases. When I first went on the bench in 1976, as far as criminal cases were concerned, our total caseload for the criminal division ran about eight thousand. When I left, the total dispositions per year were in excess of thirty thousand.

TB: From eight thousand to thirty thousand in a period of sixteen years?

WC: In a period of less than sixteen years. In a period of about fourteen years. It almost quadrupled. And half the cases then, on the call, were drug cases, so we had more than twice the number of drug cases than we had of all other kinds of cases together. During my first year, only about one-tenth of the total cases on the call were drug cases, you see, and so the total number mushroomed, and now things are really out of control. Our prisons are overloaded. The governor, I understand, is going to have a press conference today about building a new maximum-security prison. So the prison space has been multiplied, but even so, we've fallen further behind. The policies of sentencing have been misconceived. The notion that we can stamp out crime by constantly increasing the penalties without doing anything else just doesn't work. And you don't even have enough places to put people! It's hypocrisy and, I would say, a lot of hogwash, because the people involved in the system know that it doesn't work, and since we don't even have places to put people when they're sentenced, we put them in one door and have to let the same people walk out the back door.

TB: What was the racial, ethnic, and gender breakdown by percentage of the people who came before you when you first came to the bench?

WC: I would say the makeup, racially, has remained reasonably constant. At least 75 percent of the defendants are black in our felony criminal court system in Cook County. And then somewhere between 10 and 15 percent are Hispanic and somewhere between 10 and 15 percent are white Americans. The number of women coming into the system has increased. Along with some advancement of women in different ways, you also have an increasing number of women coming into the criminal court system.

TB: Bill, you have lived a very productive life.

WC: It's been a full life.

TB: You have been married for forty years, haven't you?

WC: Yes, for forty years.

TB: And you have four children?

WC: Yes, I do. And, Tim, I have a lot of satisfaction with my life. I have to say my way was not an easy way. I did not choose an easy way. I could have chosen an easy way. I could have been alderman long before I was alderman—under different circumstances. Indeed, when I ran for alderman the first time, Congressman Dawson's secretary called me at my home and said, "The congressman wants to see you." And I said, "What about?" And he said, "He wants to talk to you about the aldermanic campaign. Will you come down?" And I said, "Yes, I'll come down." So I did. I went down to the Second Ward, and I took with me the members of my executive committee!

[*Laughter.*]

We had the meeting, and the congressman said to me, "We want you to withdraw." And I said, "Withdraw? In favor of who?" And he said, "In favor of Les Bland." Well, I figured Les Bland should be withdrawing in my favor. Then the congressman said to me, "You know, you could be one of the most powerful people in this city"—that's what he said to me, or words to that effect. And I said, "Well, maybe I will be," or something to that effect. And I can tell you at this time that if I had wanted to take a position as a magistrate in a judicial office, it was mine for the asking. All I had to do was to leave the Eighth Ward open to them. But of course, even if I had wanted to become a judge then—and I didn't have a burning ambition to become a judge then, anyway—but even if I had wanted to, I would not have done so under those circumstances.

TB: As you said earlier, it would be against your nature.

WC: Yes. I would not have done it in that way. I took my executive committee with me to Congressman Dawson's office so they would know what was going on and why I was down there. Obviously, Dawson's people had taken some soundings out there in the ward and had found that the doors were closed in their faces. They probably knew more than I did, and I had a pretty good report as to what was going on throughout my candidacy, and they could see that there was no way that Les Bland was going to win that race out there!

[*Laughter.*]

So there have been satisfactions in living my life without, let's say, compromising what I conceive to be some very basic and fundamental principles. I can also say that while I was alderman I never asked the mayor for a meeting that he didn't grant. And he generally would say, "We'll see what we can do about it."

TB: Is this Mayor Richard J. Daley?

WC: Yes. The mayor, in my view, could not understand why I could not be bought into that circle.

TB: The charmed circle!

[*Laughter.*]

WC: He just couldn't understand it. That was something that he was not able to fully comprehend!

[*Laughter.*]

TB: Well, while I never attained the status of an elected office, the mayor had folks chasing after me because he didn't want a straggling voice out there against him. He wanted it to be closed off. And, then, of course, he made an example of people whom he could bring in so he could say, "See, they can all be bought." And that sort of thing discourages people, particularly young people. When they have given some admiration to certain people, and then they see those people drop by the wayside, things like that decrease the young people's ability to resist the forces of evil. So Daley sent a few people my way, and I handled it just like you did. Ed Marciniak called me and said, "The mayor wants to see you."

WC: Yes, he was the mayor's main man for a long time.

TB: Well, this was after the mayor got booed off the stand in 1963. The mayor thought I had had something to do with it, and he was right. But I said, "Well, we'll be down." And he said, "No, just you." And I said, "No, I can't come to see the mayor by myself. No." And so the meeting never happened. But then, of course, he sent one of his other agents over to me to plead his case.

WC: In the whole scheme of things, you know, respect and honor really outrank everything else.

TB: Yes, and part of that is self-respect.

WC: Oh, yes, you have to have self-respect. If you have self-respect, then you have the respect of others. That surely is more valuable than all of these other things.

March 3 and June 7, 1993

MARJORIE ECHOLS
AND HARVEY ECHOLS

SOCIAL WORKER AND HER HUSBAND

Marjorie Echols's story is a very charming one, but our conversation was painful for me because I knew she was very sick with cancer. I told her husband, Harvey, that although she had agreed to chat with me about her life in Chicago much earlier, now we should consider calling off our discussion because of the serious nature of her illness. She had Harvey call me back right away, however, to let me know that she wanted to have our chat right away because there might not be another better opportunity. So it was with deeply mixed feelings that I went to their lovely home in Chicago's Chatham community. Harvey, a professional colleague of mine at City Colleges of Chicago, was there to help her in telling the story of her life, but our conversation was focused on and is her own story as expressed in her own words.

This remarkable woman was a member of a fairly successful small-town middle-class family that was originally from Jackson, Mississippi. Her mother loved classical music and dance, but her grandfather disapproved of this "devil's music," and so her mother and her aunt had to see and hear that kind of music without his knowledge. Finally, when she had the opportunity, her mother came to Chicago and married and lived on the West Side.

Marjorie went to schools on the West Side and graduated from McKinley High School. Because of her superb academic as well as leadership qualities within what was then a mixed-race environment, she received a four-year scholarship to Howard University, where she graduated with honors. Returning to Chicago, she soon became one of the first female black employees for Illinois Bell. Later she met and married

Harvey Echols and started a family of her own. During the seventies, she returned to graduate school at the University of Illinois at Chicago and received an M.S. in social work. Before her death, she gave extensive time to HIV-infected patients and their families at Cook County Hospital.

Mrs. Echols was a truly remarkable woman who always gave her very best to her family, to her community, and to her profession. After our conversation, as I was leaving, she smiled warmly as she said good-bye to me and then closed the door. She passed the following week.

TB: Marge Echols has been living in Chicago most of her life, and I want to ask her to share some of her experiences and reflections with us today. Marge, when and where were you born?

ME: In 1929 on the West Side of Chicago.

TB: Oh, 1929, the year of the Great Depression. Where on the West Side were you born?

ME: At that time, Mother was living around Walnut Street over near Western. Now that whole area is completely industrialized, I think.

TB: That's an area of settlement which has been almost totally African-American for probably more than a hundred years. Historians mostly talk about African-American settlements on the South Side, but there were always a lot of African-American families living on the West Side as well. And where were your mother and dad born?

ME: My mother was born in Jackson, Mississippi, and she came here when she was in her early twenties. We actually knew nothing about my dad's family. He was very secretive, it seems.

TB: What year did she come to Chicago?

ME: My mother came to Chicago in 1921.

TB: Did you know any of your grandparents?

ME: I knew who they were, but I never got to meet them. Mother wrote to them, but I never got a chance to visit them in Jackson, and they never left Jackson. Both of them were in ill health. My mother also had two sisters who continued to live in Jackson, and we saw and talked with them. One or the other of them would visit Chicago regularly.

TB: But you never visited Jackson?

ME: No, I never got to Jackson.

TB: When I think of that older generation—which I'll also call my generation because I'm much older than you—for one reason or other our parents had no urge to go back south. For most of the people I've talked with whose families had left the

South, there was no attraction to return. I think the reason was based on the fact that they had left the South because things were not good for them down there.

ME: Well, my mother's reason for leaving was that, as the youngest daughter of a Methodist minister, she did not have the freedom to do a lot of things she felt should be her own decision to make. She wanted to dance. She wanted to sing. She had, in fact, appeared in several operettas. My uncle had organized a group that traveled through the South. The group was named for one of the schools in Jackson—an AME Methodist college.

TB: Well, we share that background. I came out of the AME tradition myself.

ME: My uncles were AME ministers, and because their school needed funds, my uncles organized that operetta group. They traveled throughout the South putting on operettas until my grandfather convinced my uncle that singing and dancing were sinful—even though their work supported the school. But at the time, as an AME minister, my grandfather felt that he should no longer encourage this. My mother then decided that she wanted to become a secretary, and so she learned typing and shorthand, but Grandpa wouldn't let her be a secretary because blacks couldn't afford secretaries, and he wouldn't have her working for a white man. Therefore, she simply thought that there was nothing for her to do in the South. If she came up to Chicago she thought she could at least do *something*. There were some friends of the family who had relocated here in Chicago, so Grandpa was willing for her to come here. She came to Chicago and stayed with friends and worked as a dental assistant here on the South Side. It was only after she met my father that she moved to the West Side.

TB: Now, as I remember, the West Side, at that time, did not as yet have a large number of African-Americans living there. However, there were always some living around Walnut, Warren—that area—and also on Lake Street. It's important for us to remember and understand that there have been African-Americans living on the West Side for as long as there have been African-Americans here on the South Side.

ME: There was even one area near Damen between Madison and Lake Streets in which there were about four really large black churches.

HE: And, of course, the Metropolitan, in our time, was especially important—and Provident also, if you're talking about churches that go back to the last century.

ME: I don't think that in most areas on the West Side there were many blocks that were continuous with black residents, but there were lots of pockets where black people lived.

TB: By what other ethnic groups were these pockets surrounded?

ME: Italians. Greeks. Jews. My high school graduating class at McKinley High School was, I think, predominately Greek and Italian.

TB: Who were some of the people that you remember from the West Side when you were growing up?

ME: Shanille Perry. His daughter and I were the same age. I was one of the few people that she was allowed to play with. And the Reverend Ledbetter was pastor at Metropolitan Baptist Church.

TB: Reverend Ledbetter, yes, I remember him. And the big political Policy man, Big Jim Martin, was the man that most of us knew about from the West Side. And there was his son, Sol Martin, and also Ike Sims. What elementary school did you go to, Marge?

ME: We moved around a lot.

[*Laughter.*]

TB: Like most of us!

[*Laughter.*]

ME: At the time my father died, Mother had five children. Two of them were living with my grandparents in Mississippi. Mother remarried when I was about six years old and started having children even faster! She was a good woman—she really was—but she didn't think husbands were much good.

[*Laughter.*]

She didn't make any really wise choices, and we did move a lot—mostly in the middle of the night!

TB: The good old days of the Depression! The good old days of the thirties!

ME: Even though we had moved around a good deal, we always managed to continue going to Grant School, but finally, we were just too far from it. We were living in one of Jim Martin's wife's buildings on Lake Street, and he and his wife convinced us to transfer to a closer school district, so I finished my last three years at Hayes School at Leavitt and Walnut.

HE: It has since been torn down. That whole area, now, is commercial.

TB: So you graduated from Hayes School. What was the neighborhood like back then?

ME: It was poor. Right around the school I think there were quite a few people who owned their own homes. They weren't fine homes, but at least they were owned by the people who lived in them.

HE: As a matter of fact, Billy King's restaurant was on the corner of Oak and Lake Street. He lived right down the street from his own restaurant.

ME: That was one of the first places that Nat King Cole appeared. When nobody else would listen to Cole's style, he was hired by Billy King.

HE: Billy King's is where a lot of the young men in the neighborhood used to gather. My uncle, who was a musician and who still lives on the West Side, would appear there also.

TB: Another important thing that I remember is that there were some very great Golden Gloves champions that came out of the West Side.

ME: Johnny Fagan is one of them, and his brother, Benny Fagan, is another.

TB: Well, I remember Johnny because he became, to some of us, kind of a folk hero. So when you graduated from elementary school, the neighborhood was stable, and you got to know a lot of people over a long period of time.

HE: Yes, and speaking further of the people that came out of that neighborhood, Daryl Bishop was our neighbor. Lonnie Crimm is another. And there was K. D. "King" Fleming, the great piano player.

TB: Yes, he used to travel all over the South with his band during the slow season.

ME: My sister, Betty, was best friends with King Fleming's youngest sister—so whenever he was playing here in the city, the kids would get together and go see him perform. My sister was going to see King Fleming *long* before Mother felt I was old enough to attend that type of event.

TB: Yes, he used to play at the old Parkway Ballroom. He played a lot of gigs on the South Side. In fact, he and Nat both had their own bands—large bands—and they would have a battle of the bands occasionally, at whichever ballroom where they happened to be appearing. Of course, since I knew Nat, I was always a supporter of his, but I enjoyed all the music. The music was good—on both sides.

ME: I didn't hear King Fleming play until about ten years ago. But my sister, who was only about a year older than I, had the privilege of hearing him early on.

TB: Isn't that interesting? One of the things I remember is that parents were very selective about where their daughters, in particular, went and what they did.

ME: Very much so. There had to be someone that they knew who was also going to the event. If there wasn't, you didn't go!

TB: Boys had a little more freedom, although there was still a certain amount of control, but not nearly as much as there was for the young ladies, and I can understand and appreciate that. Now, Marge, when you graduated and left Hayes School, you went on to McKinley High School. What was that like?

ME: I am probably not the best person to give you a really good picture of what it was like. For some reason, my mother never believed that I was as myopic as I really was, and she never believed that I needed stronger glasses in order to see well, so I was without proper glasses for a lot of the time. But in spite of that, I was a good student, and I enjoyed practicing—I played the flute in the band. I didn't really circulate in the neighborhood. McKinley, at the time I went there, was not predominantly black, as it later became when my sisters went there.

TB: Now, what time period is this?

ME: Well, this was 1942 to 1946. I was also many of the teachers' "pet." That way I could brush off some of the prejudice that I knew was there, but there was one teacher who was blatantly prejudiced. I don't know why they let her keep it up. She was very impressed with Shomea Perry's father's position—he was an attorney at the time. She would really butter up Shomea. But Shomea was the only female and the only black that she treated at all well. Institutionally, however, I didn't feel any prejudice in the school.

TB: What was the composition of McKinley—besides the black students?

ME: Mostly Greek and Italian. All of the young people that went there came from the neighborhood where the University of Illinois Circle Campus is now, except for a good percentage of the boys who went off to Crane Technical School.

TB: Yes, that's right. Crane, because it was technical, was an all-boys school at that time. Now, in the period we're discussing, during those years of the war, do you remember anything specifically about World War II?

ME: Well, you see, a lot of the older boys simply dropped out. Actually, at that time—with eight years of grammar school and two years of high school—a lot of people dropped out. They were sixteen and lots of jobs were available.

TB: Well-paying jobs?

ME: Yes, and so the dropout rate of the black students was even higher than that of the whites.

HE: And also many young African-Americans were being drafted.

TB: Right—just as soon as they left high school!

HE: Yes, and in some instances even before. When they would become eighteen, they would be drafted right away, but many of them signed on at seventeen.

TB: What kinds of jobs were available to young men and, increasingly, I imagine, to young women as well?

ME: Two of my sisters worked in defense plants, and one of my sisters worked at Spiegel's, the catalog company, for quite some time. I never found a job. I got to high school younger than most people did. However, I managed to work at Western Union at one time. That was fascinating. They had a great big building downtown near Union Station.

TB: Were they still carrying the telegrams by hand at that time?

ME: Yes, they were. As a matter of fact, when the messengers would come in, they would come to one central location. What I was doing, along with many other high school students, was picking up the messages and then taking them to the operators who dispatched them to the individual offices. Some of us wore roller skates, and we were running around the floor all the time because we picked up messages as they came in, and the fastest way to get them sent out was to carry them over to the other side of the building where that messenger was. We were running around on roller skates all day long! I really don't think that that was quite the picture that the public had of Western Union, do you?

[*Laughter.*]

TB: Well, I had friends who rode bicycles for Western Union. You know, after they got a message, then they would give it to the delivery boys who delivered these messages on bicycles. Can you imagine that happening today?

HE: Well, they are doing something very much like that downtown even today. I see messengers on bicycles riding around all the time.

TB: Yes, that's true. But take, for example, the Western Union office down on Seventy-ninth Street. The kid would get on his bike and ride around delivering all those messages! If you had a bike, that was one job you could always get. It was a nice job for a high school student. But the point is that our young men and young women had lots of choices about the possibility of some kind of work— even right there in the neighborhood.

HE: Well, we're talking about the forties now, but as late as 1938 and 1939, on the West Side, African-American men couldn't get any kind of a job with Western Union. It was all white back then.

TB: But at least there were "ma and pa" grocery stores where you could get jobs.

HE: We couldn't get those kind of jobs here on the West Side either!

TB: Is that right?

HE: At that time on Madison Street, which was *the* main shopping street, we weren't allowed to clerk or do anything else.

TB: Oh, is that right? As late as what date?

HE: That would be 1942. As a matter of fact, that's when they had the sit-in in order to get us clerks' positions in the Woolworth's five-and-dime store.

TB: As late as 1942! And what happened about 1942?

HE: Well, World War II had started, and help was hard to get. When you ask what kinds of jobs we got, I remember in 1942 my cousin, who had dropped out of high school, got a job in Nachman's spring factory. I don't know if you have ever heard of it.

TB: Oh, yes.

HE: Well, Nachman was building springs for use in the defense industry. But those were the only kinds of jobs you could get. You couldn't get jobs that involved any real responsibility.

TB: Well, that still doesn't happen very often!

[*Laughter.*]

Except for the highly skilled, of course, and those who are clued into connections.

HE: But there was room back then for those people who didn't have a good education, because the unskilled worker was always needed to do the backbreaking work, the kind of work that is being done today by machines.

TB: Which accounts for many of our young people having no skills as well as no jobs.

ME: In 1942, we still had ice trucks and coal trucks going through the alleys, and somebody always had to be hired to carry the ice and the coal. Mr. Lights was one of the most prominent ice and coal men on the West Side.

HE: Yes, he had three trucks, and when I was a youngster, my friends and I would all pile on the back of a truck, and it would take us out to Eighty-seventh Street and Western—the Dan Ryan Woods—or to Swallow Cliff, and we had a great time! Now laws have been passed, and you can't ride on the backs of trucks like that anymore. Mr. Lights lived in my block, so if the day was warm and if it was a Sunday, he would pass the word around, "Let's go on a picnic!" And everybody would pile onto those trucks.

ME: Mr. Light's wife's brother was our family doctor.

HE: Yes, and you see that's the difference between then and now. There were businesspeople in the neighborhood, and they lived right there with you. For instance, there were two fine doctors within walking distance of both my family and Marge's family. Dentists were also right there. Even the man that headed the draft board lived five doors east of my family.

TB: And he had to look you in the eye after he had drafted you!

[*Laughter.*]

HE: Well, those are the kinds of things we had access to that we don't have access to today.

TB: It *was* possible in that setting—aside from going outside the neighborhood—to find what you would consider a *good* job. You could live pretty comfortably within the confines of your neighborhood. This was especially true for a young person.

ME: You could hustle and be legitimate and make it.

TB: I'm speaking also of recreation.

HE: No, when my friends and I got ready to really have some recreation we always went to the South Side. There were some things happening on the West Side as well, of course, but for the real thing you always went to the South Side. It was a much larger community and had so much more to offer.

TB: What about movie houses and places like that?

HE: Now, at this time, movie houses weren't just for blacks only.

TB: No, but neither were those on the South Side. Did you have any storefront churches around?

HE: *Loads* of them. Metropolitan Baptist Church started as a storefront.

TB: But it wasn't a storefront in your day?

HE: When my parents first joined, it was still a storefront church on the corner of

Carol Avenue and LeBouchee. This was in about 1927. It was in 1929, I believe, that the church moved from there over to Ward and Western. They stayed there for years, but in 1939 they had a political rally there, and it just "happened" that the next night the church burned down!

ME: Of course what happened was politically inspired.

TB: Well, God didn't come down from heaven and do that!

HE: They eventually rebuilt it, but for several years they had to meet over at a little storefront church in the 2500 block of Lakeview. Reverend Smith was the founder of that church. Finally, around the time that the war started, about 1942, they moved back of the Metropolitan. Shortly after that, I guess about 1947 or so, Reverend Smith fell on ill times. Well, let's put it this way, he was doing some things that a minister ought not to do, and the church saw fit to relieve him of his duties. The Reverend Ledbetter came to replace him and really developed the church, and then they bought the existing Baptist church that was on the corner of Leavitt and Washington.

TB: What was Lake Street like in those days?

HE: Lake Street was very much like what Forty-third Street was like in the forties. You could find anything you wanted there. All the trouble you wanted was there as well—*if* you were looking for it. But you also could find good things there if you wanted to. It just depended on what you were looking for. If you wanted to shop, you went to Madison Street, but the taverns where we went were on Lake Street. You couldn't go into any of those taverns that were on Madison because they were white taverns. I went into them sometimes as a shoeshine boy, but I couldn't have gone in otherwise.

TB: I used to go to Jim Martin's Corner at 1900 Lake Street. That was a very, very popular place to go for *anybody*. I saw Kid Chocolate there and some of the boxers and popular figures in sports at that time.

HE: But Lake Street was the main drag.

TB: Now, Marge, you went to McKinley High School, and after you left McKinley you went to Howard University in 1947? I believe you had a scholarship to Howard. Was that an academic scholarship?

ME: Yes, it was.

TB: What was Howard like at that time?

ME: I had never seen so many black people in my life!

[*Laughter.*]

And I had *never* seen that many black men, and most of them were cute! It was an eye-opener. I really didn't know anything about Howard until I heard that I had won the scholarship.

TB: You had gone to McKinley High School, which was a mixed high school in a mixed community on the West Side, so how did Howard come about? Was the faculty also mixed?

ME: No, the faculty was all white.

TB: And the administration was all white?

ME: Yes, but not all of the teachers were prejudiced against black students, and our English teacher arranged for a group of us—the black students in the class—to take this exam. There were about five of us who were, I guess, academically oriented. I hadn't been told anything about the exam before then.

TB: Were you going away from home for the first time?

ME: Yes, for the first time in my life. I didn't even know where Washington, D.C., was! I asked one of my friends—because she had a job downtown—to buy my tickets at the railroad station. So she went to the railway station, and she bought a ticket to Seattle, Washington! But eventually I got the right ticket and went off to Howard. School was very interesting. This was at the end of World War II, and there were a lot of returning vets. They always seemed to be pretty well off, and they had plenty of money for books.

TB: Yes, we had a generous book allowance. World War II, for those of us who survived it, was pretty generous.

ME: There was always one of the vets that would turn his books over to me, and in that way I obtained the necessary books for my classes.

TB: Where did you stay?

ME: The first year I stayed on campus, but the next year there wasn't room on campus, so they farmed us out to individual homes nearby.

TB: Putting the veterans aside for the moment, what was the rest of the student body like?

ME: Snobbish. Wealthy. My freshman roommate was from Jamaica. I think a lot of the Americans resented those students from other countries. You see, they had been at the top of the class in their own countries. Back then in the British colonies you did not progress through high school and go away to college unless you were right at the top, so at Howard we were getting the cream of the crop.

TB: And then those students also probably resented the fact that they had been rejected by the British schools, but at the same time they felt culturally and intellectually superior to the American black students.

ME: Yes, they did.

TB: What was the attitude of the residents of Washington, D.C., toward Howard students?

ME: You know, we didn't have that much interaction with them. The Washington, D.C., Teachers College was about two blocks away from Howard's campus and many of the students from the Teachers College—who were predominantly D.C. students—would come up to use the facilities on Howard's campus because the facilities at the D.C. Teachers College were pretty poor. But, aside from that, the students from D.C. Teachers College really did not interact very much with the Howard students. In fact, there was a lot of resentment between the residents of Washington, D.C., and the Howard students, and I never really got to know anybody from the district that well.

TB: Did you socialize outside the school?

ME: No, everything we wanted was there on campus. Most of our activity was in and around the campus itself.

TB: Most of the entertainment that you had was on campus also?

ME: Yes. At that time the school was still held responsible for the behavior of the students. The president of Howard had kids of his own attending the school while I was there. I met him, and I shook his hand a couple of times. He would speak to us when we were going across campus, and sometimes he would just stop and pass the time of day with us—I guess to try to feel closer to the students—but it's kind of hard to feel close to the students when you're living in a great big house that's up on the hill instead of right there on campus!

TB: Was E. Franklin Frazier there at that time?

ME: Yes.

TB: What was your major, Marge?

ME: My major was psychology.

TB: So you've been pretty consistent in your entire career.

ME: Pretty much so. Actually, I started out as a sociology major, however, and then I realized that I didn't want to have that field as my profession for the rest of my life.

TB: When did you graduate from Howard?

ME: I graduated in 1951 and came back to Chicago. I really wanted to go back to school and get a master's degree but was unable to do so at that time.

TB: So you entered the field of social work. Now, around this time, you and Harvey got married. What year was that?

ME: It was in 1955.

TB: You had been living on the West Side at that time. Did you continue to live on the West Side?

ME: I was living with my sister during most of this time, over near Fulton and Kedzie. Prior to when Harvey and I decided to get married, I had moved from there because I was working on the South Side, and I found an apartment near Forty-sixth and Champlain. This was in 1954, and I had already been living there for several months at the time Harvey and I got married.

TB: What was the neighborhood at Forty-sixth and Champlain like?

ME: Well, I never really became a part of the neighborhood, but I could walk to work in ten minutes.

TB: Where did you work?

ME: I worked at Forty-third and Drexel at the telephone company.

TB: At that point, the neighborhood—Hyde Park, or Kenwood—was changing.

ME: Yes, it was changing. I will never forget a call that I got one day from an employee of the telephone company. The caller said, "Yes, we're moving. We've been here for forty years, and we're moving because the sun is setting in this neighborhood."

TB: The sun is setting!

ME: "The sun is setting, and we need to get out." My guess is that this was a very racially motivated remark. The telephone company, at that point, was segregated, and so, of course, you could not respond to a remark like that. Although people said they could tell when they were talking to blacks, they couldn't really. The thing is that although this kind of job didn't require a college education, most of the black girls that held that job were, in fact, college educated.

TB: Yes, I would imagine so.

ME: And they were selected, to some extent, for their ability to be understood on the telephone. So we didn't speak so much with the black dialect, and when whites called in, they didn't know to whom they were speaking. So, although you might want to tell them, "Look, I'm black!"—you couldn't ever do anything like that.

TB: At this time did they still have pay telephones in the homes?

ME: Yes, there were still some pay telephones in homes. I don't think there were many party lines still available, but people would still ask for one.

TB: Explain what you mean by "party lines."

ME: Well, a "party line" is where there are two telephone numbers sharing a common line. You'd have different numbers, but if the other party is using the telephone, you can't use it.

HE: In the early days there were two-party lines and four-party lines. There would be two families on a line or four families on a line. Of course, there was no privacy on those party lines, but to have a single line would have cost you a lot more.

TB: So having a one-party line was kind of prestigious!

ME: Yes, the telephone company had actually stopped installing party lines by that time. But they hadn't gotten permission, legally, not to install them anymore, so they still had to allow people to ask for a two-party or a four-party line. The customers knew the telephone company probably couldn't find anybody else to put on the party line with you, and so in that way you could get the privacy you wanted at a very low rate.

TB: Now, this indicates that at about this time, for the blacks and whites—but most certainly for the blacks—economic conditions must have gotten at least a little better.

ME: Yes, but it was far enough after World War II that employment for women had somewhat begun to level off.

TB: What do you mean by "level off"?

ME: Well, when the war ended, the flow of money abruptly stopped and all of the women who had worked during the war and who had gotten accustomed to that kind of money had to seek employment in other areas, and some of them just stayed home after they got married.

TB: Yes, the custom then was—if it could be afforded—that the wife should stay at home. Had nursery schools and day care schools emerged to any great degree at this time?

ME: No, not at all. Once you had your children you stayed home, and you took care of the children. That was your job.

TB: And if the husband had to work two jobs, then that's what he did! Now, were you still living in the same neighborhood?

ME: Yes, Harvey was living in the area of Damen and Washington, and I moved in there.

TB: What was the West Side like during this time? Were there changes coming about or were there about the same social, cultural, and economic conditions? What was happening?

ME: The flight of blacks out of the poor neighborhoods had begun.

TB: The lower end of the belt was moving south.

ME: Or to the southwest.

HE: Those people who could afford it were moving to the suburbs. Doctors and lawyers—whoever could afford to—moved away from that part of the city. The pillars of the community moved away. Those that made the neighborhood stable moved away, and those that were left were not stable.

TB: Now, just who are these people that were left behind?

ME: The ones who lacked jobs and education.

TB: Yes, but aren't there also newcomers who are now moving into these old places? Where did they come from?

HE: They came from the South—and the people that were left in the neighborhood were the ones who didn't really know how to cope very well.

TB: So all that was left was what we might loosely call "the residue"?

ME: Yes, and these new people were coming in from rural communities—people who really didn't know the ways of the city, and those people remaining in the community did not have the ability to take these newcomers in hand, like there had been when my father-in-law came to Chicago, and show them how to cope in the city. So the newcomers came up from the rural areas and proceeded to behave pretty much as they had been doing back there where they had come from. And, of course, that wasn't the way to behave in the city!

TB: That wasn't considered acceptable behavior here in the city.

ME: And another thing that happened just prior to the time we're talking about—during World War II—is that there had been an earlier great influx of people coming to Chicago from the South. This created a problem for the West Side and the South Side in that everything became grossly overcrowded. Houses and apartments were subdivided again and again. Some of the families that moved out of the area just wanted more room in which to spread out. But most of us couldn't expand out of that little area.

TB: And more people were constantly pouring in?

ME: Yes, and so it wasn't so much the middle-class flight as much as it was the problem of finding enough elbow room to be able to exist. Housing five or six families in a single-family unit is always going to cause problems. The condition of the real estate, in many instances, was really downtrodden, but this was not so much reflective of the people who were coming into the city and their mode of living as it was of the existing conditions of severe overcrowding.

HE: In 1945, when I was getting back from the army, I saw families living in storefronts that had been boarded up for years when I was a child. I never did think there would be people living in places like that because they had been abandoned for so long, but housing was so tight that now people were living in those kind of places. The area of Lake Street in the 2500 block was particularly bad.

TB: So there are a couple of factors operating here. Newcomers—strangers—that have not become urbanized or learned how to live in the cities, in addition to those kinds of challenges, now they have to face an overcrowding factor which makes living extremely uncomfortable. As you probably know, it was common at that time for two families to use the same washroom and, in some instances, even the same kitchen.

ME: Well, let me tell you this. My mom used to say this, and I think it throws a different light on the situation. She grew up in the country knowing that if you saw a blade of grass growing you went out and stamped on it and killed it because grass would take over the garden and take over your flower plot, and the quicker you killed it the better off you were. As a matter of fact, you were much better off with no grass at all—with just sweeping the dirt clean—rather than having grass growing into your okra and your mustard and turnips. When she came to Chicago, she was still being what she thought was a good citizen, and so she was stamping out every piece of green grass that came up in our front lawn, and she did that until finally somebody told her—or maybe the family just began to realize—that in the city grass is considered to be a treasure. You don't plant a garden of mustard and turnips that you need to protect out in the backyard or the front yard. But my mom thought she was being a good citizen when she stamped the grass out. Those are the kinds of things that you learn from other people, but if everybody else has moved out of the area, then you don't understand about not stamping on the grass, and if everybody else that's still left in the neighborhood is stamping on the grass, then you're going to continue doing it too. That's why, when we would go over to the West Side, there was more dirt that was visible. It was because there every time somebody would see an empty little piece of dirt they would go and plant something. But on the South Side you have backyards and vacant lots and nobody was ever doing any kind of planting.

TB: Yes, nobody on the South Side was planting potatoes or mustard greens or collard greens or tomatoes—as they had done in the South.

ME: But on the West Side it was only the second generation that learned not to do this, not the first generation.

TB: That was because nobody transferred the right kind of information to that first group.

HE: Yes, and there was a breakdown in the families as well. You see, there was not the discipline that there had been when we were growing up, and you didn't know most people very well because there were so many newcomers. So the children did not get discipline the way we had gotten discipline. I'm not going to tell you that when we were growing up everybody was free to discipline us, because they weren't. But, on the other hand, we didn't get out of line because, if they told our mothers on us, our mothers would have disciplined us themselves. So we had to be sure that the neighbors didn't see us doing any of the things that we shouldn't have been doing! But if you don't even know the neighbors' families, then you can't have that same kind of social control.

TB: And the family would not want a stranger that they didn't know or trust to start messing around with their child or even trying to give them any kind of advice.

ME: Yes, they wouldn't have believed a stranger coming in and saying, "This is what your child did."

TB: So community trust in this sense breaks down. Did you feel more comfortable with people when you returned to the South Side?

ME: Well, let's not call it a return! My little stint on the South Side was merely because that was the place that was close to my work. I walked to work. We only came here to the South Side permanently in 1970.

HE: But we weren't "getting away." We did not mistrust our neighbors on the West Side. They were nice. As a matter of fact, when we came here we found that, personally, we've lost more here than we had ever lost over there.

ME: The reason we came here and to this house is because it was owned by my sister and my brother-in-law. They were not living in this city at the time, and the lawyer they had given power of attorney to put some horrible tenants in this building who were running it down, so they urgently needed somebody to be there in the house, and at the same time we needed more space, so we didn't bother to even look at other places. Here was a house that would accommodate us in a neighborhood that we were vaguely familiar with. All we had to do was to take over the payments.

TB: Now, by this time, how many children did you have?

ME: We had all five of them, and another reason for moving into this area was that we had the statistics that showed that the school in the Chatham neighborhood was rated very high scholastically.

TB: Yes, Dodd School.

ME: That was one of the things that made us feel that this would be a good place for us, because we were beginning to be somewhat dissatisfied with the education that our children were getting in the West Side schools.

HE: Our feeling has always been that our children were going to have at least as good an education as we had, because we believe it's up to the parents to provide that. You want them to get the education in school, of course, but in case the school doesn't give them the education you want for them, then you yourself have to make up for what the school doesn't do.

TB: That's exactly right.

ME: I have always gotten access to teachers' books. I found out what was required, and if the teacher didn't teach it, I taught it. But I was looking forward to my children going to a school where their lessons would be taught in the school instead of my having to teach at five different levels at home—although I had been doing just that ever since they started school. I am a good teacher by nature. I have an ability to understand the other person's mind. I can see the path on which they're thinking. That's one of the things that makes one good at social work. It is a kind of intuitive thinking.

TB: That is very true.

ME: And I was anxious to go back to school so I would be able to continue to learn. I feel that my gifts are God-given. I have taught my children that God made many people who can hold two quarts of water, and if you suddenly realize that you can hold three quarts, it would be sinful not to fill yourself up.

TB: Yes, and so you returned to school in 1987?

ME: Well, in the meantime, I had started working because I thought I could just have my bachelor's degree and a year of psychology on a graduate level and be able to get a good job. I started working for a nominal salary, but fortunately, my first job ended after about eight or ten months, and I got another better job as the volunteer recruiter and coordinator for the Literacy Council. When I began to feel that there was no longer any room for me to grow there, I knew that I needed to prepare myself for a situation where I could grow. I was trying to wrap up things at the job so I wouldn't go off and leave undone work dangling. I knew my boss was going to have trouble hiring somebody to take over my job. This was also the summer that my son Harvey graduated from medical school and my son Erik got married. But I persevered, and I finished my master's degree in 1989. My husband, Harvey, had just had eye surgery and surgery on both of his knees and was still having some trouble moving around. I thought I would graduate, come home, get my house in order, and nurse Harvey back to health, but I was immediately offered a job with McHenry Foster Care. I didn't know anything about foster care, but I knew social work. I had my master's degree, and McHenry had not previously been hiring anybody with master's degrees.

TB: Is that right?

ME: Yes, and they were in big trouble with DCFS because of the quality of care they were giving and the lack of supervision for their workers. There were two of us who were hired to work directly with the workers. Neither of us knew foster care, but both of us had our master's degrees and so we were supervising the workers. Later the mentor that DCFS sent out took all of the kids—the wards—away from McHenry. At that point my mentor told me I would be better off taking another position as soon as possible, but I stayed there for another year. I then went over to the University of Illinois Hospital. I was with a research project there. It was called "Women and Infants Transmission Studies," and we were monitoring HIV-positive women who were pregnant when they came into the study. It was a study of the transfer of the virus from mother to child. Most of these women needed social-work support as well because about 50 to 70 percent of our women were drug users. Many were shooting drugs, and their source of contact might have been the needles they were using. Their other infections were probably from heterosexual contacts. We also had one there who was a bleeder and had gotten a bad transfusion. Another was a victim of rape, and almost all of our clients were people who needed some sort of psychological counseling in addition to medical treatment.

TB: What was the caseload?

ME: The caseload was small. I think I had about thirty-five.

TB: With that kind of specialized need?

ME: Yes. Actually, they did not give me the opportunity to do the kind of casework that I would have liked to have done—or that any of us would have liked to have done. You see, this project was funded by the National Institutes of Health, and the only way they were able to maintain us at all was that somebody had convinced them that they wouldn't lose as many of the mothers if they had social workers involved in the cases. So they hired the requisite number of social workers, but they didn't give us the kind of leeway or space or anything that we needed to perform our jobs well. If I needed to talk privately with somebody, I had to get out and walk outside the hospital because there was never any space available for private consultation. I had two families, for instance, who knew the source of contact and who needed family therapy, and I couldn't provide it for them.

TB: They were not infected though?

ME: My client was. She was infected from her ex-husband, but she didn't know it until she became pregnant with the child of her second husband. Her only other sexual contact had been with her first husband. She knew he was sick at the time she came in. She had been with her first husband for ten years. Her first husband actually died during her pregnancy. There was no question that he had been her source of contact, but she had never been tested for HIV before, and she might have gone on a lot longer without knowing she had been infected had she not agreed to the testing because she was pregnant. That's why we were meeting every pregnant woman who came in and asking her to be tested. This particular woman was a health enthusiast, and so her nutrition was excellent. She did aerobic exercises, ate carefully, and she never allowed cigarette smoking anywhere near her. She didn't drink. She was leading a very healthy lifestyle, and suddenly her second husband finds out that this beautiful young seminary student whom he has married—and who is pregnant with his child—is HIV-positive!

TB: That's devastating, I'm sure, but what can you do?

ME: You have to take a holistic approach to the family as well as to the individual, and there simply wasn't enough room for me to do this. There wasn't enough space. There wasn't enough time.

TB: Why wouldn't the funding agency, realizing the gravity of the situation—or do they even realize the gravity of the situation?—give you the resources necessary to do the best job possible?

ME: Because they're scientists.

TB: Oh, I see. They're not humanists. They don't understand the full complexity of the human situation.

ME: I think what had happened is that, in making up the initial grant, the funders had no idea of the extent to which they needed to fund these projects. But what they did see at the first site, which was in New York City, was that they were losing a lot of patients.

TB: By death?

ME: Well, they didn't even know where the patients were. The patients just didn't come back for their subsequent appointments. And NIH [National Institutes of Health] couldn't even pay them carfare! We were able at least to provide what we called "lunch and carfare"—five or ten dollars—which isn't worth what a woman has to go through to do all of this, but at least it was something.

TB: What was the general attitude at the University of Illinois toward this study? By that I mean the general attitude of the administration. Was the administration black or white?

ME: The lead social worker was white. The clients were predominantly black—about 80 percent, I would say. I got most of the black women as clients.

TB: What were the patients' attitudes toward themselves?

ME: Most of the black women had very low self-esteem—very low indeed.

TB: What about the relatives of those women that did not come forward? What is your feeling, Marge, about the general attitude of our community toward this disease that is progressing so swiftly through our people?

ME: They see it as punishment. They feel that if these women hadn't done some "bad" thing they wouldn't be being punished—and I must say, I feel so sorry for all those women.

TB: Is that kind of attitude religion-based or culture-based?

ME: Religion- and culture-based. If you caught AIDS, they thought, it was because you were doing drugs or you were sleeping with everybody. And they're right! It's because you are sleeping around and/or you are doing drugs. Those are your contact points.

TB: Therefore, you think it's divine punishment if you're religious, and if you're not religious you think you were careless and that you got what you deserved. Is there ever any sympathetic attitude toward people who have been afflicted?

ME: People can be so understanding at certain times, but they can also say one thing and then do just the opposite.

TB: It must have been very stressful for you—or was it a challenge? Or a combination or both?

ME: It was very stressful. I talked to my supervisor after I had been there several months because I was having dreams at night about the patients and their problems, and the supervisor told me to just turn it loose—to "let them go"—and I got nothing from her because I knew her reasons for being in this work were different from mine. I think that I was only able to continue because I was able to see people as individuals who happened to be ill. When you're able to see people as people who are good, or bad, or frail, or strong—when you're able to incorporate those things that make a person a human being—you can somehow continue to make unbearable work a little more bearable.

TB: And you don't want to make judgments—not those kinds of judgments anyway.

ME: Yes, I think I began this process when I was still in school. In my first-year placement, I was working with children. Later I was placed in a halfway house for men who had been released from jail. I knew people used drugs, but I had never really known any drug users personally, but as a result of working closely with a wide variety of people, I was able to see them as individuals whom society has turned its back on.

TB: When I look around to see who are the pros in the field of social work and social services—University of Chicago, Cook County Hospital, University of Illinois—I see that the need for good social workers is growing, but people like Marge Echols don't seem to be increasing proportionally. We need to have more people like you who can empathize with the patient—not just sympathize—who can put themselves almost as one, psychologically, with that person who is their patient, almost becoming that person in order to understand and begin to be able to help.

ME: Well, when I started looking closely at therapy styles, I began to realize that I am very interactive with my patients. When I am with somebody, I get so closely involved in what they are saying that, at the time I am with them, I fully accept whatever it is they are saying as reality and as gospel. Something that I learned which helped me when I was over at the University of Illinois was this: After the person I had been talking to would leave, I would sit back and either write or think out the experience. At that point I could pull myself out of that deep level of empathy, and I could become very objective and no longer have to go on feeling lost in that other person's world anymore. In other words, I didn't have to limit myself in terms of my feelings while I was with the person because that's where the bond between us comes from, but later I was able to remove myself from the situation and look and see just what was actually transpiring during that time.

TB: What is your assessment of the African-American community's needs at present? Do you think the casualty rate will stabilize or rise or stay pretty much consistent?

ME: It will take years until we are able to stabilize ourselves. Until we take ownership of our situation, we can't do anything about it. If you don't admit that your kid is stealing pennies, how can you reprimand him for taking the teacher's fountain pen? You have to note that this is a part of your life. First of all, you have to accept it. If we don't accept it, then it's not a part of our life. It's only a part of other people's lives, and so we can't begin to do anything about it.

TB: Yes, in that kind of situation, people tend to say—about a problem like that—"It's yours," and not, "It is ours."

ME: That's the reality.

TB: Yes. People can make all kinds of excuses. A mother trying to come to terms with her son's violent behavior might say, "The evidence points to my son being a killer. The killer had a .357 Magnum, and a man is dead, and my son was there. The description sounded like him. He had a .357, so maybe it was him." With that kind of reasoning she could get closer to facing the reality of the situation. Then she could come to some kind of conclusion as to whether it was him or not. But if she says, "No, it couldn't be my boy," then she would not be facing reality. I had been involved in helping people infected with the AIDS virus long before I learned that my son was infected, because I believe that I have a responsibility to help wherever I can help—universally—whenever a problem like that arises.

ME: You know, Tim, there is something that I would like to bring into our conversation here today, and it is this: I remember reading a book entitled *The Last Hundred Miles*. It talked about the changes that take place as we live our lives and how we must allow ourselves to grow through life. I know that I was a different person when I was young than the person that I am now, but if I try to hide that difference, then I can't use my difference to make a difference. It's only when I accept the fact that I'm a woman, I'm smart, and I'm black that I can live to my fullest potential. But, even so, I still have had a hard row to hoe because people did not like me as a professional because I was a woman, because I was smart, and because I was black.

TB: Yes, that's right. Even some black people might be resentful toward you!

ME: Yes, and so you have to be able to appraise yourself and think, "What am I going to do? Can I stop being black? Can I stop being a woman? Can I stop being smart? Which one of these can I stop being? Or should I just try to put myself in another mode and try to be what I'm not?"

TB: Yes, be white and not so smart!

[*Laughter.*]

ME: Well, so many people get confused because they're never able to properly identify themselves. I was very confused in my childhood. I was black in a racist society. Our young people, whether black or white, are going to have to come to grips with something in the social system that labels people like us so it can use them. Young people have got to realize that if you allow yourself to accept a certain label, you are going to behave like that label simply because you have not yet discovered your own identity.

TB: When we look at the problems in our community—violence being one, the issue of teenage pregnancies being another, and the lack of responsibility among young men being still another—we must say, "Well, how can we find solutions to these serious problems?" And if we don't face the reality that these problems exist, then we are acting as if there's no pressing need to get to a solution. AIDS is just one of the most devastating of these problems. Just the other day I asked my students two questions. I asked them, "How many of you know someone who has been either shot or killed in the streets?" Almost every student raised his hand. Then I asked, "How many of you know someone that has been infected with HIV/AIDS?" Again, almost every student raised his or her hand. Now, we can't be completely certain whether the ones that didn't raise their hands are holding back, or whether the ones that raised their hands are actually telling the truth, but at least they raised their hands. I know in my class right now I have two cases of HIV/AIDS—two of my young men. I can tell by their sickness and by the fact that they stay out of school. Both of them are home a lot. They're in real trouble, and when they do come to class, they come up to me, and we hug, and then we talk. I don't say anything or offer any kind of advice. I just know they need me, and so I give myself to them.

ME: That's right, they need you to touch them. They need to know that they're not pariahs to society. This is so important, Tim.

TB: Marge, this time I have spent today with you and your husband has been such a pleasure for me. You know, over the years, we have met and talked many times, and it has always been for me an enlightening and pleasurable experience, and I am so grateful that you agreed that I could come by today and say hello and talk for a while. Thank you very much.

ME: Thank you, Tim.

May 6, 1995

BISHOP ARTHUR BRAZIER

CHURCH FOUNDER

Bishop Arthur Brazier is one of the best-known ministers and community activists in Chicago, and he is well known and respected throughout the entire nation as well. His church, the Apostolic Church of God, is located in the 6300 block of Dorchester Avenue in the rapidly developing neighborhood of Woodlawn. His church is reputed to have a congregation of over sixteen thousand active members and provides many personal and community services on a daily basis. Under his leadership and that of his fellow pastor, Dr. Leon Finney, Woodlawn and North Kenwood–Oakland are currently undergoing dramatic and positive housing development.

I first met Bishop Brazier in 1962 when his congregation was smaller and much less deeply involved with the community than it is today. At that time he was also the president of the Woodlawn Organization (TWO), which had originally been organized by the late Saul Alinsky. Bishop Brazier was TWO's representative to the citywide civil rights advocacy group known as the Coordinating Council of Community Organizations (CCCO) whose mission was to obtain high-quality education in fully integrated public schools and open and unrestricted housing. The CCCO was the organization that brought Dr. Martin Luther King Jr. to Chicago in 1966.

From his efforts and accomplishments in TWO and CCCO, Bishop Brazier built a solid base of community support that catapulted him to local and national fame and acclaim. He graciously granted me from his crowded schedule the amount of time that was necessary for us to have this very enjoyable and enlightening conversation.

TB: Bishop Arthur Brazier is the founder and developer of a very successful church with a large congregation. Bishop Brazier, where were you born?

AB: I was born here in Chicago in Hyde Park at Fifty-second Street and Hyde Park Avenue. As you can recall, back in those days, most of us were born at home since we were not allowed in hospitals. Hospitals were totally segregated in those days, so I was born at home on the third floor of an apartment in Hyde Park.

TB: When was this?

AB: It was 1921.

TB: So Hyde Park has almost always had some black residents.

AB: Well, certainly in my time, from 1921 onward, there were small pockets of black people living in Hyde Park. When we moved out, I was very young, probably four or five.

TB: How many brothers and sisters do you have?

AB: I had three brothers and two sisters, and I was the last of the lot. My brother next to me was thirteen years old when I was born. At that time my dad was forty-eight, and I was the apple of my dad's eye. You know, back in those days when one was forty-eight that was considered to be quite old. If you lived to be fifty-five or fifty-six, you had lived a long life.

TB: Are your mom and dad from Chicago?

AB: My mother and father were from Alabama. They were born and grew up in a town about thirty miles from Birmingham called Montevallo.

TB: I was born in Birmingham. Did your parents meet in Birmingham?

AB: Well, I don't know if it was in Montevallo or Birmingham.

TB: But they lived in Birmingham. Your father was a coal miner.

AB: He was a coal miner and got caught in a mine disaster and trapped, and he tells the story that he prayed, and he said, "Lord, if you let me get out of here, I will never go back in a coal mine again." Well, of course, they were rescued, and all the other coal miners went back to work, but my father wouldn't go back. My mother couldn't understand why all the other miners went back and he didn't, but my father said, "I'm not going back because I prayed and told the Lord that if he let me out, I wouldn't go back," and I think that was the main reason for my father's leaving the South and coming to Illinois, where he settled in Chicago.

TB: Do you remember your grandparents?

AB: I don't remember my grandparents at all. In fact, my grandfather was a slave, and my father was born only eleven years after slavery was abolished in 1863.

TB: But his father had been a slave. So you are a member of the second generation.

AB: I think we have come a long way in these two generations. A lot of people today do not like to look back at those times, but we used to be proud of our history. Though discrimination had blocked us at every turn, and laws were passed in the

North as well as in the South to lock us in as close as they possibly could, in spite of all that, when you look at the obstacles that they had to overcome, we should be proud that they would never let up in their struggle.

TB: It takes strong people to survive and continue despite the onslaught. So then you moved away from Hyde Park.

AB: Yes, and we moved to Thirty-second and Ellis Avenue. I grew up there, and I didn't leave until I was drafted into the army in 1942.

TB: What was the neighborhood like back then?

AB: You know, when I think about the neighborhood, there is a lot of nostalgia in my mind.

TB: George Johnson, of Johnson Products, grew up in that same neighborhood.

AB: He did. It was a wonderful neighborhood, I always thought. It was a unique situation. You see, Lake Park Avenue ran from Twenty-ninth to Thirty-third Street and then cut off and didn't pick up again until Thirty-fifth Street. Well, between Thirty-first and Thirty-third one block was a long white block, because after that was the tracks, and no blacks was allowed to live on that block. Through my entire growing up, from 1924 when we moved in, no blacks were ever allowed to live on that block. Groveland Park was all white. Woodlawn Park was all white, but all the rest of the neighborhood was all black, and I used to wonder where did their kids go to school since all were supposed to go to the schools in our own neighborhood.

TB: Which schools were those?

AB: Doolittle and Douglas. In order to go to school, these little white kids had to come through the black neighborhood, because they couldn't go east because the IC tracks were there. They didn't go to our school. They went someplace else, and then I thought about busing. It seems like white people have been bused all the time, and busing didn't become a bad thing until they started busing black kids to better schools. That's when they started saying it was a bad thing. Another interesting thing about that neighborhood is that it was a mixed-income neighborhood. You know, the Depression was in 1929 and throughout the thirties, but yet there were people in that neighborhood who had jobs. My dad worked all through the Depression.

TB: What kind of work did he do?

AB: My dad was a maintenance mechanic in the Hyde Park Laundry Company. He kept the machinery running.

TB: Your mother was a housewife?

AB: My mother did domestic work. She went out and washed and took in laundry. She went to people's houses and did their laundry three or four days a week. We had a twelve-room house, but rent was only thirty dollars per month.

TB: We lived in an apartment on what was then called Grand Boulevard, and we had eight rooms and three baths and the rent was either thirty or thirty-five dollars per month, and all my relatives, when they came up from Birmingham, would come there to stay.

AB: Well, my aunt and her two children also lived there with us. My daughter and her husband and two children lived there with us. My cousin Walter, he also lived there with us. We had a house full of family, and it was a wonderful experience! The neighborhood had mixed income. Some people were on relief—what we call welfare today—and you pretty much knew who was on relief because the section truck would drive up to their door and deliver the food, but no one thought that was bad. It was just that some people received food. There were others who were working on the WPA, and then there were others who taught school. There were others who did social work. Others were truant officers, and we even had a few politicians in that neighborhood. I think there was a man named Gaines in that neighborhood, and he was a Republican.

TB: That was Charlie Gaines's father. I think he went to the state House. His wife's name was Irene McCoy Gaines, who also was a Republican.

AB: It was a fun time even though it was the Depression. We didn't have time for killing and shooting among kids. There were fights, and there were gangs, and once in a while somebody got cut or stabbed, but that was only once in a while. As long as you could outrun them, you were in good shape. There were a lot of businesses all up and down Thirty-first Street, Thirty-fifth Street, and Forty-seventh Street. One of the things that is very depressing to me is to see Forty-seventh and King Drive the way they are today. It makes me cry to see how it has changed from what it was back in 1939.

TB: Do you remember the Mecca Building?

AB: Of course I do. It was a beautiful piece of architecture. And the Binga Bank Building over on Thirty-fifth Street was also a beautiful building. What happened is the result of the other less positive side of integration. When the restrictive covenant broke, the blacks moved to a lot of places where they once could not previously have moved. People with better incomes began to seek better homes, which is only normal because anybody would like to live better.

TB: This was about 1947 or 1948.

AB: Yes, '48, '49, or '50. I was out of the service by then. Lake Meadows was already being developed by then, because I remember, when I got out of the service in 1945, the home that I left before the war was all boarded up.

TB: This was because of the takeover?

AB: Yes, 3168 Ellis Avenue was taken over for Lake Meadows. In fact, before I came back, my parents wrote me when I was in the army to say that they had to move.

Then, when I came back, I made my trip down to Thirty-fifth Street to see the old neighborhood, and the house where I grew up was all boarded up. I'm not complaining about it, but it was just such a big change.

TB: I used to spend some time in that neighborhood. There was a sense of unity within the community, and I used to go play softball on the Douglas playground. I also used to go there to play basketball when Hucks Bullets was around there. Chuck Walton had a gang of young folks, and I used to go with them over to the South Park Methodist Church, which was on Calumet, where one of my best friends' father, Reverend Carroll, was the pastor. The point I'm making is that for a long time I've had a special feeling and familiarity with that neighborhood. When I was down there, I used to go to the Taste and I also used to go to Pep's. Do you remember Pep's at Thirty-first and Cottage Grove?

AB: I also used to go to Pep's.

TB: There was a sense of unity in that community that was broken when New York Life bought—or basically was given—the land so that they could develop it into what became Lake Meadows.

AB: Yes, at that time a vital community that we both knew was totally destroyed. There is no question about that. I lived in Lake Meadows for twenty-seven years and the only people I knew on my floor were the neighbors that lived next door, and there were sixteen apartments on that floor! I knew nobody else on that floor, and I lived there twenty-seven years! Nobody came and knocked on my door, and I didn't knock on their door. But before that, when I was growing up in that old neighborhood, we knew everybody in the community. We not only knew the folks next door but also knew the folks across the street and down the block.

TB: And if there was trouble, it was viewed as trouble for more than one person, and a lot of people would come to your assistance.

AB: It was a wonderful neighborhood, and back in those days when you were making twenty-five dollars a week, among blacks you were considered to be in the middle class. We weren't really in the middle class. I mean, my dad was making twenty-five dollars a week, and my mother was doing laundry, but at least we weren't on relief. As a matter of fact, I had to quit school to get a job.

TB: Which schools did you go to?

AB: I went to Douglas Elementary School and to Phillips High School.

TB: When did you go to Phillips?

AB: I went to Phillips in 1937 or 1938.

TB: I was graduating from DuSable at that time, but I had been to Phillips previously.

AB: Then you are older than I am.

TB: Yes, I am seventy-four now.

AB: I'll be seventy-two this year.

TB: But we are in the same generation and have had similar experiences, because the Phillips and the DuSable guys and girls knew one another.

AB: I remember when they built DuSable. When I graduated from Douglas, I wanted to go to DuSable, but they wouldn't let me because it wasn't in my district. DuSable was all brand new.

TB: Before you went to Phillips, do you remember any of your classmates from Douglas that we might say became relatively successful?

AB: I don't know anybody who became famous. I do remember one fellow who was an artist. His name is Daniel Lucas, and the last I heard of him he was one of the cartoonists for Walt Disney.

TB: I've seen the name, but I didn't know he was black. What kind of school was Douglas at that time?

AB: I thought it was a wonderful school. Back in those days, Douglas only went up to the sixth grade, and then it started going to eighth grade when I first started going to high school. I was going to Frances E. Willard because my parents were giving a false address so I could go there. Willard was close to a friend's house, so somebody could take care of me when my parents were working. I'd go over to my aunt's house on Calumet, and then I'd go to Frances E. Willard from there, but I played a lot of hooky there, so my parents finally had to bring me back to where they had a closer control on me. I guess when I got around to the fourth or fifth grade they came up with this concept of what they call the "middle school" now but what we called "junior high school" back then. Dunbar was out at Twenty-sixth and Wabash in that red building, and they moved me into a room with a teacher named Ms. Baltimore, who has since passed away. She had a reputation of being mean, which meant that you had to learn and you couldn't fool around. I wanted to hurry up and get out of Ms. Baltimore's room. I passed into her room in 5A, but then when we went from 6A to 6B, her room also went up a grade and so I stayed right there in her room until we went up from 7A to 7B and I left her behind. Every semester after that, they moved us up a grade, and we went into a different room.

TB: Those were what were called "semester promotions."

AB: Yes, and, as you recall, on passing day we would dress up like we were going to a banquet. Everybody that was there was always dressed to kill.

TB: And showing off their best manners.

AB: Yes, sir, we were all just sitting there watching and waiting for them to call off the names to see who was passing, and a lot of them were all dressed up but didn't go nowhere! Those were some wonderful days, but times have changed quite a bit. I finally graduated from Douglas. Then they did away with the junior high school, and then I had to leave Phillips just before my second year because of the Depression, and to a lot of us, going to school just didn't seem worthwhile anymore. If you got a job you were better off, but most of the jobs that were available were only available to the whites. You couldn't drive a cab. You couldn't drive a bus. You couldn't drive a streetcar. You couldn't even be a conductor. They had a plant right in the heart of the black neighborhood, and no blacks were working there at all.

TB: Was the CCC camp still going?

AB: Yes, but I couldn't go to the CCC because my father had a job. I tried to get on the WPA, but couldn't get on for that exact same reason. You didn't have to make a lot of money—all you had to do was have a job, and, of course, that ruled your kids out as well.

TB: So when you left Phillips, what year was that?

AB: I think it was about 1938.

TB: And where did you get a job?

AB: I finally got a job bailing paper at seven dollars per week. I'd bail papers all week, then sell them myself to the junkyard.

TB: To the junkyard?

AB: Well, I'd sell them to the guy with the wagon who would come by. I'd dump these bailed-up papers on him, and he'd give me the money for them. Then I got a job on a milk wagon as a milkman's helper. No blacks were milkmen. There was Bowman's milk, Borden's milk, and no blacks at all. There were no blacks working for the phone companies. No blacks were meter readers for the gas company.

TB: What about icemen?

AB: Well, there were black guys running the ice wagons and coal wagons, but generally they were working mostly on their own. They owned a horse and wagon, you know, like the watermelon guys.

TB: They were small-scale entrepreneurs, almost like the alley hustlers.

AB: Well, the guys with a horse and wagon, they'd sell watermelon in the summer, and they'd sell coal in the winter. I used to make about two dollars a week as a milkman's helper, and I had to be there at about 4 A.M. and work until 12 noon or 1 P.M. Then I got a job delivering drugs for a drugstore. I also delivered cigarettes and things like that when I worked for Coles Drugstore, which was at Forty-seventh and Lake Park, in the building that came to a point. I delivered from there on my bicycle. That guy wouldn't let me have any lunch, so I told my dad, and he said, "Go and tell them you can't work without lunch. You have to have lunch." So I went and talked to Mr. Coles, and I said, "Mr. Coles, the way things are, I can't have lunch," and he said, "Listen, if somebody wants something and you are at lunch, you have to just stop and drop it and get ready to go." But I said to him, "My father said I don't have to work here without any break for lunch." And he said, "Well, your father don't run this store!" So I said, "In that case, I quit," and he said, "Can you at least give me two days' notice?" I said, "No, just give me my pay." So I got my little money that I had earned, and I left. I think I made something like seven dollars per week.

TB: It gave you a lot of confidence back then when you had a dad like that.

AB: Then I got a job as a dishwasher, and that was the only job I have ever been fired from! It was a restaurant at Fifty-first and Lake Park, and I worked there from nine in the morning until nine at night for eight dollars a week.

TB: How many days?

AB: Monday through Saturday, but the first week I got fired. You see, I didn't want to wash dishes.

TB: Were you hand-washing them?

AB: Yes, and I even asked the guy to give me another chance, but he said, "No, you are not going to make it." So I got fired off that job, and it wasn't too long before I got another job, which was running an elevator in the Hyde Park Laundry Company. I got that job in 1940, and it paid fifteen dollars a week.

TB: Well, fifteen dollars a week was probably quite a lot of money in that period of your life. Where was the Hyde Park Laundry located?

AB: At Fifty-first Street and Lake Park, right across the street from the medical building there, near that little shopping center that used to be a bowling alley. It was four stories with a basement, and I guess they employed about 125 people.

TB: Mostly black or white or mixed?

AB: It was mixed, but all the truck drivers were white.

TB: So you all were working inside.

AB: Yes, we were inside. I was a wringer and a tumbler man.

TB: What was the ratio between male and female?

AB: Mostly female. I worked in the washing part and in drying the laundry. Most of the women did mangle work—ironing and pressing the laundry.

TB: So, in 1941, you were making that not-very-exuberant salary of fifteen dollars per week.

AB: Yes, but, in the meantime, I had registered for the draft in 1940 and was drafted in 1942, just as soon as I turned twenty-one, and that was in July. In October I got that letter, and at that time I was making forty-one cents an hour on my job. Most of the people I talk to now just can't believe that anyone would be willing to work for forty-one cents an hour, but that's a fact.

TB: Forty-one cents an hour! Was that considered minimum wage, or did they even have a minimum wage at that time?

AB: They didn't have minimum wage. When I first started working at the laundry, they gave me a job making fifteen dollars per week, then they gave me another job making thirty-three cents per hour, and then, depending on how many hours I worked, I could make twenty-one or twenty-two dollars per week.

TB: Did you have a family at this time?

AB: No, I was not married. I didn't get married until I got out of the army in 1947.

TB: That's the same year I got married—first time around. So you got drafted in 1942.

AB: Yes, on October 26 of 1942, to be exact.

TB: Were you drafted here in Chicago?

AB: Yes, right here in Chicago.

TB: Do you know where your draft board was?

AB: My draft board was over at Thirty-first and Indiana. I had to go downtown and spend all day going over the exams. And at about four that evening they called for me to report to Thirty-first and Indiana, and when I got there, the man said, "You are now in the army."

TB: How did you feel about that?

AB: At that time I felt—well, I had some mixed feelings, but mostly I felt good about it, and I think the things I felt good about more than anything else were that I was helping, and I didn't want to be "unclassified" because that meant that something was wrong with you.

TB: Yes, there was a social stigma attached to that out in the street. Girls, especially, thought that there was something that was wrong with you.

AB: Yes, but if you had a "Section 8" that meant you had a deferment because you were working in a defense plant—someplace that they thought was necessary for the war effort, and that meant that you were all right even though you were deferred.

TB: And the idea that you were "all right" made you happy and able to accept the situation?

AB: Yes, it made me very happy, but it was also a shock because it was the first time in my life that I had ever been away from home alone. I'd been to different places with my mother when I was small, but when we got on the train and went to Camp Custer in Michigan, and when I went into the barracks, for the first time in my life I was alone, and I had to fend for myself. Before that my father was always by my side—we were very close—but now he wasn't there to protect me, and I had to adjust to that, and I adjusted quite well.

TB: How long were you at Custer?

AB: I was there a week, and from there I went to Tallahassee, where I was assigned to the air corps. We were there for a week, and then they shipped us out to a place called Ten Mile Station, just outside of Charleston, South Carolina, and when I got there, I was assigned to a quartermaster truck company.

TB: I was in the quartermaster corps as well, but I was assigned to the infantry.

AB: I was in the Fifty-second Air Service Group, and I stayed there throughout my entire career in the service.

TB: Your mission was to service the air corps—food, bombs, equipage, ammunition—the whole thing. Without the quartermaster corps, the rest of the armed forces can't do anything. They can't even get off the ground.

AB: Yes, they can't do nothing. When we were in the combat area overseas, we would take bombs right to the planes and just kick them off the truck and leave them there. Then the ordnance guys would fuse them, load them, and put them on the plane and take right off.

TB: In my experience of being in the army, we supplied the First, Third, and Ninth armies with a million rations—just pure rations—a day, plus lots of other essential stuff. When you guys would come back to where we were, you guys had special privileges. I mean, the air corps guys would move to the front of the line. There was no argument about it.

AB: I think those pilots always ate real good too. I know we were eating powdered eggs and a lot of other C rations. When the K rations came out, they were a little better than the C rations, but none of it was any good. But the day that Japan surrendered, the very next day we were eating like kings. Before then, all the best food was going to all those pilots. They were eating good all the time, but I don't have any resentment about that.

TB: Now, where did you go when you were overseas?

AB: I went to India first.

TB: You went to India? Were you there on the Burma Road?

AB: No, on the Ledo Road. The engineers built the Ledo Road from India to northern Burma to connect up with the Burma Road from the other side of the mountain because the Japanese had already captured the entire Burma Road. In order to get food to our troops, they had to build these new roads right through the jungle, right over the mountains, and it went all the way from Ledo in India over the Himalayas and into Burma.

TB: That should have been a rather interesting experience.

AB: Yes, it was. There we were going over the Himalayas, climbing over some of the highest mountains in the world, with those two-and-a-half-ton trucks.

TB: Where those six-by-fives?

AB: No, six-by-six.

TB: And you were driving?

AB: Yes, and every fifth truck had a machine gun mounted in the gallop. When the mountains really got really steep, on a clear day we could look across the horizon and see Mount Everest. It was the tallest mountain of all, with big, white peaks. Then we would come down into this place called Shingbwiyang, and then we went into another big set of mountains and came out of that into Burma, which was our destination.

TB: Now, in that area, I imagine there were quite a number of Japanese troops.

AB: Yes, there were lots of Japanese troops. The main borderline troops separating us from them were the Chinese Thirty-eighth Division and an infantry group called the Merrill's Marauders.

TB: Merrill's Marauders. I read that they were like what we call today the "Special Service."

AB: That's exactly what you would call them today.

TB: Those were the units that did the most dangerous services for the assault and combat troops that were in the field. What was the composition of these units in terms of race?

AB: All black, but the officers were white.

TB: What about the drivers of the trucks?

AB: All black.

TB: All of the real physical work was done by black soldiers. What is your assessment of the contribution of those units to victory?

AB: Without these units there wouldn't be have been any victory, because for every man that was actually in the line of combat there were ten to fifteen men in those units who gave essential support. Without what we were doing by delivering gasoline and food, how could the Allies have gotten supplies over to the Flying Tigers in China? We had to prepare them to fly on what was called their "hunt" missions. It was our job to load twenty-one drums of gasoline on each of those huge gasoline drums on those C46s—seventeen on one side and four on the other—and I thought that was an imbalance, but evidently it wasn't because of all the weight of the bombs and everything else. There was no other way you could get anything into China, because the Burma Road was closed and we were still building the Ledo Road. Of course, they had to fight the Japanese all along the way in order to clear them out of Burma.

TB: You got combat credit for some of this, didn't you?

AB: Yeah, I got two battle stars for the northern Burma campaign and the central Burma campaign. Thank the Lord for that, because those two battle stars helped me to get out of the army.

TB: Did you ever get any kind of a leave during this time, or were you just under this pressure all the time?

AB: I got a leave once, and it's a good thing that I did, because I was really going downhill. I got fifteen days in Calcutta, but that's all, and, except for that, I was in the jungle under that kind of pressure all the rest of the time.

TB: So from June or July 1942—

AB: No, that was 1943 when I went over. We docked in Bombay in September of 1943. I was in the States for nine months before I went over.

TB: During all that time for preparation, did you ever get a chance to come back home?

AB: Yes, I came home for three days and stayed for Christmas in 1942. Then a little later I was sent home for fifteen days on medical leave because I had an appendectomy.

TB: Then, when you went into combat, there was no relief once you were over in the combat zone.

AB: Well, I had these fifteen days, and then the Japanese invaded and tried to cut us off.

TB: Cut off supplies?

AB: Yes, we were in a place called Johi, and it was in the Assam Valley and the Japanese were trying to take over. They surrounded a city called Imphal and were making a hard push through there, and it looked like they were going to take it. In fact, we were all called together and told that the Japanese were taking the valley and that we would have to fight our way out of Assam over the mountains because we were trapped. But it just so happened that the Japanese didn't take the city of Imphal. It didn't fall. The British held on to it and, of course, if Imphal didn't fall, the Japanese could not take over the area. But it was a real tense period of time because those of us who never had had any real infantry training had to call upon those that did.

TB: Aside from your machine guns and your side arms, did you have any carbines?

AB: I had a fifty-caliber machine gun mounted on my truck.

TB: What were you then?

AB: I was a corporal, and like every other squad leader, I was required to carry side arms, and there was no more rest for any of us until the end of the war.

TB: Not until the end of the war?

AB: No, not until the end of the war. I was stationed in a place called Bobbili near Burma, and sometimes at night we would put on all our rain gear and boots and go out in the rain to look at a movie, but on this one particular night right in the middle of the movie, some guy yelled out, "It's all over!" and they cut off the projector. Well, at first I was sort of upset because I thought he meant that it was all over for the movie, but then suddenly everybody was jumping up and shouting, and I said, "What is wrong with you guys?" One of them said, "Man, the war is over!" and it was just unbelievable to me, because by then I had been overseas for two years.

TB: And most of that time was in combat.

AB: No, most of it was not in the combat zone. But for the last nine months it certainly was.

TB: When was this? About August?

AB: Yes, August of 1945.

TB: At that same time I was in Marseilles, France. I had been through four combat experiences, and we were in Marseilles until it was time for us to leave and go fight in Japan, but then we got the word that the Japanese had surrendered. This was after we had dropped the atomic bomb. I had mixed feelings about that; did you?

AB: No, I didn't. Some of the guys thought they should have dropped the bomb and asked me my opinion, and I said, "Yes, they should have dropped it. Why should any more of us get killed?" I didn't have any mixed feelings about it at all. Some guys did, but I was totally energized. One of the things that really was bothering me was all the shooting that was still going on all over the place when we received word that the war in the Pacific was over. I mean by that the celebration of our victory. Those guys were still firing off their rifles all over the place, and I said to myself, "I do not want to get killed now."

TB: Not now when the war was already over!

AB: Yes, the war was over, and those guys were still shooting all over the place.

TB: We had similar experiences over there in the European theater.

AB: The same thing with the European theater? Did they start shooting like that?

TB: They started shooting and didn't seem to want to stop, but now the war is over, and you leave to come back home?

AB: Yes, the war was over, and I came back home. We docked in New York on December 24, 1945.

TB: How did you feel?

AB: I felt fine. We had sailed past the Statue of Liberty and I knew I was finally coming back home. I could see the fishermen across the bay at Camp Kilmer in New Jersey, and then the next day was Christmas.

TB: What a Christmas present! This was December 24, 1945?

AB: Well, I docked December 24, and the next day was December 25, and the next day after that they shipped me to Fort Sheridan, and the following day, I was out!

TB: I also got off the boat at Camp Kilmer, and I was back here in Chicago on December 25.

AB: You were here two days ahead of me!

TB: I walked in on my mother and daddy just as they were having Christmas dinner! Boy, that was something! But then I still had to go back and get discharged.

AB: They had already discharged me, so I didn't have to go back.

TB: Well, we've practically covered that first stage of your life now. You have returned home, and you have to make a series of decisions about your life from this point on. By now you have a great deal of experience, and you have learned what it is to be away from home—the loneliness, you've been able to deal with that. You have been able to deal with emotional things and physical things on your own, so you return home now and you are a full-grown, mature man. How old are you?

AB: Twenty-four.

TB: The war matured us all very quickly. Pretty soon many of us got involved in the struggle for civil rights. When Dr. King came here to Chicago, there was a march on Cicero that was not led by Dr. King. Do you recall that or know anything about that?

AB: No, I don't. I recall that a lot of people weren't much in favor of it. It was led by Bob Lucas and another gentleman, whose name I forgot, who was the leader of a West Side organization.

TB: Was that Doug Andrews and the West Side Organization?

AB: It was not the West Side Organization. It was an organization on the West Side, but it was not the WSO. I forgot the fellow's name now, but certainly Bob Lucas was a part of it. I was also not in favor of it. Most of us were adherent to Dr. Martin Luther King's leadership, and we believed that all those people who were running around doing their own thing would undermine his leadership role. We thought that any march without Dr. King and the vast majority of black people behind it would only be a show of anger and would accomplish nothing except create more frustration.

TB: Now, Dr. King leaves Chicago, and you began to concentrate most of your time on activities in your church.

AB: When Dr. King left, I stayed president of the Woodlawn Organization until 1970, and what we did was, we began to concentrate our efforts on the gang problems that existed in the community.

TB: Gang violence had become of major importance by then?

AB: Yes, the struggle between the Blackstone Rangers and the Eastside Disciples was wrecking the community.

TB: There was physical violence.

AB: Yes, a lot of shooting and a lot of killing. The interesting thing about that, though, was that back then drugs were not involved. It was basically the turf thing that was the source of the animosity between the rival gangs. The drug situation had not yet become problematic.

TB: Most of the Blackstone Rangers, in terms of schooling, went to Hyde Park High School or the neighborhood schools.

AB: Yes, most of them did, but a lot of Eastside Disciples went to Hyde Park as well, and that's why Hyde Park High School attendance dropped so low. It was because so many of the Eastside Disciples didn't go to school.

TB: It was out of their turf.

AB: Most of them were from west of Woodlawn Avenue, and the Blackstone Rangers were mostly east of Woodlawn Avenue.

TB: Now, the person who became the nominal leader of the Blackstone Rangers, the young man I had the opportunity of having in my class when he was a freshman. His name was Jeff Fort. Do you remember him?

AB: Yes. Why did you call him the "nominal" leader? He was the leader!

TB: I don't know. You can't always tell for sure. I only know as far as my own experience with him as a student is that he was a natural leader. He was not a good student—that is, a scholar—but he and I were all right with each other. Even up until the time when he became really very well known, it was always, "Mr. Black, how are you doing?" We always had a great deal of mutual respect.

AB: I always found him to be a respectful person when he was talking to me, but I wasn't sure what his attitude really was. I was always amazed at his ability to control himself in various kinds of situations.

TB: Yes, he did have that ability. I was a teacher at Hyde Park High School at that time, but then I left to go to the Teacher Corps. At that time Hyde Park High School had a snobbish attitude toward certain students like Jeff who were considered somewhat undesirable because they lowered the academic standards. At that same time, as you may remember, there was also an increasing tension that began to develop between South Shore and Woodlawn and Hyde Park.

AB: Yes, of course, I remember that.

TB: They wanted a new high school in South Shore.

AB: And they got it.

TB: Yes, they did.

AB: And I think that was the destruction of Hyde Park [High School].

TB: I remember the kids I had in one class felt rejected, and they said, "Well, Mr. Black, if we can't go to school together, we'll just take over the school!"—that was their rationale as they expressed it to me. But the decision by people in Hyde Park was to divide those students into three separate communities.

AB: At that point in time Hyde Park and South Shore residents were sending their graduates to Hyde Park High School because they were scared that Woodlawn was rapidly becoming more of a residential community for people who were on welfare or who had very low-paying jobs. The people of South Shore and Hyde Park were more middle class. They had more money at their disposal, and they were better educated, and a lot of the kids that were on the honors track lived in Hyde Park and South Shore.

TB: Yes, but there were some honor students in Woodlawn as well.

AB: I'm sure there were some, but I'm talking about the bulk. I'm saying that when they made that decision to build Kenwood High School, and then South Shore High School, they sucked away a tremendous amount of resources, not only in students but also in teachers.

TB: Almost all the Hyde Park teachers went directly to those new high schools. Only a few of the teachers remained at Hyde Park High.

AB: It really did real damage to Hyde Park High School, and, of course, that's when we got involved in the Woodlawn Experimental Schools Project at Hyde Park in order to improve the level of education at Hyde Park High.

TB: There was another experiment that was going on at the University of Chicago. It was under the leadership of Herb and Ann Mack out of New York—two liberal whites—and I think that was called the Woodlawn Project.

AB: Yes, that was the Woodlawn Experimental Schools Project that I was talking about.

TB: Was some of the sponsorship for that from the University of Chicago?

AB: Well, there's no question about that. In fact, they wrote the original proposal, and the Woodlawn Organization protested. I wrote a letter to HUD about that, saying that this was being set up with no input from the community. That's how the community got involved. I was the one who insisted that the principal of Hyde Park High School be included, and I was also the person who insisted that the head of the Woodlawn Experimental Schools Project be Barbara Sizemore.

TB: Did you know that she is back here in Chicago now? She is the dean of the De-Paul University School of Education. As a matter of fact, she has been back here only about three months.

AB: It was a serious struggle that was going on, and we wanted teachers to testify about the conditions of the schools. The teachers who agreed to testify had to wear bags over their heads so they could remain anonymous.

TB: I remember that.

AB: Anna Kolheim was the only person who came out and stood out flatfoot and told what was happening at the school. But another reason why we wanted Barbara Sizemore was because integration was really involved in this project, and Barbara Sizemore had the reputation for being a strong and able person who would take no nonsense in regard to the advancement of black education, and we felt that her being the director of the project would legitimize the project. Those are the reasons why we insisted on those two people for the positions at the project and at the high school.

TB: I remember Tony Gibbs as also being part of that experiment.

AB: Yes, Tony was a part of the Woodlawn experiment.

TB: When I was down in Washington recently, I saw him.

AB: Tony used to work with Barbara.

TB: It was a very exciting project. After heading up the project here, Barbara went to Washington, D.C., to become the superintendent of schools. Then she went to Philadelphia and then on to Pittsburgh, where she was a professor of education at a university there. Now she is back here as dean of the School of Education at DePaul University. Wherever she has gone, she has always been an advocate of quality black education. Her position would now be generally considered Afrocentric, but she was Afrocentric in her position in a much earlier time.

AB: Well, I didn't always agree with what she did and taught, but I certainly did continue to have a high respect for her.

TB: Tell me a little about the tension which developed between the general community and the gang which became known as the Keystone Nation and then later as the El Rukn. I know they were involved in a big plan for the redevelopment of Woodlawn because I saw some of the sketches.

AB: But during that particular time, there was no plan. We couldn't make any plans like that ourselves because we were so preoccupied with the violent gangs. The Woodlawn Organization was constantly being approached by people in the community — especially by irate mothers — demanding to know what TWO was going to do about the gangs. I had one minister in Woodlawn come and ask me to contact the mayor and have him call out the National Guard, which I absolutely refused to do. At that time our belief was that these gang groups were basically turf-minded, and most of them had already dropped out of high school.

TB: Dropped out or been kicked out.

AB: One or the other. They were trying to find themselves, and we wanted to try to help them to do that. So I approached several educational institutions in this regard. The first one we approached was the Encyclopaedia Britannica to talk about setting up some kind of educational program. Then we approached the Revlon Corporation and had discussions with their educational foundation. I was advised to get in touch with a guy named Jerome Bernstein. So I wrote a letter to Bernstein and sent him an outline of what I called a "program of interest." Bernstein responded and I met with him in Washington, D.C., in 1966. Later he came to Chicago, and out of those meetings came a grant for nine hundred twenty-seven thousand dollars. I met with Mayor Daley, Bill Berry, Marshall Korshak, and others to get Mayor Daley's support. I met with O. W. Wilson, who was then the superintendent of police, and I also met with the head of the YMCA here in Chicago. After all these meetings, it was finally agreed that our program would be funded only if sixteen special conditions were accepted. I don't remember all of them, but the key ones were that the city would have the right to monitor all aspects of this program and that the executive directors of the project had to have the concurrence of the mayor of the city of Chicago. I was told that unless I agreed to these conditions that there would be no program, and so I agreed, and the program was funded. It really was a good program. It was designed so that training classes were set up in the neighborhoods where the Blackstone Rangers were and also in the neighborhoods where the Eastside Disciples were.

TB: The Eastside Disciples' territory was from where to where?

AB: I don't know exactly how far they went, but I know they were west of Cottage Grove. David Barksdale was the leader of the Disciples and Jeff Fort was the leader of the Rangers. We were supposed to have two training centers in the Blackstone Rangers' territory and two in the Disciples' territory. We hired the Xerox Corporation and their educational division to design a training program, and they transferred a man to Chicago to set it up. We hired professional people. We wanted to take the leaders of the gangs and give them some basic training, and then we hoped they would transfer that training knowledge to the youth over whom they had so much influence. All of this had nothing to do with kids who were still in school. It applied only to those who had already dropped out or had been kicked out. Since they had such influence on their fellow gang members for bad, we were trying to see if they would have influence on them for good. Part of that program was a health program which provided eyeglasses and an eye examination for everyone who needed them. It also provided physical examinations. We had a contract with the Urban League for them to help us find jobs for the young people who had been trained in this program, but there was so much negative publicity about this project that it became very difficult for the Urban League to get jobs that were in any way connected with the Woodlawn Project. We even underwent a series of investigations in the Senate under Senator McClellan. Anyway, the project lasted for a year and managed to survive all that kind of controversy. I think the project could have won. In fact, our evaluation, which was independently done, said that the project should be re-funded, but unfortunately, that is not what happened

TB: Now, during this period of time, from 1966 to 1970, Woodlawn was becoming depopulated and much of the housing structure in that area was decaying.

AB: I think that began around 1970. It may have been earlier, but it really escalated during the seventies. People began to leave the community. There were a lot of fires and vandalism, and people started moving to South Shore and into the suburbs close by. Even Oak Park had started to open up. You see, earlier on, all these suburbs had been closed.

TB: Yes, and by now black people had more options.

AB: Yes, now they had more options, and they were taking advantage of those options.

TB: So back then Woodlawn was deteriorating and becoming depopulated, and now it's in the process of doing what?

AB: Now it's in the process of being revitalized and rehabilitated, but more than that, the mayor of the city of Chicago is now interested in trying to do something about these three communities out here: Oakland, North Kenwood, and Woodlawn. His interest is not to drive black people out but rather to have a big rehabilitation program. The lead person in the city on this is Valerie Jarrett, who is the commissioner of the Department of Planning and Development.

TB: Valerie is the former daughter-in-law of Vernon Jarrett. Her grandfather was Robert Taylor.

AB: Her primary concern is how to get North Kenwood and Woodlawn to pull together in some kind of organized fashion. I was asked if I would be willing to help pull them together, and I said I'd only be willing if the mayor asked me to, so a short time later, I spoke with the mayor, and he asked me to do just that, and I began to meet with the people in North Kenwood and Woodlawn, and we put together a fund for revitalization and rehabilitation. We wrote a proposal and got funded for $1.3 million over a three-year period of time. The real key for our success is to utilize all the land in North Kenwood, Oakland, and Woodlawn that is currently vacant, a tremendous amount of which is already owned by the city. Our plan is not to move anybody out but to utilize lower-income housing and tax benefits for rehabilitation for people who live in those communities and need rent subsidies. But you can't revitalize a community with just rent subsidies. A community has to be revitalized by home ownership, and so we also talked about building new homes.

TB: What about an increase in economic development?

AB: Economic development is part of it. Along Sixty-third Street and along Sixty-seventh Street, in order for businesses to come back you have to have people that want to come back and shop there, so we are now talking about building five thousand single-family homes and rehabilitated units in Hyde Park and Woodlawn.

TB: This has always been an important community in terms of its location. If the plan you have outlined is successful, you will have played an important part in linking what is now the old downtown Loop area with the area along the lakefront to Sixty-seventh Street.

AB: Yes, I think this is a tremendous opportunity, if only we can learn to work together.

TB: And in the process you don't unnecessarily have to displace people, and the community's educational, religious, and recreational institutions, such as the YMCA, will also prove to be additional assets.

AB: I'm glad you mentioned that, because there is a piece I left out, and that is, not only are we talking about physical redevelopment when we are talking about rehabilitating the existing buildings and building new single-family homes and townhouses. I did not mention the fact, but one of our other goals is to work toward improving education in Woodlawn. We are not going to be able to redo the entire educational system in Chicago, of course, because that is beyond our capability, but certainly for these two communities in this area we are going to change things for the better. We are sincerely looking for some real know-how as to the means by which this might be best accomplished, and in this regard we are currently obtaining input from the University of Chicago. The first piece of our plan is physical, the second is educational, and the third piece is community safety. Those are the three major areas that we are going to be working with. I just believe that because of the location of these two communities and the fact that we have got a tremendous amount of open land, we will be able to succeed. We are not looking at a Lake Meadows or Prairie Shores kind of displacement situation. We are looking at a place where we can have the kind of communities that we used to have when we grew up. Where middle-class people and people on welfare will all be able to live in the same community, and you won't know which was which—that kind of community. I'm also talking about revitalizing commercial businesses like stores, supermarkets, bowling alleys, and theaters. I'm talking about creating all of this right here in Woodlawn, North Kenmore, and Oakland!

TB: You're talking about establishing a real community, a community with spirit.

AB: When you have a sense of community, that is spiritual in itself. You cannot get a real sense of community living in high-rises. A real sense of community is where people interact with one another on all possible levels. We have wonderful recreational facilities. If you are in an automobile, you are three minutes from the lake, you are three to five minutes from Washington Park on the west and from Jackson Park on the east. East of Washington Park, there are the baseball fields. Jackson Park has an eighteen-hole golf course as well as the lagoon and the marina. There are tree-lined streets in both North Kenwood and Woodlawn, and these communities are anchored by the already-established, middle-class community of Hyde Park. It's already interracial, and we've got everything we need to make this happen.

TB: Well, this is certainly something you can dream about. I can remember when I was a kid I could walk from Sixty-third and Vernon to the lake and was completely safe. I didn't need a car. I had enough energy. I just walked.

AB: This kind of danger that we have today, all of that can be done away with.

TB: When you talk about Woodlawn, are you talking about the area as far west as King Drive?

AB: No, only as far as Cottage Grove. We don't mind expanding in the future, but at the present this is our immediate target. If the people in West Woodlawn say they want to get involved in this, then they can organize and we can expand this whole thing and include them as well.

TB: But you have to have some success first.

AB: I think that if West Woodlawn wants us to help them, then they have to organize and say so, because we don't want to go into a community and have to fight folks and organizations and have them say, "Who are you?" We don't want to get involved in that kind of mess. If they need some help and want it, we'll help. What I said to the South Shore Commission when I was president of the Woodlawn Organization was, "We want to try to work with South Shore." Now, remember, at that time South Shore was all white, and I said, "We want to work with South Shore, and we want you to work with us." What I indicated to them was that you cannot isolate yourself and still be able to survive successfully with a community that is falling apart right next door to you. If you choose to ignore your responsibility to your neighbors, then you had better know just exactly what the score is and be prepared to pay the price.

April 9, 1995

DR. BARBARA BOWMAN AND DR. JAMES BOWMAN

ACADEMIC ADMINISTRATOR AND MEDICAL SCHOOL PROFESSOR

Dr. Barbara Bowman was born into a highly educated middle-class family and at-tended elite schools throughout her academic career, doing exceptionally well in all of them. She is one of the daughters of the late Robert Taylor, who advised Julius Rosen-wald, the chairman of the board of Sears Roebuck, to buy the land and build the Rosenwald Building, later to be known as the Michigan Boulevard Apartments. Ini-tially, this architectural complex was designed and built for occupancy by so-called lower-income families. Because of the great housing shortage resulting from the re-strictive covenants of that period and also because of the quality of its construction as well as the convenience of its location, however, the Rosenwald Building soon became occupied instead almost exclusively by the middle-class families of teachers, lawyers, and accountants. Later, after housing segregation eased, most of those professionally trained people and their families moved out, and the building began to fall on hard times. The Robert Taylor Homes are a public housing project that was named in honor of Barbara's father and his vision of providing affordable lower-income hous-ing, but, unfortunately, the reality experienced by those who are living in a "project" of this sort has deteriorated from that of the original dream to what has become for many a daily nightmare.

After successfully completing his own brilliant academic career at medical schools both here and abroad, Dr. James Bowman quickly discovered during his residency at old St. Luke's Hospital at Fifteenth and Michigan that he was expected to enter through the rear door of the building and was not allowed to use the hospital's dining room unless he was the guest of a white doctor or a white resident or intern. These painful experiences serve as examples of the forms of racial prejudice that even the most gifted and privileged members of African-American communities often must have to face in their professional careers as well as their personal lives.

The Bowmans have experienced a beautiful and very successful long-lived marital partnership, always encouraging and energizing each other in their separate careers and accomplishments. The Bowmans continue to be active and involved individually and together in health and social issues not only here in Chicago but also nationally and throughout the entire world. They are truly universal humanitarians who still retain "the local touch." This was a delightful and greatly enlightening conversation, and, like all the rest of these conversations with my friends and neighbors, our time together went all too quickly and was much too brief!

TB: Barbara, what was the first school you attended?

BB: Mrs. Cochran's nursery school. You didn't find anybody who lived in Chicago between 1933 and 1960 who didn't go to Anita Cochran's nursery school. Everybody went there. That's why I became a nursery schoolteacher myself. That's what started me on that aspect of my career when I was still in college. I was studying psychology, and when I got ready to graduate from college and come back to Chicago—I was in school in the East—my adviser said, "You are going to go to graduate school at the University of Chicago. Why don't you try to get a job at the University of Chicago Lab School?" When I told Anita that, she said, "Well, I taught there for summer school. Let me say a good word for you," and that's how I got my first job at the University of Chicago Laboratory School.

TB: What year was that?

BB: It was 1950. I got married and started graduate school and also had a part-time job teaching nursery school. Anita was always a wonderful mentor.

TB: She is a legend too. When you went east for your undergraduate work, which college did you go to?

BB: After I left prep school, I went to Sarah Lawrence College, and then I came back here, and Jim and I got married, and I went to graduate school while he was doing his boards and working at Provident Hospital.

TB: Provident Hospital, another legend!

BB: Yes, my father had been on their board. My grandmother had also been on their board. Provident Hospital was a major part of our lives.

TB: Dr. Diggs was our family doctor. He would come out to see us anytime, day or night, whenever we needed him. He was on the staff there, but where are his kids living now?

BB: Dr. Ned Beasly was our family doctor. Alfreda lives in New York. Her husband just died recently, and Fragena lives in California. I haven't seen her in a long time.

TB: Yeah, Dr. Beasly had his office up there in the Supreme Building.

JB: And he lived on Fifty-first or someplace nearby.

BB: Not on Fifty-first Street, but on Forrestville or Prairie or somewhere in there between Forty-seventh and Fiftieth. He lived along about in there when he was married to Alice. Then they moved over on Drexel soon after Aunt Catherine and Uncle Earl did, but when I was a kid, they lived somewhere in that space between Fifty-first and Forty-seventh, and between South Park and Cottage.

TB: Yeah, he was quite a famous person. He was the first and only black pediatrician in the city until Dr. Jefferson. So many kids don't have any feeling for these pioneers. They don't know who they are or even recognize their names. Even a name like Oscar DePriest.

BB: You know who you ought to talk to is Leonidas Berry.

TB: We know each other, but he asked me not to wear him out because he is tired. He is trying to do something for Provident. I have his book *I Wouldn't Take Nothin' for My Journey*.

BB: He's very, very old.

TB: I absolutely respect him. He told me about some of the experiences he had when he was going to the University of Chicago as a student in that medical school over there, and the kind of indignities that he was subjected to.

BB: So much of our history has been lost. I remember my mother went through my father's papers, and she threw away what she considered to be the junky things and just kept speeches, formal letters, and things like that.

TB: But all of it might have been valuable. You know, I became annoyed with myself for having so much junk around when I was living at Fifty-first and Ellis. I just put all kinds of stuff in bags, and then one day someone said, "Why don't you throw some of those bags out?" Then one day I thought, "Well, maybe they are right!" And I picked up a bag and threw it out.

BB: Without even looking at what was in it?

TB: Without looking, and then I got a call in 1970 from Arch Motley at the Chicago Historical Society, and he said, "Tim, I would like to have some of your stuff." I said, "Man, I don't have anything worth anything." He said, "Just put everything in a bag, and we'll sort it out. We'll know what's good." And I said, "Gee, I've got these letters when King and I were having some disagreements and also when A. Philip Randolph and I had another kind of disagreement. Maybe those would be worthwhile giving to somebody." But, when I went to look for the papers, I discovered that all those letters must have been in that bag I'd thrown out, and I promised myself from that point on—

BB: Never throw away another bag!

TB: At least not until I look in it, and so now I've got a room that I call a "junk room" that's full of boxes.

BB: That's what we keep doing: putting things in boxes that nobody has time to look at and sort out.

TB: Well, it all takes so much time.

BB: Yes, because you get interested, and then you stop and you look at each one. You just don't separate and organize. You simply pause and savor the past.

TB: I certainly understand what you mean. I lost my son a year and a half ago, and recently I began to try to organize his papers in some kind of way. He was a composer and arranger as well as a singer, and he had boxes of stuff because he was very prolific. Of course, there is so much grief that goes with anything like that. It is very hard. You know, he had HIV, AIDS, a disease which is devastating our community. He happened to be gay, but it is not just homosexuals. Beyond that, now we are beginning to have an increase in heterosexuals with that same disease, and yet so little is being done to educate our community and the young people who live in it.

JB: Yes, the biggest increase is now among adolescents, but it's everywhere. A couple of weeks ago there was a report about even finding it in the retirement community!

BB: Would you think you would have to be careful with a seventy-year-old?

JB: You sure wouldn't.

BB: Well, of course, you wouldn't, but now they also have it.

TB: Oh, my Lord.

BB: It is not just young people, but all of us. Old people are totally unaware of the danger, and women still are not protecting themselves. Adolescents still are not protecting themselves, and older people are not protecting themselves.

TB: I am trying to get some people in the churches to become more knowledgeable and involved.

BB: Well, good luck to you! I haven't had any luck getting the black churches to be responsive about almost anything. Certainly not about HIV. We have been trying to talk about sex education and get kids to use family planning techniques if they are going to be sexually active, but the churches absolutely will not touch that area of responsibility.

TB: I'm afraid that you're right, but, even so, we have to keep on trying. Barbara, tell me about the work you're doing. You are in administration now, aren't you?

BB: Yes, I am president of the Erikson Institute, which is a graduate program in child and family planning.

TB: Yeah, I am familiar with Erikson. Erik Erikson is one of my heroes.

BB: We do a lot of work with adolescent moms. What we are most interested in doing is prevention, and the black church is the most logical place to do that kind of prevention work because their congregations are primarily female in attendance. If you can get the moms of the community to be more supportive of family planning and other kinds of prevention techniques, then at least some of these problems can be kept from increasing.

JB: Do the young black people go to church?

BB: It doesn't really make any difference if they do or don't—*if* their mothers don't assume any responsibility.

TB: Well, if you talk about a place like Brazier's church, there are still a lot of young people who go there.

BB: Yes, but, whether the young people are there or not, their *mothers* are there, and so that would be the logical place to start a campaign against adolescent pregnancy. I am telling you, sometimes I get so angry. The last time I was at a church meeting I vowed I wasn't ever going to say anything about these problems to them anymore. They feel strongly that abortion is wrong. They feel strongly that sex before marriage is wrong, and, therefore, you should not do anything to encourage children to use contraceptives because it is morally wrong.

TB: Well, they need to seriously reexamine their theology.

BB: Beethoven Clinic was letting students have contraceptives with parental permission, and there was a big brouhaha, primarily from the Catholic community, about using public property to pass out birth control. We had a meeting with a group of black ministers because Provident was running a health clinic and trying to convince the churches that if they would become more active in distributing information about birth control you wouldn't have to teach it in school. It is the absence of that kind of information for students that we were trying to address, but their response was absolutely no. "You should not tell about it in school. You shouldn't tell about it at home. You shouldn't tell about it anywhere." Because in their opinion, young people shouldn't be engaged in sex at all, and if you tell them how to engage in safe sex, you will only be encouraging them to become sexually active, but the fact is that among adolescent women in the African-American community the rate for pregnancy is horrendously high, and if you have a baby before you are nineteen or twenty, the chances of you and your baby never getting off of welfare are just enormous. It is not like we don't have examples of what will happen right here in front of our eyes, and yet we have just an awful time convincing anyone of what needs to be done.

TB: And meanwhile the outside world, especially television, is constantly stimulating these young people to become sexually active.

BB: And so now we have twelve-year-olds, thirteen-year-olds that are having their first baby!

TB: One of my former students who works for the Chicago Board of Education was saying that they had one kid who is ten and she is already a mother, and they have another kid who is fifteen and who has two children.

BB: Two by fifteen, three by sixteen . . .

TB: And the churches aren't doing anything to change the situation.

BB: No, they certainly are not.

TB: Well, another reason that I am going after this HIV thing is because I have talked with some of the kids that have been in the County Jail, and when they come out, many of them have AIDS.

BB: Yeah, because of all of the homosexual activity that goes on in those prisons.

JB: It has been estimated that in some prisons in this country the incidence of rape is approximately 90 percent!

TB: These are still young men, and one high school—that I will not name, but is a public high school—has estimated that, because of these fellows coming out of jail with AIDS and then reengaging themselves with young girls that are still in school, about 40 percent of the girls now enrolled in that school are now infected!

JB: That is quite surprising.

TB: Not really. The reason is because those girls don't believe that the guys have AIDS. They attribute that condition to gay men, and, therefore, they think their boyfriends couldn't possibly be infected.

JB: A major problem in the Hispanic community also.

BB: Because there is much more tolerance in that community for bisexuality.

JB: Much more tolerance and also because those young men appear to be so macho that the girls don't dare ask them any questions.

TB: Now tell me about your own experience. Where did you do your internship?

JB: At St. Luke's. That meant I had to get home about one in the morning and then get up at five and rush back downtown. Well, back in 1947, when I started as a resident, blacks were not allowed to walk in the front door of St. Luke's on the Michigan Avenue side. They had to go in on the Indiana Avenue side, but I didn't know anything about any of that. I had gone in on the Indiana Avenue side for my interviews because that was the closest way to get to Dr. Hersey's office on the nineteenth floor. I had not ever heard about that restriction, so the first day I just walked right on through the front door of the hospital, and the only blacks who were there were maids and janitors, and they looked at me and told me to be more careful or I would get into trouble.

BB: And at that time they also wouldn't let you live in the interns' quarters.

JB: No, they wouldn't let me live in residents' quarters, and those who lived there could get three free meals every day, which was extremely important to me because I was only paid one hundred dollars a month, out of which I had to pay my room and board and everything else! So I would have to wait all day and then eat in the evening at Barbara's family's house. At lunch the white residents would rotate so that there were nine of us—instead of ten—and that way each day another one of them would be able to take me as his guest for lunch. That's how I got my lunch and wouldn't have to pay for it.

BB: Two days after [the Supreme Court decision on] desegregation in Washington, Jimmy's father made a reservation for us at the Shoreland Hotel. We drove up, arrived at the front desk, and they said, "We can't find your reservation." Jim was in military uniform at the time.

JB: I had come to Chicago all the way from Denver, Colorado, and then I was told that there was no reservation!

BB: They put us in a ballroom.

JB: Yes, they put us all by ourselves in a place that was about as big as the first floor of this house.

BB: And the reason for that was because they did not want us standing around there in the lobby of that hotel! Whether they were being honest and they didn't really have our reservation, I don't know, but when they took a look at us and decided we were going to raise holy Ned right there in the lobby, they decided they were going to find a place for us. They did not want to have us standing in the lobby of that hotel, and so they changed their minds and decided to say, "Just a minute please, Captain Bowman."

[*Laughter.*]

TB: Well, did you know that Dr. Ellis died? I couldn't go to the funeral.

BB: I didn't either. If I knew the family, I would have made an extra effort, but I did not know her family. I only knew Alcie.

TB: I only knew her from her advocacy for children.

BB: Oh, she and I bonded together for years on children's health issues, and we called each other regularly, but we didn't see each other socially, and so I just didn't know her family.

TB: Well, that same day I had to go to the funeral for A. P. Jackson, who was a schoolmate of mine at DuSable. In fact, his father's church used to be right across the way from the Rosenwald.

BB: What church was that?

TB: It was the Liberty Baptist Church on Forty-sixth Street between Michigan and Wabash.

BB: Off of Michigan at Forty-sixth Street there was kind of a mansion.

TB: That was the mansion that the president of the Drexel Bank used to live in.

BB: What was at the other end of the block? I can't remember what was at Forty-sixth and Wabash.

TB: That shows me that I am much older than you folks. His father, D. Z. Jackson, was the pastor at that church. A lot of people came here from the South during and after World War II, and, as a result, the churches grew tremendously, and they had to move to larger quarters. So that's when they bought those lots at Forty-ninth and South Park where there had previously been a Father Divine Mission.

BB: Oh yes, I remember a church that was right there at Forty-third and Wabash. Reverend Clarence Cobb was the minister.

TB: That was a church that embraced everybody. He took in those who would have been rejected in other circumstances and embraced them. He had a big congregation, and he became politically a pretty powerful guy.

JB: That is the type of ministry we should have today.

TB: And because of the kind of guy he was, he probably would have been much more sympathetic than others have been. Now, tell me what happened to you after you completed your residency at St. Luke's.

JB: Well, what happened is very interesting. After I finished my residency and passed my boards, Barbara finished graduate school and I was thinking about taking a job as the head of Provident Hospital. At that time Provident Hospital paid a salary of nine thousand dollars a year. All of my colleagues—the residents who were with me in my class—those white guys were starting off their careers at twenty-five thousand dollars a year. I think that the people at Provident thought that I had no other place to go, and they said, "We will pay you ten thousand dollars." Now, if they had offered me a more reasonable salary, we were prepared to come back, but also at that time Eisenhower was president, and so we decided to leave the United States. We said, "Let's look for someplace to go, and we may or may not ever come back." And so we went away.

BB: We just went.

JB: I was thinking of places like India or Africa, but I was at a meeting in Washington, D.C., and a friend of mine told me that the Iranians had built a hospital and were looking for Americans as well as Iranians to staff this brand-new hospital, and he gave me the name of a foundation which was incorporated in New York. So I wrote to them, and they sent a very nice letter back inviting Barbara and me to come out and meet them. They were having their board meeting the following month. So we went there, had a few cocktails with them at dinner, and then they offered me a job in Iran.

BB: For thirteen thousand dollars, tax free, and they would pay all our travel costs!

TB: That makes a big difference.

JB: So Barbara and I went off for what we thought would be two years. It turned out that I stayed six years because when I was there I became interested in what is called "enzyme deficiency." Then, on the basis of the work that I did there, and after I spent a year in London studying genetics and surgery, I was invited to be on the faculty of the University of Chicago.

TB: So when did you come back?

JB: In 1962.

TB: I first became acquainted with you when you were studying sickle-cell anemia. Did you run into any of that while you were in Iran?

JB: I didn't run into it there. Where we lived in southern Iran, there was some, but what I became interested in while I was there was enzyme deficiencies and hemoglobin. It was only after I came back here that I became interested in sickle hemoglobin.

TB: Have you ever gone back to Iran?

JB: Yes, I was back there last year at the invitation of the government. I was the first American to be invited back since the revolution. We were treated very well and had a great time.

BB: Except they are going crazy. I don't know what is wrong with them.

TB: You mean because of their religious fundamentalism?

JB: Yes, but, I suppose, the same thing could also happen here in the United States.

TB: Sure it could, Pat Robertson—

JB: Yes, the Pat Robertsons and all of those other guys. You just can't argue with people like that who think they can talk directly to God. There is no room for argument, and they will kill you in a minute if they think that you disagree with them. Barbara and I have been through revolutions all over. We have seen everything, but I would not go to Egypt now, and I would not go to Nigeria now.

BB: Yes, right now Nigeria is really crazy too.

JB: A lot of the world is in turmoil, but a lot of people in this country don't seem to realize that most of these violent conflicts have been going on for quite some time. In '69, when I was in Ethiopia on the border with Sudan, I stayed in a camp where the Christians from the south were fighting the Muslims from the north, and they have been fighting with each other ever since. But now, just the other day, I heard on TV that all of a sudden they have just discovered what is going on in the Sudan!

TB: Well, in situations like that, whenever people accentuate religious or ethnic differences in order to gain and maintain their own personal power, then you are going to have violent conflict.

BB: And we ought to keep that message well in mind here in this country as well.

JB: In this country we should start beginning to learn from what is going on in the rest of the world.

TB: But we don't.

JB: Of course, I try to be an optimist. I have hopes that South Africa will be able to show the way for the rest of Africa. The sad thing about it is that when you look at other African countries like Nigeria, for example, they have bright people that have been educated at Oxford and Cambridge. As well as a large population, they also have abundant natural resources such as oil, but the problem is that their leaders stole the country and its resources right after the coup. If you look at what had happened economically in Japan and South Korea and Singapore and Taiwan, in a country like Nigeria they could have accomplished that same sort of thing.

TB: Yes, but they were not in control of their economics.

JB: Yeah, but the South Koreans and the Taiwanese weren't either. Of course, those other countries may have had a longer history behind them in terms of being in control of themselves before the Europeans came and took over. In that sense you are right, but, even so, there is no excuse for somebody stealing three billion dollars from a country like that. They might steal a hundred million and still leave that country somewhat intact, but not three billion dollars! That's sheer craziness.

TB: And another sad and terrible thing that the Nigerians did was to disband their agriculture system. When I first went to Nigeria in 1960, even then, they could no longer feed themselves because they had transferred all their energy into oil production—and everybody was busy getting ready to move to Lagos.

BB: And then they didn't use that money that was earned from oil to build for themselves an infrastructure that is sustainable. And so when the oil gives out, or when the prices of oil go down, they have nothing in the infrastructure to support their economy.

TB: The people in Japan don't feed themselves either, but—

BB: But they didn't have any oil, and so they had to build from the bottom up.

JB: At the present time most of my friends who are Nigerian are out of that country. They are in Saudi Arabia or Ghana or all other kinds of places like that, but not Nigeria. They tried to change Nigeria, and they discovered that they couldn't, and then they left because it became too dangerous for them to stay.

TB: How do you stabilize a situation like that when the nations outside their borders—such as Zaire as well as France—control their economy and support those violent and destructive regimes which have provided the basis on which they have built up their own power and riches?

JB: Part of the solution is that we have get to the guys on top and somehow change the leadership structure. For example, if only Nkrumah had stayed on, but Nkrumah was considered by a lot of powerful people to be a very dangerous man. Number one, he did away with tribalism. He wanted the Africans to unite, and the Europeans didn't want anything like that to happen. So they started saying that he was a dictator, and they began complaining how "dictators" like Nkrumah were standing in the way of "progress."

TB: Yes, standing in the way of "progress" as *they* wanted to define it. What happens is that if power does not get distributed in a way that is favorable to those who already control it, wherever that happens, then they will always try to pit one group against another, just as they have done right here in Chicago.

JB: And they retain their power while all the others fight it out.

BB: Yes, but, even without those artificial distractions, it stills appears to be very hard for any society to facilitate fundamental change in an orderly fashion without resorting to some form of a repressive system. You look at China, and they are moving much more rapidly than Poland, for instance, into a free economy. Why is that? Because in China the economy is managed with an iron fist—"and if you don't do it my way, then I'll kill you."

JB: Yes, but the Poles are surprising everybody. The Poles are doing better than anyone expected.

BB: No, they aren't. They are on the edge of bankruptcy. They tried to do too much too fast without the proper controls being in place.

JB: When we left the United States and had been living overseas six or seven years, we thought we were not ever going to come back. The main reason we decided to come back was because of our daughter. Because she didn't know who she was, and we wanted her to know who she was. In those days we were called "Negroes," but when we would say to our daughter, "You are Negro," she would say, "Well, what does that mean?" We tried to explain it to her, but she said, "Everywhere I look I see lots of people with dark skin, but they are not called 'Negroes.' Why aren't they called 'Negroes?'" She would also ask us questions such as who is the shah of the United States? We would say that we don't have a shah, but finally, after trying to explain all those sorts of things to her, we said, "Well, it is time for us to go back home so she can find out who she really is."

BB: They called her a little white girl in Iran because she is very fair. In fact, in Iran she is fairer than almost everybody else, but we told her she was not white. She was Negro.

TB: You know, they have big problems with distinctions of that kind in Brazil.

JB: Yes, in a place like Brazil they have twenty different classes based on various degrees of color. But did you know that now in Brazil they also have classifications that are called "Money Might"?

TB: No, I don't know about that.

JB: Well, what that means is that a person can be born black, but he might be considered "white" if he has enough money and the right kind of education.

BB: And so now he is considered to be "white" racially as well.

TB: No, I'm sure that it's really more of a class distinction, a class kind of thing. When I go there, I still can see who does all the dirty work. I can see it very clearly by the color of their faces.

BB: And the Portuguese do the same thing. In Portuguese East Africa, if you get educated and you have enough money then you become "Portuguese," and those are the kind of black people who migrated to Portugal after the liberation of East Africa. When they got there, they mixed in with the population, and now you can't find them anymore because they have intermarried with the Portuguese and are considered to be Portuguese themselves. In other words, if you have enough money and education, then you are Portuguese—and that may be the way the whole world is going now because I understand intermarriage is really beginning to increase.

JB: But at the same time stable marriages are decreasing.

TB: Jim, your own family is from Washington, D.C., isn't it?

JB: Yes.

TB: And your dad was what?

JB: He was a dentist.

TB: And your mother?

JB: She was a high school graduate, but she did not go to college. My brothers and sisters went to college, all of them.

TB: That's the same story that I see when I look at the two migrations to Chicago. My mother finished high school, and I know my dad didn't, but all of the children of that next generation went on to college and graduated.

BB: In our family, everybody in my mother's generation went to college, and the generation before that also went to college. My grandfather, his brothers, all of their kids, and, of course, us—we all went to college.

TB: Then your family history is similar to that of Jewel LaFontant, but that kind of family history is quite a rarity.

BB: On my mother's side, my great-grandmother went to Oberlin. It was a seminary before it turned into a coeducational college, and she went there just before the Civil War when she was about sixteen or seventeen years old.

TB: During that period, my own family was in bondage on both my father and my mother's side. For us, the first generation to go to college was my generation, but we knew for certain that was what we were going to do. At first I tried to duck it, but my mama was a nagger. It was easier for me to go to school than to hang around and listen to her!

[*Laughter.*]

JB: All of my brothers and sisters went to college. My brother is a dentist. My niece is an oral surgeon.

TB: And once it is established in your family tradition, you can't escape because you are trapped unless you do something awfully bad.

JB: Or unless something awfully bad happens to you.

BB: I was talking to Irvin Harris the other day. He is a black businessman. He is also a philanthropist, and he was saying he had been over at DuSable High School, and he met with the valedictorian of the class. He was so impressed with this articulate, outgoing young man that he said, "What do you want to do?" The young man told him, "I want to go to IIT [Illinois Institute of Technology]," and Irvin said, "Well, I think that is a wonderful idea, and I encourage you to do that." So he called the president of IIT, and he said, "Look, if this young man applies for admission, I will foot the bill for his scholarship. I will pay for him to go four years, but don't tell him that I'm the one who's doing this for him." Well, about six or eight weeks later the president called, and he said, "I am sorry, but this young man can't go to IIT. His College Board scores are absolutely terrible. He can hardly read and write." "But," Irvin said, "he is the valedictorian of his class." And that was when Irvin really began to understand how much behind the eight ball these kids of today are in terms of their education. Here is a kid who is doing very well, but he still isn't doing well enough to get into a decent college. IIT is a very good school, but it is not an Ivy League school.

TB: It doesn't have the stature of MIT [Massachusetts Institute of Technology] or CIT [California Institute of Technology].

BB: No, and this kid who was his class valedictorian couldn't even matriculate into a second-class school.

TB: The best thing for many of those youngsters is to go to a two-year college and then transfer.

BB: Yes, but the problem is that, in order to be transferred, they almost have to repeat a full academic year. So the people who have the hardest time and who have the least amount of money will have to spend the most money and stay in school longer than the rest of their classmates.

TB: But if that is what they have to do, then that is what they must do. At least it is a way to get them out of where they were.

BB: But we need to build them a better support system. We need to build in a system of tutoring for them. You just can't say, "OK, just come on over here," because if they do enter, but probably won't be able to stay in.

TB: Those kids get petrified when they go off to college. They had never been in an environment that is anything like that before.

BB: When I went to Stanford, there was a young Native American woman. She came right out of the tribe, but she had spent three years at Northfield [now Carleton College], and by the end of those three years, she had learned the basic skills of studying, and so she was able to do very well at Stanford, but if she had come right off a reservation school, she would not have lasted at Stanford.

TB: Culture shock can be so devastating. I didn't realize that until I went down to visit my own kids in the colleges they went to. Because of their previous background and experience, at least it wasn't too much of a culture shock for them, but what they ran into there was a degree of racism that they had not ever experienced before.

BB: I had experienced racism before I went away to school, but, even so, it was a real culture shock for me, a little kid from the Midwest, to be going to an eastern prep school. Forget about being black! They didn't even talk the same way I talked, and then, of course, you add on being black and all the racism that went along with something like that! There were only five of us that were black in a school of a thousand students, and so for all of us that kind of racism came as a real shock.

TB: Yes, I am sure it did. What is interesting about your generation and the one that came before yours is that somehow those two earlier generations seem to have survived all of that hostility better then these kids are doing in this third generation that we have today.

BB: Yes, because we knew that it was our fate in life to be strong and that nobody would sympathize with us or ever help us out. I started elementary school out at Louis Champlain, which is at Sixty-second and Stewart, and when I went there, there couldn't have been more than thirty black kids in the whole school. Nobody would hold my hand when we would march into school after recess and after lunch. My sister was the only one who would have to hold my hand, but black kids without sisters or brothers or friends had to get used to being alone very quickly at a place like that!

JB: In talking with some of our black students here in Chicago, sometimes I cannot get that across to them, though I always try my very best. I don't just sit there. I say, "Look, I have been alone all my life just like you. You can do it on your own." But they want me to feel sorry for them, and so I say, "I can't feel sorry for you. I can't because you have to make it, and I know you can to it, but, being black, in order to compete you have to be better than the rest. You can't be just as good. You have to be better, and once you realize that and stop feeling sorry for yourself, then — and only then — you will succeed, and no one will stand in your way." You know, when I first entered medical school at the University of Chicago while I was still in my early twenties, the only black classmate that I ever had was Julian Lewis. That's when I first began to realize that you are always by yourself and must always do your best no matter what.

TB: Allison Davis came through there before you, and I'm certain that he had to go through all that you did and probably much that was even worse.

BB: And he couldn't get an apartment in the Cloisters. He couldn't join the Quadrangle Club. By the time we came along, at least we could do things like join the Quadrangle Club. The university even helped us buy an apartment in a building that they controlled. So at least some things changed a little in that fifteen years between the time that Allison was there and the time we went there.

JB: After Allison Davis, there was Chuck Long [Dr. Charles Long].

TB: Chuck Long the historian?

JB: Yes, he eventually became head of the department of the history of religion at the University of Chicago, and now he is down at Durham. There was Chuck Long, Allison Davis, and another person in the Divinity School, and that was it as far as the black population was concerned at the University of Chicago in those days.

TB: When I went into the service, I had to make another real culture adjustment. The race thing was there, of course, but at least I was somewhat prepared for and even expecting it. It was something that I knew I could abide, but when the culture shock came in was when I had to deal with my black brothers from the rural, agricultural South.

BB: That must have been quite a shock. That's a group of people that I really don't know anything much about.

TB: They are quite a bit different.

BB: My father used to say things like that all the time because he grew up in Tuskegee. He used to always say, "You don't know anything about rural black people. The people that you know about are urban blacks, and they are quite different." And when black people began to come up north after the Second World War from the Deep South, I remember he would say that it was going to be very difficult for them to assimilate. When he started the Ida B. Wells housing project, one of the things that he insisted on was that there was to be a social director whose job was to be sure that people kept their houses clean, their children clean, and also the area around their houses. The reason they needed to be trained was because he said that these are people used to just throwing their garbage out the back door, and that was because they didn't even have a window. Just a back door!

JB: I can say this about Chicago, I have been here almost thirty-two years now, and I have never—I tell my students this—I have *never* to my knowledge been confronted with an act of racism. The only thing that was ever said to me that I would consider a racist act was when a person came up to me about ten years ago—and I was a full professor by then—and he said, "Dr. Bowman, you know by now people like you are very prominent around here." That is the sort of remark that he would not have said to another professor at the University of Chicago.

TB: I suspect that he thought that he was complimenting you.

JB: Well, perhaps he thought he was, and I didn't say anything to him about it because I realized that he meant no harm, but that is the type of thing that you have to be prepared to deal with, and they never call it "racism," do they?

BB: No, and, of course, you'll never know how many opportunities you *didn't* get because of your race, and you just have to accept that as well.

TB: I remember a similar remark when I was doing casework years ago. I was doing casework with a very disturbed boy who was white. So I helped this white kid and brought him up to a level that he could get back in the community with his mother again, and she said, "Mr. Black, I am so glad for your help, and you don't know how much I appreciate what you have done. You act just like a white man."

JB: When people say things like that, they think that they are complimenting you.

BB: Well, thank goodness, nobody has ever made one of those kind of "compliments" to me. I don't like or accept compliments like that!

TB: My job was to help her kid, so I could not blame her.

BB: That's true. I only hope that if an occasion like that should ever arise, I can be as considerate as you were. I suppose that it is subtle things like that that are so hard to control. People's belief systems are so hard to change. Even when they don't mean to be prejudiced, it still comes out in little, tiny ways. It is very hard to say to somebody that I perceive that what they said was a racist thing to say, but I suppose that by now I have gotten increasingly good at doing it! I was at a meeting last week, and a guy stood up and said, "We always are so critical of ourselves here at the university, but just remember we have an illustrious history, and we have done so many wonderful things as a professional community." I said to him, "You know, I appreciate what you are saying, but you have to remember that as a black woman I was excluded from the leadership of that 'wonderful' community you are talking about, and so it is very hard for me now to think that it really was all that 'wonderful' back then. In fact, it makes me very angry when you say that it was all that 'wonderful' without recognizing that it excluded *any* black people from positions of leadership!"

TB: The value of these conversations like this, which I am recording, is that people in our community—particularly young people—need to know even those of us who have been tremendously successful have had to struggle. They have not been exposed to the kind of struggle that even the most successful of us have been through.

BB: Well, it was relatively easy for us as compared to our parents' generation.

JB: But you can never think that you have gone so far that you will not sometime be reminded of prejudice like that in some sort of way.

TB: Yes, because racism is still endemic to this social system.

BB: Well, that system is going to have to change because in 2025 the power will shift from 60 percent white and 40 percent minorities to 51 percent minorities and 49 percent white, and that shift will increase even more over the following twenty-five to fifty years. Unless something happens and we all become mixed very soon, there will be a minority of white people in this country and a majority of what are now minorities.

TB: Yes, but who will have the power?

BB: Well, that's an interesting question. If I notice correctly, what they are doing now is that they are beginning to say to the Hispanics, "You are white just like us, aren't you?"—and, of course, that's just what they would say!

TB: When I was first going to Miami in the late forties and fifties, the service jobs were all held by blacks, but today if you can't speak Spanish as well as English, you have to work for much lower pay.

BB: I understand when poor black people say, "It's not fair that I should have to work for less than the minimum wage just because there is another poor person who is willing to come in and do it." That's why you don't see any African-American taxi drivers anymore. Now they all come from Belize or Africa or India or Pakistan or Poland, and the reason that blacks today don't drive cabs is because you have to drive a cab twelve hours a day, day in and day out, in order to make a decent living, and black folks don't think they ought to have to work twelve hours a day. That's just too hard. I mean, you really have to work very hard being a taxi driver and putting in those twelve hours every day.

TB: Yes, but something like that is better than nothing, and that's what they don't seem to understand.

BB: "Nobody has nothing, and nobody does nothing"—that's the attitude so many people seem to have, and that's the problem. "Nobody has nothing," but somehow there will always be someone—either "my mama or my sister or my girlfriend"—who will always be there to take care of me and give me what I need.

TB: That represents a major shift in values because, even during the depth of the Depression, there were people like my dad who would say, "I am not going to be on welfare or take any kind of relief." His pride would say, "No, I am not going to do that!"

BB: Well, now people think that welfare is what is owed to them.

JB: And another sad thing that is going on as far as blacks are concerned is that people never talk about the *working* poor. Those are the people that don't make the newspapers and who are not seen out there on TV. When I taught at the University of Chicago, I was there one night, and the janitor came around and started talking. This man had two kids in college, and he said he was working three jobs "so that my kids will not have to do what I am doing," and there are lots of blacks like that out there working just as hard as he does. We have students at the University of Chicago who come from the West Side and from some of the most horrible conditions that you would ever think of, and who come through here and are very successful, but nobody wants to talk about that sort of thing on television.

TB: No, television doesn't ever highlight things like that, and our communities are broken down so completely that we don't see those kinds of successes with our own eyes anymore. Many years ago, when we were living at Fifty-first and Michigan, down the street from us there was where Dr. Dawson lived, and his brother was the alderman. All those successful people, you just saw them every day coming and going right by your door. Those role models were there for us to see, and we could say, "Well, that cat looks like me. I think I would like to be like that." At least you are going to try your best to succeed. But the way it is today these kids don't see any role models except maybe for some of those drug dealers who look like they are making it big. They affirm the attitude that "I don't have to live long, but at least I can live well"—and that is a dangerous and destructive thing. That is the stuff out of which violent revolutions can be made.

BB: But I don't think we have any chance of having a violent revolution in this country.

TB: Yes, but you still continue to have agitators.

BB: They agitate all over the place, and all that does is to get some more good black kids killed, and their lives totally wasted.

TB: But the agitators don't care about that.

BB: That is true. The agitators don't care.

TB: They want to prove that the system does not work.

BB: But all that it proves is that you weren't smart enough to figure out a way to make things change and still stay alive and at least have a chance that the changes you died for are going to be realized by your kids or your kid's kids. Just to throw away your life is both wasteful and unnecessary.

TB: Yes, but youngsters who see no hopeful future for themselves within the existing system can easily be duped into believing almost anything that promises to give them an opportunity to achieve some sort of recognition and prestige.

JB: And so they are led to believe that they are doing something that is "brave" or "heroic" but which is only self-destructive.

TB: In certain situations they see no alternatives.

BB: But it's not just poor kids. Middle-class youngsters are also saying, "I have got to identify with my poverty peers. I have got to act just like them. I have got to not be good in school. I don't want to speak 'standard' English. I don't even want to write 'standard' English because then it will make me look like I am trying to be uppity and as if I am trying to separate myself from my peers"—and that is the prevailing attitude even in the magnet high school!

TB: I remember when both Tim and Ermetra first went away to school. She went to Bennington, and he went to Phillips Andover—this is back in the time when they were giving a push for minority kids—and somebody called me up and asked me about my son's educational and cultural background. I said, "Well, he has been to Europe, and he speaks French. He sang with the Chicago Symphony Orchestra." And they said, "Well, then he cannot be considered as being in need of a scholarship."

BB: Yet he still needs that scholarship.

TB: And then, when he got to Phillips Andover, being reared in the way in which he was reared, he had a deep respect for women. That attitude came from seeing my dad and the way he always treated my mother. Even though his mother and I didn't stay together, we always respected each other. But then when these other tough, smart black guys came to Phillips Andover with the ABC program—some of them from Taylor Homes, and they were smart, but they were also very tough—my son quickly discovered that their way of looking at women was very different. So he was caught in the middle of trying to understand and reconcile these differences, and that is also where a lot of other kids are having serious difficulties. They are not going to change the standards that they grew up with, because those standards are too deeply embedded, but they can still be influenced, and that's when they start to get confused.

BB: Our daughter's comment about her own experience at Stanford was that when she finished she felt that she had not taken full advantage of the opportunities that were there because she had let herself be restricted by what the other black students wanted to participate in. As a consequence, there were lots and lots of experiences that she cut herself off from. She missed lots and lots of opportunities that she might have had to make new friends, to try out new ideas, to try new courses. "I've got to be just like everybody else" is what she told me.

TB: It is very hard for a young person to be in a situation like that.

JB: Yes, the pressure is tough. Most of the other black kids there at Stanford were also in that ABC [A Better Chance] program, but they were there on scholarships, and so they asked our daughter, "What about you?" She said, "Well, I am on scholarship too." Well, in a certain sense she was, because of the fact that the University of Chicago pays full tuition for a student who has a faculty-member parent to go to wherever they want to go, up to the cost of tuition at the University of Chicago. But she didn't want to tell her friends what kind of "scholarship" she had because she didn't want to be perceived as different.

BB: She went to the law school at the University of Michigan because that was where she belonged, but nobody wanted to believe that was true. Her classmates were all certain that she was there as an example of affirmative action.

TB: My son experienced the same sort of thing at Phillips, that old "aren't you glad you are here?" kind of attitude, but, being the kind of guy he was, he said to them, "Well, why should I be glad? My grandfather should have been here." That was the kind of spirit that he had, but, even so, he was much more tactful in his own way than my daughter. She would strike out. When she went to college, my daughter became very angry, and my son became more sympathetic and understanding. He did not waver from the standards, but he often had to be in the position of acting as the buffer between his friends and the administration.

BB: Where did you say that your daughter went to college?

TB: Ermetra went to Bennington.

BB: God, a black student at Bennington in those days! She must have been the only one.

TB: No, as a matter of fact, there must have been ten or eleven, and there were only about three or four hundred girls there all together. What really confused her was the fact that the civil rights movement was in full flame.

JB: Yes, during that period, a scholarship for anyone at even a place like the University of Chicago was almost completely wasted.

BB: Except that it was always easier for whites to get back on course. It was very hard for the black youngsters. They were very naïve and were misled. It is so sad. During that period, one time we had about one hundred black students over at our house that we had invited up for dinner. About six of those black kids were sitting in the library with the door closed, and one of the students said to me, "Dr. Taylor, you don't want to come in here, because we are planning a revolution." So I said, "Well, if you are planning a revolution and there are six of you in here, then probably at least two or three of you are informers." They said, "What?" Somebody quoted Che Guevara, and I said, "Don't quote Che Guevara. He is dead. He was unsuccessful. Do you really want to be like him?" There was one young man in there who was under indictment by the Philadelphia Police Department, and I could see that he was trying to poison their minds. So I said, "Look, suppose you are in a country with 90 percent black and 10 percent white, and you know that a group of whites are plotting a revolution, what would you do? Well, the first thing is you have to be smart. The way things are in this society you just can't assume that somebody in your group is not an informant, just because that person happens to be black."

TB: In the civil rights movement, we also knew that there were provocateurs in the midst of our group, and we had to learn to try to deal with them as best we could in our own little way.

BB: The kids that had strong support at home were able to rise above all that and go back to school and finish up. But, even so, we lost a lot of kids in that generation.

TB: We lost a lot of them. Some of them just broke down because of all the pressures they were under, and in that regard I often think of the courage displayed by those kids in the South that would come and pick us up at the airport and then drive with us back through the dark.

BB: You talk about courage! I was down in Mississippi, and those children would take us down these sharp, red-clay roads, and there would be a car behind us with white people in it, and I would say, "Why are they so close behind us?" "Oh, they are just trying to scare us." I said, "Well, they did. They most certainly did." Then these young people would point out a place we were passing and say, "That's the prison where we spent the night three weeks ago," and later, down the road, they would say, "And that's the prison we slept in two nights ago." By then I was a total wreck, and I said, "I have been through revolutions all over the world, and I don't know when I have ever been as scared as I am right now."

TB: When I went to Birmingham, before I went over to the Sixteenth Street Baptist Church, I called one of my cousins who lived there, and I said, "I am in town." He said, "Don't come down here. We don't want to see you." Well, I understood what he meant and also why he said it. Anyhow, when it was all over, my cousins were the recipients of the benefits of what we were doing, and my cousins now will admit that it was because of Dr. King that life finally got better for them. But those kids who took the actual blows, they got very little out of it. Those kids believed that they were going to be moving into the utopia of their dreams just as soon as this struggle was over, and they are the ones who were left with disappointment. They were the ones who became psychologically broken.

JB: You know, several years ago I heard a speech by Farrakhan, and he was preaching that one of these days we are going to have to have a country of our own—a separate territory—here in the United States where all of us blacks can go to live and be together. He kept repeating that same message over and over, so finally I stood up and said, "You know something? You are not nearly as radical as I thought you were. You don't even know your history—what *really* happened—and, therefore, you do not know just how racist this country really is." Then I told him, "If we were to put all the blacks in one separate place, number one, the land which they would let us have would not be any good, and so we would be at an automatic disadvantage—and, number two, one day all of a sudden we would see a plane fly over this 'wonderful' place where we were all living together, and that plane would drop something on us, and what it would drop would most likely be a hydrogen bomb!"

BB: That's right. To gather us together like that would only make it easier for them to oppress us.

TB: And isn't what he's asking for what the ghetto already is? Didn't we already have to pay a "color tax" to those who forced us to live in a separate restricted area more or less just like the one that Farrakhan was describing?

JB: What happens is that someone like Farrakhan gets so wrapped up in his own rhetoric that he doesn't seem to realize that anybody who is in power wants to stay in power, and they are going to find ways to oppress any group of people who are in opposition to them, however that opposition might happen to be defined. I sometimes tell my students that the only people in the history of the world that I know of who have never oppressed anybody are the Eskimos, the Bushmen in the Kalahari, and the Australian Aborigines—and the reason *why* they have never oppressed anybody is because they never had the opportunity!

TB: Speaking for myself, I've spent too much time trying to help this country to just give up and give it back to them. At this point I really don't want to say I am going to go somewhere else and just give up the struggle. When I was in the service, I enrolled in the Sorbonne, and I thought seriously for a little while of not coming back home, but then I began to think of my mother and my father and all my friends, and I began to get to feeling lonely, and I decided I'd better go back. So I came back and got into trouble trying to do the little bit that I could do to begin to change things around.

JB: We have lived in two foreign countries and have worked in about six or seven of them and traveled to about thirty-five others, and so I have seen a lot of the world, but I really can't think of a place, as a black person, that I would rather live than the United States.

TB: I came to that same conclusion in that same kind of way, moving around and making comparisons and thinking about how could I adjust to this, that, or the other, and then I always came back here to Chicago. I have been to nice little towns in this country, but I always say, "Oh, Lord, this is so boring. Let me go back to where there is some excitement." At least let me be where I can get to it if I want to! But the point is that you become acclimated to all of this, both the good and the bad, and eventually you become adjusted. I used to say to my students when I was teaching high school that when things begin to get you really down, you should learn to get yourself some good rest and some good books. Learn to live alone if you need to, and then, when things start to get bad, turn your records off, pick up a book, and lose yourself in what you are reading.

BB: That's certainly one of the best ways to handle stress. It is much better than just getting drunk or something like that, because if you can lose yourself in a book, if you can lose yourself in music — whether it is gospel or jazz or classical — whatever turns you on, you can redeem yourself so much better than if you have the drink. You will also feel much better when you wake up!

JB: You have to develop a sense of perspective. When we lived overseas, oftentimes we would get the *New York Herald Tribune, Time* magazine, *Newsweek* at least two weeks late. We also listened to the Voice of America and the BBC, and what we were hearing really started to get us worried and upset about the world situation. But, when you get something two weeks late and you read about how everybody is excited about something, then suddenly you remember that all of this is something that happened two weeks ago, and nothing really bad has happened. From a perspective like that, you are able to obtain a very useful sense of history.

BB: And if it happened two weeks ago and nothing "bad" has happened since then, then maybe what happened was actually for the good.

TB: Yes, but it's like those old papers that I've got to throw away one day. Why didn't I throw them out earlier? They aren't worth anything, but somehow all that history keeps coming back at you.

BB: Yes, that is also quite true.

TB: In regard to history, Barbara, your dad left a legacy in terms of the public housing that bears his name, the Robert Taylor Homes, and I have said it before and I am going to say it again, why don't you folks sue the city to get your dad's name taken off that monstrosity that still exists over there?

BB: My feeling about it is that there are so many more important things we ought to be concerned about. Dad doesn't know what happened, what those buildings have become. He had no idea that they named that housing project after him to begin with. Mother was a little angry toward the end, and I think she did a newspaper interview a year or two ago in which she said they ought to tear them down. I guess that she began to feel a little more defensive about my father's name being associated with a place like that. My own feeling about it is that I have got so many other things on my plate that are more important that to make a big fuss about a place like that just seems like it would probably be more effort than it's worth.

TB: Barbara, why don't you tell me a little about the work you are doing over at the Erikson Institute?

BB: Well, it is a graduate school affiliated with Loyola University, but we are independently funded. We have a master's program and two teacher certification programs. We have a number of specific projects we are working on. For instance, I work in four Chicago public schools. We also do a lot of violence prevention and abuse prevention for the courts and for the Department of Children and Family Services, where we provide the training for child protective workers. We work a lot with Head Start and day care programs in the city. In other words, we are a combination of graduate school and research facility.

TB: You approach these social problems from a psychological and psychiatric point of view?

BB: What we do is to take a very holistic view of child development, and so all of our students take an interdisciplinary program. We talk about health and physical development. We talk about culture. We talk about psychometrics. We talk about emotional development, but we also talk about cognitive development. We talk about education of both children *and* their families. So we are looking not just at kids as if they existed in isolation like they do in most teacher education programs when they talk about the development of the child. We talk about the child in a family *and* in a community *and* in relation to all the factors that impinge on that child's life and play a role in how you plan for that child's education and in how you help support that particular child's family.

TB: How much faculty and how many students do you have?

BB: We have seven full-time what you would call "tenured" faculty. We also have about fourteen others that we call "project associates" or assistant professors, and we have about 150 students, some of whom are one-year students and some are two-year students and some are three-year students.

TB: These are mostly graduate students?

BB: They are all graduate students.

TB: And you are now president of the institute?

BB: Yes.

TB: And in your role as president, you are the one who runs the "joint"?

BB: Yes, I run the "joint"!

[*Laughter.*]

JB: She was just elected president.

BB: I have been running the academic part for about twenty years now, but now our last president was no longer interested in the administrative aspect, and he kind of wanted to get away from it. I don't really mind administration. I am a good fiscal manager. I am a good organizer. I have done the presidency once before, but that was only for a year. This time I have agreed to take it on for three to five years and see how it goes.

TB: When you first started, was there any kind of controversy because Erikson's theories are somewhat different from those of Freud and some of the others?

BB: No, not really, because we have always been established as an accredited graduate program, but what I suppose you are really asking is why we are called the "Erikson" Institute?

TB: Yes.

BB: Well, Erik Erikson was a very good friend of Maria Piers, who was our first dean. When we first started the institute, he came frequently and gave a series of public lectures for us, and he was extremely supportive of this new young venture of ours. Many people assumed that we named the institute for Erik because of his "eight stages." You probably know about the "eight stages" of child development, but, actually, that is not it. The real reason was that he was one of the first psychologists who took seriously the interface between culture and development. What he said was that people are not only the result of their intrapsychic experiences within their own home but are also products of the times and social contexts within which they live. His book *Young Man Luther* and his book about Gandhi were examples of how he took what was happening to somebody personally and intrapsychically and embedded that information within a larger social context. The Gandhi book showed that Gandhi was a product of his family, but he was also a product of what was happening in India at the time in which he lived.

TB: And, before that, a product of his experience with racism in South Africa.

BB: Yes, that is right. He moved to South Africa before he returned to India, but, on the other hand, he wasn't as perturbed when he lived in South Africa about the oppression of blacks as he was about the oppression of Indians in that particular situation. Why? Well, who he was at that time in South Africa was very different from who he was when he returned to India somewhat later. That's really what Erikson's contribution helps us to understand. He thought about people not just as Freud had done, as being products of the conflicts in their own homes and of their emotional lives, but as individuals who live in a larger social setting and who use that larger social setting to both ameliorate their intrapsychic problems and also exacerbate them. So it is no longer just the question of what is good or bad — it is now the question of recognizing a person as being embedded in a specific social context that provides certain important opportunities for growth. An example that I often use with my students is that for those of us in my generation there was a certain pride that we took in confronting racism. Because it was so hard, we thought about ourselves as being made stronger by the struggle. We were looked at from the outside like, "Oh, you poor little dears, how awful it must have been to be sent off to an eastern prep school and to have nobody there to comfort and protect you" — whereas we ourselves viewed what we were doing as an opportunity to test and develop our personal strength. For us, it was another example of how wonderful we are that we were able to do something as hard as this and be able to be successful at doing it!

TB: You had a sense of mission.

BB: My grandmother always kept telling us that they cannot make you uncomfortable—only you can make yourself uncomfortable. My grandmother who raised me could have been accepted as white, but she took pride in being black, and I also took pride in being black.

JB: Barbara says that when our daughter, Valerie, was at Stanford, she called up and said, "I have the opportunity to live in a black house," and Barbara told her, "Well, dear, you've already lived in a black house all of your life, haven't you?"

BB: Yes, we took enormous pride in the fact that we were black. My great-grandmother, she took her stick, and she would say, "You know you are a Negro. You should always be proud of that."

TB: That was an important lesson that she taught you.

BB: I don't know whether you have read one of the books that was written by a psychiatrist named Robert Coles, but he wrote about the children in the generation that desegregated the school systems in the South and all the traumas that they suffered as a result of those experiences. Well, in talking to him about it later, I said, "You saw one part of it, but what you didn't see was the other side and the sense of pride in their community that was instilled in these children and how that compensated for the unpleasantness of their experience. No question about that, they did experience traumas, but they also experienced a pride in their community and in what they were doing which far outdistanced all the pain. So, sure, they remember the pain, but you didn't think to ask them to tell you about their pride."

TB: And how that pride helped them get over the pain.

BB: That's right. Charlayne Hunter-Gault is a perfect example of that attitude. Her painful experiences only made her more arrogant and determined!

TB: They sure did! I remember the guys who went to the University of Illinois in the late twenties and early thirties. My brother was among them. They had comfort in one another. Most of them stayed at the Kappa house. They had a sense of mission, and if you have that to carry you, and you also have a little music and some books to read, the outside world really doesn't bother you all that much. It doesn't bother you because it can't touch the presence of the God that is within you. I once heard a South African woman saying that she was living in Zion and had been placed there because that is where she had a job to do.

JB: And *here* is where we have a job to do!

TB: Barbara, in terms of doing the work we need to do, why hasn't the approach that Erik Erikson advocated been more widely accepted? When I first heard Erik

Erikson in the forties, what he said made a lot of sense to me back then, and now it still does. Why is it that his theories have not taken root in the minds of educators working in the public schools? Why weren't they taken on? It seems to me that what he said makes so much sense.

BB: I think the reason is because the mainstream world of psychology didn't see the entire point that he was making. All that they could see were the "eight stages" of development and how they could relate to the kind of conflict that ordinary individual human beings have to go through. That aspect of what he said rang quite true to them, and it was quite easy for them to think about the "identity crisis" or about the problems of preschool children separating from their parents and having to go to school alone and all of those other specific aspects of Erikson's work. What I'm saying is that I think the conventional world of psychology more easily could see what he was getting at when he talked about the "eight stages" because they were accustomed to looking at intrapsychic issues, and they were much less able to see what he was talking about on the culture developmental interface because that area was outside of their realm. It has taken the anthropologists to raise this aspect both in cognitive psychology and interpersonal psychology, and it has really only been within the last ten or fifteen years that this perspective has begun to move into the mainstream of psychological thinking. Until then, psychology moved increasingly from the 1930s through the 1960s toward a treatment modality as opposed to establishing a deep field of knowledge about human development. In other words, the emphasis had become much more on training people to treat other people who have emotional difficulties than on generating a base of knowledge as to why people act the way that they act.

TB: What was the name of that psychologist at the University of Chicago who wanted to put everybody into treatment?

BB: Carl Rogers. He believed that everybody needed treatment, and everybody back then believed him because the focus of psychology at that time was on treatment.

TB: Did he make any positive kind of contribution?

BB: Well, he was wrong about almost everything, but he did make a significant contribution because his theories made all of us start thinking about new questions and gathering new kinds of information. After all, any theory is nothing but a combination of ideas that is useful only just as long as it continues to be useful and productive. It is only something that you use to get more information on the basis of which you can then develop new theories. So at least Rogers provided us with a very useful set of ideas which enabled us to obtain more information, and then we were able to develop new and more useful theories of our own—but, of course, Rogers had a very Eurocentric perspective on development, and, there-

fore, his theories had certain built-in limitations. There are many other culture groups, for instance, whose conception of moral development is that in the process of maturation the individual must learn to reflect the moral consensus which, in fact, defines the community in which that person lives. Someone like Piaget, of course, would place a person like that at a lower level on their scale of moral development than a Western European who learns to arrive at moral decisions through the exercise of "pure" reason alone. Well, but, if you lived in a consensual society, and if you said, "I am going to think this matter over and make a decision about it all by myself, and I don't care what anyone else thinks is right or wrong," the other people in that community would not think that you were operating on a much higher moral level. They would just think you were crazy!
[*Laughter.*]

BB: Starting back in the early sixties, the anthropologists began to talk about culture differences and the relation of these differences to our understanding of cognitive development. That's when they came up with something called "situated cognition," but by then Erikson's message had already been out there for so long and he was such an old man that he wasn't able to be as influential as he should have been.

TB: Well, even so, I still don't understand why haven't Erikson's theories entered public education more. You could at least take a specific district and say, "Let's see whether this theory of his works or not."

BB: Well, partly because the developmental process is so very complex, it's hard to test theories like his in a specific setting because none of those settings exists entirely in isolation. What we do now know, however, is that, although seemingly all children have quite similar potential abilities, as soon as a child is born into a particular society, the culture of that society begins to shape how you use your abilities, and, in order to switch societies and use your abilities in a different way, you are required to build "bridges," and it is very hard for anyone to build "bridges" of that kind. Let me give you an example. A very nice study was done on children's responses to test questions. These were second- and third-grade children, and the black children who participated in this study tended to give answers to a direct question that were referential or analogous and that usually referred to themselves as the referent in it—whereas the white children in that same study tended to either label or to define as their response to the same kind of question. So, for example, if I held up a banana, and I said to the children, "What is this?" The black child would be apt to say, "My grandmother gave me one." The white child would be more likely to say, "It is a fruit that grows on trees." OK, both children could also make the other kind of answer. After all, the black kid also knows that a banana is a kind of fruit, and the white kid could easily say his father bought some of those at the supermarket. Both of them could make both kinds of answers, but because one group of children grew up in a culture that tends to think about things as being personally related, and the other grows up in a culture that focuses on the external aspects of things, each group tends to give the kind of an answer that they are most comfortable with. Well, all right, but then what happens in school is that only *one* kind of answer is considered to be correct, and the "correct" answer is always the kind of answer that middle-class white kids grow up with, and it is not the kind of answer that most poor black kids grow up with.

TB: What about other ethnic minorities?

BB: There is no question that some Asian cultures are even more attuned to that kind of "objectivized" thinking than the white middle-class culture. So it is not just a question of what some people can do and what some people can't. What you learn is based on what the people around you practice, and, as long as you make the test so that it is responsive in a positive way only to what a certain group of people practice, then that kind of testing is not ever going to work in a manner that is fair.

JB: You know the sad thing that goes on today in regard to young blacks is that they are worried that even if they do well, maybe the whites will still think that the only reason they have been able to do well at all is *because* of affirmative action, and, as you know, that simply is not true. I remember we were at a conference at the University Club several years ago, and one of the speakers said that affirmative action has *never* worked here in the United States. I said, "Yes, affirmative action has worked. It has been *eminently* successful for whites ever since 1619, which is when the first black came to the United States!

[*Laughter.*]

BB: And I always say if you really want to ace out most middle-class white kids, you would just have to go to the inner city. You go there and get an understanding of their current vocabulary, and then you ask those middle-class white kids what exactly do some of those words and expressions mean, and in that kind of situation most of them would fall all over the place. Some would learn more than the others, of course, because they all have the same potential, but what you learn and how you express what you have learned are determined within the social context of what you are accustomed to doing.

TB: I remember one time standing outside of Farren School at Fifty-first and State Street during the height of the traffic and watching those kids negotiate that traffic!

BB: A middle-class white kid would probably have a great deal of difficulty in a situation like that.

TB: Kids like that can go to the store and buy food, get the right amount of change, cross that busy street, and get back home safely, but when they go to school the next day, the teacher gives them a problem such as what is seventy-six minus forty, and that same child cannot do it. Why can't he do it? He can do it at the store, but he can't do it in the school!

BB: They have some wonderful studies that were made by observing Brazilian street children. Evidently, they buy cigarettes and candy from a wholesaler, and then they sell it for a profit by bargaining out on the street, and in their heads they can figure whether two for a dime is better than three for twenty-five cents and other things like that. Those are the kind of things that most people would need a pencil and paper to figure out, but they are able to do all of that in their heads, and yet they fail in school. Why? Well, there is another nice study that was made by observing the behavior of people out at the racetrack, and they discovered that certain people without much formal education are able to figure out the pari-mutuel betting percentages before the officials can even put those figures up on the pari-mutuel form. They seem to know what's going to go up there before it ever goes up. How do they do that? The reason is because there are other ways at arriving at knowledge than the standard accepted procedures. Boys pitching pennies learn how to triangulate in order to figure out who is closer to the line. When they play a game, they can do something like that almost automatically, but when they go to school, they can't pass geometry!

TB: I was in the army with a guy who could look up at a building and pretty accurately tell you just how many bricks there were in that entire building, and yet I would have needed a calculator to be able to come even reasonably close.

BB: Any form of knowledge is very context-specific, and so if you ask me to bring forth my knowledge and apply it in an entirely new situation, it's going to be extremely hard for me. I would have to try a series of different strategies, and sometimes I might just cast around or use trial and error, but whatever I might choose to do, I probably won't seem to be acting at all reasonably because now you have placed things in a new context which I don't quite understand. Let me give you another good example of what I'm talking about. Sylvia Esther Warren talks about the behavior of kids in school. In Appalachia the parents only ask children questions when the parents themselves don't know what the answers are. "Where are those shoes?" "What is your brother doing?" So then, when that child comes to school, the teacher holds up a round, red ball and says to the child, "What is this?" The child doesn't know how to articulate the "correct" response. The child doesn't know because the child hasn't learned how to answer a question like that. Now, of course, the child *knows* that the teacher knows what it is that the teacher is holding, and the child also *knows* that the teacher knows that he knows what it is, but then, "Why is she asking me what it is? What does she want me to say?" We've had situations just like that over and over again in Head Start. The teachers would say, "What's your name?" and the child would say, "Robert," and the teacher would interpret this as meaning, "Ah, that poor kid doesn't even know what his last name is." But if you had asked that same child what was his *other* name, he would have told you right away what his last name was. But, in terms of his prior experience, in his neighborhood everybody knew him as "Robert." His family also knew him as "Robert," and for him "Robert" was what you meant when you asked him for his name.

TB: You know, just yesterday I was at our annual Fifty-eighth Street Picnic. My friends there are very different kinds of guys, and they have their own way of saying things, and so in that kind of situation I guess I had to build a little "bridge" of my own.

BB: Yes, of course, you need to build "bridges" that are very different over there, but someone like you seems to be able to build "bridges" like that in every direction.

TB: But, Barbara, how do you teach someone to build those kind of "bridges" if they don't already know how? For example, my brother tries hard, but he can't build those kind of "bridges." He grew up with the Tilden Tech crowd and the University of Illinois crowd and the Kappa crowd—

BB: And so what he knows, he only knows in that one kind of way.

TB: So when he gets with the Fifty-eighth Street guys, he is completely out of place. But there are guys just like him, such as Arnie Byrd, who went to the same schools, and yet Arnie is able to fit right in.

BB: Yes, and some people like Jesse Jackson are able to do something that most other people can't do. You can't switch over suddenly to "black" English can you?

TB: Not easily. Sometimes I have to work at it.

BB: Well, Jesse Jackson can talk "black" English and then turn right around and talk "standard" English. Very few people can do that.

TB: And he also knows exactly when it is the right time for him to do it.

BB: That's even more important, of course, but the point is that most of us can't do it at all.

TB: King could also do that. He could do it because he was keenly aware of the importance of cultural factors. I heard him preach in his own church, and the way he spoke—

BB: He used a sort of black church rhythm, didn't he? But most of us speak either "standard" English or we speak the patois. Very few people can speak both the standard form and the patois with equal dexterity.

TB: But the problem here is that if you speak only the patois, then, from the viewpoint of those who have been trained to speak "standard" English, you are often seen as someone who is not *capable* of speaking correctly.

BB: Yes, and, of course, the perception is that if you don't talk like me, then you must not be as intelligent as I am, and if you make any sort of grammatical errors, then you can't be terribly bright, but every language changes, and what was a grammatical error fifty years ago by now may have become the new "standard" practice—and yet, even so, we all still act like "standard" English has somehow been cut in stone.

TB: Particularly if an "error" of that type comes from a black person.

BB: Oh, that is absolutely true.

TB: That kind of grammatical error has a stigma that is associated with it because it is used to support a preexisting prejudice. But, when you have mispronunciations or grammatical errors of that same sort that come from another ethnic group which happens to be European, then they are more or less acceptable. They are sometimes even considered to be "cute."

JB: Yes, but also in many ways blacks are getting whiter and whites are getting blacker. In fact, the influence of blacks on whites is absolutely fantastic, particularly in entertainment. Even such a simple thing as wearing your cap on backward suddenly creates a style that everyone wants to copy.

BB: Jimmy almost had a fit when our granddaughter came in the other day with her hat turned around backward.

JB: Well, yes, it surprised me, but now I see all these white college kids coming to class, and the hats they're wearing are also turned around backward on their heads!

TB: The reason that they are compelled to copy things like that is because black culture is so extremely fertile. It has such a high degree of creativity that there is always a certain level of surprise and excitement which it continues to provide for everyone who comes into any kind of contact with it.

BB: Yes, even the poorest kids in the inner city, every time I go down there, I am absolutely entranced with how creative they are linguistically. I mean they can say things that absolutely shatter me.

TB: Maybe sometimes they even surprise themselves!

June 21 and July 19, 1994

CONCLUSION

Bridges of Memory has as its mission the task of extracting from a variety of African-American people from different walks of life their own memories of growing up in Chicago. In terms of structure, this project has been designed to capture these personal memories across three generations that span nearly an entire century.

What you have just finished reading in this first volume are edited conversations that I had the pleasure of participating in with forty-one individuals whose experiences reflect their varying social, economic, cultural, religious, and political perspectives. What they all have in common is that they are African-Americans who have spent most of their lives in Chicago—and for all of them their experiences with racial prejudice provide a continuing and often defining theme.

The second volume of *Bridges of Memory* will continue with additional narratives from that first generation, such as that of the eminent lawyer and public figure, Jewel Stradford Rogers LaFontant-MANkarious, the famous civil rights and feminist movement lawyer, Benjamin Duster, who also happens to be the grandson of Ida B. Wells, as well as many others who, though they may not be as well known, have just as fascinating stories of their own to tell. These conversations with the oldest generation will weave and blend into a series of conversations with members of the next (or "second") generation, such as the scientist Hunter Adams, and the pioneer of rhythm-and-blues music Jerry "Iceman" Butler, who still continues his singing career while diligently serving as a commissioner on the Cook County Board of Trustees. Though most of the interviewees from these two generations do not know one another personally, their narratives reveal the distinct connection that exists on the basis of a common cultural heritage and the necessity for developing "strategies of survival" because of the continuing pressures of racial discrimination. These same themes with just as many (if not more) variations will also be seen in the narratives of the current (or "third") generation, whose narratives will be included in the final volume.

Taken together in their entirety, the conversations in these three volumes present a tapestry of the experiences of African-Americans living in Chicago, extending from the turn of the last century to the beginning of the new, from the living memory of those whose parents or grandparents were born into slavery to the as-yet-unresolved problems and possibilities of the present generation. It is my hope that these "bridges of memory" will continue to instruct and inspire future generations as well as those of the present.

INDEX

Bush, Harry, 484
Butler, Jerry, 23, 188, 601
Butterbeans, 171
Bynum, Marshall, 374
Byrd, Arnie, 598
Byrne, Jane (Mayor), 381–82, 383, 458

"Cadillac Bob" (club owner), 453
Caldwell, Carl "Carlos the Cool," xi
Caldwell, Daniel, 234
Caldwell, Louis, 259–65
California Eagle, 103
Calloway, Cab, 396
Camel Boosters (athletes), 208
Campbell, Clifford, 349
Campbell, Floyd, 198
Campbell, Kenneth "Ken," 15, 479–80
Canty, Virgil "Fess," 388, 394
Carey, Archibald (Bishop), 59, 111, 121
Carey, Archibald Jr. "Arch" (Judge), 59, 121, 270, 486
Carney, William H. (Sergeant), 94
Carone, Duke, 392
Carroll, Larry, 512
Carroll, Reverend (at South Park Methodist Church), 551
Carroll, Robert "Bob," xi
Casey, Eddie, 35
Cavanaugh, Dave, 203
Cayton, Horace, vii, ix, 125
CCC (Civilian Conservation Corps), 61, 125, 553
Census Bureau, U.S., 327, 517
Chamberlain, Neville, 473
Chandler, Horace, 498–99
Chandler, Pete, 150
Charles, Ray, 201
Cheiken, Mr. (district attorney), 511
Chew, Charles, 514–15
Chicago Bar Association (CBA), 513
Chicago Board of Education, 324; blacks on, 83, 84, 319, 409; picketed, 3, 236
Chicago Conservatory, 169
Chicago Daily News, 486
Chicago Defender, 22, 67, 70, 110, 116, 278, 400,

454–55; boys selling, 23–24, 282
Chicago Herald Examiner, 282
Chicago Historical Society, 20, 110, 182, 570
Chicago Housing Authority (CHA), 442, 460–61
Chicago Police Department, black members of, 73–75, 444, 447; prominent people, 294, 403, 415–20, 421–42, 448–61
Chicago Public Library, 110
Chicago Race Relations Committee (CRRC), 414
Chicago Symphony Orchestra: hiring policy, 188–89; performers with, 154, 586
Chicago Tribune, 282, 514
Chusis, Bill, 183
Civil War, U.S., 47–49, 77–78, 92–94, 96, 223; GAR (Grand Old Army of the Republic), 93
Clark, Irma, 134–41
Clark, John, 373
Clark, Joyce, 233–34
Clark, Mark (General), 474
Clay, Robert, and Clay family, 92
Clayburn, Dr. (dentist), 178
Clayton, Joe, 483
Cleveland Plainview, 110
Clifton, Sweetwater, 271
Clubs. *See* DeLisa; Rhumboogie "'Boogie"
Cobb, Arnett, 180, 251
Cobb, Clarence (Reverend), 575
"Mr. Coca-Cola," 42
Cochran, Anita, 569
Cole, Eddie, 148
Cole, Mr. (entrepreneur), 331
Cole, Nat King, 148, 153, 203–4, 213, 215, 529; early days, 32, 162, 186, 193, 197, 247, 350, 528
Cole family, 148
Coleman, Oliver, 167, 200
Colemon, Johnny, 247
Coles, Dr. Robert, 593
Coles, Mr., and Coles Drugstore, 553–54
Coles, Mrs. Robert, 32
Colin, Robert "Bob," 67–75
Colin, Mrs. Robert (Mattie), 67
Collins, Ernie, and Collins family, 326
Collins, Harvey, 130
Colter, Cyrus, 474–75

Harlem Globetrotters, 24, 122, 130, 169, 179, 197

Harlem Renaissance, Chicago equivalent to, 205

Harness, Bob, 74, 448, 449–50, 457

Harper, Ravel "Ghost," 122

Harris, Irvin, 237–38, 580

Harrison, Richard B., 109

Harth, Ray, 487

Hartman, Hermene, 242, 249, 253–56, 258

Hartman, Johnny, 165, 242, 249, 498

Hathaway, Donny, 188

Hauser, Johnny, 167

Hawkins, Coleman "Hawk," 211, 213, 214, 216, 251

Hawkins, Erskine, 211

Hayes, Charley, 10

Hayes, Rutherford B., 48–49

Helson, Mr. (fundraiser for Provident Hospital), 108

Henderson, Bill, 348

Henderson, Fletcher, 162

Henderson, Horace, 162

Herald (church group), 58

Herald Examiner (later *Herald American*), 348

Herrick, Mary, 134–35, 140, 167, 181

Hersey, Dr. (at St. Luke's), 573

Higginbotham, Jay C., 201–2

"Hi-Jinks" productions. *See* Dyett, Walter Henri (Captain)

Hindon, Louie, 392

Hines, Charles, 180

Hines, Earl "Fatha," 160, 169–70, 191, 242; as performer, 21, 39, 162, 251; performers with, 16, 179, 186

Hines brothers, 180

Hinton, Milt, 179, 180, 202, 350

Hitler, Adolf, 473, 474

Hofeld, Al, 384

Holiday, Billie, 161, 202, 205, 242, 268, 395, 399; and drugs, 450–51; John Levy with, 199, 200

Holman, Claude, 486

Holman, Miss (teacher), 469

Holman, Mr. (president of insurance company), 295

Horne, Lena, 14, 112, 161, 202, 252

Hornsby, Miss (teacher), 469

Howard Swing Masters, 183

Howling, James "Jesse James," 406

Hubbard, Freddie, 203

Hubbard, Mrs. Freddie "Burgie," 203

Hudson, Roosevelt "Rosey," 24

Hunter, Lurlean, 213

Hunter-Gault, Charlayne, 593

Hurston, Zora Neale, ix

Hutchinson, Willie "Hutch," 21

Incres, Mr. (railroad man), 38

Ingram, Albert "Al," xii

Inowa, Erskine, 294

Insull, Samuel, 479

Isbell, James "Jack," 31, 216, 280–301, 329

Isbell, Mrs. James (Ann), 286, 288, 290

Isbell, Robert "Bob," 280

Ish, Jefferson, 261

Jaber (Johnson Products competitor), 358

Jackson, A. P., 574

Jackson, D. Z., 575

Jackson, Jesse, 9, 278, 317, 372, 598

Jackson, Michael, 253

Jackson, R. G., and Jackson Jubilee Singers, 105

Jackson, Reverend (at Olivet Church), 58

Jacobs, Donald, 271

Jacobs, Warren, 313

Jamal, Ahmad, 220, 453

Jarrell, Boyd, 296

Jarrett, Valerie, 565

Jarrett, Vernon, 565

Jeeter, Howard, 485, 486

Jefferies, Herb, 250

Jefferson, Dr. (pediatrician), 570

Jeffries, James J., 109

Jenkins, Tom, 119

Jessye, Eva, 106, 108–9, 112

Jet magazine, 364

Jock (pimp), 392

Johnson, Al, 229, 266, 382

Johnson, Eddie, 33, 162, 173, 199, 207–20

Johnson, Mrs. Eddie (Clara), 214

Johnson, Fred, 207, 208, 451

Moten, Etta. *See* Barnett, Etta Moten
Moten, Freeman (Reverend), 99–104, 108, 109
Moten, Mrs. Freeman (Ida), 99–100
Motley, Arch, 570
Moton, Dr. Robert R., 111, 113
Mullin, Miss (teacher), 469
Mulvihill, Mr. (landlord), 281
Murchison, Ira, 321
Murphy, George and Chester, 25
Murphy, Miss (teacher), 469
Murray, Harold, 469, 470
Murray, Wilbur, 470
Musak, Mr. (bank official), 377
Muse, Clarence, 109
Mussolini, Benito, 473

NAACP (National Association for the Advancement of Colored People), 3–4, 103, 316, 508
Nachman (factory owner), 531
NALC (Negro American Labor Council), 302
Nance, Raymond "Ray," 162, 214, 242; early days of, 179, 193, 212, 247, 350, 408–9
Nash family, 491
National Guard, 293–94, 431, 480, 487–89, 508–11, 563
National Institutes of Health (NIH), 541, 542
National Lawyers Guild, 513
NBA (National Basketball Association), 271
NBC (National Broadcasting Company), 330
N'Digo magazine, 242
Neal, Earl, 512
Nealy, John, 165
Negro Chamber of Commerce, 259, 263
Negro Digest, 359
Nelson, Carl, 448–49
Nelson (George Johnson's partner), 358
Nettles, Geneva, 81
Newman, Mr. (grocery store owner), 147–48
New York Life Insurance Company, 76, 85–86, 299–300
NFL (National Football League), 321
Nimocks, Dr. Rudy, 420, 421–41, 448, 454
Nixon, Richard, 279
Nkrumah, Kwame, 578
Nolan, Sam, 419, 456, 458

Noone, Jimmie, 202
Norman, Octavia, 100
Norman, Sarah, 100
NRA (National Rifle Association), 431, 432
NYA (National Youth Administration), 61, 308–9

O'Donoghue, Miss (teacher), 118
O'Hara, Denny, 478–79
Olive, Milton II, 94–95
Olive, Mrs. Milton II (Antoinette), 94–95
Olive, Milton III, 94
Oliver, Joe "King," 196, 223
Olympics, 109, 171
Ormandy, Eugene, 208
O'Shield, LeRoy, 422
Overton family, 141, 261
Owens, Jesse, 109

Pace, Harry, 261
Palmer House, 7–8, 189, 229
Palmer, Lu, 222, 236
Palm Tavern, 161, 268
Parham, Alonzo, 116–28
Parsons, James (Judge), 108
Partee, Cecil, 189, 268
Passmore, Juanita, 382
Patterson, Fred, 111, 113
Payne, Aaron, 483
Pegou, Maria Sofia, 90, 91
Perkins, Donald, 271
Perry, Richard, 109
Perry, Mr. (Shomea's father), 528
Perry, Shomea, 530
Perry, Theodore, 122
Pershing, John "Black Jack" (General), 46, 223
Petain, Henri (Marshal), 46
Peters, Cortez, 411
Petrillo, James, 188
Phillips Cite (school newspaper), 249
Piaget, Jean, 595
Pickett, Wilson, 365
Pierce, Mr. (teacher), 121–22
Piers, Maria, 592
Pinkart, Charlie, 374
Piper, Scotty, 44, 226, 250

Thompson, Big Bill, 38

Thurman, Howard, 241

Tilden, Samuel J., 48–49

Tojo, Hideki (General), 473

Tootie's, 389–91, 395

Tortorelli, Mr. (coach), 321

Tough, Dave, 262

Touhy, William (Judge), 481–82, 483–84

Travis, Dempsey, 10, 249, 324

Truman, Harry S, 302, 478, 503, 508

Tubman, William, 114

Tucker, Juanita, 221–41, 322

Tung Brothers, 169

Turk (friend of Jimmy Ellis), 163

Turner, Ollie, 86

Turner, R. A. S., 514

"Two-Gun Pete" (policeman). *See* Washington, Sylvester

Tyler, Lionel "Chinkie," 388, 393

Tyler, Ruben, 393

UAW (United Automobile Workers), 3, 303, 315, 316, 317

Underground Railroad, 90, 159

University of Chicago, 59, 421; blacks at, 82, 173, 582–83, 587, (restrictions on) 17; and Woodlawn Organization, 87; and Woodlawn Project, 562, 566

Upshaw family, 80

Urban League, 259, 333, 340, 369, 380, 512, 564

VA (Veterans Administration), 278

Vallas, Paul, 238

Vaughan, Sarah, 199, 200, 205, 242, 251

Vendome, the, 205; stars at, 17, 347

Vernon, Bishop, 103

Vietnam War, 127, 509

Waldo, Raymond, 200

Walker, Madame C. J., 31

Walker, Earl, 389

Walker, Mr. (Olympic contestant), 109

Walker, T-Bone, 251

Wallace, Henry A., 107

Waller, Fats, 247

Walton, Chuck, 551

Warren, Sylvia Esther, 597

Washington, Booker T., 42–43, 44, 111; daughter of, 176; granddaughter of, 159

Washington, Dinah, 26, 185, 202, 350

Washington, Harold (Mayor), 63, 187, 249, 268, 270, 272, 384, 457, 520; appointments by, 458, 460; supporters of, 33, 266, 303, 319, 330, 380, 381–83

Washington, Sylvester "Two-Gun Pete," 14–15, 164, 349, 391, 449, 456

Waters, Ethel, 21, 106, 110

Watkins, Nugie, 28

Watt, Garland, 514

Webb, Chick, 347

Webster, Mr. (musician), 216

Wells, Charles, 232

Wells, Ida B., 232, 601

Wells, Willie, 95

Weltsen, Dr. Frances, 83–84, 88

West, Frank, 183

Westbrook, Mr. (lawyer), 486

West Point, 116, 123

West Side Organization (WSO), 560

White, Charles, xi, 469

White, Jeremy, 272

White, Mary, 388

Wilkins, J. Ernest, 512

William Morris Agency, 201, 202

Williams, A. W., 323, 478

Williams, Billy, 63

Williams, Cootie, 214

Williams, Dr. Daniel Hale, 222

Williams, Danny, 193, 207, 211, 214

Williams, Eddie, 331

Williams, Joe, 186, 193, 200, 202, 204, 284; early days of, 183, 212, 251

Williams, L. K. (Reverend), 20, 57–59

Willis, Benjamin, 3

Willkie, Wendell, 58

Wilson, Kenneth, 268, 270

Wilson, Mrs. and Miss (teachers), 410

Wilson, Nancy, 186, 193, 200, 202, 204, 205

Wilson, O. W., 451, 454, 456, 459, 563

Wilson, Teddy, 34, 223

COVER PHOTOGRAPHS

FRONT

Top: Outside a movie theater (Russell Lee, Library of Congress, Prints and Photographs Division, FSA/OWI Collection, LC-USF34-038808-D, 1941)
Bottom: Roller-skating exhibition (Russell Lee, Library of Congress, Prints and Photographs Division, FSA/OWI Collection, LC-USF34-038594-D, 1941)

BACK

Top: The prominent Williams family: Morris, Annie, Morris Jr., Levi, and Willa (Chicago Historical Society, ICHi-26565 [cropped and duotoned], ca. 1920)
Bottom: In line for the movies (Edwin Rosskam, Library of Congress, Prints and Photographs Division, FSA/OWI Collection, LC-USF33-005148-M1, 1941)
Author photo: Vivian G. Harsh Research Collection, Woodson Regional Library, Chicago

SPINE

Top: Jumping rope in the Black Belt (Edwin Rosskam, Library of Congress, Prints and Photographs Division, FSA/OWI Collection, LC-USF33-005163-M4, 1941)
Bottom: Nile Queen Costumes shipping room (Chicago Historical Society, ICHi-17328 [cropped and duotoned], 1917)